Ethnic Groups
in Conflict

Ethnic Groups in Conflict

Donald L. Horowitz

UNIVERSITY OF CALIFORNIA PRESS
Berkeley · *Los Angeles* · *London*

University of California Press
Berkeley and Los Angeles, California
University of California Press, Ltd.
London, England
© 1985 by
The Regents of the University of California
Printed in the United States of America

1 2 3 4 5 6 7 8 9

Library of Congress Cataloging in Publication Data

Horowitz, Donald L.
  Ethnic groups in conflict.

  Includes index.
  1. Ethnic relations.   2. Social conflict.
3. Developing countries—Ethnic relations.
4. Ethnic groups—Political activity.   I. Title.
GN496.H67 1985   305.8   84–8914
ISBN 0–520–05385–0

The publisher gratefully acknowledges the support of
the Ford Foundation in the publication of this book.

For Judy

Contents

PART FOUR: MILITARY POLITICS
AND ETHNIC CONFLICT

PART FIVE: STRATEGIES
OF CONFLICT REDUCTION

Tables and Figures

TABLES

FIGURES

Preface

The importance of ethnic conflict, as a force shaping human affairs, as a phenomenon to be understood, as a threat to be controlled, can no longer be denied. By one reckoning, ethnic violence since World War II has claimed more than ten million lives,[1] and in the last two decades ethnic conflict has become especially widespread. Ethnicity is at the center of politics in country after country, a potent source of challenges to the cohesion of states and of international tension. Connections among Biafra, Bangladesh, and Burundi, Beirut, Brussels, and Belfast were at first hesitantly made—isn't one "tribal," one "linguistic," another "religious"?—but that is true no longer. Ethnicity has fought and bled and burned its way into public and scholarly consciousness.

As the rediscovery of ethnicity has proceeded apace, so has the availability of information about it. What has emerged is a plethora of more or less parochial material on ethnic conflict in scores of countries. What has not yet emerged is a comprehensive set of generalizations that fits the material and into which new material can be fitted. There is still, for example, no general treatment of such a central subject as the relationship of ethnicity to party politics in severely divided societies. We no longer lack basic data on ethnicity. We lack explanation—principles by which to classify cases, depictions of the structure and texture of group relations, an understanding of patterns of conflict—explanation that will hold cross-culturally. There is, in the main, too much knowledge and not enough understanding, too much evidence chasing after too few categories.

The aim of this book is to explore systematically and comparatively the politics of ethnic group conflict in severely divided societies. I am concerned to answer such general questions as the following:

1. Harold R. Isaacs, *Idols of the Tribe: Group Identity and Political Change* (New York: Harper & Row, 1975), 3.

On ethnic affiliations and their importance: What is it about ethnic affiliations that makes them conducive to severe conflict? Why does ethnic conflict tend to be more intense and violent in Asia and Africa than in Europe and North America? Are groups defined by color differences or religious differences essentially the same as groups defined by linguistic differences?

On the sources of conflict: What exactly are the goals of ethnic conflict, and what relationship does ethnic conflict bear to social-class conflict? Is it cultural difference that drives ethnic groups into conflict, is it ignorance, or is it a realistic divergence of interest? Why do ethnic groups attempt secession, even when it appears they would have much to gain by remaining in the undivided state and much to lose by leaving it? Why are there many attempted ethnic secessions but few irredentas?

On party politics: Why do political parties in severely divided societies split along ethnic lines, even when that means perpetual minority status for one of them? Why are there so few multiethnic political parties in ethnically divided societies of Asia and Africa? What would it take to produce multiethnic parties or coalitions?

On military politics: Why do ethnically based military coups frequently occur in developing countries at just the time when their politics seem most competitive and democratic? After their coups, how did leaders such as Idi Amin of Uganda and Hafez Assad of Syria come to preside over regimes representing ethnic groups comprising 10 percent or less of their populations? Is coup-proofing possible in an ethnically divided society?

On interethnic accommodation: What can be done to reduce the severity of ethnic conflict and maximize the likelihood of interethnic cooperation? What are the major techniques of conflict reduction, and exactly how do they work? When do such occasions for constructive policies arise, and what are the major pitfalls to be avoided? What are the prospects for democratic multiethnic politics in severely divided societies?

This by no means exhaustive list, which parallels the organization of the book, is a representative sample of the concerns dealt with in this work. As the questions show, my focus is on the logic and structure of ethnic conflict and on measures to abate it. The assumption, abundantly justified by the materials, is that ethnic conflict embodies regularities and recurrent patterns that are, in principle, discoverable. A further assumption, best laid on the table at the outset, is that ethnicity is one of those

forces that is community-building in moderation, community-destroying
in excess. It is, as I shall suggest, both fruitless and undesirable to attempt ⎫
to abolish ethnic affiliations, but not at all fruitless to attempt to limit ⎬ 0
their impact.   ⎭

The book is concerned, then, with theories, patterns, and policies. To
begin with, it aims to understand the nature of ethnic affiliations and to
devise an explanation of ethnic conflict that will fit the observed regularities of that conflict. The next and largest portion of the book then centers
on that most significant task of comparative analysis—pattern identification—taking as its focus ethnic politics, both civilian and military. The
remainder of the volume is an effort to evaluate policies of conflict reduction. For reasons I shall explain in Chapter 1, my primary focus is on Asia
and Africa, with secondary attention to the Middle East and Caribbean.
The conclusions, however, should also have applicability in severely divided societies elsewhere—societies such as Northern Ireland.

Understanding ethnic conflict and conflict reduction is an ambitious
task. No two analysts would go about it in quite the same way. As I hope
the entire volume demonstrates, a profitable route to understanding this
phenomenon lies in a judicious combination of careful cross-national
comparison, on the one hand, and immersion in the intricacies of paradigm cases, on the other. Extensive comparison is useful for mapping
patterns across space, and intensive case study is helpful for tracking
mechanisms and changes over time.

The approach of this book is, then, to get the hands dirty, in the double
sense of dealing with the often seamy side of ethnic politics and of looking
closely at the details of actual cases. The raw material of the book is what
politicians and their followers have done, and much of what they have
done is cruel and violent and disturbing and far from democratic. The rise
of ethnic conflict has gone hand in hand with the decline of democracy in
Asia and Africa. As these pages will amply show, the problems of reducing
ethnic conflict are at many points connected to the problems of fostering
democracy, so much so that success in the one will probably mean a
measure of success in the other as well.

This work had its gestation many years ago at the Harvard Center for
International Affairs, where I benefited from the unstinting support of
Samuel P. Huntington. It began to take shape when I was a joint fellow of
the Woodrow Wilson International Center for Scholars and the Council
on Foreign Relations. At these two institutions, Benjamin H. Read and
John Temple Swing, respectively, facilitated my work. Much of the actual

writing was done at the Smithsonian Institution, under grants from the National Institutes of Health, the Ford Foundation, and the Institute for Educational Affairs, as well as a fellowship from the Rockefeller Foundation. The National Science Foundation, the Center for International Affairs, and N.I.H. supported my field research in Malaysia and Sri Lanka. A small stipend from the American Philosophical Society helped with some work in Nigeria and Ghana. To all of these grantors, I owe a considerable debt of gratitude.

Portions of two chapters were presented in lecture form at McGill University, where I was privileged to deliver the McDonald-Currie Memorial Lectures in 1980. For the fine hospitality shown to me on that occasion, I express my thanks to my hosts and particularly to Barbara G. Haskel.

At Duke, where the manuscript was completed, I have profited in innumerable ways from the supportive environment created by Dean Paul D. Carrington. I was also fortunate to have superlative help in research and revision from Neil McFeeley. Francesca Piemonte typed most of the original draft, and Joan Ashley did a splendid job of turning out a final product from my scratchy revisions.

Along the way, my path has been smoothed by resourceful librarians, above all Linda Carlson at the Johns Hopkins School of Advanced International Studies, Jack Marquardt at the Smithsonian, and Bessie Carrington, Ilene Nelson, and Jane Vogel at Duke. It is also a pleasure to record my thanks to friends and colleagues who have provided intellectual support or cleared away an obstacle at a crucial moment. Prominent among these are Michael J. Lacey, Joan M. Nelson, and Brian Weinstein.

Barbara Ras, my editor at the University of California Press, worked long hours with skill and grace to make the book meet exacting professional standards.

I would like to convey my appreciation to my children, Bruce, Karen, and Marshall Horowitz, for their indulgence during the time this book was being written. They and the book grew up together.

Finally, I want to express my deepest gratitude to my wife, Judy, who has studied ethnicity with me for nearly twenty years on four continents and put up with all the travail that goes into producing a book of this scope. Every author should have at least one such spouse.

Donald L. Horowitz

PART ONE

Ethnic Relations and Ethnic Affiliations

CHAPTER ONE

The Dimensions of Ethnic Conflict

Not so long ago, the proposition was advanced that increased political consciousness could be expected to consolidate the unity of states with homogeneous populations and "strain or destroy" the cohesion of states with diverse populations.[1] At the time, the observation seemed even-handed enough, but in the interval it has become clear that few states are homogeneous and many are deeply divided. Ethnic conflict is a world-wide phenomenon.

The evidence is abundant. The recurrent hostilities in Northern Ireland, Chad, and Lebanon; secessionist warfare in Burma, Bangladesh, the Sudan, Nigeria, Iraq, and the Philippines; the Somali invasion of Ethiopia and the Turkish invasion of Cyprus; the army killings in Uganda and Syria and the mass civilian killings in India-Pakistan, Burundi, and Indonesia; Sikh terrorism, Basque terrorism, Corsican terrorism, Palestinian terrorism; the expulsion of Chinese from Vietnam, of Arakanese Muslims from Burma, of Asians from Uganda, of Beninese from the Ivory Coast and Gabon; ethnic riots in India, Sri Lanka, Malaysia, Zaire, Guyana, and a score of other countries—these comprise only the most violent evidence of ethnic hostility. There are many less dramatic manifestations. In country after country, political parties and trade unions are organized ethnically. There are movements to expropriate ethnically differentiated traders and expel long-resident workers of foreign origin. Armed forces are frequently factionalized along ethnic lines. Separatist referenda in Quebec and the Swiss Jura, a painful division of Belgium into zones for Flemings and Walloons, the protests of Berbers in Algeria and of Croats in Yugoslavia all serve to mark the potent political

1. Karl W. Deutsch, "Social Mobilization and Political Development," *American Political Science Review* 55 (Sept. 1961): 493–514, at 501.

force of ethnicity in the politics of both developing and industrialized states.

Ethnic conflict is, of course, a recurrent phenomenon. Shifting contexts make ethnicity now more, now less prominent. The international environment plays a part in its emergence and remission. Often overshadowed by international warfare and masked by wartime alliances, ethnic allegiances are usually revived by the wartime experience or emerge again soon afterward, as they did after the First and Second World Wars. In their periodic reemergence, ethnic sentiments have been supported by the widespread diffusion of the doctrine of "national self-determination."[2] This doctrine, traceable to eighteenth-century conceptions of popular sovereignty, flowered with the burst of nationalism in nineteenth-century Europe and the building of states like Germany and Italy out of more parochial units. The twentieth-century version, on the other hand, entailed the dismemberment of empires and large states in favor of smaller units, beginning after World War I, when the Wilsonian espousal of self-determination helped remake the map of Eastern Europe.

The process was repeated after World War II, with the termination of colonial control in Asia and Africa. Decolonization set in motion a chain. reaction, the ultimate impact of which has yet to be felt. The movements that sought independence from the colonial powers were not always wholly representative of all the ethnic groups in their territories. Some groups that were not so well represented attempted, with varying degrees of success, to slow down the march to independence or to gain special concessions or even a separate state. But, with some exceptions, ethnic differences tended to be muted until independence was achieved.

Following independence, however, the context and the issues changed. No longer was the struggle against external powers paramount. No longer was colonial domination the issue. Self-determination had been implemented only to the level of preexisting colonial boundaries. Within these boundaries, the question was to whom the new states belonged. As some groups moved to succeed to the power of the former colonialists, others were heard to claim that self-determination was still incomplete, for they had not achieved their own independence. "The discontinuance of a sin," wrote Anthony Trollope in 1860, "is always

2. See Walker Connor, "Self-Determination: The New Phase," *World Politics* 20 (Oct. 1967): 30–53.

the commencement of a struggle."[3] In a large number of ex-colonial states, the independence rally gave way to the ethnic riot.

As these issues began to emerge, the independence of Asia and Africa was being felt in Europe and North America. The grant of sovereignty to the former Belgian territories in Africa (Zaire, Rwanda, and Burundi) helped stimulate ethnic claims among Flemings in Belgium itself. If, they said, tiny Burundi can have an autonomous political life, why should the more numerous Flemish population be deprived of the same privilege? The emancipation of Africa also had an impact on Afro-Americans, and it probably made racial discrimination seem anomalous to many other Americans. In Canada, some French-speaking Quebeckers cited African independence as a precedent for their own, and some identified the position of Afro-Americans as analogous to theirs, calling themselves "*Nègres blancs d'Amérique*."[4] The latest large-scale exercise in self-determination—decolonization—thus had reverberations across oceans. Although international conditions cannot create a conflict where one does not exist—for contagion is not the source of ethnic conflict—they can create a setting in which ethnic demands seem timely and realistic.

Certain worldwide ideological and institutional currents have also underpinned the growth of ethnic conflict. The spread of norms of equality has made ethnic subordination illegitimate and spurred ethnic groups everywhere to compare their standing in society against that of groups in close proximity. The simultaneous spread of the value of achievement has cast in doubt (and self-doubt) the worth of groups whose competitive performance seems deficient by such standards. Finally, the state system that first grew out of European feudalism and now, in the post-colonial period, covers virtually the entire earth provides the framework in which ethnic conflict occurs. Control of the state, control of *a* state, and exemption from control by others are among the main goals of ethnic conflict.

In consequence of all these developments, ethnic conflict possesses elements of universality and uniformity that were not present at earlier times. The ubiquitous character of ethnic conflict opens opportunities

3. *The West Indies and the Spanish Main* (London: Chapman & Hall, 1860), 63.
4. Pierre Vallières, *Nègres blancs d'Amérique* (Montreal: Editions Parti pris, 1968). If "peoples hardly emerged from the Stone Age" can have independence, surely "a people issued from the great French civilization" can. Frank L. Wilson, "French-Canadian Separatism," *Western Political Quarterly* 20 (Mar. 1967): 116–31, at 121, quoting a separatist leader.

for groups and movements to become part of a broad and respectable current, learning from each other and in so doing becoming similar in their claims and aspirations. The profusion of ethnic claims is in fact expressed in a distinctly parsimonious common rhetoric. Its terminology is the language of competition and equality, a remarkably individualistic idiom for claims that are advanced on a collective basis. The ubiquity of the phenomenon provides the basis for comparative analysis, for ethnic conflict has common features.

THE LONG REACH
OF ETHNIC AFFILIATIONS

If few states have been impervious to ethnic divisions, the new states of Asia, Africa, the Middle East, and the Caribbean have been particularly susceptible. The importance of ethnicity in these states is indicated by the results of sample surveys. Open-ended questions that ask "Who are you?" "What is your nationality?" or "What is your country?" overwhelmingly elicit ethnic responses, even when the "set" before the question is fixed on "national" rather than ethnic identity.[5] Children as well as adults respond in these terms; in a Philippine study, children as young as six were aware of their ethnic identity and by the age of ten provided strongly ethnic responses.[6] Questions about appropriate political behavior also elicit responses cast in ethnic terms, responses sometimes startlingly ethnocentric. Thus, in the Philippines, it is "better" to vote for someone "from your own home region."[7] In Nigeria, a person's loyalty "should be to his region rather than to his country," and a child "should

5. Otto Klineberg and Marisa Zavalloni, *Nationalism and Tribalism Among African Students* (Paris and The Hague: Mouton, 1969), 131; Howard Schuman, "Social Change and the Validity of Regional Stereotypes in East Pakistan," *Sociometry* 29 (Dec. 1966): 428–40, at 429–30; Filipinas Foundation, *An Anatomy of Philippine Muslim Affairs* (n.p., mimeo., 1971), 116; Maria Fe Jamias, Renato Y. Pablo, and Donald M. Taylor, "Ethnic Awareness in Filipino Children," *Journal of Social Psychology* 83 (Apr. 1971): 157–64, at 162–63; Donald L. Horowitz, unpublished data from Guyana and Trinidad, 1965, on file with the author. Cf. Marshall H. Segall, Martin Doornbos, and Clive Davis, *Political Identity: A Case Study from Uganda* (Syracuse: Maxwell School of Citizenship and Public Affairs, Eastern Africa monograph 24, 1976), 87–109, 166 n.1.
6. Jamias, Pablo, and Taylor, "Ethnic Awareness in Filipino Children," 164.
7. Rodolfo A. Bulatao, *Ethnic Attitudes in Five Philippine Cities* (Quezon City: Univ. of the Philippines Social Research Laboratory, 1973), 39. Likewise, a clear majority of Ashanti respondents in Ghana believe in the appropriateness of some form of Ashanti-based political organization. Minion K. C. Morrison, *Ethnicity and Political Integration: The Case of Ashanti Ghana* (Syracuse: Maxwell School of Citizenship and Public Affairs, African Series, no. 38, 1982), 86.

be taught to protect the welfare of his own people and let other tribal groups look out for themselves."[8] In Ghana, many people expect favorable treatment at the hands of bureaucrats belonging to their own ethnic group and unfavorable treatment at the hands of bureaucrats belonging to other ethnic groups.[9] In one country after another, other ethnic groups are described in unflattering or disparaging terms.[10] In general, ethnic identity is strongly felt, behavior based on ethnicity is normatively sanctioned, and ethnicity is often accompanied by hostility toward outgroups.

Nowhere, of course, is politics simply reducible to the common denominator of ethnic ties. Even in the most severely divided society, there are also other issues. Nor do ethnic affiliations govern behavior in all situations. If they did, the bonds across ethnic lines that make a multiethnic society possible could not develop. Everywhere there exist buyers and sellers, officials and citizens, co-workers, and members of professions; all of these roles are to some degree independent of the ethnic origin of their incumbents.

The degree of this independence, however, varies widely. It tends to be smallest in those societies that are most riven. Although ethnic affiliations can be compartmentalized—that is, their relevance can be limited to some spheres and contexts—there is nonetheless a tendency to seepage. In deeply divided societies, strong ethnic allegiances permeate organizations, activities, and roles to which they are formally unrelated. The permeative character of ethnic affiliations, by infusing so many sectors

8. *New York Times*, Monthly Supplement (Mar. 1967), reporting on a survey of 600 Northern Nigerians, age seventeen, 74 percent of whom agreed with the first quoted statement and 69 percent of whom agreed with the second.

9. Robert M. Price, "The Pattern of Ethnicity in Ghana: A Research Note," *Journal of Modern African Studies* 11 (Sept. 1973): 470–75.

10. See, e.g., Marilynn B. Brewer and Donald T. Campbell, *Ethnocentrism and Intergroup Attitudes: East African Evidence* (New York: John Wiley, 1976); Klineberg and Zavalloni, *Nationalism and Tribalism Among African Students*, 140–64; Bulatao, *Ethnic Attitudes in Five Philippine Cities*, 56–68; Vaughn F. Bishop, "Language Acquisition and Value Change in the Kano Urban Area," in John N. Paden, ed., *Values, Identities, and National Integration: Empirical Research in Africa* (Evanston: Northwestern Univ. Press, 1980), 188; Brian M. du Toit, "Ethnicity, Neighborliness, and Friendship Among Urban Africans in South Africa," in du Toit, ed., *Ethnicity in Modern Africa* (Boulder, Colo.: Westview Press, 1978), 143–74; A. F. A. Husain and A. Farouk, *Social Integration of Industrial Workers in Khulna* (Dacca: Univ. of Dacca, 1963), 46–49; Peter Osei-Kwame and Paul P. W. Achola, "A New Conceptual Model for the Study of Political Integration in Africa," *Journal of Developing Areas* 15 (July 1981): 585–604, at 596–98; Roberta E. Mapp, "Cross-National Dimensions of Ethnocentrism," *Canadian Journal of African Studies* 6 (Winter 1972): 73–96; George Henry Weightman, "A Study of Prejudice in a Personalistic Society," *Asian Studies* (Manila) 11 (Apr. 1964): 87–101.

social life, imparts a pervasive quality to ethnic conflict and raises sharply the stakes of ethnic politics.

The permeative propensities of ethnic affiliations in divided societies are easily demonstrated. In severely divided societies, ethnicity finds its way into a myriad of issues: development plans, educational controversies, trade union affairs, land policy, business policy, tax policy. Characteristically, issues that elsewhere would be relegated to the category of routine administration assume a central place on the political agenda of ethnically divided societies. Hydroelectric power and logging have been bones of violent ethnic contention in the Philippines. The status of private schools has been an ethnic issue in Malaysia and Tanzania. In Guyana, an upsurge of ethnic tension between East Indians and Africans brought demands for segregated field gangs on sugar estates. Malays in Thailand have opposed the settlement of Thai Buddhists in the interior of Southern Thailand. Kurds in Iraq have opposed the settlement of Arabs in their areas. Ceylon Tamils have opposed the settlement of Sinhalese in the East of Sri Lanka, and the Mahaweli irrigation scheme, supported by international aid donors, is controversial because it is supposed that the scheme will attract Sinhalese colonists. In Ethiopia, a major effect of a land reform was to take land away from Amhara and distribute it to Galla, and for a time the revolution was suspected of being a Galla plot.[11] While Nigeria was under civilian rule in the early 1960s, ethnicity entered into court-martial practice. Army officers accused of misappropriating funds could only be tried if men of other ethnic groups were also standing trial.[12] These examples lend support to the frequently heard refrain in divided societies that almost any issue, any phenomenon, can suddenly "turn ethnic" or "turn communal."

The salience of ethnicity is reflected, too, in the segmented organizational structure of ethnically divided societies. This applies to the structure of economic organization, as it does to political organization.

Capital and labor are often organized on ethnic lines. Fukienese entrepreneurs in Hong Kong, Malayalee clerks in Bombay, and Ibo plantation laborers in Equatorial Guinea were all mobilized into their economic activity on the basis of ethnic affinity. Consequently, it comes as no surprise that, in Malaysia, for example, there are separate Malay Chambers of Commerce and Chinese Chambers of Commerce or that, in sev-

11. Blair Thomson, *Ethiopia: A Diary of the Revolution* (London: Robson Books, 1975), 130–31.
12. J. M. Lee, *African Armies and Civil Order* (New York: Praeger, 1969), 78.

eral countries, cooperative societies are usually controlled by one or another ethnic group; if they are not, internal tensions may soon make them so.[13] Trade unions are also commonly monoethnic, especially if an occupation or craft is dominated by a single group. In Fiji, the mineworkers' union is mainly Fijian; the canegrowers' federation, mainly Indian; and there are two teachers' unions, one for each group.[14] Unions that start out multiethnic are subject to schism along ethnic lines. In Kenya, waterfront workers from Coastal ethnic groups left the Luo-led Dockworkers' Union to form their own union; in Zimbabwe, where a railwaymen's union was led by a Ndebele, branches representing Shona workers assumed their dues were "lining Ndebele pockets in Bulawayo, and they rebelled and broke away."[15] In Jos, Northern Nigeria, the first miners' unions were Ibo-dominated. Later, Hausa and Birom workers formed separate unions corresponding to the occupations in which each group was clustered and paralleling the political party preferences of each group.[16]

As this also suggests, organizational pluralism is strongly reflected in party systems. In name or in fact, ethnically based parties have grown up, often with perfectly irreconcilable aims. By the time of independence, there were essentially Ibo, Yoruba, and Hausa-dominated parties in Nigeria, East Indian and Creole parties in Guyana and Trinidad, Sinhalese and Tamil parties in Sri Lanka, Malay and Chinese parties in Malaysia. Perhaps more revealing of the permeative character of ethnic affiliations is the tendency of avowedly nonethnic parties to be captured by one or another ethnic constituency. The tendency affects parties all along the political spectrum. The Communist Party has been dominated by Ansaris in the Sudan, by Sinhalese in Sri Lanka, by Javanese in Indonesia, by Greeks in Cyprus, and by Chinese in Malaysia. In various Indian

13. See, e.g., R. S. Milne, "Guyana's Co-Operative Republic" (unpublished paper, Univ. of British Columbia, n.d.), 15, 22–23, pointing out that cooperatives are dominated by Afro-Guyanese. In Tanzania, rural cooperative societies were often torn apart by ethnic factions competing for benefits. The "villagization" policy of the government was adopted, in part, to eliminate this ethnic competition. Interview, Dar es Salaam, Jan. 1980.

14. R. S. Milne, *Politics in Ethnically Bipolar States: Guyana, Malaysia, Fiji* (Vancouver: Univ. of British Columbia Press, 1981), 129–30.

15. Richard Stren, "Factional Politics and Central Control in Mombasa, 1960–1969," *Canadian Journal of African Studies* 4 (Winter 1970): 33–56, at 40–41; Arthur Turner, "The Growth of Railway Unionism in the Rhodesias, 1944–55," in Richard Sandbrook and Robin Cohen, eds., *The Development of an African Working Class* (London: Longman Group, 1975), 85.

16. James Pagano, "Patterns of Ethnic Conflict in African Trade Unions" (unpublished paper, Johns Hopkins Univ. School of Advanced International Studies, Nov. 27, 1979).

states, the Communists have appealed to various ethnic constituencies. In Punjab, the Communists have been a party of Sikhs, especially of the prosperous Jat caste; in Kerala, a party of the poorer Ezhava; in Assam, a party of Bengalis; and in Tripura, alternately a party of indigenous hill people and later of Bengali migrants, but never of both.[17] The Socialists have had the same experience. When there was party competition in Guinea, the Socialists were Fulani; in the Ivory Coast, they were Bété; and in Congo (Brazzaville), they were Mbochi.[18] All of these parties were affiliated with the French Socialists, but the local ethnic context was crucial in determining the limited scope of their support. And so it has been for Muslim political parties. Although Pakistan and Indonesia are overwhelmingly Muslim countries, support for Muslim parties has been ethnically differentiated, strongest among Urdu-speakers in Pakistan and among certain Sumatran groups in Indonesia.[19] Ethnic affinities constitute an obvious organizational link in divided societies. By the same token, ethnic antipathies dictate that a party identified with one ethnic group repels members of antagonistic groups, who are then attracted to other parties.

Revolts and insurgencies, although ostensibly inspired by class ideology, have sometimes derived their impetus from ethnic aspirations and apprehensions instead. The independence movement in Guinea-Bissau was a movement of Balante, with no appreciable support among the Fula. The core of Mozambique's anti-colonial army was recruited from the Makonde in the North of the country, while the political leadership of the movement came heavily from the Shangana of the South. The Angolan movement was split three ways, among the Kumbundu of the Center, who gained power, and the Bakongo of the North and Ovambo of the South, who continued their guerrilla fighting after independence. In Namibia, SWAPO is also a movement of Ovambo, and in Zimbabwe

17. Paul R. Brass, *Language, Religion and Politics in North India* (New York: Cambridge Univ. Press, 1974), 389–92; Lloyd I. Rudolph and Susanne Hoeber Rudolph, *The Modernity of Tradition: Political Development in India* (Chicago: Univ. of Chicago Press, 1967), 72 n.14; M. S. Prabhakar, "The 'Bongal' Bogey," *Economic and Political Weekly* (Bombay), Oct. 21, 1972, pp. 2140–42; *Far Eastern Economic Review* (Hong Kong), Apr. 10, 1981, p. 36. Cf. Marcus F. Franda, "Communism and Regional Politics in East Bengal," *Asian Survey* 10 (July 1970): 588–606, at 591–96.

18. Ruth Schachter Morgenthau, *Political Parties in French-Speaking West Africa* (New York: Oxford Univ. Press, 1964), 181; Virginia Thompson and Richard Adloff, *The Emerging States of French Equatorial Africa* (Stanford: Stanford Univ. Press, 1960), 485.

19. Dilip Mukerjee, "Pakistan's Growing Pains," *Times of India*, July 17, 1972; J. D. Legge, *Sukarno: A Political Biography* (New York: Praeger, 1972), 267. See also Stephen A. Douglas, *Political Socialization and Student Activism in Indonesia* (Urbana: Univ. of Illinois Press, 1970), 39, 183; Edward M. Bruner, *The Expression of Ethnicity in Indonesia* (New York: The Asian Society, SEADAG Papers, mimeo., 1972), 11.

the bulk of Robert Mugabe's support is from the Shona majority, while most of Joshua Nkomo's is from the Ndebele minority.[20] In Laos, the Pathet Lao relied heavily on the hostility of hill tribes to the Mekong Lao,[21] and the Cham Muslims of Cambodia gave only equivocal support to the Khmer Rouge. The organization and behavior of the rebellious *Union des populations du Cameroun* in the late 1950s were greatly influenced by the "widely differing tribal cultures and structures" of its main participants, the Bassa and the Bamiléké.[22] In composition, spirit, and leadership, the Communist insurrection in Malaysia was a Chinese movement,[23] just as the Huk rebellion in the Philippines was confined to the Pampangan ethnic group of Central Luzon.[24] The Kwilu revolt in Zaire possessed, in addition to its millenarian social objectives, an element of ethnic deprivation.[25] Close analysis of the 1971 insurgency in Sri Lanka reveals significant ethnic elements. Though fighting was extensive, no major incidents occurred in the Tamil areas of the North and East, for few Tamils participated. Nor did Sinhalese Christians participate in proportion to their numbers, since the revolt was almost entirely conducted by Sinhalese Buddhists. The Karava caste, disproportionately Christian, was likewise underrepresented, but a powerful rebel leader was Karava, and it seems "he made rather subtle attempts to build up a leadership based on loyalty to the Karava caste."[26] The participants in

20. See, e.g., *Africa Research Bulletin*, May 15, 1976, p. 3999. There are, in addition, pertinent subethnic differences. The Karanga subgroup, a majority of the Shona, is most influential in Mugabe's party, driving some of the Zezuru subgroup to align with Nkomo's heavily Ndebele party.

21. Charles W. Anderson, Fred R. von der Mehden, and Crawford Young, *Issues of Political Development*, 2d ed. (Englewood Cliffs, N.J.: Prentice-Hall, 1974), 72. Cf. *Far Eastern Economic Review*, May 27, 1977, p. 27.

22. Willard Johnson, "The *Union des populations du Cameroun* in Rebellion: The Integrative Backlash of Insurgency," in Robert I. Rotberg and Ali A. Mazrui, eds., *Power and Protest in Black Africa* (New York: Oxford Univ. Press, 1970), 679.

23. See Lucian W. Pye, *Guerrilla Communism in Malaya* (Princeton: Princeton Univ. Press, 1956).

24. Edward J. Mitchell, "Some Econometrics of the Huk Rebellion," *American Political Science Review* 62 (Dec. 1969): 1159–71. For a similar pattern on Samar Island, see *Far Eastern Economic Review*, Aug. 11, 1978, p. 23.

25. Renée C. Fox, Willy de Craemer, and Jean-Marie Ribeaucourt, "The Second Independence: A Case Study of the Kwilu Rebellion in the Congo," *Comparative Studies in Society and History* 8 (Oct. 1965): 78–109; Crawford Young, *Politics in the Congo* (Princeton: Princeton Univ. Press, 1965), 577.

26. "Politicus," "The April Revolt in Ceylon," *Asian Survey* 12 (Mar. 1972): 259–74, at 268. See also Gananath Obeyesekere, "Some Comments on the Social Backgrounds of the April 1971 Insurgency in Sri Lanka (Ceylon)" (unpublished paper presented at the 1973 annual meeting of the Association for Asian Studies), 8–12. Six months before the revolt, the rebel organization had made a demand for the exclusion of 150 Tamil students admitted to study engineering at the University of Ceylon. *Washington Post*, May 23, 1971.

the Azahari revolt in Brunei (the aim of which was to oppose the creation of Malaysia and to create instead a larger Brunei) were predominantly Coastal Kedayans: "In fact the whole area covered by the 1962 rebellion can be placed on the map and exactly fitted in with the distribution of Kedayans."[27] The particularism of all these movements is at once a source of organizational cohesion and an important limitation on their ability to generalize their support.

In societies where ethnicity suffuses organizational life, virtually all political events have ethnic consequences. Where parties break along ethnic lines, elections are divisive. Where armed forces are ethnically fragmented, military coups, ostensibly to quell disorder or to end corruption, may be made to secure the power of some ethnic groups at the expense of others. Whole systems of economic relations can crystallize around opportunities afforded and disabilities imposed by government policy on particular ethnic groups. In Fiji, for example, Indians, about half the population, are not permitted to own land. Consequently, they must lease agricultural land from Fijians. "The growing pressure on the better leases meant that some of these were sub-let at very high rents, or were transferred under the burden of premiums which forced the incoming tenant to over-farm the land in order to get his money back. Hence, the system brought indebtedness and bad agriculture."[28] In such societies, even despotism assumes an unmistakably ethnic form. When Macias Nguena Biyogo of Equatorial Guinea began a reign of terror that resulted in the flight of nearly half the population, the violence, like that of Idi Amin in Uganda and Jean-Bédel Bokassa in the Central African Republic, was directed by a militia drawn from his own ethnic group, and the victims were ethnically defined.[29]

In divided societies, ethnic conflict is at the center of politics. Ethnic divisions pose challenges to the cohesion of states and sometimes to peaceful relations among states. Ethnic conflict strains the bonds that sustain civility and is often at the root of violence that results in looting, death, homelessness, and the flight of large numbers of people. In divided societies, ethnic affiliations are powerful, permeative, passionate, and pervasive.

27. Tom Harrisson, *Background to a Revolt: Brunei and the Surrounding Territory* (pamphlet; n.p. [Brunei?], 1963), 21.
28. Adrian C. Mayer, *Indians in Fiji* (London: Oxford Univ. Press, 1963), 62.
29. Randall Fegley, "Minority Oppression in Equatorial Guinea," in Georgina Ashworth, ed., *World Minorities*, vol. 2 (Sunbury, England: Quartermaine House, 1978), 80–84.

THE CASE FOR
COMPARATIVE ANALYSIS

The increasing prominence of ethnic loyalties is a development for which neither statesmen nor social scientists were adequately prepared. Here and there, as the colonialists departed the new states, constitution-makers accorded protections to minorities, and in one or two notable cases concluded that the only adequate protection was political separation. But generally such proposals were rejected on the ground that they would foster rather than heal enmities. Rarely was it anticipated that the ethnic cleavage might become a principal line of political division, one that could preempt other cleavages. Especially after the experience of World War II, it was thought that the industrialized countries had outgrown political affiliation based on ethnicity, and anti-colonial movements elsewhere had created an appearance of unity that was slow to dissipate even after independence was won. When the force of ethnic affiliations was acknowledged, ethnic conflict was often treated as if it were a manifestation of something else: the persistence of traditionalism, the stresses of modernization, or class conflict masquerading in the guise of ethnic identity.

Part of the explanation for the many shortcomings in our understanding of ethnicity is the episodic character of ethnic conflict itself. It comes and goes, suddenly shattering periods of apparent tranquility. The suddenness of the phenomenon helps explain the lag in understanding it. As scholarship is reactive, the spilling of ink awaits the spilling of blood.

Yet, some share of the burden must also rest with what Walker Connor has delicately called "the predispositions of the analyst."[30] The study of ethnic conflict has often been a grudging concession to something distasteful, largely because, especially in the West, ethnic affiliations have been in disrepute, for deep ideological reasons I shall elaborate at a later point. Until recently, the field of ethnic relations has been a backwater of the social sciences, and the first response to the rising tide of ethnic conflict was to treat it as an epiphenomenon.

The need for comparative analysis is compelling, not merely because events have overtaken our ability to understand them—though that is reason enough—and not merely because ethnic conflict has been viewed through the lenses of categories that tend to blur the phenomenon by

---

30. "Nation-Building or Nation-Destroying?" *World Politics* 24 (Apr. 1972): 319–55, at 354.

treating it as part of something else. It is compelling on quite independent practical and intellectual grounds.

In practical terms, the need for policy to ameliorate ethnic conflict has come close on the heels of the need for theory to explain it and to elaborate its many patterns. Unfortunately, models of integration have tended to precede concepts of conflict, and policy prescriptions have been dispensed without regard for the character of the ailment they were designed to treat. Everything, from partition to income redistribution and the rectification of economic imbalances among the ethnic groups, has been proposed to resolve ethnic conflict. Sometimes these remedies have been put forward as academic exercises, sometimes as serious advice to policymakers.

Many of the proposals have a distinctly rationalistic and materialistic bias. For example, it has been argued that, to solve ethnic problems, policymakers should "organize rewards in such a way that everyone will have expectations of increasing gains."[31] I leave to one side the sheer difficulty in any society of organizing rewards so that everyone can expect increasing gains, the more so if these are to be material rewards in an economy of scarcity or in a growing economy that, because of rapid change, inflicts losses as well as gains on some sectors of the population.[32] For present purposes, the important point is the assumption that ethnic conflict is motivated by rational calculations of gain. Needless to say, the proposal will at best be utterly without effect—and at worst may exacerbate what it aims to heal—if the conflict is not motivated by such calculations, or if the rewards sought lie in the area of psychic gratification, or if the calculations of the participants are so relative that no benefit is considered a gain unless it comes at the expense of an opponent.

In intellectual terms, ethnic relations has been a field rife with dogma and yet lacking in agreement on first principles. There has been, for example, a common failure to distinguish between types of ethnic relationships. In study after study, it has been assumed that ethnic relations are necessarily relations between superiors and subordinates. Schooled in slavery and Jim Crow, "a great many American sociologists, immured in their own society, have developed a sort of pathos of minorities as

---

31. This suggestion belongs to Karl Deutsch, who made it in a faculty seminar at Harvard University in 1970.
32. See Mancur Olson, Jr., "Rapid Growth as a Destabilizing Force," *Journal of Economic History* 23 (Dec. 1963): 529–52.

'victims,' conceptualizing the relations between subordinate and dominant groups in such a way that the former are invariably oppressed and
exploited."[33] In fact, many ethnic groups *are* enmeshed in a system of
subordination. But the relations of many other ethnic groups—on a
global scale, most ethnic groups—are not accurately described as supe-
rior-subordinate relations. The dogma of the inevitability of ethnic subordination has clouded out a significant set of relationships. Worse still,
cross-national studies of conflict based on the premise of subordination
usually involve unwitting comparison of like and unlike cases.

The comparable dogma of the supremacy of social class asserts that
common class interests will (or, at any rate, should) overtake ethnic
interests.[34] On the other hand, it is asserted that the competition for
scarce values and material goods is exactly what propels people to see
themselves as members of distinct ethnic groups, whose interests conflict
with those of other ethnic groups.[35] Even if we grant *arguendo* that
competition for scarce resources is what divides groups, this hardly explains why they are led to perceive and organize themselves along ethnic
lines, rather than some other lines, such as social class. Theories of ethnic
conflict need to specify what the groups are fighting over—which is not
as obvious as it seems—and why ethnic lines of conflict are so important.

It is also argued that one or another factor is the key element in ethnic
conflict—that a common religion or a common language is what "knits
people together"[36] and that its absence is what pulls them apart. This,
despite the presence of ethnic conflict in countries where there is a common language or religion. Likewise, it is frequently asserted and (less
frequently) denied that there is something especially atavistic or at least
distinctive about conflicts founded on color differences. Thus, on the one
hand, it is argued that "inter-racial strife" is not "just another form of
inter-ethnic conflict," for "qualitative differences distinguish race and
ethnicity."[37] On the other hand, while it is granted that "so-called 'racial'

33. R. A. Schermerhorn, *Comparative Ethnic Relations* (New York: Random House,
1970), 8.
34. See, e.g., Mayer, *Indians in Fiji*, 130.
35. R. William Liddle, "Ethnicity and Political Organization: Three East Sumatran
Cases," in Claire Holt, ed., *Culture and Politics in Indonesia* (Ithaca: Cornell Univ. Press,
1972), 172; cf. Malcolm Cross, "Colonialism and Ethnicity: A Theory and a Comparative
Case Study," *Ethnic and Racial Studies* 1 (Jan. 1978): 35–59.
36. Hugh Tinker, *India and Pakistan: A Political Analysis* , rev. ed. (New York: Praeger, 1968), 125.
37. Onkar S. Marwah and James H. Mittelman, "Alien Pariahs: Uganda's Asians and
Bangladesh's Biharis" (unpublished paper presented at the 1975 annual meeting of the
African Studies Association), 4.

differences make populations so divided more physically recognizable," this, it is urged, "does not necessarily make the politics of ethnic conflict, in which skin color adds to other differences, analytically distinct from those in which it does not." Any conflict can be described by its participants as "racial," whether or not physical differences divide the groups. Unless it can be shown that calling a conflict racial "adds to its intensity, the distinction should be dropped altogether."[38] And, as if this 180-degree difference were not enough, it is sometimes contended that "prejudice" arises from "assumed belief dissimilarity," and so "distinctions among the groups based on belief systems . . . are all more elemental than the distinction based on race (skin color)."[39] Hence, even the scope of the subject matter is at issue, for to say that one kind of conflict is more elemental than or qualitatively different from another is also to question whether the two are properly considered together or whether they are different phenomena.

As these debates make clear, the problem of comparability in cross-national studies of ethnic conflict is likely to be substantial. Giovanni Sartori's characterization of the field of party politics fits ethnic politics as well: the more we know, "the more we are faced with a proliferation of threads, and the less we seem capable of pulling them together."[40] What we need is not more data but what Sartori aptly calls "data containers," categories that "own sufficient discriminating power."[41] To categorize, to synthesize, and to discriminate require at the threshold clear criteria for the scope of the inquiry. The class of cases needs careful delimitation, for the simple reason that comparison requires comparability. Delimitation is a task that entails substantive as well as prudential judgment.

THE SCOPE OF THE COMPARISON

All comparative studies must face at the outset a vexing question: the appropriate scope of comparison. It is a dilemma without a wholly satisfying answer. To sweep broadly risks including like and unlike cases,

38. Richard Ned Lebow, "Communal Conflict," *Journal of International Affairs* 27 (Spring–Summer 1973): 122–25.
39. Russell A. Jones and Richard D. Ashmore, "The Structure of Intergroup Perception: Categories and Dimensions in Views of Ethnic Groups and Adjectives Used in Stereotype Research," *Journal of Personality and Social Psychology* 25 (Mar. 1973): 428–38, at 438.
40. *Parties and Party Systems*, vol. 1 (Cambridge: Cambridge Univ. Press, 1976), 66.
41. "Concept Misformation in Comparative Politics," *American Political Science Review* 64 (Dec. 1970): 1033–53, at 1039.

entangling the analysis in unnecessary complexity, and in the end probably diluting the power of the explanations that emerge.[42] To slice narrowly risks leaving little to compare; a small number of observations will probably not yield answers to a large number of questions.[43] Comparability does not imply perfect identity or even very close similarity, but rather a restricted range of difference.

Accordingly, I have taken a judicious first cut, designed to pare away some of the grossest differences among cases. The materials in this book are drawn from cases that possess certain baseline characteristics in common.

First, the states with which we are concerned all encompass severely divided societies in Asia, Africa, and the Caribbean. With few exceptions, they are states that received their independence during or after World War II.

Second, the ethnic groups in conflict do not stand in a hierarchical or ranked relationship to each other. Rather, they are parallel or unranked groups, divided by a vertical cleavage. This excludes, for example, relations between Hutu and Tutsi in Rwanda and Burundi, where ethnic conflict has revolved around systems of ethnic stratification; but it includes relations among such groups as Hausa, Ibo, and Yoruba in Nigeria, Sinhalese and Tamils in Sri Lanka, and Malays, Chinese, and Indians in Malaysia.

Third, the groups are relatively large and therefore interact at the center of politics rather than in isolated local pockets. Tanzania, where most groups are small and scattered, is generally excluded, whereas Nigeria, Sri Lanka, and Malaysia, with major groups meeting at the center, are included.[44]

Fourth, the groups are defined by ascriptive differences, whether the indicium of group identity is color, appearance, language, religion, some

42. Ibid., 1050–52.
43. As Arend Lijphart points out, as soon as the first few distinctions among cases are made, the number of cases becomes "too small to permit systematic control . . . ." The difficulty is, as Lijphart calls it, "many variables, small N." "Comparative Politics and the Comparative Method," *American Political Science Review* 65 (Sept. 1971): 682–93, at 684.
44. Included also are certain ethnically divided Indian states, such as Punjab and Assam. The interactions of large ethnic groups at the state level of politics in India resemble the interactions of groups at the center elsewhere. The point that in many respects Indian states comprise political systems comparable to national political systems elsewhere is made in Myron Weiner's introduction to his edited volume, *State Politics in India* (Princeton: Princeton Univ. Press, 1968).

other indicator of common origin, or some combination thereof. This is an inclusive conception of ethnicity.

THE CLASS OF STATES

Limiting the study to the developing countries has a number of practical advantages. With few exceptions, these countries share a common experience of colonialism and, in the post-colonial period, have had to cope with similar problems of building new institutions and relating component ethnic groups to them. Whereas politics in the West antedates the present period of ethnic conflict and political institutions have a certain autonomy and resilience, the same is less true in the new states, where serious conflict preceded the firm establishment of ways of coping with problems. The commonality of their political experience is suggested by the frequency across boundaries of such phenomena as military rule. Not least important, the problems of post-colonial politics have been treated in a large and still-growing literature on the new states, a literature with a common vocabulary and one that can readily be tapped when necessary.

There is a more important conceptual reason for confining a study to Asia, Africa, and the Caribbean. Ethnic conflict is a problem in Western Europe and North America, too, but there are three important differences that impart to ethnicity in the West a generally less urgent character.

In the first place, there is an important overarching level of identity in the West. A survey of Switzerland that tapped levels of identity found that, in spite of ethnic differences, about half of all respondents identified themselves as Swiss.[45] Only 25 percent of French Basques surveyed called themselves Basques; 20 percent called themselves French, and the remaining 55 percent responded with Basque-French or French-Basque.[46] In the Netherlands, only 11 percent of voters who were asked what role their legislators should play responded that legislators should protect the interests of their group, whereas 30 percent said legislators should look after the interests of the Dutch people as a whole.[47] Survey

45. Henry H. Kerr, Jr., *Switzerland: Social Cleavages and Partisan Conflict* (Beverly Hills: Sage Professional Papers, Contemporary Political Sociology Series, no. 06–002, 1974), 21. The Swiss identity figure is even higher among youth. Ibid., 23.

46. James E. Jacob, "Two Types of Ethnic Militancy in France" (unpublished paper presented at the 1978 annual meeting of the International Studies Association).

47. Arend Lijphart, *The Politics of Accommodation: Pluralism and Democracy in the Netherlands* (Berkeley and Los Angeles: Univ. of California Press, 1968), 154.

data from Austria likewise show a growing sense of Austrian national-ism.[48] As we have already seen, these are not findings that could be obtained in Guyana, Nigeria, or Malaysia. When David H. Marlowe declares that "there is no such thing as a 'Burmese' since there is no structural incorporation of the separate entities—Burmans, Kachins, Karen, Chin, and so forth,"[49] we are not surprised, but a comparable declaration even for ethnically divided Belgium would hardly go unchallenged. Supraethnic identities tend to have a salience in the West that they do not generally have in Asia and Africa.

Second, there is not only an overarching layer of identity; there are also alternative identities at the same level. Belgium, for all its Fleming-Walloon differences, has religious and class differences that compete for attention with ethnic differences. Switzerland has linguistic, class, religious, and cantonal differences. Canada has class, regional, and religious conflicts in addition to Anglophone-Francophone conflict. The differences show up in party organization, voting behavior, and the structure of divisive issues. In multiethnic societies of Asia, Africa, and the Caribbean, wherever free elections prevail, parties tend to be organized along ethnic lines; in Western Europe and North America, they do not. In Belgium, for instance, the three main parties long bridged the Flemish-Walloon cleavage, and one of them, the Liberal Party, with its distinctly nonethnic perspective, actually increased in support as ethnic issues gained in prominence. Ethnic issues have never wholly preempted others in Belgium. Rather, a "triple-issue spectrum"—language, class, and religion—characterizes political debate, with each issue changing the alignment of forces and to some extent neutralizing the others.[50] Consistent with the Belgian pattern, a study in Switzerland shows that language is no stronger a predictor of party preference than is class, though it is somewhat stronger than is religion.[51] Ethnicity in the West typically does not displace all other forms of group difference.

48. William T. Bluhm, *Building an Austrian Nation* (New Haven: Yale Univ. Press, 1973), chap. 8.
49. "In the Mosaic: The Cognitive and Structural Aspects of Karen-Other Relationships," in Charles F. Keyes, ed., *Ethnic Adaptation and Identity: The Karen on the Thai Frontier with Burma* (Philadelphia: Institute for the Study of Human Issues, 1979), 203.
50. George A. Kelly, "Belgium: New Nationalism in an Old World" (unpublished paper, n.d.), 9. For a comparable phenomenon in the Netherlands, see Lijphart, *The Politics of Accommodation*, 118.
51. Kerr, *Switzerland*, 13. Cf. Arend Lijphart, "Religious vs. Linguistic vs. Class Voting: The 'Crucial Experiment' of Comparing Belgium, Canada, South Africa, and Switzerland," *American Political Science Review* 73 (June 1979): 442–58.

Underlying this multifaceted configuration of cleavages are a number of historical developments unique to the Western world. The Reformation gave rise to Protestant-Catholic cleavages that in most linguistically divided countries did not coincide with linguistic cleavages. The Enlightenment laid the foundation for a secular reaction to religious parties of any kind. And the Industrial Revolution created working classes of all groups with a political agenda of yet another sort. The moving forces of European history can be described broadly in terms of religion, nationalism, and class. No such description would be apt for Asia and Africa. The residue of these developments in the West is a complex pattern of alternating issues that prevents preemption by ethnic affiliation.

Third, there is inferential evidence that the intensity of ethnic conflict is somewhat lower in the West than in Asia and Africa. In Switzerland, survey data show that the French and Italian minorities are actually *more* satisfied with Swiss government and politics than is the German-speaking majority.[52] In Austrian politics since 1966, there has been a decline in the rigidity and predictability of party allegiances and a concomitant increase in the number of floating voters.[53] Such phenomena are incompatible with strong ascriptive loyalties. Where ethnically based parties have any degree of electoral success in the West, it tends to be attributable to their willingness to reach out beyond ethnic issues.[54] Patterns of violence point in the same direction. Ethnic violence in the West nearly always takes the form of terrorism, as in Northern Ireland or the Basque country; in the non-West, ethnic riots, directed against the persons and property of members of other ethnic groups, and usually accompanied by mutilations, are far more common.[55] What such riots signify is the intensity of mass ethnic sentiment.[56]

52. Harold E. Glass, "Ethnic Diversity, Elite Accommodation and Federalism in Switzerland," *Publius* 7 (Fall 1977): 31–48, at 38.

53. Bluhm, *Building an Austrian Nation*, 97, 100. Compare Chapter 7, below.

54. French Basque politicians, appealing solely to Basque sentiment, have achieved little popular support, whereas Occitanian politicians, recognizing the weakness of Occitanian identity, have turned to ecologists and similar dissenting movements to bolster their position. Jacob, "Two Types of Ethnic Militancy in France." In a survey of activists of the Scottish National Party, 62 percent reported that purely Scottish issues were insufficient by themselves to have caused the respondents to join the party. John E. Schwarz, "The Scottish National Party: Nonviolent Separatism and Theories of Violence," *World Politics* 22 (Oct. 1970): 496–517, at 513–14.

55. For some examples, see Donald L. Horowitz, "Direct, Displaced, and Cumulative Ethnic Aggression," *Comparative Politics* 6 (Oct. 1973): 1–16; Horowitz, "Racial Violence in the United States," in Nathan Glazer and Ken Young, eds., *Ethnic Pluralism and Public Policy: Achieving Equality in the United States and Britain* (London: Heinemann, 1983), 187–211.

56. Erik Allardt makes the related point that, in the West, ethnic claims are directed

In the divided societies of the West, then, there is generally a more complex pattern of group loyalties than in Asia and Africa. Ethnic loyalties are less exhaustive, for they compete with an array of other politically important loyalties, reflected in mixed party systems and complex issue configurations. The level of ethnic hostility has generally not been so great as to threaten the state itself. To these generalizations, there are prominent exceptions—notably, Northern Ireland—but the overall thrust of the distinctions is sufficiently clear to justify an effort to deal with Asian and African ethnic conflict separately. Once in a while, however, I shall break this rule by referring, for instance, to the Belgian party system or to Basque separatism, where it is useful to do so to illustrate a point or highlight a contrast.[57]

I should emphasize, however, that separating out ethnic conflict in the West is a conceptual convenience, not a conceptual imperative. It would be possible, though assuredly more difficult, to produce a cogent comparative study that embraced Afro-Asian and Western conflicts; they are members of the same family of conflict. I do not subscribe to the notion that African and Asian systems are too "fluid" to be compared fruitfully with Western systems or that the "ethnic identity of a Hutu or an Ibo" is necessarily "of such profoundly different psychological quality and social consequence" from ethnic identity in the West "that the subjective states involved are scarcely of the same order."[58] There are differences in configurations of ethnic politics, and we should not shrink from identifying them; but, as I hope to make clear, the underlying phenomenon of group identity is at bottom the same.

THE STRUCTURE OF GROUP RELATIONS

The relationship between ethnicity and class has been subject to great confusion.[59] Much of the confusion can be dispelled by recognizing a

against governments, rather than against other groups: "Instead of expressing their aggressivity directly toward other ethnic groups and toward the national majority population, the minority can approach the state, which, in terms of its own policy goals, is forced to take them seriously." "Implications of the Ethnic Revival in Modern Society" (unpublished paper, Woodrow Wilson International Center for Scholars, May 22, 1979), 29.

57. For studies of ethnicity in the West, see Uri Ra'anan, ed., *Ethnic Resurgence in Modern Democratic States* (New York: Pergamon Press, 1980); Milton J. Esman, ed., *Ethnic Conflict in the Western World* (Ithaca: Cornell Univ. Press, 1977).

58. Sartori, *Parties and Party Systems*, vol. 1, chap. 8; John Porter, "Ethnic Pluralism in Canadian Perspective," in Nathan Glazer and Daniel P. Moynihan, eds., *Ethnicity: Theory and Experience* (Cambridge: Harvard Univ. Press, 1975), 292.

59. The distinctions elaborated in the following two sections were first presented in a much more cryptic form in Donald L. Horowitz, "Three Dimensions of Ethnic Politics," *World Politics* 23 (Jan. 1971): 232–44. Copyright © 1971 by Princeton University Press, to which I am indebted for permission to use this material.

22

FIGURE I. Ranked and Unranked Ethnic Systems

Ranked Groups

Unranked Groups

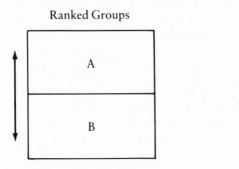

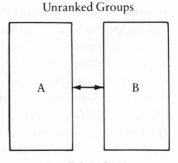

Hierarchical Ordering

Parallel Ordering

Arrows indicate the direction of ethnic conflict.

simple distinction between ranked and unranked ethnic groups. The distinction rests upon the coincidence or noncoincidence of social class with ethnic origins. Where the two coincide, it is possible to speak of *ranked* ethnic groups; where groups are cross-class, it is possible to speak of *unranked* ethnic groups. This distinction is as fundamental as it is neglected. If ethnic groups are ordered in a hierarchy, with one superordinate and another subordinate, ethnic conflict moves in one direction, but if groups are parallel, neither subordinate to the other, conflict takes a different course.

Figure 1 depicts the two systems. The diagram, which is greatly simplified, obviously represents ideal types rather than actual systems. It also assumes, for the sake of clarity, that there are only two ethnic groups, *A* and *B*, though in most systems there are more than two.

As the figure shows, stratification in ranked systems is synonymous with ethnic membership. Mobility opportunities are restricted by group identity. In such systems, political, economic, and social status tend to be cumulative, so that members of Group *B* are simultaneously subordinate in each of these ways to members of Group *A*.[60] Relations between the groups entail clearly understood conceptions of superordinate and subordinate status. Interactions partake of caste etiquette and are suffused with deference. The systems of race relations founded on African slavery in the Western Hemisphere were archetypical cases of ranked ethnic systems, but there are many others: relations between Hutu and

60. F. G. Bailey, "Closed Social Stratification in India," *European Journal of Sociology* 4 (May 1963): 107–24, at 119.

Tutsi in Burundi, between Burakumin and other members of Japanese society, between Rodiya and other Sinhalese in Sri Lanka, between Osu and other Ibo in Nigeria, to name just a few.

In unranked systems, on the other hand, parallel ethnic groups coexist, each group internally stratified. Unlike ranked ethnic groups, which are ascriptively defined components of a single society, parallel groups are themselves incipient whole societies and indeed may formerly have constituted more or less autonomous whole societies.[61] Language suggests this: parallel groups in the Netherlands are aptly described as separate "pillars" (*zuilen*) and in Austria as "tribes" (from *Stämme*, meaning stems or tree trunks).[62] Although the question of group superiority is far from irrelevant in such a system, it is not settled. The groups are not definitively ranked in relation to each other, certainly not across the board. The term *polydomainal* has been applied to such a society.[63] The position of a group varies from one domain to another, none of them decisive in establishing superordination or subordination. Accordingly, transactions can occur across group lines without necessarily implying anything about a hierarchy of ethnic groups. In ranked systems, by contrast, roles are not merely consistent from one domain to another, but really comprise "a single role"; an actor "is never subordinate in one [domain] and superior in another."[64]

A similar distinction between ranked and unranked systems has been drawn by Max Weber. Weber uses "caste structure" to refer to hierarchically ordered groups and "ethnic coexistence" to denote parallel groups, and he notes some of the major differences:

. . . the caste structure transforms the horizontal and unconnected coexistences of ethnically segregated groups into a vertical social system of super- and subordination. Correctly formulated: a comprehensive societalization integrates the

---

61. Gerald D. Berreman draws a similar distinction: ". . . castes are ranked components in a larger society comprised of analogous components. Tribes contrast to caste in that they are relatively independent and homogeneous systems of their own." "Structure and Function of Caste Systems," in George De Vos and Hiroshi Wagatsuma, eds., *Japan's Invisible Race* (Berkeley and Los Angeles: Univ. of California Press, 1966), 287. This is not the place to enter the debate over whether caste, in the precise usage of the term, is unique to India, for there is no doubt that ranked systems exist in many countries. Here and elsewhere in the text, wherever the word *caste* appears in a quotation, it is used in a sense equivalent to ranked ethnic groups. See ibid., 275. In India, of course, there are castes that have become essentially unranked groups, as Bailey, among others, has pointed out ("Closed Social Stratification," 119). This is one reason to adhere to the ranked-unranked terminology, rather than using a word like *caste*, which is now less precise.

62. Lijphart, *The Politics of Accommodation*; Bluhm, *Building an Austrian Nation*.

63. Marlowe, "In the Mosaic," 195.

64. Bailey, "Closed Social Stratification in India," 119.

ethnically divided communities into specific political and communal action. In their consequences they differ precisely in this way: ethnic coexistences condition a mutual repulsion and disdain but allow each ethnic community to consider its own honor as the highest one; the caste structure brings about a social subordination and an acknowledgement of "more honor" in favor of the privileged caste and status groups.[65]

As Weber suggests, the distribution of honor or prestige is a key difference.[66] In ranked systems, the unequal distribution of worth between superiors and subordinates is acknowledged and reinforced by an elaborate set of behavioral prescriptions and prohibitions. In unranked systems, relative group worth is always uncertain, always at issue.

Ranked and Unranked Systems in Practice

The distinction between these two types of systems is blurred in practice. Ranking is a pervasive aspect of social relations, which creeps into relations between individual members of unranked groups. A trader from unranked Group A may defer to an aristocrat from unranked Group B, while a servant from Group B may be subordinate to the same trader from Group A. What is more, ascriptive patterns of recruitment to these roles may develop. Merely because an unranked group has a full complement of statuses does not mean that its status pyramid has the same shape as that of other groups in the society or that every role is filled by a group member. Some unranked groups have larger elites than others; some have more intragroup social mobility; some leave particular functions to be performed by outsiders. Unranked systems assume elements of ranking, and, though for most purposes ethnic groups within them exist almost as autonomous societies, in some respects they are also interdependent parts of a common society.

Conversely, a subordinate ethnic group in a ranked system may produce an elite that defies the rules of ascriptive stratification. Clearly, the functional integration of ranked groups into a single society is far

65. H. H. Gerth and C. Wright Mills, eds., *From Max Weber: Essays in Sociology* (New York: Free Press, 1958), 189.
66. Following Weber, Berreman ties caste to "criteria of intrinsic worth, honor, or purity," stating that "the fact that the paramount virtue is accorded differentially to birth-ascribed groups in a society is a common and distinctive characteristic of caste systems." "Structure and Function of Caste Systems," 281. Similarly, Bryce Ryan identifies caste with a system of ranks based on the hereditary distribution of "honor." *Caste in Modern Ceylon* (New Brunswick: Rutgers Univ. Press, 1953), 59.

stronger than it is for unranked groups. Yet even here there are areas of ethnic autonomy. Neither type of system is pure, and both are usually in a process of change, about which more shortly.

Despite the blurring, nearly all ethnic relationships can be identified as ranked or unranked. A key question is whether each group has a full complement of statuses or, to put the point differently, whether each of the groups in contact possesses a legitimately recognized elite. If so, the system is unranked.

Consider the case of Malaysia. There are high-status Malays who are members of the royalty or aristocracy and others who are members of the modern bureaucracy. There are high-status Chinese among the descendants of early traders and among the newer industrialists, professionals, and intellectuals. Although in the modern sectors there may be certain common criteria of stratification, there are also separate criteria for rank and prestige among the two groups. Each group has its own elite strata, so that the groups do not stand in a generalized hierarchical relation to each other. Each of these subsocieties can and does, as Weber suggested, consider its own "honor" to be the highest.

The clearest indicator of subordination, on the other hand, is the logical impossibility of an acknowledged upper class among the subordinate group.[67] That is not to say that all members of a superordinate group are of upper-class standing. This is most unlikely, and the line in Figure 1 that puts all members of Group A in a class above all of Group B is a distortion. In fact, any ideal-type conception that puts all members of a superordinate group in an economic class above all members of a subordinate group is something of a distortion. Within limits, a system of subordination can survive some dissonance between the economic status of the groups and that of its individual members, especially members of the superordinate group. For example, in Jamaica, traditionally stratified by color groups, the relatively few poor whites were viewed by their poor black neighbors as aberrations, rather than as glaring evidence of the equality of all.[68] Likewise, members of a subordinate group can and do acquire elite credentials acknowledged within their own community but not across ethnic lines. Carried far enough, however, either of these dissonant conditions can prove destabilizing to a ranked system:

67. See, e.g., John Dollard, *Caste and Class in a Southern Town*, 3d ed. (Garden City, N.Y.: Anchor Books, 1957), 65–67.
68. Fernando Henriques, *Family and Colour in Jamaica* (London: Eyre & Spottiswoode, 1953).

inferior members of a superordinate group threaten the myth of its superiority, and the growth of an elite among a subordinate group sooner or later creates aspirations for mobility and recognition incompatible with strictly ascriptive hierarchy.

Leadership selection constitutes another operational test of whether a ranked system exists. The leadership of a subordinate group must be acceptable to the superordinate group, which is usually in a position to reject unacceptable leaders. Influence or prestige within the subordinate group by itself is not enough. Lack of group autonomy in leadership selection is a sure sign of ethnic subordination.[69]

Unranked groups, on the other hand, select their leaders with relative autonomy, although the need to engage in bargaining across ethnic lines sometimes sets external limits on the selection. Because of this autonomy, unranked Groups A and B may throw up quite different types of leaders, in terms of social background, educational qualifications, personality, and relationship with their following. The relations of dissimilar ethnic elites can become a significant problem if they must interact on a regular basis.

The operating assumptions of the two types of systems, and the behavior appropriate to each, are vastly different. Ranked systems typically have ritualized modes of expressing the lower status or contamination of the subordinate groups. These may include restrictions on eating, dress, touching, sex, marriage, and social contact.[70] In Sri Lanka, the Rodiya are the closest thing the Sinhalese have to an outcaste group. Formerly, Rodiya women were required to go bare-breasted and, when this rule was abandoned, were forbidden to wear jackets.[71] Restrictions on education and occupation are also common. Stereotypes reflect the denial of prestige to subordinate groups, who are often depicted as a "contrast conception,"[72] the embodiment of all the vices disdained by the superordinate group. The Burakumin of Japan, whose earlier name, *Eta*, means "full of filth," are said to be "intellectually dull, disorderly, sexually

69. See Lewis C. Copeland, "The Negro as a Contrast Conception," in Edgar Thompson, ed., *Race Relations and the Race Problem* (Durham: Duke Univ. Press, 1939), 167.

70. Martin R. Doornbos, "Kumanyana and Rwenzururu: Two Responses to Ethnic Inequality," in Robert I. Rotberg and Ali A. Mazrui, eds., *Protest and Power in Black Africa* (New York: Oxford Univ. Press, 1970), 1090; Ryan, *Caste in Modern Ceylon*, 59, 74–75; George A. De Vos, *Japan's Outcastes: The Problem of the Burakumin* (London: Minority Rights Group, Report no. 3, 1971), 6.

71. Ryan, *Caste in Modern Ceylon*, 132–34.

72. Copeland, "The Negro as a Contrast Conception."

loose, rude, violently aggressive and physically unclean."[73] The term *Rodiya* also means "filth," and the Rodiya, like other such groups in Asia, are said to have originated because of contact with "unclean activities," such as carrying corpses, slaughtering animals, or eating beef.[74] In Sulu, in the Southern Philippines, Tausug regard their subservient neighbors, the Samal Luwaan, as repulsive. The word *luwaan* means "that which was spat out," that is, rejected by God. There are myths that justify the low status of the Luwaan, including some stating that the Luwaan and the monkeys "come from the same race."[75] And, in Japan, Burakumin are sometimes referred to as *Yottsu*, meaning four and connoting four-legged beasts. Whether or not there is an attempt to deny the common humanity of the subordinate group, the stereotype of such a group generally depicts it as irremediably slow, violent, lazy, unmannered, and dirty. Indeed, such groups often do the dirty work.

Unranked groups obviously do not require methods of reinforcing and rationalizing ethnic subordination. Instead, a parallel group in contact and competition with others develops elaborate ways of reaffirming the superiority of its own culture, even while conceding limited spheres of cultural superiority to other groups. Malays, for example, admire the business skill of the Malaysian Chinese, but often regard Chinese behavior as crude and uncultured.[76] Creoles in Guyana and Trinidad readily grant the greater solidarity, thrift, and shrewdness of East Indians; yet Indians are referred to by the pejorative term *coolie* and are denied possession of certain traits that are highly valued in Creole society.[77] Indians, for their part, concede the physical strength of Creoles, but do not acknowledge the moral worth of presumed Creole behavioral patterns in general.[78] The Nigerian Kanuri likewise "are ambivalent about Ibo. In general, Ibo are disliked, mistrusted, and even despised . . . . Yet

73. De Vos, *Japan's Outcastes*, 7; John Donoghue, "The Social Persistence of an Outcaste Group," in Melvin Tumin, ed., *Comparative Perspectives on Race Relations* (Boston: Little, Brown, 1969), 110–11.

74. Nandasena Ratnapala, *Sarvodaya and the Rodiyas* (Colombo, Sri Lanka: Sarvodaya Research, mimeo., 1979), 1–2.

75. Thomas M. Kiefer, *The Tausug: Violence and Law in a Philippine Moslem Society* (New York: Holt, Rinehart & Winston, 1972), 22–23.

76. Peter J. Wilson, *A Malay Village and Malaysia* (New Haven: HRAF Press, 1967), 25–29, 36.

77. Elliott P. Skinner, "Group Dynamics and Social Stratification in British Guiana," *Annals of the New York Academy of Sciences* 83 (Jan. 20, 1960): 904–12.

78. Morton Klass, *East Indians in Trinidad: A Study of Cultural Persistence* (New York: Columbia Univ. Press, 1961), 244.

Kanuri grudgingly admire Ibo for their Western education, salaried jobs, and higher standards of living . . . ."[79] Stereotypes reflect these mixed evaluations. The Ceylon Tamils, for example, are seen by Sinhalese as poor and dirty, but also as thrifty and diligent.[80] Such mixed evaluations contrast vividly with the unmitigated denial of prestige and even of humanity that is reflected in stereotypes of subordinate groups in ranked systems.

Despite the common rigidity of ethnic stratification, relations between ethnic superiors and subordinates usually embody at least some elements of social cohesion and shared expectations, in addition to coercion and conflict. There may be a more or less explicit "premise of inequality,"[81] some degree of consensus on the aptitudes, rights, and obligations of the respective groups. In many settings, religion plays a role in legitimizing the ethnic hierarchy. Furthermore, there are elements of reciprocity and clientage that underpin the system. Typically, there is an exchange of protection of the subordinate for service rendered the superior. Benefits, such as increased personal security and even limited leeway for maneuver among competing superiors, usually accrue to those of subordinate status who accept the premise of inequality.[82] Adaptive behavior by the subordinate group to the requirements of its status is therefore common, and a substantial measure of predictability in relationships follows.

Relations among members of unranked ethnic groups are far less predictable. Characteristically, there is a lack of sufficient authority to establish a high level of reciprocity premised on inequality. Misunderstandings and misperceptions abound.[83] As there is less generalized domination, so there is also less generalized collaboration.

79. Ronald Cohen, "Social Stratification in Bornu," in Arthur Tuden and Leonard Plotnicov, eds., *Social Stratification in Africa* (New York: Free Press, 1970), 243.
80. W. Howard Wriggins, *Ceylon: Dilemmas of a New Nation* (Princeton: Princeton Univ. Press, 1960), 232–33.
81. Jacques J. Maquet, *The Premise of Inequality in Ruanda* (London: Oxford Univ. Press, 1961). See Donoghue, "The Social Persistence of an Outcaste Group," 120–21.
82. For example, see C. C. Stewart, "Political Authority and Social Stratification in Mauritania," in Ernest Gellner and Charles Micaud, eds., *Arabs and Berbers: From Tribe to Nation in North Africa* (Lexington, Mass.: Lexington Books, 1972), 383; René Lemarchand, "Power and Stratification in Rwanda: A Reconsideration," *Cahiers d'Etudes africaines* 6 (Dec. 1966): 592–610, at 602–05; Dollard, *Caste and Class in a Southern Town*, 179, 212, 262, 282; Kenneth M. Stampp, *The Peculiar Institution: Slavery in the Ante-Bellum South* (New York: Random House, 1956); see also Michael Banton, *Race Relations* (New York: Basic Books, 1967), 87.
83. For an example, see Everett C. Hughes, *French Canada in Transition* (Chicago: Univ. of Chicago Press, 1943), 86.

Ranked ethnic systems thus may possess more social cement than unranked at some stages of their development. This observation is consistent with experimental evidence that much potential aggression against superiors is inhibited, habits of deference as well as fear being what they are; more aggression against peers tends to be expressed.[84] But when the cement cracks in a ranked system, the edifice usually collapses: when ethnic hierarchies are undermined, they may undergo fundamental transformations, as we shall soon see.

The characteristics of ranked and unranked systems flow from their differing origins. In general, ranked systems are produced by conquest or capture. The ensuing domination lends itself to the establishment of upper and lower ranks, clientage relations, and an ideology of inferiority for the subordinate groups. The highly stratified ethnic system of Central Rwanda was the result of invasion and conquest, as were some equally stratified systems of Southern Africa and the Southern Philippines.[85] Slavery in North and South America was made possible by the equivalent of conquest: the forced transportation of Africans to the New World. On the other hand, unranked systems are produced by invasion resulting in less than conquest, by more or less voluntary migration, or by encapsulation within a single territorial unit of groups that formerly had little to do with each other—or by some combination of these. Invasion short of conquest produced parallel groups in Nigeria and Sri Lanka, for neither Hausa-Fulani nor Ceylon Tamils were able to control the whole territory. Economically induced migration also created unranked systems in Malaysia, once Chinese and Indians arrived to mine tin and tap rubber, and in Guyana and Trinidad, where East Indians succeeded African labor on the sugar estates. And, in many cases, colonial rule brought together unranked groups that had had no previous contact, as well as those that had met on the battlefield or in the mines, shops, plantations, tea gardens, and other enterprises attracting ethnically differentiated work forces. Accordingly, their interactions were not those of clearly ranked superiors and subordinates but of unranked strangers.

Hierarchical groups are generally fairly well intermixed geographi-

---

84. Leonard Berkowitz, *Aggression: A Social-Psychological Analysis* (New York: McGraw-Hill, 1962), 76–78; Frances K. Graham et al., "Aggression as a Function of the Attack and the Attacker," *Journal of Abnormal and Social Psychology* 46 (Oct. 1951): 512–20, at 516.

85. Lemarchand, "Power and Stratification in Rwanda"; I. Schapera, *Government and Politics in Tribal Societies* (New York: Schocken Books, 1967; originally published in 1956), 128; Kiefer, *The Tausug*, 22.

cally. It seems evident that ranked subordination cannot long be sustained without a measure of spatial proximity to enforce it.[86] Parallel groups, however, may be either intermixed or regionally discrete. Typically, migration generates more geographic intermixture than does incomplete conquest.

Migration and incomplete conquest also give rise to different kinds of lingering historical grievances. A group whose conquest has been thwarted may nourish unfulfilled territorial ambitions, while a group whose land has been partly conquered may develop a domestic version of *revanche*.[87] An indigenous group that was colonized and forced to abide the entry of ethnic strangers for colonial economic purposes may later regard their presence as illegitimate *ab initio*.[88]

By now it should be clear that ranked and unranked systems are susceptible to different forms of ethnic conflict. Because the boundaries of ranked ethnic groups largely coincide with class lines, conflict in ranked systems has a class coloration. When warfare occurs, it takes the form of a social revolution.[89] The two post-independence changes of regime in Africa that can plausibly be called revolutionary—Rwanda in 1959 and Zanzibar in 1964—were both the outgrowth of systems of ranked ethnic subordination.[90] (Ethiopia and Liberia are more debata-

86. This is quite different from the position that, in the absence of a clear "rank sign," subordination is only possible on a localized basis. Compare Bailey, "Closed Social Stratification in India," 113, 120, discussed below. So long as geographic intermixture exists, large-scale systems can be ranked.

87. In Nigeria, the advent of British rule interrupted a Hausa-Fulani invasion southward, and after independence "many Southerners feared that the departure of the British had opened the way for its continuance"—a fear reinforced by occasional Hausa-Fulani utterances. Walter Schwarz, *Nigeria* (New York: Praeger, 1968), 76. See Richard L. Sklar, *Nigerian Political Parties* (Princeton: Princeton Univ. Press, 1963), 98 n.25. In Sri Lanka, Tamil invasions had resulted in a de facto partition of the island centuries before colonial rule. But the teaching of Sinhalese history kept the issue alive and gave it periodic political significance. In 1957, when the prime minister agreed to a decentralization that would have devolved considerable power on Tamil local authorities in the North and East, the opposition toured the country, displaying maps with a black footprint over the areas to be "ceded" to the Tamils. Robert N. Kearney, *Communalism and Language in the Politics of Ceylon* (Durham: Duke Univ. Press, 1967), 117–18.

88. See, e.g., Elliott P. Skinner, "Strangers in West African Societies," *Africa* 33 (Oct. 1963): 307–20.

89. See Lemarchand, "Power and Stratification in Rwanda," 609–10.

90. See ibid.; René Lemarchand, "Revolutionary Phenomena in Stratified Societies: Rwanda and Zanzibar," *Civilisations* 18 (Mar. 1968): 16–49; Michael Lofchie, *Zanzibar: Background to Revolution* (Princeton: Princeton Univ. Press, 1965); John Okello, *Revolution in Zanzibar* (Nairobi: East African Publishing House, 1967); M. Catharine Newbury, "Colonialism, Ethnicity, and Rural Political Protest: Rwanda and Zanzibar in Comparative Perspective," *Comparative Politics* 15 (Apr. 1983): 253–80.

ble, but they, too, might fit the description.) The result was the overthrow of the former superordinates.

It is entirely different with unranked systems. They, too, are susceptible to serious conflict and violence, but with different goals. Unranked ethnic groups "act as if they were states in an international environment."[91] Interethnic elite relations partake of diplomacy. Ethnic leaders "form alliances that might remind the diplomatic historian of Renaissance Italy, and they deal with one another on the basis of sovereign equality."[92] They even make treaties: the Poona Pact and the Lucknow Pact in India, the Bandaranaike-Chelvanayakam Pact in Sri Lanka. The analogy to the international system is suggestive, not only with respect to alliance formation and negotiation across group lines, but also with respect to conflict and warfare. During the Sri Lanka riots of 1958, for example, the "refugee population, both Tamil and Sinhalese, was soon exchanged as hostages of war would be exchanged."[93] Unlike ranked groups, which form part of a single society, unranked groups constitute incipient whole societies.[94] It is not so much the politics of subordination that concerns them, though they are ever alert to threats of ethnic subordination, but rather the politics of inclusion and exclusion. These shadow societies often speak in the idiom of nations, referring, for example, to "the Dagomba nation" or to "Assamese nationalism." When ethnic violence occurs, unranked groups usually aim not at social transformation, but at something approaching sovereign autonomy, the exclusion of parallel ethnic groups from a share of power, and often reversion—by expulsion or extermination—to an idealized, ethnically homogeneous *status quo ante*.[95]

The confused relationship of class to ethnicity is now much clearer. On the one hand, it has often been stated that ethnic conflict is really

91. Michael C. Hudson, *The Precarious Republic: Political Modernization in Lebanon* (New York: Random House, 1968), 9.

92. Ibid., 135. James O'Connell refers to ethnic interaction as "international relations without safeguards." "Authority and Community in Nigeria," in Robert Melson and Howard Wolpe, eds., *Nigeria: Modernization and the Politics of Communalism* (East Lansing: Michigan State Univ. Press, 1971), 634–37.

93. Tarzie Vittachi, *Emergency '58: The Story of the Ceylon Race Riots* (London: André Deutsch, 1958), 91.

94. Cf. Clifford Geertz, "The Integrative Revolution: Primordial Sentiments and Civil Politics in the New States," in Geertz, ed., *Old Societies and New States* (New York: Free Press, 1963), 109–11.

95. For illustrations, see Lemarchand, "Power and Stratification in Rwanda," 609–10; Wilson, *A Malay Village and Malaysia*, 50.

class conflict. On the other, it has been said that ethnic conflict is an alternative or a barrier to class conflict. Both are true, but not in the broad way in which they have been asserted. Ethnic and class conflict coincide when ethnicity and class coincide—in ranked systems. Class conflict, notes Ralf Dahrendorf, always entails "the arrangement of social roles endowed with expectations of domination or subjection,"[96] and this description applies equally to conflict between ranked ethnic groups. Ethnic conflict, however, impedes or obscures class conflict when ethnic groups are cross-class, as they are in unranked systems. There is, under those circumstances, a strong tendency to reject class conflict, for it would require either interethnic class-based alliances or intraethnic class antagonisms, either of which would detract from the ethnic solidarity that unranked ethnic conflict requires. Ethnic conflict in unranked systems usually goes hand in hand with conservative politics.[97]

Change in Ranked and Unranked Systems

Neither ranked or unranked ethnic systems are static. Among the engines of change is ethnic conflict itself.

Virtually all ranked systems of ethnic relations are in a state of rapid transition or of increasing coercion by the superordinate group to avert change. On a global scale, ethnic subordination is on the decline. Eroded "by the spread of universalistic, egalitarian, achievement-oriented values,"[98] by international contact, and by the diffusion of education, ethnic stratification is ideologically obsolete.[99] Among subordinate groups, economic and educational change has repeatedly given rise to new leaders, including "intellectuals who debunk the myths of the racial order,

96. *Class and Class Conflict in Industrial Society* (Stanford: Stanford Univ. Press, 1959), 165.
97. See, e.g., Myron Weiner, *Sons of the Soil: Migration and Ethnic Conflict in India* (Princeton: Princeton Univ. Press, 1978), 173; Samuel Decalo, *Coups and Army Rule in Africa* (New Haven: Yale Univ. Press, 1976), 177–78; Stein Rokkan, "Geography, Religion, and Social Class: Crosscutting Cleavages in Norwegian Politics," in Seymour M. Lipset and Stein Rokkan, eds., *Party Systems and Voter Alignments: Cross-National Perspectives* (New York: Free Press, 1967), 403, 423; Raymond E. Wolfinger, "The Development and Persistence of Ethnic Voting," in Lawrence H. Fuchs, ed., *American Ethnic Politics* (New York: Harper & Row, 1968), 180; Ed Cairns, "Intergroup Conflict in Northern Ireland," in Henri Tajfel, ed., *Social Identity and Intergroup Relations* (Cambridge: Cambridge Univ. Press, 1982), 281.
98. Lemarchand, "Power and Stratification in Rwanda," 609.
99. See the interesting prognosis of Herbert G. Blumer, "Reflections on the Theory of Race Relations," in Andrew W. Lind, ed., *Race Relations in World Perspective* (Honolulu: Univ. of Hawaii Press, 1955), 13–17.

who advance new definitions, and who agitate on their behalf."[100] Mechanisms previously utilized to create exceptions to the principle of ascriptive subordination for unusually talented or wealthy members of the subordinate group and to lift them into the superordinate group[101] are generally unable to adapt fast enough to absorb the new elites. Consequently, subordinate groups and the frustrated, aspiring elites they produce aim to destroy the principle of subordination that impedes their mobility and limits their dignity.

In the leadership of these movements are educated members of the subordinate group, often professionals whose careers are handicapped by their origins, as well as some educated members of the superordinate group, whose change of political allegiance is reminiscent of the defection of the intellectuals from the Old Regime that is said to presage the great revolutions.[102] In many cases, there is a round of name changes. The Eta became the Shin-heimin or "new citizens" in 1871 and today are the Burakumin (roughly, village people), as the untouchables of India became Harijans or "children of God." It is characteristic of stigmatized groups to demand adoption of "a softer social label for the category in question"[103] or even one that converts the stigma into a badge of pride.

The battle of labels occurs in unranked systems as well, but it has a different significance. In Thailand, the term *khaek*, used for Malays who inhabit the Southern provinces, means "visitor," though the visit has lasted since time out of mind. *Khaek* is pejorative, not because it connotes utter inferiority—though it also means "dark" (cf. "khaki") and thus refers to skin color—but because to call the Malays visitors is to undercut their legitimate place in the country. The official counterpart, which affirms their legitimacy, is "Thai Islam." The term *Moro* in the Philippines means Moor and has an obvious Spanish origin. Used by Christian Filipinos to describe Muslims in the South, it is hardly flatter-

100. Ibid., 16. See Bailey, "Closed Social Stratification in India," 122; Donoghue, "The Social Persistence of an Outcaste Group," 117–18.

101. See note 146, below.

102. F. G. Bailey, *Politics and Social Change: Orissa in 1959* (Berkeley and Los Angeles: Univ. of California Press, 1963), 133; Kusum Nair, *Blossoms in the Dust* (New York: Praeger, 1961), 155–56; Donoghue, "The Social Persistence of an Outcaste Group," 117. See Crane Brinton, *The Anatomy of Revolution* (New York: W. W. Norton, 1938).

103. Erving Goffman, *Stigma: Notes on the Management of Spoiled Identity* (Englewood Cliffs, N.J.: Prentice-Hall, 1963), 24, citing "hard of hearing" as a replacement label for "deaf." Cf. "senior citizen" and "elderly" for "old" and "illegitimate child" for "bastard." On ethnic labels, see the interesting treatment by Harold Isaacs, *Idols of the Tribe: Group Identity and Political Change* (New York: Harper & Row, 1975), 71–92.

ing. Yet it has been adopted by Muslim leaders themselves, because it serves to unite the various Muslim ethnic groups of the South, who are otherwise divided. It then becomes possible to speak of a "Moro nation" (*bangsa Moro*) in the Philippines, whereas the "Islamic nation" is too widely spread to be the basis of so particularistic a movement. For unranked groups, then, terminology is a tool of group cohesion and legitimacy in the country rather than a weapon in the battle against continuing subordination.

Theoretically, a ranked system can move in one of four directions. Subordinate groups can attempt to displace superordinate groups; they can aim at abolition of ethnic divisions altogether; they can attempt to raise their position in the ethnic hierarchy without denying the legitimacy of that hierarchy; or they can move the system from ranked to unranked.

There are models for each type of change. First, in Rwanda and arguably in Zanzibar, superordinate groups were displaced by subordinate groups using revolutionary violence. Second, it is conceivable that some ranked ethnic systems may become largely nonascriptive class systems. This apparently began to occur in post-war Liberia, long dominated by the Americo-Liberian group.[104] Certainly, a nonascriptive system is the official goal for white-black relations in the United States and intercaste relations in India. More prevalent in India, however, is the third possibility: the assertion by subordinate groups of entitlement to a different and higher rank in the hierarchy. To support such claims, caste histories are rewritten, stigmatizing occupations are abandoned, and practices signifying ritual purity (abstention from meat, alcohol, and widow remarriage) are adopted.[105] Collective mobility thus becomes possible without destruction of the system of ranks. This flexibility within rigidity is possible in India because the hierarchy is so complex and contains so many groups that it can withstand changes in rank that are accomplished one group at a time. From change in rank, it is a short step to the fourth possibility, converting a ranked system to an unranked system. This, too, is happening in India (and elsewhere) as formerly subordinate groups develop elites that lead them into a measure of collective autonomy and prestige they had not formerly known and also into "competition with

    104. Merran Frankel, *Tribe and Class in Monrovia* (London: Oxford Univ. Press, 1964), 224–29.
    105. Tinker, *India and Pakistan*, 131–32; Rudolph and Rudolph, *The Modernity of Tradition*, pt. I.

their former masters."[106] This process, the horizontalization of previously vertical relationships, is perhaps the most likely of the changes ranked systems can undergo.

Whatever the direction of change, rarely will it be possible, without the application of considerable coercion, to maintain a system of ethnic stratification. The killing of many thousands of Hutu in Burundi in 1972 is evidence that violence can be used to maintain ethnic subordination. But everywhere there is a growing conviction of the illegitimacy of such systems, and powerful forces are deployed, internally and internationally, to bring practice into line with egalitarian ideology.

Unranked systems do not suffer from the same ideological disabilities. They therefore have much more ability to survive. Since there is no ascriptive bar to social mobility, the structure is not tainted by the obvious illegitimacy that attaches to rigidly ranked systems. There are generally opportunities for mobility within the ethnic group. One need not choose between his mobility aspirations and his group membership, whereas in ranked systems elite status is possible for members of a subordinate group only if they are willing and able to renounce their origins by passing into the superordinate group. This does not mean, of course, that each unranked group has proportionate numbers of its members in all strata or that mobility opportunities are proportioned to the demand. Discrepancies in the status profile of the respective groups typically constitute an irritant in group relations. But disproportionate representation is not the same fatal defect as an ascriptive bar to any elite representation whatever.

Still, there are forces for change in unranked systems. There is typically strong pressure for educational and occupational proportionality by ethnic group. There are also frequent demands for the building of a wholly nonascriptive system, and proportionality is often depicted as a necessary way station toward a society in which ethnic divisions are not significant. Then, too, as we have seen, the existence of two or more incipient societies in a single territory is a discomforting condition, conducive to periodic, sometimes violent, attempts to restore homogeneity or, alternatively, to subordinate previously unranked groups, thereby turning the system into a ranked system.

The burden of this extended contrast is that there is a theoretically

106. Bailey, *Politics and Social Change*, 231. See Bailey, "Closed Social Stratification in India," 119; Marlowe, "In the Mosaic: The Cognitive and Structural Aspects of Karen-Other Relationships," 203–04.

important distinction between ranked and unranked systems. The distinction has far-reaching consequences for ethnic conflict. The two types differ in their origin, structure, operation, and disintegration.

It should be stressed that, in any given country, there may be numerous groups, some ranked in relation to others and some unranked. In Guyana and Trinidad, for example, there have long been ranked color groups (white, brown, and black) alongside the unranked East Indian group. In Mauritania, the Moors consist of a variety of ranked groups juxtaposed with several unranked black African groups. If ranked and unranked systems exist in the same state, they tend to interact with each other. Ranked subordinates sometimes displace their aggression onto unranked parallel groups.[107] Societies that are divided into ranked as well as unranked groups—Sri Lanka, with its caste-class and ethnic divisions, is another example—may experience more conflict between unranked groups than societies not doubly divided in this way. By the same token, a subordinate group may align politically with—or even attempt to forge a common ethnic identity with—a parallel group so as to escape domination by superordinates. There are several examples of low-caste groups in South Asia that have made such attempts. Sikh Harijans have periodically aligned with Hindus to avoid domination by Sikh Jats in the Punjab, and so-called minority Tamils in Sri Lanka have gained leverage by associating with Sinhalese political parties.[108] Despite the interaction, ranked and unranked systems are conceptually different, and it is a great mistake to lump them indiscriminately together for comparison. Consequently, although I have no intention of ignoring the importance of ranking—where, for example, ranked subgroups have an impact on party politics—the focus of this work is on the political relations of ethnic groups that do not stand in a ranked relation to each other but exist side by side as separate subsocieties, whether regionally discrete or geographically intermixed.

THE LOCUS OF GROUP RELATIONS

If the distinction between ranked and unranked systems is conceptually clear, the distinction between ethnic conflict that takes place at the center

107. Horowitz, "Direct, Displaced, and Cumulative Ethnic Aggression."
108. Baldev Raj Nayar, *Minority Politics in the Punjab* (Princeton: Princeton Univ. Press, 1966), 50–51; Robert N. Kearney, *The Politics of Ceylon (Sri Lanka)* (Ithaca: Cornell Univ. Press, 1973), 189–91. Cf. Urmila Phadnis, "Neo-Buddhists in India and Ceylon," *Economic and Political Weekly*, Dec. 6, 1969, pp. 1897–98.

of politics and that which takes place in dispersed pockets is conceptually much less clear. It is, nonetheless, important in practice.

Every ethnic group operates, to some extent, at all levels of the political system of which it is a part. A group may simultaneously strive to win local elections, seek a larger share of patronage from an intermediate governmental body (such as a state in a federal system or a district in a unitary system), and demand linguistic recognition in the country as a whole and local autonomy for its own area. But some groups are so small in size and so geographically concentrated that it makes little sense for them to devote energy to political activity much beyond their locality. Other groups, however, may be large and influential enough to make plausible claims to power at the center. In general, there is a propensity for groups to concentrate their efforts on the highest level of activity that seems to promise success.

Several Asian and African states embrace a large number of dispersed ethnic groups, none of them large or powerful enough to threaten to dominate the center. Excepting perhaps the Hindu-Muslim cleavage, India is such a state.[109] Because of the large number of scattered groups, it would be preposterous to suggest that politics at the center in India revolves around the rivalry of, say, Gujaratis, Bengalis, Oriyas, and Telugus, though not at all preposterous to conclude that politics in many Indian states revolves around comparable rivalries: Assamese and Bengalis in Assam; Hindus and Sikhs in Punjab; Nairs, Christians, Ezhava, and Muslims in Kerala. Similarly, in Tanzania, with its frequently cited figure of some 120 ethnic groups,[110] no single group can make credible claims to power at the center, although even in such a dispersed system some relatively advantaged groups, such as the Chagga and the Wahaya, are disproportionately represented in Tanzanian institutions despite their small numbers.[111] In such states, needless to say, governments encounter problems of coordination and uniformity, for a profusion of dispersed groups means a society composed of multiple particularisms moving in different directions simultaneously.

From the standpoint of ethnic conflict, however, much of the pressure

109. Brass, *Language, Religion and Politics in North India*, 12.
110. Such figures, based on some objective and often arbitrary measure of group separateness rather than a subjective measure of group consciousness, need always to be taken as much less than conclusive. See Paul Puritt, "Tribal Relations," in *Two Studies of Ethnic Group Relations in Africa: Senegal, United Republic of Tanzania* (Paris: UNESCO, 1974), 122.
111. Ibid., 128.

is off the center. In dispersed systems, group loyalties are parochial, and ethnic conflict is localized; it "could put one of a series of watertight compartments out of order, but it could not make the ship of state sink . . . ."[112] Furthermore, there are incentives in dispersed systems against carrying ethnic extremism too far. The principal incentive stems from political ambition. Parties and politicians concerned solely with parochial ethnic conflicts find themselves unable to expand their influence beyond the locality. The Shiv Sena, for example, which was identified with the cause of Maharashtrians in Bombay against migrant South Indians, did very well in the late 1960s in Bombay electoral politics; but its showing elsewhere in Maharashtra state, where conflict with South Indians was not prominent, was negligible. Not surprisingly, the Shiv Sena moved to more moderate ground.[113] In this respect, it followed in the footsteps of several other parochial parties in India eager to share power at levels of politics higher than the level at which their motivating conflicts subsist. These incentives are not inexorable, for some political organizations will find the parochial conflict of overwhelming significance, but in such a case the compartmentalization of the conflict is a safeguard against its engulfing the entire political system.

In such circumstances, the center usually has some flexibility. The demands of one group can sometimes be granted without injuring the interests of others. Often such demands are made at the expense of the center, rather than at the expense of ethnic competitors. Even when they are not, it may be possible to satisfy ethnic aspirations by concessions from the central pool, particularly if these take the form of opportunities for social mobility that are in scarce supply in a given region.[114] The plurality of groups ordinarily enables the center to deal with one conflict at a time, thus providing some assurance that the entire state will not experience destabilizing upheavals simultaneously. (Some claims, however, though made by one group, will quickly be seen as having wide applicability and precedential value, even in a dispersed system, and then flexibility contracts.[115]) A further limit on conflict in a dispersed system

112. Doornbos, "Kumanyana and Rwenzururu," 1136.
113. See Ram Joshi, "The Shiv Sena: A Movement in Search of Legitimacy," *Asian Survey* 10 (Nov. 1970): 967–78, at 974–75; "Poona: Jan Sangh vs. Shiv Sena," *Economic and Political Weekly*, Special Number, July 1968, p. 975. See generally Mary Fainsod Katzenstein, *Ethnicity and Equality: The Shiv Sena Party and Preferential Policies in Bombay* (Ithaca: Cornell Univ. Press, 1979).
114. See Doornbos, "Kumanyana and Rwenzururu."
115. Claims to divide an existing Indian state into two (as in the case of the Telangana and Andhra movements) have generally been viewed this way in New Delhi, though even

is provided by the possibility of composing the armed forces in such a heterogeneous way that on any given issue the center has the certain ability to enforce its will.[116] Above all, in civilian politics, a profusion of dispersed groups usually creates such great ethnic heterogeneity at the center that when the center intervenes it may do so as a neutral arbiter.[117]

A different pattern of demands and tensions prevails in those states where a few groups are so large that their interactions are a constant theme of politics at the center. Then the claims of one group tend to be made at the expense of another: "mutually exclusive demands characterize political debate."[118] The exigencies of political organization pull in opposite directions in the two types of system. A leader at the center in India or Tanzania can hardly afford to rely on the support of one or two ethnic groups; a leader at the center in Guyana, Lebanon, or Malaysia can hardly do otherwise. The structure of dispersed ethnic systems abets interethnic cooperation, while the structure of centralized ethnic systems impedes it.[119]

A centrally focused system possesses fewer cleavages than a dispersed system, but those it possesses run through the whole society and are of greater magnitude. When conflict occurs, the center has little latitude to placate some groups without antagonizing others. Conflict is not easily compartmentalized, and problems cannot be dealt with one at a time; they involve the whole state. In dispersed systems, the relationship between group and group is mediated by the relationship between the locality and the center. In centralized systems, one group confronts another directly, generally in a competitive framework. If the major malaise of the ethnically dispersed polity is inertia and difficulty of central coordination, that of the ethnically centralized polity is constant tension and

---

then exceptions have been made for compelling reasons (the division of the Punjab in 1966, for example).

116. See Stephen P. Cohen, *The Indian Army: Its Contribution to the Development of a Nation* (Berkeley and Los Angeles: Univ. of California Press, 1971), 196.

117. For illustrations, see Doornbos, "Kumanyana and Rwenzururu"; Martin R. Doornbos, "Protest Movements in Western Uganda: Some Parallels and Contrasts," in Raymond L. Hall, ed., *Ethnic Autonomy—Comparative Dynamics* (New York: Pergamon Press, 1979), 263–82; Nayar, *Minority Politics in the Punjab*, 283; Selig S. Harrison, *India: The Dangerous Decades* (Princeton: Princeton Univ. Press, 1960), 238–43; Joan V. Bondurant, *Regionalism versus Provincialism: A Study in Problems of Indian National Unity* (Berkeley and Los Angeles: Univ. of California Press, 1958), 118.

118. Wriggins, *Ceylon*, 460. See K. J. Ratnam, *Communalism and the Political Process in Malaya* (Kuala Lumpur: Univ. of Malaya Press, 1965), 170.

119. By "centralized systems," I do not mean, of course, systems in which political power is gathered at the center as opposed to those in which it is dispersed. My use of the terms "central" and "dispersed" refers solely to the locus of ethnic group interactions.

an overheated political system. The center is not a neutral arbiter for conflicts originating elsewhere. On the contrary, the center is itself a focal point of competition. To the extent that contending groups succeed in controlling it, the center becomes an actor as much as an arbiter in ethnic conflict.

Whether ethnic politics is more parochial or more central is mainly a function of group size relative to state size. Group size in many cases depends on the ability of subgroups to forge a common identity. This, in turn, depends heavily on perceived similarities among subgroups *vis-à-vis* other groups they confront. Given the dependence of group identity on felt distance from other groups, it is not surprising that states with large groups relative to state size have often experienced intensely hostile relations among the groups. Extensive amalgamation of subgroups is often a sign of a great chasm between them and others. Consequently, to focus on centralized polities is generally to be concerned with intense conflict.

Not all states can be classified easily as either ethnically dispersed or centralized. Some are at various points between the two. Likewise, most countries with a centralized ethnic politics also contain within their boundaries smaller groups whose relations with their neighbors are mainly local. Before the Nigerian coups of 1966, each region experienced constant tension between its dominant group and the regional minorities. The Borneo states of Malaysia contain similar compartmentalized relationships, not replicated in peninsular Malaya. The Ceylon Tamils are an important minority in Sri Lanka politics, but in the Eastern Province they are a plurality and the Ceylon Moors are an important provincial minority. Nevertheless, in all of these states the major focus of politics at the center has been the rivalry of a few large groups.

In judging whether a system is central or dispersed, it is important not to be misled by objective indicators of ethnic group identity, such as the distribution of certain cultural traits. The groups that emerge as participants in ethnic conflict define their own boundaries, which may or may not match those of outside observers attuned to cultural inventories. "We anthropologists thought that tribes were small in this area," confessed a young Frenchman about Congo (Brazzaville). "But the rise of local political organization seems to have stimulated the re-emergence of larger tribal associations than we had ever identified."[120] Moreover, it

120. Quoted in Gwendolen M. Carter, *Independence for Africa* (New York: Praeger, 1960), 90.

does not take overwhelmingly large numbers for a group to make its influence felt at the center. The Ibo and Yoruba in Nigeria are both groups with less than 20 percent of the total population; so are the Kikuyu in Kenya and the Ceylon Tamils in Sri Lanka. Yet all have been participants in conflict at the center. And, to complicate matters even further, there are certain circumstances in which very small groups can become contestants at the center, displacing larger groups that were essentially knocked out of effective political competition. In Chapter 12, we shall examine such transformations.

From what has already been said, the dispersion model would seem to be an appealing one for conflict reduction. Perhaps there are ways that policymakers interested in reducing ethnic conflict can work to make their political systems resemble those of India and Tanzania. I shall deal with these issues in Chapters 14 and 15. In the meantime, the large number of ethnically centralized systems offers many opportunities for the observation and understanding of severe ethnic conflict.

THE INDICATORS OF ETHNIC IDENTITY

We have been so busy drawing distinctions that I have not yet had a chance to explain what I mean by ethnicity. It may seem that we have gotten ahead of ourselves, but in fact the omission was intentional. The conception of ethnicity that I intend to put forward is rendered more understandable once the distinctions, especially between ranked and unranked systems, have been drawn.

Do we again wish to draw distinctions? Shall we separate "race" from "ethnicity," reserving race for differences of color?[121] Shall we sort out groups based on religion from those based on language or "nationality"? Although comparison is impeded by lumping together ranked and unranked cases or cases of conflict at the center with cases of conflict in dispersed pockets, comparison is facilitated by an inclusive conception of ethnicity that embraces differences identified by color, language, religion, or some other attribute of common origin.

The case for inclusiveness also rests on the contextual and in some ways accidental determination of attributes of difference. Group *A* speaks a language different from that of Group *B*, so language becomes

---

121. For the separate treatment of color differences, see Harold R. Isaacs, "Color in World Affairs," *Foreign Affairs* 47 (Jan. 1969): 235–50; Isaacs, "Group Identity and Political Change: The Role of Color and Physical Characteristics," *Daedalus* 96 (Spring 1967): 353–75.

the indicator of group identity in that relationship. But if, instead of Group *B*, the environment contained only Groups *A* and *C*, then religion or color or place of origin might differentiate the groups. In a typical multigroup environment, moreover, different attributes are invoked for differing group interactions. Indeed, it is apt to describe the attribute as belonging to the interaction as much as it belongs to the group. I shall explain boundary definition in more detail in the next chapter.

The suggestion that color-group relations necessarily differ in kind from other types of ethnic-group relations is generally based on one of two barely articulated assumptions: (1) that color differences are capable of arousing uniquely intense emotions and loyalties among the participants or (2) that color differences serve as unusually reliable signs of individual identity.[122] Neither of these assumptions can be supported, though the origin of each can readily be surmised.

The argument that color-group relations are especially conducive to hostility presumably derives from the aftermath of African slavery in the Western Hemisphere and perhaps also from the history of Western colonialism, which entailed subjugation of "non-white" by "white" peoples. To be sure, color preferences can be found in many parts of the world.[123] Quite often, color forms part of the imagery invoked in conflict relations. We have already seen this in the use of the word *khaek* for Malays in Southern Thailand, and there are comparable examples available for India, Sri Lanka, and Malaysia, all cases in which there is much color overlap among groups. But this is far from demonstrating the supposedly unique effects of color differences on group antipathy and cohesion.

What seems to have happened is that, because of the historical association of color differences with subordination and the conflict-laden efforts to overcome it, color differences are assumed to give rise to subordination and in general to severe conflict. In other words, the attempt is to explain the special harshness of a ranked system, such as slavery and Jim Crow, by the presence of somatic differences. Because it occurs in a context in which color has been linked with rigid stratification, the explanation mistakes the indicator for the substance of the relationship.

Elsewhere, as we have seen, hierarchical ethnic systems have been

122. For yet another distinction, see D. John Grove, "The Race vs. Ethnic Debate: A Cross-National Analysis of Two Theoretical Approaches," University of Denver Center on International Race Relations, *Studies in Race and Nations*, vol. 5, no. 4 (1973–74): 1–44, at 35.
123. See the contributions to the issue, "Color and Race," *Daedalus* 96 (Spring 1967).

possible without color differences: between Tutsi and Hutu in Burundi (though there are other physical differences between those groups), between Tausug and Luwaan in the Philippines, between Burakumin and other Japanese in Japan, and between Osu and other Ibo in Nigeria. By the same token, the peculiar passions supposedly aroused by color differences can also be generated without them. The Chinese penchant for the consumption of pork can be seized upon by the abstemious Malays as a sign of the uncleanliness and crudeness associated with the Chinese[124] in somewhat the same way as blackness became a symbol of pejorative traits associated with Africans in the New World. And, where there are alternative ways to divide groups up, color is not necessarily the preemptive differentiator. In Mauritania, for example, black Africans have attempted to forge political alliances with the so-called black Moors or Hartani, descendants of slaves who form a subordinate segment of the Moorish group. Not only have the appeals been unsuccessful, but in the ethnic riots of 1966 Hartani were in the vanguard of Moorish mobs that attacked black Africans.[125] Differentiators other than color were obviously more important.

The thesis that color-group relations are especially conducive to group cohesion and intergroup hostility is not merely insupportable in comparative terms; it is also historically inadequate. In the Western Hemisphere, slavery and its successor institutions did come to be identified with color. But color did not initially possess the stigma that it later did. In seventeenth-century North America, the English were originally called "Christians," while the African slaves were described as "heathens." The initial differentiation of groups relied heavily on religion. After about 1680, however, a new dichotomy of "whites" and "blacks" supplanted the former Christian and heathen categories, for some slaves had become Christians. If reliance had continued to be placed mainly on religion, baptism could have been employed to escape from bondage.[126]

124. Wilson, *A Malay Village and Malaysia*, 25.
125. For the background, see *Le Monde*, Feb. 19, 1966; Mokhtar Ould Daddah, "Rapport moral," presented at the Congrès ordinaire du Parti du Peuple, Aioun, Mauritania, June 24–26, 1966 (mimeo.), p. 9. I am also indebted to conversations with several Mauritanians. For a report on the status of the Hartani (sing. Haratin), see the *Washington Post*, May 31, 1981.
126. See Winthrop D. Jordan, *White Over Black: American Attitudes Toward the Negro, 1550–1812* (Chapel Hill: Univ. of North Carolina Press, 1968), 91–98. See also Jeffrey R. Brackett, *The Negro in Maryland* (Baltimore: Johns Hopkins Univ. Press, 1889), 32, 38.

Color provided a "barrier" seemingly both "visible and permanent"[127] and therefore apt for maintaining a degrading and hereditary system of forced labor. To the extent that Christianity was a voluntary affiliation, the special place of color in American ethnic relations seems to have originated in the special desire of the slaveholders for a permanently servile group.[128] That purpose could be accomplished by redefining the indicia of ethnicity.

The distinction between color and other forms of ethnic identification thus derives largely from the failure to distinguish between ranked and unranked systems of ethnic relations. The most significant way in which color differs from other varieties of ethnicity is its apparent immutability. But this characteristic is far more important in systems of ethnic stratification, where there is likely to be some attempt by members of the subordinate group to escape their identity, than it is in unranked systems.[129] Moreover, color had the comparative advantage in this respect only because the slaveholders regarded religion as mutable. Had they not held this view, had they refused to recognize the baptism of slaves, they would not have needed to resort to color. And, even then, the North American system of slavery, which placed such a premium on the visibility and permanence of the signs of identity, was obliged to resort to evidence of ancestry in the case of mulattoes who claimed to be descended of a free mother.[130] Even color can be changed in the course of generations.

This brings us to the second of the grounds on which color-group relations are asserted to be different from other types of ethnic relations: that color, because it is visible and permanent, is the most reliable indicator of identity. On this score, F. G. Bailey has argued that the visibility of color makes a hierarchical system based upon color differences easier

127. Jordan, *White Over Black*, 96.
128. Cf. Dollard, *Caste and Class in a Southern Town*, 61, for the apocryphal story of a Negro found in a railroad car reserved for whites on a Southern train. Asked to move to the Jim Crow car, he announced he had "resigned" from the "colored race." Obviously, the reply sounds absurd in the Southern context only because color was an immutable indicator of subordinate identity. There is a double impossibility, physical and social: (1) color-group membership is fixed; (2) even if it were not, movement from one group to the other cannot be at the choice of a member of the subordinate group in a system of ethnic stratification.
129. The distinction made by Laponce between "minorities by force" and "minorities by will" is suggestive in this connection. J. A. Laponce, *The Protection of Minorities* (Berkeley and Los Angeles: Univ. of California Press, 1960), chap. 1. By the former, Laponce seems to refer mainly to subordinate groups in hierarchical systems; by the latter, to parallel groups excluded from political power.
130. Kenneth M. Stampp, *The Peculiar Institution*, 195–96.

to maintain over a large territory than is a hierarchical system based on nonvisible signs of difference.[131] Caste, according to Bailey, can only operate on a small scale, for, without a visible "rank sign," such as color, the caste origins of individual group members cannot be ascertained reliably for purposes of caste etiquette and avoidance.

This view seems plausible enough, but it can be shown to be inaccurate. What it reflects is the extent to which we think we depend on our eyes when in fact we depend as much or more on stimuli processed by the other senses. What we see is not always reliable, and what we hear and feel is not always less reliable than what we see. Moreover, even within the realm of what is visible, there is more than merely what is given at birth.

Bailey himself casts the first seeds of doubt, for he refers to the well-known phenomenon of collective caste mobility or even a shift for certain castes from ranked to unranked status. The impetus for this frequently occurred "when persons of humble caste achieved professional status as a lawyer or a Government servant," for they then "found themselves in difficulties with colleagues, most of whom belonged to higher castes."[132] Their response was to refuse to be subordinate and to claim a higher status for their caste. But then it is necessary to ask why persons of humble caste found themselves in such difficulty if indeed caste identification is impossible in a large-scale society. The answer seems plain: even in a government office or a bar association, far from village life, caste origins could easily be detected without a visible "rank sign."

This, in fact, is generally true. Where there are ambiguities of group membership, ways are found to make accurate identifications as fast as necessary. Color and phenotype are not the only visible cues, and in any case reliance need rarely be based on visible cues alone. In a North Indian village area, shopkeepers, using posture, bearing, gesticulation, clothing, and grammatical usage, in addition to physical features, were able, rapidly and rather reliably, to single out low-caste strangers for discriminatory service.[133] In the Nigerian riots of 1966, Northern mobs in search of Ibo sorted out Yoruba by their dress.[134] In Hindu-Muslim violence,

131. "Closed Social Stratification in India," 113, 120. See also Bailey, *Politics and Social Change,* 126.
132. "Closed Social Stratification in India," 122.
133. James M. Sebring, "Caste Indicators and Caste Identification of Strangers," *Human Organization* 83 (Fall 1969): 199–207.
134. See the official Eastern version of the riots, *Nigerian Pogrom: The Organized Massacre of Eastern Nigerians* (Enugu: Eastern Regional Government, 1966), 15, 19.

circumcision is usually the definitive test of identity for male victims.[135] In the absence of so decisive a differentiator, Sinhalese mobs in the Sri Lanka riots of 1958 had to use a variety of indicators to identify Tamils. Methodically, they looked for men "who wore their shirts over their *vertis*, Tamil fashion," who had earring holes in their ears (a Tamil sign of "early parental affection"), or who could not on the spot "read and explain a piece from a Sinhalese newspaper."[136] Calling into operation as they did the wrath of the mob, these alternative tests of identity constitute a grim caution against acceptance of the figment of the pigment.

As the examples suggest, there is a continuum of cues, from visible to nonvisible. Among visible cues, there are, first of all, those that are birth-determined and bodily, such as color, physiognomy, hair color and texture, height, and physique. Then there are those that are not determined at birth but are also bodily: circumcision and earring holes, as we have seen, and also scarification, which indicates ethnic group and subgroup in parts of Africa, modification of earlobes in parts of Asia and Africa, the filing or removal of certain combinations of teeth among Masai, Luo, and Luhya in East Africa,[137] or the staining of teeth among Chagga in Tanzania from the brown water they drink. Still visible but behavioral rather than bodily, and certainly not determined by birth, are posture, bearing, gestures, dress, grooming, and display.[138] Perhaps in the same category are the short beards that identify Ahmadis in Pakistan, for, though bodily, they are not indelible, as holes, scars, and circumcision are. Finally, there are the nonvisible cues, many of which derive from language and culture: grammar, syntax, vocabulary, accent, and reading facility, to begin with, but also differences in names, as in Northern Ireland and the Punjab,[139] as well as food habits and mastery of the standard cultural repertoire, which may include such arcane items as the ability to recall Buddhist stanzas in their original Pali version, as commonly learned by Sinhalese children.[140]

135. See Manohar Malgonkar, *A Bend in the Ganges* (New Delhi: Orient Paperbacks, 1964), 367.
136. Vittachi, *Emergency '58*, 54.
137. R. D. Grillo, "Ethnic Identity on a Kampala Housing Estate," in Abner Cohen, ed., *Urban Ethnicity* (London: Tavistock Publications, 1974), 177.
138. See ibid.
139. Harold Jackson, *The Two Irelands—A Dual Study of Inter-Group Tensions* (London: Minority Rights Group, Report no. 2, 1971), 4; Khushwant Singh, *Train to Pakistan* (Bombay: IBH Pub. Co., 1970), 143. See also John Darby, "Group Interaction in Northern Ireland: The Literature" (unpublished manuscript, Colraine, Northern Ireland, 1982).
140. Vittachi, *Emergency '58*, 49.

On the average, perhaps, the more visible and the closer to birth, the more immutable and therefore reliable the cue. A name can be changed, a language learned, and clothing altered, but scars and height are more difficult to undo. Even here, the association is not perfect, for many of the birth-bodily cues are merely probabilistic, and cultural inventory items like speech patterns may be even more probative of identity. But this is a rather abstract way of putting the matter, for it is the combination of cues that constitutes the authoritative differentiator. Groups will use that mix of cues which they find most reliable. In Andhra Pradesh, Andhras often wear scarves around their necks, whereas Telanganas do not; Telangana speech has many Urdu words, Andhra speech fewer; Telangana food is more like Muslim food than the Andhra cuisine is; Telanganas prefer tea, Andhras coffee.[141] Of such small differences are identifications compounded, and the indicators of separate identity then also come to represent as symbols the traits said to be associated with the groups.[142]

No cue or combination of cues is wholly reliable. In one study, for example, physiognomy proved to be a reliable cue to Jewish identity on a more than random basis, but physiognomy, speech, and gestures together were less reliable than physiognomy alone. When names were added to these cues, accuracy increased sharply.[143] There is some suggestion that the more salient the cleavage, or the more intense the conflict, the more accurate the identifications are likely to be.[144] Under acute conflict conditions, it will be more important to locate those cues that differentiate the largest number of members of the respective groups. But, even under the most severe conflict conditions, such as violent encounters in which rioters have the power to test ethnic identity systematically, mistakes are occasionally made.[145]

141. Weiner, *Sons of the Soil*, 240.
142. Gordon W. Allport, *The Nature of Prejudice* (Garden City, N.Y.: Doubleday Anchor Books, 1958), 133–34.
143. Leonard D. Savitz and Richard F. Thomasson, "The Identifiability of Jews," *American Journal of Sociology* 64 (Mar. 1959): 468–75.
144. Cf. Launor F. Carter, "The Identification of 'Racial' Membership," *Journal of Abnormal and Social Psychology* 43 (July 1948): 279–86. Erving Goffman has emphasized the distinction between visible and nonvisible stigmata (often handicaps), arguing that persons with visible stigmata are "discredited," whereas persons with nonvisible ones are merely "discreditable" and can sometimes avoid being discredited by controlling information about themselves. *Stigma*, 48. If this distinction holds, it is only because most stigmata are probably not highly salient; if they were, the control of relevant information would be more difficult.
145. Vittachi, *Emergency '58*, 49; Aswini K. Ray and Subhash Chakravarti, *Meerut Riots: A Case Study* (New Delhi: Sampradyikta Virodhi Committee, n.d.), 11.

Partly because ambiguities and mistakes in membership occur, individual changes in identity become possible. These can be temporary or permanent and more or less covert.

In the course of violence, members of a victim-group often attempt to pass as members of an attacker-group or bystander-group. They do this by miscueing. In 1966, some Ibo were able to escape death by taking refuge with Yoruba neighbors, who dressed them as Yoruba. In 1970, some Vietnamese were provided with sarongs by Cambodian Cham Muslims to protect them from violence inflicted by Cambodian Buddhists. At the time of the Indian partition riots in 1947, Hindus, Sikhs, and Muslims used dress and other ruses in attempts to escape detection by mobs that dominated the territory they were fleeing. The fear of mistake, however, sometimes induces members of a bystander group to reemphasize their distinctive identity. When Moors killed black Africans in Mauritania in 1966, Wolof wore small Senegalese flags to make sure they would not be confused with Fulani, whom they tended to resemble and whom the Moors had especially targeted for violence. There are many Wolof in Senegal, so the ethnic meaning of the flag was clear.

Like temporary passing at times of violence, permanent passing may occur either with or without the knowledge and assent of the receiving group. Where it becomes useful, particularly in order to absorb successful or potentially troublesome members of ranked subordinate groups, superior groups may conveniently "forget" the origins of individuals or families.[146] Elsewhere, ranked subordinates or members of groups who

---

146. In the ranked system of Eastern Rwanda, for example, Tutsi were superordinate and Hutu subordinate. "Yet, the evidence shows that in some cases the strength of the local Hutu lineages was such that the Tutsi found it expedient to absorb these meddlesome 'upstarts' into their own caste. In a fascinating discussion of the power struggle which took place in Remera, Gravel notes that 'the Hutu lineages which have been *in situ* longest have acquired some sort of priority of rights on the hill. Their members are respected and the heads of the lineages have much influence on their neighbors, and have an important voice in local administration. . . . The powerful lineages keep the power of the [Tutsi] chieftain in check. If, however, they become powerful enough to threaten the chieftainship they are absorbed into the upper caste. Their Hutu origins are "forgotten." ' " Lemarchand, "Power and Stratification in Rwanda," 604–05, quoting Pierre Gravel, "The Play for Power: Description of a Community in Eastern Rwanda" (Ph.D. diss., 1962), 229.

There is a parallel in the completely different context of slavery in the British West Indies, where children of mulatto origin, three steps removed from their African ancestry, were by statute considered white. In exceptional cases, usually involving wealthy or well-connected mulattoes, the Jamaican Assembly sometimes passed private bills to confer on individuals without the requisite generational removal all the legal rights of whites. See Bryan Edwards, *The History, Civil and Commercial, of the British Colonies in the West Indies*, 4th ed., vol. 2 (London: John Stockdale, 1807), 20–23. For the more recent practice, see Henriques, *Family and Colour in Jamaica*, 49–50. Certain Indian high-caste

sense some advantage in passing may, with varying degrees of success, attempt to change their identity. Their degree of success is a function of their ability to miscue. If names are reliable cues to Jewish identity, Jews seeking to change their identity may change their name.[147] But, where ethnic identity is significant in social life, passing is never easy.

Visibility and color do not determine whether passing succeeds. There is no appreciable physical difference between Burakumin and other Japanese, and a few Burakumin manage to conceal their identity if they are prepared to take elaborate precautions against discovery. But many are detected, because their place of origin becomes known, or their distinctive speech and behavior give them away, or their conspicuous anonymity in a society knitted together by kinship ties and pedigrees puts them at a disadvantage in employment, marriage, and social relations.[148] Success in miscueing is not determined by the objective character of the traits that differentiate groups, but rather by how salient ethnic identities are and thus by how much trouble people will take to insure accurate individual identifications. When enforcement of boundaries becomes lax, change becomes possible, color differences or not. In Sri Lanka, Goyigama are indisputably high caste, just as, in the color stratification systems of the Western Hemisphere, whites were at the apex of the status pyramid. However, there are "Colombo Goyigama,"[149] just as there are "Jamaican whites," and in each case the adjective means that only in Colombo or only in Jamaica would the claim to such group membership be honored, for there are genealogical doubts.

If "heathens" can become "blacks" (just as, on Cyprus, Greeks and Turks were formerly referred to as Orthodox and Muslims[150]), and if it

---

groups have also demonstrated a capacity to assimilate members of lower castes. Rudolph and Rudolph, *The Modernity of Tradition*, 118–19 n.24. In Zanzibar, the Arab community gained a large number of members by the absorption of "Swahilis," descendants of slaves of Afro-Arab origin. Lofchie, *Zanzibar: Background to Revolution*, 74–76. And in Liberia aspiring "tribesmen" were incorporated into the dominant "Americo-Liberian" group by intermarriage or adoption, a process which included the severance of their former ethnic connections and a change of name. Frankel, *Tribe and Class in Monrovia*, 224. Comparable passing into the Creole group has been reported in Sierra Leone. John S. Sinclair, "Perceptions of Social Stratification Among the Sub-Elite of Sierra Leone" (unpublished paper, Manchester Univ., 1971), 13–14.

147. See Leonard Broom, Helen P. Beem, and Virginia Harris, "Characteristics of 1,107 Petitioners for Change of Name," *American Sociological Review* 20 (Feb. 1955): 33–39.

148. De Vos, *Japan's Outcastes*, 12–13; Donoghue, "The Social Persistence of an Outcaste Group," 116, 120.

149. Ryan, *Caste in Modern Ceylon*, 319.

150. Adamantia Pollis, "Intergroup Conflict and British Colonial Policy: The Case of Cyprus," *Comparative Politics* 5 (July 1973): 575–99.

is the mix of attributes that denotes group differences, then it is clearly a mistake to seize on one or another attribute and impute decisive significance to it.[151] It is not the attribute that makes the group, but the group and group differences that make the attribute important.

The emphasis that has sometimes been put on linguistic differences as a special source of tension is, then, as misplaced as the emphasis put on color. Linguistic differences may or may not be regarded as demarcating different ethnic groups. In Greece and Norway, language differences have signified rural-urban, parochial-cosmopolitan, and social-class differences without ethnic overtones. Conversely, in Guyana and Trinidad, there has been much conflict between groups that speak the same language but view themselves as permanently distinctive. Language can be changed, but where it is identified with ethnicity it is likely to be enduring. In the Philippines, the language a child learns creates an ethnic identification that "persists for 19 out of 20 people."[152] What counts, once again, is not whether objective differences are present, but whether they are used to mark one group off from another.

The same possibilities attach to religion. The modern Western notion is that religion is voluntary or affiliational, an act of faith. As a delayed result of the Reformation and a direct result of the Enlightenment and the French Revolution, the right to choose one's religion was recognized. Religion passed into the realm of affiliations one could enter or leave at will. Even then, most people identified with the religion given them at birth. Outside the West, religion remained an ascriptive affiliation. For many groups, religion is not a matter of faith but a given, an integral part of their identity, and for some an inextricable component of their sense of peoplehood. When missionaries began their work in colonial Burma and Java, the early reaction of the subject peoples was that the conversions produced fundamental changes in identity: "The Sundanese (or, for that matter, the Javanese or any other group)," wrote a contemporary observer, "consider conversion identical with *masuk Belanda* (becoming Dutch), with a change of *bangsa* (people)."[153] For groups like the Syrian Alawi, descendants of mountain dwellers who blended Shiite doc-

151. Compare Claire Palley, *Constitutional Law and Minorities* (London: Minority Rights Group, Report no. 36, 1978), 5: ". . . regional, caste, cultural and tribal differences are generally less divisive than are racial, linguistic and nationality differences."
152. Bulatao, *Ethnic Attitudes in Five Philippine Cities*, 169.
153. Quoted by Fred R. von der Mehden, *Religion and Nationalism in Southeast Asia* (Madison: Univ. of Wisconsin Press, 1963), 174.

trine with nature worship, religion and ethnicity are coterminous.[154] The same is true in neighboring Lebanon, where "sectarian affiliations are communal and sect affiliation has a corporate aspect."[155]

Alternatively, the sense of belonging to an ethnic group may transcend religious differences within it. In Africa, ethnic groups are frequently divided between adherents of Christianity and Islam, Protestantism and Catholicism, or one of these and an indigenous religion. The Muslim-Christian cleavage runs right through the Yoruba, as it does through the Melanau in Sarawak and the Batak in Sumatra. The Karens in Burma include both Christians and Buddhists. In such cases, the overarching identification is usually more closely linked with the presumed origins of the group and hence is felt to be more fundamental to group identity. Further, where competing confessions threaten to divide a group, there are frequently important reasons to define the group to encompass members of more than one religion, thereby avoiding schisms and a loss of group members that might weaken the group in a multiethnic setting. The response to religious change depends in part on what other groups are in the environment. Especially where religious differentiation is relatively recent, the common but not invariable pattern is for religion to form the basis for subgroups rather than for wholly separate groups.[156]

THE CONCEPT
OF AN ETHNIC GROUP

In attempting to come to grips with the attributes that differentiate ethnic groups, I used some phrases that begin to define the concept of an ethnic group. I spoke of "genealogical doubts" when group members try to pass, of groups that see each other as "permanently distinctive," of a "sense of peoplehood," and of the "corporate aspect" of sectarian affiliations. I also noted that when a change of identity occurs, it is often because a person's origins have been conveniently forgotten.

If this usage makes any sense at all, it is because ethnicity is connected

---

154. Tabitha Petran, *Syria* (New York: Praeger, 1972), 27.
155. Hudson, *The Precarious Republic*, 21. See also Cairns, "Intergroup Conflict in Northern Ireland," 281.
156. See, e.g., William John Hanna and Judith Lynne Hanna, "The Political Structure of Urban-Centered African Communities," in Horace Miner, ed., *The City in Modern Africa* (London: Pall Mall Press, 1967), 158.

to birth and blood, but not absolutely so. Individual origins count, but exceptions are made. Ethnic identity is relatively difficult for an individual to change, but change sometimes occurs. Group origins also are important, for the corporate aspect means that the group is intergenerational, ongoing, and independent of its present members. Hence, ethnic identity is established at birth for most group members, though the extent to which this is so varies. Ethnicity is based on a myth of collective ancestry, which usually carries with it traits believed to be innate. Some notion of ascription, however diluted, and affinity deriving from it are inseparable from the concept of ethnicity.[157]

Many of the innumerable definitions of ethnicity that have been proposed embody these same elements.[158] The terms the groups themselves employ stress the ascriptive element. Physical anthropologists can show that ethnic groups that are regarded as fundamentally different from or opposed to each other have, over time, drawn on the same gene pool, as inferred from cranial dimensions, nasal profiles, and stature measurements.[159] In part, the disparity between this physical evidence and group conceptions reflects different time frames. Groups that were once one may have split centuries before, with each of the resulting groups remaining largely endogamous, thus producing opposed but physically similar populations.[160] In part, the disparity reflects recognition of individual group membership by other than birth criteria—conversion, intermar-

157. Compare Abner Cohen, *Custom and Politics in Urban Africa: A Study of Hausa Migrants in Yoruba Towns* (London: Routledge & Kegan Paul, 1969), 4: ". . . an ethnic group is an informal interest group whose members are distinct from the members of other groups within the same society in that they share a measure of . . . 'compulsory institutions' like kinship and religion, and can communicate among themselves relatively easily." Note that this leaves out ascription, emphasizes cultural differences, and puts the basis of group cohesion on political interest.

158. See, e.g., Blumer, "Reflections on the Theory of Race Relations," 5; Robert Ezra Park, *Race and Culture* (Glencoe, Ill.: Free Press, 1950), 114; Copeland, "The Negro as a Contrast Conception," 166; Nelson Kasfir, "Cultural Sub-Nationalism in Uganda," in Victor Olorunsola, ed., *The Politics of Cultural Sub-Nationalism in Africa* (Garden City, N.Y.: Anchor Books, 1972), 62; U.N. Secretary-General, "Definition and Classification of Minorities," U.N. Document E/CN.4/Sub.2/85, Dec. 27, 1949 (Lake Success, N.Y.: U.N. Publications, 1950); Bailey, "Closed Social Stratification in India," 121; Berreman, "Structure and Function of Caste Systems," 279.

159. Harry L. Shapiro, *The Jewish People: A Biological History* (Paris: UNESCO, 1960); Fay-Cooper Cole, *The Peoples of Malaysia* (New York: D. Van Nostrand, 1945), 324–37.

160. This would certainly be consistent with early findings that the Javanese, the Minangkabau, the Perak Malay, several Filipino groups, and even the Southern Chinese show strong physical similarities. Cole, *The Peoples of Malaysia*, 329.

riage, passing, "forgetting" origins, and the like—as well as the merger of subgroups.[161] In this way, genetically different but proximately located populations become physically less different over time. Taking account of the disparity between physical evidence and group conceptions requires a concept of ethnicity that is somewhat elastic. On this score, Enid Schildkrout's does as well as any: "The minimal definition of an ethnic unit . . . is the idea of common provenance, recruitment primarily through kinship, and a notion of distinctiveness whether or not this consists of a unique inventory of cultural traits."[162] This is close to Max Weber's conception of "a subjective belief" in "common descent . . . whether or not an objective blood relationship exists."[163] To this I would add a minimal scale requirement, so that ethnic membership transcends the range of face-to-face interactions, as recognized kinship need not. So conceived, ethnicity easily embraces groups differentiated by color, language, and religion; it covers "tribes," "races," "nationalities," and castes.[164]

This concept of ethnicity means that ethnic conflict is one phenomenon and not several. To be sure, that conflict takes different courses, depending on whether relationships between groups are ranked or unranked and on how groups are distributed in relation to territory and state institutions. But, as I shall explain in the next chapter, the putatively ascriptive character of ethnic identifications imparts to ethnic con-

161. Evidence of past intermixture of groups now deemed wholly separate is abundant. On Cyprus, there was much intermarriage and conversion between Greeks and Turks, and there are Turkish names among the Greeks. Pollis, "Intergroup Conflict and British Colonial Policy," 583. In Sri Lanka, Sinhalese-Tamil contacts were many, as evidenced by Tamil loan-words in Sinhala, intermarriages at the Sinhalese royal court, and the incorporation of Tamil-speaking subgroups as new Sinhalese castes. S. Arasaratnam, *Ceylon* (Englewood Cliffs, N.J.: Prentice-Hall, 1964), 97, 103; Ryan, *Caste in Modern Ceylon*, 104.

162. "The Ideology of Regionalism in Ghana," in William A. Shack and Elliott P. Skinner, eds., *Strangers in African Societies* (Berkeley and Los Angeles: Univ. of California Press, 1979), 184 n.4.

163. Weber, "Ethnic Groups," in Guenther Roth and Claus Wittich, eds., *Max Weber, Economy and Society: An Outline of Interpretive Sociology* (New York: Bedminster Press, 1968), 389.

164. Caste, however, will rarely figure in the analysis of this book. This is not because it fails to conform to a proper conception of ethnicity or because it fails to "pose the same kind of potential threat to the nation-state that tribes, religious communities, and linguistic groups do." Rudolph and Rudolph, *The Modernity of Tradition*, 67. Rather, it is because castes are so commonly involved in ranked systems, which are beyond the scope of this work. As noted earlier, however, some castes have become essentially unranked groups, and some comprise subgroups of unranked groups. Where castes are not ranked, I shall refer to caste interaction.

flict its intense and permeative qualities. It also accounts for some special difficulties ethnic conflict poses for democratic politics. And ascription is what makes interethnic compromise so difficult in divided societies, for those who practice compromise may be treated "with the bitter contempt reserved for brothers who betray a cause."[165]

165. Hudson, *The Precarious Republic*, 177.

CHAPTER TWO

A Family Resemblance

Many of the puzzles presented by ethnicity become much less confusing once we abandon the attempt to discover the vital essence of ethnicity and instead regard ethnic affiliations as being located along a continuum of ways in which people organize and categorize themselves. At one end, there is voluntary membership; at the other, membership given at birth. We like to think of birth and choice as mutually exclusive principles of membership, but all institutions are infused with components of both. There are birth elements in associations purporting to be founded on choice. These emerge, for example, when a person's origins govern whether he will be accepted into a social club. There are also choice elements in birth associations. The family, the very fount of blood relationships, is perpetuated by the contract of marriage. Virtually everywhere provision is made for giving a person the status of child of another by adoption, and in many societies it is common for non-kin to become members of a kinship group through longstanding joint residence or close association.[1] Both principles of membership—birth and choice—are capable of accommodating fictive elements. Language reflects the interweaving of the two principles in practice. The term *affiliation*, now widely used for membership by choice, originally signified acknowledgment of paternity.

Ethnic groups can be placed at various points along the birth-choice continuum. But there is always a significant element of descent. Most people are born into the ethnic group in which they will die, and ethnic groups consist mostly of those who have been born into them. We have

---

1. See, e.g., H. Arlo Nimmo, *The Sea People of Sulu* (San Francisco: Chandler, 1972), 94; Thomas Rhys Williams, *The Dusun: A North Borneo Society* (New York: Holt, Rinehart & Winston, 1965), 51; McKim Marriott, "Little Communities in an Indigenous Civilization," in Marriott, ed., *Village India* (Chicago: Univ. of Chicago Press, 1955), 177–78.

already established, of course, that individuals may alter their ethnic identity, and we shall soon see that groups sometimes do the same. Ethnic groups differ in the fluidity they are prepared to tolerate at the margin and in the alacrity with which they adapt their identity to changing conditions. The Karen along the Thai-Burmese frontier, for example, are willing to recognize as Karen men from outside the group who marry Karen women and conform to a few key Karen behavioral rules.[2] Nevertheless, most Karen become group members by being born to Karen parents. In other cases, however, the choice element in membership looms so large as to make claims to ethnicity seem spurious. But this can change as a group closes its boundaries. Sikhism, as an offshoot of Hinduism, has traditionally relied on accessions from the Hindu community to augment its ranks, but the Sikhs in the Punjab have increasingly acted as if they were a separate descent group. Some decades ago, Sikh leaders attempted, with some success, to sever the traditional ties of Sikhs to Hindus.[3] They apparently believed that by ending the long history of religious interchange, conversion, and intermarriage, they would put the Sikhs on a more solid—because more ascriptive—political foundation.[4] Other groups that at first cohered on a wholly nonascriptive religious or linguistic basis, such as Ahmadis in Pakistan or Waswahili in Tanzania, have evolved into at least somewhat endogamous and self-conscious entities.[5] These are borderline cases, no doubt, but it is a useful borderline that reminds us we are dealing with a continuum and not a dichotomy.

It is nonetheless true that ethnic membership is typically not chosen but given. The meaningfulness of ethnic identity derives from its birth

2. See David H. Marlowe, "In the Mosaic: The Cognitive and Structural Aspects of Karen-Other Relations," in Charles F. Keyes, ed., *Ethnic Adaptation and Identity: The Karen on the Thai Frontier with Burma* (Philadelphia: Institute for the Study of Human Issues, 1979), 179, 190. See also I. Schapera, *Government and Politics in Tribal Societies* (New York: Schocken Books, 1967; originally published in 1956), 26, 154, 156, 175, 186–87, 199–200, 202; Michael Moerman, "Ethnic Identification in a Complex Civilization: Who Are the Lue?" *American Anthropologist* 67 (Oct. 1965): 1215–30, at 1222.
3. Baldev Raj Nayar, *Minority Politics in the Punjab* (Princeton: Princeton Univ. Press, 1966), 57–74. See also Virginia R. Dominguez and Richard G. Fox, "The Determinants of Ethnicity" (unpublished paper, Duke Univ., Sept. 1981), 23–39.
4. This course was divisive within the Sikh community. See, e.g., Sant Singh Sekhon, "The Problem of a Punjabi State," in *Punjabi Suba: A Symposium* (n.p., n.d. [1966?]), 29.
5. See Spencer Lavan, *The Ahmadiya Movement* (Delhi: Manohar Book Service, 1974?); W. Arens, "The *Waswahili*: An Emerging Ethnic Group" (unpublished paper presented at the 1972 annual meeting of the American Anthropological Association).

connection—it came first—or from acceptance by an ethnic group *as if* born into it. In this key respect (the primacy of birth), ethnicity and kinship are alike.[6]

THE KINSHIP WITH KINSHIP

To view ethnicity as a form of greatly extended kinship is to recognize, as ethnic groups do, the role of putative descent. There are fictive elements here, but the idea, if not always the fact, of common ancestry makes it possible for ethnic groups to think in terms of family resemblances—traits held in common, on a supposedly genetic basis, or cultural features acquired in early childhood—and to bring into play for a much wider circle those concepts of mutual obligation and antipathy to outsiders that are applicable to family relations.

The language of ethnicity is the language of kinship. Group members often call each other brothers and call distantly related groups cousins. Harmonious relations among groups are referred to as brotherhood, a term with a figurative meaning: the word connotes the condition of being like brothers but not actually brothers. The behavior of ethnic groups is often justified on the basis of a family idiom. When the Fang of Gabon and Cameroon embarked on a movement to reunite their diverse clan and dialect clusters, they explained their former disunity in terms of family quarrels.[7] The Nigerian Yoruba, searching for commonality against a background of intragroup strife, turned to the myth of a common ancestor for all the subgroups.[8] One of the key indications of the conceptual underpinnings of a behavioral phenomenon is the language of justification, which, in the case of ethnicity, is heavily familistic.

The connections between ethnic relations and family relations are well illustrated by the importance placed on indigenousness or prior occupation of territory, wherever large-scale immigration of ethnic strangers occurs. Confronted with immigrants, a good many ethnic

6. For a quite different treatment of this relationship (one resting on sociobiology), see Pierre L. van den Berghe, *The Ethnic Phenomenon* (New York: Elsevier, 1981), 15–36.

7. James W. Fernandez, "The Affirmation of Things Past: Alar Ayong and Bwiti as Movements of Protest in Central and Northern Gabon," in Robert I. Rotberg and Ali A. Mazrui, eds., *Protest and Power in Black Africa* (New York: Oxford Univ. Press, 1970), 427–57.

8. William Bascom, "Comment: African Arts and Social Control," *African Studies Bulletin* 5 (May 1962): 24.

groups have taken to referring to themselves as "sons of the soil," or some equivalent; they base claims to priority on that status.[9] Prior occupation is also important in relations between families. Among certain fishing groups in the Southern Philippines, for example, some families are "recognized as the first, or leading, kin group. In most cases, this first group is the one that originally began mooring at the place. Others who began to moor there later recognized the priority of the first group. . . . Certain rights and prestige are enjoyed by these 'first families.' In the event of quarrels, others are often chastized as being outsiders, even though they may have moored there for many years."[10] A comparable phenomenon is observable within families. The right of ownership based on having been there first, on being indigenous, is said to be derived from rivalry between older and younger siblings.[11] Here, then, is an example of clearly parallel behavior at the intrafamily, interfamily, and interethnic levels. And, as Erik H. Erikson has pointed out, when prior ownership is contested by a claim to equality, the contradiction is "not easily reconciled either in systems of child training or in political systems."[12]

The mechanism by which connections are made among these various levels of relations probably entails the transference of conceptions and behavior developed at one level onto another. A category of person or a situation seems to resemble another, typically one in which some pattern of appropriate behavior has already been well learned. Something like this is implied by the admittedly too-simple statement that ethnic strangers can be perceived as "symbols of one's baby brother."[13] The transference of habits of behavior is partly due to the difficulty of learning, compartmentalizing, and invoking at appropriate moments altogether different patterns for different relationships. Harry Eckstein has posited a tendency to reduce incongruity between the family and political spheres. Such incongruities, he argues, might produce strain by requiring that similar roles be performed in different ways at different levels.[14]

9. See, e.g., Myron Weiner, *Sons of the Soil: Migration and Ethnic Conflict in India* (Princeton: Princeton Univ. Press, 1978).
10. Nimmo, *The Sea People of Sulu*, 40.
11. Erik H. Erikson, *Childhood and Society*, 2d ed. (New York: W. W. Norton, 1963), 412.
12. Ibid.
13. Gordon W. Allport, *The Nature of Prejudice* (Garden City, N.Y.: Anchor Books, 1958), 369.
14. *A Theory of Stable Democracy* (Princeton: Princeton Univ. Center for International Studies, Monograph no. 10, 1961).

If transference does occur from one level to another, then it is reasonable to surmise that many of the conflictual and cooperative aspects of intrafamily and interfamily life will be reflected in ethnic relations. Freud's view of the family as the unconscious prototype of all human groups is especially appropriate for ethnic groups, with their birth element. Cultural variations in family patterns may be felt in the arena of ethnic conflict. Norms of equality in family life might, for instance, have a bearing on the emergence of a liberal pattern of ethnic relations. Cultural variables of this sort will not receive much attention here, for in a wide-ranging, cross-regional study of this kind, culture has to be held more or less constant. Nonetheless, there are interesting hints in the country-focused literature of the relevance of particular patterns of relations between parents and children and among siblings to relations between in-group members and members of other groups.[15] The apparent spillover of one sphere into another is what Erikson refers to when he speaks of "those configurational analogies between family life and national mores which are hard to fit into a theoretical pattern but seem of utmost relevance."[16]

The connections of kinship to ethnicity are not exhausted by the common ascriptive character of the two affiliations or by the merely analogical influence of family on ethnicity. There are more direct connections between the two. As an ascriptive affiliation, ethnicity is defined by congeries of family relationships, and ethnic ties are therefore pyramided on family ties, often with little consciousness of any distinction between the two. Some small ethnic groups are nothing more than agglomerations of kinship clusters, and many larger groups are aptly described as composites of subgroups—based on caste, region, or dialect, for example—which consist in turn of networks of extended families.[17]

The whole matter has been put nicely by Joshua A. Fishman. Kinship, he says, "is the basis of one's felt bond to one's own kind. It is the basis of one's solidarity with them in times of stress. It is the basis of one's right to presume upon them in times of need. It is the basis of one's

15. See Hyman Rodman, *Lower Class Families: The Culture of Poverty in Trinidad* (New York: Oxford Univ. Press, 1971), 93–99; Murray A. Straus, "Childhood Experience and Emotional Security in the Context of Sinhalese Social Organization," *Social Forces* 33 (Dec. 1954): 152–60.

16. *Childhood and Society*, 316.

17. See Schapera, *Government and Politics in Tribal Societies*, 202; Janice Jiggins, *Caste and Family in the Politics of the Sinhalese, 1947–1976* (Cambridge: Cambridge Univ. Press, 1979), 96.

dependency, sociability and intimacy with them as a matter of course."
And, concludes Fishman, "ethnicity may be the maximal case of socie-
tally organized intimacy and kinship experience."[18] The ethnic tie is
simultaneously suffused with overtones of familial duty and laden with
depths of familial emotion.

There are no bright lines to be drawn between kinship and ethnicity,
especially in societies where the range of recognized family relationships
is wide and the importance of kinship ties is great. The wider the family
network extends, the more likely does it seem that what appears to
insiders as the fulfillment of a specific family obligation, say to a distant
cousin, will appear to outsiders as a form of diffuse, ethnically based
preference or discrimination. The common use of kinship networks to
find jobs, for example, is sometimes interpreted by observers in ethnic
terms instead.[19] Which interpretation is put on the transaction matters,
for the one is morally compelled as help to a kinsman in need, whereas
the other is seen as an invidious instance of favoritism and even injury to
those who lack recourse to such help. In the modern world, nepotism is
generally regarded as more understandable and less reprehensible than
ethnic discrimination is. The two shade into each other repeatedly. As
David Parkin has noted, "one of the problems confronting many ethnic
groups is how to promote or defend its interests in a manner which is
discreet and hidden, so to speak, from wider disapproving authorities. A
people's interests can be advanced through seemingly 'harmless' kinship
relations."[20]

Blurring the line further is the reported tendency for kinship obligations in urban areas to be "broadened to include fellow village dwellers
and even persons from other villages and districts; and the language of
relationships, such as the use of putative kin terms, is broadened to
suggest this expansion," so that "a mythology of consanguinity"
emerges.[21] Such a conceptual extension is no sharp deviation. The range

18. Fishman, "Language and Ethnicity" (unpublished paper presented at a conference
on ethnicity in Eastern Europe, Univ. of Washington, June 1976), 5 (footnote omitted).
19. Judith Djamour, *Malay Kinship and Marriage in Singapore* (London: Athlone
Press, 1959), 49–50; R. D. Grillo, "Ethnic Identity and Social Stratification on a Kampala
Housing Estate," in Abner Cohen, ed., *Urban Ethnicity* (London: Tavistock Publications,
1974), 167.
20. David Parkin, "Congregational and Interpersonal Ideologies in Political Ethnicity,"
in Cohen, ed., *Urban Ethnicity*, 122.
21. Robert H. Bates, "Ethnic Competition and Modernization in Contemporary Africa," *Comparative Political Studies* 6 (Jan. 1974): 457–84, at 468–69.

of recognized kinship is variable over time to begin with, and, as already noted, in many parts of Asia and Africa it is customary to extend kinship terms and treatment to selected nonkinsmen. This extension of kinship is merely a wholesaling of what was previously done retail.

To put the point succinctly, in a society where fictive kinship is accepted and aid to extended kinsmen is commonplace, the supplicant who runs out of cousins to help him would seem likely to turn, as a matter of course, to persons of the same ethnic background. Ethnicity and kinship thus overlap in a quite direct, operational way: the former builds on the latter, the one is often confused with the other, and behavior in one sphere is extended into the other.

In politics, the line between ethnicity and kinship is repeatedly blurred, just as it is in other sectors. Time and again, regimes that are ethnically limited exhibit a reliance for their most crucial functions on family ties, as we shall see when we deal with narrowly based military regimes. Perhaps the apogee of this reliance was achieved in Kenya at the death of Jomo Kenyatta in 1978. Two factions vied for the succession. Both were dominated by Kikuyu, although other ethnic groups tended to cluster around one or the other faction. Beyond this, the factions were divided by Kikuyu subgroup, based on region of origin. One of the factions, in addition, was composed largely of close relatives of Kenyatta, including his son, nephew, brother-in-law, and son-in-law. This faction was popularly called "The Family." Here was a straight line from ethnic group to subethnic group to kinship group.

To emphasize the overlap with kinship is to make aspects of ethnicity clear that are not clear without the kinship connection. Three stand out: (1) the dependence of ethnicity on strong family ties; (2) because of this, the generally greater power and permeativeness of ethnic affiliations in Asia and Africa than in the West; and (3) the intensity of ethnic conflict when it occurs.

The ethnic group is dependent on the family. A strong sense of ethnic identity is difficult to maintain without strong family ties. These include, most prominently, marriage within the group, for completely free choice of marriage partners would undermine the birth basis of the ethnic group.[22] It is not uncommon, as ethnic conflict accelerates, to observe a sharp decline in exogamy. As Kikuyu-Luo political relations grew more

22. For a clear statement of this connection, see Bryce Ryan, *Caste in Modern Ceylon* (New Brunswick: Rutgers Univ. Press, 1953), 25–32.

tense in Kenya, there was a virtual end to Kikuyu-Luo cohabitation and intermarriage.[23] In all of Sri Lanka in 1949, there were only 167 marriages between Sinhalese and Ceylon Tamils.[24] Rates of exogamy for severely divided societies typically run below 10 percent of all marriages, and probably lower if only unions between the most-conflicted groups are counted. In a Kampala, Uganda, survey, the rate of exogamy was 8.2 percent, and no marriage crossed the major fault lines of the society.[25] In Singapore, the rate in the 1960s was 5.1 percent, but Malay-Chinese unions were much rarer.[26] Exact figures are not available for Lebanon before the civil war of the mid-1970s, but there is enough evidence to show that exogamy ran much below 10 percent.[27] Where ethnic loyalties are strong, marriage is even more urgently than usual a family matter.

Societies with more moderate levels of ethnic conflict generally have somewhat higher rates of exogamy.[28] Ghana has overall exogamy rates in the 8 to 18 percent range, depending on how groups are counted.[29] In Philippine cities, exogamy runs as high as 15 or 20 percent.[30] Yet, in Morocco, with its mythology of relatively tolerant ethnic relations, by one count only 11.3 percent of all marriages crossed Arab-Berber lines.[31] Virtually everywhere in Asia and Africa, endogamy is the norm.

As ethnicity is an extension of family, however imperfect, some of the hostility manifested in interethnic relations can be an extension of hostility expressed in interfamilial relations. Ali A. Mazrui has contended that, in traditional African societies, one was either a kinsman or a potential

23. Parkin, "Congregational and Interpersonal Ideologies in Political Ethnicity," in Cohen, ed., *Urban Ethnicity*, 141–42.

24. Ryan, *Caste in Modern Ceylon*, 139.

25. Grillo, "Ethnic Identity and Social Stratification on a Kampala Housing Estate," in Cohen, ed., *Urban Ethnicity*, 168.

26. Riaz Hassan, *Interethnic Marriage in Singapore: A Study in Interethnic Relations* (Singapore: Institute of Southeast Asian Studies, Occasional Paper no. 21, May 1974), 12.

27. David R. Smock and Audrey C. Smock, *The Politics of Pluralism: A Comparative Study of Lebanon and Ghana* (New York: Elsevier, 1975), 92.

28. Where the level of conflict is much more moderate, intermarriage may be far more common. For European immigrant groups in the United States, exogamy rates ranged between 30 and 60 percent by the 1960s. Leonard Dinnerstein and David Reimers, *Ethnic Americans: A History of Immigration and Assimilation* (New York: Harper & Row, 1975), 147.

29. Smock and Smock, *The Politics of Pluralism*, 307; Enid Schildkrout, "Ethnicity and Generational Differences Among Urban Immigrants in Ghana," in Cohen, ed., *Urban Ethnicity*, 209–10.

30. Rodolfo Bulatao, *Ethnic Attitudes in Five Philippine Cities* (Quezon City: Univ. of the Philippines Social Research Laboratory, 1973), 34.

31. Lawrence Rosen, "The Social and Conceptual Framework of Arab-Berber Relations in Central Morocco," in Ernest Gellner and Charles Micaud, eds., *Arabs and Berbers: From Tribe to Nation in North Africa* (Lexington, Mass.: Lexington Books, 1972), 163.

enemy; there was no intermediate category, such as fellow citizen.[32] From this Mazrui deduces that there are formidable barriers to building tolerant, multiethnic societies on such traditional foundations. One needs to be skeptical of such continent-wide cultural generalizations, but such sharp discontinuities between kin and non-kin are not uncommon.[33] In the Philippines, where ethnic endogamy is strongly favored,[34] the same term that is used for outsiders to the village is used for ethnic strangers, and "antipathy to the Chinese (or any other ethnic group) embodies elements of antipathy to the non-kin."[35]

The power and permeativeness of ethnicity in the developing world owe much to the considerable strength of kinship ties in Asia and Africa. In the West, most tasks outside the home are performed by organizations not based on kinship.[36] The same is simply not true in Asia and Africa or is only accurate with a great deal of qualification, recognizing that formally impersonal institutions are actually infused with personal considerations of several kinds; and this is particularly the case with kinship. One reason for the difference is capacity: extended families are able to help their members in more transactions than nuclear families are. Reciprocally, the need and expectation of help strengthen the bonds of the extended family. They are ties it pays to keep in good repair. In the West, on the other hand, the expectation that impersonal criteria will generally (though not always) be applied to formally impersonal transactions weakens the ties of extended kinship. Conversely, the predominance of the nuclear family strengthens the role of impersonal criteria.

Where extended kinship is well established as an affiliation invoked across an array of social, political, and economic transactions, it is a small matter to take the next step and call upon ethnicity—kinship greatly extended—in those transactions. The use of ramified kin networks as underpinnings of ethnic group affiliation makes it easy to communicate "information about matters of common ethnic interest, thus

32. *Soldiers and Kinsmen in Uganda: The Making of a Military Ethnocracy* (Beverly Hills: Sage, 1975), 67.
33. See, e.g., M. M. Green, *Ibo Village Affairs* (London: Sidgewick & Jackson, 1947), on the dangers of stepping outside one's home village in Eastern Nigeria in the early part of the twentieth century.
34. Bulatao, *Ethnic Attitudes in Five Philippine Cities*, 39.
35. George Henry Weightman, "A Study of Prejudice in a Personalistic Society: An Analysis of an Attitude Survey of College Students—University of the Philippines," *Asian Studies* (Manila) 11 (Apr. 1964): 87–101, at 90.
36. George C. Homans, *The Human Group* (London: Routledge & Kegan Paul, 1950), 265.

keeping people alert to the possibility of more mobilized, collective action."[37] Kinship ties, in short, facilitate ethnic political organization. Where, on the other hand, extended kinship is not well established, the invocation of ethnicity is less in conformity with expectations and more apt to be viewed as a breach of the impersonal rules.

Because ethnic affiliations are putatively birth affiliations, their compelling power in conflict is also understandable. If group members are potential kinsmen, a threat to any member of the group may be seen in somewhat the same light as a threat to the family. To call ethnicity a kinlike affiliation is thus to call into play the panoply of rights and obligations, the unspoken understandings, and the mutual aspiration for well-being that are so characteristic of family life in most of Asia and Africa. And to take seriously the myth of ancestry and modal traits in common implies that, within group boundaries, there is something of ourselves in each other.[38] In this light, identification with an ethnic group takes on a much more serious meaning, for it literally involves becoming one with the group.

GROUP BOUNDARIES AND THE NATURE OF ETHNIC AFFILIATIONS

The interplay of givens and chosens in ethnicity is nowhere better revealed than in changes that occur in the scope of group boundaries. As ethnic groups vary in the extent to which individual membership can be acquired solely by birth, so do they vary in the extent to which their boundaries change over time. Here, too, ethnicity parallels kinship. The range of kinship also varies from culture to culture, varies with context within a culture, and varies over time in the same culture. People who are recognized as relatives under some conditions would find their kinship unrecognized under other conditions, and the same is true for recognition of ethnic identity.

ETHNOGENESIS: ASSIMILATION AND DIFFERENTIATION

Ethnic groups can become more or less inclusive. Some small ethnic groups merge with or absorb others, or are absorbed by them, producing

37. Parkin, "Congregational and Interpersonal Ideologies in Political Ethnicity," in Cohen, ed., *Urban Ethnicity*, 149.
38. I owe this formulation to Joshua Fishman, who presented this view at a conference on ethnicity in Eastern Europe, University of Washington, June 1976.

TABLE I   PROCESSES OF ETHNIC
FUSION AND FISSION

Assimilation		Differentiation	
Amalgamation	*Incorporation*	*Division*	*Proliferation*
A + B→C	A + B→A	A→B + C	A→A + B
Two or more groups unite to form a new, larger group	One group assumes the identity of another	One group divides into two or more component parts	One group or more produces an additional group from within its ranks

larger, composite groups. Larger groups, on the other hand, may divide into their component parts, or a portion of such a group may leave it to form a new, smaller group. Group boundaries thus grow wider or narrower by processes of assimilation or differentiation. New groups are born, though old groups do not always die when this occurs. These changes are summarized in Table 1, and I shall provide examples in just a moment.

It will be noted from the table that amalgamation and division are opposite processes, just as incorporation and proliferation are. To say that these are opposites is also to imply that each is potentially reversible. In point of fact, ethnic identity typically embraces multiple levels or tiers, so that it is possible for an individual to claim more than one identity. In the case of amalgamation, for example, members of the new Group C need not renounce completely their membership in one of what are now the component subgroups, A and B. At appropriate times, these lower levels of identity may be invoked again. From the family to the lineage or clan to the regional subgroup to the ethnic group—this is a common progression of increasingly inclusive group memberships.

I have analyzed patterns of ethnic fusion and fission elsewhere,[39] and there is no need to reiterate the details here. But the outlines of the processes of boundary change are important to a proper understanding of

39. Donald L. Horowitz, "Ethnic Identity," in Nathan Glazer and Daniel P. Moynihan, eds., *Ethnicity: Theory and Experience* (Cambridge: Harvard Univ. Press, 1975), 111–40.

ethnic conflict and of prospects for accommodation. Group boundaries are made of neither stone nor putty. They are malleable within limits. The mutability of boundaries does not mean that ethnic affiliations are merely "strategic," that they can be called forth whenever it is convenient to do so in the quest for competitive advantage or can be willed into being in the service of economic interest. On the other hand, boundaries do change, and it is possible to consider the design of measures to utilize shifts in group identity in the interest of conflict reduction. What is necessary, therefore, is a sense of the mutability of group boundaries and yet their dependence on antecedent affinities that are not easily manipulated. To overemphasize the one is to mistake the bases of conflict; to overemphasize the other is to miss important opportunities for policy innovation.

An appropriate starting point is the contextual character of ethnic identity. Group boundaries tend to shift with the political context. Among the most important features of that political context are the size and significance of territorial boundaries. Territorial boundaries help shape the level of group identity that emerges as most salient. The wider the effective territorial boundaries, the wider the ethnic boundaries are likely to be; the narrower the territorial boundaries, the narrower the ethnic boundaries, all else equal. Thus, in the former undivided state of Madras in India, with large Tamil and Telugu populations, cleavages within the Telugu group were not very important. As soon as a separate Telugu-speaking state was carved out of Madras, however, Telugu subgroups—caste, regional, and religious—quickly formed the bases of political action. When many other people in the territory were Tamils, it was vitally important whether one was a Tamil or a Telugu. But when virtually everyone is a Telugu, being Telugu is less important than being, say, Kamma or Reddi, Telangana or Coastal, Muslim or Hindu. The territorial boundary, in short, frames the context in which group interactions occur.

The colonial period in Asia and Africa was, overall, a time during which territorial horizons became larger and, concomitantly, an enormous amount of subgroup amalgamation took place. The colonialists often created territories out of clusters of loosely linked villages and regions. Out of this welding together of local environments a great many new groups appeared, among them the Malays in Malaysia, the Ibo in Nigeria, the Kikuyu in Kenya, the Bangala in Zaire, and the Moro in the Philippines. Some such groups were "artificial" creations of colonial authorities and missionaries, who catalyzed the slow merger of related peoples into coherent ethnic entities. They did this by the way they categorized those they encountered and by the incentives they established to consummate the amalgamation, recruiting soldiers or clerks, for example, from among the newly forged group.[40] Some amalgams emerged because older, lower-level identities were no longer apt, though many such groups also retained the older identities as alternatives, available for frequent invocation in appropriate circumstances. The Malays and Kikuyu, both very cohesive amalgams, can still divide up by ancestral place of origin. Everywhere, however, participants in the process of amalgamation had to adjust their identity upward to conform to the new and larger environment.

They changed their identity by a process of shifting and sorting among the range of peoples they now confronted. The colonial territory contained ethnic strangers perceived as possessing varying degrees of likeness and difference. If a man from Owerri, in Eastern Nigeria, went to Lagos to seek a job, he had to decide whether his new neighbor, who hailed from Onitsha and spoke roughly the same language, was like himself or different. The question would not have arisen back home in Owerri. There an Onitsha man was clearly a stranger. But it was a serious question in Lagos, hundreds of miles from Owerri, for the new environment was heterogeneous. In the immediate vicinity, perhaps there lived members of groups as disparate as the Hausa, Kanuri, Tiv, Yoruba, and Efik. In this context, it became obvious that the Owerri man was related to the Onitsha man, whereas the Muslim Kanuri, who came from a distant region, spoke a quite different language, and behaved quite differently, surely was not. And the Onitsha-Owerri commonality would be even more obvious if those others in the environment made no distinctions between the two, which was likely the case. In such circumstances, a sense of "Ibo" identity was forged through the interplay of self-definition and definition by others.

The process of forging new identities was principally a perceptual one. The principles of social judgment theory help us to understand how it worked.[41] In the experimental literature, the relevant phenomena are

40. For a subtle treatment, see Crawford Young, *Politics in the Congo* (Princeton: Princeton Univ. Press, 1965), chap. 11.

41. See Muzafer Sherif and Carl I. Hovland, *Social Judgment: Assimilation and Contrast Effects in Communication and Attitude Change* (New Haven: Yale Univ. Press, 1961). Also helpful is Henri Tajfel's concise statement, "Perception: Social Perception," in David Sills, ed., *International Encyclopedia of the Social Sciences*, vol. 11 (New York: Macmillan, 1968), 570.

called assimilation and contrast effects. In a heterogeneous environment, a series of stimuli, such as weights or heights or colors, will be sorted out perceptually so that those stimuli that are closely related to each other in value—say, two weights a few ounces apart, compared to others pounds apart—will be merged or assimilated, that is, will appear to the senses to be the same value. More distant stimuli will be contrasted; they will appear to be even more different in value than they actually are. So a complex environment is simplified by a process of judgment that declares relatively similar stimuli to be essentially the same and divergent stimuli to be quite different.

For this simplifying process to occur, there must be a range of difference represented in the environment. The colonial territory did indeed broaden the range of difference by bringing groups into contact that had not had contact, or at least simultaneous contact, before. Of course, the new identities did not necessarily hold for all seasons or all purposes. Just as Ibo subgroups seemed quite similar in the heterogeneous setting of Lagos, so might they again have seemed very different in an all-Ibo environment in Eastern Nigeria. Still, for political purposes, the colony-wide, heterogeneous environment came to be increasingly important. And, as it did, the broader identities it fostered among groups that started out with only limited affinities were solidified. The Malays, for instance, comprised varied groups from as far afield as Sumatra, the Celebes, Borneo, and Java, as well as Malaya, but they developed a highly cohesive, overarching identity *vis-à-vis* the substantial number of Chinese immigrants who appeared in their midst.[42]

If assimilation involves the simplification of identities in a more heterogeneous environment, differentiation entails drawing fine distinctions among people in a less heterogeneous environment. With changes in context, groups can adjust their identity downward as well as upward. This is especially possible if lower (subethnic) levels of identity provide a preexisting basis of cohesion to which a group can repair when the context seems to shrink. One instance of downward shifts in identity, already mentioned, was the heightened salience of divisions among the Telugus as soon as a Telugu-speaking state was carved out of Madras. An even more dramatic downward shift followed the partition of India and Pakistan along what were thought to be hard-and-fast Hindu-Mus-

42. See Judith Nagata, "In Defense of Ethnic Boundaries: The Changing Myths and Charters of Malay Identity," in Charles F. Keyes, ed., *Ethnic Change* (Seattle: Univ. of Washington Press, 1981), 88–116.

lim lines. Barely had this been accomplished when ethnic divisions within Pakistan became prominent, culminating in the emergence of Bangladesh in 1971. Changing context can work for fission as easily as for fusion, and lower and higher levels of identity can coexist and be activated as territorial boundaries change. These are behavioral propensities quite relevant to the design of structures to reduce ethnic tensions.

To depict the process of boundary change in these terms is to understand why it makes no sense to ask abstractly whether groups based on language are more cohesive or more separatist or more prone to conflict than, say, groups based on religion. For, as I indicated in Chapter 1, it is not the particular differentiating characteristic that matters for such questions. That is largely an accident of context and contact. The differentiating characteristics that become prominent will be defined in terms of what traits an emerging group has in common as against other groups with whom it finds itself in a single environment. It is, in the end, ascriptive affinity and disparity, and not some particular inventory of cultural attributes, that found the group.

In fact, there may be quite a wide range of cultural difference represented even among the subgroups within an ethnic amalgam. Among the Malays, only the Minangkabau are matrilineal. Among the Nigerian Yoruba, there have been considerable differences of language from one traditional kingdom to another. In both cases, culture has tended to follow boundaries rather than defining them. So the Minangkabau tend to accommodate to general Malay cultural standards, and a standard dialect has been emerging among the Yoruba. As group cohesion grows, cultural deviations and rough edges get smoothed off. Culture is important in the making of ethnic groups, but it is more important for providing *post facto* content to group identity than it is for providing some ineluctable prerequisite for an identity to come into being.

There is no need to impute predetermination to this whole process. Although the perceptual side of boundary change bears emphasis, it is, of course, not entirely an unguided process of stimulus and response. Political choices are also made by group leaders as assimilation and differentiation proceed. Consider the Fang of Gabon, who developed a rivalry with the better-educated Mpongwé people during the colonial period. The Fang sensed that, in a political conflict, their clan and dialect divisions were a disadvantage, and they set about recreating their former unity. A prominent part in the Fang revival was played by a legend of common origin and migration, which rested on genuine genealogies but also contained new elements, of dubious historical accuracy.[43] Strategic judgments of this sort, about the shape and scope of group boundaries necessary for competition, are not incompatible with more spontaneous perceptual judgments. Rather, deliberative strategic judgments are made possible by prior perceptual judgments about other groups in the same environment. They presuppose, in other words, the sifting process by which group affinities and disparities are discerned.

In general, therefore, leaders cannot call into play an identity that is not founded on judgments of relative likeness and difference. If the perceptual context changes so as to reactivate some higher or lower level of group or subgroup identity formerly regarded as highly salient, such changes in identity may happen quickly. But, for the rest, the process of sifting and sorting takes time. Wholly new ethnic groups do not come into being overnight. There can be no "big bang" theory of ethnogenesis.

CULTURAL MOVEMENTS
AND BOUNDARY REINFORCEMENT

Group boundaries must be underpinned by a suitable apparatus of myth and legend, which cannot be generated spontaneously. Cultural movements, ranging from mild literary, religious, and historical revivals to full-fledged crisis cults, gradually shape and reshape the contours of ethnic myth and legend. A common source of cultural movements is concern about potential shifts in group boundaries. The colonial period was filled with such movements. The form they took was largely a response to the direction of boundary change underway, to growing differentiation or assimilation. An ethnic group fragmented into subgroups that threatened to overtake the larger group identity might react by reinforcing elements of common culture and common ancestry, suppressing, for example, differences in dialect or stressing descent from a single ancestor. On the other hand, a group that found itself losing its distinctive identity by absorption in another ethnic group might respond by emphasizing its cultural uniqueness, selectively recalling ancient glories, resuscitating all that distinguishes group members from others, destroying all that links them to others. It is appropriate, then, to speak of *movements of assimilation* and *movements of differentiation*, depending on whether affinity or disparity is being emphasized. Either way, how-

43. Fernandez, "The Affirmation of Things Past."

ever, the progress of cultural movements to support boundary maintenance or reconstruction was measured in decades, for they entailed the
reorientation of collective beliefs and practices, religious, linguistic, and
historical.[44]

Movements of Assimilation

Groups such as the Fang of Gabon and Cameroon, the Yoruba of Nigeria, the Lozi of Zambia, and the Bakongo of Zaire, Angola, and Congo
(Brazzaville) all experienced movements of assimilation. In each case,
the movement was a reaction to internal differentiation. These were
groups whose unity was precarious. Sometimes their subgroups had
fought each other. Often their languages had drifted apart. During the
colonial period, efforts were made by group leaders to unite them, efforts
that stressed a glorious past and legends of common origin. They were
often accompanied by measures to standardize language and in other
ways to minimize cultural differences among the subgroups.

Typically, these efforts were spurred by the recognition that, as colonialism waned, the group would face ethnic competition in which its
fragmentation would put it at a disadvantage. A group vulnerable to
subgroup fission was liable to divide its support "uneconomically"
among several political parties unless a foundation were laid for ethnic
reunification. Movements that aimed to unify fragmented groups like
the Fang and the Yoruba were generally utilized by party leaders to
mobilize the groups for effective political action. The Yoruba movement,
the *Egbe Omo Oduduwa* (Society of the Children of Oduduwa, the
Yoruba mythical ancestor), was closely linked to the Yoruba party, the
Action Group; there was much overlapping membership.

Attempts to reconstitute a group by amalgamating its subgroups met
with a considerable measure of success. Still, the reconstitutive process
left room for backsliding. The Yoruba, for example, managed to surmount internal differences and participate in politics on a broader group
basis, but at various points Yoruba subgroups competed with the all-
Yoruba identification. The persistence of subgroup identities was reflected in Yoruba party politics. Despite the quest for commonality, the
Action Group was rent by subgroup factionalism.

44. For a fuller treatment than is possible here, see Donald L. Horowitz, "Cultural
Movements and Ethnic Change," *The Annals* 433 (Sept. 1977): 6–18. The discussion in
the remainder of this section is drawn from this article.

Movements of Differentiation

Whereas groups threatened with differentiation turn to the past to reduce their internal diversity, groups threatened with assimilation resort to their history to affirm their distinctiveness from those around them. Often begun by group members who are furthest along in the individual assimilation process, these movements commonly result in an explosive and violent assertion of group separateness.

The Bakonjo in Western Uganda, the Kurds in Iraq, Syria, Iran, and Turkey, the Basques in Spain, and the Sikhs in the Indian Punjab all went through such movements of differentiation. In each case, the boundary between them and a group in close proximity was porous. Acculturation to the norms of the neighboring group was common. This might include abandonment of one's own language or religious practices. Changes in individual ethnic identity might follow. In this way, elites were lost to the group, and the language and culture of the group were frequently disparaged. Bakonjo borrowed Batoro rites and language, Kurds in Iraqi cities underwent Arabization, Basques became Castilianized, and the line between Sikhs and Hindus was uncertain.

The cultural revivals that emerged in response reflected an awareness of the danger of a fading group identity. They tended to emphasize the history of separateness and even hostility between the groups. Memories of insults were recalled. Languages were "purified" of words that derived from the language of the neighboring group.[45] Religious practices were cleansed in the same way, in the name of returning to some former state of orthodoxy that may or may not have existed. Group identity was thus infused with a new or revived cultural content that served to demarcate the lines between groups more clearly, thereby reducing the ease with which individuals could cross group boundaries.

Concomitant with the sharpening of group differences was an increase in intergroup hostility. Movements that went furthest in asserting the distinctiveness of groups believed to be in danger of assimilation ultimately became strongly separatist. The Bakonjo and the Kurds both participated in secessionist insurgencies. The Basque country of Spain has experienced separatist terrorism. The Sikhs have conducted separatist agitations on several occasions—most recently in the 1960s, before a Sikh-majority state was carved out of the Punjab, and in the 1980s in

45. See Brian Weinstein, *The Civic Tongue: Political Consequences of Language Choices* (New York: Longman, 1983), 65.

behalf of an independent Sikh state, "Khalistan." As movements of assimilation are geared to transcend subgroup identities to facilitate effective group participation in the wider politics of the whole territory, so movements of differentiation lend themselves to separatist political claims. The violent character of these responses to the feared loss of group distinctiveness is a powerful point in the case against assimilationist policies of nation-building.

Cultural Movements and Conflict

A common result of cultural movements of assimilation and of differentiation, as well as of movements that began as anti-colonial cultural revivals, was the infusion of cultural demands into post-colonial politics. The ethnocentric cultural functionaries who rewrote the grammars, histories, and scriptures often emerged in a position to condition their political support on state recognition and patronage. In Burma, Buddhism was made the state religion. In Sri Lanka, Sinhala was made the official language. Where a language was recognized as official, language institutes were often created, and cultural functionaries were converted into state officials producing new lexical, literary, and instructional materials. Typically, there was heightened attention to language as a basis of group identity. At the same time, demands for state patronage and official adoption of ethnic symbols were seen as exclusivist by members of other ethnic groups. Concessions to such demands precipitated secessionist movements by non-Burmans in Burma and ethnic violence in Sri Lanka. Culture, revived to support group identity, became a public issue between groups.

CULTURE, BOUNDARIES, AND CONFLICT

Ethnic boundary change and cultural movements illustrate several general characteristics of ethnicity. Underlying all of them is the interactive quality of the variables related to group identity: culture, boundaries, conflict, and the policy outcomes of conflict.

Discourse about ethnic conflict is replete with assumptions about how wholly formed, unchanging cultural inventories give rise to the emergence of ethnic groups. Ethnic groups are said to be based on shared cultures, histories, traditions. In turn, it is assumed, groups with firmly fixed boundaries enter into conflict with each other. From this conflict, policy outcomes emerge. The common notion is that these are watertight, sequential, and unidirectional processes: each must precede the next.

No doubt it is often necessary to speak of things in flux as if they were static. In most of this book, I, too, shall speak as if ethnic conflict occurs between groups with fairly firm boundaries.

Yet, even as conceptual convenience often demands a static idiom, it needs to be remembered that the phenomena are reciprocal rather than unidirectional. First, the construction and reconstruction of group boundaries are not processes wholly prior to ethnic conflict; they take place partly in anticipation of conflict. Second, as ethnic conflict proceeds, it can influence the shape and firmness of the boundaries, by such means as heightened pressure for endogamy. Third, group boundaries are not simply the product of common culture. Emerging boundaries can alter cultural patterns by, for example, homogenizing them as amalgamation proceeds. Fourth, policy is not merely an end product of ethnic conflict, for it reacts in turn upon conflict and upon boundaries and culture. In all of this, there is ample evidence that phenomena which our mind's eye tends to keep separate are parts of a system.

THE UTILITY OF
ETHNIC AFFILIATIONS

From what has already been said, it is not difficult to infer that ethnic affiliations typically fulfill needs that might otherwise go unmet. What some such functions might be is hinted at in a general way by the conception of an ethnic group as a fictive, greatly extended family, a unit that provides blood solidarity and personalistic help in an increasingly impersonal environment—in short, ascription in an ostensibly nonascriptive world.

Previous writers have occasionally asked whether the recurrent importance of ethnic ties indicates that ethnic groups do somehow derive their strength from the functions they perform. Having approached the question, however, they generally draw back from it, for one of two reasons. Functional interpretations are in disfavor, because they are regarded as teleological and biased toward the status quo: something is—therefore, it must be. Alternatively, the question has sometimes been cast in an unfortunate way: are ethnic affiliations "natural"?[46] To this, an answer has been given. Ethnicity, it is argued, entails a mistaken version of a natural process. The mistake is "pseudospeciation," the treatment

46. See, e.g., Anthony D. Smith, *The Ethnic Revival in the Modern World* (Cambridge: Cambridge Univ. Press, 1981), 85–86.

of members of other groups as if they were members of different species, which manifestly they are not.[47] Denial of common humanity has produced unspeakable brutality against members of other ethnic groups. And so the question of function has gone by default, because, on the one hand, it seems to conjure up functional*ism* and, on the other, it seems to lead directly to some of the great, potentially lethal, false cognitions of the human species.

The question, however, is deserving of more serious treatment. It is possible to identify some functions of ethnicity without succumbing to teleology and without getting derailed on the spurious survival value of "pseudospeciation" or the denial of a common humanity to members of other ethnic groups.

The ubiquity of ethnic loyalties suggests the existence of needs to which they respond. The sensitivity of group boundaries to changing territorial context in Asia and Africa provides help in identifying those needs in a concrete way. As I explained earlier, one of the most powerful influences on the scope and shape of "we" and "they" has been the scope and shape of political boundaries. For the most part, as I said, movement during the colonial period was upward—toward larger territories and more inclusive, frequently amalgamated, ethnic groups. It is worth looking a bit more closely at the impact of territory on ethnicity, for it is apparent that territorial unification, besides shaping perceptual judgments of ethnic affinity and disparity, created new conditions and opportunities that emerging ethnic groups were suited to meet.

There has been much misleading talk and writing about the artificiality of colonial territorial boundaries. The Europeans, it is said, drew arbitrary lines on maps to suit their own interests, heedless of their effect on ethnic groups. Some ethnic groups were thereby divided between territories, and some were included in the same territory along with others with whom they had little in common. These arguments are greatly exaggerated. The boundary-drawing process frequently took ethnic interests into account, and boundaries were often redrawn later by colonial powers in response to ethnic demands.[48] Any boundaries of significant scale, no matter how they were drawn, would have been arbitrary, for most Asian and African groups of the time were clustered at

47. Erik H. Erikson, *Dimensions of a New Identity* (New York: W. W. Norton, 1974), 28.
48. Saadia Touval, *The Boundary Politics of Independent Africa* (Cambridge: Harvard Univ. Press, 1972), 3–17.

the village level or in somewhat larger kingdoms, generally not of a highly centralized sort. To draw any line to pull 200,000 or 300,000 square miles into a single territory was necessarily to throw together a great many stranger-groups and to divide other groups. What is remarkable is not that some former kingdoms, such as the Bakongo, were apportioned to several colonies, but that many others, including the Sinhalese and Baganda kingdoms and the Malay and Indonesian sultanates, were not divided.

What the colonialists did that was truly profound, and far more important for ethnicity, was to change the scale of the polity by several fold. The colonies were artificial, not because their borders were indifferent to their ethnic composition, but because they were, on the average, many times larger than the political systems they displaced or encapsulated.

Parallel to this political-territorial expansion were comparable economic developments, especially in the export sector. International commerce in minerals and cash crops required networks of labor recruitment, production, and transport that far transcended, in distance and complexity, established trading patterns. Of course, the long-distance trade antedated the European arrival; indeed, it attracted the Europeans. But the scale of trade made possible by an infrastructure of new roads and ports and markets, the new credit networks established for it, the number of people brought into the trading vortex, the new mobility it created as labor migrated in response to opportunity, the growth of urban centers—all were enormously expanded under colonial rule. As there was a new superstate imposed, so, too, was there a new supereconomy.[49]

In both, the network of transactions grew in scale out of all proportion to the reach of preexisting sentiments of community. With migration, trade, and a central bureaucratic structure, among other things, it became necessary to establish social relations far beyond the village or locality. Later, with national elections, the need became even more exigent. To respond to the new opportunity structure imposed by the Europeans required assurances of predictability, trust, reciprocity, fair deal-

49. Some of the consequences in the field of labor migration are depicted in Immanuel Wallerstein, ed., *Social Change: The Colonial Situation* (New York: John Wiley, 1966), pt. II. For the general tendency of colonialism to increase the scale of transactions, see Peter Duignan and L. H. Gann, "Introduction," in Duignan and Gann, eds., *Colonialism in Africa, 1870–1960*, vol. 4: *The Economics of Colonialism* (Cambridge: Cambridge Univ. Press, 1975), esp. 3, 8, 17. See also Duignan and Gann, "The Pre-Colonial Economics of Sub-Saharan Africa," in ibid., 42, 52, on the limits of pre-colonial economic structures.

ing, and help in the event of need in strange surroundings. From what source could appropriate social arrangements be fashioned?

One possibility was the evolution of an impersonal conception of citizenship that would transcend particularistic identifications, minimize uncertainty, and facilitate relations among strangers.[50] In providing physical security and some measure of legal recourse, the colonial powers took the first steps along these lines, alleviating some inhibitions on taking up new opportunities. But a full-blown apparatus of citizenship was precluded by the obvious fact that colonials were not citizens but subjects. In Western Europe, by contrast, citizenship rights had developed along with conceptions of popular sovereignty. Even had that not been so, the European ideological developments that produced doctrines of equality and impersonal treatment had evolved over the course of centuries and were not susceptible to wholesale transplantation within the time frame required to respond to new colonial opportunities. In Asia and Africa, the transactional problem was measured in years and decades.

Far more apt a response was the adaptation of preexisting social institutions, particularly informal ones that neither threatened the colonial regime with a new panoply of rights nor taxed its strictly limited administrative machinery. Most notable among these institutions were kinship and ethnicity. Some ethnic groups had earlier been active in controlling particular trade routes or occupations, and much economic activity had been organized along kinship lines. By itself, however, the reach of extended families or of existing ethnic groups was generally not great enough to cover the span of the new transactional networks. Yet it is not surprising that the familiar hand of kinship should reach out and expand into these new domains, through the medium of the extended family but more often through the medium of that greatly extended and expansible family, the ethnic group.[51]

The point has been put in concrete form by Joseph M. Kaufert for urban Africa:

Among non-elites in African cities, kin groups may not possess sufficiently broad networks of influence or sufficient economic power to fulfill the same functions

---

50. Cf. T. H. Marshall, *Citizenship and Social Class* (Cambridge: Cambridge Univ. Press, 1950); Reinhard Bendix, *Nation-Building and Citizenship* (New York: John Wiley, 1964).

51. See, e.g., Gerald M. Meier, "External Trade and Internal Development," in Duignan and Gann, eds., *Colonialism in Africa*, vol. 4, pp. 444–46.

for the urban migrant that they did in the rural environment. A single family may have insufficient resources, for example, to pay the bribe, or contact the distant cousin in order to find employment for the migrant, or get a younger brother into a secondary school. Members of extended families having few elite linkages may not be very successful at resocializing their newly arrived relatives into the intricacies of the urban environment. In such cases more inclusive ethnic groups take on some of the functions of the extended family, thus diminishing the number of situations in which narrower kinship ties are important.[52]

Kaufert notes that several students in his Ghanaian sample were called upon to play the role of "brother" or "uncle" for more and more distantly related people in the city and that kinship terms have tended generally to be transferred to members of the broader ethnic group.

Ethnicity, then, is functionally continuous with kinship. The process of shifting from one to the other has not been studied comprehensively, but there are interesting glimpses from which mechanisms of change can be discerned. Consider briefly two examples, one contemporary, urban, and African, the other historical, rural, and Asian. In both, ethnicity takes over a range of new interactions where kinship leaves off, and it does so using a kinship idiom.

The stretching of earlier kinship forms and obligations to meet the new transactional needs is exemplified by Mossi migrants from Upper Volta to Kumasi, Ghana. First-generation Mossi migrants have few kinsmen in Kumasi. Nevertheless, they quickly become part of the Mossi community and create fictive family relationships with other Mossi "which they can rely upon as they could rely upon kinship relationships 'at home.' They come to town with kinship concepts but without kin."[53] Unrelated Mossi assume the specific roles and obligations of family members. The Mossi headman in Kumasi is treated by migrants just as a lineage head would be treated in Upper Volta. He is accorded authority to settle a wide range of what would otherwise be regarded as family disputes. The Mossi in Kumasi transfer, broaden, and apply their kinship concepts to the ethnic arena with alacrity, illustrating Meyer Fortes' more general point (for the culturally similar Tallensi) that "all social

52. Joseph M. Kaufert, "Situational Ethnic Identity in Ghana," in John N. Paden, ed., *Values, Identities and National Integration: Empirical Research in Africa* (Evanston: Northwestern Univ. Press, 1980), 59.
53. Enid Schildkrout, "Ethnicity and Generational Differences Among Urban Immigrants in Ghana," in Cohen, ed., *Urban Ethnicity*, 204.

relations implying mutual or common interests tend to be assimilated to those of kinship."[54]

Second-generation Mossi in Kumasi are in a different position. Unlike new migrants, they have real kin to assume kinship roles and obligations. For them, ethnicity is no longer a substitute for kinship. Overlaying kinship relations is a network of explicitly ethnic associations devoted to advancing Mossi political interests in the competitive environment of Kumasi.[55]

The interplay of kinship and ethnicity thus changes as the generationally defined situation of the Mossi in Kumasi changes. In the first instance, kinship provides the bridge to ethnic membership. This is achieved by ignoring actual consanguinity in establishing relationships. Then kinship recedes to its previous dimensions, based on consanguinity. Ethnic membership, inclusively defined and broader in Kumasi than in Upper Volta, where Mossi society is subdivided, becomes important in coping with the problems of collective existence in a multiethnic city far from the Mossi homeland. The initial stretching of kinship so as to disregard actual consanguinity facilitates the later representation of the Mossi as a single, undifferentiated community by their political associations. From adaptations of this sort, it becomes possible to see how the scale of group interactions could expand with the effective size of the territory, permitting people to go further afield and redressing what would otherwise have been an imbalance between the scope of transactions and the scope of social relations required to consummate the new transactions.

The Asian example, drawn from Malaysia, involves an analogous extension of kinship to the wider ethnic community, but it entails a different sequence of changes.[56] In the nineteenth century, Malay rural life in the Sik district of Kedah state was centered on *padi*-growing villages, virtually all of whose inhabitants were kindred. Kinship was the source of aid in the event of destitution, of easy and trusting personal relations, of certainty in dealings, and of popular support for aspiring

54. Meyer Fortes, *The Web of Kinship Among the Tallensi* (London: Oxford Univ. Press, 1949), 19, quoted in ibid.
55. Schildkrout, "Ethnicity and Generational Differences," 214.
56. See Conner Bailey, *Broker, Mediator, Patron and Kinsman: An Historical Analysis of Key Leadership Roles in a Rural Malaysian District* (Athens, Ohio: Ohio Univ. Papers in International Studies, Southeast Asia Series, no. 38, 1976); David J. Banks, "Changing Kinship in North Malaya," *American Anthropologist* 74 (Oct. 1972): 1254–75.

leaders. As rice cultivation is a labor-intensive and cooperative enterprise, the extended family was also an economic unit in subsistence production. With the advent of rubber tapping and a vastly improved system
of roads in the early twentieth century, however, there was a great influx
of strangers, most of them also Malays, into Sik. The developing cash
economy also put Malays into contact with Chinese shopkeepers. The
need to earn money, rather than merely grow rice, reduced the general
ability to help distant kin. Rubber tapping required less social cooperation than rice farming. The net result of these developments was to dilute
somewhat the kinship basis of village organization, to foster a wider
sense of being Malay, and to heighten the importance of the nuclear
family at the expense of the extended family.[57]

As the twentieth century wore on, the population in Sik had grown so
rapidly that land shortage became prevalent. Many Malays inherited no
land and were forced to leave their home villages for rubber tapping jobs
far away. With this development, the "importance of filial ties declined
in the lives of many,"[58] so that the nuclear family became more distant
as out-migrants were thrown upon their own resources for sustenance.
The former village antinomy between "familiars" and "strangers" was
broken by the whole sequence of in-migration and out-migration, and
there emerged "a wider community of concern with other peoples possessing different accents who are all now simply Malays and opposed to
Chinese and other groups . . . ."[59] Kinship defined by strict consanguinity had not been supplanted but supplemented by kinship defined in
inclusive ethnic terms. The case of Sik "shows a dispersion of kinship
outside of the immediate nucleus of parental-filial and sibling relations
to include various kinds of bonds, with friendship, contractual, and
blood components. People must look for kinship everywhere now"[60]—
that is, everywhere in the Malay community. As the range of intrafamil-
ial interactions contracted, the range of intraethnic interactions widened, and the targets of family-like claims for emotional and material
help were broadened accordingly.

In both Kumasi and Sik, modern transport, colonial administration,
and a cash economy created opportunities to which people responded.
An effective response was not possible within the literal confines of the

57. For parallel developments in an urban Malay community, see Djamour, *Malay
Kinship and Marriage in Singapore.*
58. Banks, "Changing Kinship in North Malaya," 1268.
59. Ibid., 1271.
60. Ibid.

prevailing genealogical kinship system, for an effective response entailed migration far from identifiable relatives. Such a response was possible, however, by substituting fictive kinship for genuine kinship, conferring kin or kin-like relationships on members of the same ethnic groups, and recognizing a broader role for the ethnic group in the lives of individuals. The route to this outcome was not the same in Kumasi and in Sik, but in both cases there was a disposition to see ethnicity and kinship as functionally related structures. The balance between them could be altered and obligations from one transferred to the other. The willingness to mold elements of the two structures to meet the exigencies posed by a broader transactional network suggests that the functions of ethnicity and kinship in the new setting may not be so different from those of kinship alone in the old.

Among the most important needs met by ethnicity is the need for familiarity and community, for family-like ties,[61] for emotional support and reciprocal help, and for mediation and dispute resolution—for all the needs served by kinship, but now on a larger canvas. And, because the scale is changed, some new functions also have to be performed. Transactions with people not previously encountered become more frequent. Common ethnicity enhances the predictability of their behavior and imposes a set of normative obligations on transactions. Encounters with the state and its ostensibly impersonal apparatus are also necessary. Common ethnicity can create bonds between bureaucrats and citizens. If impersonal criteria of fair treatment and impartiality are novel, suspect, or imperfectly understood, then protection deriving from the very partiality of ethnicity can provide a cushion against arbitrariness. Ethnicity, moreover, provides a convenient handle for political organization to press claims on government and to interpret government to group members. Knowledge that a group's leaders are guarding group interests can impart a sense of security to group members. In short, members of an ethnic group need not face a new environment, an untested system of relations, or a situation requiring help all alone.

No doubt the degree to which ethnicity performs these functions, or does so to the exclusion of other affiliations, is highly variable. For example, in interactions with strangers, common ethnic membership calls

---

61. Ethnicity counters "the structured and artificial isolation of persons who must act and interact with one another within legitimated boundaries restricted to the differentiation of roles in complex societies. If alienation is a malfunction of modern society, ethnicity is an antidote." Ronald Cohen, "Ethnicity: Problem and Focus in Anthropology," *Annual Review of Anthropology* 7 (1978): 379–403, at 401.

up abstract qualities that transcend the individual qualities of individual members and cue the behavior of others on the basis of social placement and supposedly innate characteristics. But the degree to which ethnicity entails such abstraction varies with, among other things, the cultural disposition to think about others in categorical rather than personal terms. In Bali, to take one instance, that disposition is strong, and so ascriptive identity is paramount.[62] In Morocco, categories are less important than are the attributes of individual personality. Consequently, ethnic identity is used in personal relations only to establish probable traits, which, combined with individually established traits, provide the basis for interpersonal judgments.[63] Cultural variations of this sort, which I shall generally suppress, do not detract from the broader point that ethnicity provides a convenient way to simplify reality in unfamiliar circumstances by avoiding the necessity to make wholly individual judgments with every new encounter.

The view I have advanced here of the utility of ethnic affiliations in the wider transactional networks of the colonial and post-colonial state contrasts with the commonly held notion in the early years after independence that there was a need for a massive shift of loyalties from the ethnic group to the state in the interest of "nation-building."[64] The assumption was that ethnic loyalties subsisted at a lower level and lagged behind the development of the modern state. What we have seen shows this assumption to be unfounded. More often than not, ethnic groups are the product of altered levels of loyalty and are already keyed to the state level. That they are not inclusive of everyone within the state is not due to any lag in development but to the powerful role of contrast in the growth of group identity. In view of the functions ethnicity performs, supplanting ethnic loyalties is at once less realistic and less attractive a goal than is the more modest object of reducing ethnic conflict.

There is another issue raised by identification of the functions of eth-

---

62. See Clifford Geertz, *Person, Time, and Conduct in Bali: An Essay in Cultural Analysis* (New Haven: Yale Univ. Southeast Asia Series, Cultural Report no. 14, 1966), 43, 53–54.

63. See Rosen, "The Social and Conceptual Framework of Arab-Berber Relations in Central Morocco," 167, 171.

64. For other views on the functions of ethnicity, see Lloyd I. Rudolph and Susanne Hoeber Rudolph, *The Modernity of Tradition: Political Development in India* (Chicago: Univ. of Chicago Press, 1967); Immanuel Wallerstein, "Ethnicity and National Integration in West Africa," *Cahiers d'Etudes africaines* 3 (Oct. 1960): 129–38; Chandra Jayawardena, "Religious Belief and Social Change: Aspects of the Development of Hinduism in British Guiana," *Comparative Studies in Society and History* 8 (Apr. 1966): 211–40.

nicity, and it is best clarified sooner rather than later: the relationship between the needs met by ethnic ties and the emergence of ethnic conflict. That relationship is not straightforward. To understand the functions of ethnicity is not necessarily to know anything much about ethnic conflict. To be sure, in a great many countries the functions I have identified have not only been performed but overperformed. Some groups have been given so much security as to make others uneasy and suspicious. Organization has generated counterorganization, familiarity a sense of exclusion in others, ethnic allocations a feeling of discrimination and grievance. Yet it remains true that many of the needs I have identified are met by private activity that does not impinge on intergroup relations or by action that culminates in a tacit apportionment of ethnic spheres of influence, as we shall see in the case of job competition. The quest for community, which leads to clustering by ethnic groups, can actually retard the growth of intergroup conflict. The utility of ethnic affiliations cannot be gainsaid, but it need not and should not give rise to a wholly utilitarian or instrumental theory of ethnic conflict.

ETHNIC AFFILIATIONS AND THE INSTITUTIONS OF THE MODERN STATE

I have insisted on describing ethnic affiliations as involving descent. The principle of ethnic membership is typically the birth principle, however much it may be diluted in practice by fictive extensions. What I have not done is to say what difference ascription makes in ethnic politics. The difference can be shown dramatically with a single, revealing example of the interaction of ascriptive affiliations with the formal institutions of the modern state.

Suppose the population of a country is divided into two ethnic groups, A and B. Group A comprises 60 percent; Group B, 40 percent. The two groups have equal rates of natural increase and similar age structures. Political parties form along ethnic lines, as they tend to do in ethnically divided societies. Members of Group A uniformly support Party A. Members of Group B support Party B. Both groups are cohesive, so that no third party emerges in this bipolar society. In parliamentary elections, the parties bring to the polls the vast majority of their respective supporters. The country is divided into single-member territorial constituencies of equal population. The two ethnic groups are spread through the country in such a way that Group A forms a majority in 60 percent of the constituencies and Group B a majority in 40 percent. (Note that if the two groups were distributed evenly through the territory, Group A would form a majority in all of the constituencies.)

Under these conditions, Party A will always form the government. As a matter of fact, Party A will form the government under a number of variations on these conditions as well. Whether the rule of decision is majority vote or first-past-the-post, Party A will secure 60 percent of the seats. Likewise, if the election were conducted on the basis of proportional representation, with the whole country as a single constituency, Party A would also win 60 percent of the seats. It is possible to introduce uncertainty into the result, but to do so would require rather drastic and elaborate electoral engineering. The contrivances needed to make the result uncertain would quickly begin to undermine the legitimacy of the electoral process, because they would inevitably mean that a party with a nationwide voting majority might nevertheless be deprived of office. In short, the predictable and "reasonable" result of party preferences distributed as I have specified is the victory of Party A and Group A.

The implications for Group B are ominous. It has not lost just one election. Absent some dramatic change in group demography or in the cohesion of Group A, the result of this election is likely to hold for the next election and for every election thereafter. Group B will forever be excluded from power and its rewards and even from the ability to influence the exercise of power. In such a predictable system, what electoral incentives do Group A and Party A have to be moderate toward Group B? Perhaps the only reason to be moderate is to discourage members of Group B from being driven to extreme strategies of opposition.

It will come as no surprise that where the interaction of ethnic demography, party alignments, and electoral systems produces results of this sort, Group B often resorts to violence. In the example given, the two groups are spread through the country, so secessionist violence is highly unlikely; but where the groups are territorially concentrated, that possibility is not to be excluded. Two other forms of violence are possible. Members of Group B may vent their sense of permanent exclusion through rioting against members of Group A that is more or less spontaneous or more or less directed by the leaders of Party B. Alternatively, members of Group B in the armed forces may decide that something is fundamentally wrong with the electoral process and that a fairer way of allocating power is to seize it.

It will at once be objected that the specifications given in the problem are unrealistic. There are never only two ethnic groups in a single society. Each group rarely throws its support to only one party. If it does, the groups will nonetheless vary in their electoral participation rates. Rates of natural increase are ethnically variable. Ethnic groups are not so distributed through a territory as to permit the drawing of constituencies to produce a parliamentary majority mirroring the ethnic composition of the whole population. The fixity of the result in the example is an artifact of rigidly specified demographic, party-political, and electoral conditions.

It is certainly true that the politics of every country is more complex than the politics I have conjured. But the example, albeit an ideal type, remains far more realistic than might be supposed. The variations that have been adduced do not assure a more satisfying or tranquil outcome.

This is the business of later chapters, and I can only indicate enough here to show that the example is merely a pristine case of a much larger category of cases. Generally, there are more than two groups, but sometimes they nonetheless choose up sides in what becomes a bipolar confrontation. Where bipolarity does not take over, the presence of third groups opens the possibility that the largest group, though able to muster a plurality of the vote for its party, will be excluded from power by the configuration of votes and seats obtained *in toto* by the other groups. If the excluded group is the largest, the degree of dissatisfaction may be greater than in the simple 60–40 situation. An even more extreme result can be produced by party fragmentation. If Group *A*, with 60 percent of the population, divides its support between two parties, it is open to Group *B* or to *B* and *C*, with 40 percent but only one party, to form a government that excludes the majority group. This it can do by winning a majority of seats by repeated pluralities in three-way contests. Likewise, rates of natural increase often do vary, but the variation, while making the group with the lower rate more anxious about the future, does nothing to change ascriptive party politics. In polarized polities, ethnic variations in rates of voting participation are rarely great, because parties mobilize their supporters. Variations in the territorial distribution of population or in the apportionment of constituencies, though common, have as their principal effect the widening of the gap between votes cast by an ethnic group and seats won by that group. If Group *A*, with 60 percent of the total vote, wins 80 percent of the seats, the outlook for Group *B* is even gloomier. If, however, Group *B*, with 40 percent of the vote, gains 51 percent of the seats, then Group *A*, a nominal majority, is reduced to minority status. None of the variations does much to soften the rigidity of ascriptive party politics. There are, however, some deliberate policies, dealt with in Chapter 15, that may have some impact.

If we ask what went wrong with this election, there are at first plausible grounds for saying nothing went wrong. The election was democratically conducted. The results are in conformity with the principle of majority rule. But that is the sticking point. Majority rule in perpetuity is not what we mean by "majority rule."[65] We assume the possibility of shifting majorities, of oppositions becoming governments, of an alterable public opinion. All this is foreclosed by the ascriptive character of the majority that voted for Party A. The election, intended to be a vehicle of choice, was no such thing and will be no such thing in the future; it registered, not choice, but birth affiliation.[66] This was no election—it was a census.

I shall show later that elections of this general type are a major—though not the only—reason for the decline of democracy in Africa, Asia, and the Caribbean. Such elections have much to do with the outlawing of opposition, the rigging of future elections, and the incidence of military coups. But that is not the drum I wish to beat here. Here I want to argue that the source of the unsatisfying outcome of the election resides in the antinomy between two principles of human organization. At the outset of this chapter, I called attention to the continuum of ways in which people organize and categorize themselves, with voluntary membership at one end and birth membership at the other. Actually, birth membership is an anchor on more than one such continuum: territorial proximity, for example, is another competing way in which people organize themselves. These principles of organization—birth and choice, birth and territory, birth and function—are not merely alternatives. Occasionally, they collide, and some of the mysteries of ethnic politics are explicable in terms of the collision. In this election, there was a collision of birth and choice.

---

65. For example, one of Dahl's rules promulgated to keep conflict low enough for "polyarchy" is that no group should indefinitely be denied the opportunity to participate in government. Robert A. Dahl, *Polyarchy* (New Haven: Yale Univ. Press, 1971), 114–21.

66. For the centrality of choice in thinking about the electoral process, see Barry Holden, "Liberal Democracy and the Social Determination of Ideas," in J. Roland Pennock and John W. Chapman, eds., *Nomos XXV: Liberal Democracy* (New York: New York Univ. Press, 1983), 307–09.

This sort of antinomy arises because the institutions of the modern liberal state—institutions such as democratic elections—tend to be biased against birth. These institutions have their roots in the ideological heritage of the post-Enlightenment West, and that heritage is heavily individualistic in its assumptions. We like to think that states are composed of congeries of free-floating individuals, each of whom is endowed with a kit of basic rights and immunities and each of whom is available for those tasks and associations that fit his talents and preferences. The rules of equality in treatment by government officials, merit in employment, the Utilitarian standard of the greatest good for the greatest number (of individuals), and even the vote itself all presume that the effective unit of action is the individual person. Ascription, on the other hand, connotes fixed social placement, based on abstract categories transcending the personal qualities of individuals. Ascriptive membership was distrusted by Enlightenment political theorists. For them, the birth principle signified the chains of the feudal estates; their individualism was an alternative both to feudal immobility and to the centralized autocracy of the monarchical state. Now, as then, the birth principle of membership introduces a qualification on the free-floating availability of individuals for tasks and associations according to individual talent and preference. It is for very good historical reasons that Western individualism is hostile to birth affiliations.[67]

Liberalism, however, is at its weakest when it comes to constructing bonds of community.[68] Community, which is based on diffuse affinities among people, is difficult to rest on the multiple networks of functionally specific, compartmentalized ties that the liberal state fosters. Of the three pillars of the French Revolution, liberty-equality-fraternity, fraternity has fared least well in the West.[69] It is here that ethnicity comes in, for, even in the West, ethnicity continues to be an organizing principle of community, supplementing the weak bonds of egalitarian individualism. The individualistic assumptions of Western thought are modified in

---

67. See Wilson Carey McWilliams, *The Idea of Fraternity in America* (Berkeley and Los Angeles: Univ. of California Press, 1973), 4, 10; Guido de Ruggiero, *The History of European Liberalism*, trans. R. G. Collingwood (Boston: Beacon Press, 1959; originally published in 1927).

68. See Carl J. Friedrich, "The Concept of Community in the History of Political and Legal Philosophy," in Friedrich, ed., *Nomos II: Community* (New York: Liberal Arts Press, 1959), 3–24; Dante Germino, "The Crisis in Community: A Challenge," in ibid., 80–98.

69. See McWilliams, *The Idea of Fraternity in America*.

practice by the collective instincts of everyday behavior and by what is at root the need for family and family-like ties. Outside the West, as I have argued, this is all the more true.

The individualistic assumptions of Western thought have, however, had a powerful influence on formal political institutions, an influence that extends far beyond the West. The election, based on individual choice, is one such institution. The rise of the modern territorial state, with its principle of membership by proximity, is also part of this heritage. The modern state, which in the short span of a few centuries has come to cover the globe, is founded on territorial inclusiveness: it necessarily encompasses everyone within its boundaries. There was a time when it was thought, with Sir Henry Sumner Maine, that in primitive societies "kinship in blood is the sole possible ground of community in political functions."[70] Maine argued that the territorial basis of political community was a revolutionary innovation, a conception entirely alien to primitive antiquity. It now seems clear that even the simplest peoples can possess territorially based political systems.[71] The perfect dichotomy of kinship and territory has been pierced.

Yet the dialectical relationship between consanguinity and contiguity as organizing principles of community persists. Often the two coexist uneasily, neither displacing the other. Even the political systems of preliterate peoples commonly embrace groups of unrelated strangers. Various arrangements are worked out to manage relations among the component groups.[72] The organization of heterogeneous descent groups in a territorially based political system is, in short, always a complicated matter. Rarely, if ever, is territory alone sufficient to give rise to uniform treatment of all who reside within it.

This analysis has a number of implications for our understanding of ethnic conflict. For one thing, it helps explain our reluctance to acknowledge the importance of ethnicity in politics. To the considerable extent that ethnic ties reflect the birth principle, they fall within the curtilage of

70. Maine, *Ancient Law* (London: Oxford Univ. Press, 1931; 1st ed., 1861), 106. Maine touched off a lengthy debate. See Lewis Henry Morgan, *Ancient Society* (New York: Holt, 1877); Robert H. Lowie, *The Origin of the State* (New York: Harcourt, Brace, 1927); Robert M. MacIver, *The Web of Government* (New York: Macmillan, 1947); Lucy Mair, *Primitive Government* (Harmondsworth: Penguin Books, 1962).
71. Schapera, *Government and Politics in Tribal Societies*.
72. Ibid., 19, 198–200.

those disagreeable phenomena disfavored by our ideals and therefore capable of securing only the reluctant attention reserved for distasteful subjects.

Then, too, to understand that consanguinity and contiguity are competing principles of organization is to appreciate that ethnic groups can appeal now to one, now to the other of these principles. Whereas territorial proximity is an inclusive principle—all within the territory are to be treated equally—ascription can be an exclusive principle. Politics in severely divided societies needs to be understood as reflecting this competition of principles. If kinship is not the sole basis of political community, neither has it been wholly displaced by territory. There is no clear path from the principle of blood to the principle of proximity, any more than there was from status to contract.

To suggest that formal institutions are predicated largely on choice and territory, whereas the realm of informal behavior is suffused with birth allegiances, is not at all to concede that formal institutions are unimportant. Many states make special, discriminatory provision for one group or another in the polity. It is testimony to the worldwide power of Enlightenment ideals that such provision is usually justified as an exception, a temporary expedient, often with a specified time limit. Because the acknowledged norm remains equal treatment of all individuals in the territory, such measures carry a heavy presumption of illegitimacy. In short, the gap between the theory of formal institutions and the practice of ethnicity is not evidence of the insignificance of the theory. The world of ethnic relations would be quite different—and, I believe, less civil than it already is—were it not for the pervasive importance of individualist thought. The equal treatment of individuals is the touchstone by which deviations from it are measured.

ETHNIC AFFILIATIONS AND CLASS AFFILIATIONS

In Chapter 1, I pointed out that ethnicity is not just a mask for social class conflict; in Chapter 3, I shall argue that ethnic affiliations are not just a convenient vehicle by which elites satisfy their own class aspirations. Here I intend to show why ethnicity is so often a more compelling and preemptive affiliation than social class is. That conclusion has often been reached,[73] but remains in need of explanation. Although a full-scale comparison of ethnicity with social class is beyond the scope of this book, it is possible to understand the generally greater conflict potential of ethnic affiliations than of class affiliations in Asia and Africa by considering a few central features of each.

A good way to do this is to utilize Marxist assumptions against Marxist conclusions. Ralf Dahrendorf has aptly summarized the conflict-producing attributes of class identity as conceived by Marx. The key is Marx's belief that class identity is ascriptive, that a person's class position is his "inherited and inescapable fate."[74] One's position in society is determined by his parents' position. For Marx, social classes are closed conflict groups, permanently composed, and that, above all, makes class the affiliation that supersedes all others.

Had Marx been right about the closed character of class affiliations, he would surely have been describing an explosive conflict situation. The lines between contestants would be hard and fast, the stakes high. Mediating attachments between classes would be few. Conflict groups would be solidary and polarized, their memberships fixed, clear-cut, exclusive, and relevant in a wide range of contexts.

The Marxian prophecy of class conflict in Western industrial society was, however, undermined by the inaccuracy of this characterization of class affiliations. First of all, class membership is not wholly inherited and inescapable. Social mobility, both within single lifetimes and across generations, mitigates the ascriptive character of class affiliations, and in the West the degree of social mobility has been considerable.[75] As Dahrendorf suggests, "the weight and intensity of manifest group interests within the individual personality decrease as social mobility and the openness of conflict groups increase. The easier it is for the individual to leave his conflict group, the less likely is he to engage his whole personality in group conflict . . . ."[76] Dahrendorf goes so far as to postulate "an

73. See, e.g., Weiner, *Sons of the Soil*, 173; Kathleen A. Staudt, "Sex, Ethnic, and Class Consciousness in Western Kenya," *Comparative Politics* 14 (Jan. 1982): 149–67; Onigu Otite, "Ethnicity and Class in a Plural Society: Nigeria," in Cora Bagley Marrett and Cheryl Leggon, eds., *Research in Race and Ethnic Relations*, vol. 1 (Greenwich, Conn.: JAI Press, 1979), 87–107.

74. Dahrendorf, *Class and Class Conflict in Industrial Society* (Stanford: Stanford Univ. Press, 1959), 60.

75. See, e.g., Peter M. Blau and Otis Dudley Duncan, *The American Occupational Structure* (New York: John Wiley, 1967).

76. Dahrendorf, *Class and Class Conflict in Industrial Society*, 191.

inverse relation between the degree of openness of classes and the intensity of class conflict."[77] Second, class position is not utterly determinative in arenas of life removed from the workplace. Contrary to the Marxian conception of class as the central social affiliation, class position is "merely one of a plurality of social roles."[78] Indeed, concludes Dahrendorf, "occupation has been confined to a set place in the life of the worker, just as industry has been confined to a set place in the structure of society."[79] And so the fluidity of class membership and the plurality of social roles both act to reduce the prevalence of class conflict.

Data on social class are less reliable for Asia and Africa than they are for the West. What is available, however, suggests that social mobility is likely to mitigate the emotive component of class affiliations. Summarizing a variety of studies of social mobility in developing countries, Joan M. Nelson finds that a significant fraction of the urban poor manages to improve its material condition substantially.[80] Intergenerationally, a majority of people whose fathers were unskilled manual workers become skilled manual workers, nonmanual workers, and in some cases administrators, businessmen, or professionals. Even within generations, she concludes, "there is widespread though modest upward mobility across the span of individual working lives," and in addition many "who fail to climb the occupational ladder may nonetheless manage to increase their incomes."[81] Where overall rates of occupational mobility are modest, the composition of modern-sector elites tends to be quite open to persons of various social backgrounds. This is largely due to the powerful influence of schooling in regulating access to elite positions and the tendency of secondary schools to draw students from a broad spectrum of the population, including the peasantry.[82] Given such patterns, it comes as no surprise that interclass hostility is far more rarely expressed in surveys than is the desire for emulation of those of higher status.[83] Moreover, social class affiliations, though sometimes important, appear to be as

77. Ibid., 222.
78. Ibid., 60.
79. Ibid., 269.
80. Nelson, *Access to Power: Politics and the Urban Poor in Developing Nations* (Princeton: Princeton Univ. Press, 1979), 43–47.
81. Ibid., 46.
82. See Remi Clignet and Philip Foster, *The Fortunate Few: A Study of Secondary Schools and Students in the Ivory Coast* (Evanston: Northwestern Univ. Press, 1966), 201–09.
83. Nelson, *Access to Power*, 160.

readily compartmentalized in developing countries as in industrialized countries.[84] The Marxian concept of class as an inherited and determinative affiliation finds no support in these data.

Marx's conception applies with far less distortion to ethnic groups. Ethnic membership is generally given at birth. The ethnic group has a certain "position" in society. As Marx postulated that class affiliations penetrate every pore of social life, ethnic group membership has ramifying effects; its significance is not confined to a single narrow realm. If class and family are disconnected in a way Marx did not envision, ethnicity and family are indeed connected. For this "Marxian" reason, ethnic affiliations have considerable power to generate conflict. They are not exact replicas of the class affiliations Marx had in mind, but their properties bear resemblance in ways central to Marx's argument. In much of Asia and Africa, it is only modest hyperbole to assert that the Marxian prophecy has had an ethnic fulfillment.

84. Robert Melson, "Ideology and Inconsistency: The 'Cross-Pressured' Nigerian Worker," *American Political Science Review* 65 (Mar. 1971): 161–71.

PART TWO

The Theory of
Ethnic Conflict

CHAPTER THREE

Conflict Theory
and Conflict Motives

The obstacles to a theory of ethnic conflict are formidable. Until lately, conflict theory has been an impoverished category of analysis in the social sciences.[1] Many of the recent attempts to redress this deficiency and develop conflict theory in political science have been made in connection with international relations. The notoriously treacherous intellectual terrain of international relations, however, has of necessity made this a halting enterprise. Although a number of important similarities can be identified between international relations and interethnic relations, attempts to base a theory of ethnic conflict on theories of international conflict seem likely to end by resting one unknown upon another.

Among the elusive elements in ethnic conflict theory is an acceptable definition of conflict. Most definitions embody an element of struggle, strife, or collision, and in this way distinguish conflict from competition. Some go further and suggest that conflict entails the struggle for mutually exclusive rewards or the use of incompatible means to a goal. Although much ethnic conflict is properly described in these terms, mutually exclusive ends or means nevertheless need not be intrinsic to all conflict. For me, a version of Lewis Coser's definition serves well.[2] Conflict is a struggle in which the aim is to gain objectives and simultaneously to neutralize, injure, or eliminate rivals. This leaves the nature and incompatibility of objectives and methods open to investigation rather than closed by definitional fiat.

Despite the slow start that conflict theory had, as ethnic conflict has

---

1. See Jessie Bernard, "The Sociological Study of Conflict," in International Sociological Association, *The Nature of Conflict* (Paris: UNESCO, 1957), chap. 1. For ethnic conflict in particular, see Joseph Rothschild, *Ethnopolitics* (New York: Columbia Univ. Press, 1981), 19–24.

2. Coser, *The Functions of Social Conflict* (Glencoe, Ill.: Free Press, 1956), 8.

gathered worldwide momentum, theoretical statements have been advanced to explain it. Some of these statements have gained a measure of acceptance.

The theories provide a useful starting point—and not just because they afford us a glimpse of the state of the art against which to develop new conceptions. Most current theories of ethnic conflict are derivatives of other concerns. They have often grown out of a fascination with an ongoing process (such as "modernization"), to which they have attempted to relate ethnic phenomena, or out of commitment to a broader theoretical perspective (such as class analysis), under which ethnic conflict might be subsumed. The subsidiary origins of these theories have virtually guaranteed them a partial character: they fit certain aspects of ethnic conflict much better than they fit other aspects. Furthermore, at key points these differing perspectives are mutually inconsistent. Although existing theories are not wholly satisfying, their deficiencies cast what needs to be explained in rather bold relief. In particular, their points of difference raise some basic issues about conflict motivation. My effort to construct a coherent explanation of ethnic conflict begins, therefore, with a critical but highly selective review of the state of the art.

TRADITION AND MODERNIZATION

Naturally enough, the dominant concern in studies of developing countries has been the process of change, particularly those interrelated changes in thought and experience that can be labeled "modernization."[3] Ethnicity has often been studied in the context of modernization.

There are three ways of relating ethnic conflict to the modernization process. The first is to view ethnic conflict as a mere relic of an outmoded traditionalism, doomed to be overtaken by the incursions of modernity. The second is to regard ethnic conflict as a traditional but unusually stubborn impediment to modernization. The third is to interpret ethnic conflict as an integral part—even a product—of the process of moderni-

---

3. For an introductory treatment, see Myron Weiner, ed., *Modernization: The Dynamics of Growth* (New York: Basic Books, 1966). For some of the intellectual history associated with the concept, see Samuel P. Huntington, "The Change to Change: Modernization, Development, and Politics," *Comparative Politics* 3 (Apr. 1971): 283–322. For a reassessment, see Lucian W. Pye, "Political Modernization: Gaps Between Theory and Reality," *The Annals* 442 (Mar. 1979): 28–39.

zation itself.[4] In important respects, each of these approaches is at odds with the other two.

ETHNICITY AND TRADITION

The optimism that pervaded the first studies of the new states made it easy to perceive ethnic allegiances as purely vestigial affiliations, survivals of a traditionalism whose lack of contemporary utility would be made apparent by the onslaught of modern forces. The same innovative strata associated with modernization in general—educated elites, urban dwellers, and army officers—were asserted to be the most "detribalized" sectors of society as well.[5] Surely they would lead the movement away from traditional ethnic loyalties.

The strength of ethnic affiliations and the status of many who held tight to them have made it impossible to regard ethnic conflict as an anachronism on the verge of disappearance. The very elites who were thought to be leading their peoples away from ethnic affiliations were commonly found to be in the forefront of ethnic conflict. Militantly ethnic political parties sometimes had their deepest roots among educated elites,[6] ethnic violence flared up in urban areas all over the developing world, and armies were divided by ethnic tensions that led to coups and killings. An upsurge of ethnic sentiment in Western countries demonstrated that ethnicity could not be explained solely in terms of a fading traditionalism that the West had outgrown.[7]

Perhaps, on the other hand, ethnic conflict is the result of an extraordinary persistence of traditional antipathies so strong that they can sur-

4. A variant of the first and third ways of relating ethnic conflict to modernization is to see this conflict as part of the "stresses and strains" of moving away from traditionalism, but as a purely transitional phenomenon. Cf. Harold A. Gould, "Religion and Politics in a U.P. Constituency," in Donald Eugene Smith, ed., *South Asian Politics and Religion* (Princeton: Princeton Univ. Press, 1966), chap. 3.

5. See David E. Apter, *Ghana in Transition*, 2d rev. ed. (Princeton: Princeton Univ. Press, 1972), 148; Lucian W. Pye, *Aspects of Political Development* (Boston: Little, Brown, 1966), 179–80.

6. See, e.g., Myron Weiner, *Sons of the Soil: Migration and Ethnic Conflict in India* (Princeton: Princeton Univ. Press, 1978), 274–93; Mary Fainsod Katzenstein, *Ethnicity and Equality: The Shiv Sena Party and Preferential Policies in Bombay* (Ithaca: Cornell Univ. Press, 1979), 63–81; Craig Baxter, "The Jana Sangh," in Smith, ed., *South Asian Politics and Religion*, chap. 4.

7. In the West, too, survey research has shown that support for ethnic movements often increased with education, income, and high-status occupations. See, e.g., Erwin C. Hargrove, "Nationality, Values, and Change: Young Elites in French Canada," *Comparative Politics* 2 (Apr. 1970): 474 n.1.

vive even the powerful solvent of modernization. If so, it becomes possible to explain the persistence of ethnic allegiances even among modern elites and modern countries.[8] From time to time, ethnic conflict has been regarded as peculiarly potent when it reflects ancient enmities, and it has sometimes been dismissed as artificial or ephemeral where no such longstanding antagonism could be identified.[9] A corollary of such a view may be that the strength of ethnic conflict is proportional to the depth of its traditional origins.

It is true, of course, that some ethnic antagonisms are of long duration. Memories of earlier, lapsed conflicts, centuries and sometimes millennia old, can be revived to fit contemporary conditions. The Sinhalese and Tamil kingdoms fought recurrently in ancient Sri Lanka (Ceylon),[10] as did Mende and Temne in pre-colonial Sierra Leone and Maronites and Druze in what is now Lebanon. The Acholi and Langi clashed intermittently in pre-colonial Uganda,[11] and the Assamese king, Chakradhvaj Singha, "fought for independence with the war cry, 'Better death than submit to the Bengalis.' "[12] These old hostilities are all significant again. The role of historical memory in contemporary ethnic relations is perhaps further suggested by survey evidence indicating that African university students from groups which boast a glorious (and generally monarchical) past—Baganda, Bakongo, Ashanti, Yoruba—seem to possess somewhat more ethnocentric attitudes and behavior patterns than do their fellow students from other groups.[13]

Nevertheless, ethnic conflict is not just the persistence or recrudescence of earlier antagonisms. As we have seen in Chapter 2, many ethnic groups are rather new creations. As the groups are not themselves traditional, they could not have had traditional rivalries among themselves. Whether or not recently formed, many groups encountered each other for the first time during colonial rule. Their relationship, obviously, is the product of this relatively recent encounter. Finally, just as some tra-

8. See Michael Parenti, "Ethnic Politics and the Persistence of Ethnic Identification," *American Political Science Review* 61 (Sept. 1967): 717–26.

9. See, e.g., Robert I. Rotberg, "Tribalism and Politics in Zambia," *Africa Report*, Dec. 1967, pp. 29–35.

10. S. Arasaratnam, *Ceylon* (Englewood Cliffs, N.J.: Prentice-Hall, 1964).

11. Nelson Kasfir, "Cultural Sub-Nationalism in Uganda," in Victor A. Olorunsola, ed., *The Politics of Cultural Sub-Nationalism in Africa* (Garden City, N.Y.: Anchor Books, 1972), 70.

12. Hugh Tinker, *India and Pakistan: A Political Analysis*, rev. ed. (New York: Praeger, 1968), 15.

13. Otto Klineberg and Marisa Zavalloni, *Nationalism and Tribalism Among African Students* (Paris and The Hague: Mouton, 1969), 77–81.

ditional antipathies persist, others lose their relevance. The Maharash-trian Hindu folk hero, Shivaji, who led the armed struggle against the Muslims in the seventeenth century, was invoked once again in the twen-tieth, in the form of the Shiv Sena (Army of Shivaji). But this militant Maharashtrian movement directed its animus mainly against recently arrived migrants to Bombay—not Muslims, except secondarily, but South Indian Hindus. Here, then, is an adaptation of historical memory to fit a wholly new conflict. History can be a weapon, and tradition can fuel ethnic conflict, but a current conflict cannot generally be explained by simply calling it a revived form of an earlier conflict.

ETHNICITY AND MODERNIZATION

More frequent and more systematic statement has been given to the view that ethnic conflict is a by-product of modernization itself. The mere statement that ethnic conflict is a by-product of modernization might invite the rejoinder that such a theory is necessarily timebound.[14] How can it explain ethnic conflict in the pre-modern period, unless perhaps the term *modernization* is given a capricious meaning that makes it the equivalent of all change or unless ethnic conflict is given an unduly nar-row meaning that limits it to the modern period? There is something to this skepticism about the ahistorical quality of modernization theories. Yet this limitation need not be decisive if such theories are not to be taken as explaining all aspects of ethnic conflict—and I shall so interpret them.

Karl W. Deutsch first advanced the idea that "social mobilization" was related to ethnic conflict. Social mobilization was conceived as "an overall process of change, which happens to substantial parts of the population in countries which are moving from traditional to modern ways of life."[15] It involves the substitution of new patterns of behavior for old, and it includes "involvement in mass politics."[16] The compo-nents of this process are exposure to mass media and changes in literacy, residence (especially from rural to urban), occupation (especially from agricultural to non-agricultural), and other characteristics that break

14. For a useful corrective, see John A. Armstrong, *Nations Before Nationalism* (Chapel Hill: Univ. of North Carolina Press, 1982).
15. "Social Mobilization and Political Development," *American Political Science Review* 55 (Sept. 1961): 493–514, at 493. See also Deutsch, *Nationalism and Social Communication* (Cambridge: M.I.T. Press, 1953).
16. Deutsch, "Social Mobilization and Political Development," 494.

down "commitments to traditional ways of living . . . ."[17] Deutsch suggested that ethnic conflict is the product of something analogous to a race between rates of social mobilization and rates of assimilation. The proportion of mobilized but unassimilated persons is "the first crude indicator" of group conflict.[18]

These views have subsequently been given more explicit theoretical formulation.[19] Social mobilization, it is argued, fosters ethnic competition especially in the competitive modern sector, for "it is the competitor within the modern sphere who feels the insecurities of change most strongly and who seeks the communal shelter of 'tribalism,' "[20] even as he seeks the many new rewards brought by modernization. Educated, urban elites "organize collective support to advance their position in the competition for the benefits of modernity."[21] Indeed, it is even said that

Ethnic groups persist largely because of their capacity to extract goods and services from the modern sector and thereby satisfy the demands of their members for the components of modernity. Insofar as they provide these benefits to their members, they are able to gain their support and achieve their loyalty.[22]

The fundamental assumption underlying modernization theories has been articulated in terms of converging aspirations:

People's aspirations and expectations change as they are mobilized into the modernizing economy and polity. They come to want, and to demand, more—more goods, more recognition, more power. Significantly, too, the orientation of the mobilized to a common set of rewards and paths to rewards means, in effect, that many people come to desire precisely the same things. Men enter into conflict not because they are different but because they are essentially the same. It is by making men "more alike," in the sense of possessing the same wants, that modernization tends to promote conflict.[23]

17. Ibid.
18. *Nationalism and Social Communication*, chap. 6. Deutsch, however, has not been wholly consistent on this subject. See the careful review of his writings by Walker Connor, "Nation-Building or Nation-Destroying?" *World Politics* 24 (Apr. 1972): 319–55.
19. See especially Paul R. Brass, "Ethnicity and Nationality Formation," *Ethnicity* 3 (Sept. 1976): 225–41; Robert Melson and Howard Wolpe, "Modernization and the Politics of Communalism: A Theoretical Perspective," *American Political Science Review* 64 (Dec. 1970): 1112–30; Robert H. Bates, "Ethnic Competition and Modernization in Contemporary Africa," *Comparative Political Studies* 6 (Jan. 1974): 457–84. For a comparative application, see R. S. Milne, *Politics in Ethnically Bipolar States* (Vancouver: Univ. of British Columbia Press, 1981), 83–105.
20. Melson and Wolpe, "Modernization," 1115.
21. Bates, "Ethnic Competition," 468.
22. Ibid., 471.
23. Melson and Wolpe, "Modernization," 1114.

Here one is reminded of Francis I, who, when asked to identify the differences that made for constant warfare between him and Charles V, replied: "None whatever. We agree perfectly. We both want control of Italy!"[24]

Whereas ethnic conflict was conceived earlier as a vestige destined to disappear and then as a vestige stubbornly resistant to change, recent theories of conflict view it as no vestige at all, but as part and parcel of the very process of becoming modern. With this, we may have exhausted the logical possibilities, but have we moved ahead?

In two ways, certainly, we have. Theories that stress the relationship between ethnic conflict and modernization are quick to call attention to two important themes in ethnic conflict: the role of elite ambitions and the role of the differential modernization of ethnic groups in fostering conflict.

The modern middle class, rather than playing the detribalizing role earlier assigned to it, often furthers its interests by invoking ethnic support. The point here is that elites *have* distinctive interests that relate to the benefits of modernity: good jobs, urban amenities, access to schools, travel, prestige. The many bitter stories that circulate in the developing world about those new tribes, the Wabenzi (those who drive the Mercedes), and the Beentos (those who have "been to" Europe or America), suggest a prominent differentiation of class interests. But if this is reflected in ethnic conflict, it gives rise to two further questions: (1) why should nonelites render their support? and (2) why are class interests so strongly reflected in ethnic tensions which, after all, usually cross-cut class lines? Both questions require attention.

MODERNIZATION: LEVELS, RATES, AND DISPARITIES

Modernization theories of ethnicity commonly also stress that the benefits of modernity are not equally spread among ethnic groups.[25] This uneven distribution of economic and educational opportunities in the modern sector is an important source of group tensions. How and why?

One answer given by modernization theories is that, because some groups gain a headstart in the competition for the rewards of the modern world, the social classes that emerge tend to overlap and reinforce ethnic

24. Quoted in Kenneth N. Waltz, *Man, The State, and War* (New York: Columbia Univ. Press, 1959), 187–88.
25. Brass, "Ethnicity and Nationality Formation," 231–32; Melson and Wolpe, "Modernization," 1115–17; Bates, "Ethnic Competition," 462–64.

group boundaries, thereby making ethnic group confrontations more intense. "The fewer the cross-cutting socio-economic linkages, the more naked such confrontations and the greater the likelihood of secessionist and other movements of communal nationalism."[26]

Another answer, not inconsistent, puts the matter in terms of class resentment. Ethnic groups that "are more wealthy, better educated, and more urbanized tend to be envied, resented, and sometimes feared by others; and the basis for these sentiments is the recognition of their superior position in the new system of stratification."[27]

Is it adequate to cast the significance of differential modernization, as these theories do, in terms of reinforcing cleavages or social stratification—in other words, in terms of class? I intend to show in the next chapter that ethnically differential modernization is a highly useful starting point for analyzing the collective psychology of ethnic conflict. But its importance is not captured in straight social class terms. Partly, the facts alone suggest this: the opportunity structure in the modern sector may be skewed in favor of one group or another, but it rarely approaches being completely closed to particular groups. In any event, the modern sector is, of course, not the only determinant of stratification. Then, too, and most important, more than just incipient class feeling lies behind the envy, resentment, and fear of those groups which seem to be benefiting unduly from modernization. To mark the issue as one worthy of pursuing at length, rather than to pursue it just now, I shall simply state my view that the basis of this envy, resentment, and fear is to be found, not in the ethnic distribution of opportunities and benefits *per se*, but in what this indicates about relative group capacities and what it portends for group relations across the board.

Modernization theories place most of their emphasis on modern elites, the modern stratification system, and the modern sector of developing societies in general. I noted a moment ago that these theories tend to give insufficient attention to the conflict motives of nonelites, whose stake in the benefits being distributed is often tenuous at best. The same point needs to be made across countries as across classes. In those countries, as in those sectors within countries, where modernization is not far advanced, this theoretical perspective proves inadequate. Thus, modernization theory provides no convincing way to explain why so much ethnic conflict (and so much ethnic conflict that has gone as far as civil war)

26. Melson and Wolpe, "Modernization," 1116.
27. Bates, "Ethnic Competition," 462.

has occurred in some of the least modernized areas of the world: Chad, Ethiopia, the Southern Sudan, Mauritania, the mountainous areas of Iraq, Northeast India, the periphery of Burma, and Papua New Guinea. These are not just deviant or exceptional cases. They are in many ways quite central and typical, of ethnic secessionist movements, for example, as Chapter 6 will show. It is no surprise, therefore, that empirical efforts to confirm the role of modernization level as an intervening variable between ethnic diversity and political instability have come to nought.[28]

The possible solutions to the poor fit between modernization theory and conflict among less modernized populations and countries only compound the problem. Deutsch, for example, accords at least as much importance to *rates* of social mobilization as to absolute levels. Naturally, if all else is equal, rates of change are higher where starting levels are lower. Therefore, rates of social mobilization may be relatively high in the least modernized parts of the developing world. But this proves too much. In such countries—particularly in the least modernized areas of such countries, where ethnic resentments seem to be concentrated— the fraction of the population that could be considered socially mobilized would still remain very low, too low to rest an explanation for an entire conflict on it. Here it is worth recalling Deutsch's early formulation that the proportion of mobilized but unassimilated persons is "the first crude indicator" of group conflict. Though rates of change may be high in the areas and countries just mentioned, this critical proportion remains quite low. It is therefore difficult to avoid the conclusion that an explanation that relies on social mobilization or modernization would not be sufficient to account for conflicts as widespread and serious as the ones that have been named.

Unless, of course, what counts is neither absolute levels nor rates of modernization but the span of ethnic *differences* in either or both of these variables. That is, ethnic conflict may be a function of a "modernization gap" between ethnic groups or a function of the rate at which such a gap is being widened. But in that case it is not adequate to frame the explanation in terms of modernization or in terms of everyone's

---

28. Donald G. Morrison and H. Michael Stevenson, "Cultural Pluralism, Modernization, and Conflict: An Empirical Analysis of Sources of Political Instability in African Nations," in John N. Paden, ed., *Values, Identities, and National Integration: Empirical Research in Africa* (Evanston: Northwestern Univ. Press, 1980), 11–23; Lynn F. Fischer, "Mass Education and National Conflict in Thirty African States," in ibid., 265–68; Walter L. Barrows, "Ethnic Diversity and Political Instability in Black Africa," *Comparative Political Studies* 9 (July 1976): 139–70, at 164.

becoming "more alike," because in key respects the differences between groups may remain constant or may increase. Certainly, neither version of the gap explanation would necessarily postulate that everyone is becoming significantly "more modern": what would count, according to such explanations, is not the overall level or rate of modernization in a society but the distance between groups on some specified attribute or attributes. Such a gap might exist at levels of modernization so low as to render explanations in terms of the global modernization process tortured and artificial at best, misleading at worst. There are, then, basic differences among explanations for ethnic conflict founded, respectively, on overall levels of modernization, overall rates of modernization, and group disparities in levels or rates of modernization. Modernization theories have not been very clear about the implications of these various explanations.

To the suggestion that modernization is not sufficient to account for severe ethnic conflict in unmodernized parts of the world, modernization theorists might rejoin that the elites in those areas, small though they may be, are disproportionately important. It is their ambition that ignites the conflict. As we have seen, such an assumption is already present in modernization explanations of ethnic conflict. But this assumption leaves open, once again, the insistent question of why the masses follow. One is left to surmise either that elite manipulations can, without more, induce mass action or that the masses follow only so long as there is a payoff. Recall the statement that "groups persist largely because of their capacity to extract goods and services from the modern sector and thereby satisfy the demands of their members for the components of modernity." Ethnicity, in the words of a cynic, entails not the collective will to exist but the existing will to collect.

The assumption that nonelites follow because there is a payoff in goods and services runs into difficulty as soon as we recognize that there are losing as well as winning groups in ethnic politics. Those groups which are increasingly excluded from the "extractive" process usually do not cease to exist. They may, on the contrary, fight to the death. Ethnicity has a much more frail basis than most observers would grant it if ethnic groups really did wax and wane with their capacity to extract goods and services. That tangible benefits alone might be the basis of ethnic solidarity is belied by the intense passions that ethnic allegiances regularly elicit. The ethnic group is not just a trade union.

The alternative assumption—that elite machinations and deceptions bring the masses along—requires a leap of faith, and a far-reaching one at that. What it suggests is that nonelites are suffering from a case of "false consciousness," for they are serving interests other than their own. Such an argument, implicit in modernization writings, has also been advanced quite explicitly: ". . . tribal movements may be created and instigated to action by the new men of power in furtherance of their own special interests which are, time and again, the constitutive interests of emerging social classes. Tribalism then becomes a mask for class privilege."[29]

It is important to be clear on what is at stake at this point. Plainly, middle-class careerist interests have been a prominent part of ethnic conflict. The question is why others follow. One answer is that the others have been misled. Such an explanation presumes that enormous masses of people in country after country do not have a sound conception of what concerns them. This is a presumption difficult to square with mounting evidence that nonelites in Asia and Africa are far from ignorant about politics.[30] Before jumping to an explanation based on manipulation, it would seem incumbent to exhaust all other plausible explanations that do not require such a presumption. For I presume instead that if elites pursue a policy of deflecting mass antagonisms onto other ethnic groups, such a policy must strike roots in mass sentiments, apprehensions, and aspirations in order to succeed. By failing to attend to the "unmodernized" strata, modernization theories of ethnic conflict tend to neglect the potential heterogeneity of conflict motives. This is a paradoxical omission for a theory that starts from the premise that populations are undergoing profound, and yet uneven, changes.

ECONOMIC INTEREST

Ethnic conflict has generally been an embarrassment to proponents of class politics and of the class analysis of politics. Ethnic groups and social classes rarely overlap perfectly; ethnic affiliations generally seem

29. Richard L. Sklar, "Political Science and National Integration—A Radical Approach," *Journal of Modern African Studies* 5 (May 1967): 1–11, at 6. Compare Sklar's earlier views, expressed in Sklar, *Nigerian Political Parties* (Princeton: Princeton Univ. Press, 1963), 474–80; and in Sklar and C. S. Whitaker, Jr., "Nigeria," in James S. Coleman and Carl G. Rosberg, Jr., eds., *Political Parties and National Integration in Tropical Africa* (Berkeley and Los Angeles: Univ. of California Press, 1964), 620, 646–47.

30. Fred M. Hayward, "A Reassessment of Conventional Wisdom About the Informed Public: National Political Information in Ghana," *American Political Science Review* 70 (June 1976): 433–51; Joel D. Barkan, "Comment: Further Reassessment of 'Conventional Wisdom': Political Knowledge and Voting Behavior in Rural Kenya," ibid., 452–55; Marvin L. Rogers, "The Politicization of Malay Villagers," *Comparative Politics* 7 (Jan. 1975): 202–25.

to elicit more passionate loyalty than do class allegiances; and certainly there has been no marked trend in the developing world for class interests across ethnic lines to supersede ethnic ties. For all of these reasons, class theories of ethnicity have not been richly developed.[31]

Still, economic interests may play a role in ethnic conflict, and the economic underpinning of group hostility has been a persistent undercurrent in the literature of ethnic conflict.[32] Only recently has the theme been given more explicit statement. Several variants can be identified.

The first I have already touched on. According to this view, ethnic conflict is artificial. Belief in the importance of distinct ethnic interests constitutes part of an ideology (in the Marxist sense) that masks class interests and diverts the working classes from pursuing their interests. Ethnic conflict amounts to "challenging nonexistent or barely dangerous enemies" and avoiding "the real issues" and the real enemies, namely "the ruling class."[33]

A second version of materialist theory stresses, not irrational mass submission to elite manipulation, but rational working-class competition. There may be manipulation here, too, but also discernible competitive interests. Employers use the labor of one ethnic group to undercut the price of labor of another group. Higher-paid laborers are, of course,

threatened by the introduction of cheaper labor into the market, fearing that it will either force them to leave the territory or reduce them to its level. If the labor market is split ethnically, the class antagonism takes the form of ethnic antagonism. . . . [W]hile much rhetoric of ethnic antagonism concentrates on ethnicity and race, it really in large measure (though probably not entirely) expresses this class conflict.[34]

Ethnicity, then, is not an artificial diversion from economic interests, but a faithful reflection of those interests.

31. The class theory has, however, been developed in the case of something approaching "ethnic caste," that is, rigidly ranked systems. See Oliver C. Cox, *Caste, Class and Race* (New York: Modern Reader, 1948); Marvin Harris, *Patterns of Race in the Americas* (New York: Walker, 1964).

32. See, e.g., Tamotsu Shibutani and Kian M. Kwan, *Ethnic Stratification: A Comparative Approach* (New York: Macmillan, 1965), 168, 196–97, 380–82; Richard G. Fox, Charlotte H. Aull, and Louis F. Cimino, "Ethnic Nationalism and the Welfare State," in Charles F. Keyes, ed., *Ethnic Change* (Seattle: Univ. of Washington Press, 1981), 198–245; Nancy L. Snider, "What Happened in Penang?" *Asian Survey* 8 (Dec. 1968): 960–75.

33. M. S. Prabhakar, "The 'Bongal' Bogey," *Economic and Political Weekly* (Bombay), Oct. 21, 1971, pp. 2140–42. See also Okwudiba Nnoli, "Ethnicity as a Counter Revolutionary Force," *Africa Review* 7 (1977): 1–12.

34. Edna Bonacich, "A Theory of Ethnic Antagonism: The Split Labor Market," *American Sociological Review* 37 (Oct. 1972): 547–59, at 553.

A third formulation of economically based ethnic conflict focuses on tensions between "middleman minorities" and their "host societies."[35] Middleman minorities are said to concentrate in trade and commerce and often to act as intermediaries "between producer and consumer, employer and employee, owner and renter, elite and masses."[36] The Chinese in Southeast Asia, the Asians in East Africa, and the Jews in prewar Europe are among the groups referred to in these terms.

Trading minorities, it is argued, come into conflict with business rivals of other ethnic groups. Conflict occurs, not merely because of ordinary business rivalries, but because immigrant minorities are able to undercut their rivals by the use of their own credit institutions, their guild techniques of restraining competition among themselves, and their use of cheap, usually family, labor. Their interests also collide with the interests of those with whom they transact business: consumers, tenants, clients. Finally, because trading minorities have the ability to obtain their own cheap labor, they depress the prospects for labor in the host society. The tractable character of labor in middleman minority firms insures that rising wages in competing businesses would not be accompanied by similar increases for workers of minority firms. A competing firm in the host society that granted a wage increase would find itself priced out of the market. Eventually, workers in host society firms come to identify immigrant businesses and the low wages they pay as the source of the low wages paid in the economy generally.

"The middleman and the host society come into conflict because elements in each group have incompatible [economic] goals."[37] Even the most extreme measures taken against such groups can largely be explained on this basis. So powerful, economically and organizationally, are the trading minorities that they are

extremely difficult to dislodge. . . . The difficulty of breaking entrenched middleman monopolies, the difficulty of controlling the growth and extension of their economic power, pushes host countries to ever more extreme reactions. One

35. Edna Bonacich, "A Theory of Middleman Minorities," *American Sociological Review* 38 (Oct. 1973): 583–94. For other statements, see Pierre van den Berghe, *The Ethnic Phenomenon* (New York: Elsevier, 1981), 137–56; Sheldon Stryker, "Social Structure and Prejudice," *Social Problems* 6 (Spring 1959): 340–54; Irwin D. Rinder, "Strangers in the Land: Social Relations in the Status Gap," *Social Problems* 6 (Winter 1958–59): 253–60; Onkar S. Marwah and James H. Mittelman, "Alien Pariahs: Uganda's Asians and Bangladesh's Biharis" (unpublished paper presented at the 1973 annual meeting of the African Studies Association).

36. Bonacich, "A Theory of Middleman Minorities," 583.

37. Ibid., 589.

finds increasingly harsh measures, piled on one another, until, when all else fails, "final solutions" are enacted.[38]

This attempt to place genocide on a solid economic foundation raises a host of interesting questions which it might be tempting to pursue. Here, however, I shall simply deal with the extent to which ethnic conflict rests on realistic economic competition.

Unlike modernization theories of conflict, class theories may acknowledge the diversity of conflict motives among various classes. In fact, they attribute to different classes different economic reasons for ethnic hostility. At least three levels of competition have been identified: businessman versus businessman, businessman versus customer, and worker versus worker, where each of these roles is occupied by members of opposing ethnic groups. These economic rivalries unquestionably exist. From time to time and from country to country, they may become significant, as we shall soon see. Nevertheless, their frequency and severity are in general far less pronounced than might be imagined. Diverse though these conflict motives may be, together they do not add up to the extent or level of ethnic hostility they purport to explain.

ECONOMIC RIVALRY AND THE ETHNIC DIVISION OF LABOR

The fundamental deficiency of the class theory of ethnic conflict is that it credits with conflict-producing power every rationally competitive interest that can conceivably be identified, while ignoring all of the forces that work against the emergence of such competitive interests. In fact, there are many forces that operate to inhibit competitive relationships and therefore blunt the impact of economically based conflict.

Foremost among these forces is the ethnic division of labor. By this phrase I mean ethnic specialization of occupation in general; the phenomenon is not confined to "labor" in the narrow sense. The concentration of particular ethnic groups in particular sectors of the economy and in particular occupations within sectors is a feature of many societies, but it reaches its apogee in the ex-colonial countries. There ethnic-occupational differentiation may be elaborately organized. A trade, a department of a factory, or a government office is not infrequently the preserve of a group completely unrepresented in a related trade, a neighboring department, or the next office.[39]

38. Ibid., 592.
39. See, e.g., Burton Benedict, *Mauritius: The Problems of a Plural Society* (London: Pall Mall Press, 1965), 19–20, 26; Adrian C. Mayer, *Indians in Fiji* (London: Oxford Univ.

The origin and ongoing support of the ethnic division of labor are to be found in a network of interrelated conditions. Colonial policy often played an important part. Sometimes, but not always, specialization resulted from migration, internal or international. Colonial governments recruited or opened the door to immigrants whose services were thought indispensable to the performance of certain economic tasks. In Malaysia, Chinese were encouraged to enter to mine tin and to trade, Indians to tap rubber, Ceylonese to run the railroads. In Trinidad, Guyana, Fiji, and Mauritius, Indians were imported to cut sugar cane. Intracolonial migration for new economic ventures was also encouraged, and, because distances were shorter and boundaries did not have to be crossed, internal migration was easier to accomplish. At all events, much occupational specialization began in the colonial period, when, after all, many new occupations opened up. To a perhaps surprising extent, this specialization continues today.

The initial rationale for using ethnic specialists was generally economic. Quite often the migrants came from deprived backgrounds and deprived homelands, so that they were receptive to working in occupational ventures that others had no comparable incentives to enter or, much less frequently, receptive to working in established enterprises in need of cheaper labor. In Guyana and Trinidad, for example, conditions in the world sugar market made it difficult to pay the wages demanded by emancipated African labor; the importation of Indians was designed to depress wages or, as it was more delicately phrased, to provide "a fresh labouring population, to such an extent as to create competition for employment."[40] In that objective, it succeeded admirably, driving large numbers of Africans from the canefields to the towns and to the neighboring villages. Cane-cutting remains a largely Indian occupation.

Press, 1963), 94–95, 132; Hugh Tinker, *India and Pakistan: A Political Analysis*, rev. ed. (New York: Praeger, 1968), 155, 167; Morris David Morris, "The Effects of Industrialization on 'Race' Relations in India," in Guy Hunter, ed., *Industrialization and Race Relations* (London: Oxford Univ. Press, 1965), 146–52; Leonard Plotnicov, *Strangers to the City: Urban Man in Jos, Nigeria* (Pittsburgh: Univ. of Pittsburgh Press, 1967), 51; T. G. McGee, "The Cultural Role of Cities: A Case Study of Kuala Lumpur," *Journal of Tropical Geography* 17 (May 1963): 178–96, at 190–91; John F. Cady, "Burma," in Lennox A. Mills et al., eds., *The New World of Southeast Asia* (Minneapolis: Univ. of Minnesota Press, 1949), 135–36, 146; Leo A. Despres, *Cultural Pluralism and Nationalist Politics in British Guiana* (Chicago: Rand McNally, 1967), 141–43, 164; Merran Fraenkel, *Tribe and Class in Monrovia* (London: Oxford Univ. Press, 1964), 227–28.

40. "Resolutions of the House of Commons Committee on the West India Colonies," July 25, 1842, in Kenneth N. Bell and W. P. Morrell, eds., *Select Documents on British Colonial Policy, 1830–1860* (London: Oxford Univ. Press, 1928), 422.

Africans who work on the estates tend to be employed in the sugar factories, rather than in the fields.

Despite the economic rationale for the recruitment of ethnically specialized functionaries, justifications based on the alleged special qualifications of the group being recruited were prominently advanced. A dogma of ethnic skills developed, which asserted, for example, that, in Guyana and Trinidad, Indians had the right combination of thrift, industriousness, and docility for field work at low wages, that Malayalees made the very best clerks on Malaysian rubber estates, and that, in Bombay textile mills, Pathans and Punjabis were most suitable for heavy labor, Sikhs were the most outstanding artisans, and Muslims were the most accomplished weavers.[41] These assessments of special ethnic aptitudes have survived. In this way, the residue of colonial policy is felt in sentiment, as well as in the perpetuation of early occupational specialties, long after the initial economic rationale has disappeared.

A variety of public policies and private practices impinging on credit, savings, land tenure, education, and bureaucratic recruitment also supports occupational specialization. If it is difficult for Chinese in Southeast Asia to acquire the land to become *padi* farmers, they will channel their energies in other directions. If the Lebanese in West Africa found it easier than Africans to get bank loans,[42] this was a business advantage they could build on. If, on the other hand, South Indian Brahmins are prevented from obtaining civil service posts in proportion to their educational attainments, they will turn their attention to the private sector.[43] And, finally, it would seem that if wages can slowly be built into savings by plantation laborers, they may have an advantage over peasants in their ability to enter those business opportunities that require some small accumulation of capital.[44] (Indeed, one is tempted to postulate ethnic differences in paths to social mobility on this basis: laborers become traders, whereas peasants become bureaucrats.)

Cementing the ethnic division of labor is the preeminent role of ascriptive ties in economic relations in the developing world. Family and close friends—certainly members of the same ethnic group—tend to be instrumental in locating economic opportunities for kinsmen. Job-finding is by no means the impersonal search that it tends to be depicted as

41. Morris, "The Effect of Industrialization on 'Race' Relations in India, " 154.

42. R. Bayley Winder, "The Lebanese in West Africa," in L. A. Fallers, ed., *Immigrants and Associations* (The Hague: Mouton, 1967), 122.

43. Tinker, *India and Pakistan*, 150.

44. See, e.g., Mayer, *Indians in Fiji*.

in the West. Families may hire relatives or steer them to friendly sources of employment. Job-finding is one of the most important functions performed by ethnic associations throughout the developing world. In part, of course, this may reflect a preference for ethnically homogeneous places of work. In any case, the result is exactly the kind of ethnic homogeneity of occupation and workplace that was noted earlier. Recruitment is often, therefore, to established occupational niches on an ascriptive basis.

For these reasons, certain occupations, certain offices or shops, become well known as the preserve of one ethnic group or another. Partly as a cause, partly as a consequence of these occupational preserves, aspirations are channeled accordingly. A sample of final-year secondary-school students in the Basque city of San Sebastian, Spain, revealed, for example, that 90 percent aimed at a career in the private sector, while *none* wished to enter the public service.[45] Presumably, these clear-cut preferences have something to do with both Castilian domination of the civil service and the many opportunities open to Basques in business.[46] Moreover, ethnically differentiated aspirations can be quite persistent. Business is a family tradition among non-Malay Muslim businessmen in Penang, Malaysia, but not among Malay businessmen. When both groups of businessmen were asked their aspirations for their children's future, 83 percent of the non-Malay Muslims preferred a business career for their children, but 78 percent of the Malay businessmen preferred salaried (including civil service) employment.[47] The preference for a secure salaried job survived even the entry of these respondents into business.

Many studies have documented ethnic differences in patterns of motivation and aspiration, as well as ethnic differences in the grading of occupational prestige.[48] The point would scarcely be worth making again, were it not so often overlooked in theories of ethnic conflict. Ethnic groups often have distinctly preferred occupational paths that are

45. Juan J. Linz and Amando de Miguel, "Within-Nation Differences and Comparisons: The Eight Spains," in Richard L. Merritt and Stein Rokkan, eds., *Comparing Nations* (New Haven: Yale Univ. Press, 1966), 304–06.
46. See Kenneth Medhurst, *The Basques* (London: Minority Rights Group, Report no. 9, 1972), 6.
47. Judith A. Nagata, "Ethnic Differentiation Within an Urban Muslim Mercantile Community in Malaysia," *Ethnicity* 4 (Dec. 1977): 380–400. The sample, however, was small.
48. See, e.g., Andrew M. Greeley, *Ethnicity in the United States: A Preliminary Reconnaissance* (New York: John Wiley, 1974), 178–85.

related to the structure of opportunities and to differences of culture and history. In Calabar, Nigeria, for example, Ibo were once slaves and Efik were once slave traders. Occupational differentiation persisted right up to the 1960s: Ibo were traders, clerical workers, and self-employed artisans; Efik tended to be farmers or salaried laborers. These differences were supported by divergent orientations toward education and work. Ibo, more than Efik, regard education as a means to a career, and Ibo believe work to be an important goal. Efik, on the other hand, regard education as an end more than a means. They have a more discriminating attitude toward work, distinguishing sharply between "slave" work and "respectable" work, eschewing occupations they regard as demeaning.[49] Similar distinctions are made by Guyanese Africans, eager to avoid economic behavior that is commonplace among neighboring East Indians, behavior which, if adopted by Africans, might involve backsliding to a lower status. Indians, it is said, are hardworking and thrifty, indeed excessively so: they "work cheap, eat cheap, and save and save. Black people can't punish themselves so. If we punish ourselves like coolieman [the Indian], we slaves again."[50]

The point can be put more generally. Every group has defenses against certain kinds of work. Among the major sources of such defenses is the association of particular occupations with ethnic strangers whose ways seem unenviable. A clear example of this is reported from the Nowgong district of Assam, where Bengali peasants settled both before and after the partition of India in 1947. In this district, Muslim Bengalis from Mymensingh (now in Bangladesh) are said to be more proficient farmers and "more hard working than the native Assamese—even the cow of the Mymensingh peasant yields more milk than that of the local farmer," and only the Bengalis grow vegetables for commercial sale, "usually at inordinately high prices. But the local [Assamese] population refuses to follow suit and share in the profits. And it is not because they are unaware of it; the example is at their doorstep."[51] The reason, according to Kusum Nair, is that Bengali farmers carry their vegetables to market on their heads, a method the Assamese find incompatible with their "dignity." For the same reason, the Assamese decline employment on the tea

49. W. T. Morrill, "Immigrants and Associations: The Ibo in Twentieth Century Calabar," in Fallers, ed., *Immigrants and Associations*, 154–87.

50. Quoted in Despres, *Cultural Pluralism and Nationalist Politics in British Guiana*, 93.

51. Kusum Nair, *Blossoms in the Dust: The Human Factor in Indian Development* (New York: Praeger, 1962), 139–40.

estates, leaving that field, too, to immigrants from other states.[52] Clearly, non-economic calculations intrude into occupational choices in rural as well as urban areas.

These, then, are the bases of the continuing ethnic division of labor: policy, both colonial and contemporary; stereotypes of group qualifications for particular kinds of work; ascriptive factors in economic relations; and ethnic aspirations based on existing patterns of economic activity as well as on culturally conditioned preferences. The net result of the ethnic division of labor is greatly to reduce the occasions for economic competition and to channel competition within trades and occupations in an intraethnic direction.

BUSINESS RIVALRIES

To the extent that the ethnic division of labor produces occupational monopolies, of course some people will resent them. Inasmuch as it represents some groups disproportionately in some trades and constricts opportunities for other groups at points of entry, it can be a source of friction. But, at the same time, the division of labor limits (by definition) the competition of members of different ethnic groups who are in the same business. The business rivals envisioned by theories that predicate ethnic conflict on economic competition among members of opposing ethnic groups are far fewer than imagined. Specifically, the division of labor inhibits the growth of resentment of undercutting and other competitive practices allegedly based on the trading minorities' access to credit on favorable terms, their ability to restrain their own competition, and their use of cheap labor. And, while the division of labor skews the structure of economic opportunities, the very fact that it exists tends, as we have seen, to propel ethnic groups in the direction of complementary rather than competitive occupations. Except at times when great changes seem possible in the entire economic structure, a principal effect of all the ingredients that go into dividing occupations along ethnic lines is to make it "natural" to go into an established trade and "unnatural" to break into a wholly new one. In ethnic conflict, the ethnic division of labor is more a shield than a sword.

Moreover, when the division of labor breaks down as a result of convergence in occupational socialization, it does so primarily because of common educational experience. Among the sectors exposed to this—

52. Ibid., 140 n.5; B. G. Verghese et al., *Situation in Assam: Report of a Study Team* (New Delhi: Gandhi Peace Foundation, mimeo., 1980), 14.

the educated elites of the developing world—business is by no means the preferred occupational choice. In Trinidad, where there are data on the career preferences of upwardly mobile secondary students, business is the stated choice of only one percent of both black and East Indian male students.[53] In Sri Lanka, soon after independence, a sample of university entrants and a sample of males finishing secondary school were asked in different ways about occupational goals.[54] Only 3.8 percent of the first group preferred work in a private firm; while 15.6 percent favored self-employment, most of these were speaking of professional practice. Business was not a highly esteemed prospect. But government was: in the second group, the preference for government ranged between 75 and 99.9 percent, depending on the province. Nearly three-quarters of a Malaysian secondary-school sample preferred professional and technical careers. Less than a fifth chose "proprietor, manager, or executive," a category that mixed salaried employment with independent business careers.[55] A survey of secondary-school students in the Ivory Coast found that business was among the least preferred occupations. Job security was the most important criterion of occupational desirability. Accordingly, government was the employer preferred by more than 80 percent of all students.[56]

No doubt more than a handful of such students actually end up in business, whatever their initial preferences. But business is not the career in which competitive energies are invested by educated elites.[57] For the most part, the aspirations of the new elites produced by the schools of the developing societies are turned not toward entrepreneurship but toward careers in the bureaucracy.

To say that there are significant defenses against the emergence of

53. Vera Rubin and Marisa Zavalloni, *We Wish To Be Looked Upon: A Study of the Aspirations of Youth in a Developing Society* (New York: Teachers College Press, 1969), 77.

54. Murray A. Straus, "Family Characteristics and Occupational Choice of University Entrants as Clues to the Social Structure of Ceylon," *University of Ceylon Review* 9 (Apr. 1951): 125–35; T. L. Green, "Education and Social Needs in Ceylon," *University of Ceylon Review* 10 (Oct. 1952): 297–316.

55. Yoshimitsu Takei et al., "Aspirations and Expectations of West Malaysian Youth: Two Models of Social Class Values," *Comparative Education Review* 17 (June 1973): 216–30.

56. Remi Clignet and Philip Foster, *The Fortunate Few: A Study of Secondary Schools and Students in the Ivory Coast* (Evanston: Northwestern Univ. Press, 1966), 152–63.

57. Henry Bienen, *Kenya: The Politics of Participation and Control* (Princeton: Princeton Univ. Press, 1974), 143–49; Donald Rothchild, "Kenya's Africanization Program: Priorities of Development and Equity," *American Political Science Review* 64 (Sept. 1970): 737–53.

competitive rivalries between ethnically differentiated groups of businessmen is not to imply that such rivalries do not exist. But, where business rivalries of this kind emerge, it is typically after the division of labor has broken down and a new class of ethnically differentiated entrepreneurs or traders has arisen, a class significant enough to have organized itself politically.

There are examples of this, but by no means everywhere. In Sri Lanka, a former activist of the extremist Sinhalese organization, the *Jathika Vimukthi Peramuna* (National Liberation Front), has recounted that its main financial support came from small businessmen in Colombo. These merchants often had Tamil rivals or had experienced difficulty obtaining credit from banks in which they sensed disproportionate Tamil influence.[58] In Uganda, the commodity boom of the 1940s helped create a new class of African petty traders, the overwhelming majority of them Baganda. These traders were vociferously anti-Indian. But, as would be expected from an ethnic division of labor, when a boycott of non-African businessmen was organized in 1959–60, few Africans except Baganda supported it, and many actively opposed it.[59] In Kenya, many of the restrictive measures enforced against Indians in the areas of trade and commerce have been sponsored by an active interest group of African entrepreneurs, the Kenya African Wholesalers and Distributors.[60] The Marwari business community all over India has encountered resistance to its presence where there is a well-organized class of indigenous commercial competitors, such as the Christian merchants in Kerala and the Chettiars in Madras.[61] Similarly well-organized Filipino entrepreneurs, represented by the Philippine Chamber of Commerce, have been the source of governmental action against Chinese merchants in the Philippines.[62] But all of these examples must be matched against the numerous counterexamples of little or no hostility as a result of business rivalry,

58. Here and at later points in this chapter, I am drawing on my earlier paper, "Multi-racial Politics in the New States: Toward a Theory of Conflict," in Robert J. Jackson and Michael B. Stein, eds., *Issues in Comparative Politics* (New York: St. Martin's Press, 1971), 164–80.

59. Dharam P. Ghai, "The Bugandan Trade Boycott: A Study in Tribal, Political, and Economic Nationalism," in Robert I. Rotberg and Ali A. Mazrui, eds., *Power and Protest in Black Africa* (New York: Oxford Univ. Press, 1970), 758, 765–66.

60. Donald Rothchild, "Citizenship and National Integration: The Non-African Crisis in Kenya," *Studies in Race and Nations*, vol. 1, no. 3 (1969–70): 1–32, at 30 n.44.

61. Selig S. Harrison, *India: The Dangerous Decades* (Princeton: Princeton Univ. Press, 1960), 114–22. See also Thomas Timberg, *The Marwaris* (New Delhi: Vikas, 1978).

62. Gerald A. McBeath, "Political Behavior of Ethnic Leaders," *Comparative Politics* 10 (Apr. 1978): 393–417.

including Lebanese in West Africa, Parsis and Marwaris elsewhere in India, Isma'ilis in Pakistan, Minangkabau in Indonesia, Dioula in West Africa, Moors in Senegal, and Hausa in Equatorial Africa. Business rivals are a prerequisite for business rivalries.

Sometimes the emergence of a new class of ethnically differentiated businessmen is not so much the cause as the effect of political action. That may have been the case with the Northern Nigerian traders, merchants, and contractors who, in the 1950s and '60s, gave their vigorous support to the regional government's policy of "Northernization."[63] This program was designed to free the North of dependence on Southern Nigerian civil servants and businessmen by giving preference in employment, contracts, scholarships, land, and loans to Northerners. The program flowed from a broad set of apprehensions about the prospects of Southern domination of Northern Nigerian life.[64] Early Northern businessmen were proponents of Northernization, from which they stood to gain. Yet the policy did not rest on anything so narrow as business rivalries. Indeed, what gave rise to it was not the existence of a powerful class of eager but resentful Northern businessmen, chafing at their inability to compete on equal terms, but a general perception that the *absence* of such a significant class was harmful to Northern interests as a whole. And the Northernization policy spurred the growth of such a class.

Much the same sequence could be documented for other countries that have adopted programs to give priority to businessmen of a particular ethnic group. The very purpose of such programs, as for example in Malaysia, is to break the ethnic division of labor and bring a new class of entrepreneurs into being by holding out competitive advantages for them. Such programs are not properly interpreted as the result of commercial rivalries. Instead, the commercial rivalries are the result of the programs. But, once begun, the programs are supported by emerging business rivals.

TRADERS AND CUSTOMERS

So far we have discussed only the rivalries asserted to exist between "middleman minorities" and their business competitors of other ethnic groups. While sometimes present and occasionally severe, these rivalries

63. Sklar, *Nigerian Political Parties*, 327–29; Walter Schwarz, *Nigeria* (New York: Praeger, 1968), 240.
64. James S. Coleman, *Nigeria: Background to Nationalism* (Berkeley and Los Angeles: Univ. of California Press, 1958), 360–63.

are not universal. Their incidence and importance have been exaggerated. I shall suggest later some reasons other than business rivalry for the hostility sometimes directed at trading minorities. Before moving from the business class to the working class, it is necessary to consider the tensions that are supposed to inhere in relations between businessmen belonging to one ethnic group and consumers, tenants, and clients belonging to another.

Here there is some evidence, much of it rural and most of it counterintuitive. What it suggests, by and large, is that the supposed economic resentments of businessmen by their customers often do not exist. A major reason they do not exist is that non-economic values intrude into the calculations that customers and tenants are supposed to make. There are intervening variables between economic position and economic conflict along ethnic lines.

One of the persistent themes of the "middleman minority" literature is that alien traders who settle in rural areas to buy produce and sell seed and staples exploit the peasantry with whom they deal and build up a reservoir of hostility toward themselves. Yet, rather than resenting alien rural traders, peasants often welcome them. Partly, this is because trade is generally not an esteemed occupation in village society, despite its relatively high rewards. Then, too, it is easier to trade at arm's length with an ethnic stranger. And these traders provide highly valued services that, villagers have found from experience, less well-capitalized shops owned by members of their own ethnic group or by the government are in no position to provide. Among these services are transportation to get the crop to market, gunny sacks in which to transport it, and, perhaps most important, cash advances in anticipation of harvest.[65]

These services may seem trivial to outsiders, but they are the lifeline tying peasant society to the cash economy. Stranger-groups in a position to meet these needs have often thrived unmolested in rural areas. The Arabs of Indonesia and the Indians of Burma are classic cases. Rural traders and moneylenders, the Arabs long served as the contact point of the Indonesian villager with the market. Supplying peasants with cash before harvest, buying their surplus crop after harvest, the Arabs charged usurious rates of interest. Yet Indonesian peasants tended to prefer the Arabs to alternative credit and marketing institutions offered by the government, which, while "reasonable" (especially in interest rates),

65. For the importance of some of these services to peasants, see Nair, *Blossoms in the Dust*, 77, 140.

were also more rigid. The Arabs were flexible in the amount they were willing to advance, more prepared to take risks, and more willing to lend money at the right moment to meet the cash exigencies of birth, marriage, and circumcision.[66] Similar reports emanate from Burma, where the government displaced Indian middlemen. "In the old times," complained a Burman farmer, "I sold my rice to an Indian trader. When I needed money for fertilizer or seed I could borrow. Now I must deal with the government. They refuse loans," and in addition their doors are not always open, as the Indian trader's shop was.[67]

Anthropological field studies in Malaysia support the same conclusions and provide some detail on the quality of relations between Chinese middlemen and Malay peasants. Antagonism toward the Chinese in Malaysia has been formidable. Repeatedly, foreign observers and sections of the Malaysian elite have perceived widespread economically based discontent in the Malay villages. There surely has been antipathy and violence (though most of it in towns). But precisely what has been the role played by Malay envy of Chinese affluence and resentment of the trading class? Peter J. Wilson in his village study summarized the prevailing attitude:

... the Malays of Jendram Hilir readily admit the superiority of Chinese in economic affairs and, on the whole, they do not begrudge or envy the Chinese his paramount position. That many Chinese are wealthy whereas most Malays are poor is indeed a topic of concern and self-pity for Malays, but the skill of Chinese businessmen and their ability to meet all the demands placed on them is often the subject of admiration on the part of village Malays. In the same way, the evident ability of the Chinese to work harder than the Malays is admitted and admired.[68]

Malays frequently prefer to deal with Chinese shopkeepers who, because of their strong financial position and wholesale relationships, can provide customers with goods on credit, small loans, lower prices, and a wider variety of goods than many Malay shopkeepers are able to provide. Similar considerations also account for the frequent preference

66. See Justus M. van der Kroef, "The Arabs of Indonesia," *Middle East Journal* 7 (Summer 1953): 311–17.
67. Quoted in the *Washington Post*, Oct. 9, 1978. To the same effect regarding Indian traders in South Africa, see Leo Kuper, *An African Bourgeoisie: Race, Class, and Politics in South Africa* (New Haven: Yale Univ. Press, 1965), 300.
68. *A Malay Village and Malaysia: Social Values and Rural Development* (New Haven: HRAF Press, 1967), 26.

of Malay peasants for Chinese commodity dealers to market their produce.[69]

It is quite widely felt by Malays that Chinese success comes at a high moral price. The Chinese emphasis on economic activity is seen as excessively single-minded. It ignores religious values and requires sacrifices that prevent the maintenance of both ritual cleanliness and personal cultivation. Chinese are only rarely classified as *halus* (civilized, refined, or cultivated). Usually they are regarded as *kasar* (crude or uncultured).[70] There has not been much desire in the villages either to emulate or expropriate the Chinese. When a Malay politician was attempting to persuade a group of *padi* farmers that a state marketing authority would bring them benefits, he was met with the persistent question, "Will it provide gunny sacks the way the Chinese do?"[71]

Malay village society possesses a number of mechanisms that operate to limit economic aspirations, including those that might put Malays in economic conflict with Chinese. Since work relations are also personal relations,[72] there are important satisfactions besides profit to be derived from them. Economic success, moreover, is only partly viewed as a function of individual effort; the concept of *rezeki*, or resignation to one's economic fate, attributes a large part of success or failure to divine ordination. Much of the remainder is attributed to the action or inaction of government. Finally, there is a decided ambivalence about change, which manifests itself in the parental desire to see children succeed without taking extensive risks or really abandoning village ways for a new lifestyle.[73] This conservatism has the effect of restricting the range of ambitions for social mobility and, concomitantly, of retarding ethno-economic conflict.

The studies that suggest these conclusions were not carried out in particularly remote or isolated villages. All of them were conducted on the relatively modernized West Coast of Malaya, where contact with the Chinese is quite regular and not always friendly. One of the older studies was carried out in the Batu Pahat district of Johore state—an area where

---

69. M. G. Swift, *Malay Peasant Society in Jelebu* (New York: Humanities Press, 1965), 71–72; Kenelm O. L. Burridge, "Racial Relations in Johore," *Australian Journal of Politics and History* 2 (May 1957): 151–68, at 157.

70. These themes run through both Wilson, *A Malay Village and Malaysia*, and Burridge, "Racial Relations in Johore."

71. Interview, Alor Star, Malaysia, Jan. 11, 1968.

72. Wilson, *A Malay Village and Malaysia*, 106–07, 132, 147–48.

73. Ibid., 106; Swift, *Malay Peasant Society in Jelebu*, 28–30, 161–62.

fierce ethnic rioting occurred in 1945. Discussing the hostility in Batu Pahat, K.O.L. Burridge points out that "only those Malays who have come into significant contact with European thought—those with long experience in the administration, or those who have been educated in the United Kingdom—feel, or see, that Chinese control of commerce and economic life creates an issue between Chinese and Malays."[74] The ethnic violence, however, was the work of others:

As far as the evidence goes those who were capable of appreciating the economic issues had no hand in making the incidents. On the contrary, they seem to have been taken by surprise and thereafter did their utmost to restore order. And action was taken by the peasants themselves, the Malays and Malaysians, who thought little of economics and who felt that other more important issues were at stake.[75]

Burridge notes, quite accurately, that this situation presents a paradox only because in the West "it has become increasingly relevant to seek the economic issues which are considered to lie 'below' a conflict capable of being expressed in a variety of other terms."[76]

The point about Malay aspirations can be generalized. We have been unduly accustomed to think of economic ambition as being unaffected by countervailing values like sociability, resignation, and the fulfillment of religious obligations. We are also inclined to think of aspirations for improved status and income as being boundless. In point of fact, there is much evidence to suggest that economic aspirations among peasants and urban workers in the developing world are generally quite modest, certainly far more modest than those of their middle-class counterparts.[77] Moderate aspiration levels tend to inhibit resentment of the more advantaged ethnic strangers with whom they deal.

Even in conditions of extreme instability, groups bent on violence have often avoided inflicting injury on "middleman minorities." Greek traders in the Southern Sudan were left completely unharmed in the

74. Burridge, "Racial Relations in Johore," 157.
75. Ibid., 159. "Malaysians" here refers to Malays of Indonesian origin. This is different from the later usage, in which the term includes citizens of Malaysia irrespective of ethnic origin.
76. Ibid., 157.
77. See the evidence assembled by Joan M. Nelson, *Migrants, Urban Poverty, and Instability in New Nations* (Cambridge: Harvard Univ. Center for International Affairs, Occasional Paper no. 22, 1969), 45–53; Nair, *Blossoms in the Dust*, 29, 31; Raymond T. Smith, *The Negro Family in British Guiana* (London: Routledge & Kegan Paul, 1956), 205. Compare aspirations of upwardly mobile secondary-school students reported by Rubin and Zavalloni, *We Wish To Be Looked Upon*.

widespread rioting of 1955.[78] If there had been old scores to settle against this trading minority, there was ample opportunity to do so then. When Indians were attacked in Burma in the severe riots of 1938, the main victims were Indian Muslims, despite the fact that the landlord class in Lower Burma was heavily composed of Indian Hindus who had profited inordinately from the depression.[79] Assamese have rioted against Bengalis in Assam on a number of occasions since independence. So serious has this violence often been that in 1960 some 45,000 Bengalis were forced to flee Assam for other states, and in 1972 some estimates of homeless ran to 25,000 or more.[80] In the most severe violence of 1979–83, thousands of Bengalis were killed.[81] There is some evidence of Assamese-Bengali rivalry in the professions, government service, and, in some localities, small-scale trade.[82] For such reasons, the conflict has been viewed as "essentially economic."[83] But Marwaris, not Bengalis, control Assam's wholesale trade, industry, rice mills, oil mills, godowns, and tea marketing.[84] Yet this trading minority *par excellence* has not (with some minor exceptions) been the victim of Assamese violence in any way comparable to that inflicted on the Bengalis. Participants in ethnic violence have more often than not passed up the chance to attack trading minorities.

From time to time, however, ethnic groups with a strong position in trade and commerce have been the victims of mass violence. But the available evidence suggests it is a distortion to attribute these attacks to economic resentment. What emerges from the data with much greater frequency is political resentment against the groups so attacked. When for once the Marwaris were the victims of a very mild Assamese assault, in 1968 (compared to the fierce attacks on Bengalis, this scarcely qualified as a riot), it was Assamese grievances against the central government, with which the Marwaris were identified, that formed the most

78. Government of Sudan, *Report of the Commission of Inquiry into the Disturbances in the Southern Sudan During August 1955* (Khartoum: Government of Sudan, 1956), 78.

79. Government of Burma, *Final Report of the Riot Inquiry Committee* (Rangoon: Government Printer, 1939), Appendix XI.

80. *The Statesman* (Calcutta), Oct. 19, 1972; ibid., Oct. 30, 1976.

81. In one month of 1983 alone, 3,600 Bengalis were killed. *Far Eastern Economic Review* (Hong Kong), Mar. 24, 1983, p. 5.

82. Charu Chandra Bhandari, *Thoughts on Assam Disturbances* (Rajghat, India: A. B. Sarva Seva Sangh Prakashan, 1961), 12–14.

83. K. C. Chakravarti, "Bongal Kheda Again," *Economic Weekly* (Bombay), July 30, 1960, p. 1193.

84. For figures, see Bhandari, *Thoughts on Assam Disturbances*, 19.

prominent theme.[85] The identification of the Biharis of Bangladesh with the West Pakistanis is what aroused the Bengalis against them,[86] much as the open identification of the Chinese in Thailand with the Kuomintang regime helped bring on the violence against them in Bangkok in 1945.[87] The anti-Chinese violence in Indonesia that followed the attempted coup of 1965 was linked to the support given by some Chinese to the Indonesian Communists and to their alleged ties to China at a time when China was greatly feared.[88] Anti-Chinese violence in Malaysia has been connected to elections and other political events with ethnic overtones,[89] and the great anti-Bengali violence in Assam that began in 1979 was precipitated by the calling of elections in which it was feared that Bengalis from Bangladesh would have a disproportionate impact. These cases all partake of political apprehension, often with a foreign component, far more than they evidence mass economic jealousy. If patterns of violence reflect the "inevitable conflict of interest between buyer and seller, renter and landlord, client and professional,"[90] they have yet to exhibit this relationship.[91]

Attitudinal data seem to show the same gap between mass and elite sentiments toward commercial minorities that evidence of actual behavior suggests. African university students, questioned about the trading minorities in their countries—Indians in Uganda, Lebanese in Nigeria, Ghana, and Senegal, Armenians in Ethiopia—were generally hostile toward them, most often on economic grounds.[92] Even here, there is unevenness in the responses: a significant fraction of the Ethiopian sample attributed various positive traits to the Armenians.[93] Still, these univer-

85. Dilip Mukerjee, "Assam Reorganization," *Asian Survey* 9 (Apr. 1969): 297–311, at 308.
86. Marwah and Mittelman, "Alien Pariahs: Uganda's Asians and Bangladesh's Biharis."
87. G. William Skinner, *Chinese Society in Thailand* (Ithaca: Cornell Univ. Press, 1957), 278–79.
88. Cynthia H. Enloe, *Ethnic Conflict and Political Development* (Boston: Little, Brown, 1973), 196 n.15.
89. Horowitz, "Multiracial Politics in the New States," 177–78.
90. Bonacich, "A Theory of Middleman Minorities," 589.
91. There is a possible exception in the only example of violence cited by Bonacich: the anti-Indian riots in Durban, South Africa, in 1949. However, much more was at work in Durban than shopkeeper-customer tension. See Maurice Webb and Kenneth Kirkwood, *The Durban Riots and After* (pamphlet; Johannesburg: South African Institute of Race Relations, n.d.); Union of South Africa, *Report of the Commission of Enquiry into Riots in Durban* (Cape Town: Cape Times, Ltd., 1949); Kuper, *An African Bourgeoisie*, 301.
92. Klineberg and Zavalloni, *Nationalism and Tribalism Among African Students*, 183–87.
93. Ibid., 185, 304.

sity students tended to dislike the trading groups they were asked about, and usually described them as "exploiting," "money-minded," or "dishonest."

There are no cross-national data to test the extent to which these elite attitudes are shared by members of other social classes, who are likely to come into contact with commercial groups solely as customers and without having been educated to believe, as Burridge puts it, that "control of commerce and economic life creates an issue" between ethnic groups. There is, however, a nonelite survey of ethnic relations in Sierra Leone that casts light on this question.[94] It provides extensive data on attitudes toward Syrian and Lebanese traders and toward other Africans.

Because of the Lebanese "tendency to monopolize commercial activities," John Dawson hypothesized before he conducted his survey "that attitudes to Syrians and Lebanese might be unfavorable."[95] Responses to the social distance scale Dawson administered did indeed rank the Syrians and Lebanese very low, indicating the reluctance of Africans to enter into relationships involving intimacy with those groups.[96] Nevertheless, the general attitude displayed toward Syrians and Lebanese was markedly friendly. Well over half of all African respondents evinced favorable attitudes toward the Syrians and Lebanese, citing their propensity to learn local languages, marry African women, provide financial assistance, and to deport themselves in ways calculated to gain social approval, despite their relative affluence.[97]

Dawson asked a much smaller sample of Sierra Leone Africans, "Which group causes the most trouble?"[98] Twenty-four respondents agreed that the Temne did; five (all Temne) suggested the Mende; and only three named the Lebanese and Syrians. Dawson lists about a dozen more or less typical reasons cited: the Creoles (descendants of repatriated former slaves) were seen as too haughty, the Mende too exclusive and domineering, the Temne too aggressive. Not one of the listed responses referred to economic grievances against any named ethnic group.

The hypothesis that trading minorities and their clienteles have an

94. John Dawson, "Race and Inter-Group Relations in Sierra Leone," part 2, *Race* 6 (Jan. 1965): 217–321.
95. Ibid., 218.
96. Ibid., 224. For the unusual rank order of statements in Dawson's study, see ibid., 223.
97. Ibid., 218.
98. Ibid., 219–22.

"inevitable conflict of interest" thus rests on a number of dubious assumptions. Among these are the assumptions that traders are seen by their customers as exploiters rather than as expediters, that those customers are motivated by economic goals that outweigh other kinds of goals, and that their aspirations are so strong as to impel them to resentment. There is a certain woodenness about these assumptions, postulating as they do rather automatic reactions to a given economic situation.

In fact, ethnically differentiated traders appear to thrive in the developing world because they are seen as more useful than harmful, because aspirations are limited, and because economic motives are not necessarily the mainsprings of all ethnic action—a point we have noted in various ways for the Efik, the Assamese, the Guyanese Africans, the Malays, and the various Sierra Leoneans. Ethnic conflict traceable to the divergent interests of merchant and customer, dealer and farmer, even landlord and tenant, seems relatively rare, in spite of the assessments of Western theorists and educated elites in the developing countries themselves that these are (or ought to be) conflict-prone relationships.

WORKING-CLASS COMPETITION

If there is little evidence of economically motivated hostility between traders and their customers, there would seem to be more reason to expect economic competition among urban working classes in ethnically divided societies. Here, after all, the conflict motive is competitive rather than redistributive. Workers are presumably competing for the same scarce jobs and wages, just as businessmen compete among themselves for the same opportunities. Aspiration levels need not be very high for collisions of ethnic interests to occur. All that is required is for members of opposing ethnic groups to be in the same labor market, especially if one group is preferred by employers over another because it sells its labor cheaper or performs some task more efficiently (which amounts to the same thing).

The problem with this line of argument is that this simple precondition is very often absent. Competing labor pools, each ethnically based, do not generally exist. Significant ethnic disparities in wage rates are particularly difficult to find. If business rivalries are not a pervasive source of ethnic conflict, working-class rivalries are even less so.

To be sure, competing labor pools and ethnic wage differentials did exist historically, in the nineteenth and early twentieth centuries. During that period, in the industrial countries and in the colonies, migrant labor was used to undercut existing supplies of indigenous labor. Consequently, it is possible to identify ethnic hostility that was clearly grounded in working-class rivalry. For example, in Guyana, as we saw earlier, East Indian indentured labor was imported to depress wages on the sugar plantations and later in other enterprises. By the turn of the twentieth century, about half of the Indians lived off the estates. There they were used as cheaper alternatives to urban black labor.[99] Among the results were a serious riot by black laborers in Georgetown in 1905 and a protest movement against further Indian immigration.[100] The Guyanese case was exceptionally blatant, because of the mercantile origins of the colony and the extent to which the British equated the welfare of the colony with the welfare of the sugar estates. Nonetheless, other colonial and Western examples of labor importation and manipulation can be found during the same period.[101] In Burma, for example, the British had used Indian Telugu longshoremen on the Rangoon docks. Serious violence occurred in 1930 when British employers brought in Burman labor to replace the striking Telugus.[102]

After about the 1930s, however, this kind of engineered competition everywhere became much more difficult to arrange. Restrictions on emigration and immigration, some of the latter restrictions due to pressures like those emanating from the Afro-Guyanese, constricted the supply of tractable competitors available for undercutting. The growth of trade unions in a number of countries bolstered the power of those already employed and standardized at least some wage rates. The opening up of new economic opportunities, to which members of previously competing ethnic groups could gravitate, permitted ethnic specialization and inhibited undercutting. Rarely can one now identify competing ethnic labor pools or the kind of ethnic conflict associated with undercutting on a large scale.

Rarely does not, however, mean never. The conflict between Ivorians and Mossi immigrants in the Ivory Coast is a legacy of colonial labor policy. Imported from Upper Volta by the French, the Mossi are em-

---

99. See, e.g., *The Creole* (Georgetown), Jan. 27, 1906.
100. Ibid., Dec. 30, 1905; ibid., Apr. 28, 1906. During these riots, there were proposals to use East Indians against black rioters.
101. The examples cited by Bonacich, "A Theory of Ethnic Antagonism," are nearly all from this period.
102. Maurice Collis, *Trials in Burma*, 2d ed. (London: Faber & Faber, 1945), 141–47; E. L. F. Andrew, *Indian Labour in Rangoon* ([Calcutta?]: Oxford Univ. Press, 1933), 279–92.

ployed in a wide range of low-level occupations, as agricultural workers and urban menials and domestics. So numerous are they and so prevalent throughout the lowest rungs of urban wage labor that laborers of other ethnic groups could scarcely avoid meeting competition from the Mossi, who are regarded as especially hardworking and reliable. In 1969, they were attacked in Abidjan. The attacks were led by associations of unemployed Ivorian laborers.[103] Significantly, the riot followed a dispute at an employment exchange, where a prospective employer, a Frenchman, had apparently stated a preference for a Mossi employee.

This, then, was a clear case of ethnically defined, competing labor pools and of violence flowing from the competition. But such cases are exceptional. The 1969 violence in the Ivory Coast is the only post-colonial ethnic riot I have found that can be attributed to working-class economic competition. Such competition is occasionally reported, usually involving group rivalries over jobs in modern sector enterprises, in factories and on the docks.[104] But what is surprising is not that such competition exists, but that it is not the major and most intense theme of urban ethnic politics. After all, cities in the developing world are growing at rates of 5 to 8 percent annually, labor forces generally even faster.[105] Virtually everywhere, modern sector urban employment is growing at slower rates, generally not exceeding 5 percent per annum. It might be expected that the job scarcity reflected in the gap between these two rates of growth would give rise to a significant incidence of economically based ethnic conflict. Yet the evidence for such a development is conspicuous by its paucity. As I have said, such competition rarely breaks out into violence, although urban ethnic violence is by no means uncommon in Asia and Africa. Similarly, working-class job competition rarely plays a prominent part in urban ethnic movements, although these move-

103. J. L., "New Developments in French-Speaking Africa," *Civilisations* 20 (Winter 1970): 270–78. I have discussed this riot in Donald L. Horowitz, "Direct, Displaced, and Cumulative Ethnic Aggression," *Comparative Politics* 6 (Oct. 1973): 1–16, at 10.

104. See David Parkin, *Neighbours and Nationals in an African City Ward* (London: Routledge & Kegan Paul, 1969), 31–33; J. S. La Fontaine, *City Politics: A Study of Leopoldville, 1962–63* (Cambridge: Cambridge Univ. Press, 1970), 114–15; Richard Stren, "Factional Politics and Central Control in Mombasa, 1960–1969," *Canadian Journal of African Studies* 4 (Winter 1970): 33–56, at 40–41.

105. Joan M. Nelson, *Access to Power: Politics and the Urban Poor in Developing Nations* (Princeton: Princeton Univ. Press, 1979), 48; Nelson, "The Urban Poor: Disruption or Political Integration in Third World Cities?" *World Politics* 22 (Apr. 1970): 393–414. I am indebted to Joan Nelson for a helpful discussion of urban migration and employment.

ments, too, are not uncommon. The ethnic concerns of urban working classes typically run to other matters.

These concerns are heavily symbolic. They relate particularly to the "symbols of prestige,"[106] such as the name of a town and whether it connotes "ownership" by one group or another.[107] Such matters are especially significant as between groups stamped, respectively, as indigenous and immigrant. There are high rates of rural-to-urban migration in Asia and Africa. Due to internal or previous international migration, indigenous groups in many cities feel swamped by immigrants. Indigenous-minority cities include, for example, Bombay, Freetown, Karachi, Abidjan, Phnom Penh, Mombasa, Kuala Lumpur, Kumasi, Singapore, Jos, Bangalore, and Kinshasa. A common preoccupation in urban politics is the relationship of groups to the locale, with indigenes claiming the right to be free of "domination" by immigrants (and sometimes the right to expel them) and immigrants claiming the right to equal treatment (and sometimes communal autonomy or exemption from certain uniform requirements).[108] The relationship of groups to the city is often expressed symbolically. In one Nigerian town, an issue that divided ethnic groups was "the choice of armorial bearings"; those claiming indigenous status preferred the crossed swords of their traditional ruler, while their rivals wanted "an emblem symbolizing all the three major ethnic groups."[109] Exactly the same issue—the coat of arms—divided Fijians and Indians on the other side of the globe in the town of Suva, in Fiji.[110]

Such themes of ethnic inclusion and exclusion emerge far more prominently and uniformly than any issue of labor competition. Summing up the situation of Indian cities with nativist movements, Mary Fainsod Katzenstein concludes: "Conspicuous by its absence in all localities is

106. William John Hanna and Judith Lynne Hanna, "The Political Structure of Urban-Centered African Communities," in Horace Miner, ed., The City in Modern Africa (New York: Praeger, 1967), 155.

107. Ibid., 155–56; P. C. Lloyd, "Ethnicity and the Structure of Inequality in a Nigerian Town in the Mid-1950s," in Abner Cohen, ed., Urban Ethnicity (London: Tavistock, 1974), 242–44.

108. La Fontaine, City Politics, 27; Aristide R. Zolberg, One-Party Government in the Ivory Coast (Princeton: Princeton Univ. Press, 1964), 41, 202–05; Lloyd, "Ethnicity and the Structure of Inequality in a Nigerian Town," 240–44; Stren, "Factional Politics and Central Control in Mombasa," 40; Peter C. W. Gutkind, "Accommodation and Conflict in an African Peri-Urban Area," Anthropologica, n.s., 4 (1962): 163–74, at 169; Abner Cohen, Custom and Politics in Urban Africa: A Study of Hausa Migrants in Yoruba Towns (London: Routledge & Kegan Paul, 1969), chap. 5.

109. Lloyd, "Ethnicity and the Structure of Inequality in a Nigerian Town," 241.

110. Milne, Politics in Ethnically Bipolar States, 129–30.

any organized protest between ethnic groups over factory and working-class jobs."[111] A major reason is the segmented labor market that results from the ethnic division of labor.[112] What this means, as suggested earlier, is that workers of different ethnic groups are often steered by helpful friends, patrons, kinsmen, and ethnic associations toward employment in enterprises where members of the same group already have a foothold. Job competition is likely to be intraethnic.[113] The evidence is abundant that interethnic contacts and ties are concentrated in the upper and middle classes.[114] At the working-class level, neighborhoods tend to be particularly clustered along ethnic lines, friendships to be intraethnic, marriage endogamous. All of the interpersonal relationships that might lead to new employment opportunities tend, like the workplace itself, to ethnic concentration. That is not to say that any of these relationships is ethnically watertight. But the ethnic insularity of working-class life in the developing world is a strong impediment to interethnic competition. And even where such interethnic competition does emerge, it is not usually in all sectors in a given stratum, as in the rivalry with the Mossi in Abidjan, but rather in a single line of work or even a single factory. In an ethnically divided society, the labor market is ethnically segmented.

There is a further factor cushioning job competition. Rates of rural-to-urban migration in most of Asia and Africa are high, and in most

111. Katzenstein, *Ethnicity and Equality*, 198. In Bombay, where the Shiv Sena, a strong "nativist" movement, emerged in the 1960s, employment data showed the indigenous Maharashtrians to be overrepresented in manual jobs. Katzenstein, "The Consequences of Migration: Nativism, Symbolic Politics, and National Integration" (unpublished paper presented at the 1973 annual meeting of the American Political Science Association), 16–18. There may have been job competition at work in Bombay, but not at the working-class level.

112. Cf. Ozay Mehmet, "Manpower Planning and Labour Markets in Developing Countries: A Case Study of West Malaysia," *Journal of Development Studies* 8 (Jan. 1972): 277–89.

113. A study of the workings of the Massachusetts Commission Against Discrimination sheds some interesting light on ethnic competition for jobs. The Commission acted only on the basis of complaints about job discrimination. The study found that the complaints did not at all mirror the structure of the whole labor market. Rather, the complaints were disproportionately aimed at firms that already had a substantial black labor force. These, after all, were the firms in which black job-seekers would know of and look for opportunities. Leon Mayhew, *Law and Equal Opportunity* (Cambridge: Harvard Univ. Press, 1968), 159, 165.

114. See, e.g., William J. Hanna and Judith Lynne Hanna, "Polyethnicity and Political Integration in Umuahia and Mbale," in Robert T. Daland, ed., *Comparative Urban Research* (Beverly Hills: Sage, 1969), 179; R. D. Grillo, "Ethnic Identity and Social Stratification on a Kampala Housing Estate," in Cohen, ed., *Urban Ethnicity*, 173; A. F. A. Husain and A. Farouk, *Social Integration of Industrial Workers in Khulna* (Dacca: Univ. of Dacca, 1963), 47, 129.

countries migrants retain their ties to rural areas.[115] In much of Africa, the intention is usually to return home after meeting economic goals. Visits are paid to home villages. Land may be retained in the village, families left there. Under these circumstances, the commitment to staying in the city is conditional, and an economic failure in the city may not be disastrous. In Mbale, Uganda, where many Kenyans are employed in manual labor, "they have preempted some jobs, [but] the indigenes have not been seriously hurt economically because they can easily return to farming."[116] In the words of a Ugandan civil servant, "The people here don't have to work; they go dig."[117] The same is said of non-Kikuyu residents of Nairobi, which is viewed as a Kikuyu city. They "perceive the necessity to have an alternative in the rural areas if they should lose jobs in the city (or be forced to leave)."[118] The continuing availability of rural employment for urban dwellers who do not fare well in job competition in town is a prospect that prevents job competition from being a major source of working-class ethnic conflict.

Here, however, we are back to the same puzzle regarding working-class behavior. If the motivation for ethnic conflict at the mass level is not primarily economic, then what is the motivation? For it is quite clear that the working class engages in ethnic conflict. Most ethnic riots, for example, are urban, and many of the participants are working class.[119] What moves them to political action, peaceful or violent, against ethnic strangers?

The issue is presented sharply by an essay of Peter C. Lloyd, describing ethnic politics in the Nigerian town of Warri in the mid-1950s.[120] This was the town in which ethnic groups contested the choice of armorial bearings. After noting the absence of ethnic tensions in factories and offices, Lloyd proceeds to pinpoint the divisive issues in Warri, which rather clearly relate to whether the indigenous Itsekiri Yoruba still

115. See Joan M. Nelson, "Sojourners Versus New Urbanites—Causes and Consequences of Temporary Versus Permanent Cityward Migration in Developing Countries," *Economic Development and Cultural Change* 24 (July 1976): 721–57.

116. Hanna and Hanna, "The Political Structure of Urban-Centered African Communities," 167.

117. Quoted in ibid.

118. Marc Howard Ross, *Grass Roots in an African City: Political Behavior in Nairobi* (Cambridge: M.I.T. Press, 1975), 131.

119. See, e.g., the *Times of India* (New Delhi), Apr. 16, 1969, for an occupational breakdown on participants in the Bombay riots of February 1969. See also Ghanshyam Shah, "Communal Riots in Gujarat," *Economic and Political Weekly*, Annual Number, Jan. 1970, p. 197.

120. "Ethnicity and the Structure of Inequality in a Nigerian Town."

"own" the town as against their migratory competitors, the Urhobo Edo and the Ibo. One dispute was over whether the traditional Itsekiri ruler should be given a title that might imply he "was paramount ruler over the entire Province—there being no Urhobo or Ibo ruler of comparable status."[121] This dispute flared into violence when Urhobo mobs attacked an Itsekiri procession.

The intensity of these conflicts Lloyd finds it difficult to explain. He is especially at a loss to understand "What had the Itsekiri common man to gain from these struggles?"[122] Itsekiri fears of "Urhobo superiority"[123] seemed greatly exaggerated, if measured by the current threat posed by the Urhobo. There was "little immediate likelihood that the Itsekiri would lose their ethnic identity. . . . But they were encouraged to believe that a diminution in status of [their ruler] and his chiefs would be a substantial threat to their own separate identity. It is such fears which seem to produce mob violence—violence which expresses no specific or well articulated interests, at least of the mob."[124]

Clearly, the motives of the Itsekiri mob puzzle Lloyd, but he senses a resolution of his puzzlement, which he expresses in a concluding sentence: ". . . one ought always to look closely to see which individuals gain from exploiting this tension and study the means by which they seek to gain their ends."[125] In Lloyd's account, the principal gainers have been the Itsekiri ruler and his chiefs.[126] Like other writers, Lloyd seems to feel obligated to choose between realistic economic competition and elite manipulation as explanations for ethnic hostility. Ultimately, he puts the puzzling behavior of "the Itsekiri common man" down to his susceptibility to manipulation by his rulers.

As I have suggested earlier, such a conclusion is really in the nature of a presumption about mass political motivation, one which ought not to be indulged lightly. I do not pretend to know, of course, what was troubling the Itsekiri common man, but his situation and behavior seem to have much in common with the situation and behavior of the common man of many other ethnic groups. There are clues to alternative explanations for Itsekiri behavior.

Two features of the Itsekiri reaction to the Urhobo threat particularly

121. Ibid., 244.
122. Ibid., 248.
123. Ibid.
124. Ibid., 249.
125. Ibid., 249–50.
126. Ibid., 248.

trouble Lloyd. The Itsekiri seemed to be expressing ethnic hostility out of all proportion to the danger that actually confronted them, and they seemed to focus heavily on what the future might hold for them. Their fears, in other words, were not realistic. This leads Lloyd to infer that the Itsekiri elite had incited its ethnic followers and used them to defend narrow interests that were not really their own. Yet the presence of reactions out of all proportion to the threat that arouses them and the singularly pessimistic concern about what seemingly insignificant present circumstances portend are data that may point in a quite different direction. These apprehensions are strong signs that the roots of mass antagonism may reside in the domain of psychology, rather than in the realm of material interest.

This is not the time to pursue this line of argument any further. I intend to explore the whole subject of group anxieties, returning to Lloyd's dilemma, in the next chapter. What is important now is simply to hold open the prospect of alternative explanations for mass ethnic behavior and to avoid making premature judgments about the motivation of the "common man" that must rest ineluctably on either economic competition or elite manipulation.

GROUP SACRIFICES OF ECONOMIC INTERESTS

If, instead of examining the conflict behavior of particular social strata or classes within unranked ethnic groups, we shift our attention to the actions of groups as a whole, it remains difficult to tie significant aspects of ethnic conflict to economic interests. On the contrary, what emerges quite clearly is the willingness of ethnic groups to sacrifice economic interest for the sake of other kinds of gain.

Consider, for example, the extensive economic sacrifices ethnic separatists are frequently prepared to make for their goals. As we shall see in Chapter 6, most secessionist movements in Africa and Asia have involved regions that stood to lose economically from autonomy or independence. Nor is this phenomenon confined to the developing world. The statement of a French Canadian separatist would be echoed heartily by ethnic separatists in many countries: "English Canada puts up with a lower standard of living in order to remain independent of the United States. Why don't they credit us with the same sort of pride?"[127]

Of course, many ethnic separatist movements would gain in strength

127. Quoted by Mordecai Richler, "Quebec Oui, Ottawa Non," *Encounter*, Dec. 1964, p. 83.

if secession promised economic as well as political benefits. Survey data in some potentially secessionist regions in the West suggest that among the factors preventing separatist movements there from gaining majority support are the anticipated economic costs of secession.[128] But the more important point for present purposes is not that economic considerations may hamper ethnic separatism, but rather that many separatist groups all over the developing world have proceeded to fight for ethnic autonomy *despite* the costs.

Now, to be sure, we can also analyze secessionist movements by strata. When we do, we may find that, whereas the secessionist region as a whole often stands to suffer a decline in per capita income if it goes its own way, the secessionist elite stands to gain from the many new opportunities that will open up. Once again, it is easier to explain elite behavior on the basis of straightforward rational interest than to understand the wellsprings of mass motivation. But before we abandon ourselves to the conclusion that elite interests alone are decisive, perhaps we ought to consider a case in which elite interests were overridden by mass concerns that ran counter to them.

The case concerns the regional autonomy controversy in Sri Lanka. There, in the 1950s and '60s, the Ceylon Tamils, concentrated in the North and East of the island, were demanding some form of regional autonomy in their areas. The demand was a reaction to the growth of a powerful Sinhalese ethnic movement that had resulted in the imposition of Sinhala as the official language. There was a growing sense among Tamils that they were about to lose their advantages in government employment and in other activities where their educational head-start had placed them in a favorable position. Accordingly, they hoped at least to be able to gain control over their own areas and, by running their own administration, to have positions available for civil servants they thought would be displaced from the South.[129]

---

128. See, e.g., *Maclean's* surveys cited in ibid., 79. Cf. H. M. Begg and J. A. Stewart, "The Nationalist Movement in Scotland," *Journal of Contemporary History* 6 (1971): 135–52, at 150; Manfred W. Wenner, "A Comparative Analysis of Modern Separatist Movements: Examples from Western Europe and the Middle East" (unpublished paper presented at the 1969 annual meeting of the American Political Science Association), 12.

129. For general treatments of ethnic politics in Sri Lanka, see Robert N. Kearney, *The Politics of Ceylon (Sri Lanka)* (Ithaca: Cornell Univ. Press, 1973); W. Howard Wriggins, *Ceylon: Dilemmas of a New Nation* (Princeton: Princeton Univ. Press, 1960); S. Arasaratnam, *Ceylon* (Englewood Cliffs, N.J.: Prentice-Hall, 1964); B. H. Farmer, *Ceylon: A Divided Nation* (London: Oxford Univ. Press, 1963); Robert N. Kearney, *Communalism and Language in the Politics of Ceylon* (Durham: Duke Univ. Press, 1967). This discussion of the regional autonomy controversy is drawn from interviews I conducted in Colombo in 1968 and again in 1980.

Beginning with S.W.R.D. Bandaranaike, who rode to power in 1956 on a wave of militant Sinhalese nationalism, Sinhalese politicians have been attracted by the idea of "solving" the "Tamil problem" at a stroke by various schemes of decentralization. Implicit in many of these schemes was a grant of *de facto* linguistic autonomy in the Tamil areas and probably a return of Tamil government servants to those areas.

Educated Sinhalese, of whom there are many—Sinhalese literacy is nearly universal—might ordinarily welcome such a decentralization, because it would open many government and private-sector jobs previously filled by Tamils. The image of Tamils migrating from Colombo to Jaffna, instead of in the other direction, was surely one calculated to whet the appetites of a large number of aspiring Sinhalese.

On several occasions, beginning with the so-called Bandaranaike-Chelvanayakam Pact in 1957 and ending with the District Councils Bill in 1968, the two major Sinhalese parties attempted to effect a decentralization to meet the demands of the Tamils. Each time the government in power was on the verge of implementing such a measure, it was forced by Sinhalese mass opinion, led by politically active Buddhist monks, to repudiate the underlying agreement with the Tamils. Faced with opposition from the villages to decentralization proposals that would allegedly "divide the nation" and "deprive the Sinhalese of their legitimate place in the country,"[130] first Bandaranaike and then Dudley Senanayake were compelled to withdraw proposals already drafted. In 1968, government party members of parliament were so fearful of running for reelection if their party implemented the district councils plan that backbench rebellions were in progress when the plan was abandoned. Only in 1980, after a new constitution made backbench opposition far more difficult, was a devolution scheme finally adopted.

Why was the opposition so fierce? One hypothesis is that competition between the two major Sinhalese parties limited the options of the government in each case. When the Sinhalese party in power attempted to decentralize, the other opposed; and vice versa. But in each case the opposition was so effective only because it aroused such passion at the local level. In short, the opposition was able to take advantage of the issue because feeling on it was so intense in the villages.

There would seem to be no way of accounting for the intensity—indeed, the virulence—of Sinhalese mass opposition to regional autonomy on economic grounds. Actually, there is good reason to think that

130. Opponents of the district councils proposals, quoted in the *Times of Ceylon* (Colombo), Mar. 30, 1968; ibid., Nov. 19, 1967.

the arid, unproductive Tamil areas might suffer economically from such a decentralization, depending, of course, on how autonomous the regions would in fact become. (That the Tamils nevertheless demanded extensive autonomy suggests, incidentally, that they are another ethnic minority that is willing to pay an economic price for separatism.) The Senanayake proposals carefully circumscribed the powers of the regional councils and placed them under the "direction and control" of the central government.[131] The concession to the Tamils was more symbolic than substantial; and, as we have seen, on economic grounds alone, there is every reason to think that the articulate, Sinhala-educated middle class would have benefited from the exodus of Tamil government servants, company clerks, and traders from the Sinhalese South. It can only be concluded that other, highly salient values—cast in terms of political control of the whole country—intervened at the mass level to prevent popular Sinhalese approval of these rather modest decentralization proposals.

ECONOMIC COMPETITION AND ETHNIC GOALS

I have been at some pains to show that straightforward relationships between economic rivalry and ethnic conflict are difficult to establish. Such relationships are not wholly absent. But economic antagonism explains much more about conflict at the top than at the bottom of developing societies. Beyond that, the pursuit of economic interests in ways that might lead to ethnic conflict is actually impeded by certain features of ethnic pluralism itself. Ethnic diversity usually results in a segmented labor market and to some extent a segmented economy in general, thereby inhibiting the emergence of competitive rivalries. Ethnic differences in culture, history, preferences, and imputed aptitudes often lead groups to pursue their rewards in different spheres. Ethnicity thus inhibits the development of a common currency of gratification that would foster economic competition along ethnic lines. Much more obviously, economic theories cannot explain the extent of the emotion invested in ethnic conflict. As Ed Cairns has pointed out for Northern Ireland, in terms that apply more generally, the passions evoked by ethnic conflict far exceed what might be expected to flow from any fair reckoning of

131. See the text of the bill and accompanying explanation in *Proposals for the Establishment of District Councils Under the Direction and Control of the Central Government* (Colombo: Government Press, 1968).

"conflict of interest."[132] Finally, materialist theories leave unexplained the striving for such goals as domination (or autonomy), a "legitimate place in the country," and "the symbols of prestige," all of which may take precedence over economic interest in determining group behavior.

CULTURAL PLURALISM

Ethnic conflicts are often labeled cultural conflicts, because cultural differences are among the differences that usually divide ethnic groups. But what has been the role of cultural divergence in fostering ethnic conflict? Is there any reason to believe that the more pronounced the cultural differences that exist between groups, the greater the ethnic conflict? There has been no shortage of offhanded assertions that cultural differences engender ethnic conflict. But as in the case of economic theories of conflict, systematic statements of the relationship are more difficult to find. The theory of the plural society, developed by J. S. Furnivall and refined by M. G. Smith, contains some conceptions of the role of cultural differences in the politics of ethnic relations.[133]

Furnivall's theory grew out of the colonial experience in Southeast Asia. There the coexistence of large indigenous Asian, immigrant Asian, and European populations within the same political unit led him to emphasize the separateness of the peoples who reside in a plural society. The constituent groups had been brought together fundamentally for commercial ends. As Furnivall saw it, they met only in the marketplace. The community of interest between groups was limited to their few common economic interests. Furnivall's plural society is therefore characterized by cultural divergence, the limitation of cross-cultural contacts to economic relations, economic specialization by cultural sectors (an ethnic division of labor), a lack of shared values, and the absence of a "common will." Such a society is held together by dint of the force

132. Cairns, "Intergroup Conflict in Northern Ireland," in Henri Tajfel, ed., *Social Identity and Intergroup Relations* (Cambridge: Cambridge Univ. Press, 1982), 277.
133. J. S. Furnivall, *Colonial Policy and Practice* (London: Cambridge Univ. Press, 1948), 303–12; M. G. Smith, *The Plural Society in the British West Indies* (Berkeley and Los Angeles: Univ. of California Press, 1965); Leo Kuper and M. G. Smith, eds., *Pluralism in Africa* (Berkeley and Los Angeles: Univ. of California Press, 1969). For a good sample of the controversy surrounding the plural society concept, see Vera Rubin, ed., "Social and Cultural Pluralism in the Caribbean," *Annals of the New York Academy of Sciences* 83 (Jan. 20, 1960): 761–916. For an attempt to weave cultural differences into a more general explanation of ethnic conflict, see Talcott Parsons, "Racial and Religious Differences as Factors in Group Tensions," in Lyman Bryson, Louis Finkelstein, and Robert M. MacIver, eds., *Approaches to National Unity* (New York: Harper, 1945), 182–99.

supplied by the colonial power.[134] It is inherently a precarious and unstable social form.

In M. G. Smith's formulation, the emphasis on the economic roots of cultural pluralism is no longer present. The emphasis is instead on cultural differences, regardless of the origin of the plural society. Cultural pluralism consists of the coexistence within a single society of groups possessing "mutually incompatible" institutional systems. By institutional systems, Smith means social structures, value and belief patterns, and systems of action; these form the "core" of any culture. Cultural pluralism, in his view, is more than mere cultural heterogeneity. A society is truly culturally plural only when "there is a formal diversity in the basic system of compulsory institutions."[135]

The main characteristics of Smith's cultural pluralism are clear enough. First, because "any institutional system tends toward internal integration and consistency, each of these differentiated groups will tend to form a closed socio-cultural unit."[136] Second, "where culturally divergent groups together form a common society, the structural imperative for maintenance of this inclusive unit involves a type of political order in which one of these cultural sections is subordinated to the other."[137] Since a society ordinarily requires a "community of values,"[138] a society embracing groups displaying wide cultural differences can only be held together through subordination. Third, plural societies are "defined by dissensus and pregnant with conflict . . . ."[139] Linking dissensus and conflict makes it clear that cultural incompatibility is at the heart of the instability that threatens the plural society.

A society is a "plural society," in this view, only when one of the cultural sections dominates the others. If each section were to carry on its cultural practices freely, each would constitute a separate society. In addition, the absence of consensus requires, as Furnivall also thought, regulation by force. Consequently, plural societies, in Smith's view, tend strongly toward the ethnic hierarchies or ranked systems discussed in Chapter 1.[140] In such cases, there is an identifiably dominant segment—

134. J. S. Furnivall, "Some Problems of Tropical Economy," in Rita Hinden, ed., *Fabian Colonial Essays* (London: Allen & Unwin, 1945), 161–84.
135. Smith, *The Plural Society in the British West Indies*, 82.
136. Ibid., 88.
137. Ibid., 62.
138. Ibid., xi.
139. Ibid., xiii.
140. Smith, "Institutional Political Conditions of Pluralism," in Kuper and Smith, eds., *Pluralism in Africa*, 33, 38, 53–54; Kuper, "Plural Societies: Perspectives and Problems," in ibid., 10–16.

dominant, that is, socially and politically. So strong was Smith's insistence on equating pluralism with the existence of a dominant segment that in the early formulations of Smith's theory, Weber's "ethnic coexistences," the widely prevalent unranked systems which form the subject of this book, were treated as a null category, apparently a logical impossibility.

This omission was later redressed, for Smith distinguishes "differential incorporation" (his earlier plural society), in which one group dominates, from "consociational incorporation," in which there is explicit pluralism without clear-cut domination, and from "uniform incorporation," in which individuals hold their citizenship directly rather than through ethnic-group identifications.[141] In ethnic terms, these three forms correspond roughly to ranked systems, unranked systems, and systems in which ethnic groups do not interact *qua* groups in politics.

Nevertheless, Smith still argues that where there is ethnic pluralism, there is a strong tendency toward domination by one of the groups.[142] The existence of a tendency to hierarchy has a theoretical foundation. It is the incompatibility of institutions and values among the groups that gives rise to the need for domination. "Whatever the form of the political systems, the differing sectional values within a plural society are a profound source of instability."[143] The instability that characterizes culturally plural systems thus seems to be the result of the clash of values. As Smith suggests in another essay, "the moral axioms of one section are not the axioms of another," so that similar events evoke differing interpretations. "The need to express these differences of value and morality governs and reflects intersectional relations, and this insistence on the incompatibility of the sectional moralities is incessantly activated by the differing sectional reactions to common events, especially of course those which involve intersectional relations."[144]

Although the plural society framework was originally designed to explain conditions of instability,[145] the theory lacks a mechanism of conflict. When and exactly how are group "differences of value and

141. Smith, "Some Developments in the Analytic Framework of Pluralism," in ibid., 434. The term *consociation* as used by Smith is not synonymous with the usage of the same term by political scientists. Compare Arend Lijphart, *Democracy in Plural Societies* (New Haven: Yale Univ. Press, 1977).
142. Smith, "Some Developments in the Analytic Framework of Pluralism," 446.
143. *The Plural Society in the British West Indies*, 90.
144. Ibid., 174. See also ibid., 14.
145. See especially ibid., xiii, 56, 90–91, for Smith's dissatisfaction with earlier theorizing which had postulated cultural integration and minimized the significance of instability.

morality" expressed in conflict behavior? The theory of cultural pluralism embodies an undifferentiated conception of culture, for surely not all aspects of institutional and value incompatibility affect intersectional relations equally. In particular, how far will uniformity of specifically political institutions and values go in mitigating conflict? Need such consensus have any particular content?

Value dissensus may lead to conflict, Smith suggests, if one group infringes the precious norms of another. But value dissensus may equally impede conflict, as we have already seen, by focusing the ambitions of various groups on alternative sources of gratification, thereby preventing them from impinging on each other. Moreover, by emphasizing dissensus, cultural pluralism theory tends to neglect those institutions and beliefs that are held in common. Such elements of shared culture in plural societies may occupy only a small fraction of the total cultural sphere, but they may be among the most highly relevant elements as regards relations among the component parts of such societies.

Just as dissensus may foster or retard conflict, so consensus may be integrative or disintegrative. The colonial experience, for example, may have provided the formerly subject peoples with a shared conception of the purposes of government and politics. If the groups espouse the notion that politics is the art of domination, that shared norm may abet unrestrained strife. On the other hand, if the colonial experience imparts common conceptions of legitimacy, it may generate moderation.

An example will help make this point. In Malaysia, not long ago many Chinese shared the view that the Malays, by virtue of their indigenousness, should be *primus inter pares* in the political system. This view changed only slowly. For many decades, colonial policy, the conditions of Chinese immigration, and the Chinese desire ultimately to return to China all promoted its acceptance. Even after independence, Chinese moderation was manifested in the assumption of party leaders that political legitimacy lay in associating with a Malay political group, if possible, rather than organizing on an explicitly Chinese basis. In the early years after independence, this deference to Malay legitimacy helped allay Malay fears about Chinese intentions and limited the conflict that would likely have arisen from an unrestrained Chinese challenge based on numbers and an uncompromising demand for immediate political equality.

Neither in Malaysia nor in any other severely divided society have shared norms of this sort provided absolute protection against intense conflict. Still, they highlight three features of ethnic politics that are neglected by cultural pluralism theory.

First, they show that very slender threads of consensus can, depending on their content, mitigate severe conflict. Consensus in a limited but crucial sphere—appropriate political behavior—may have an influence out of all proportion to its narrow scope or to the narrow stratum of relevant actors it embraces. If we were merely to search indiscriminately for incompatible "moral axioms" among ethnic groups, we might be led to assume that the groups interact on equal terms, save for obvious disparities of numbers or power. We would miss the impact of unevenly distributed legitimacy, deriving, in the Malaysian case, from indigenousness. Such pretensions to legitimacy may affect profoundly the demands made and the methods adopted by the respective group leaders. The exact content of norms and beliefs probably counts for more than merely whether they are convergent or divergent.

Second, the plural society model has generally tended to denigrate the importance of political variables, envisioning the interaction of whole "cultural sections" in a rather leaderless, extemporaneous fashion.[146] The Malaysian example, simple as it is, nonetheless shows the importance of political forms and of leadership.

Third, since plural society theory focuses on whole groups, it ignores the specific contributions that elites make to ethnic conflict, just as it ignores their contribution to norms of moderation. In the Philippines, for example, there is good evidence that ethnic prejudice is most marked among the professional and salaried middle class, "those elements who constitute the most Westernized portion of Philippine society."[147] If ethnic conflict is produced by the meeting of incompatible values, there is no explanation of why so much ethnic conflict occurs among strata of the various ethnic groups that are culturally and socially most similar: the "modern" elites that, in education and in occupational life, have typically engaged in the greatest amount of contact and interchange.

TOWARD MORE INCLUSIVE THEORY

It should be apparent that theories invoked to explain ethnic conflict are premised on opposite assumptions. Where the theory of cultural plural-

146. See the criticism by Leo Despres, "The Implications of Nationalist Politics in British Guiana for the Development of Cultural Theory," *American Anthropologist* 66 (Oct. 1964): 1051–77.

147. George Henry Weightman, "A Study of Prejudice in a Personalistic Society," *Asian Studies* (Manila) 11 (Apr. 1964): 87–101, at 96. See also Rodolfo A. Bulatao, *Ethnic Attitudes in Five Philippine Cities* (Quezon City: Univ. of the Philippines Social Science Research Laboratory, 1973), 126, 129.

ism conceives of ethnic conflict as the clash of incompatible values, modernization and economic-interest theories conceive of conflict as the struggle for resources and opportunities that are valued in common. Where cultural pluralist theory stresses separation and isolation of the groups, modernization and economic-interest theories stress contact and competition. Where one speaks of divergence and dissensus, the others speak of convergence and consensus.

Theories with such different premises also focus on different features of ethnic conflict. Modernization and economic-interest perspectives are useful in highlighting the role of elites in conflict. Cultural pluralists neglect the role of elites, particularly elites with convergent goals and aspirations. On the other hand, modernization and materialist theories encounter difficulty in explaining why nonelites take part in the conflict at all.

All the theories canvassed here imply that ethnic conflict in unranked systems will be persistent and difficult to manage. For the modernizers and materialists, this is because people are becoming more alike and tangible interests are increasingly in conflict. For the pluralists, it is because unranked systems are inherently vulnerable to dissolution or to the domination of one group. None of the theories, however, addresses the significance of symbolic issues in ethnic conflict. None deals with the important role of ethnic-group anxiety and apprehension, to which Lloyd's study inadvertently commends our attention.[148] None treats the intensity and violent character of ethnic conflict as specially worthy of explanation.

I suggested at the outset of this chapter that careful examination of prevailing theories might help reveal what still needs to be explained. Indeed, it does. Attention needs to be paid to developing theory that links elite and mass concerns and answers the insistent question of why the followers follow. The role of apprehension and group psychology needs specification, as does the importance of symbolic controversies in ethnic conflict. The sheer passion expended in pursuing ethnic conflict calls out for an explanation that does justice to the realm of the feelings. It is necessary to account, not merely for ambition, but for antipathy. A bloody phenomenon cannot be explained by a bloodless theory.

148. For a refreshing exception, see Rothschild, *Ethnopolitics*, 60–66. Cf. Michael Banton, *Racial and Ethnic Competition* (Cambridge: Cambridge Univ. Press, 1983).

CHAPTER FOUR

Group Comparison and the Sources of Conflict

In *The Village in the Jungle*, a novel about life in colonial Ceylon, Leonard Woolf describes an incident that cuts to the heart of ethnic relations in country after country. To appreciate the implications of the story is to have a very good start on the sources of ethnic conflict.

The episode involves a Hindu god, Kandeswami, whom the Buddhist Sinhalese came to venerate. One day, as Kandeswami sat in his abode overlooking a river,

the wish came to him to go down and live in the plain beyond the river. Even in those days he was a Tamil god, so he called to a band of Tamils who were passing, and asked them to carry him down across the river. The Tamils answered, "Lord, we are poor men, and have travelled far on our way to collect salt in the lagoons by the seashore. If we stop now, the rain may come and destroy the salt, and our journey will have been for nothing. We will go on, therefore, and on our way back we will carry you down, and place you on the other side of the river, as you desire." The Tamils went on their way, and the god was angry at the slight put upon him. Shortly afterwards a band of Sinhalese came by: they also were on their way to collect salt in the lagoons. Then the god called to the Sinhalese, and asked them to carry him down across the river. The Sinhalese climbed the hill, and carried the god down, and bore him across the river, and placed him upon its banks under the shadow of the trees, where now stands his great temple. Then the god swore that he would no longer be served by Tamils in his temple, and that he would only have Sinhalese to perform his ceremonies; and that is why to this day, though the god is a Tamil god, and the temple a Hindu temple, the kapuralas [temple custodians] are all Buddhists and Sinhalese.[1]

The tale is told from the Sinhalese viewpoint. It is biased accordingly. Sinhalese devotion to a Tamil god is not explained in terms of cultural transfer but in terms of moral evaluations of Tamil and Sinhalese behav-

1. Woolf, *The Village in the Jungle* (London: Edward Arnold, 1913), 105–06.

141

ior. The Tamils, by this account, are no doubt hardworking. Indeed, they are altogether too single-minded about work, leaving them no time to perform meritorious service, even for their own god. The Sinhalese, on the other hand, understand the nature of religious service, and their sincerity is demonstrated by their unselfish conduct. They will even put important work aside to serve a Hindu god not their own, thereby making good the deficiency of the Tamils in fulfilling their obligations. The generosity of the Sinhalese stands in marked contrast to the narrow calculativeness of the Tamils. Plainly, as Kandeswami himself concluded, the Sinhalese are morally worthy people.

That the Sinhalese version of the episode has a more general meaning for ethnic relations is apparent from the congruence of the story with studies of stereotypes conducted in Ceylon.[2] Sinhalese respondents considered themselves to be kind, good, and religious, albeit twice as lazy as the Tamils, whom they viewed as cruel and arrogant as well as diligent and thrifty.

How such views come to be held is a subject to which I shall soon return, but I want now to examine the more general moral of Kandeswami's tale, which is to be found in the domain of group comparisons. The version we are given demonstrates that groups are felt to have different mixes of attributes. Group attributes are evoked in behavior and subject to evaluation. The groups are in implicit competition for a favorable evaluation of their moral worth. The competition derives from the juxtaposition of ethnic groups in the same environment, here represented by ethnically differentiated but otherwise indistinguishable bands of salt collectors. Responding to an identical request, they reveal markedly different qualities. Their responses lead immediately to judgments of merit, for the request to which they respond has a morally imperative character that leaves no room for cultural relativism, with its exasperating inconclusiveness. The judgments of merit are entirely comparative. The Sinhalese response is contrasted with the earlier Tamil response. The responses are rendered separately, so there is no question of interaction between the groups. Competition results as much from being in the same environment as from being in relationships with each other.

The evaluation that ensues has a clear moral dimension: the Tamil response actually offends the god. Kandeswami then renders a conclusive judgment of relative group worth. Who, after all, can quarrel with

2. W. Howard Wriggins, *Ceylon: Dilemmas of a New Nation* (Princeton: Princeton Univ. Press, 1960), 232–33.

the judgment of a god, especially a Tamil god pronouncing judgment against Tamils? The episode shows that, for two groups in the same environment, the question of relative group worth was salient, the answer uncertain and in need of authoritative determination by the standards of a superior third party.

Kandeswami's parable is in a wider sense the tale of unranked ethnic groups in general—of Malays and Chinese, Hausa and Ibo, Maronites and Druze, Creoles and East Indians. When two or more such groups are placed in the same environment, no two groups are seen to possess the same distribution of behavioral qualities. Stereotypes crystallize, and intergroup comparisons emerge. Since each group has a distinctive inventory of imputed traits, appeals are made to alternative criteria of merit: as the Sinhalese reward was based on unselfish religious service, so a Tamil appeal might be predicated on diligence and industry. The apportionment of merit is an ongoing process, the interim outcomes of which have important consequences for ethnic relations.

Of course, one could delve further into the symbolism of Kandeswami as a father pronouncing judgment on brothers. The motif is familiar, and it is significant for ethnic relations. But more pertinent for the moment is the character of the story as wish fulfillment. Kandeswami's decision to reward the Sinhalese for their meritorious service was pleasingly permanent. In the real world of ethnic relations, there is no Kandeswami to pronounce final judgments of group worth. Group worth remains enduringly uncertain. And group worth is important, for self-esteem is in large measure a function of the esteem accorded to groups of which one is a member—the more so for memberships central to personal identity, as ethnic membership tends to be in Asia and Africa. The assessment of collective merit, we shall see presently, proceeds by comparison. In the modern state, lacking a Kandeswami, the sources of ethnic conflict reside, above all, in the struggle for relative group worth.

CLEAVAGE AND COMPARISON

Group allegiances and comparisons are a fundamental aspect of social life. There is now a rapidly accumulating body of evidence that it takes few differences to divide a population into groups. Groups can form quickly on the basis of simple division into alternative categories. Once groups have formed, group loyalty quickly takes hold. In interactions between groups, favoritism toward ingroups and discrimination against outgroups are demonstrated. What group members seem to desire is a positive evaluation of the group to which they belong. A favorable evaluation is attained by comparison to other groups in the environment.

Most of the evidence for these propositions is experimental, but there is a suggestive account in Raymond Firth's study of the 1,200 Tikopia living on a remote Pacific island.[3] What he found was a remarkable tendency to cleavage even in an isolated, culturally uniform setting. There was a significant division based on residence in one or the other of two main areas of the island, one leeward, the other windward. Each group was said to differ somewhat in talents, temperament, and behavior, much as ethnic groups are said to differ on these dimensions. Members of each approached the others with a tinge of formality, suspicion, and rivalry. Each was prepared to make disparaging remarks about the other. These were essentially congeries of clans, living in closest proximity under identical conditions and yet displaying rudiments of separate peoplehood and a propensity to invidious comparison.

Long after Firth studied the Tikopia, the psychologist Leon Festinger postulated the existence of a human drive to evaluate one's abilities by comparing them with the abilities of others.[4] Comparisons tend to be made with those judged to be relatively similar to oneself. Where discrepancies in abilities are manifested by performance, efforts are made to reduce discrepancies by improving performance or by controlling the superior performance of a competitor. The Festinger thesis and supporting experiments applied, however, to individual subjects, not to groups.

The tendency to cleave and compare—now explicitly on a group basis—forms the theme of a series of experiments by Henri Tajfel and his associates at Bristol.[5] Unlike Festinger or Firth, Tajfel began with an interest in ethnic group relations, but he used for his subjects unrelated individuals who were assigned by the experimenter to categories. What the experiments showed was a marked propensity to form groups on the

3. Firth, We, The Tikopia, 2d ed. (London: Allen & Unwin, 1957).
4. Festinger, "A Theory of Social Comparison Processes," Human Relations 7 (May 1954): 117–40.
5. Tajfel, "Intergroup Behavior, Social Comparison and Social Change" (Katz-Newcomb Lectures, Univ. of Michigan, Ann Arbor, mimeo., 1974); John C. Turner, "Social Comparison and Social Identity: Some Prospects for Intergroup Behaviour," European Journal of Social Psychology 5 (1975): 5–34; Tajfel, "Experiments in Intergroup Discrimination," Scientific American 223 (Nov. 1970): 96–102; Michael Billig, "Normative Communication in a Minimal Intergroup Situation," European Journal of Social Psychology 3 (1973): 339–43; Michael Billig and Henri Tajfel, "Social Categorization and Similarity in Intergroup Behavior," European Journal of Social Psychology 3 (1973): 27–52. The literature is well summarized by Michael Billig, Social Psychology and Intergroup Relations (London: Academic Press, 1976), 343–52.

basis of the most casual differences and then to behave in a discriminatory fashion on the basis of the new group identity. There are many
variations on the experiments, but they generally involve subjects assigned to a category on the basis of trivial differences, no differences, or
a conspicuous toss of a coin. Once assigned, group members experienced
no face-to-face interaction with other ingroup or outgroup members,
and there was no effort to instill ingroup loyalty or outgroup hostility.
Given the opportunity to apportion rewards, subjects nevertheless
discriminated so as to favor ingroup members and disfavor outgroup
members.

The minimal basis of group differentiation needs to be underscored.
What produces group feeling and discrimination is simple division into
categories. In subsequent experiments, some subjects continued to be
assigned to categories randomly, while others were assigned on the basis
of demonstrated similarity in artistic preferences among ingroup members. In both cases, there was a strong tendency to discriminate in favor
of ingroup members. In another experiment, subjects who were not
placed into categories were accorded an opportunity to discriminate in
apportioning rewards among other subjects with similar artistic preferences, dissimilar preferences, and no known preferences at all. This produced no statistically significant tendency to discriminate on the basis of
similarity. Plainly, what counts is group membership and not demonstrated similarity.[6]

More remarkable than these findings is the exact nature of the discrimination practiced by the groups. The initial experimental design
permitted the apportionment of rewards in any of three ways. Subjects
could (1) maximize the joint profit of ingroup and outgroup, (2) maximize the total profit of their ingroup, or (3) maximize the difference
between the profit of the ingroup and the profit of the outgroup. The act
of apportionment, in other words, involved no necessary conflict of
group interests, for positive-sum outcomes were possible. Nevertheless,
maximum joint profit had hardly any appeal to the subjects. The outcome that appealed most was maximal differential between groups, even
when this meant less profit for ingroup members than they could have
obtained by pursuing one of the other modes of apportionment. In short,
"in distributing money between two other people, one from the ingroup
and one from the outgroup, the subjects were consistently sacrificing to
some extent the advantages of a greater profit in absolute terms for

6. Tajfel, "Intergroup Behavior, Social Comparison and Social Change," 20–25.

members of their group and a greater profit in absolute terms for all the subjects in order to achieve a *relatively* higher profit for members of their ingroup as compared with members of the outgroup."[7] Not only did ingroup loyalty take hold quickly, but it produced a desire, above all, for relative ingroup advantage. This proposition holds even when there is no necessary conflict between groups in the rewards to be allocated and even when relative advantage can be achieved only by sacrificing something in absolute terms. These findings have now been replicated and have a solid basis in the experimental literature.

The powerful pull of group loyalty, the quest for relative ingroup advantage, and the willingness to incur costs to maximize intergroup differentials are all findings that have significance for ethnic group relations. In interpreting the findings, Tajfel and his collaborators have posited the existence of a group drive to obtain positive social identity by competition and comparison with other groups.[8] Social groups, they argue, can only be evaluated comparatively. This produces intergroup competition quite apart from whether there is any rivalry for material rewards. Groups aim at distinguishing themselves from others, on some positively valued dimension. The experiments enabled them to do this by pursuing a course of conduct that was not instrumentally "rational"—that is, it did not maximize profit, but it did maximize differentiation. Concludes John C. Turner: "there is evidence for the utility of a conception of social competition as distinct from instrumental competition (conflict of interest)."[9]

The results of the Tajfel experiments should be viewed in conjunction with an earlier experiment involving subjects randomly assigned to groups for performance of a task.[10] Despite instructions that eliminated any hint of competition, each group injected intergroup competition into the task and aimed to do better than the others. Moreover, in confidential post-task evaluation of the products of other groups, there was a tendency to disparage them, even when they were clearly superior. Subjects aspired to belong to a group with a favorable comparative evaluation.

7. Ibid., 48 (emphasis in the original).
8. Billig, *Social Psychology and Intergroup Relations*, 350; Henri Tajfel, *Human Groups and Social Categories* (Cambridge: Cambridge Univ. Press, 1981), 226, 268–76.
9. Turner, "Social Comparison and Social Identity," 31.
10. Charles K. Ferguson and Harold H. Kelley, "Significant Factors in Overevaluations of Own Group's Product," *Journal of Abnormal and Social Psychology* 69 (Aug. 1964): 223–28.

These findings shed light on some questions discussed earlier. The secondary role of similarity in predicting behavior—compared to the powerful role of group membership quite apart from similarity—reinforces doubts about the part played by cultural similarities and differences in ethnic conflict. The willingness of group members to sacrifice economic gain for comparative advantage is redolent of ethnic group behavior that casts doubt on materialist theories of conflict. The experiments thus square with aspects of what we have seen of the behavior of ethnic groups. But in one respect the experiments perhaps prove too much. If such casually formed groups so readily become the sorts of units that feel the need for positive social identity, perhaps what the experiments suggest is that anyone can form an "ethnic" group; and, if so, ethnicity is not a separate phenomenon deserving of separate explanation.

It should not be disturbing that ethnicity involves propensities to comparison and competition that extend beyond ethnic groups. If ethnic groups did not share fundamental behavioral tendencies with other human groups, something would be amiss. True, the Tikopia account and the Tajfel experiments show that there seems to be a strong and easily evoked tendency for populations to divide up and for the component parts to behave in exclusive ways. Ethnic groups partake of this tendency, but they tie their differences to affiliations that are putatively ascriptive and therefore difficult or impossible to change. The outcome of interethnic comparisons thus becomes singularly important, far more important than the outcome of comparisons between casually assembled groups. Since ethnic groups do not compete in merely one task or one game but in lifelong games, the competition has an urgency, a centrality, that the experiments do not capture. To lose out in competition and comparison to others who are differentiated on a birth basis is to be afflicted with an apparently permanent disability. Our materials will amply capture the emotive quality of the competition for group worth in the post-colonial state.

THE EMERGENCE OF
ETHNIC COMPARISONS

An ethnic contrast that has produced an extraordinary amount of conflict in many African, Asian, and Caribbean states is the juxtaposition of "backward" and "advanced" groups. There are a number of ways to be "advanced"—and hereafter I shall omit the quotation marks, although I am obviously reporting rather than endorsing the labels applied by participants. A group may be advanced because it is disproportionately educated and represented in the civil service and the independent professions; or it may be advanced because it is disproportionately wealthy and well represented in business. A group may be backward because it is disproportionately rural, or disproportionately in the subsistence rather than the cash economy, or disproportionately poor or uneducated. There are many variations on this juxtaposition, and the terms *backward* and *advanced* are not always used (frequent alternatives are *traditional* and *progressive*). The specific history of group encounters dictates the configuration in any given case. Overall, however, to be advanced means to be interested in education and new opportunities, to be tied into the modern sector; to be backward means to have some inhibition on taking up new opportunities and to be somewhat apart from full participation in the modern sector of the economy. It is a powerful juxtaposition that is an ever-present influence on group relations, because it is so obviously central to conceptions of group worth.

In speaking of group juxtapositions in such broad terms, I am not implying that advanced groups are uniformly advantaged. Among the Malaysian Chinese, for example, there are nearly a million poor vegetable farmers, and many more eke out a living mining tin, hawking soup, or tapping rubber. The wealthy Chinese businessman or professional is a minority figure in his own community. And this is typical of so-called advanced groups, for the concept is entirely a matter of relative advantage and average levels of education, income, and representation in the modern sector of the economy.

The comparison of backward and advanced groups proceeds from their juxtaposition in a common environment. To understand the character of these comparisons, it is necessary to understand the way in which that common environment was created and group relations were shaped within it. For most ethnic comparisons in Asia and Africa, this requires an excursion into the colonial origins of group juxtapositions. Many groups had rivalrous relations with each other antedating the colonial arrival, but many others did not. For most groups, the colonial period transformed the quality of group interactions, over and above the impact of colonialism in transforming group boundaries and creating new functions for ethnic groups to fulfill. What I shall show is that colonial rule made it easier to compare group attributes and simultaneously made ethnic identity a more important matter than it might otherwise have been; that colonial purposes entailed differential recruitment of ethnic groups into new roles; and that, as a result, new standards of group evaluation emerged that carried over long after the colonial departure.

THE FRAMEWORK FOR GROUP
COMPARISONS: A PREFATORY NOTE

Colonial policy inadvertently helped sharpen group juxtapositions and clarify the field in which comparisons were made. Measures taken by European rulers to make sense of a new environment, to create order, and to facilitate colonial administration had the effect of sharpening the contrasts and evaluations that emerged with group disparities. To be sure, the colonial territory did not constitute a field permitting comparisons quite as sharp as those made at Kandeswami's abode or in Tajfel's laboratory. But ethnic contrasts that might otherwise have been perceived only dimly were perceived all too clearly after the colonialists cleared the field for comparison.

European rule in Asia and Africa was by no means uniform. A brief note like this can only take account of a few major trends. One of the most prevalent was the simplification of preexisting political arrangements as the Europeans proceeded to sort out who the inhabitants were and how they might be administered. This entailed the strengthening of ethnic as against other allegiances. Virtually everywhere, colonial rule introduced a measure of centralization and coherence, at least up to the regional level, if authority was exercised through regional governments, and to the center, if the territory was administered from the capital. So strong was the centripetal impact that people like the Nigerian Ibo and the Tanzanian Chagga, whose political life had been fragmented into local clusters (there had been seventeen Chagga subgroups[11]), found themselves pulled together into a single administration that might have been more appropriate for a small kingdom. These unified administrations were in some cases modeled on neighboring kingdoms, for the British in particular found the monarchical form congenial to centralized control.[12] In Chapter 2, I noted that the broadened territorial horizons

---

11. Paul Puritt, "Tribal Relations," in *Two Studies of Ethnic Group Relations in Africa* (Paris: UNESCO, 1974), 126.

12. Nelson Kasfir, "Cultural Sub-Nationalism in Uganda," in Victor A. Olorunsola, ed., *The Politics of Cultural Sub-Nationalism in Africa* (Garden City, N.Y.: Anchor Books, 1972), 71; James S. Coleman, *Nigeria: Background to Nationalism* (Berkeley and Los Angeles: Univ. of California Press, 1958), 52; Leslie Rubin and Brian Weinstein, *An Introduction to African Politics* (New York: Praeger, 1974), 40–41.

produced by colonialism fostered subgroup amalgamation among previously decentralized groups. The cohesion of such groups was also
strengthened by centralized administration, and so was the sharpness of
lines between them and others.

The characteristic colonial concern for order also had the effect of
reducing intraethnic divisions. In Malaya, for example, the British
brought peace where formerly there had been warfare, much of it among
Malay contenders for the various sultanates and the Malay subgroups
they mobilized for support. To bring peace, the British had to decide
who had title to state thrones. Decisions recognizing pretenders or confirming incumbents solidified the precarious position of the Malay rulers
and at the same time undercut incentives that contenders for thrones
previously had to form alliances with rival gangs of Chinese tin miners
who fought alongside them.[13] Once thrones were guaranteed by the
British, cleavages within the Malay and Chinese communities began to
fade. Ultimately, each group was able to see the other whole.

British rule similarly strengthened the Fulani emirs of Northern Nigeria, protecting them from challenges and healing fractures that threatened the peace. The Asantehene, ruler of Ashanti in Ghana, was also
helped to consolidate and centralize his power. The same course was
followed in Uganda, where "[g]reater unity within the ruling ethnic
groups in the kingdoms became possible, because the British refused to
tolerate military rivalries for the throne."[14] Though the record of the
French was more mixed, they sometimes had the same consolidating
effect on the power of the rulers they encountered. The result was to
undercut a principal source of intraethnic division, to solidify the ethnic
group for whom the ruler spoke, and to facilitate group-to-group
comparisons.

Where the British practiced "indirect rule," the mechanism was designed explicitly to make use of traditional ruling authorities—in other
words, traditional ethnic leadership—for the transmission and enforcement of policy. In the process, "it sanctioned the notion that an ethnic
group was a valid basis for an administrative unit . . . and provided an
institutional expression for cultural unity."[15] Building colonial administration on a substructure of ethnic government helped insure that disparities would be interpreted through the lens of ethnicity and made it easy
to see who the participants were.

13. J. M. Gullick, *Malaya* (New York: Praeger, 1963), 29–37.
14. Kasfir, "Cultural Sub-Nationalism in Uganda," 72.
15. Ibid., 72–73.

The colonial rulers also developed techniques for governing various ethnic groups along different lines. These I shall deal with in a later section, for they have as much to do with the precise character of group disparities as with creating a clear field for comparing the disparities that were to emerge. In general, the colonialists sorted out the peoples being ruled and centralized groups that had formerly been scattered, simultaneously clarifying and strengthening previously murky ethnic affiliations. Colonial administration tended to force "unfused elements increasingly into a single ecology . . . ."[16]

THE ETHNIC DISTRIBUTION OF COLONIAL OPPORTUNITY

The dichotomy between backward and advanced groups arose during the colonial period out of the differential distribution of and response to opportunities among ethnic groups. Environmental and cultural forces both had an impact. Location, soil, and population pressure all were important; and so were self-selection for migration, education, and employment. Dichotomous characterizations of ethnic groups are a consequence of what has come to be called differential modernization.

The location of an ethnic group's home territory often provided a head start. Groups located near the colonial capital, near a rail line or port, or near some center of colonial commerce—the siting of which was usually determined by capricious factors, such as a harbor or a natural resource to be exploited—were well situated to take up opportunities as they arose. Such groups frequently were to be found in the schools, government offices, and commercial houses established there. The Yoruba in Nigeria, the Kikuyu in Kenya, the Baganda in Uganda, and the Hawiye and Isaq in Somalia are all groups that found themselves fortuitously situated near centers of colonial activity. And the differences can be sliced even finer: among the Yoruba, the Ijebu subgroup, located just north of Lagos, was well located to monopolize trade between Lagos and the North. As a result, the Ijebu are heavily represented in commerce and industry.[17]

To some extent, locational influences correspond to the distinction between center and periphery. Coastal areas were more often centers of

---

16. Guy Hunter, *South-East Asia: Race, Culture, and Nation* (London: Oxford Univ. Press, 1966), 69.

17. E. O. Akeredolu-Ale, "A Sociohistorical Study of the Development of Entrepreneurship Among the Ijebu of Western Nigeria," *African Studies Review* 16 (Dec. 1973): 347–64.

colonial activity than inland areas, so that, in Orissa, India, for example, the coast, occupied by the British, developed professional and administrative functionaries, whereas the hills, governed by local rajas, did not.[18] In West Africa, coast and inland meant south and north, and Northerners in Nigeria, Ghana, Togo, Benin, the Ivory Coast, and Sierra Leone all ended up backward. With a population of more than half the country, Northern Nigeria in 1966 had only 9 percent of the university students; it also had 11 percent of the eligible age cohort enrolled in primary school, compared to 58 percent for the rest of the country, and 1 percent in secondary school, compared to 6 percent in the East and 10 percent in the West.[19] In Ghana around 1960, Northerners had one-fifth the number of students in school that their share of the population would have predicted; in the Ivory Coast, North-South differentials in primary-school enrollment varied by a factor of eight for some districts; in Sierra Leone, where the disparities were somewhat less pronounced than elsewhere, the Mende districts still had nearly twice the number of primary school places per thousand of population that the Northern districts had.[20] Given the overlay of territory and ethnicity, each of these disparities has a clear ethnic meaning. In the Ivory Coast, for example, the Senufo-Lobi, some 19 percent of the population, had only 6 percent of the male secondary students, while the Agni, under 6 percent of the population, had 16 percent.[21]

Natural endowment of the home area could compensate for disadvantageous peripheral location. The Chagga of Tanzania live on the fertile slopes of Mount Kilimanjaro, where coffee grows abundantly. They are not only prosperous coffee farmers but successful businessmen, students, and bureaucrats.[22] Poor natural endowment, on the other hand, was not necessarily conclusive. Conspicuous among advanced

18. F. G. Bailey, *Politics and Social Change: Orissa in 1959* (Berkeley and Los Angeles: Univ. of California Press, 1963), 173–77.

19. Gaston V. Rimlinger, *Communalism and the Gains from Development: The Case of Nigeria* (Houston: Rice Univ. Program of Development Studies, Paper no. 74, 1976), 36, 43.

20. Philip J. Foster, "Ethnicity and the Schools in Ghana," *Comparative Education Review* 6 (Oct. 1962): 127–35; Remi Clignet and Philip Foster, *The Fortunate Few: A Study of Secondary Schools and Students in the Ivory Coast* (Evanston: Northwestern Univ. Press, 1966), 42; John Cartwright, "Party Competition in a Developing Nation: The Basis of Support for an Opposition in Sierra Leone" (unpublished paper presented at the 1971 annual meeting of the Canadian Political Science Association), 5 n.4.

21. Clignet and Foster, *The Fortunate Few*, 52.

22. Kathleen M. Stahl, "The Chagga," in P. H. Gulliver, ed., *Tradition and Transition in East Africa* (Berkeley and Los Angeles: Univ. of California Press, 1969), 209–22.

groups are some whose home region is infertile and overpopulated. The Tamils of Sri Lanka, the Bamiléké of Cameroon, the Kabyle Berbers of Algeria, the Kikuyu of Kenya, the Toba Batak of Indonesia, the Ilocano of the Philippines, the Malayalees of Kerala in India, and the Ibo of Nigeria all come from regions too poor to support their populations, and all have unusually high rates of migration to areas outside their regions, where they have taken up a variety of opportunities in the modern sector. By the time of independence, about two out of every five Kikuyu lived outside their home region.[23] Well over 10 percent of Bamiléké lived away from their home areas, and they dominated petty trade and transport in Cameroonian cities.[24] As of 1960, 20 percent of all Ilocano lived outside Ilocos.[25] In the 1950s, nearly one-fifth of the population of Algiers was born in the Kabylia region.[26] Before the Biafra war, Ibo were to be found in schools, businesses, and government offices all over Nigeria. Push migrants, whose home regions have poor soil or insufficient rainfall, have strong incentives to succeed and send remittances home.

Educational opportunity interacted with location and migration. Ethnic groups located near schools or willing to migrate to such areas gained educational advantages. The siting of mission schools was not a wholly unplanned process, but it was often the result of ethnically random factors, such as the rivalries between Christian churches. The Baganda became the most highly educated people in Uganda, largely because mission schools were for a long time confined to the Kampala area, where the Baganda are located.[27] At the time of independence, on the other hand, the Northern districts of Uganda had only one secondary school. The results showed up all through the educational system. As late as 1959–60, the Kakwa and Lugbara, groups from the North, had between them a single student enrolled in Makerere University, at a time when 281 Uganda Africans were enrolled there; the Baganda, though only 16

23. Henry Bienen, *Kenya: The Politics of Participation and Control* (Princeton: Princeton Univ. Press, 1974), 99.

24. Victor T. LeVine, *The Cameroon Federal Republic*, 2d ed. (Ithaca: Cornell Univ. Press, 1971), 51–54.

25. Peter C. Smith, "The Social Demography of Filipino Migrations Abroad," *International Migration Review* 10 (Fall 1976): 307–53, at 319.

26. Jeanne Favret, "Traditionalism Through Ultra-Modernism," in Ernest Gellner and Charles Micaud, eds., *Arabs and Berbers: From Tribe to Nation in North Africa* (Lexington, Mass: Lexington Books, 1972), 319. See also William B. Quandt, "The Berbers in the Algerian Political Elite," in ibid., 289.

27. Audrey I. Richards, *The Multicultural States of East Africa* (Montreal: McGill-Queens Univ. Press, 1969), 45–46; Kasfir, "Cultural Sub-Nationalism in Uganda," 76.

percent of the population, had nearly half the Uganda-African student population.[28] The Bakongo of Congo (Brazzaville), the Ewe of Togo, and the Mpongwé of Gabon, all centrally located, were beneficiaries of missionary education, as were the Nyanja in Zambia. All of them converted educational advantages into clerical jobs under colonial rule and bureaucratic preeminence later.[29]

Some groups actively sought out mission schools, whereas others were reticent about missionary education. In Zaire, the Kasai Baluba put themselves under the protection of Christian missions, beginning with their flight from slave traders in the late nineteenth century; the Lulua, with whom they were in close contact, avoided mission schools.[30] The Baluba ended up with high rates of educational attainment and bureaucratic employment; the Lulua did not. In Mauritania, the Moors, often nomadic, proved unreceptive to French education. But the black minority, the Kewri, was a sedentary population, and it accepted French education eagerly. The result was significant black overrepresentation in the civil service and the teaching profession.[31] Where education was undertaken by Christian missions, Muslims were often—but not always—wary of it.

Cultural attributes have been invoked to explain the success of some groups, deemphasized in favor of locational or situational advantages in the case of others. Whole theories have been spun about Ibo social structure and how it has made the Ibo receptive to change.[32] The theories often stress the egalitarian, open, achievement-oriented character of Ibo society. Similar arguments have been made for the Kikuyu.[33] Some students of the Ibo go further and suggest that the achievement motive is peculiarly individualistic and anti-authoritarian.[34] In cross-cultural per-

28. Kasfir, "Cultural Sub-Nationalism in Uganda," 130.

29. See, e.g., Dennis L. Dresang, "Ethnic Representation and Development Administration: A Comparative Study of Kenya and Zambia" (unpublished paper presented at the 1974 meeting of the American Political Science Association), 6, 9; Samuel Decalo, Coups and Army Rule in Africa (New Haven: Yale Univ. Press, 1976), 89.

30. Jules Chomé, Le Drame de Luluabourg, 3d ed. (Brussels: Editions de Remarques Congolaises, 1960), 16.

31. Alfred G. Gerteiny, "The Racial Factor and Politics in the Islamic Republic of Mauritania," Race 8 (Jan. 1967): 263–75.

32. Simon Ottenberg, "Ibo Receptivity to Change," in William R. Bascom and Melville J. Herskovits, eds., Continuity and Change in African Cultures (Chicago: Univ. of Chicago Press, 1959), 130–43.

33. Stanley Meisler, "Tribal Politics Harass Kenya," Foreign Affairs 49 (Jan. 1970): 111–21.

34. Robert A. LeVine, Dreams and Deeds: Achievement Motivation in Nigeria (Chicago: Univ. of Chicago Press, 1966), 92–94.

spective, this seems very doubtful. Of the Bamiléké, often described as the Ibo of Cameroon, it is said that the reason for their pronounced success is a hierarchical social structure that accustoms group members to climb ladders in order to succeed; and there is no doubt that Bamiléké chiefs are powerful and overbearing.[35] Similarly, Baganda students, who also score high on achievement motivation, were favorably disposed toward traditional authority.[36] Achievement motivation seems compatible with a variety of social structures, hierarchical as well as egalitarian.

Some cultural features, however, do seem conducive to success in the modern sector. Thrift and a willingness of families to pool capital for education or to pool labor resources for managing business are among them. Primogeniture among the Bamiléké and matrilineal inheritance among the Minangkabau of Indonesia have contributed powerfully to the propensity of males from both groups to migrate out of their home region in search of opportunity.[37] Customary law can contribute to push migration just as surely as poor soil, insufficient rainfall, or overpopulation.

More generally, although I have enumerated good location, push migration, and facilities for education as the main ingredients, the conditions overlap each other. The Chagga had good soil, and they also had missionary education; the Kabyle had high population density that induced them to migrate to Algiers, but they also had missionary schools in their areas. And, as the Yoruba and Ibo cases show, differing combinations of conditions can produce more than one advanced group in the same country.

The case of the Tamils of Sri Lanka neatly illustrates the blending of chance, necessity, and perhaps cultural conditioning in the creation of an advanced group. In the early nineteenth century, soon after the British had conquered Ceylon, Christian missionaries entered the island. Like the colonial administration, the British missionaries established themselves in the South of Ceylon, where colonial commercial and agricultural interests lay and where the Sinhalese reside. The American Missionary Society, when it arrived, was relegated to the arid Jaffna

35. LeVine, *The Cameroon Federal Republic*, 54. Cf. Jean Hurault, "Essai de synthèse du système social des Bamiléké," *Africa* 40 (Jan. 1970): 1–24.

36. Otto Klineberg and Marisa Zavalloni, *Nationalism and Tribalism Among African Students* (Paris and The Hague: Mouton, 1969), 223, 234–35, 317. See also Decalo, *Coups and Army Rule in Africa*, 177–80.

37. Mochtar Naim, *Causes and Effects of Minangkabau Voluntary Migration* (Singapore: Institute of Southeast Asian Studies, Occasional Paper no. 5, 1971).

Peninsula, a Tamil area in the far North. The main missionary activity was education, and the Americans proved unusually efficient at setting up English-medium schools all over Jaffna. Later, as clerical jobs opened up in the colonial government and in the commercial houses, Ceylon Tamils, more often literate in English, moved south to take up a disproportionate number of them. They had every incentive to do so. Jaffna was an inhospitable land, and the Tamils were unable to support their population from the land alone. Consequently, the Ceylon Tamils came to play a large role in the economy and administration of Ceylon.

The various conditions underlying Tamil success can hardly be separated from each other. Had the British treated the American missionaries as well as they treated their own, by permitting them to operate in the South, would the Ceylon Tamils have gained the head start they acquired? Had the Jaffna Peninsula been less arid, would the Tamils have moved out of it in such large numbers? Had the English language not been the *sine qua non* for a bureaucratic job, would the Tamils have excelled in something else? These imponderables show how difficult it would be to track down the part played by various causal elements.

Similar tales can be told, of course, for dozens, probably hundreds, of groups. Whatever the exact mix of causal factors, it is abundantly clear that ethnic groups have not had uniformly distributed opportunities and have not performed uniformly even when the opportunities have existed. The result is that groups are unequally advantaged.

COLONIAL POLICY AND THE PROMOTION OF GROUP DISPARITY

I have mentioned colonial institutions and the response to them, but I have not yet mentioned the causal role of colonial policy and practice except in creating the environment for sharp group comparisons. To a considerable extent, the differential modernization of ethnic groups fostered by colonialism was simply an accident of location. Some groups were in the path of economic and educational development, and some were passed by. Some saw opportunity thrust upon them where they were; some rejected it when it appeared; and some were willing to migrate long distances to respond to opportunities awaiting their arrival. The disparities that emerged were as much a matter of ethnic groups using foreign rule to alter their condition as of foreign rulers using the groups. The relationship between colonialism and ethnicity cannot be captured by sweeping notions of "divide and rule."

Neither, however, were the Europeans indifferent to ethnicity. Colonial rule handled ethnicity inconsistently and unevenly. The same government that imposed a legal system to treat people impartially, according to specified, impersonal rules of decision, nonetheless incorporated ethnic criteria into some of those rules. Neither in precept nor in practice did colonial administrations stand unequivocally for distinctions founded on ethnic ties or for the "modern" values of equality, achievement, and general indifference to ascriptive criteria. They stood for both.

There were times when colonial governments actively promoted differential treatment of ethnic groups as a matter of policy. The clearest examples are the encouragement of immigration, protection of some groups from others, and employment of certain groups for colonial administrative purposes.

The epithet "divide and rule" finds its most accurate application in colonial labor policy. Labor migration, particularly international migration, was alternately organized, encouraged, or restricted according to the needs of the economic enterprises that employed labor. After the emancipation of the slaves, as noted previously, indentured East Indian labor was imported for some decades into Guyana and Trinidad, because sugar estates were unable to pay the wage that free labor demanded. In Fiji and Mauritius, Indians were also brought to grow cane; in Sri Lanka, Indian Tamils were imported to work the tea estates; and in Malaysia, Chinese were encouraged to mine tin and Indians were brought to tap rubber. Occasionally, in such cases, there was deliberate use of one group against another, as when Creole police were used to thwart East Indian protest in Guyana and Trinidad or when cheap Indian labor was used to keep Creole wage demands in check.

The rationale of immigration was either to cut wage rates below the level required to induce indigenous groups to perform the labor or to encourage large-scale production in a tightly controlled way, usually on estates. But the justification for the employment of immigrants was couched in terms of moral qualities. Certain jobs became the preserve of specific groups, who were said to possess attributes that fitted them uniquely for the functions they performed. In Malaysia, immigration was said to be necessary because the Malays were "unquestionably opposed to steady continuous work."[38] Creoles in Guyana and Trinidad were also regarded as possessing insufficient inclination to "continuous

38. Frank Swettenham, *British Malaya*, rev. ed. (London: Allen & Unwin, 1948; originally published in 1906), 247.

labor."[39] While the immigrants were generally not viewed by colonial administrators as legitimate long-term residents, they were at the same time held up as possessing a laudable work ethic and encouraged to accumulate wealth. Whether they succeeded or not depended largely on the purpose of the trip. Groups that came to work sugar plantations in Fiji, Guyana, Trinidad, and Mauritius were later able to find opportunities off the plantations. Groups that came to work tea or rubber estates, however, rarely found social mobility possible. Hence, the Indian Tamils who came to work the tea estates in Ceylon are not at all comparable to the Ceylon Tamils, as the Indians who came to work the rubber estates of Malaysia are not comparable to the Chinese who originally came to trade and mine tin; and the Biharis and Oriyas who work the tea estates of Assam in India are not in the advantageous position of the Marwaris who came to trade or the Bengalis who came to farm and to work in offices.

Overall, however, immigrant groups tended to be in the same advanced category as groups who had benefited from fortuitous location, missionary education, or push migration. In fact, there is an overlap, for international migrants from China and India frequently came from infertile, overpopulated regions comparable to those inhabited by the Ibo, the Toba Batak, and the Ceylon Tamils.

The rights and obligations of hosts and immigrants were specified by the colonial authorities. Immigrants were often prevented from holding land in certain reserved areas[40] and were sometimes governed by separate administrations, their children educated in separate schools. Overlaying the disparity between backward and advanced groups was that created between indigenous and immigrant groups.

Internal migration was sometimes regulated as well, typically as part of a policy of "protecting" the inhabitants of one region from incursions by migrants from another. The policy of protecting Southern Sudanese from Northerners, Karens from Burmans, Nagas from the plainsmen of Assam, and Karamoja from Southerners in Uganda had a variety of purposes. Some groups were to be protected from traders of other groups, some—generally Muslims—from missionaries, and some from ethnic strangers eager for land. The protected groups were felt to be at a

39. J. Chamberlain to J. A. Swettenham, Sept. 10, 1903, in *Further Correspondence Relating to Disturbances in British Guiana*, Cd. 3026 (London: H.M.S.O., 1906), 109.
40. See Adrian C. Mayer, *Indians in Fiji* (London: Oxford Univ. Press, 1963), 31–32; Rupert Emerson, *Malaysia: A Study in Direct and Indirect Rule* (Kuala Lumpur: Univ. of Malaya Press, 1964; originally published in 1937), 478–80.

competitive disadvantage, and it was also believed that special protection would be repaid by loyalty to the colonial power. This expectation generally proved correct. Protected peoples tended to stay aloof from anti-colonial movements, and some—the Karens and the Nagas—fought tenaciously for the British against the Japanese. After independence, several such groups became strongly separatist.

Protection implied separate development, and it was accompanied by separate administration and specialized administrators who developed distinctive biases. "A frequently heard quip was that if all the Africans were to leave Nigeria the northern and southern administrations would go to war."[41] The quip reflected the British impulse to treat Northern Nigeria on a different basis from the rest of the country. For Northern Nigerians, as for other protected groups, there was a certain encouragement to sit supine and not to change cultural orientations too much in order to adapt to colonial opportunities. In Benin, for example, the French protected the North, impeding travel to Northern *cercles* and simultaneously concentrating investment in the South.[42] Protection emphasized and accentuated the backwardness of backward groups.

If the deliberate colonial recognition and employment of ethnic distinctions is visible in immigration and protection policies, it is all the more visible in the felt necessity of the Europeans to govern their vast territories with the aid of local people they found to be particularly capable. Ruling as they did with little manpower, all the colonial powers from time to time designated members of particular groups as their agents. The Germans, for example, were explicit about the future of the Ewe they encountered in Togo as junior partners in a German African Empire.[43] When the French succeeded the Germans in Togo, the Ewe were among those exported for administrative tasks in French colonies. Among those employed by the British were the Baganda, who helped rule Uganda, and the Bengalis, who saw service all over Northeast India. In both cases, the impact of delegated authority was profound. The Bengalis insisted that the languages of Assam and Orissa were mere dialects of Bengali. They and the Baganda patronized the people they helped to rule. The result was to build up a fund of resentment among the subject peoples and pretensions among the agents of colonial rule,

41. Coleman, *Nigeria*, 47.
42. Samuel Decalo, "Regionalism, Politics, and the Military in Dahomey," *Journal of Developing Areas* 7 (Apr. 1973): 449–77, at 451.
43. Decalo, *Coups and Army Rule in Africa*, 89.

both of which were slow to dissipate.[44] More to the present point, groups like the Ewe, the Baganda, and the Bengalis all became highly educated and advanced compared to the people among whom they found themselves.

No doubt, policy regarding immigration, protection, and the use of agents did in a deliberate way what location, push migration, and access to missionary education all did in a largely fortuitous way—namely, create or accentuate disparate positions of ethnic groups in the colonial opportunity structure. Descendants of immigrants and of colonial agents swelled the ranks of advanced groups; protected peoples ended up backward. Although the balance of these forces varied from colony to colony, overall the response of the groups themselves to opportunities that opened up seems to have been more influential in producing disparities than was anything the colonial rulers did by way of disparate treatment of groups.

COLONIAL EVALUATIONS
OF IMPUTED GROUP CHARACTER

As important as objective ethnic disparities were the subjective characterizations that followed in their train. Colonial views of group virtues and vices added a crucial evaluative dimension to ethnic differences. So enduringly influential were these views that, to appreciate the full impact of group juxtapositions on ethnic conflict, it is as necessary to understand the relations of the respective groups to the colonial power as it is to grasp their relations to each other.

The fundamental premise of colonial rule was the felt unfitness of the ruled to manage their own affairs. In the colonial situation, no group, whatever its imputed characteristics or its manifest behavior, was permitted to approach the European balance of virtues, lest it imperil the European right to rule. Even the most advanced ethnic groups among the colonized peoples were denigrated. Their perceived industriousness and adaptability met with colonial approval at one level, since they served colonial purposes. But on another it was simultaneously thought that such groups were too aggressive or too acquisitive. Despite the belief that the spread of Western education was a basic component of imperial

44. Bailey, *Politics and Social Change: Orissa in 1959*, 161–62; Charu Chandra Bhandari, *Thoughts on Assam Disturbances* (Rajghat, India: A. B. Sarva Seva Sangh Prakashan, 1961), 5–8; J. B. Kripalani, *Minorities in India* (pamphlet; Calcutta: Manoranjan Guha, n.d.), 9–10; Kasfir, "Cultural Sub-Nationalism in Uganda," 72; Richards, *The Multicultural States of East Africa*, 48–50.

"trusteeship," the British in particular reserved their severest scorn for the "educated native." As James S. Coleman states for Nigeria in terms that would hold for other British colonies, "the characteristic attitude of resident Europeans toward the educated African was one of contempt, amusement, condescension or veiled hostility . . . . Many Europeans felt that educated Africans were insulting, assertive, and 'uppity' . . . ."[45] Backward ethnic groups, which had been bypassed by the colonial educational and economic system and hence remained tied exclusively to the land, also received a mixed evaluation. To the extent that they preserved traditional ways, such groups were seen as a true embodiment of indigenous culture, as possessing a nobility and pureness of heart denied to their compatriots who had been "spoiled" by the cash economy or by education in a Western language. Yet these same groups, for all the solicitous paternalism they received, were also seen as slothful and unmotivated, lacking the quality of striving that was a necessary accoutrement of civilized man. The advanced groups were disparaged because they were imitators, and the backward groups were disparaged because they were not.

To some extent, French colonialism reversed the biases of the British. "For the British, the educated African was a gaudy, despised imitator of European ways,"[46] whereas the French, with their policy of *assimilation*, held out the possibility that, through education and acculturation, a subject could "evolve" into a Frenchman, provided he could prove adoption of a "European way of life." In practice, however, very few French subjects were able to achieve *évolué* status, and the French maintained their distance.[47] Although the French had somewhat better relations than the British with educated groups, the French, too, were given to disparagement. If the British disliked the aggressiveness they found in the Ibo, the French were equally hostile to the "arrogance" they sensed in groups like the Bakongo.[48]

Foreign rule rested on some mix of presumed racial superiority and differences in levels of "civilization." Such premises had an ambivalent impact on the colonial evaluation of ethnic groups. On the one hand, the

45. Coleman, *Nigeria*, 145, 147.
46. Michael Crowder, *West Africa Under Colonial Rule* (Evanston: Northwestern Univ. Press, 1968), 399.
47. Pierre Alexandre, "Social Pluralism in French African Colonies and in States Issuing Therefrom," in Leo Kuper and M. G. Smith, eds., *Pluralism in Africa* (Berkeley and Los Angeles: Univ. of California Press, 1969), 199–201, 204.
48. Decalo, *Coups and Army Rule in Africa*, 126.

"civilizing mission" of the Europeans argued for encouragement of behavior that seemed to approach the Western model of modern man, for
approval of the virtues of education, competitiveness, and achievement.
And so, at various times, such virtues were applauded. The French approved of the Kabyle Berbers, whom they found "reasonable, hardworking, and enterprising. . . ."[49] The Belgians flattered the Kasai Baluba "for
their advancement" and evaluated the Lulua "negatively for their passivity."[50] The British found the Yoruba to be "sophisticated, orderly, and
vigorous."[51] On the other hand, backward groups were said to possess a
desirable trait that the striving, advanced groups were accused of lacking. It was variously described as dignity, character, or simply good
manners.[52] The Malays, the Hausa, the Fijians, and other groups with a
hierarchical social structure were especially believed by the British to
possess such a quality. And when the British perceived a group to be
energetic and dignified *and* attached to its own (preferably aristocratic)
institutions—as they found the Yoruba and the Baganda to be—British
approbation was transparent.[53]

The exigencies of the colonial economy and administration also
pointed to ambivalent evaluation. European commercial purposes required encouragement of advanced groups, and so did the need for
trained personnel in the administration. From the standpoint of the colonial economy, there was no avoiding recognition that, in colonial eyes,
the Chinese were "cleverer," "more industrious," and "more enterprising," while the Malays were "indolent and improvident," as well as
unambitious; that the Bengalis in Assam were energetic, whereas the
Assamese were lazy and excessively proud; that the East Indians in Guyana and Trinidad were hardworking and thrifty, while the Creoles were
lethargic and thriftless; that the Kikuyu, the Ibo, the Baluba, the Ewe,
and the Ceylon Tamils were all possessed of a dynamism conducive to
achievement, while the Kamba, the Hausa, the Lulua, the Northerners

49. Quandt, "The Berbers in the African Political Elite," 323.
50. Thomas Turner, "Congo-Kinshasa," in Olorunsola, ed., *The Politics of Cultural Sub-Nationalism in Africa*, 270 n.74.
51. Margery Perham, *Native Administration in Nigeria* (London: Oxford Univ. Press, 1937), 161.
52. For examples, see W. R. Crocker, *Nigeria: A Critique of British Colonial Adminis-tration* (London: Allen & Unwin, 1936), 208; L. Richard Wheeler, *The Modern Malay* (London: Allen & Unwin, 1928); Ian Morrison, *Malayan Postscript* (London: Faber & Faber, 1942), 29.
53. Perham, *Native Administration in Nigeria*, 271; Richards, *The Multicultural States of East Africa*, 44–46.

in Togo and Ghana, and the Kandyan Sinhalese were all, in these terms, unduly inclined to let things happen rather than make things happen.[54] The necessity to uphold European superiority, however, tempered such evaluations. Moreover, insofar as the advanced groups found their way into commerce, there was something of the disdain commonly felt by government servants for those engaged in "trade." The advanced groups were a bit too clever, too cunning, too materialistic, and assuredly too self-important.[55]

The need for security and for foot soldiers also counseled a favorable view toward the generally more compliant backward groups. Where, however, there was reason to expect greater loyalty from advanced groups, prudent policy was to propitiate them. The French thus accorded a special position to the Maronites in Lebanon, as the British did to the Baganda, but these were the exceptions. Policies of protecting backward groups, as I have mentioned, had security goals in view, although they also arose out of consideration for the felt unfitness of the protected groups to compete. Since backward groups were usually slower to develop anti-colonial sentiment—for this flowered more readily near the centers of colonial power—special relationships that grew up between them and the colonizers had a calculative side to them. The Europeans showed solicitude toward those who threatened their interests less. This surely was the case with Belgian favoritism for the Lulua of Zaire in the late colonial period and French favoritism for the Moors in Mauritania.[56] Such relationships were accompanied by appropriate evaluative mythology. Although disinclined to achievement, the backward groups had offsetting personal qualities: loyalty, tact, politesse, integrity. This was something to weigh in the balance of group virtues and vices.

The emergence of advanced and backward groups often entailed a reshuffling of group position. Antecedent relations were altered in one direction or another. An initial advantage gained by a group before the advent of colonial rule was sometimes consolidated, as it was for the

54. See, e.g., R. O. Winstedt, *Simple Malay* (London: Longmans, Green, 1938), 9; Cuthbert Woodville Harrison, *The Magic of Malaya* (London: John Lane, 1916), 89, 108, 121–26, 132, 168, 200–01; L. Crookall, *British Guiana* (London: T. Fisher Unwin, 1898), 150; B. H. Farmer, *Ceylon: A Divided Nation* (London: Oxford Univ. Press, 1963), 51.

55. See Donald Rothchild, "On Becoming *Bwana* in Kenya," *Transaction*, Jan. 1972, pp. 23–30, at p. 25.

56. Chomé, *Le Drame de Luluabourg*, 20–21; interviews with Mauritanians, Washington, D.C., Aug. 1971.

Baganda. The self-confidence of other groups, such as the Hausa-Fulani, was, however, shaken by the colonial experience. As advantages were either preserved or lost, disabilities were also either perpetuated or eradicated by the vicissitudes of colonial occupation. The Ibo, formerly slaves to the Efik of Calabar, became heirs to a European commercial and bureaucratic legacy and rulers of a region that included Calabar itself. The black minorities of the Sudan and Mauritania also had a history of servitude to their Arab or Moor neighbors. But whereas the Mauritanian Kewri emerged from the colonial period entrenched in the schools and the state apparatus, and evaluated by the French as "closer than the [Moorish] nomad to our world and especially to our industrial age,"[57] the Southern Sudanese were left by the British relatively as backward as before. The Western impact thus was to make available new opportunities differentially distributed and to superimpose on them new standards of group evaluation that might be highly dissonant with antecedent standards.

The colonialists thus set in motion a comparative process by which aptitudes and disabilities imputed to ethnic groups were to be evaluated. Those evaluations, solidly based in the group disparities that emerged, could not be dismissed as the irrelevant invention of a foreign overlord. Like the new polity and economy in which the disparities were embedded, the evaluations took hold.

Among unranked groups, no one emerged from colonial rule untouched by the new standards of group evaluation. Even after the colonialists departed, colonial standards of value, and those of the West more generally, remained the standards to which all groups in some considerable measure paid obeisance.[58] These standards were fortified by the continuing role of Western systems of education and the emergence of something like worldwide norms of development and achievement. To be sure, there were alternative paths to group worth, especially where colonial judgments had been fairly evenly balanced. No group could lay unequivocal claim to approbation or superiority on the basis of imputed personal qualities; in some cases, close contests were possible. A colonial report on Gabon referred to two claimants to power, "one [the Mpongwé] by virtue of its intellectual superiority, and the other [the

57. Robert Gauthier, "Mauritania—A Country of Change," *Le Monde Diplomatique*, March 1966, p. 2.

58. J. P. Nettl and Roland Robertson, *International Systems and the Modernization of Societies* (New York: Basic Books, 1968), 63–127.

Fang] because of its greater vitality and numbers."[59] In Guyana and Trinidad, acculturation to Western ways was clearly further along among Creoles than among East Indians. Even though Indians were placed in the industrious-diligent category, Creoles were better educated and found their way into the colonial civil service. In making group comparisons, Creoles could cleave to their affinity for Western culture, while Indians could cite their possession of the virtues valued by the West. A comparable division of virtue—acculturation versus dynamism—was visible in the relations between Efik and Ibo in Eastern Nigeria.[60]

Comparisons based on such standards suggest the pertinence of an observation by both psychologists and psychoanalysts that an unseen third party plays a role in prejudice directed from one party to another: "the cause in any case of prejudice should be looked for not only in the relationship existing between the subject and the object of prejudice, but mainly the cause should be looked for in an unsuspected rivalrous relationship to a third party—a more fortunate or desired third party."[61] Typically, for individuals, such a third party is a parent. In a deep and pervasive way, the colonialists and their standards played this Kandeswamian role in the group conflicts of Asia and Africa. Thus, Creoles in Guyana, frustrated by what they saw as colonial favoritism, early on referred to the East Indians as the "darlings" of the European parents and expressed bitter disappointment that Creole devotion to "British justice" and to the king was not requited.[62] Many groups evoked a similar idiom, redolent of sibling rivalry, expressing resentment of groups protected by the colonial power as spoiled children. The sibling analogy is indeed apt, and it has been noted by others. The new society promised by Francophone Quebec terrorists, interviewed by Gustave Morf, "would at last be that paternal home where all the children had the same rights, the same security, and the same recognition."[63]

59. Quoted in Georges Balandier, The Sociology of Black Africa (New York: Praeger, 1970), 236.

60. W. T. Morrill, "Immigrants and Associations: The Ibo in Twentieth Century Calabar," in L. A. Fallers, ed., Immigrants and Associations (The Hague: Mouton, 1967), 177–81.

61. Brian Bird, "A Consideration of the Etiology of Prejudice," Journal of the American Psychoanalytic Association 5 (July 1957): 490–513, at 494. See also John Dollard, Caste and Class in a Southern Town, 3d ed. (Garden City, N.Y.: Anchor Books, 1957), 434–46; George C. Homans, The Human Group (London: Routledge & Kegan Paul, 1951), 248.

62. See The Creole (Georgetown), May 26, 1906; ibid., July 14, 1906.

63. Morf, Terror in Quebec (Toronto: Clarke, Irwin, 1970), 69.

As some groups deplored the favoritism of the colonialists, others undertook to follow in their footsteps. The Baganda and the Bakongo, who sensed no need to share virtue with other groups, emulated the colonizers, took it as their mission to lead—or "civilize"—others, and, in the Baganda case, referred to other groups as "natives" and to themselves as "Europeans."[64] The Ibo likewise "modelled themselves after their masters . . . ."[65] The terminology, of course, changed after independence, and the Europeans, as people, dropped out of the picture. But their standards of merit did not. Thenceforward, the most important criterion of group evaluation remained proximity to or distance from the Western model of achieving man. Few groups went as far as the Baganda or the Ibo in their pretensions, but many, displaying dynamism, diligence, and competitiveness, could on that account claim what they regarded as an appropriate adjustment to the modern world. Consequently, although all groups were in some measure disparaged under European rule, the backward groups, who could not make the same claim, had to bear a heavier burden in the quest for group worth.

INVIDIOUS COMPARISON AND
THE DISTRIBUTION OF GROUP WORTH

The cutting edge of comparison and conflict is the juxtaposition of backward and advanced groups. For certain groups, the discovery that ethnic strangers had mastered the modern skills associated with the colonial rulers more completely than they themselves had, compounded and perpetuated the humiliation of the colonial experience. It seems to have made such groups determined not to yield prestige or power whenever it was in their grasp, and it has shaped their behavior in myriad ways. There is much evidence that so-called backward groups are more frequent initiators of ethnic violence and advanced groups more frequent victims. To see this, one needs only to examine repeated sequences of rioting involving Hausa and Ibo, Malays and Chinese, Assamese and Bengalis, Sinhalese and Tamils, Lulua and Baluba. More than this, however, the sense of backwardness is a profoundly unsettling group feeling. It means that strangers are "wresting from one's people mastery over

64. Richards, *The Multicultural States of East Africa*, 45; Virginia Thompson and Richard Adloff, *The Emerging States of French Equatorial Africa* (Stanford: Stanford Univ. Press, 1960), 479.
65. Paul Anber, "Modernization and Political Disintegration: Nigeria and the Ibos," *Journal of Modern African Studies* 5 (Sept. 1967): 163–79, at 170.

their own fates."[66] To entertain such a feeling is for group members to be subject to anxiety-laden perceptions of intergroup relations and to pressures to end the state of backwardness by transforming their personal qualities. At the same time, the unflattering images of group characteristics generated by the comparison give rise to powerful efforts to use the political system for the confirmation of group worth. An effort to understand the politics of group comparison must begin with the subjective quality of group sentiment.

TO BE BACKWARD

To be backward is, first and foremost, to feel weak *vis-à-vis* advanced groups. The Assamese, remarks Myron Weiner, see themselves as so weak that they do not believe they could compete with the Bengalis, asserted to be superior in skills and motivation, in a free labor market.[67] Likewise, a leader of a backward group in Bihar told Weiner that members of his group are "not very bright. They have limited intelligence so they cannot do well in school," just as Telanganas told him they were "no match for the Andhras."[68] The same was said by Karens, who felt they could not keep up with the more "sharp-witted" and "aggressive" Burmans.[69] Backward groups in general feel at a competitive disadvantage as they compare their imputed personal qualities with those imputed to advanced groups.

The nature of these feelings can be understood better by examining the stereotypes groups hold about each other. Although there is much regularity from one situation to another, the precise configuration of stereotypes of course varies. I have therefore assembled a composite list of adjectives employed by backward and advanced groups to describe each other. In stereotype studies, there is typically a moderate to high level of agreement between self-stereotypes and other-stereotypes,[70] es-

66. Everett C. Hughes, *French Canada in Transition* (Chicago: Univ. of Chicago Press, 1943), 3.
67. Weiner, *Sons of the Soil: Migration and Ethnic Conflict in India* (Princeton: Princeton Univ. Press, 1978), 47, 113.
68. Ibid., 167, 238.
69. Ba Maw, *Breakthrough in Burma: Memoirs of a Revolution, 1939–1946* (New Haven: Yale Univ. Press, 1968).
70. See J. M. F. Jaspars and Suwarsih Warnaen, "Intergroup Relations, Ethnic Identity and Self-Evaluation in Indonesia," in Henri Tajfel, ed., *Social Identity and Intergroup Relations* (Cambridge: Cambridge Univ. Press, 1982), 354–57; Joseph C. Finney, "Judgments of Ethnic Groups," *Journal of Psychology* 68 (Mar. 1968): 321–28; Erich Reigrotski and Nels Anderson, "National Stereotypes and Foreign Contacts," in Louis Kriesberg, ed., *Social Processes in International Relations* (New York: John Wiley, 1968), 67, 79;

pecially on group ratings of "dynamism," but groups tend to strike different balances between favorable and unfavorable traits. Usually, they attribute more favorable traits to their own group than to outgroups.[71] This list, which consists of outgroup characterizations, is therefore heavier on the pejorative side than would be a list that included self-stereotypes.

Several other observations are in order before examining the stereotypes. It will be apparent that imputed qualities are heavily influenced by the economic roles played by the respective groups. But they go beyond this, for they clearly reflect felt differences in acculturation to modern ways. Finally, although it is important to bear in mind that these are composites drawn from many cases of group comparison, the most obvious comparison dimension of the opposite clusters is passive-uncompetitive versus active-competitive. All of these observations also find support in the general literature on stereotypes.[72]

Here, then, is the list, culled from systematic stereotype studies as well as less systematic accounts.[73] The attributes make it painfully clear why—and how—backward groups feel weak:

Donald T. Campbell, "Stereotypes and the Perception of Group Differences," *American Psychologist* 22 (Oct. 1967): 817–29, at 822–23; Rodolfo Bulatao, *Ethnic Attitudes in Five Philippine Cities* (Quezon City: Univ. of the Philippines Social Science Research Laboratory, 1973), 101.

71. See, e.g., Jaspars and Warnaen, "Intergroup Relations, Ethnic Identity and Self-Evaluation in Indonesia," 354–55; Marilynn B. Brewer and Donald T. Campbell, *Ethnocentrism and Intergroup Attitudes: East African Evidence* (New York: John Wiley, 1976), 143.

72. Russell A. Jones and Richard D. Ashmore, "The Structure of Intergroup Perception: Categories and Dimensions in Views of Ethnic Groups and Adjectives Used in Stereotype Research," *Journal of Personality and Social Psychology* 25 (Mar. 1973): 428–38, at 435; Campbell, "Stereotypes and the Perception of Group Differences," 826–27; LeVine, *Dreams and Deeds*.

73. Sources: Marc Howard Ross, *Grassroots in an African City: Political Behavior in Nairobi* (Cambridge: M.I.T. Press, 1975), 131; Bulatao, *Ethnic Attitudes in Five Philippine Cities*, 57–62, 169; Akeredolu-Ale, "A Sociohistorical Study of the Development of Entrepreneurship Among the Ijebu of Western Nigeria," 351; Decalo, *Coups and Army Rule in Africa*, 177–80; A. A. Castagno, "Somali Republic," in James S. Coleman and Carl G. Rosberg, Jr., eds., *Political Parties and National Integration in Tropical Africa* (Berkeley and Los Angeles: Univ. of California Press, 1964), 532; Alvin Rabushka, "Racial Stereotypes in Malaya," *Asian Survey* 11 (July 1971): 709–16; Herbert Feldman, "The Communal Problem in the Indo-Pakistan Subcontinent: Some Current Implications," *Pacific Affairs* 42 (Summer 1969): 145–63, at 159; Walter Schwarz, *Nigeria* (New York: Praeger, 1969), 215, 251–53; Alfred G. Gerteiny, *Mauritania* (New York: Praeger, 1967), 151; Klineberg and Zavalloni, *Nationalism and Tribalism Among African Students*, 140–64; B. G. Verghese et al., *Situation in Assam: Report of a Study Team* (New Delhi: Gandhi Peace Foundation, mimeo., 1980), 14; Elliott P. Skinner, "Strangers in West African Societies," *Africa* 33 (Oct. 1963): 307–20, at 314; Fred R. von der Mehden, *Religion and Nationalism*

BACKWARD		ADVANCED	
Poor	Feudal	Enterprising	Clannish
Lazy	Polite	Aggressive	Nepotistic
Traditional	Submissive	Ruthless	Tribalistic
Inefficient	Unintelligent	Money-hungry	Progressive
Ignorant	Lacking	Industrious	Crafty
Leisurely	initiative	Shrewd	Frugal
Indolent	Proud	Successful	Avaricious
Docile	Dependent	Stingy	Pushy
Easygoing	Spendthrift	Arrogant	Efficient
		Cunning	Thrifty
		Intelligent	Ambitious
		Energetic	Coarse
		Resourceful	Miserly
		Serious	Clever

Two dimensions of comparison need to be highlighted. The more obvious is individual competitiveness. By this reckoning, backward groups must compete against people whose personal qualities are better adapted to competition, both educational and economic. Less obvious but equally important is the collective side. Backward groups very often believe advanced groups to be more cohesive, better organized, more given to mutual cooperation and collective effort—including ingroup favoritism—than backward groups are.

To take a few examples: A. H. E. Sanderatne, a Sinhalese, accounting for the success of Tamils in gaining government positions in Sri Lanka early in the twentieth century, stresses their "hard work, shrewdness, and a capacity for pleasing their superiors," but he goes on to claim that

in Southeast Asia (Madison: Univ. of Wisconsin Press, 1963), 193; Herschelle Sullivan Challenor, "Strangers as Colonial Intermediaries: The Dahomeyans in Francophone Africa," in William A. Shack and Elliott P. Skinner, eds., *Strangers in African Societies* (Berkeley and Los Angeles: Univ. of California Press, 1979), 73; Eyo B. E. Ndem, *Ibos in Contemporary Politics: A Study in Group Conflict* (Onitsha, Nigeria: Etudo, 1961); Weiner, *Sons of the Soil*, 240–41; Wriggins, *Ceylon*, 217, 232–33; Campbell, "Stereotypes and the Perception of Group Differences," 826–27; Onkar S. Marwah and James H. Mittelman, "Alien Pariahs: Uganda's Asians and Bangladesh's Biharis" (unpublished paper presented at the 1973 annual meeting of the African Studies Association), 7; Hugh Gray, "The Demand for a Separate Telangana State in India," *Asian Survey* 11 (May 1971): 463–74, at 464; Dilip Mukerjee, "Pakistan's Growing Pains: Language Riots in Sind," *Times of India* (Bombay), July 17, 1972; K. C. Barua, *Assam: Her People and Her Language* (Gauhati, Assam: Lawyer's Book Stall, 1960), 12–13.

the Tamils "were united, and they did everything they could to help their brethren of the North." In contrast, the Sinhalese

did not present a united front, seeking only to safeguard their own personal interests. They hardly went out of their way to help their own people. Once a Tamil [government] officer assumed a position of power and influence, it was the invariable policy of his to safeguard the interests of the Tamils and do everything possible for their advancement. The Sinhalese on the other hand were rather callous about the questions of unity . . . .[74]

Creole views of East Indians in Guyana are similar. Indians are felt to be single-mindedly devoted to work and accumulation, and they are regarded as solidary and well organized for cooperation. Indians "are more together"; Creoles "don't help each other": these are typical expressions,[75] in spite of much evidence of greater cooperation and organizational life among Creoles than among Indians, the latter preoccupied with loyalty to family more than to ethnic group.[76] In East Bengal, before Bangladesh, survey data showed that Bengalis, who generally disliked Biharis, nevertheless admired, above all, their "unity among themselves."[77] Maharashtrians in Bombay also "berated themselves for being 'less educated,' " and they claimed not to have enough "ambition, guile, sense for gain, or the capital to take up business"; but over and above this they asserted that the South Indians, with whom they compared themselves, were clannish and hired only their own people.[78] Similarly, the Vokkaliggas of Karnataka state, in India, see themselves at a disadvantage in competition with their rivals, the Lingayats, because the latter are ostensibly more cohesive and well organized.[79] Not only are advanced groups allegedly endowed with superior individual traits, but also with superior collective attributes.

The totality of these self-stereotypes on the part of backward groups resembles very closely the psychoanalytic depiction of a "compliant" personality, characterized by an unassertive, unambitious demeanor, a

74. Sanderatne, *Glimpses of the Public Services of Ceylon During a Period of Transition, 1927–1962* (Colombo: Sam Printing Works, 1975), 9, 43.
75. Leo A. Despres, *Cultural Pluralism and Nationalist Politics in British Guiana* (Chicago: Rand, McNally, 1967), 93, 98. Quotations are from Donald L. Horowitz, unpublished data on Guyana and Trinidad, 1965, on file with the author.
76. Despres, *Cultural Pluralism and Nationalist Politics in British Guiana*, 116.
77. A. F. A. Husain and A. Farouk, *Social Integration of Industrial Workers in Khulna* (Dacca: Univ. of Dacca, 1963), 48.
78. Mary Fainsod Katzenstein, "Origins of Nativism: The Emergence of Shiv Sena in Bombay," *Asian Survey* 13 (Apr. 1973): 386–99, at 389.
79. Interviews, Bangalore, June 1975.

feeling of being "weak and helpless," and an assumption that others are more intelligent, better educated, and "more worthwhile."[80] Members of groups that feel this way are likely to view themselves as the major obstacle to their own advancement. The available evidence, by no means conclusive, indicates that this is so. In a survey of Trinidad secondary-school students, there were clear findings that East Indians located threats to their success in the external world, whereas Creole students to a much greater extent located such threats internally, revealing self-doubt.[81] Much the same experience is reported by Malaysian psychoanalysts: Chinese externalize obstacles; Malays more often internalize obstacles.[82]

What we have, then, is a stylized set of group juxtapositions based on folk views of group character. Groups are, so to speak, assigned psychological positions in the environment of intergroup relations.

"CATCHING UP":
A MATTER OF EMULATION

In Hugh MacLennan's novel about French-English relations in Canada, a Francophone protagonist deplores "the incessant jabbering noise of the outside world which bombarded [the Francophones'] own idea of themselves, roaring that they were weak, unimportant, unprogressive, too backward . . . ."[83] There are, in fact, two sources of this bombardment: the presence of ethnic strangers and the accusations of a group's own elite.

The presence of ethnic strangers, remarks Weiner, may be "psychologically threatening, since their very success may imply a defect in character on the part of local people. Are outsiders more successful because they work harder, have more skills, are more education minded, more punctual and efficient in their work, better attuned to the market requirements of the outside world?" Group members ultimately must decide whether to emulate the behavior of the ethnic strangers in order to compete. Ethnic strangers, Weiner continues, often create an unwelcome

80. Karen Horney, *Our Inner Conflicts* (New York: Norton, 1945), 53.
81. Vera Rubin and Marisa Zavalloni, *We Wish To Be Looked Upon* (New York: Teachers College Press, 1969), 59, 108–09.
82. Interview, Kuala Lumpur, July 16, 1975. See also David J. Banks, *Malay Kinship* (Philadelphia: Institute for the Study of Human Issues, 1983), 173–74: Malay peasants "admitted that they have not been frugal enough, not progressive enough in their pursuit of higher education for their children, but they have also blamed the Chinese . . . ."
83. MacLennan, *Two Solitudes* (New York: Popular Library, 1945), 149.

"compulsion for change"—unwelcome because, although necessary for competition, "the very notion of changing oneself to compete may be anathema." Moreover, the specific qualities perceived as the reasons for the strangers' success may be qualities group members "would prefer not to emulate—such as working hard or long hours, following more punctual work habits, taking fewer holidays, or adopting . . . a more aggressive personal style."[84]

This alone might be tolerable, and there is much evidence, already cited, that backward groups regard the success of advanced groups as not worth achieving because it entails behavior regarded as unacceptable. But there is now an additional ingredient: the educated elites of backward groups. They enjoin backward group members to change and specifically to emulate the behavior of advanced groups.

There is a litany to these injunctions. Backward groups are said to partake of unacceptable lethargy. Their attitude of "never mind" or "take it easy" is disparaged. In the Southern Sudan, it is *maalesh*, an expression connoting a fatalistic "too bad" when a job does not get done. Southern Sudanese leaders have been on a campaign to end *maalesh* and "encourage the work ethic."[85] The Assamese, with an attitude of *lahe-lahe*, meaning "slowly, slowly," are, it is said, "a leisurely people," thereby indirectly responsible for the importation of vast numbers of immigrants into their state.[86] The Malays use the expression *tidak apa*—"never mind"—and they are recurrently accused of "tidak apathy." The accusations do not come from ethnic strangers but from their own leaders, who admonish them to rouse themselves from their lethargy and adopt a competitive spirit.

These injunctions began with the Europeans in the colonial period. "Thus, the Iteso [of Uganda] were urged to grow more cotton and collect more taxes so as not to fall behind the Langi."[87] Creoles were told to work as hard as East Indians. Now, however, the admonitions are louder, more urgent, and more universal. A bootstrapping effort is recommended. Backward groups must "catch up" with their competitors by taking lessons from them. The Tamil "farmers of Jaffna," said a Sinhalese district minister, are "a hard-working and persevering lot who make maximum use of every inch of land available in their area, and the

84. Weiner, *Sons of the Soil*, 353–54.
85. James E. Sulton, Jr., "Regional Autonomy in the Southern Sudan: A Study in Conflict Regulation" (Ph.D. diss., Johns Hopkins Univ., 1980), 274–75.
86. Verghese et al., *Situation in Assam*, 14.
87. Kasfir, "Cultural Sub-Nationalism in Uganda," 73.

Sinhalese should follow the example set by the farmers of Jaffna."[88] In 1966, the military governor of Northern Nigeria, a prominent Hausa-Fulani, castigated his people for their passivity, which made it difficult to "catch up": "This attitude of idleness and fatalism has made the people backward and weak."[89] Maharashtrians have been told repeatedly that they are unable "to meet the demands of the age," that they need to learn new skills "so that they can compete with the Tamils."[90] Fijians have been repeatedly exhorted to use their lands as well as Indians,[91] and Creoles in Guyana have been told to emulate Indian work and savings habits, more provident than their own. Comparable injunctions have been addressed by group leaders to the Lulua of Zaire, various Northern Ugandans, Indian Muslims, and the Assamese, among others.[92]

This syndrome has several features. Group cultural values are under attack. Without a change in personal qualities, the group will fall permanently "behind." The way to change is to learn from more diligent ethnic adversaries. Malaysian and Maharashtrian admonitions have been perhaps most explicit on this score. To take two of many Malaysian examples, the chief minister of Perak state publicly "advised Malays living near Chinese neighborhoods to emulate their industrious way of life," and the then-prime minister told a Malay party meeting: "We [Malays] cannot be jealous of the success of the other communities [Chinese and Indians] who are way ahead of us. If we are in the clouds, negligent and sluggish, we cannot expect other communities to come to a standstill to wait for us."[93] The Malays are advised daily of the need for "hard work" and "discipline."[94] Maharashtrian laborers are also told to "awaken" and follow the example of "clever and very hard work-

88. *Ceylon Daily News* (Colombo), Apr. 7, 1980.

89. Hassan Katsina, quoted in *West Africa*, June 11, 1966, p. 668.

90. Kapilacharya, *Shiv Sena Speaks* (pamphlet; Bombay: V. D. Limaye, 1967), 47; Weiner, *Sons of the Soil*, 354.

91. Mayer, *Indians in Fiji*, 82.

92. See, e.g., Chomé, *Le Drame de Luluabourg*, 16; Henri Nicolai, "Conflits entre groupes africains et décolonisation au Kasai," *Revue de l'Université de Bruxelles* 12 (1960): 131–44; Cherry Gertzel, *Party and Locality in Northern Uganda, 1945–1962* (London: Athlone Press, 1974), 82; S. N. Faridi, *Economic Welfare of Indian Moslems* (Agra: Ram Prasad, 1965), 58, 88; Paul R. Brass, "Muslim Separatism in the United Provinces: Social Context and Political Strategy Before Partition," *Economic and Political Weekly*, Jan. 1970, pp. 167–86, at pp. 168–69.

93. *Straits Times* (Kuala Lumpur), May 17, 1968; *Far Eastern Economic Review*, June 10, 1977, p. 24.

94. See, e.g., *New Straits Times* (Kuala Lumpur), Mar. 29, 1980; Mahathir bin Mohamad, *The Malay Dilemma* (Singapore: Donald Moore, 1970), 60, 108. For the impact of the compulsion to change as felt in villages, see M. G. Swift, *Malay Peasant Society in Jelebu* (London: Athlone Press, 1965), 91, 158.

ing" South Indian laborers in their midst. The same advice is dispensed
to businessmen by a Maharashtrian party magazine. According to the
title of an article, "Losing a Customer Is a Specialty of Marathi Shop-
keeper." Maharashtrians, concludes Mary F. Katzenstein, "are being
urged to acquire the characteristics exhibited by the 'outsiders' " whom
their leaders oppose.[95]

The message of all of these elite injunctions is that the qualities that
formerly served to distinguish a group from the undesirable ways of
ethnic strangers are now themselves seen to be undesirable. There is no
longer consolation in the argument that, while ethnic strangers may
achieve more, their behavior is unenviable. Now they achieve more precisely because their behavior is more worthy. Inexplicably, one's own
elites say so.

All ambivalence has gone out of group evaluations. The sentimental-
ity of the former colonial rulers for the "dignity, politeness, and nobility"
of the backward groups finds no echo in the views of leaders of those
groups. Politeness, it is said, is not conducive to achievement; aggressiveness is better. That elites should feel this way—and that it should create
stress—are both understandable. There is some evidence that people
with more foreign contact are more critical of their own group and its
attributes—such broader horizons would certainly characterize ethnic
elites—and there is also evidence that less advanced groups tend to be
somewhat more prejudiced toward outgroups.[96] The two together add
up to conflicting pulls on members of backward groups. Ingroup attributes are denigrated, and the models advanced for emulation are the
very outgroups that are especially disliked.

The whole matter is made more difficult by the fact that backward
groups usually claim, and often receive, preferences of one kind or another. Compensatory measures are demanded to offset the presumed
superior ability of advanced groups to compete. Backward groups demanding them are convinced of their inability to compete on equal
terms. Our sons, notes a Telangana in support of preferences, "are not
as ambitious as theirs. So how can we ever catch up?"[97] On this basis,
Lulua and Sinhalese have received preferences in university admissions,

95. All quotes are from Katzenstein, "The Consequences of Migration: Nativism, Symbolic Politics, and National Integration" (unpublished paper presented at the 1973 annual
meeting of the American Political Science Association), 8.
96. Reigrotski and Anderson, "National Stereotypes and Foreign Contacts," 72, 74;
Bulatao, *Ethnic Attitudes in Five Philippine Cities*, 84, 130, 144, 146.
97. Quoted in Weiner, *Sons of the Soil*, 251.

Malays have been beneficiaries of a variety of preferential programs, Maharashtrians and Telanganas have been accorded preferences in (ployment. "If," explains a Maharashtrian government leader, "you have two plants, one with hardy roots and broad leaves and the other with only weak roots and small leaves, they can not drink the water, the soil nutrients, or absorb the sun's energy with the same efficiency. The weak plant needs more attention so that it can catch up and one day produce beautiful fruit."[98] Preferences, said a proponent, are "medicine"—it "cannot be withdrawn if a patient continues to be sick."[99]

The key is indeed catching up, for now it is taken as given that collective equality is an important good and also that the presence of achievement motivation is ground for moral approbation, its absence ground for deprecation. There is tension between these two—collective equality and achievement motivation—and both have been pursued. "The Government's policy," said a Northern Nigerian official, "is to support merit, but at the same time to protect the weak."[100]

But it does not end there. Elites recognize that preferential policies are a deviation from norms of equal treatment, typically rationalized as a temporary expedient. Consequently, groups that receive preferential treatment are under constant pressure from leaders to justify their benefits by performance. Performance is felt to entail rejection of the very traits that come with one's ethnic identity and adoption of those possessed by people who, at bottom, are believed unworthy of emulation. Early socialization sends one message to group members; political elites send another, quite dissonant message.

THE FEAR OF EXTINCTION

There is a race-against-time element in the felt necessity to catch up. A backward group needs to catch up fast, because, as just noted, preferences cannot be justified forever, and the group must also catch up "before it is too late." The future looks uncertain. In fact, backward groups have frequently exhibited severe anxiety about threats emanating from other groups. One form this anxiety takes is apprehension about being dominated and being turned into "hewers of wood and drawers of water."[101] Conciliatory leaders are depicted as being excessively gener-

---

98. Quoted in Mary Fainsod Katzenstein, *Ethnicity and Equality: The Shiv Sena Party and Preferential Policies in Bombay* (Ithaca: Cornell Univ. Press, 1979), 28.
99. Quoted in Weiner, *Sons of the Soil*, 250.
100. *West Africa*, June 4, 1966, p. 639.
101. Kapilacharya, *Shiv Sena Speaks*, 13.

ous in granting concessions to ethnic strangers, whose intentions are, allegedly, to take control of the country and subordinate the backward group. Every issue can then become a survival issue. A common formulation is that if a certain political demand is not granted, the group "will cease to exist." To take two examples among many: At the time of the Sinhala Only legislation in Sri Lanka in 1956, there was a fear among certain Sinhalese that there would be a compromise with the Tamils. Sinhala language activists called Buddhist priests to agitate against this prospect, telling them "that if they didn't do something there would be no more Buddhism and no more Sinhalese—they'd all be Hindu priests, speaking in Tamil."[102] The same was said at the time of the compromise language legislation in Malaysia in 1967. If the Malays do not "stand up," the "Malay race will disappear and sink from our own land!"[103]

Survival is not meant metaphorically. Strikingly, a great many backward groups entertain a fear of extinction, usually expressed by reference to the fate of the "Red Indians of America." Here is what they say:[104]

Fiji: The *raison d'être* of the Fijian National Party "was to prevent Fijians from succumbing to competition, as the North American Indians, Hawaiians, and Maoris had done."

Sind, Pakistan: Sindhis "do not want to be turned into Red Indians . . . ."

Malaysia: "More than one [Malay party branch] leader expressed concern that the Malays might become 'like the Red Indians in America,' an analogy frequently repeated in the Malay press."

Punjab, India: "Either the Sikhs must live as equals or accept virtual extinction."

102. Interview, Colombo, Aug. 17, 1968. See also Robert N. Kearney, *Communalism and Language in the Politics of Ceylon* (Durham: Duke Univ. Press, 1967), 62–63, 73.
103. *Bangsa Melayu Akan Hilang Di-Dunia* (pamphlet; Kuala Lumpur, Feb. 1967), 1.
104. The following are quoted in R. S. Milne, *Politics in Ethnically Bipolar States* (Vancouver: Univ. of British Columbia Press, 1981), 97; *Far Eastern Economic Review*, July 1, 1972, p. 12; Marvin L. Rogers, "The Politicization of Malay Villagers," *Comparative Politics* 7 (Jan. 1975): 202–25, at 217; Baldev Raj Nayar, *Minority Politics in the Punjab* (Princeton: Princeton Univ. Press, 1966), 117; Weiner, *Sons of the Soil*, 167; Ba Maw, *Breakthrough in Burma*, 187; Filipinas Foundation, *An Anatomy of Philippine Muslim Affairs* (n.p., mimeo., 1971), 149; Bernard K. Gordon, *The Dimensions of Conflict in Southeast Asia* (Englewood Cliffs, N.J.: Prentice-Hall, 1966), 54; "A Comma in the Refinery Movement," *Economic and Political Weekly*, Nov. 8, 1969, pp. 1771–73, at p. 1771; Wriggins, *Ceylon*, 240, quoting N. D. Wijesekera, "Dynamism of Traditional Cultures," in R. Pieris, ed., *Traditional Sinhalese Culture* (Peradeniya: Univ. of Ceylon, 1956), 21–22.

Bihar, India: If tribals do not have their land, "then they will become extinct like the American Indians."

Burma: Many Karens "believe that a Burmese-dominated nation . . . will mean their gradual extinction as a community or at least permanent neglect and inferiority to the Burmese."

Philippines: "This feeling of urgency and fear of eventual extinction [on the part of Philippine Muslims] should be understood by those in power . . . ."

Cambodia: Khmers fear they may lose their identity as a people, "like the Cham," a people of the ancient Champa Kingdom absorbed centuries ago by the Vietnamese.

Assam, India: "The Assamese think that their individuality is in danger of being wiped out by foreign and non-Assamese elements . . . ."

Sri Lanka: "Lacking a strong culture, the people, too, are considered vulnerable. 'For have not certain societies where traditional cultures were abandoned become extinct within our living memory? Some of the South Sea Islands have become depopulated.' "

Vamik D. Volkan notes a comparable fear of "dying off" among Turkish Cypriots—"within fifty years no Turk will be left on the island"—and connects it to a low group "self-concept."[105] Among groups in the West that have used the same language of extinction are the Basques and the French Canadians.[106]

To a considerable extent, such apprehensions reflect demographic insecurity. The Philippine Muslims and the Assamese have experienced extremely high rates of in-migration of ethnic strangers in recent decades, and the Assamese are in close proximity to East and West Bengal, with, between them, a Bengali population fifteen times the Assamese population. The Fijians are outnumbered by the Indians in their midst. The Sikhs, a bare majority in the Punjab, are surrounded by a sea of Hindus outside the Punjab. The Sinhalese, a large majority in relation to the Tamils in Sri Lanka, are a minority in relation to the Tamils in India. Comparable observations have been made about the Flemings and Wal-

105. Volkan, *Cyprus—War and Adaptation: A Psychoanalytic History of Two Ethnic Groups in Conflict* (Charlottesville: Univ. Press of Virginia, 1979), 105.
106. Milton M. da Silva, "Modernization and Ethnic Conflict: The Case of the Basques," *Comparative Politics* 7 (Jan. 1975): 227–51, at 230; Robert Chodos and Nick Auf der Maur, eds., *Quebec: A Chronicle, 1968–1972* (Toronto: Lewis & Samuel, 1972), 79; Hughes, *French Canada in Transition*, 152.

loons in Belgium and the Protestants and Catholics in Northern Ireland. Majorities within a country become minorities within an international region, depending on how the region is conceived. Political space is not a fixed concept. This is another way of saying that the environment of group juxtapositions may be broader than that created by formal territorial boundaries. When once this is conceded, it becomes obvious that there is a realistic component to group anxiety.

But the realism is strictly limited. The Philippine Muslims who have engaged most vigorously in separatist warfare are the Tausug, whose islands are practically unaffected by in-migration. The Fijians have rates of population growth at least as high as those of the Indians. Fearful as they are of extinction, the Sikhs have had in recent decades the highest rate of population increase of any group in the Punjab, a rate one-third higher than the all-India rate. The Malay population has a significantly higher rate of growth than the more urbanized Chinese population and is in close proximity to kindred peoples in Indonesia. Neither the Hausa in Northern Nigeria nor the Telanganas in Andhra Pradesh had reason to fear becoming a minority, much less becoming extinct, but they, like the Malays, spoke of being overcome by ethnic strangers:[107]

Nigeria: "the less well-educated people of the North will be swamped by the thrusting people of the South."

Telangana: There "seems to be [an] apprehension felt by the educationally-backward people of Telangana that they may be swamped and exploited by the more advanced people of the coastal area."

Malaysia: "Malaysia has far too many non-Malay citizens who can swamp the Malays the moment protection is removed."

These apprehensions about survival, swamping, and subordination reflect the enormous importance accorded to competitive values: a group that cannot compete will be overcome or will die out. Such sentiments have tended to be uttered at times when the groups entertaining them have been politically in a strong position.

107. The following are quoted in *West Africa*, June 11, 1966, p. 647; *The Telangana Movement: An Investigative Focus* (Hyderabad: Anand Rao Thota, for the Telangana University and College Teachers' Convention, 1969), 43; Mahathir, *The Malay Dilemma*, 31.

GROUP ANXIETY AND ETHNIC CONFLICT

To an outside observer, the fear of succumbing to the superior numbers or capacities of another group and disappearing must be regarded as extreme and irrational. Still, these apprehensions persist, coloring group relations in many ways. How to explain them?

First of all, the fear of subordination needs to be marked as a characteristic feature of life in unranked ethnic systems. These resemble two or more societies in one environment, and for this reason they give rise to inevitable uncertainty and discomfort that I shall treat more carefully later.

Second, the fear of extinction and swamping in particular can be identified technically as an anxiety-laden perception. Anxiety reactions are characterized by a "disproportion between the external stimulus and the response," and in extreme cases that disproportion is also extreme.[108] Whereas fear flows from a recognizable danger and gives rise to a proportionate response, anxiety flows from a diffuse danger of exaggerated dimensions; it limits and modifies perceptions, producing extreme reactions to modest threats.[109] It has often been remarked that ethnic politics in severely divided societies is characterized by extreme demands. To understand the context of group anxiety from which such extreme demands emanate is to make the politics of such societies far more comprehensible.

Third, there are relationships among self-esteem, anxiety, and prejudice. Prejudice allows a discharge of hostility, thereby reducing anxiety.[110] A correlation has also been found between lack of individual self-esteem and degree of hostility toward outgroups,[111] and the same relationship should hold for group self-esteem. Aggression, says Volkan of the Cyprus case, can be "ego-syntonic" for a group, "a means by which to gain a sense of worth."[112] The exaggeration of threats, more-

108. Ernest Jones, "The Psychopathology of Anxiety," in Jones, Papers on Psychoanalysis, 5th ed. (Boston: Beacon Press, 1961), 295. See Charles Rycroft, Anxiety and Neurosis (Baltimore: Penguin Books, 1968).
109. Erik H. Erikson, Childhood and Society, 2d ed. (New York: Norton, 1963), 406–07; Ross Stagner, "The Psychology of Human Conflict," in Elton B. McNeil, ed., The Nature of Human Conflict (Englewood Cliffs, N.J.: Prentice-Hall, 1965), 56.
110. Bruno Bettelheim and Morris Janowitz, Social Change and Prejudice (New York: Free Press of Glencoe, 1964), 54.
111. Leonard Berkowitz, Aggression: A Social Psychological Analysis (New York: McGraw-Hill, 1962), 278; Bettelheim and Janowitz, Social Change and Prejudice, 53–55, 70.
112. Volkan, Cyprus—War and Adaptation, 117.

over, serves another function. Since "it is incompatible with his self-esteem to realize that he is waging a war of persecution," a person hostile to outgroups "sometimes invents the existence of a powerful and threatening conspiracy aimed at his own well-being."[113] The fear of extinction is a powerful threat, more readily understood as a rationale for hostility.[114]

Fourth, the fear of extinction needs to be viewed against the specific content of the exclusivist demands made by the groups entertaining such fears. As in the Sinhala Only demand, for example, the thrust of the claim is to pursue a policy designed as if the country contained only the Sinhalese—that is, as if it were homogeneous. As I noted a moment ago, two or more incipient societies in a single state is an uncomfortable situation, and it often produces impulses to make the society homogeneous, by assimilation, expulsion, or even extermination. This leads me to speculate that the fear of extinction is actually a projection. Projection is a psychological mechanism by which unacceptable impulses felt by oneself are imputed to others, often the very targets of those impulses. If the thought is that "we wish to overcome or extinguish them," it may be expressed as "they wish to overcome or extinguish us."[115] This is called direct projection. Its relevance here is reinforced by patterns of violence initiation. As noted earlier, backward groups are overwhelmingly initiators and advanced groups are targets of ethnic riot behavior. So much hostility can only be justified if there is a large threat emanating from the targets of the aggression. Experiencing an emotion without the presence of an adequate stimulus commonly results in a quest for justification by projection of that emotion onto others.[116]

We are now in a position to explain the conflict behavior of nonelites, to sense what was troubling "the Itsekiri common man"[117] and common men of other ethnic groups. It will be recalled that Lloyd was puzzled by the tendency of the Itsekiri to exaggerate threats out of all proportion to the actual dangers confronting them, to apprehend the future with foreboding, and to engage in mob violence over issues in which they

113. Bettelheim and Janowitz, *Social Change and Prejudice*, 138.
114. As Jones says, anxiety always has guilt behind it. Jones, "Fear, Guilt, and Hate," in Jones, *Papers on Psychoanalysis*, 304–05.
115. See Alexander Mitscherlich, "Psychoanalysis and the Aggression of Large Groups," *International Journal of Psychoanalysis* 52 (May 1971): 161–67, at 162–63.
116. See the classic study by Henry A. Murray, Jr., "Fear and Estimates of the Maliciousness of Other Personalities," *Journal of Social Psychology* 4 (Aug. 1933): 310–29, at 324. See also Erikson, *Childhood and Society*, 164.
117. See Chapter 3, pages 129–31, above.

apparently had little material stake. In particular, Itsekiri nonelites were concerned that they might lose their ethnic identity, despite very few indications that this might actually occur.

It seems clear now that the Itsekiri, like the Sinhalese, the Hausa, the Malays, the Fijians, the Telanganas, the Assamese, and a good many other groups, were troubled by invidious group comparisons with the "dynamic" Urhobo in their midst. Disdainful of manual work, inclined to consumption expenditure, and stereotyped as lazy, the Itsekiri acknowledged the Urhobo propensity to hard work but consoled themselves with a view of the Urhobo as uncultured and dirty. The Itsekiri were given to anxiety-laden perceptions—for that is precisely what their exaggeration and foreboding connote: they are textbook symptoms—and they were also inclined to conflict behavior based on their anxiety. Understandably, their view of the situation did not appear to Lloyd to be realistic, and that is why he searched for an explanation in the realm of leadership manipulation and deception. A more fruitful explanation, however, lies in the disparaging evaluations of group worth to which the Itsekiri and comparable groups were subject, evaluations that led them to want to do something to retrieve their self-esteem. The participation of nonelites in the conflict, hard to explain on the basis of narrow group "interests," is easy to explain on the basis of invidious comparison. Since the individual "sense of identity is the feeling of being a worthy person because he fits into a coherent and valued order of things,"[118] ego identity depends heavily on affiliations. A threat to the value of those affiliations produces anxiety and defense.[119] For this reason, people often express hostility toward those who create uncertainty about the correctness of their own behavior and that of the groups to which they belong,[120] and they often do so out of all proportion to the character of the threat that presently confronts them.

A POSITIONAL GROUP PSYCHOLOGY

The sources of ethnic conflict are not to be found solely in the psychology of group juxtapositions, but they cannot be understood without a psychology, an explanation that takes account of the emotional concomi-

---

118. Alan O. Ross, *Ego Identity and the Social Order: A Psychological Analysis of Six Indonesians* (Washington, D.C.: American Psychological Association, Psychological Monographs, no. 542, 1962), 27.

119. Ibid., 32.

120. Berkowitz, *Aggression*, 171–72.

tants of group traits and interactions. To ask purely objective questions, such as whether increasing intergroup contact accelerates or retards conflict, is to miss the decisive impact of the quality of that contact.[121] It is also to close one's ears instead of attending carefully to what groups say about themselves and others. Without feelings of antipathy, there can be no ethnic conflict.

By the same token, the backward-advanced dichotomy is not the only possible dimension along which conflict-producing comparisons can be made, but it is obviously the most powerful and widespread dimension, given the history of group interactions in Asia and Africa and the fact that imputed traits are the currency of intergroup comparison. Without this dichotomy, ethnic conflict would be much less important in the contemporary world.

Dichotomization as a result of juxtaposition and comparison helps clarify an otherwise puzzling phenomenon in ethnic conflict: why is it that, despite the plurality of groups in an environment (rarely are there only two), polarity frequently emerges? Two groups are counterpoised, and the participation of other groups in the conflict tends to be minor. If there are three major groups, the three reduce to two. Malays and Chinese, more than Indians; Hausa and Ibo, more than Yoruba; Sinhalese and Tamils, more than Moors; Telanganas and Andhras, but not Ryalaseemas; Ashanti and Ewe; Kikuyu and Luo; Assamese and Bengalis: the examples are plentiful, though there is no iron law of duality. An argument can be made for an economy of antipathy. It is dangerous to have multiple enemies and more efficient to concentrate on the main problem. But there is something beyond this. Group juxtapositions and comparisons and elite injunctions all emphasize the dichotomous aspect of interactions, since they call attention to perceived polar types of behavior. Pairs of antagonists emerge as comparative reference groups.

Implicit in all of this is a modification of a commonly articulated proposition derived initially from Freud's narcissism of small differences. It is often said that the greatest conflict arises between groups that are only slightly different from each other. Comparison is then thought to be more plausible; small differences are an implied criticism of ourselves.[122] Of course, groups compare themselves only with those be-

121. See ibid., 61–62; Yehuda Amir, "Contact Hypothesis in Ethnic Relations," *Psychological Bulletin* 71 (May 1969): 319–42.
122. See, e.g., Martin R. Doornbos, "Protest Movements in Western Uganda: Some Parallels and Contrasts," *Kroniek van Afrika*, May 1–Aug. 1, 1970, pp. 213–29; Gordon Allport, *The Nature of Prejudice* (Garden City, N.Y.: Anchor Books, 1958), 132.

lieved, in relevant respects, to be "comparable,"[123] but that does not limit the field to small differences. Larger differences, even polarities, may form the basis of comparison, especially if authoritative voices repeatedly make exactly that comparison.

In treating group comparisons, I have moved between formulations at the individual and collective level, so far avoiding several consequential issues. Is there an autonomous domain in which group psychology operates, or is group psychology merely the aggregate of individual reactions? If there is a group psychology, can it be understood without exploring the idiosyncratic recesses of each individual culture from which it springs? And how separate from individual psychology is it? Erikson remarks, for example, that the Sioux are emotionally healthy people as individuals but are a sick group.[124] And Freud once asked, "may we not be justified in reaching the diagnosis that . . . some civilizations, or some epochs of civilization—possibly the whole of mankind—have become 'neurotic'?"[125] The implication of these suggestions, acknowledged by Freud, is that there is room for development of a separate group psychology if the socialization processes of groups can be specified as they have been for individuals.

There the matter stands. The individualist bias of psychoanalytic and social-psychological thought has been deplored.[126] We know much about the psychology of the prejudiced individual but little about the psychology of the prejudiced group. Freud's one systematic effort in collective psychology unfortunately was limited to regressively formed groups—in other words, crowds.[127]

Whatever the ultimate direction of group psychology in general, sev-

123. See Festinger, "A Theory of Social Comparison Processes."

124. *Childhood and Society*, 131.

125. Sigmund Freud, *Civilization and Its Discontents*, trans. and ed. James Strachey (New York: Norton, 1961; originally published in 1930), 91.

126. Fred Weinstein and Gerald M. Platt, *Psychoanalytic Sociology* (Baltimore: Johns Hopkins Univ. Press, 1973), 5; Robert Waelder, "Psychoanalysis and History: Application of Psychoanalysis to Historiography," in Benjamin B. Wolman, ed., *The Psychoanalytic Interpretation of History* (New York: Basic Books, 1971), 17; Alfred H. Stanton, "Comparison of Individual and Group Psychology," *American Psychoanalytic Journal* 6 (Jan. 1958): 121–30, at 123; Donald M. Taylor, "Stereotypes and Intergroup Relations," in R. G. Gardner and R. Kalin, eds., *A Canadian Social Psychology of Ethnic Relations* (Toronto: Methuen, 1980), chap. 9; Tajfel, *Human Groups and Social Categories*, 3–8.

127. Sigmund Freud, *Group Psychology and the Analysis of the Ego*, trans. and ed. James Strachey (New York: Liveright, 1967; originally published in 1921). See also Franco Fornari, *The Psychoanalysis of War*, trans. Alenka Pfeifer (Garden City, N.Y.: Anchor Books, 1974), 145–52. Jung took much the same approach. See C. G. Jung, *Collected Works*, trans. R. F. C. Hull (New York: Pantheon Books, 1959), vol. 9, pt. 1, pp. 125–27.

eral observations are pertinent to our specific concerns. No doubt some cultural patterns have a special bearing on interethnic relations. Volkan suggests that childhood in an extended family is conducive to development of anxiety and use of ethnic strangers as targets for externalization.[128] The extended family is, of course, a common institution in many of the most severely divided societies. There is also evidence of borrowing of motifs from interpersonal relations in interethnic relations, as remarked in Chapter 2. As ethnicity is connected to family, ethnic conflict has an aspect of playing out of sibling rivalry. In Kandeswami's parable and in the colonial situation, I have noted the role of superior third-party "parents" in judging group merit. Ethnic rivals often speak in a sibling idiom. It is not possible to write childhood experience out of ethnic conflict altogether.

Yet so strong are the structural similarities among culturally disparate groups like the Assamese, the Hausa, the Sinhalese, the Lulua, and the Malays that a focus on culturally conditioned processes like childhood development makes no sense for understanding ethnic conflict. A regularity cannot be explained by a variable. Nor does it make sense to seek a causal link between phenomena like collective anxiety and anxiety at the individual level, which need not be present. Without question, there are certain distinctively collective elements at work in intergroup psychology. Striking parallels in the idiom and behavior of groups far apart in geography, social structure, and emotional life, and sharing only commonality of interethnic situation, indicate some considerable degree of independence of group processes from individual processes. The threat that ethnic juxtapositions pose to the group self[129] and the behavior that flows from that threat can be understood within a framework of what Erving Goffman calls "normal psychology"—or what I would call a positional psychology—meaning that people or groups situated in a similar position "respond in an appreciably similar way."[130]

128. Volkan, *Cyprus—War and Adaptation*, 53–73.
129. Ibid., 96; John E. Mack, "Foreword," in ibid., xi.
130. Goffman, *Stigma: Notes on the Management of Spoiled Identity* (Englewood Cliffs, N.J.: Prentice-Hall, 1963), 130. See also Robert Melson, "A Theoretical Inquiry into the Armenian Massacres of 1894–1896," *Comparative Studies in Society and History* 24 (July 1982): 481–509, at 496 n.44.

CHAPTER FIVE

Group Entitlement and the Sources of Conflict

"The English lessened him," sensed MacLennan's Quebec extremist. "Merely by their existence, they lessened a man. You could become great and powerful only if your own people were also great and powerful. But what could his people do when the English constantly choked them?"[1] On that thought hangs a clue to the politics of ethnically divided societies. If the need to feel worthy is a fundamental human requirement, it is satisfied in considerable measure by belonging to groups that are in turn regarded as worthy. Like individual self-esteem, collective self-esteem is achieved largely by social recognition.[2] Everywhere, but especially in developing countries, where the sphere of politics is unusually broad and its impact powerful, collective social recognition is conferred by political affirmation. For this reason, struggles over relative group worth are readily transferred to the political system.

Political affirmation confers something else that ethnic groups seek. That something can be described as ethnic identification with the polity. Identification can be cast in terms that are exclusive or inclusive. Some groups claim that the country (or the region or the town) is or ought to be theirs and that the political system should reflect this fact by being constituted along essentially homogeneous lines. Other groups merely claim the right to be included on equal terms. The struggles over armorial bearings recounted in Chapter 3 evoked these conflicting claims, for the alternatives proposed signified domination by a single group or equal participation by all groups in the environment.

1. Hugh MacLennan, *Two Solitudes* (New York: Popular Library, 1945), 172.
2. On individual self-esteem, see Hadley Cantril, *The Psychology of Social Movements*, 2d ed. (New York: John Wiley, 1963), 46; Edward E. Jones et al., *Some Determinants of Reactions to Being Approved or Disapproved as a Person* (Washington, D.C.: American Psychological Association, Psychological Monographs, no. 521, 1962).

The claim to inclusion or exclusion is not dependent on the contest for group worth in the psychological sense described in Chapter 4. It derives instead from a quite general urge to be in harmony with one's surroundings, to belong in a territory, to be comfortable and at home. But the two quickly link up. Where invidious comparisons are strong and the struggle for relative group worth is powerful, the quest for ethnic inclusion and exclusion seems to be all the more important in politics. If the presence of ethnic strangers provides an unflattering contrast with one's own group, that is a good reason to emphasize demands for exclusion of the strangers. Homogeneity would remove the irritating comparison. Furthermore, claims to group legitimacy provide alternative ways of measuring worth. If a group suffers by invidious comparison along the dimension of achievement motivation, it may nonetheless have a special connection with the land that furnishes an alternative basis for relative group evaluation. Groups that do suffer from such comparison tend, therefore, to make stronger claims to priority by virtue of legitimacy, so as to make up on one front what they have lost on another.

Relative group worth and relative group legitimacy thus merge into a politics of ethnic entitlement. Otherwise inexplicable characteristics of ethnic conflict—such as the overwhelming concern of ethnic groups with the goal of political domination and the high symbolic content of ethnic politics—can be explained in terms of the politics of entitlement in both of its aspects. The contest for worth and place is the common denominator of ethnic conflict among unranked groups.

A POLITICS OF DOMINATION

Processual theories of politics, developed in the United States at a time when ethnic claims were largely dormant, contain an inadvertent bias that impedes the understanding of ethnic politics. These theories hold that politics is a process for deciding "who gets what." The theories acknowledge that holding power provides a sense of satisfaction, and so power is sometimes a goal in itself. Nonetheless, following Hobbes, they conceive of power principally as a "means to some future apparent good." For the most part, says V. O. Key, "power is a means, an indispensable means, to other ends"; in this, influential writers like David B. Truman concur.[3]

3. Key, *Politics, Parties and Pressure Groups*, 3d ed. (New York: Crowell, 1956), 7; Truman, *The Governmental Process* (New York: Knopf, 1951), 264.

To understand ethnic conflict, it is necessary to reverse this emphasis. Power is, of course, often an instrument to secure other, tangible goods and benefits, including benefits for members of an ethnic group, but power may also *be* the benefit. Power is the main goal at both ends of a spectrum. At one end, power is sought purely for its value in confirming a claimed status. To attain the status, power need hardly be exercised; the main thing is to gain it. At the other end, power is sought as a means to goals so diffuse, so remote, so difficult to specify, that attainment of power becomes, again, an end in itself. This latter case depicts many situations in international politics, where power is sought to prevent the emergence of dire but distant and dimly perceived consequences. So critical and dangerous are those feared consequences that it is deemed vital to take steps to avert them far in advance of their likely occurrence. In short, power may be desired, not only for the lesser things it can gain, but for the greater things it reflects and prevents. Power in these two latter senses—confirming status and averting threat—usually entails an effort to dominate the environment, to suppress differences, as well as to prevent domination and suppression by others.

In this respect, unranked ethnic systems resemble the international system. The fear of ethnic domination and suppression is a motivating force for the acquisition of power as an end. And power is also sought for confirmation of ethnic status. Broad matters of group status regularly have equal or superior standing to the narrow allocative decisions often taken to be the uniform stuff of everyday politics. Fundamental issues, such as citizenship, electoral systems, designation of official languages and religions, the rights of groups to a "special position" in the polity, rather than merely setting the framework for politics, become the recurring subjects of politics. Conflicts over needs and interests are subordinated to conflicts over group status and over the rules to govern conflict. Constitutional consensus is elusive, and the symbolic sector of politics looms large.

THE STRUGGLE FOR PREEMINENCE

I shall have more to say about the politics of ethnic status later in this chapter. At this point, it is necessary to explore what Gaetano Mosca calls the "struggle for preeminence."[4]

Evidence that control of the state is a central ethnic conflict objective

---

4. Mosca, *The Ruling Class*, ed. Arthur Livingston, trans. Hannah D. Kahn (New York: McGraw-Hill, 1939).

is abundant. Dov Ronen's description of the meaning of politics in Benin is typical: "for one of the three chief political leaders [of regional ethnic groups] not to be 'in power'—mere representation and participation in government do not count—means for his supporters not only to be 'out of power,' but also to be ruled by another region or regions which are in power; it means not only to be 'out,' but also to be 'under'; it means . . . to be politically overpowered by 'others.' "[5]

The timing of ethnic conflict was usually in lockstep with the approach of independence. The transfer of power raised the cardinal question of who would rule. Self-government thus brought in its train a "wildly speculative atmosphere generated by the uncertainties of the transfer of power."[6] In this atmosphere of uncertainty, the greatest group anxiety was to avoid trading an old colonialism for a new one, and there remains a strong current of fear that an unranked system may be transformed into a ranked system, with clear superordinates and subordinates.

The fear of domination by ethnic strangers can be documented in an array of states. Northern Nigerians suspected that "in a self-governing Nigeria the north would in effect be a backward protectorate governed by southerners. . . . [T]he threat of southern domination, fancied or real, was the major stimulant in the northern awakening."[7] So, too, "in Zanzibar widespread awareness of the imminence of independence engendered in all communities a ubiquitous fear that the end of colonial domination might be the beginning of domination by one community over another."[8] In Sri Lanka, there was talk of deciding whether the country "belongs to" the Sinhalese or the Tamils. "The gradual transfer of power from foreign to Ceylonese hands quickly created concern for the relative political strength of the various communities. The basic assumption upon which this concern rested was that the share of political power held by members of one community would be used for the exclusive benefit of that community or to the detriment of other communities."[9] In Leba-

5. Ronen, *Dahomey: Between Tradition and Modernity* (Ithaca: Cornell Univ. Press, 1975), 188.

6. James S. Coleman and Carl G. Rosberg, Jr., eds., *Political Parties and National Integration in Tropical Africa* (Berkeley and Los Angeles: Univ. of California Press, 1964), 690.

7. James S. Coleman, *Nigeria: Background to Nationalism* (Berkeley and Los Angeles: Univ. of California Press, 1958), 360, 363.

8. Michael Lofchie, "Party Conflict in Zanzibar," *Journal of Modern African Studies* 1 (June 1963): 185–207, at 188.

9. Robert N. Kearney, *Communalism and Language in the Politics of Ceylon* (Durham: Duke Univ. Press, 1967), 21.

non, the Maronites demanded a state with a "Christian character."[10] Michael C. Hudson reports that strong Maronites "regard Mount Lebanon as their territory, and their creed includes a claim to domination over it; similarly, many Sunnites feel an affinity with the Arab-Muslim world around them and identify with Arab nationalist and unity movements. Mutual insecurity results in incessant competition for power— the scarcest and dearest value; political tension is the final product."[11] In Mauritania, Chad, and the Sudan, all of which lie, as Lebanon does, between two "worlds," the question was similarly put: was the state to be "Arab" or "African"? And the derivative question, of course, was who would rule it, Arabs or Africans?[12] The imminence of independence in Uganda aroused "fears of future ill-treatment" along ethnic lines.[13] In Kenya, it was "Kikuyu domination" that was feared; in Zambia, "Bemba domination"; and, in Mauritius, "Franco-Mauritians, Creoles and Muslims began to fear they will be overshadowed by the more populous Hindus."[14] Everywhere the word *domination* was heard. Everywhere it was equated with political control. Everywhere it was a question of who were "the real owners of the country"[15] and of who would rule over whom.

The incidence of ethnic violence also reflects the motivating force of fears of domination. Some of the most serious episodes of ethnic riot behavior have occurred when an ethnic group engages in conflict signifying its apparent intention to capture the state for itself. The anti-Ibo riots of May 1966, for example, came after a military regime headed by Ibo issued military promotion lists that seemed to favor Ibo officers; promulgated a decree unifying the regional civil services, a move that would open the Northern civil service to an influx of Ibo; and then

10. Ralph Crow, "Religious Sectarianism in the Lebanese Political System," *Journal of Politics* 24 (Aug. 1963): 489–520, at 518.

11. Hudson, *The Precarious Republic: Political Modernization in Lebanon* (New York: Random House, 1968), 21–22.

12. See, e.g., Alfred G. Gerteiny, "The Racial Factor in the Islamic Republic of Mauritania," *Race* 8 (Jan. 1967): 263–75; William H. Lewis, "Francophone Africa," *Current History* 60 (Mar. 1970): 142–45, 177–78; Keith Kyle, "The Southern Problem in the Sudan," *The World Today* 22 (Dec. 1966): 512–20.

13. Nelson Kasfir, "Cultural Sub-Nationalism in Uganda," in Victor A. Olorunsola, ed., *The Politics of Cultural Sub-Nationalism in Africa* (Garden City, N.Y.: Anchor Books, 1972), 87.

14. George Bennett and Carl G. Rosberg, Jr., *The Kenyatta Election: Kenya 1960– 1961* (London: Oxford Univ. Press, 1961), 30–43, 150; Ian Scott and Robert Molteno, "The Zambian General Elections," *Africa Report*, Jan. 1969, pp. 42–47; Burton Benedict, *Mauritius: The Problems of a Plural Society* (London: Pall Mall Press, 1965), 67.

15. Lawrence Fellows, "The Duka-Wallas Are Outcasts in Africa," *New York Times Magazine*, June 25, 1967, p. 26.

indicated its intention to abolish the regions altogether. These were policies favored by Ibo, feared by Northerners, and interpreted as an Ibo conspiracy "to colonize the North."[16] Five days later, fierce attacks on Ibo began in Northern cities.

The themes of colonization, subjugation, and extermination recur in such events. Southern Sudanese inferred from a long series of affronts that "Northerners want to colonize us for another hundred years."[17] When Northern troops were flown to the South, to be used, as many thought, "for the extermination of the Southerners,"[18] and Southern troops were to be withdrawn to the North as independence approached, there was violence against Northerners in the South and ultimately civil war.

Comparable events occurred in Burma and Malaysia during and after World War II. The Karens and the Malays, respectively, resisted with violence what they took to be tantamount to colonial impositions by ethnic antagonists. The Karens suggested that a Burmese effort to disarm them was part of "a plan to rob and exterminate" the Karen community.[19] The Malays, responding to an attempt by Chinese guerrillas to control parts of Malaysia, articulated a sense of utter degradation. The Chinese, they said, "want to swallow the people."[20] The events made a lasting impression on Malay consciousness.[21] Similar fears of subjection can be found in violent episodes in Congo (Brazzaville), Guyana, Zanzibar, certain Indian states, and Cyprus, to name a few.

No doubt the theme of domination was especially prominent during the war and at the time of independence. Times of transition are often times of ethnic tension.[22] When it looks as if the shape of the polity is being settled once and for all, apprehensions are likely to grow.[23] For this reason, many ethnic groups preferred a continuation of colonial rule to

16. Ruth First, *Power in Africa* (Harmondsworth: Penguin, 1972), 311.

17. Quoted in Sudan Republic, *Report of the Commission of Inquiry into the Disturbances in the Southern Sudan During August, 1955* (Khartoum: Government of Sudan, 1956), 114.

18. Ibid., 120.

19. Ba Maw, *Breakthrough in Burma: Memoirs of a Revolution, 1939–1946* (New Haven: Yale Univ. Press, 1968), 188.

20. Kenelm O. L. Burridge, "Racial Relations in Johore," *Australian Journal of Politics and History* 2 (May 1957): 151–68, at 163.

21. Ibid., 161–65; M. G. Swift, *Malay Peasant Society in Jelebu* (London: Athlone Press, 1965), 85.

22. Tamotsu Shibutani and Kian M. Kwan, *Ethnic Stratification: A Comparative Approach* (New York: Macmillan, 1965), chap. 14.

23. Aristide R. Zolberg, "The Structure of Political Conflict in the New States of Tropical Africa," *American Political Science Review* 62 (Mar. 1968): 70–87, at 74.

independence or, in some cases, preferred a separate independence. Groups with such preferences were far more numerous than the anti-colonial rhetoric of the time might have implied.

I suggested at the beginning of this chapter that the quest for group worth and the quest for political inclusion and exclusion join together to form a politics of entitlement. Opposition to independence provides an excellent example of the conjunction. Predictably, a good many backward groups were reluctant to accede to the transfer of power. Well into the 1950s, Northern Nigerians, fearful of an independence that would benefit Southerners, wanted slow progress toward that goal.[24] Philippine Muslims preferred continued American administration, or a separate independence, to a unified, independent Philippines, and later they expressed hope for a return of the Americans.[25] Mainland Africans in Zanzibar wanted to delay independence until more education enabled them to compete with Arabs on equal terms; they asked for "time to learn."[26] Karens in Burma flatly preferred British rule to independence and occasionally ran the Union Jack up after capturing some territory from the Burmese government.[27] The Sab cultivator groups in Somalia preferred Italian rule to an independent state they thought would be controlled by the "more adept and intelligent" Samaale pastoralists.[28] The Lulua in Zaire, tribals in Bihar and Northeast India, various pastoral groups in Kenya, highlanders in Papua New Guinea, and Fijians in Fiji are among the backward groups who asked for "time to catch up with [their competitors], both economically and politically, before there is a devolution of power."[29] Invidious comparisons color political positions.

But where some backward groups felt that independence would accentuate their predicament, other backward groups actively sought in-

24. Elliott P. Skinner, "Strangers in West African Societies," *Africa* 33 (Oct. 1963): 307–20, at 314.

25. Thomas M. Kiefer, *The Tausug: Violence and Law in a Philippine Muslim Society* (New York: Holt, Rinehart & Winston, 1972), 135; Peter G. Gowing, "Muslim Filipinos Between Integration and Secession" (unpublished paper presented at the 1973 annual meeting of the Association of Asian Studies), 8; *Far Eastern Economic Review* (Hong Kong), Mar. 18, 1974, p. 27.

26. Michael F. Lofchie, *Zanzibar: Background to Revolution* (Princeton: Princeton Univ. Press, 1965), 167.

27. Hugh Tinker, *The Union of Burma*, 4th ed. (London: Oxford Univ. Press, 1967), 351–52.

28. A. A. Castagno, "Somali Republic," in Coleman and Rosberg, eds., *Political Parties and National Integration in Tropical Africa*, 524, 527, 529, 532–34; I. M. Lewis, *The Modern History of Somaliland* (New York: Praeger, 1965), 146–48.

29. Adrian C. Mayer, *Indians in Fiji* (London: Oxford Univ. Press, 1963), 133.

dependence. Numbers have something, but not everything, to do with this. Majorities, like the Indians in Mauritius, the Sinhalese, the Malays, the Northern Sudanese, and some pluralities, like the Javanese in Indonesia and the Darood in Somalia, tended to seek independence, even if they were relatively backward, particularly if they had some claim to priority in the country. And some advanced groups, such as the Lozi in Zambia, the Maronites in Lebanon, the Tamils in Sri Lanka and in India, and the Chinese in Malaysia, were distinctly ambivalent about independence. Group inclinations in this respect turned to some extent on position in the civil service. Groups well represented there, even if not in a majority in the country, tended to believe that their future position would be assured and enhanced by independence. Consequently, the Creole minority in Surinam, the Creole majority in Trinidad, the Ibo, the Bemba in Zambia, and the Malays were enthusiastically for independence.

Backward or advanced, groups that were not in favor of early independence either collaborated with the colonialists or demanded formal guarantees. The Ceylon Tamils asked for balanced ethnic representation in parliament; the Foulah in Guinea voted to remain in the French Community; the Fijians demanded a separate electoral roll; Indians in Surinam sought quotas in the armed forces and proportional representation in elections; in Indonesia, the Sundanese, fearful of Javanese domination, agreed with the Dutch, as other groups did, to set up a nominally independent state in West Java; and Creoles in Mauritius and some Batak in Indonesia preferred continued colonial association.[30]

There was, then, a tradeoff between backwardness and political advantage. On the whole, advanced groups were more active anti-colonialists, but this could be turned around if a backward group were so favorably positioned that it forecast a politically dominant position in the independent state. Groups that made the opposite forecast and acted on it helped to widen differences between them and the anti-colonial groups after independence. In some cases, notably the Karens in Burma, the

30. See, e.g., Kearney, *Communalism and Language in the Politics of Ceylon*, 69, 73; Robert L. Hardgrave, Jr., "The Riots in Tamilnad: Problems and Prospects of India's Language Crisis," *Asian Survey* 5 (Aug. 1965): 399–407, at 403; R. William Liddle, "Ethnicity and Political Organization: Three East Sumatran Cases," in Claire Holt, ed., *Culture and Politics in Indonesia* (Ithaca: Cornell Univ. Press, 1972), 143; Adele Smith Simmons, "Politics in Mauritius Since 1934: A Study of Decolonization in a Plural Society" (Ph.D. diss., Oxford Univ., 1969), chap. 8; Yogendra Malik, *East Indians in Trinidad: A Study in Minority Politics* (London: Oxford Univ. Press, 1971); Edward Dew, "Surinam's Balance of Power Politics" (unpublished paper presented at the 1977 annual meeting of the International Studies Association).

Ambonese in Indonesia, and the Foulah in Guinea, these differences had profound and enduring effects on intergroup relations, some of which we shall examine in Chapters 11 and 12.

The struggle for domination and the sharply opposed positions taken by ethnic groups on independence and constitutional arrangements reflect, not merely the anxiety-laden perceptions of backward groups, but also a more general phenomenon of distrust. As colonial rule heightened the importance of the state—and of controlling it—it did nothing to further belief in the impartiality of institutions.[31] "Never stand behind a horse or in front of an official," runs a Punjabi proverb, conveying the flavor of attitudes in many countries. There is now a mountain of evidence that, in Asian and African states, distrust of institutions, suspicion of the intentions of other ethnic groups, and a negative evaluation of politicians and their functions are all widespread.[32] Marvin L. Rogers comments that the Malays "have been mobilized into politics without being socialized to support a genuinely democratic, multiethnic political system."[33] Hudson describes Lebanese groups as "mutually suspicious, and they do not trust the formal institutions to be powerful or impartial enough to protect their local interests."[34] Robert Melson remarks of Nigerians that, "as a member of this or that ethnic group or region, the same worker who denounced all politicians in one breath, supported *his* man in the next."[35] Politically alienate responses are common in surveys of Asia and Africa.[36]

31. On the colonial role in attitude formation, see Aristide R. Zolberg, *One-Party Government in the Ivory Coast,* 2d ed. (Princeton: Princeton Univ. Press, 1969), 145; Robert I. Rotberg, "Origins of Nationalist Discontent in Africa," *Journal of Negro History* 48 (Apr. 1963): 130–41, at 139–40.

32. For a summary, see Samuel P. Huntington, *Political Order in Changing Societies* (New Haven: Yale Univ. Press, 1968), 28–31. See also Crawford Young, *Politics in the Congo* (Princeton: Princeton Univ. Press, 1965), 576; Baldev Raj Nayar, *Minority Politics in the Punjab* (Princeton: Princeton Univ. Press, 1966), 129; Hudson, *The Precarious Republic,* 18, 34, 256; James C. Scott, *Political Ideology in Malaysia: Reality and the Beliefs of an Elite* (New Haven: Yale Univ. Press, 1968), 69–72; Marvin L. Rogers, "The Politicization of Malay Villagers," *Comparative Politics* 7 (Jan. 1975): 205–25, at 223; Chandra Jayawardena, *Conflict and Solidarity in a Guianese Plantation* (London: Athlone Press, 1963), 60–63; F. G. Bailey, *Politics and Social Change: Orissa in 1959* (Berkeley and Los Angeles: Univ. of California Press, 1963), 15; Robert Melson, "Nigerian Politics and the General Strike of 1964," in Robert I. Rotberg and Ali A. Mazrui, eds., *Power and Protest in Black Africa* (New York: Oxford Univ. Press, 1970), 786–87.

33. Rogers, "The Politicization of Malay Villagers," 223.

34. Hudson, *The Precarious Republic,* 9.

35. Melson, "Nigerian Politics and the General Strike of 1964," 787 (emphasis in the original).

36. See, e.g., Otto Klineberg and Marisa Zavalloni, *Nationalism and Tribalism Among African Students: A Study of Social Identity* (Paris and The Hague: Mouton, 1969), 53–60; Filipinas Foundation, *An Anatomy of Philippine Muslim Affairs* (n.p., mimeo., 1971),

This attitudinal configuration affects interethnic behavior. It has long been known that general attitudes of distrust are correlated with interethnic antipathy.[37] What is more, suspicion is acted upon. In Sri Lanka, for example, a common Sinhalese view that Tamil graders were giving extra marks to Tamil papers helped produce a policy of ethnic weighting of grades, and I have heard a grader in Malaysia admit to ethnic favoritism, on the assumption that graders from other groups were doing the same: "everyone favors his own race." In an array of societies, it is believed that officeholders will use their authority for the exclusive or disproportionate benefit of their own ethnic groups.[38] In the concise language of a Guyanese survey respondent: "Indian for Indian—black for black." If there is such suspicion, coupled with an absence of faith in the impartiality of public institutions and a belief that those institutions are nonetheless inordinately important in shaping the fortunes of ethnic groups, it becomes vital to capture them. Politics becomes urgent, and it is not easy to fashion institutions that can mediate group claims.

WINNING THE CENSUS

As an entitlement issue, the census is a splendid example of the blending of group anxiety with political domination. On the one hand, it is common to encounter anxiety-laden perceptions of the fecundity or illegal immigration of competing groups; these produce considerable overestimates of the population of outgroups.[39] In this sense, the census is related to the fear of extinction discussed in Chapter 4. On the other hand, since numbers count in the quest for political domination, the hope of a group is to enlarge its relative share of the population. Numbers are an indicator of whose country it is. As ingroups fear higher rates of natural increase on the part of outgroups, they simultaneously aim for a gener-

---

131. My own survey results from Guyana and Trinidad in 1965 are similar. Compare Gabriel Almond and Sidney Verba, *The Civic Culture: Political Attitudes and Democracy in Five Nations* (Princeton: Princeton Univ. Press, 1963), 101–04.

37. Leonard Berkowitz, *Aggression: A Social Psychological Analysis* (New York: McGraw-Hill, 1962), 152; Gordon W. Allport, *The Nature of Prejudice* (Garden City, N.Y.: Anchor Books, 1958), 382; George Henry Weightman, "A Study of Prejudice in a Personalistic Society: An Analysis of an Attitude Survey of College Students—University of the Philippines," *Asian Studies* (Manila) 11 (Apr. 1964): 87–101, at 99.

38. See, e.g., Hudson, *The Precarious Republic*, 18, 34; Kearney, *Communalism and Language in the Politics of Ceylon*, 138; Walter Schwarz, *Nigeria* (New York: Praeger, 1968), 14.

39. See, e.g., Michael Poole, "The Demography of Violence," in John Darby, ed., *Northern Ireland: The Background to the Conflict* (Belfast: Appletree Press, 1983), 159.

ous count of ingroup members. The census is therefore no dreary demographic formality to be left to experts.[40]

Disputes over census results in ethnically divided societies are common. Nigeria had such disputes in 1962, 1963, and 1973, and in each case the question was whether the Hausa, Yoruba, or Ibo had been overcounted or undercounted. Kenya had such a dispute in 1981, when census results indicated that the Kikuyu population had increased by 50 percent in a decade, twice the Luo rate of growth. In Baluchistan, in Pakistan, Pathans complain that the Baluchi numbers are inflated. In Mauritania, results of the 1978 census were not published, and Kewri suggested that a Moor-dominated government was suppressing the news that the Kewri are now a majority. It comes as no surprise, then, that in Tanzania ethnic questions have been left off the census since 1978; that Kurdish demands for a new census in Iraq were ignored; that the Belgians cannot agree on how to phrase the ethnic question; and that the Lebanese, fearful that changed ethnic ratios would upset the quotas on which state institutions were founded, have conducted no census since 1932.

It is not merely what is asked and how the results are to be interpreted that counts. Individual answers are also manipulable, since there is an element of self-definition in ethnic affiliation. In one pre-independence census in India, the division of the Punjab into Muslim, Hindu, and Sikh states was at stake. The Hindu versus Sikh question was closely contested, with many Punjabi-speaking Hindus telling census enumerators that their language was really Hindi, so as to leave the Punjabi-speaking Sikhs in a minority and repel the demand for a separate state.[41] In Assam, Bengali Muslims had routinely declared Assamese to be their language, partly because it rendered them eligible for certain land rights reserved for indigenes. But then shifts in census responses produced small changes in the proportion of Bengali to Assamese speakers that in the early 1970s "aroused the anxieties of many Assamese"[42] and paved the way for their violent reaction to enlarged Bengali electoral rolls later in the decade.

40. See generally James F. Guyot, "Who Counts Depends on How You Count: The Political Consequences of Census Counting for Ethnic Minorities" (unpublished paper presented at the annual meeting of the Population Association of America, mimeo., n.d.).

41. See G. D. Khosla, A Taste of India (Bombay: Jaico, 1970), 144–49.

42. Myron Weiner, "The Political Demography of Assam's Anti-Immigrant Movement," Population and Development Review 9 (June 1983): 279–92, at 286. See also Charu Chandra Bhandari, Thoughts on Assam Disturbances (Rajghat, India: A. B. Sarva Seva Sangh Prakashan, 1961), 17.

The census shows nicely the capacity of ethnicity to stand ordinary processes on their head. In a severely divided society, we have seen that an election can become an ethnic head count. Now it is clear that a census needs to be "won." So the election is a census, and the census is an election.

THE ASYMMETRY OF GROUP CLAIMS

Group claims are not necessarily equal. Some groups seek domination, not the mere avoidance of it. Some seek to exclude others from the polity altogether, and some seek merely to be included on equal terms. If all groups merely wanted inclusion, distrust and anxiety would still make ethnic conflict serious, but more tractable than it is. What makes it intractable is that claims to political inclusion and exclusion have an area of mutual incompatibility.

Consider the Pushtuns (Pathans) of Afghanistan: "As a vigorous and aggressive people, they have felt that they are destined to rule and have never for a moment doubted the rightness of their occupancy of the pinnacles of power. They have not wanted to share power with other groups or to accommodate their soaring ambitions."[43] For inclusion, parity of power would be sufficient. To achieve the exclusion of others, however, confining them to parity is inadequate.

Ethnic conflict is often in the zero-sum category, but not always. Claims may not be perfectly incompatible. The claim to exclude need not be absolute; it may only be a claim to priority. Political claims can therefore be scaled, from equality to priority to exclusivity. Still, even priority can be gained only at the expense of political equality.

The asymmetry of the claims means that they are also relative. What is sought is not necessarily some absolute value but a value determined by the extent to which it reduces another group's share. Demands are often cast in relative terms, and conflict-reducing proposals that involve expanding the pool of goods available to all groups typically have little appeal.[44] Not "how many?" but "what fraction?"—that is the key ques-

43. Leon B. Poullada, "Afghanistan Searches for Unity" (unpublished paper presented at a Colloquium on Afghanistan, U.S. Department of State, Sept. 1973), 13.
44. See, e.g., *Far Eastern Economic Review*, July 11, 1980, p. 11, reporting a Malay leader's demand for controls on the economic progress of non-Malays. Proposals to expand the number of Malay university students simply by increasing the number of places were also opposed by Malay back-benchers on the ground that relative, not absolute, numbers counted. Interview, Kuala Lumpur, Feb. 29, 1968.

tion, just as it was for Tajfel's experimental subjects, who emphasized maximum intergroup differential more than maximum payoff alone. Just as relative group worth is at issue, so is relative group power. "Tell me who is rubbing his hands in glee," declares the Basque separatist Telesforo de Monzon, "and I'll tell you who should cry." Ethnic conflict is, at bottom, a matter of comparison.

The position of a group claim on the scale from equality to priority to exclusivity is not rigidly fixed, but contingent. Movement along the scale is possible and frequent. Demands first cast in terms of parity can ripen into demands for priority or exclusivity. That is the history of language demands in Sri Lanka, which rapidly moved from *Swabasha*, a claim for the recognition of both indigenous languages, Sinhala and Tamil, to Sinhala Only. This change went hand in hand with popular slogans like "Ceylon for the Sinhalese."[45] The growing narrowness of Sinhalese conceptions of nationalism through this century has been chronicled by Michael Roberts.[46] It is a process replicated in one severely divided society after another. But narrowness is not the only direction in which claims move. Largely as a function of political opportunities, constraints, and incentives, claims may soften as well as harden, as we shall see when we deal with party politics and military politics. Ethnic claims respond to the political market, which in democratic countries is heavily structured by the electoral process and elsewhere by the balance of force.

Nevertheless, ethnic exclusivism is quite common, and it takes a number of forms. As Sinhala Only implies, one form is to treat other ethnic groups (here, Tamils) as if they are not included in the political community. Another form is to seek their formal exclusion from the polity, by disfranchisement or some equivalent. Homogeneity is an exclusivist goal with a powerful appeal. In any struggle between two societies, "the victorious society as a rule fails to annihilate the vanquished society, but subjects it, assimilates it, imposes its own type of civilization upon it."[47] Mosca is of course referring to the conquest of one nation by another, but the statement is equally evocative of intrastate ethnic conflict between unranked groups, so much do the two types of conflict have in common.

Mosca concludes that "every social type"—he might have said every

45. Tarzie Vittachi, *Emergency '58: The Story of the Ceylon Race Riots* (London: André Deutsch, 1958), 33.
46. Roberts, "Ethnic Conflict in Sri Lanka and Sinhalese Perspectives: Barriers to Accommodation," *Modern Asian Studies* 12 (July 1978): 353–76.
47. Mosca, *The Ruling Class*, 29.

unranked ethnic group—"has a tendency to concentrate into a single political organism,"[48] to draw a territorial boundary around its conception of "the people" and to include only that people within it. As an ineluctable tendency to homogeneity, the proposition is doubtful, but a good many groups behave as if it were true. One fate, one state.

The means by which homogenization is attempted are various. Most Tamils of Indian origin in Sri Lanka (not the Ceylon Tamils) were deprived of their citizenship in 1949. The same aim was rejected for Chinese and Indians in Malaysia, but it has been accomplished elsewhere. Expulsion has been fairly widely practiced. In 1964, India and Sri Lanka agreed to "repatriate" hundreds of thousands of so-called Indian Tamils to India, which most of them had never seen. This was a more orderly exodus than was produced by the expulsion of Chinese from Vietnam, Bengalis from Burma, or Asians from Uganda. Subjugation is also frequently attempted. The Ahmadis of Pakistan were targets of a long campaign to stigmatize them as non-Muslims and to subject them to legal and social disabilities signifying subordination. Punctuated by violence, the campaign came to fruition in 1974, when the Pakistani parliament officially declared the Ahmadis to be non-Muslims.

Violence and expulsion are alternative ways to homogeneity, the two often operating in tandem. In the Ivory Coast riots against Dahomeyans and Togolese in 1958, some victims were offered the "choice" between departing the country and death.[49] Some Ahmadis were offered a comparable choice in 1953: conversion or death.[50] The role of the partition riots in India and Pakistan in homogenizing both sides of the Punjab, by slaughter and exodus, is well known. In Zaire, attacks by Lulua on Baluba in 1959 were preceded by assertions of Lulua control over the territory in which the city of Luluabourg is located. There were suggestions of disenfranchising the Baluba and of sending them back to their region of origin. When the Lulua did attack, perhaps a million Baluba fled homeward to South Kasai.[51]

Ethnic slogans adopted at the time of rioting make clear the common

48. Ibid., 103.

49. Gwendolen M. Carter, *Independence for Africa* (New York: Praeger, 1960), 113. See also Peter J. Wilson, *A Malay Village and Malaysia* (New Haven: HRAF Press, 1967), 50.

50. Government of Punjab, *Report of the Court of Inquiry Constituted Under Punjab Act II of 1954 to Enquire into the Punjab Disturbances of 1953* (Lahore: Government Printer, 1954), 3–4, 140.

51. Thomas Turner, "Congo-Kinshasa," in Olorunsola, ed., *The Politics of Cultural Sub-Nationalism in Africa*, 222–23.

connection between violence and efforts at expulsion. When Bengalis resisted the imposition of Assamese as the sole language of state government, extensive violence was perpetrated against them, and a movement gained ground to expel them from the state. *Bongal Kheda*—"Drive the Bengalis out"—was the motto of the movement.[52] "Get rid of the Mossi" (Ivory Coast, 1969), "upcountry people to their home areas" (Kenya, 1962), "Muslims Quit India" (Ahmedabad, 1969), "Fiji for the Fijians"—these are some of the many slogans of ethnic exclusion, most of them linked to episodes of violence.[53]

Short of eliminating ethnic diversity in the physical sense, exclusionary groups seek to impose a homogeneous identity on the state and to compel acknowledgment of their preeminence in it. It is as if a part claimed to be the whole. Members of other groups are relegated to the status of "guests"—a term frequently heard—with the implication that the rules of the "household" are to be laid down by the "host." Before the violence of 1959, Lulua demanded that Baluba recognize their primacy and submit to their political authority or else return "home."[54] Guest status and an idiom appropriate to it are particularly common where the guests can be placed in the category of international or interregional migrants, no matter how far removed in time the migration occurred.

Acknowledgment of preeminence implies destruction of the evidence of diversity, a particularly appealing course when the diversity is associated with invidious comparison. When, for example, the Bengali population of Assam was enlarged by an influx of refugees from East Bengal upon the partition of India, Assamese leaders declared it their wish "that the outsiders living in our state should identify themselves with the indigenous people. They may live among us as we do."[55] Assamese were deeply resentful of Bengali-medium schools, and were on occasion wont to object to the use of the Bengali language in public places, such as

---

52. K. C. Chakravarti, "Bongal Kheda Again," *Economic Weekly* (Bombay), July 30, 1960, pp. 1193–95.

53. Efrem Sigel, "Ivory Coast: Booming Economy, Political Calm," *Africa Report*, Apr. 1970, pp. 18–21; Richard Stren, "Factional Politics and Central Control in Mombasa, 1960–1969," *Canadian Journal of African Studies* 4 (Winter 1970): 33–56, at 40; Ghanshayam Shah, "Communal Riots in Gujarat," *Economic and Political Weekly* (Bombay), Jan. 1970, pp. 187–200; R. S. Milne, *Politics in Ethnically Bipolar States* (Vancouver: Univ. of British Columbia Press, 1981), 72.

54. Jules Chomé, *Le Drame de Luluabourg*, 3d ed. (Brussels: Editions de Remarques Congolaises, 1960), 23.

55. Ambikagiri Ray Choudhury, quoted in the *Assam Tribune* (Gauhati), July 17, 1950.

buses, and in times of tension to force Bengali women to wear only Assamese dress.[56] The model of appropriate Bengali behavior that was held up was nothing short of abandonment of Bengali identity. Where exclusionary groups form only a minority in urban areas, a common complaint is that the cities seem to the eye, ear, and nose to be "centers of alien life."[57]

The desire to extirpate diversity seems greatest in states that are among the most heterogeneous. Few unranked groups view the freedom from uncomfortable entanglement with ethnic strangers without a certain longing. Policies of homogenization are commonly portrayed as part of an attempt to restore a homogeneous *status quo ante*. Some groups actually were separate societies. But many groups seeking "restoration" of homogeneity have not had a homogeneous past. Some groups were in constant contact with ethnic strangers, for ethnic heterogeneity is by no means solely a modern phenomenon,[58] and others, of course, had no long-standing, previous corporate existence. It is notable that some fairly recent or loosely bonded amalgams—Sinhalese, Assamese, Malays, Kikuyu—are among the most exclusivist, often the most preoccupied with the fate of their "nation." The maintenance of boundaries viewed as precarious may impel groups to assume exclusive postures.

If claims are asymmetrical, it follows that exclusivism produces a reaction among those to be excluded. Typically, however, exclusivist groups are politically strong; otherwise the claim would not be plausible. Accordingly, the reaction to exclusivist claims must be framed rather carefully. An Aesopian rhetoric of exclusion and inclusion develops. Even in two countries as far apart as Algeria and Malaysia, the themes of this rhetoric are demonstrably similar.

As the anti-colonial movement grew in Algeria during the 1940s, two slogans—and two visions—contended. One was *"l'Algérie arabo-musulmane,"* an Arab Algeria that took no account of the Berbers. The other was *"l'Algérie algérienne"*—literally, an Algerian Algeria.[59] Trans-

56. Bhandari, *Thoughts on Assam Disturbances*, 20–23, 36.

57. Weiner, "The Political Demography of Assam's Anti-Immigrant Movement," 286. See Government of Uganda, *Report of the Committee on Africanisation of Commerce and Industry in Uganda* (Entebbe: Government Printer, 1968), 3.

58. See I. Schapera, *Government and Politics in Tribal Societies* (New York: Schocken Books, 1967), 19, 198–99.

59. H. J. R. Roberts, "The Economics of Berberism: The National Basis of the Kabyle Question in Contemporary Algeria," *Government and Opposition* 18 (Spring 1983): 218–35, at 227.

lated, this means an Algeria not limited to Arabs and therefore one inclusive of Berbers. With the growth of ethnic conflict again in the 1970s and '80s, triggered by a new Arabic language policy, Kabyle Berbers have demanded linguistic parity, and the slogan "Algerian Algeria" has been heard again in the Kabylia.[60]

Around the time of Malaysian independence, citizenship for the non-Malays had to be negotiated, and out of the bargain the Malays gained recognition of their "special position," modified by the "legitimate interests" of the Chinese and Indians. When Singapore was incorporated in Malaysia in 1963, Lee Kuan Yew, chief minister of Singapore, entered Malaysian politics, adopting as his slogan "A Malaysian Malaysia." The slogan proved explosive, for it implied, as it was intended to imply, to the Chinese and Indians that the Malaysia they lived in was becoming an exclusively "Malay Malaysia."

In each case, a turn toward what was perceived as exclusivism was met by an innocuous-sounding and therefore lawfully expressed demand, not for separatism, but for political inclusion on equal terms. Despite the different setting, the demand sounds the same and has the same power to attract adherents. "Algerian Algeria" and "Malaysian Malaysia" are magnetic appeals for equality of treatment. The asymmetry of group claims means precisely that demands for priority confront demands for parity.

GROUP LEGITIMACY:
THE BASIS OF ETHNIC CLAIMS

Ethnic claims to priority or exclusion are supported by appeals to moral principles. The principles are invoked to justify departures from strict equality. The moral basis of ethnic claims lies in group legitimacy within a territory. Legitimacy is asserted to be distributed unevenly among ethnic groups.

To understand the concept of group legitimacy, it is necessary to link it to ownership. Legitimacy goes to one's rightful place in the country. To be legitimate is therefore to be identified with the territory. Georg Simmel shrewdly notes that the ethnic stranger is "no 'owner of the soil'—soil not only in the physical but also in the figurative sense of a life-substance which is fixed, if not in a point in space, at least at an ideal

60. Hugh Roberts, "Towards an Understanding of the Kabyle Question in Contemporary Algeria," *Maghreb Review* 5 (Sept.–Dec. 1980): 115–24, at 123.

point of the social environment."[61] As patrimony confronts equality, group legitimacy provides a foundation for the recurrent psychological denial that another group owns an equal share in the land.[62]

THE FOUNDATIONS OF GROUP LEGITIMACY

As there are several ways to acquire ownership of property, so there are several sources of legitimacy. I may acquire property and the right to exclude others from it because I inherited it, or because I purchased or squatted on it, or because I built it from scratch by my toil, or because I annexed it to adjacent property that I own. If the property is really mine, then the claim of another to the same property is nothing more than theft. Access to enjoyment of the property will be granted or withheld on my terms. The same applies to ownership of the country.

Prior Occupation

By far the most common claim to legitimacy is predicated on indigenousness. Among groups that regard themselves as indigenous *vis-à-vis* ethnic strangers are the Malays, the Sinhalese, the Assamese, the Fijians, the Muslims of Southern Thailand, the Kannadigas of Karnataka state in India, the Lepchas of Sikkim, and the Bakonjo and Baamba of Western Uganda. Indigenousness is an exclusive principle asserted in cities as well as in regions and states. In Jos, Northern Nigeria, the Birom claim to be indigenous; in Calabar, in Eastern Nigeria, the Efik do; in Kinshasa, in Zaire, the Bakongo claim indigenousness; in Luluabourg, the Lulua do; and in Lumumbashi, the Lunda do.

Indigenousness has some clear-cut consequences. To be indigenous means to "own the country,"[63] and to own it even if, as in Sikkim, the indigenous Lepchas and Bhutias comprise a small minority of the population, compared to the Nepalese, who constitute 70 percent.[64] Indigenousness may justify special electoral arrangements to perpetuate or inflate the power of the indigenes, in Fiji and Sikkim for example, and it typically produces claims to reserve employment, restrain the alienation of land, and in other ways secure for "the local people a pride of place in

---

61. Simmel, *The Sociology of Georg Simmel*, trans. Kurt H. Wolff (Glencoe: Free Press, 1950), 404.

62. Vamik D. Volkan, *Cyprus—War and Adaptation: A Psychoanalytic History of Two Ethnic Groups in Conflict* (Charlottesville: Univ. Press of Virginia, 1979), 11.

63. Astri Suhrke, "The Muslims in Southern Thailand: An Analysis of Political Developments, 1968–78" (unpublished paper, Washington, D.C., Dec. 1978), 1.

64. *Far Eastern Economic Review*, July 11, 1980, pp. 30–32.

their own land."[65] To be indigenous, however, does not always mean literally to have arrived first, and to be immigrant does not mean to have arrived last or even recently. This is not a matter of the actual history of migration but of ideas about migration. In Sri Lanka and Malaysia, the Veddas and the Orang Asli are aboriginal peoples whose arrivals long antedate those of the Sinhalese and the Malays, respectively. By the same token, a good many Chinese can trace their roots in Malaysia much further back than the roots of fairly recent Indonesian immigrants who are assimilated to the Malay identity. The Ceylon Tamils, who arrived, on average, perhaps a thousand years ago, can hardly be regarded as immigrants, even though the Sinhalese arrived, on average, earlier. Nepalese are discriminated against in Sikkim, although they arrived in the eighteenth and nineteenth centuries.

Similar ambiguities surround the concept of the locality and how precisely it is to be located. In Durban, South Africa, there was an influx of Africans, who settled on Indian-owned land after World War II. The African "was the newcomer, but he regarded himself as the son of the soil and the Indian as the interloper,"[66] because Durban alone was not viewed as the relevant field. A comparable difference in perspective affected Zanzibar. Arabs believed it to be an Arab country. Mainland African migrants saw Zanzibar as part of Africa, the Arabs as "immigrants," and themselves as "sons of the soil."[67] Geography is as important as history in producing claims to indigenousness. Political space is not a fixed concept.

Despite the doubtful quality of many claims to indigenousness, relative time of arrival is a common basis of distinctions among people, but it does not always foster exclusivism. In a small New England town studied in the 1930s, "Yankees" (Protestant descendants of the original settlers) were identified as the "Charter Group." They had a sense of proprietorship and superiority, and descendants of immigrants tended to acknowledge their pride of place, so that the claim was mildly asserted and met with some deference.[68] That is not the way indigenousness is

65. "Appeal [by] Shiv Sena Loksabha Candidate [Manohar Joshi]," election handbill, Bombay, 1971. On indigenousness and demands for reserved employment in Karnataka, see *Indian Express* (Bombay), Apr. 21, 1980.

66. Union of South Africa, *Report of the Commission of Enquiry into Riots in Durban* (Cape Town: Cape Times, 1949), 13.

67. Michael F. Lofchie, *Zanzibar: Background to Revolution* (Princeton: Princeton Univ. Press, 1965), 128–29, 166, 168.

68. Elin Anderson, *We Americans* (Cambridge: Harvard Univ. Press, 1937), 21–24.

played out in severely divided societies, where it accentuates the gulf between groups. In such societies, the association of people with places is utilized to create myths of occupation, thereby limiting recognition of the perennial, worldwide movement of peoples.

It is not, then, an objective question of who actually came first, or who is acknowledged to have come first, that governs the strength of claims to indigenousness. Rather, it is the political context of such claims and the uses to which they can be put that matter.

Special Mission

Equally identified with the soil are those groups that believe they have a special mission to perform in the territory. Typically, that mission has a religious character. Maronites see Lebanon as the home of Maronite Christianity, as Amhara see Ethiopia as the home of "the only authentic Christians in the world,"[69] Coptic Christians. Sinhalese regard Sri Lanka as "the island destined to preserve and propagate the Buddha's doctrine."[70] The Sinhalese arrival in Sri Lanka is said to have coincided with the death of the Buddha, so the destinies of the Sinhalese and Buddhism are interwoven. In addition, Sri Lanka is the only home the Sinhalese have, whereas Tamils also have a homeland in India. Unique identification with the land can thus relate to the mission of preserving a home for the people as well as for the faith. Either way, it has exclusivist overtones. Tamils appear in Sinhalese mythology as a challenge to Buddhists and to the Sinhalese people. "If the Tamils get hold of the country, the Sinhalese will have to jump into the sea," apprehends a Buddhist monk, graphically uniting the theme of the single homeland with the fear of extinction.[71] Amhara, Maronites, and Sinhalese have all insisted on at least preeminence in the state.

Traditional Rule

Several groups have made claims to preeminence that originate in earlier domination. The Sikhs once controlled much of Northwestern India and parts of Pakistan, fighting first the Moghuls and then the British. The declaration of the tenth Sikh Guru, Gobind Singh, "The *Khalsa* [Sikh

69. Donald N. Levine, "Ethiopia: Identity, Authority, and Realism," in Lucian W. Pye and Sidney Verba, eds., *Political Culture and Political Development* (Princeton: Princeton Univ. Press, 1965), 254.

70. Kearney, *Communalism and Language in the Politics of Ceylon*, 41.

71. Quoted in Roberts, "Ethnic Conflict in Sri Lanka and Sinhalese Perspectives," 367.

community] shall rule," evokes an earlier glory.[72] Maharashtrians equally look back to the great Maratha empire with a nostalgia that informs contemporary claims.[73] Pathans seized the Afghan throne early on and held it thereafter. Moors in Mauritania have a long-standing claim to the Senegal River valley inhabited by Kewri, black Africans whom the Moors consider "people under their suzerainty."[74] Several West African groups had aspirations to conquest, some thwarted by the arrival of Europeans. The Fang were conquerors of large parts of Equatorial Africa, and a Hausa-Fulani march southward in Nigeria was interrupted by the British. Such historical movements color politics at and after independence. "If the British had not come," said an Ashanti weaver in Ghana, "the Ashanti would have taken over the whole country."[75] Influential Northern Nigerians, including the Sardauna of Sokoto and the first prime minister of Nigeria, spoke openly of the possibility of continuing the "interrupted conquest to the sea."[76] All such memories constitute dimly or not-so-dimly felt pretensions to dominion that are difficult to reconcile with the claims of other groups to equality. Acting on the basis of such memories, however, is not at all the same as pursuing traditional enmities, particularly since historical and contemporary antagonists are so often not the same group.

The Right to Succeed the Colonial Power

Prior occupation, special mission, and traditional rule all relate to precolonial history. The right to succeed the Europeans, on the other hand, is a prerogative grounded in events of the colonial period itself.

Acculturation and close relations with the colonizers can produce pretensions to fill their shoes. The Baganda are a group favored by the British from an early date. Buganda had a special status deriving from treaty, and Baganda were employed in the administration of other areas.

72. Baldev Raj Nayar, "Sikh Separatism in the Punjab," in Donald Eugene Smith, ed., *South Asian Politics and Religion* (Princeton: Princeton Univ. Press, 1966), 156–57; Khushwant Singh, "Sikh, Singh, Sardarji," in Rahul Singh, ed., *Khushwant Singh's India* (Bombay: IBH, 1969), 140.
73. See Mary Fainsod Katzenstein, *Ethnicity and Equality: The Shiv Sena Party and Preferential Policies in Bombay* (Ithaca: Cornell Univ. Press, 1979).
74. Alfred G. Gerteiny, *Mauritania* (New York: Praeger, 1967), 117, 152.
75. Quoted in Maxwell Owusu, "Politics in Swedru," in Dennis Austin and Robin Luckham, eds., *Politicians and Soldiers in Ghana, 1966–1972* (London: Frank Cass, 1975), 259.
76. Tafewa Balewa, quoted in Richard L. Sklar, *Nigerian Political Parties: Power in an Emergent Nation* (Princeton: Princeton Univ. Press, 1963), 98 n.25.

At independence, the Baganda, who clearly felt superior to others as a result of their historical relationship with the British and their strong educational position,[77] obtained some short-lived special privileges for Buganda as well as the position of head of state for their traditional ruler.[78] But they were forced to abandon their claim to primacy in the country as a whole.[79]

Creoles in Guyana and Trinidad did advance such a claim, but its roots were more complex. Like the Baganda, the Creoles were acculturated and "Westernized." Descendants of emancipated African slaves whose place on the sugar estates was taken by indentured East Indians, Creoles felt that they had priority by virtue of their much earlier arrival. In addition, Indians continued to return to India well into the twentieth century, thereby solidifying the contrast between putatively "permanent" Creoles and "transient" Indians. So there is an element of prior occupation as well as prior and more complete adoption of British culture. Beyond this, however, when government positions were opened up to non-whites, Creoles qualified and functioned in government offices for decades before Indians were seen in them. And when local elections came to Guyana early in the century, Creoles but not Indians were in the electorate. Finally, emancipation was to be a genuine and permanent liberation. Its logical fruition was a hold on political power upon the departure of the British more than a century later. That hold was threatened by the entry of the Indians into mass politics.[80]

To sense the complexity of the Creole claim—a claim far more often felt than articulated publicly—is to see why pretensions to succeed the colonialists on grounds of acculturation or historical relationship are not very common. It appears more reasonable to all participants for a group to claim legitimacy on grounds that, first, antedate the colonial arrival and, second, establish a connection with the soil rather than with departed and no longer legitimate rulers.

77. See Klineberg and Zavalloni, *Nationalism and Tribalism Among African Students*, 94.

78. May Edel, "African Tribalism: Some Reflections on Uganda," *Political Science Quarterly* 80 (Sept. 1965): 357–72; James C. Akins, "Problems of Federalism in Uganda," *Public Policy* 13 (1964): 369–94.

79. Audrey I. Richards, *The Multicultural States of East Africa* (Montreal: McGill-Queen's Univ. Press, 1969), 48–50.

80. For distinctions between Creoles and Indians along these several lines, see J. N. Brierley, *Trinidad: Then and Now* (Port-of-Spain: Franklin's Electric Printery, 1912), 294; *The Creole* (Georgetown, British Guiana), Jan. 10, 1873; *Memorandum Prepared by the Elected Members of the Combined Court of British Guiana in Reply to the Report of the British Guiana Commission* (Cmnd. 3047; London: H.M.S.O., 1928), 39–41.

Prominence in the Anti-Colonial Movement

Groups that played a leading role in gaining independence—such as the Bemba in Zambia, the Bakongo in Congo (Brazzaville), and the Ibo—have occasionally asserted a right to preeminence as a matter of just desert. And the other way round: compared to groups that held back or sought colonial protection, the claim seems all the more justified. Hindu extremists in India have said that the Muslims' "contribution in the fight for national emancipation has not been creditable."[81] Bemba have "argued that they were the people who had fought hardest against colonialism. . . . At that time, what were the Lozi doing?"[82] Merely squabbling among themselves. When Bemba power was reduced in the 1970s, the complaint was often heard that those who did the most for the country were not being rewarded adequately.

More often than not, such claims were muted, and they dissipated with time. The ideology of independence made it hard to assert that it was acceptable to reward some groups disproportionately, absent some other special basis of group legitimacy. An exception, however, is the case of groups that actually fought for independence. The Burmans and the Kikuyu clearly inferred from their struggle that a special place was due them.[83] These claims have ripened over time—in the first case because most other groups joined armed insurrections against the new state soon after independence, leaving the Burmans in charge, and in the second because the actual struggle, with its suffering and its secret oaths, left the Kikuyu "with a sense of identity so much stronger that it would be difficult to subordinate to a larger nationalism."[84] That difficulty remains.

COLONIAL RECOGNITION
OF GROUP LEGITIMACY

This brief survey of the foundations of group legitimacy makes clear that some principles of ethnic legitimacy are stronger than others. The claim to primacy by dint of indigenousness is both widespread and powerful;

81. Quoted in Harold A. Gould, "Religion and Politics in a U.P. Constituency," in Donald Eugene Smith, ed., *South Asian Politics and Religion* (Princeton: Princeton Univ. Press, 1966), 60.
82. Richard Hall, *The High Price of Principles: Kaunda and the White South* (New York: Africana, 1970), 199.
83. Tinker, *The Union of Burma*; Carl G. Rosberg, Jr., and John Nottingham, *The Myth of "Mau Mau": Nationalism in Kenya* (New York: Praeger, 1966), chap. 7.
84. Cherry Gertzel, *The Politics of Independent Kenya, 1963–8* (Evanston: Northwestern Univ. Press, 1970), 16.

the term "sons of the soil" is used in a great many countries of Asia and
Africa. Special historical mission is less frequent but an important motive force where it exists. Historical claims and aspirations to rule the
territory, and claims deriving from association with or struggle against
the colonial power, are usually not quite as strong. In general, the closer
the identification of the group with the soil, the more powerful the
pretension.

One reason lies in the colonial tendency to recognize the legitimacy of
those with close ties to the land. The Malays, the Sikhs, the Maronites,
the Zanzibar Arabs, and the Mauritanian Moors were all confirmed in
their sense of priority by action the British or French took. Recognition
of the "special position" of indigenous groups in the face of large immigrant populations was a manifestation of colonial readiness to temper
their approval of advanced groups. Chinese in Malaysia, Indonesia, and
Burma, Indians in Sri Lanka, Fiji, Malaysia, and Burma were all regarded as people whose real home was somewhere else and who could
not justly claim parity of status with those who occupied the country
before the arrival of immigrants.[85] Security had something to do with
this. By such recognition, a group opposed to immigration was given
offsetting priority that made the influx of foreigners bearable. A good
many backward groups, confronted with immigrants, achieved some
recognition of their pride of place in spite of perceived deficiencies in
group virtues and aptitudes. The implication of colonial policy was that
the immigrants, though somehow more fit for the evolving competitive
life of the country, did not quite belong.

Conceptions of primacy recognized by the Europeans were well entrenched and were not discredited by the colonial departure. After independence, there was frequently sentiment that the importation of immigrants by the colonialists was an illegitimate act, an historical error
committed during the "slumber" of the indigenes. Ironically enough,
this sentiment was fed by earlier colonial recognition of the legitimacy of
the indigenous groups, but the obsolete character of that recognition
hardly mattered. Periodically, demands were made for the deportation
of immigrant groups to homelands they had never seen. As we have
observed in Chapter 1 and again in this chapter, expulsion and repatria-

85. See, e.g., Frank Swettenham, *British Malaya*, rev. ed. (London: Allen & Unwin,
1948), 342; F. J. West, "Problems of Political Advancement in Fiji," *Pacific Affairs* 33
(Mar. 1960): 23–37.

tion have been carried out in many countries, with aggregate effects on millions of people.

Colonial rule had an equally confirmatory effect on claims to control regions and localities. As district boundaries were commonly drawn to coincide with ethnic boundaries, groups that controlled a district under the practice of indirect rule were given authority over ethnic strangers who had migrated there. One of the benefits local authorities controlled was the distribution of land, for colonial administrators generally believed that permanent rights to land were traditionally controlled by groups indigenous to an area.[86] Apart from heightening the divergence of interest between indigenous and migrant groups, the result of their policies was to recognize the political legitimacy of the indigenes. This practice, too, had enduring effects.

THE POLITICAL CONSEQUENCES OF DIFFERENTIAL LEGITIMACY

A pretension to legitimacy can have a number of consequences for the group asserting it and the group responding to it. The structure of political claims and counterclaims is heavily conditioned by the strength and degree of acknowledgment of group legitimacy.

Indigenes and Immigrants: Legitimacy and Alienage

A group that asserts legitimacy by virtue of prior arrival is likely to entertain vestigial perceptions of the foreign ties of the "immigrant" group. Generations after the Chinese settled in Malaysia, some Malays are wont to say that Chinese tend to be loyal to China, a country to which most Chinese no longer have links. Fijians continue to speak of the prospect of deporting Indians to India. Creoles in Guyana and Trinidad sometimes express the belief that Indians have enduring attachments to India. This, despite the facts that, in both Guyana and Trinidad, nearly 100 percent of the population was locally born, that Indians were as frequently born locally as were Creoles, and that in response to a survey

86. Kasfir, "Cultural Sub-Nationalism in Uganda," 70–72; Philip J. Foster, "Ethnicity and the Schools in Ghana," *Comparative Education Review* 6 (Oct. 1962): 127–35, at 129; Paul Mercier, "On the Meaning of 'Tribalism' in Black Africa," in Pierre L. van den Berghe, ed., *Africa: Social Problems of Change and Conflict* (San Francisco: Chandler, 1965), 493; Robert H. Bates, "Ethnic Competition and Modernization in Contemporary Africa," *Comparative Political Studies* 6 (Jan. 1974): 457–84, at 465–66.

question about whether "things would be better" in another country, only small minorities of both Indians and Creoles believed they would.[87]

Cross-national survey data also suggest that external ethnic affinities are more likely to be perceived by outgroup members than by ingroup members.[88] The extreme lengths to which such perceptions can proceed is illustrated by occasional comments on the part of Sinhalese that Ceylon Tamils are really Indians. Speaking of a then-recent period of ethnic tension, a columnist wrote that "a dangerous communal atmosphere was created and permanently sustained in which every Tamil, even if his ancestor had come to the island one to two thousand years ago, was made to feel that he was just another *kallathoni*."[89] A *kallathoni* is an illegal Indian immigrant to Sri Lanka.

If an "immigrant" group undergoes a cultural revival, the revival may have the effect of reinforcing perceptions of alienage. This is so even when the revival is triggered by the impending loss of the cultural heritage through long residence in the adopted country and lack of contact with the ancestral homeland. The contrived and often inaccurate character of the revived culture matters less than the fact that what is now emphasized seems alien. When, for example, Indians in Guyana, Trinidad, and Mauritius undertook to resuscitate abandoned practices, construct mosques and temples, and begin religious education of their children, all of these efforts took place against a background of cultural change that had brought Indian beliefs into substantial conformity with the prevailing Creole cultural pattern.[90] The principal significance of these religious movements was to assert that Indians no longer felt the need to abandon Indian culture in order to become full-fledged participants in their society and polity. But, paradoxically, by making such a statement, Indians conveyed the quite erroneous impression that their ties to India were still strong.

For an indigenous group to entertain vestigial perceptions of the alienage of another group is rewarding in the political and moral senses. If "we" arrived here first *and*, in addition, "they" have not yet severed their

87. Survey data from 1965, on file with the author.
88. Klineberg and Zavalloni, *Nationalism and Tribalism Among African Students*, 70–76.
89. *Ceylon Daily News* (Colombo), May 15, 1970.
90. Chandra Jayawardena, "Religious Belief and Social Change: Aspects of the Development of Hinduism in British Guiana," *Comparative Studies in Society and History* 8 (Jan. 1966): 211–40, at 223; Daniel J. Crowley, "Cultural Assimilation in a Multi-racial Society," *Annals of the New York Academy of Sciences* 83 (Jan. 20, 1960): 850–54; Simmons, *Politics in Mauritius Since 1934*, 212–19.

loyalty to another country, then it may not be wrong to discriminate on this basis, for aliens must have lesser rights than those who are native to the soil and single-mindedly loyal to its institutions. Comparable justifications for exclusivist practices on behalf of groups that struggled for independence can easily be imagined.

Legitimacy and Moderation

A group claiming priority may feel more or less strongly about the claim. The Malay claim to legitimacy by virtue of indigenousness is far more strongly felt than the claims of the Creoles in Guyana and Trinidad. Unlike the Malay claim, the Creole claims were not recognized by the colonial power—the British went out of their way to refuse such recognition—and the time of arrival of Creoles and Indians in the territory was not so far apart. By the same token, the Sinhalese claim was not recognized by the British, and the Ceylon Tamils arrived much earlier than the Malaysian Chinese, making Sinhalese son-of-the-soil claims less plausible.

On the other side of the equation, I indicated in Chapter 3 that for a long time Malaysian Chinese conceded the priority of Malay claims. This served to restrict conflict. For example, when the British proposed to alter the structure of government in late-colonial Malaya, in a direction disadvantageous to the Malays, a storm of Malay protest arose; later, when the British revised their plans in a direction unfavorable to the Chinese and Indians, protest was much milder. If the pretension to legitimacy is acknowledged by other groups, the latter are likely to pursue moderate strategies. Indians in Fiji, although a majority, have generally acquiesced in a variety of measures that operate to their political disadvantage. The same has been true of Bengalis in Assam, aware as they are of their immigrant status: "a mother [namely, Bengal] who has begotten too many children and is not in a position to accommodate and rear them all in her own house and has to depend upon her neighbors to accommodate and bring them up should have humility in all respects in dealing with them."[91] (The statement, of course, is notable not merely for its depiction of guest status but for its familial allusions.) Moderation of this sort limits the assertion of ethnic claims to full equality.

Acknowledged legitimacy is not the only basis for the moderation of group demands. Economic interests that can be advanced by political

91. Bhandari, *Thoughts on Assam Disturbances,* 42.

concessions promote moderate strategies, as the behavior of many trading minorities attests. A propensity to moderation is also visible among groups that are demonstrably weak, in numbers, organization, or representation in the instrumentalities of state force. But relative group legitimacy is still a powerful influence, as a comparison of Chinese behavior in Malaysia with Indian Tamil and Ceylon Tamil behavior in Sri Lanka shows. The Malaysian Chinese have been fairly moderate. The Indian Tamils, historically isolated on Sri Lankan tea estates, have a less pronounced sense of their rightful place in Sri Lanka, and their disfranchisement in 1949 met only with "muted protest."[92] The Ceylon Tamils, however, have been far less tolerant of discrimination against them than either the Malaysian Chinese or the Indian Tamils have been. Since the Ceylon Tamils did not arrive a mere century ago, they do not accord the Sinhalese any claim to indigenousness. The other prong of the Sinhalese claim—the special mission to provide a home for Buddhism—has no influence whatever on the predominantly Hindu Tamils, so on neither count is there acknowledged priority.

Indeed, on the latter point, special religious mission is generally unlike indigenousness. Whereas prior arrival may command acknowledgment on the part of fairly recent immigrant groups, especially if a group's indigenousness was recognized by the colonial power, special religious mission is unlikely to have any moral force across the lines of ethnic groups not sharing the religious persuasion. The guest idea is different, based as it is on a universal and familiar principle. As a Batak leader, initiating new migrants to West Java, the Sundanese homeland, counseled: "we must adapt to their standards. . . . After all, we Batak are émigrés in an alien land . . . ."[93] Of all the foundations of legitimacy, prior occupation is most likely to compel respect across group lines.

If the acknowledgment of legitimacy is conducive to moderation on the part of other groups, it is also true that legitimate groups threatened with a loss of power are often given to extreme strategies. Creoles in Guyana resorted to violence in 1962, so unnatural did they find their exclusion. Sikh claims in the Punjab are immoderate largely because of pretensions to legitimacy. When new electoral rolls in Assam made it appear that Assamese might be outnumbered by Bengalis, Assamese

92. S. Arasaratnam, "Nationalism," in Philip Mason, ed., *India and Ceylon: Unity and Diversity* (London: Oxford Univ. Press, 1967), 262.

93. Quoted in Edward M. Bruner, *The Expression of Ethnicity in Indonesia* (New York: The Asia Society, SEADAG Papers, mimeo., 1972), 15.

embarked on an anti-Bengali campaign lasting several years, costing thousands of lives, and producing more than 280,000 refugees.[94] Malays, Sinhalese, Fijians, Kikuyu, and Mauritanian Moors are among the other groups that have reacted with great sensitivity to relatively mild threats to their political position. In each case, it continues to be unthinkable that these groups should be anywhere other than at the center of power, and the reason is their strong claim to legitimacy.

If there are several bases of legitimacy, it follows that one group may claim priority on one ground, another on another ground. Where claims based on history and geography clash, as they did in Zanzibar, moderation will be in short supply. And virtually everywhere an alternative claim, albeit not a claim to priority, lurks fairly close to the surface: the claim symbolized by "Malaysian Malaysia" and "Algerian Algeria," the claim contesting the right of the indigenous Birom to control the town of Jos when the Ibo introduced "the Western and alien concept that any part of Nigeria belongs to *all* its people,"[95] the claim, in short, that equality precludes priority for any group.

GROUP LEGITIMACY AND GROUP WORTH

The contest for group worth and the contest for group legitimacy are not wholly separate: as I have said, the two join together in a politics of entitlement. A claim to group legitimacy may be put forward by either a backward or an advanced group. The Bemba, Kikuyu, and Maronites are all advanced groups claiming legitimacy. Where, however, backward groups put forward such claims, they are often very strongly articulated and disproportionately predicated on indigenousness. The reason is straightforward. Where there is a split between indigenous and immigrant groups, it tends to coincide with the split between backward and advanced groups. Backward-indigenous groups "feel under siege in their own home,"[96] a powerful feeling that often calls up determined and violent political activity. Where backwardness and indigenousness conjoin, the configuration of political claims and responses is predictable.

First, there is likely to be a demand for preferences in education, employment, or business, justified alternately on both grounds. An indigenous group deserves preferential treatment if it is backward, for

94. Weiner, "The Political Demography of Assam's Anti-Immigrant Movement."
95. Leonard Plotnicov, "Who Owns Jos? Ethnic Ideology in Nigerian Urban Politics," *Urban Anthropology* 1 (Spring 1972): 1–13, at 11 (emphasis in the original).
96. B. G. Verghese et al., *Situation in Assam: Report of a Study Team* (New Delhi: Gandhi Peace Foundation, mimeo., 1980), 16–17.

otherwise the "sons of the soil," at the mercy of immigrants who prefer their own people, will be "dispossessed in their own country."[97] The refrain is similar from Fiji to Maharashtra, to the Ivory Coast, to Malaysia, to Assam, to various regions and localities in Nigeria and in Zaire.

Second, the same is true for political exclusion. Indigenous, backward groups argue that to confer power on equal terms on advanced, immigrant groups is to risk leaving the sons of the soil, already "behind" in the modern sector of the economy, with nothing at all.

Third, just as legitimate groups out of power behave immoderately, so do backward groups out of power. The violent Northern Nigerian response to what looked like an Ibo exclusivist government in May 1966 is one example; the violent response of Northerners in Benin to the prospect of Southern-dominated governments is another.[98] Groups claiming to be both legitimate and backward will be doubly immoderate if they face the prospect of exclusion from power.

Fourth, backward groups sometimes entertain an almost revolutionary bitterness about the past and the hand it dealt them. They tend to lament what they see as historical errors committed during their "slumber." The Sardauna of Sokoto, a powerful leader of the Hausa-Fulani, publicly regretted the unification of Northern and Southern Nigeria under the British, and he held unification responsible for the predicament of his people.[99] The major historical error emphasized by backward, indigenous groups is the decision to permit the earlier immigration. Many Malay intellectuals have viewed large-scale Chinese and Indian immigration into colonial Malaya as part of a British policy that undermined the cultural, artistic, entrepreneurial, and technological development of the Malays.[100] The Sinhalese have regarded Indian immigration as a mistake to be rectified, even generations later, by repatriation. Where repatriation is not possible, the legitimacy of thinking about it taints the reception accorded the claims of advanced, immigrant groups to equal treatment almost before they are made. In the eyes of indigenes, it is an act of grace that they are permitted to remain at all.

Fifth, the response of advanced, immigrant groups to exclusivist de-

97. Milne, *Politics in Ethnically Bipolar States* (manuscript version), chap. 7, p. 37.
98. See Ronen, *Dahomey*, 196.
99. Richard L. Sklar and C. S. Whitaker, Jr., "Nigeria," in Gwendolen M. Carter, ed., *National Unity and Regionalism in Eight African States* (Ithaca: Cornell Univ. Press, 1966), 47.
100. Mahathir bin Mohamad, *The Malay Dilemma* (Singapore: Donald Moore, 1970), 25–27.

mands and policies is also based on two grounds. The first, the universal principle of equality, we have already encountered. The second is an argument that the group "has earned the right to enjoy equal status,"[101] because its hard work and its skill have built the country; without immigrants, there would be nothing for the indigenes to claim possession of. Immigrants whose function was central to economic development of the territory are especially likely to focus on this ground of group desert.

The grounds that support exclusion and inclusion, respectively, are mutually reinforcing and invoked alternately for quite specific reasons. Indigenousness is a useful foundation for exclusion, because it traverses the question of group worth. In this respect, it is doubly valuable because, where indigenous status was recognized by the colonialists, a Western principle—ownership—can be used to counter calculations of merit deriving from group achievement, another Western and now universal principle. Thus, as invidious comparison makes the question of group worth urgent, doubts about relative group worth also make political power urgent. To be both backward and out of power is truly to risk subordination. And if power is urgent for this reason, then the claim to ownership will be emphasized all the more. On the other side, equality is, in the contemporary world, an influential principle to which advanced groups can appeal. But, even if equality is traversed or superseded by a claim of backward indigenes based on patrimony, the advanced groups are still not wholly without an answer. To some extent, the claim of ownership by virtue of prior occupation can be offset by an appeal to a share in that ownership by virtue of the disparate contribution of advanced groups to the quality or productivity of the land. There is, in short, a debate going on in severely divided societies. The structure of appeals made by each side is conditioned by the moral power of the appeals made by the other side.

The intensity of any conflict is, in large part, a function of the relative strength of group claims. The more invidious the intergroup comparison and the larger the area of unacknowledged claims to group legitimacy, the more intense the conflict, all else being equal. The "all else" that is sometimes not equal includes, most importantly, political party systems, to be dealt with in Part Three. In Guyana, for example, what might have been only a moderately severe conflict was made more severe by the party system. The same has been true in Sri Lanka. Conversely, the

101. Mayer, *Indians in Fiji*, 22.

difficult Malaysian conflict has been moderated by the party system. What we have been discussing, therefore, is the "raw" (or pre-institutional) conflict situation, comprised as it is of contested legitimacy and uncertain group worth, elements that combine to produce a politics of group entitlement.

SYMBOLIC POLITICS
AND ETHNIC STATUS

Santayana once spoke of the "deadly significance of symbols." How apt the depiction is for symbolic conflict in severely divided societies. Issues such as the status of languages, the names of towns and states, the identity of incumbents in honorific positions, national anthems, cow slaughter (in India), and the right (or sometimes duty) to wear particular garments have been significant and deadly at various times. In Kenya, public attention was riveted on the issue of whether a Kikuyu or a Luo became principal of the University of Nairobi, for its outcome seemed to foreshadow the general future of non-Kikuyu.[102] Loss of a similar job by an Ibo in Nigeria some years earlier had also become a *cause célèbre*. When it was proposed to change the name of Mysore state in India to Karnataka, there was bitter opposition. Karnataka was a name associated with the Lingayats, whose domination of the state was feared by others. When there were complaints that Malaysian Chinese were refusing to rise as the national anthem was played in theaters, parliament imposed criminal penalties.[103] In every case, what might have been seen as a minor issue involved deeper disputes over group status.

Demands for the symbolic recognition of status are not confined to multiethnic polities or to Asia and Africa. Insecure, declining, or rising groups frequently lay claim to a favorable distribution of prestige through the official invocation of symbols. Claims of this kind need have no direct effect on the distribution of tangible resources among the contending groups, but they usually connote something about future treatment: who will be discriminated against and who will be preferred. Although all political systems must cope with some such claims, in a multiethnic society the size and intensity of the symbolic sector,

102. *Africa Report*, Apr. 1970, pp. 10–11.
103. I witnessed the parliamentary debate on the National Anthem Bill in Kuala Lumpur in 1968.

as a fraction of all demands, constitute an excellent indicator of malintegration.

In a study of the temperance movement in the United States, Joseph R. Gusfield has articulated the objectives of symbolic conflict in terms of status politics.[104] The origins of such a movement Gusfield finds in the propensity of groups to derive "prestige and self-respect" from the harmony "between their norms and those which achieve dominance in the society."[105] When status uncertainties exist, efforts are made to obtain authoritative allocations of prestige. Since the distribution of prestige is partly determined by the symbolic action of public officials who " 'act out' the drama in which one status group is degraded and another is given deference," groups make "demands upon governing agents to act in ways which serve to symbolize deference or to degrade" opposing groups.[106] Politics thus constitutes one of the important "rituals by which status is determined."[107]

Politics has a commanding position for determining group status in post-colonial societies, for two reasons. First, non-political institutions have been relatively weak in such societies and cannot compete effectively with the state in the allocation of prestige. Second, under colonial rule, attributes and emoluments of ethnic status became matters of state policy. Standing above the groups, the colonial state became the arbiter of ethnic relations. In so doing, it displaced frequently less visible, *ad hoc*, more dispersed methods of handling such matters. The state became the focal point for ethnic claims, a role inherited by the post-colonial state. The imprimatur of government is therefore indispensable to satisfactory ethnic status.

The objective of symbolic demands is a public affirmation of legitimacy where legitimacy is contested. The precise issues chosen for symbolic emphasis depend on the issues that demarcate the contestants. The temperance issue illustrates this point, for the conflict-symbol—drink—was chosen for its utility in distinguishing nativist, Protestant, small-town groups from immigrant, Catholic, urban groups. Symbolic conflicts, however, also accentuate points of difference between the groups and generate countersymbols around which opposition to a symbolic claim can coalesce. In India, for example, as Hindu demands for cow

104. Gusfield, *Symbolic Crusade: Status Politics and the American Temperance Movement* (Urbana: Univ. of Illinois Press, 1963).
105. Ibid., 68.
106. Ibid., 167.
107. Ibid., 180.

protection increased, Muslim demands for the right to slaughter cows also intensified, and the Muslim Kurbani festival, at which cows were slaughtered, grew in importance.[108] Status conflicts can help shape group culture.

THE ETHNIC USES OF SYMBOLIC DISCOURSE

Symbolism is effective in ethnic conflict, because it clothes ethnic claims in ideas and associations that have acknowledged moral force beyond the particular conflict, thereby masking something that would otherwise be controversial. As "Malaysian Malaysia" calls forth all the power of egalitarian principles diffused on a worldwide basis, so "sons of the soil" evokes the sanctity of the home against intrusion. The larger principles in which a demand is cast provide justification and render it more difficult to deny the validity of the demand. The pursuit of conflict through symbols thus obscures their segmental character by linking them with universals and simultaneously avoids running afoul of prevailing local ideology. When, for example, "communal," including religious, demands were said to be illegitimate in India, the Sikhs, differentiated on the basis of religion, avoided the prohibition by casting their demands in terms of the Punjabi language instead. In politics, as in literature, the crux of any symbol lies in its ambiguity,[109] and that is also its value in conflict. Symbolism permits the purposeful confusion of meaning, so as to conflate segmental claims with a wider political morality.[110]

Viewing ethnic politics through the prism of status claims, several things become clearer. Foremost among these is the relationship of status to psychological elements in ethnic conflict. Status discontents, notes Gusfield, appear when the prestige accorded to a group is less than group members believe is merited.[111] Since social recognition affects self-esteem, much political behavior aims at bringing objective (or official) recognition into harmony with subjective or aspirational recognition.[112]

108. Anthony Parel, "The Political Symbolism of the Cow in India," *Journal of Commonwealth Political Studies* 7 (Nov. 1969): 179–203, at 188.
109. Harold D. Lasswell and Abraham Kaplan, *Power and Society: A Framework for Political Inquiry* (New Haven: Yale Univ. Press, 1950), 104; Victor Turner, "Symbolic Studies," *Annual Review of Anthropology* 4 (1975): 145–61, at 145, 158.
110. Opposition to a demand advanced in terms of universal principles "proceeds by contraction of its symbols: the groups in whose name and for whose benefit the demand is made are alleged to be as narrow as possible, and the values demanded are formulated in specific and particular terms, dissociated from the general and universal perspectives under which they have been subsumed." Lasswell and Kaplan, *Power and Society*, 107.
111. Gusfield, *Symbolic Crusade*, 17–18.
112. Cantril, *The Psychology of Social Movements*, 46.

Mass "restiveness occurs when the state is not symbolically aligned with those who feel threatened."[113] Status discontents flow, therefore, from a challenge to self-esteem or to place in a territory. Consequently, it can be expected that groups whose personal worth has been cast in doubt will be most vigorous in seeking authoritative reassurance. Group status and group psychology are not severable. They meet in struggles over the symbols of prestige and dominance. Similarly, those whose full membership in the polity is placed in doubt by exclusionary policies and symbols that connote exclusion are likely to advance their own symbolic claims to equality.

THE POLITICS OF LANGUAGE
AND THE LANGUAGE OF POLITICS

Jayakan Bahasa Kebangsaan—"Glorify the National Language"—read a neon sign in Kuala Lumpur. The national language referred to was Malay. It may seem odd to persuade people to glorify a language. It seems more appropriate, perhaps, to encourage them to learn and use it. But "glorify" is an antonym for "denigrate," and the Malay language had occasionally been denigrated. In any case, more than just language was at stake. Under the colonial regime, the language of administration was the language of the ruler, and the status of the language denotes the status of the group that speaks it. In Assam, when Bengalis and hill people opposed making Assamese the official language of the state, a placard in their procession read "Assamese is a donkey's language." An Assamese counterprocession declared Bengali to be "a goat's language." A slur on the language is a slur on the people, and a "glorified" language is a glorified—or at least securely positioned—people.

Language, then, is a symbol of domination. Groups claiming priority—Assamese, Malays, Sindhis, Sinhalese, Mauritanian Moors, Maharashtrians—demand that their language be given what they invariably call "its rightful place,"[114] by which they mean exclusive official status. For groups uncertain about their worth, the glorification of the language is also intended to reflect a revised or aspirational evaluation. The status of the language is a symbol of newfound group dignity. Claims for official status for a language are typically demands for an authoritative

113. Murray Edelman, *The Symbolic Uses of Politics* (Urbana: Univ. of Illinois Press, 1964), 167.
114. See, e.g., Mary Fainsod Katzenstein, "Origins of Nativism: The Emergence of Shiv Sena in Bombay," *Asian Survey* 13 (Apr. 1973): 386–99 ("proper place"); *Sunday Statesman* (Calcutta), July 9, 1972 ("rightful place").

indication "that some people have a legitimate claim to greater respect, importance, or worth in the society than have some others."[115] And conversely for resistance to official status: for many years, Somalia had no official script because Osmania, the leading script for Somali, was identified with the Darood who previously used it.

In more directly competitive terms, official status may aid group performance. For example, it has been commented that the Assamese language movement grew out of "a deep feeling of mortification among Assamese-speaking people at the relative excellence of Bengali-speaking people, who surpassed them in the economic field and outdid them in competitive examinations, including university examinations. . . . It was thought that, once Assamese emerged as the official language, the Bengalis, for want of their efficiency in it, would automatically be put at bay."[116] And so language issues are symbolically capable of weaving together claims to exclude others with claims to shore up uncertain group worth. Language is the quintessential entitlement issue.

Groups on the receiving end of such demands respond accordingly. The Bengalis demanded that Bengali be recognized as an alternative official language. Until a prohibition on such debate took hold in Malaysia, Chinese were wont to speak of multilingualism. Berbers in Algeria and Tamils in Sri Lanka have claimed linguistic "parity." All such demands go much beyond language. As the demand for a single official language reflects the desire for a tangible demonstration of preeminence, so linguistic parity is transparent code for equality more generally.

The matter of group worth finds its way into linguistic counterdemands as well. An advanced group, commanded to study, be examined, and work in the language of a backward group, quickly calls attention to the inadequacy of the language sought to be made official—to its simplicity, its shallow literary tradition, its underdeveloped grammar and vocabulary, the paucity of textbooks in the language, the unsuitability of the language for use in technical fields, and its general inferiority to the colonial language it is supposed to displace. The suitability of a language for official purposes and the degree to which it is in need of upgrading are measured by comparison to the European language that formerly held sway, just as the respective groups are measured in the same way. Whether the counterclaim is for multilingualism or parity, or

115. Gusfield, Symbolic Crusade, 172.
116. Sushil Kumar, "Panorama of State Politics," in Iqbal Narain, ed., State Politics in India (Meerut: Meenakshi Prakashan, 1967), 41.

for retention of the colonial language (as in Mauritania and India), the galling thing for advanced groups is to trade what is in their eyes a richer linguistic heritage for a poorer one. The Bengali statement on this is typical of that of Mauritanian Kewri, Malaysian Chinese, and Tamils in Sri Lanka and India: "Those concerned with academic standards may, of course, still wonder if the Assamese language can adequately cope with advanced teaching . . . ."[117] For a Bengali to have to work in Assamese is, from his perspective, to be demeaned.

The more the Bengalis object, the more the Northern Sudanese deprecate the contribution of the Southern tongues to human culture, the more the Tamils flaunt their Dravidian heritage, and the more the Kewri make sarcastic comparisons of Arabic to French, the more firmly do the denigrated groups insist on official status for their language. The objections raise the issue of worth more sharply.

Moreover, the backward groups have a rejoinder to these arguments. They may agree that their language is inadequate and in need of help, just as they agree that they themselves are inadequate and in need of help. Without official status, Sinhala will lose out to Tamil, it is said; and without a bootstrapping effort to improve and "catch up," neither the people nor the language can adapt to the competitive milieu. The inadequacy of the language becomes a point in favor of official status and especially in favor of the creation of language institutes to coin new terms, propagate correct usage, and in general enrich the language and cultivate the intellectuals who work in it (as well as employ them). If cultural superiority is in doubt, that, too, is something the state has the power to rectify. Politics can be used not only to confirm group status but to enhance it.

Consequently, in an array of states, the so-called vernacular intelligentsia has been in the front ranks of language policy proponents and language policy beneficiaries: Malay teachers and Chinese teachers, Moorish teachers and Kewri teachers, students and writers and filmmakers. And, as the hotbed of Malay language demands was the Malay language and literature institute, so the hotbed of Arabic language demands in Mauritania was the institute of Islamic studies.[118]

The role of such institutes and their personnel provides a further

117. Editorial, *Statesman* (Calcutta), Oct. 26, 1972. See also Gerteiny, *Mauritania,* 151–52; Hugh Tinker, *India and Pakistan: A Political Analysis,* rev. ed. (New York: Praeger, 1968), 143.

118. Brian Weinstein, "Language Strategists: Redefining Political Frontiers on the Basis of Linguistic Choices," *World Politics* 31 (Apr. 1979): 345–64.

insight into the conflict-generating power of linguistic issues. Symbolic issues may transcend subethnic differences if symbols are selected for their breadth. Language often has this ethnic cohesion-building capacity. It is directly related to middle-class job and promotion prospects in the civil service and secondarily in the private sector. But it reaches far beyond the middle class and those dependent on it, to ordinary people "far removed from rivalry over urban white-collar jobs," as Robert N. Kearney points out of the Sinhala Only movement. "The individual Sinhalese tended to identify his fortunes with those of his language and to see the status of his language reflected in his own sense of dignity and self-respect."[119]

Language is therefore a potent symbolic issue because it accomplishes a double linkage. It links political claims to ownership with psychological demands for the affirmation of group worth, and it ties this aggregate matter of group status to outright careerism, thereby binding elite material interests to mass concerns. Needless to say, language is not the only issue that can do this. Official religion served the same function in Burma. At first, the "special position of Buddhism" was "recognized," but in 1961 this equivocal phrasing was repealed by a State Religion Act that made Buddhism the official religion. The Act required the Public Service Commission, in recruiting candidates for government employment, to accord the same weight to a knowledge of Pali, the liturgical language, as to other subjects, a provision which reflected the careerist motivations of some proponents.[120] But the main support for the state religion movement came from the countryside, a fact which cannot be explained without reference to the significance of the state religion as a symbol of Burman hegemony. This is precisely the way it was interpreted by minorities, especially the Kachins and Chins. Religion, then, can sometimes link elite and mass concerns. But clearly it is more plausible to think that fluency in the working language of a bureaucracy will become an issue more often than will facility in scripture.

Language is so often an issue, in other words, not because there is something special about linguistic difference or something mystical and therefore conflict-producing about the process of communication. The reason is more mundane: in a multilingual state, there has to be a language policy to decide trivial and important issues of linguistic choice.

119. Kearney, *Communalism and Language in the Politics of Ceylon*, 73.
120. Donald Eugene Smith, *Religion and Politics in Burma* (Princeton: Princeton Univ. Press, 1966), chap. 7.

What language will be spoken in parliament? Will letters sent to government offices in one language rather than another be returned? If not, what will be the language of reply? What about road signs? Such issues find their way to the symbolic agenda wherever linguistic differences coincide with ethnic differences and so can be used as a measure of group status. Where there is no such coincidence, other issues can and will be found. Land is a common issue that tests claims to primacy and equality. As the Guyanese are fond of saying, "he who owns the land owns the country."[121]

There is another side to language conflict, not captured by my analysis of the ethnic symbolism of language. Policy choices have consequences, not just for careers of members of one or another ethnic group, but for social-class mobility, for bureaucratic effectiveness, and for international contact. To opt for multilingualism usually means perpetuating the colonial language as the interethnic "link," thereby preserving the advantages of the advanced group, with its greater mastery of that language, and also preserving ties to universities in the former metropole. To choose an indigenous language is to make job recruitment more egalitarian classwise, but to discriminate ethnically, and also to diversify international educational contacts (since French or English is no longer the "natural" second language, students may choose university training in a variety of countries). All of these consequences raise serious issues, not likely to be resolved by a careful process of weighing tradeoffs once symbolic claims are made.[122]

Far more likely is the imposition of a language over violent opposition or the imposition of an unsatisfying compromise: common formulae are to make one language "national" and another "official" or to except minority regions from the sway of the official language. Where civilian governments rule, the configuration of party competition or its absence will have much to do with the choice. Where military regimes rule, the ethnic composition of the regime will usually be determinative.

This much, however, is very clear. Symbolic claims are not readily amenable to compromise. In this, they differ from claims deriving wholly from material interest. Whereas material advancement can be measured both relatively and absolutely, the status advancement of one ethnic

121. Leo Despres, *Cultural Pluralism and Nationalist Politics in British Guiana* (Chicago: Rand, McNally, 1967), 93.

122. See Robert B. Kaplan, "Language and Science Policies of New Nations," *Science* 221 (Sept. 2, 1983): 913.

group is entirely relative to the status of others. That is an important reason for being precise about what is at stake in ethnic conflict. Ethnic claims are expressed in moral language and are not quantifiable. How does a policymaker divide up the "glorification" of the national language? Some leaders have been notably more skillful than others at splitting symbols in ethnic conflict. But the task is inherently frustrating. That is why compromise outcomes are more likely in political systems that provide countervailing incentives for politicians and their followings to behave moderately in the assertion of group claims.

ECONOMIC DEMANDS AND SYMBOLIC SATISFACTIONS: THE CIVIL SERVICE ISSUE

Wherever there is conflict between unranked ethnic groups, there has been a middle-class careerist component, revolving around competition for lucrative, prestigious positions in the civil service. The power and perquisites associated with the instruments of colonial rule have generally attached to the successor institutions. Government is a leading employer in many Asian and African countries, and in some countries civil servants absorb 50 to 60 percent of the annual budget. A sinecure in government is, as shown in Chapter 3, a rather common aspiration of educated young people in Asia and Africa. Since the ethnic proportions of the bureaucracy are susceptible to political intervention, there is hardly an ethnically divided state without its "civil service issue."

In strictly proportional terms, the problem is intractable. Since the groups rarely approach parity in both numbers and educational attainment, there is bound to be a less satisfied group, no matter what the proportions in the government service are. A group may feel deprived because it is underrepresented by numerical criteria or by merit criteria, and occasionally by both. In Mauritania, the educationally advanced Kewri have been overrepresented in proportion to their numbers, but underrepresented in proportion to their share of the educated population. On the former ground, there is discontent among the Moors; on the latter, discontent among the Kewri. This is not atypical. Backward groups want proportionality or, if they have an exclusionary claim, more than a proportional share. Advanced groups want admission to the bureaucracy based on educational criteria and examinations, provided the examinations are not in someone else's language.

Differential visibility of various government bodies compounds perceptions of deprivation. Ceylon Tamils formerly had a majority of positions in the Audit and Accountants' Services of Sri Lanka, but very much less than a majority in the generalist Ceylon Civil Service. The Tamils were often said to be better represented than they really were overall. In Malaysia, Chinese and Indians are well represented in the professional and technical services, giving Malays the impression that their 4:1 quota in the generalist Malaysian Administrative and Diplomatic Service is a chimera. In Assam and other Indian states, "sons of the soil" who now predominate in state government offices do not necessarily predominate in central government offices and public sector enterprises in their state. What group members see depends on where they look.

When the Ibo scholar K. O. Dike declared in the 1960s that "the educated Nigerian is the worst peddler of tribalism," he was referring to careerist struggles for position and promotion in government employment, including the universities. There is no doubt whatever that educated elites have used ethnic sentiment in pursuit of their own career aspirations. There is much doubt, however, on two other matters.

The first is whether educated elites are in fact generally more ethnocentric or antipathetic to other groups than are less educated masses. On this, the evidence is simply not yet definitive.[123] What is clear is that educated elites meet members of other ethnic groups in school and work settings, where anxieties about ability to compete against potentially superior, shrewder, or more industrious rivals can easily be expressed in appeals to group solidarity.

The second matter is simply this. That educated elites make use of ethnic antipathy for their own economic purposes does not mean that ethnic conflict is fundamentally about jobs and perquisites. The elites could not use the antipathy for their own ends unless ethnic feeling were already strong. I drove this point home at length in Chapter 3, and now it is time to explain exactly what permits elites to use the antipathy of others in this way. The economic component to ethno-bureaucratic conflict is the tail and not the dog. The dog responds when the tail wags,

---

123. See, e.g., Brian M. du Toit, "Ethnicity, Neighborliness, and Friendship Among Urban Africans in South Africa," in du Toit, ed., *Ethnicity in Modern Africa* (Boulder, Colo.: Westview Press, 1978), 161–62; Robert M. Price, "The Pattern of Ethnicity in Ghana," *Journal of Modern African Studies* 11 (Sept. 1973): 470–75; Roberta E. Mapp, "Cross-National Dimensions of Ethnocentrism," *Canadian Journal of African Studies* 6 (Winter 1972): 73–96. See also R. D. Grillo, "Ethnic Identity and Social Stratification on a Kampala Housing Estate," in Abner Cohen, ed., *Urban Ethnicity* (London: Tavistock, 1974), 173; William John Hanna and Judith Lynne Hanna, "Polyethnicity and Political Integration in Umuahia and Mbale," in Robert T. Daland, ed., *Comparative Urban Research* (Beverly Hills: Sage, 1969), 179.

because, apart from whatever crumbs may trickle down to a few relatives and retainers of civil servants, the composition of the civil service is an important indicator of who owns the country as well as of how groups are doing in the struggle for worth.

In this respect, the civil service issue at the mass level resembles a number of other issues. Since unranked ethnic groups are cross-class in composition, ethnic prestige can be derived from the success of wealthier or higher-status group members. A compelling illustration is the case of village Malays, whose attachment to their sultans derives from the symbolic importance of Malay royalty. "The wealth and pomp of the sultanate are topics of conversation and subject for pride among many in the village, and the Sultan is viewed as a representative of Malay power, culture, and wealth in opposition to the Chinese. Closely tied to this view is the high regard with which the [King] is held as a symbol of the primacy of the Malays in the land."[124]

Because of the element of derivative prestige, the symbolic claims of unranked ethnic groups tend to be consonant with the ambitions of their elites. It is a point of recurrent befuddlement and frustration among politicians on the Left, but it is undoubtedly the case that vicarious satisfaction plays an important part in the attribution of significance to the ethnic composition of the civil service. And the quest for this symbolic satisfaction is no chimera. In his work on symbolic politics, Gusfield is at pains to demonstrate what ethnic group members—but not always outside observers—are quick to sense: the distribution of prestige is a real and rational object of conflict. Symbols have substance.

THE TWO IMPERATIVES
IN ETHNIC CONFLICT

At the end of Chapter 3, I argued that an adequate theory of ethnic conflict should be able to explain both elite and mass behavior. Such a theory should also provide an explanation for the passionate, symbolic, and apprehensive aspects of ethnic conflict. Group entitlement, conceived as a joint function of comparative worth and legitimacy, does this—it explains why the followers follow, accounts for the intensity of group reactions, even to modest stimuli, and clarifies the otherwise mysterious quest for public signs of group status.

124. Wilson, *A Malay Village and Malaysia*, 112.

To conceive of conflict between ethnic groups as a matter of entitlement is to build on Weber's insight, quoted in Chapter 1, that in unranked systems "honor" is uncertain and each group can consider its own honor to be the highest. Viewed in this way, ethnic conflict does not occur because groups are becoming more alike. Nor does it derive from the mere fact of group differences. Ethnic conflict arises from the common evaluative significance accorded by the groups to acknowledged group differences and then played out in public rituals of affirmation and contradiction.

Worth and legitimacy are not magic keys to ethnic conflict, unlocking every mystery. There are features of conflict behavior that group comparison and entitlement do not really explain by themselves. One missing feature is the very large area of ethnic group behavior that takes place within the confines of a constraining institutional framework. Earlier, I mentioned the political party system as comprising such an arena, in which group claims are mediated through the logic of the particular system in which partisan actors, however loyal to the interests of their ethnic group, happen to find themselves. That logic will, of course, require separate explanation, and it will not always conform to what I called previously "raw" ethnic sentiment. Such sentiment is more faithfully reflected in more spontaneous behavior, such as interethnic violence.

Another feature missing from the discussion so far is variability within ethnic groups. Just as I have dealt with pre-institutional ethnic conflict, so have I dealt to this point with groups as wholes, ignoring subethnic divisions. Consequently, nothing I have said bears on a problem such as the geography of ethnic extremism, the common variability of antipathy toward outgroups on the part of territorially differentiated subethnic groups. For example, the demand for Pakistan in pre-independence India was most strongly felt in Muslim-minority—that is, highly heterogeneous—provinces. In Sri Lanka, on the other hand, the strongest anti-Tamil attitudes are often encountered among Sinhalese in the South, around Galle and Matara, cities furthest removed from Tamil population centers. In some cases, then, those subgroups most removed from contact with ethnic strangers are most passionately hostile, while in others proximity has bred antipathy.

Neither worth nor legitimacy can explain these irreconcilable tendencies completely. It turns out they are shaped, in part at least, by the party system and by the identity of those who organize the hostility. In Malay-

sia, the relatively homogeneous state of Kelantan has a history of supporting an anti-Chinese party, but that is because the party also has had
a religious appeal and the state is well endowed with influential religious
functionaries. Indeed, there is good ground for thinking that anti-
Chinese sentiment is not stronger in Kelantan than it is elsewhere in
Malaysia.[125] So what look like variations in raw hostility may be variations in institutional structures.

There are therefore two imperatives in ethnic conflict: the spontaneous and sentiment-driven versus the institutionally constrained. The
more spontaneous the conflict behavior, the more pertinent will be the
elements of group entitlement; the more tied into institutional constraints, the more we shall have to probe institutional arrangements. The
tension between these two imperatives can result in the violent overthrow of the institutional system when it fails utterly to reflect ethnic
sentiment.

The theory of group entitlement cannot by itself answer a question
such as when will an interethnic coalition be formed, but it can put flesh
on otherwise skeletal empirical observations about group position.
Merely to know the position of a group, in terms of worth and legitimacy, is probably to be able to forecast what political claims it makes,
what idiom it speaks in, what issues divide it from others, what counterclaims the others make, and generally how each will behave in and out
of power. As a matter of fact, a test of the utility of this perspective is at
hand. We have seen that some groups try to make states ethnically homogeneous by expelling members of other groups, and we shall not be
surprised if some territorially separate groups try to achieve homogeneity by withdrawing from the state. The predictive uses of a theory based
on group position will become apparent in examining the logic of secessionist movements.

125. Douglas Raybeck, "Ethnicity and Accommodation: Malay–Chinese Relations in
Kelantan, Malaysia," *Ethnic Groups* 2 (Jan. 1980): 241–68.

CHAPTER SIX

The Logic of Secessions and Irredentas

Around the time of Asian and African independence, there was talk of the "artificiality" of territorial boundaries imposed by colonial powers. Many ethnic groups had been divided between two or more colonies. With few exceptions, the new states accepted independence within existing boundaries, but there was much speculation that "troublesome irredenta[s]"[1] were in store for them.

At the same time, the success of anti-colonial movements had diverted attention from ethnic divisions within the new states. With the accent on "nation-building," scant attention was paid to the possibility of ethnic secession, at least until the Katanga secession of 1960; and even that tended to be viewed as *sui generis*.[2]

Events have belied these expectations in the most dramatic way. Troublesome irredentas have been few and far between, whereas troublesome secessions have been abundant. The few irredentas that have broken into warfare have been virulently fought, as have many of the wars of secession. Yet almost none of the secessionist or irredentist movements has achieved its goals.

These developments raise several interesting questions. What accounts for the emergence of secession? What kinds of groups attempt to secede and under what circumstances? What accounts for the success of such movements, and what effects does success have, both in the secessionist state and in the rump state? Similar questions can be asked for irredentas.

1. Rupert Emerson, *From Empire to Nation* (Cambridge: Harvard Univ. Press, 1960), 105.
2. In part, this was because Europeans in Katanga were thought to be behind the movement. But see note 61, below. Some, however, saw Katanga as portentous. See note 8, below.

PATHS TO SECESSION

Despite its frequency, secession is a variable phenomenon. Some movements emerge early in the life of a new state, seemingly with little provocation. Others develop only after a prolonged period of frustration and conflict. Some movements simmer for years, even decades, and in the end may come to nothing, whereas others burst quickly into warfare. But many movements never even reach a slow simmer, much less a quick boil.

To discern patterns of secession, it is necessary to recognize that this is a special species of ethnic conflict, but a species nonetheless. Though modified by their territorial character, secessionist conflicts partake of many features that ethnic conflict in general exhibits. Calculations of group interest play their part, although some ethnic groups opt for secession when it does not appear to be in their interest to do so. In decisions to secede, group interest is alloyed with enmity and offset by apprehension. The roots of those decisions are to be found in the texture of group relations.

One fairly firm rule of thumb can be laid down at once. Whether and when a secessionist movement will emerge is determined mainly by domestic politics, by the relations of groups and regions within the state. Whether a secessionist movement will achieve its aims, however, is determined largely by international politics, by the balance of interests and forces that extend beyond the state. Occasionally, considerations of means available to support secessionist movements, including external assistance, may modify secessionist sentiment—though separatists are often surprisingly heedless of such prudential constraints. Occasionally, too, external relations reinforce separatist proclivities, as for example when Kurds and Southern Sudanese took exception to pan-Arabist activities in Baghdad and Khartoum. Secession lies squarely at the juncture of internal and international politics, but for the most part the emergence of separatism can be explained in terms of domestic ethnic politics.

To this broad rule of thumb, there is a major exception. A group that might otherwise be disposed to separatism will not be so disposed if its secession is likely to lead, not to independence, but to incorporation in a neighboring state, membership in which is viewed as even less desirable than membership in the existing state. The cases in which this is likely to occur involve irredentism, where an international boundary divides members of a single ethnic group. The Baluch and Pathans of Pakistan, for example, are likely to limit their separatist activity to the extent that it makes them vulnerable to incorporation in Afghanistan or, in the Baluch case, Iran.[3] The Ewe of Ghana are not likely to do anything that would risk merger into Togo. Similar considerations, however, will not restrain the Malays of Southern Thailand, many of whom might indeed prefer to join Malaysia. This does not indicate under what conditions irredentism will occur; it merely highlights what is, in at least a few important cases, a limitation on domestically generated collective inclinations.

At this point, a definitional issue intrudes, one well illustrated by the limited goals of some of the groups just mentioned. Should the terms *separatism* and *secession* be confined to movements aiming explicitly at an independent state or extended to movements seeking any territorially defined political change intended to accord an ethnic group autonomous control over the region in which it resides? Conceived in the latter way, separatism would include ethnic demands for the creation of separate states within existing states or for a broad measure of regional autonomy, short of independence.

There is some ground for thinking that groups demanding complete independence may have the strongest sense of grievance. The contrast between Catalan and Basque claims in Spain is revealing on this score. Catalan ethnic sentiment runs as deep as Basque sentiment does, and it probably has broader support. But Basque political organizations have more frequently turned to violence and more frequently demanded independence, whereas Catalan organizations have aimed at autonomy within Spain. Franco's severe repression of the Basques, many of whom had supported the Republicans, probably helps explain the unyielding character of some Basque organizations. (So, too, may the fact that Basques also reside on the French side of the border, making independence a more attractive goal.) In the Basque case, at least, there seems to be a clear and direct linkage between ethnic antipathy and declared political objectives.

In many other cases, however, this linkage is more tenuous. The Kurds in Iraq consistently denied that their objective was independence. Even as they fought and died in the 1960s and '70s, they eschewed anything

3. "No one in Baluchustan wants to break away [from Pakistan]. All the Baluchis want is not to lose their identity," commented a Baluch spokesman. "Who in his right mind would want to join Afghanistan? We'd be worse off there than we are in Pakistan." *Washington Post*, Feb. 8, 1976. This is also the theme of Khalid B. Sayeed, "Pathan Regionalism," *South Atlantic Quarterly* 63 (Autumn 1964): 478–506.

beyond regional autonomy. The reason, presumably, was tactical: had they declared independence as their goal, the Iraqi Kurds would have engendered hostility from neighboring regimes in Syria, Iran, and Turkey, all of which have Kurdish minorities. In the 1974 warfare in Iraq, Iran supplied arms, food, and cross-border facilities for the Kurdish fighters, and this support particularly insured that the movement demanded only autonomy.

Demands can also shift from autonomy to independence and back again, depending on the state of negotiations between central governments and separatists. The Moro National Liberation Front in the Philippines moved from autonomy demands to demands for separate statehood after the Philippine government adopted a decentralization plan the MNLF found wanting.[4] The Mizo National Front in India followed the same path, agreeing to a solution within the framework of Indian federalism in 1976 but, after a cease-fire broke down three years later, returning to warfare to achieve independence.[5] Other movements, such as the Southern Sudanese, equivocated on their demands, using ambiguous terms like "self-determination" to cover internal differences.[6] The Chad National Liberation Front, presumed to be fighting a war for the secession of the North, long refused to declare its objectives, and eventually most of the country, including the capital, was in rebel hands. Tactics play a large role in the statement of objectives.

The often tactical nature of demands, their elasticity, even fickleness, the willingness of independence movements to settle for much less than statehood, and the occasional interest of secessionists in capturing the whole state if that proves possible—all of these argue for an inclusive conception of separatism and secession, terms I shall therefore use interchangeably. Such a conception should embrace movements seeking a separate region within an existing state, as well as those seeking a separate and independent state.[7]

4. *Far Eastern Economic Review* (Hong Kong), Aug. 17, 1979, p. 28.
5. Ibid., Sept. 14, 1979, p. 30.
6. See Keith Kyle, "The Southern Problem in the Sudan," *The World Today* 22 (Dec. 1966): 512–20. An article in the journal published by the Southern Sudan Association in Britain during the Sudanese civil war illustrates the point: "What, then, are we fighting for? We are fighting for freedom; freedom to unite with the North; freedom to federate with the North; freedom to reject the North; freedom for the people of the South Sudan to determine their own future without interference from the Arabs or any other people." Jacob J. Akol, "What We Are, and Are Not, Fighting For," *The Grass Curtain* (London) 2 (Oct. 1971): 25–26, at 26. When a settlement was suddenly reached, such formulations could readily be invoked in justification of it. See ibid., 2 (May 1972): 1.
7. For an equally inclusive conception, see Joane Nagel, "The Conditions of Ethnic Separatism: The Kurds in Turkey, Iran, and Iraq," *Ethnicity* 7 (Sept. 1980): 279–97.

OF GROUPS AND REGIONS

"Inevitably," wrote Immanuel Wallerstein at the time of the Katanga secession, "some regions will be richer (less poor) than others, and if the ethnic claim to power combines with relative wealth, the case for secession is strong. . . . [E]very African nation, large or small, federal or unitary, has its Katanga."[8] Wallerstein was right to link the ethnic claim with the character of the region from which the ethnic group springs. These are the two conditions that matter most. But he limited the potential for secession unduly when he confined it to relatively wealthy regions. In point of fact, there are several paths to secession, and rich regions are not the leading secessionists. They are far outnumbered by regions poor in resources and productivity. Despite strong feelings of alienation—or worse—neither Ashanti in Ghana nor the Western Region of Nigeria nor Buganda in Uganda, all prosperous regions, made a serious effort to secede. By contrast, wars have been fought by peoples in the poor regions of, among many others, the Southern Sudan, the Southern Philippines, and Northern Chad. Why this is so we shall soon see.

Table 2 provides a simple matrix of potential secessionists. It includes groups that have and have not attempted to secede. The variables are straightforward. They are based on the positions of ethnic groups and regions relative to others in the state.

Separatist ethnic groups are characterized as "backward" or "advanced" for shorthand purposes, in accordance with our earlier discussion of group juxtapositions. An advanced group is one that has benefited from opportunities in education and non-agricultural employment. Typically, it is represented above the mean in number of secondary and university graduates, in bureaucratic, commercial, and professional employment, and in per capita income. As we have seen, certain stereotypes are commonly associated with these attributes. Advanced groups are generally regarded by themselves and others as highly motivated, diligent, intelligent, and dynamic. Backward groups, less favorably situated on the average in terms of educational attainment, high-salaried employment, and per capita income, tend to be stereotyped as indolent, ignorant, and not disposed to achievement. Just as group position and the putative qualities associated with it are potent factors in ethnic conflict

8. Wallerstein, *Africa: The Politics of Independence* (New York: Vintage, 1961), 88. See also Peter Alexis Gourevitch, "The Reemergence of 'Peripheral Nationalisms': Some Comparative Speculations on the Spatial Distribution of Political Leadership and Economic Growth," *Comparative Studies in Society and History* 21 (July 1979): 303–22.

TABLE 2   POTENTIAL SECESSIONISTS, BY
GROUP AND REGIONAL POSITION

	Backward Groups	Advanced Groups
Backward Regional Economies	Southern Sudanese Karens, Shans, others in Burma Muslims in the Philippines Muslims in Chad Kurds in Iraq Nagas and Mizos in India Muslims in Thailand Bengalis in Pakistan Northerners in Ghana[a]	Ibo in Nigeria Tamils in Sri Lanka Baluba (Kasai) in Zaire Lozi in Zambia[a] Kabyle Berbers in Algeria[a]
Advanced Regional Economies	Lunda in Zaire Bakonjo in Uganda Batéké in Gabon[a]	Sikhs in Indian Punjab Basques in Spain Yoruba in Nigeria[a] Baganda in Uganda[a]

[a]Denotes groups that have not had a strong secessionist movement.

generally, so do they condition collective orientations to the possibility of secession.

Separatist regions are characterized as backward or advanced by the relative economic position of the region, as measured by regional income per capita excluding remittances from other regions (which would likely be terminated or reduced in the event of secession). I say "measured by," but in fact data on regional income per capita are only sporadically available, and rarely available on a reliable basis for Asian and African countries. While this excludes the possibility of analysis based on precise degrees of regional backwardness, advancement, or disparity between the two in given countries, identification of backward and advanced regions is not difficult. The same is true, of course, regarding group position.

This characterization of both regions and groups ignores some common complexities. The table assumes the existence of geographically concentrated ethnic groups that may or may not become separatist. However, many groups that possess a geographically identifiable homeland are no longer geographically concentrated. Large numbers of group members may live outside the home region, a circumstance likely to have some impact on the emergence of separatism. Conversely, a secessionist region often contains more than one major ethnic group, and the groups may differ in their position relative to groups outside the region. Likewise, the measurement of regional position by per capita income may obscure important elements of intraregional difference. Eritrea, for example, has had industrially developed cities but an exceedingly poor countryside: which is the politically relevant reality? Then, too, although I shall speak of a backward region and an advanced region, as if any state had only two regions, rarely is a state so clearly bifurcated. I shall deal with some of these complexities at later points, but for the moment it is best to proceed with a simpler framework.[9]

The interplay of relative group position and relative regional position determines the emergence of separatism. In stressing this interplay, I mean to reject direct causal relationships between regional economic disparity and ethnic secession. If degree of regional economic disparity alone determined the emergence of separatism, it would be reasonable to expect the preponderance of such movements in those states occupying the middle-income levels, for in such states regional economic disparities seem to be greatest.[10] But no such tendencies can be identified. Secession is attempted in low-income states like Ethiopia and Chad, as well as in the Philippines and Nigeria, countries with incomes four to six times higher; and, needless to say, it is an issue in a number of economically developed countries, too. Relative regional position is a causal element in the emergence of secession, not because it predicts separatism in any straightforward way, but because it conditions the claims ethnic groups make and their response to the rejection of those claims.

The four categories of potential secessionists depicted in the table differ from each other in several major respects. The demands the groups advance before separatist sentiment crystallizes, the events that move the groups to secession, the calculations that attend the decision to separate, and the timing of the decision all vary according to whether the group is

9. The framework advanced in this section was first presented in Donald L. Horowitz, "Patterns of Ethnic Separatism," *Comparative Studies in Society and History* 23 (Apr. 1981): 165–95.

One complexity of which I shall not take adequate account concerns differences of opinion within given ethnic groups on the advisability of secession. Sometimes secessionist sentiment is virtually unanimous, but very often there are debates on whether to secede. See, e.g., B. J. Dudley, "Western Nigeria and the Nigerian Crisis," in S. K. Panter-Brick, ed., *Nigerian Politics and Military Rule: Prelude to the Civil War* (London: Athlone Press, 1970), 106–08, identifying at least five Yoruba opinion strains *circa* 1966–67. More often than not, I shall ignore such differences, dealing instead with central tendencies or merely with the outcomes of such debates.

10. Jeffrey G. Williamson, "Regional Inequality and the Process of National Development," *Economic Development and Cultural Change* 13 (July 1965): 3–84, at 14, 17.

considered backward or advanced and whether it resides in a backward or advanced region. Table 2 does not provide an exhaustive enumeration of movements, of which there have been dozens, if not hundreds, in the post-colonial period. Furthermore, the table includes some non-secessionist groups for comparison. Even so, the table suggests the prevalence of backward regions among secessionists. In part, this may be a function of the coincidence of regional backwardness with geographic distance from the center. Economic backwardness is more common on the periphery. In states where the span of governmental control is limited, peripheral areas might more readily contemplate secession.[11] Yet the logic of secession comprehends much more than just the difficulty of the center in exerting control. Distance is but a minor factor in the overall prevalence of backward regions among secessionists. Indeed, there is more than one rationale for the secession of a backward region. There are four different paths to ethnic secession, which correspond to the four different cells of the table.

BACKWARD GROUPS IN BACKWARD REGIONS

By far the largest number of secessionists can be characterized as backward groups in backward regions. These groups are typically early seceders. They often attempt to secede rather soon after independence or after rejection of the claims they advance. They conclude rapidly that they have a small stake in preserving the undivided state of which they are a part. In fact, some such groups had earlier doubts: Moros in the Philippines, Nagas in India, Karens in Burma, and Southern Sudanese were among those groups that asked for a prolonged colonial period, a

11. See Charles W. Anderson, Fred R. von der Mehden, and Crawford Young, *Issues of Political Development*, 2d ed. (Englewood Cliffs, N.J.: Prentice-Hall, 1974), 75. When the Uganda government refused to accede to demands for a separate district, the Rwenzururu movement in Western Uganda became secessionist very quickly, for reasons that are probably related to span of control. "The Ruwenzori mountain areas are extremely inaccessible; effective administration had never become established in the higher altitudes and, in a sense, anybody could set up an independent government there without facing the consequences for at least some time." Martin R. Doornbos, "Protest Movements in Western Uganda: Some Parallels and Contrasts," in Raymond L. Hall, ed. *Ethnic Autonomy— Comparative Dynamics* (New York: Pergamon Press, 1979), 274. But the emergence of the movement in the first place had little to do with these geographic conditions. Distance, of course, is a condition that can cut both ways. While great distance may make secession easier—or at least make its suppression more difficult—distance may also reduce the intrusiveness of central government penetration of peripheral areas.

separate independence, or special arrangements to protect them after independence. All of them feared competition with their neighbors within the bounds of a single political arena.

Fears of this kind were not merely based on numerical inferiority, but on a sense of weakness *vis-à-vis* more "efficient," "aggressive," "sharp-witted," "dynamic," "industrious," and better educated members of other ethnic groups.[12] Sensing competitive incapacities, backward groups in backward regions at first tend to demand representation in politics and the public service in proportion to their numbers. Inevitably, this demand is unmet, for relative group backwardness implies a shortage of eligible candidates for such positions. When the denial of such opportunities is coupled with clear signs that the state is dominated by members of other groups, backward groups in backward regions choose to opt out.

Quite often the swirl of conflicts is reflected in a bewildering succession of separatist organizations, each with more uncompromising demands than the one that preceded it. This was the case in the Southern Sudan, in the Karen areas of Burma, in the Toro Kingdom of Uganda, and in other such regions as well. The rapid passage of leadership and the escalation of demands reflect the character of the calculations such groups make. They see little choice.

Often these are deficit regions that receive a subsidy from the center.[13] Consequently, the decision to secede is taken despite the economic costs it is likely to entail. This willingness to sacrifice, together with the rapid-

12. See, e.g., Ba Maw, *Breakthrough in Burma: Memoirs of a Revolution, 1939–1946* (New Haven: Yale Univ. Press, 1968), 187; Fred R. von der Mehden, *Religion and Nationalism in Southeast Asia* (Madison: Univ. of Wisconsin Press, 1963), 193; Rodolfo Bulatao, *Ethnic Attitudes in Five Philippine Cities* (Quezon City: Univ. of the Philippines Social Science Research Laboratory, 1973), 57–62; Hugh Gray, "The Demand for a Separate Telengana State in India," *Asian Survey* 11 (May 1971): 463–74, at 464.

13. For example, in Southern Thailand, "Narathiwat, which is not atypical, collected $1.25 million in local revenue in 1970, while the [Narathiwat] budget as subsidized by the central government totalled $5.87 million, excluding capital investment effected directly under central administration offices." Astri Suhrke, "The Thai-Muslim Border Provinces" (unpublished paper presented at the seminar on contemporary Thailand, Australian National Univ., Sept. 6–9, 1971), 12–13. In wealthier states, however, even this subsidy may not be enough to bring per capita spending in poor regions up to levels proportionate to their share of the state's population. In such a case, a demand for per capita proportionate spending is likely to be received most unsympathetically by the center. See, e.g., Charles M. Benjamin, "The Kurdish Non-State Nation" (unpublished paper presented at the 1975 annual meeting of the International Studies Association), 6.

ity with which such movements get going, is evidence of the sense of desperation backward groups feel in assessing their ability to compete in the undivided state.

Elite and mass economic interests, however, generally diverge at the moment of decision. Whereas the region as a whole stands to suffer if it opts for secession, educated elites stand to gain from the creation of new opportunities in a smaller, albeit poorer, state. This includes those high positions from which these elites, with their generally lower seniority, would be excluded in the undivided state. Secession creates new positions, while reducing the pool of competitors. Advanced segments of backward groups do not resist but generally lead the movement.[14]

Nonetheless, the frequency, enthusiasm, and violence of separatist movements among backward groups in backward regions can scarcely be put down to selfish elite motives alone. It is true that, whereas secession enables leaders to eliminate the interethnic competition they previously faced, many other people may be adversely affected by an end to revenue subsidies and the severance of the backward economy from the state. Yet the formal divergence of interest is just that: by the time the movement gets underway, calculations of sacrifice and opportunity are invariably overwhelmed by an avalanche of ethnic sentiment that the undivided state is intolerable. It is instructive to examine more concretely how such sentiments develop.

Time and again, it is the civil service issue that highlights grievances. Not only do backward groups in backward regions receive a dramatically smaller share of government positions than their share of the population, but, in addition, civil servants are imported from more advanced regions into theirs. Kurdish demands in Iraq reflect this dual grievance very well. They recurrently embody proposals for proportional representation in the Iraqi civil service, cabinet, and national assembly and for

14. See, e.g., von der Mehden, *Religion and Nationalism in Southeast Asia*, 171; Rasheeduddin Khan, "Political Participation and Political Change in Andhra Pradesh (India)" (unpublished paper, Osmania Univ. Department of Political Science, June 1969), 33.

In some cases, even elites that were ahead of ethnically differentiated competitors saw separatism as a way of reducing the competition. The agitation for a separate Pakistan in the 1930s and '40s was disproportionately led by Muslims in what was then called the United Provinces (U.P.). As a whole, Indian Muslims were backward, and they feared domination by educationally more advanced Hindus. But in the United Provinces, Muslims were ahead of Hindus in government employment, the professions, and the modern private sector. Still, U.P. Muslim elites feared their minority position in an undivided India, and they demanded a separate state to protect their position. Paul R. Brass, "Muslim Separatism in United Provinces: Social Context and Political Strategy Before Partition," *Economic and Political Weekly* (Bombay), Jan. 1970, pp. 167–86.

the exclusion of non-Kurds from government service in Kurdish areas.[15] The dual character of the demands indicates that the issue is not merely one of ethnic representation; it has shifted to domination. In the Sudan, for example, Southerners, more than one quarter of the population, received only six of 800 civil service openings at independence, and they were slighted in other ways as well. They held only three of forty-three seats on a constitution-drafting committee. Their position in other government bodies was equally poor: less than 3 percent of post-independence army commissions, 4 percent of newly gazetted police officers, and so on.[16] The Southern elite was small, but it had great expectations that were quickly thwarted. Moreover, British civil servants in the South were usually replaced by Northerners. By all accounts, the new administrators were not attuned to Southern sensibilities. It took little beyond this to convince Southerners that a new colonialism had arrived: imposition of Arabic for certain official purposes in the South, hints of alignment with Arab Egypt, hostility toward Christian missionaries. Concluded two Southern leaders: "the administration, the army, the police, the judiciary and trade in the South [are] all in Arab hands; Arabic is the official national language as well as the medium of instruction; Friday is the day of rest, etc. Could domination be better expressed?"[17]

Civil service appointments and postings have been prominent accelerators of separatist sentiment among a variety of backward groups in backward regions, ranging from Chad to Baluchistan to Nagaland to the Telangana region of Andhra Pradesh. With the French departure from Chad in 1960, Southerners, better educated in French, were able to claim the best civil service positions. Like Northern Sudanese sent to administer the backward South, Southern Chadians were sent to govern the backward North, which they did with scant regard for Northern local

---

15. Lorenzo Kent Kimball, *The Changing Pattern of Political Power in Iraq, 1958 to 1971* (New York: Robert Speller, 1972), 141–42; Abdul H. Raoof, "Kurdish Ethnic Nationalism and Political Development in Republican Iraq" (unpublished paper presented at the 1971 annual meeting of the Middle East Studies Association), 10. So conscious are the Kurds of their backwardness that these demands sometimes make provision for exceptions when no qualified Kurds can be found for particular positions.

16. Mohamed Omer Beshir, *The Southern Sudan: Background to Conflict* (London: C. Hurst, 1968), 72; Richard Gray, "The Southern Sudan," *Journal of Contemporary History* 6 (1971): 108–20, at 117.

17. Joseph Oduho and William Deng, *The Problem of the Southern Sudan* (London: Oxford Univ. Press, 1963), 14. For reports of similar sentiments, see Kyle, "The Southern Problem in the Sudan," 513; I. William Zartman, *Government and Politics in Northern Africa* (New York: Praeger, 1963), 140; Robert O. Collins and Robert L. Tignor, *Egypt and the Sudan* (Englewood Cliffs, N.J.: Prentice-Hall, 1967), 147–64.

authorities. This, perhaps more than the arrest of Northern politicians, prompted rebellion. Within a few years of independence, there was fighting.[18] Similarly, estimates gave Baluch only 5 percent of civil service positions in their province, and almost none at the highest levels.[19] In Nagaland, non-Naga Indian officials replaced the British, and "a change in the spirit of administration, if not yet in the pattern, was immediately felt by the Nagas."[20] By 1951, the Nagas had issued a declaration of independence. And when Andhra Pradesh was created out of a mosaic of Telugu-speaking areas in 1956, well-qualified Coastal Andhras moved into Telangana to take civil service positions in Hyderabad. Aspiring Telangana students were outraged by what seemed a theft of their opportunities. On top of this, it was said that a shortage of "skilled" Telangana public service applicants existed, and Telanganas were told they were "indolent," that their "Urduized" Telugu was impure and that their habits were "feudal."[21] In each case, a backward region inhabited by a backward group was, it seemed, "colonized" by administrators from a more advanced region and a more advanced group.

In economic terms, of course, the actions that precipitate separatist activity can be viewed as merely the equilibration of factors of production between two unequally developed regions.[22] Regions with a surfeit of human resources export them to regions with a deficit. The same is true of investment. In Telangana, to cite one case, cheap but fertile land was purchased by ambitious Coastal Andhra farmers. A single state implies a single, unbounded market for labor and capital. And there, precisely, is the rub, for the market may be unbounded, but its populations are encapsulated within ethnic and psychological boundaries. Telangana farmers thus resented the more efficient, productive Coastal

18. Robert Pledge, "France at War in Africa," *Africa Report*, June 1970, pp. 16–19; John A. Ballard, "Four Equatorial States," in Gwendolen M. Carter, ed., *National Unity and Regionalism in Eight African States* (Ithaca: Cornell Univ. Press, 1966), 272–74; William H. Lewis, "Francophone Africa," *Current History* 60 (March 1971): 142–45, at 143; René Lemarchand, "Sisyphus in Chad: The MRA as a Development Partnership" (unpublished paper, Univ. of Florida, n.d., ca. 1973), 4; *Africa Report*, Nov. 1969, pp. 10–12.

19. Robert G. Wirsing, "The Protection of Frontier Minorities: The Case of the Baluch of Pakistan," in Wirsing, ed., *Protection of Ethnic Minorities: Comparative Perspectives* (Elmsford, N.Y.: Pergamon Press, 1981), 293. These estimates were as of 1972.

20. Neville Maxwell, *India and the Nagas* (London: Minority Rights Group, Report no. 17, n.d.), 9.

21. Gray, "The Demand for a Separate Telengana State." I shall deal in more detail below with separatism in Telangana (both spellings are used).

22. See Williamson, "Regional Inequality and the Process of National Development."

farmers who migrated there, even though their activity presumably raised the value of Telangana land.

Typically, developments that occur within separatist regions are paralleled by actions at the center that are unfavorable to the backward group. These include abandonment of promises of special concessions—for example, ignoring repeated pledges to consider federalism in the Sudan or failing to enforce arrangements for local job preferences in Telangana. They also include policies that augur homogenization, such as adoption of a single state language in Assam and the Sudan, of a single state religion in Burma, or of pan-Arabist doctrine in the Sudan and Iraq.[23] Groups like the Karens, the Nagas, the Mizos, the Southern Sudanese, the Philippine Muslims, and the Kurds, with a keen sense of weakness, are easily convinced by such policies that their only hope of resisting domination lies in some form of separation. As I shall show, advanced groups are not so readily persuaded to withdraw from competition within the unified state.

It may seem paradoxical that poor regions, benefiting from association with more prosperous regions, should want to terminate the arrangement. Yet the desire recurs. Occasionally, the economic costs of separatism are tempered by the prospect of claiming some resource located in or near the secessionist area, such as oil on the fringes of Iraqi Kurdistan. But this is rarely decisive. Many groups without such opportunities simply choose to pay whatever price is required. In the secessionist idiom of the Northern Nigeria of 1966, "What does money matter when it is a question of honour?"[24] For backward groups in backward regions, secessionist sentiment is weak when political debate still revolves around predictions of whether secession would entail an economic loss and, if so, whether the political gain would be worth the economic sacrifice.

Finally, it is necessary to take account of some exceptions. Why, for

23. C. P. Cook, "India: The Crisis in Assam," *The World Today* 24 (Oct. 1968): 444–48, at 446; Collins and Tignor, *Egypt and the Sudan*, 159; Donald Eugene Smith, *Religion and Politics in Burma* (Princeton: Princeton Univ. Press, 1966), 230; Zartman, *Government and Politics in Northern Africa*, 140; Eric J. Hooglund, "Cross-Current Nationalism: A Study of Kurdish Insurgency, 1961–1969" (unpublished paper, Johns Hopkins Univ. School of Advanced International Studies, Nov. 1970).

24. Quoted in Walter Schwarz, *Nigeria* (New York: Praeger, 1968), 249. For an explanation, cast in terms of welfare economics, of "why even individuals who will probably lose in terms of tangible rewards through increased political autonomy may nevertheless be willing to invest in its attainment," see Douglas G. Hartle and Richard M. Bird, "The Demand for Local Political Autonomy: An Individualistic Theory," *Journal of Conflict Resolution* 15 (Dec. 1971): 443–56, at 455.

example, did East Bengal remain in Pakistan for almost twenty-five years before seceding? Why did Northern Nigeria edge toward secession in 1966, only to pull back again?

The East Bengalis, particularly the Bengali Muslims, were clearly a backward people in a backward region. At $63, per capita income in East Bengal before secession was just half that of West Pakistan. At independence, only three Bengali Muslims, of a total of about 100 members of the Indian Civil Service, chose to serve Pakistan.[25] Poorly represented in the civil administration, in the army, and in business, the Bengalis were said to be rich only in politicians.[26] The Bengalis contended that expenditure per capita was skewed toward West Pakistan, where development investment would presumably bring a higher rate of return. In addition, they could claim something backward regions are usually in no position to claim: that they made a disproportionate contribution to export earnings because of jute production. As in other cases, even the East Bengal administration was filled with West Pakistanis, and Bengali was only grudgingly recognized as an official language. If backward groups in backward regions have a low threshold for separatism, why were the Bengalis, having similar characteristics, such late seceders?

For one thing, the great distance between East and West Pakistan, which was so often said to have rendered the unity of the country precarious, may instead have contributed to its durability. Distance may have made complete domination of the East by the West more difficult and may have limited irritating contact between people in the two wings. More important for present purposes, however, the East Bengalis were a very large group, more than half the total population. Unlike backward minorities, they could and did, right up to the eve of secession, entertain a hope that their numbers might be translated into sufficient political power at the center to compensate for their competitive disadvantages. This was reason enough to be patient, at least until the majority finally won by the Bengali party, the Awami League, in the 1970 elections was decisively rebuffed by the armed forces.

For the Nigerian Hausa, the strategy was the same. Despite their competitive weakness, they embarked on a course of pan-regional poli-

25. Richard D. Lambert, "Factors in Bengali Regionalism in Pakistan," *Far Eastern Survey* 28 (Apr. 1959): 49–58, at 54. Hugh Tinker, *India and Pakistan: A Political Analysis*, rev. ed. (New York: Praeger, 1968), 167, reports that none of Pakistan's share of the former Indian Civil Service was Bengali.

26. Crawford Young, *The Politics of Cultural Pluralism* (Madison: Univ. of Wisconsin Press, 1976), 482.

tics, because the Northern region gave them formidable numerical resources to do so and also because they had an historic aspiration, antedating the British conquest, to march south to the sea. For some years after independence, Hausa politicians ruled at the center by skillful exploitation of differences among Southerners. When military rule reversed this political ascendancy, there was separatist sentiment expressed by some Hausa, but it was quickly checked. After the Northern counter-coup of July 1966, nothing further was heard of it.[27]

The East Bengalis and the Hausa traveled in different directions, to be sure, but the animating forces were the same. The Bengalis waited a long time but finally chose to leave Pakistan. The Hausa clearly contemplated leaving Nigeria but reversed course. In both cases, urges to secede were propelled by the same fears that underlay the actions of backward groups in backward regions elsewhere. In each case, however, these were offset by the prospect of exerting hegemonic power in the undivided state. What distinguished the Hausa and the Bengalis from comparable groups in other countries was their large numbers, which afforded them a chance to resist domination and perhaps even impose their own. That is why neither chose an early secession. Regardless of advancement or backwardness, groups with substantial political power in the undivided state will prefer to remain in it rather than secede.

ADVANCED GROUPS IN BACKWARD REGIONS

In sharp contrast to the secessionist activity of backward groups in backward regions is the behavior of advanced groups in backward regions. Where backward groups are early seceders, advanced groups are late seceders. Where backward groups often sought colonial protection, a postponement of independence, or special arrangements once independence seemed inevitable, advanced groups were, more often than not, in the forefront of the anti-colonial movement.[28] Where backward groups

27. The Biafrans suggested that influential foreigners (presumably the British) discouraged the idea of a Northern secession. *Nigerian Crisis 1966* (Enugu: Eastern Regional Government, n.d.), 41–42, 49. Ruth First, *Power in Africa* (Harmondsworth: Penguin Books, 1970), 320, attributes the suppression of secessionist sentiment to a group of Northern civil servants, British and American diplomats, and Middle Belters in the army "who saw in Northern secession the danger that they would be a perpetual and unbearable minority in the North."

28. Though not invariably so. Before independence, the Ceylon Tamils, for example, sought additional parliamentary representation to compensate for their numerical weakness. See W. Howard Wriggins, *Ceylon: Dilemmas of a New Nation* (Princeton: Princeton Univ. Press, 1960), 91.

seek proportionality in government employment, advanced groups seek only assurances of nondiscrimination. Where backward groups attempt to keep ethnic strangers from government service in their region, advanced groups affirm the principle of unrestricted mobility. Where backward groups attempt secession as soon as their competitive fears seem confirmed, advanced groups attempt secession only when all hope of salvaging their position in the country is dashed. Where backward groups in backward regions attempt to separate despite the economic costs of secession, advanced groups in backward regions decide on separation only when the advantages of remaining in the unified state are much reduced and the costs of remaining seem perilously high. Advanced groups in backward regions have a much higher threshold of tolerance for political events inimical to their interests than backward groups do.

Initially, most groups try to remain in the undivided state, but how hard they try is a function of how able they feel to compete in it. After the first serious rebuffs, the Southern Sudanese moved rapidly from an equivocally federalist to an openly secessionist position, though there was never perfect agreement in the declarations of the various organizations. It took little to push them out. By contrast, the Ibo went through serious collective violence at Jos in 1945 and at Kano in 1953, their nationalism unimpaired. It took two massacres in 1966, separated by a Northern coup in which many Ibo officers and men lost their lives, before the Ibo embarked on Biafra. Thus did the Nigerian-nationalist Ibo become secessionists and the Northern secessionists become preservers of a single Nigeria. The Ceylon Tamils have also been patient. They endured the riots of 1956 and 1958, Sinhala-Only legislation, and discrimination against them in government employment, without demanding anything more than a mild federalism. Then, in 1972, came a new constitution that ignored their demands and conferred state patronage on Buddhism, the religion of most Sinhalese. This was followed by sharp discrimination against Tamil university applicants and by the anti-Tamil violence of 1977, 1981, and 1983. Only in 1976 did Ceylon Tamil leaders unequivocally declare for a separate state, and since 1978 there have been very serious incidents of separatist terrorism. The Tamils could still go either way.

Because advanced groups in backward regions secede only as a last resort, many advanced groups in backward regions, even when severely frustrated, do not reach the point of choosing separatism. The Lozi in Zambia are such a group, aggrieved but not inclined seriously toward secession. The Lozi homeland, Barotseland, was administered separately by the British. At independence it was agreed that Barotseland would have a special status within Zambia.[29] This arrangement was soon abrogated by the Zambian government, which treated Barotseland as just another province, restricting the powers of the Lozi monarch and abolishing the Barotse legislature. Periodically, there has been violence between Lozi and Bemba. Following the restrictions imposed by the central government, Barotseland turned decisively away from the Zambian nationalist party and toward the opposition. Each time the central government has acted to limit provincial power, secession has been on the lips of the Lozi aristocracy. But it has gone no further. Secession has had no real support from educated Lozi elites and has produced no coherent movement. Despite provocation, important elements of the Lozi community still prefer a unified Zambia.

The position of advanced groups in backward regions makes it clear why their threshold of tolerance is so much higher than that of backward groups. Advanced groups in backward regions are generally population exporters. Barotseland has poor soil. Jaffna, the heartland of the Ceylon Tamils, is dry and unproductive. Iboland, having suffered soil erosion, is also infertile. In each case, group survival has depended upon the search for opportunities outside the region, upon push migration. Barotseland exported Lozi labor to South African gold mines and white-collar workers to the Zambian Copperbelt. Lozi also sought education far out of proportion to their numbers; they were the largest group of students at Lusaka's premier secondary school on the eve of independence. This opened the way to opportunities all over Zambia.[30] As we have seen, the same applies to the Ceylon Tamils, who took advantage of educational opportunities and migrated to the South of Sri Lanka as traders, bureaucrats, and professionals.[31] Ibo, too, settled all over Nigeria; Ibo clerks, traders, and laborers were to be found in every urban area.[32] Each of these backward regions thus came to depend on remittances from the sons it had exported to other regions of the country.

This explains why the Ibo became the apostles of pan-Nigerian na-

29. Gerald L. Caplan, *The Elites of Barotseland, 1878–1969* (London: C. Hurst, 1970), chaps. 6–8; Caplan, "Barotseland: The Secessionist Challenge to Zambia," *Journal of Modern African Studies* 6 (Oct. 1968): 343–60; Margaret Rouse Bates, "UNIP in Post Independence Zambia" (Ph.D. diss., Harvard Univ., 1971).

30. Caplan, *The Elites of Barotseland*, 175–76.

31. Wriggins, *Ceylon: Dilemmas of a New Nation*, 234.

32. James S. Coleman, *Nigeria: Background to Nationalism* (Berkeley and Los Angeles: Univ. of California Press, 1958), 332–34.

tionalism and the implacable opponents of compartmentalizing the country. "The Ibo, as well as the Ibibio, had strong personal economic reasons for wanting Nigeria to be a nation with freedom of movement and enterprise."[33] The educated Lozi elite, especially but not only those outside Barotseland, took an equally strong position in favor of a united Zambia.[34] And the Ceylon Tamils preferred "fruitful participation in national affairs instead of being cramped and cribbed in the arid and overcrowded Jaffna Peninsula."[35] One undivided, nationwide field of opportunity seemed in each case to be at the heart of ethnic interest.

Whereas for backward groups, unable to compete outside their home region, the question is whether they will govern themselves or be governed by carpetbaggers, for advanced groups the issue is whether they will be accepted outside their own region. For an advanced group, widely distributed throughout the country, secession would have the clearest disadvantages. It would dry up vital extraregional income sources and trigger a return of talented but unemployed group members to the homeland. Alternatively, it would leave large segments of the secessionist ethnic group outside the homeland, where they would be vulnerable to discrimination and attack and where their own income and their remittances to the home region would also be jeopardized. Advanced groups do not feel unable to compete—indeed, others often sense in them excessive confidence. Unlike backward groups, therefore, advanced groups are unwilling to disregard these formidable economic costs of secession in order to free themselves from disagreeable competitive relationships. Hence their extreme wariness of abandoning the national system for a more parochial secessionist region, with its greatly restricted opportunities.

Backward groups are, of course, not troubled by these inhibiting considerations. One reason for their ability to make such a quick judgment in favor of secession is that they need worry less often about the presence of large numbers of their kinsmen outside their home region. There are exceptions, to be sure: the majority of Karens, for example, do not live in the core Karen area, and it was not easy for Karen secessionists to stake out a contiguous territory that would embrace an acceptable number of Karens.[36] But the usual situation of backward groups is different.

33. Ibid., 338–39.
34. Caplan, *The Elites of Barotseland*, 194.
35. Wriggins, *Ceylon: Dilemmas of a New Nation*, 146.
36. Brian Crozier, *The Rebels: A Study of Post-War Insurrections* (Boston: Beacon Press, 1960), 89.

Often lacking education and marketable skills, they are less likely to migrate in large numbers out of their region.[37] Migration out of their region is inherent in the situation of advanced groups from backward regions, as it is not for backward groups.

It is their diaspora, then, and the nationwide field of opportunity that inhibit secessionist impulses among advanced groups from backward regions. Still, the Ibo did fight a war of secession, the Kasai Baluba of Zaire did set up their own state, and the Ceylon Tamils have threatened to do the same. What forces overcame their inhibitions?

If the dispersion of group members and the advantages of a single, unbounded, nationwide field of opportunity impede the growth of secessionist sentiment among population-exporting groups, then clearly the reversal of these conditions can provide a real fillip to separatism. When the national system begins to break down because of regional parochialism or because of discrimination against advanced groups, the advantages of "one Nigeria" or "one Sri Lanka" can readily be called into question. When a population-exporting region experiences an in-gathering of its scattered exiles, inhibitions on secessionist impulses can be swept aside. This is all the more so because push migrants from backward regions do not return home *en masse* unless something dramatically unfavorable has happened to them. The two unfavorable things that happen most often are discrimination that curtails their opportunities and violence that threatens their lives. The two sometimes go together, and they are the most common precipitants of secession among advanced groups in backward regions.

Advanced groups from population-exporting regions are disproportionately victims of ethnic violence. This explains the paradox of their position: reluctant separatists yet not infrequently pushed to the point of seceding. The most severe episodes of such violence produce massive back-migration that fosters secession. In Zaire, in 1959, when Lulua killed Baluba in Luluabourg in Central Kasai, some 50,000 Baluba fled back to South Kasai. Gradually, Baluba from all over Central Kasai

37. This is not an inflexible rule, of course, but it does hold for large parts of the developing world, especially less industrialized countries. Often the migration such groups undertake is temporary or seasonal, as in the case of agricultural labor. That tendency is altered, however, as industrialization proceeds, creating a need for large, unskilled and semi-skilled labor forces. In Spain, for instance, the poor Southern region of Andalusia exports much unskilled labor to Northern industry. The distribution of the population of backward groups may be a major difference—with implications for secession of backward regions—between developing and developed countries.

followed suit. By 1963, the population of South Kasai had quadrupled. The result of this flight, which signified an end to Baluba opportunities outside their own region, was the attempted secession of South Kasai.[38]

This was the Ibo case in microcosm. The Nigerian violence of 1966 spurred a similar eastward movement of Ibo. Many Ibo fled after the May riots, then later returned to the North. But the September-October killings were more organized and extensive. These riots generated a flood of refugees, some of them maimed. Their arrival in the East inflamed sentiment there. Perhaps a million Ibo returned to the East, convinced that it was dangerous to be an Ibo elsewhere in Nigeria.

The violence was the culmination of a long process of whittling away Ibo opportunities. The process began, in formal terms, with the "Northernization" of administration and business pursued by the Northern Regional Government in the 1950s.[39] Discrimination was practiced against Ibo government servants and businessmen in employment, contracts, and licenses. The process accelerated in the 1960s, with attacks on alleged Ibo nepotism and concerted struggles to remove Ibo from high government and university positions. The victims of violence who fled eastward were joined by those who felt that Ibo prospects in other regions were no longer salvageable. The Ibo, it was said, had built the country but would not be permitted to reap the rewards.[40]

Thus far, the Ceylon Tamils have been spared the massive violence of an episode comparable to Nigeria in 1966. But they have increasingly been victimized in widespread riots. At such times, refugees from the South have carried back credible tales of lack of protection for Tamils in Sinhalese areas.

More than this, the Tamil position in the country has time and again failed to receive the official recognition the Tamils demand. The relegation of the Tamil language to a distinctly secondary place in official business resulted in a decline in opportunities for Tamil government servants without a knowledge of Sinhala. The 1972 constitution reinforced the position of Sinhala, accorded a "foremost place" to Sinhalese

38. Thomas Turner, "Congo-Kinshasa," in Victor A. Olorunsola, ed., *The Politics of Cultural Sub-Nationalism in Africa* (Garden City, N.Y.: Anchor Books, 1972), 217–24.

39. Richard L. Sklar, *Nigerian Political Parties* (Princeton: Princeton Univ. Press, 1963), 327–28.

40. K. Whiteman, "Enugu: The Psychology of Secession, 20 July 1966 to 30 May 1967," in Panter-Brick, ed., *Nigerian Politics and Military Rule: Prelude to the Civil War*, 117; Young, *The Politics of Cultural Pluralism*, 467–68; Victor A. Olorunsola, "Nigeria," in Olorunsola, ed., *The Politics of Cultural Sub-Nationalism in Africa*, 35–36.

Buddhism, and denied Tamil claims for regional autonomy.[41] The constitution was a decisive symbolic rebuff.

Then came a policy of "standardizing marks," a system of weightage in grades to offset the superior performance of Tamil students in academic examinations. The result was a dramatic decline in Tamil representation in higher education, a decline that had begun earlier. Reductions of 30 to 40 percent in Tamil enrollment, depending on the field, were experienced in a period of one to three years.[42] In the decade between 1963 and 1973, the percentage of Ceylon Tamils with university education fell from 2.2 to 0.6, below the Sinhalese level.[43] Tamil prospects in government service and the professions dwindled.

For the Tamils, as for the Ibo—but to a lesser degree—repeated failure to acknowledge the Tamil position in the country, the steady contraction of opportunities in the South, and periodic violence have all contributed to a growing willingness to forgo opportunities in an undivided state if those opportunities could be exchanged for expanded opportunities in a smaller, sovereign Tamil state. For most Tamils, this willingness remains equivocal, partly because many Tamils remain in the South. Recurrent anti-Tamil violence, such as the serious riots of 1983, may change this, but so far, like other advanced groups in backward regions, the Tamils are still reluctant secessionists.

ADVANCED GROUPS IN ADVANCED REGIONS

As indicated previously, the vast majority of secessionist regions are economically backward. Advanced regions are far less inclined to separatism. But just as backward and advanced groups in backward regions have different reasons for choosing a separatist course, so, too, do the paths traversed by groups inhabiting advanced regions differ from each other.

The calculations of advanced groups in advanced regions are easy to fathom. In the nature of things, they are likely to have a regional economic grievance. Advanced regions usually generate more income and

41. Robert N. Kearney, "Language and the Rise of Tamil Separatism in Sri Lanka," *Asian Survey* 18 (May 1978): 521–34. See also Urmila Phadnis, "Keeping the Tamils Internal," *Far Eastern Economic Review*, Mar. 25, 1972, pp. 21–22; W. A. Wiswa Warnapala, "Sri Lanka in 1972: Tension and Change," *Asian Survey* 13 (Feb. 1973): 217–30.

42. Kearney, "Language and the Rise of Tamil Separatism in Sri Lanka," 531; Walter Schwarz, *The Tamils of Sri Lanka* (London: Minority Rights Group, Report no. 25, 1975), 12–13.

43. *Report on the Survey of Consumer Finances*, part 1 (Colombo: Central Bank of Ceylon, 1974), 32.

contribute more revenue to the treasury of the undivided state than they receive. They believe that they are subsidizing poorer regions. The Basque and Catalan cases in Spain are an extreme example of this, well documented and worth discussing even though not in Asia and Africa. The Basque country and Catalonia are industrialized regions, with per capita incomes far above the national average—in the Basque case, more than twice that average. In the late 1960s, Catalonia paid 31 percent of all of Spain's taxes, but received only 13 percent of all expenditures. The Basque region paid 13 percent of all taxes but obtained only 5 percent of all expenditures.[44] Myths have grown up in the Basque country that the hardworking Basques are supporting less productive peoples and regions of Spain. A Basque protest song characterizes Spain as "a cow with its muzzle in the Basque country and its udder in Madrid."[45] From this standpoint, separatism would permit productive regions like the Basque country to retain their revenues and to control and limit migrants from other regions who are attracted to advanced industrial regions because of economic opportunities there.

If this were all there were to it, there would be many more separatist advanced regions than there are. There are, however, countervailing considerations that stem the growth of secessionist activity among advanced groups in advanced regions.

To begin with, such groups are likely to export surplus capital and population outside their region. Their prosperity generates investment that does not respect regional boundaries. Their education creates a talent pool in search of opportunities. Like the Ibo, but less out of necessity than out of opportunity, the Yoruba sent their sons all over Nigeria, and particularly to the North, where they were engaged in business and in government service. When the Ibo created Biafra, the Yoruba did not follow suit. There are several reasons for this,[46] but surely one of the most prominent is that the Yoruba were well positioned, by dint of qualifications and seniority, to move into opportunities in Nigeria vacated by the Ibo. And this they did. In Uganda, the Baganda were vastly

44. Willliam T. Salisbury, "Some Aspects of the Regional Issue in Contemporary Spanish Affairs" (unpublished paper presented at the 1976 annual meeting of the International Studies Association), 6, drawing on data developed by Juan Linz.
45. William A. Douglas and Milton da Silva, "Basque Nationalism," in Oriol Pi-Sunyer, ed., *The Limits of Integration* (Amherst: Univ. of Massachusetts Department of Anthropology, Research Report no. 9, 1971), 149–50. For the underlying resentments, see also Kenneth Medhurst, *The Basques* (London: Minority Rights Group, Report no. 9, 1972), 5.
46. For some of these, see Dudley, "Western Nigeria and the Nigerian Crisis," 109.

overrepresented in the civil service during the 1960s.[47] They also were overrepresented in business and the professions, and they had a long history of taking up opportunities all over the country. This favorable position no doubt had much to do with overcoming initial Baganda reluctance to join an independent Uganda. Ultimately, the Baganda ruler did threaten secession, but only after the prime minister, A. Milton Obote, had reneged on the independence agreement, removed the ruler as head of state, and forced through a new constitution.[48] For the Yoruba and the Baganda, the attractions of exerting influence and reaping rewards in a large, undivided state were stronger than the temptations of a more homogeneous, contracted homeland. Perhaps the same will hold true for the Sikhs in the Indian Punjab, even after the widespread anti-Sikh riots of 1984, unless further violence triggers a wave of refugees returning to the home region. The Sikhs are heavily represented in the transport business all over India and in the Indian army.[49] The effect of investment and employment not tied to the home region is to create among advanced groups from advanced regions outward-looking interests that retard their enthusiasm for secession.

There is something beyond this that is not present in the situation of advanced groups in backward regions (such as the Ibo). The economic development of advanced regions almost inevitably leads to claims of revenue imbalance of the sort described earlier, but this may mask the enormous economic advantages that inhere in the undivided state. If the advanced region produces for the domestic market of the undivided state, it is not certain that regional prosperity will survive separation. Some 90 percent of the production of the Basque provinces, for example, is purchased within Spain under a protectionist economic policy in aid of Basque products that would not be competitive on the international market.[50] Once the Ibo returned home, the economic interest of Iboland in the undivided state was practically at an end. But this would not be

47. Nelson Kasfir, "Cultural Sub-Nationalism in Uganda," in Olorunsola, ed., *The Politics of Cultural Sub-Nationalism in Africa*, 123–28.

48. On the Baganda, see Young, *The Politics of Cultural Pluralism*, 149–56.

49. See Dalip Singh, *Dynamics of Punjab Politics* (New Delhi: Macmillan India, 1981), 52–53; Satinder Singh, *Khalistan: An Academic Analysis* (New Delhi: Amar Prakashan, 1982); Paul Wallace, "Religious and Secular Politics in Punjab: The Sikh Dilemma in Competing Political Systems," *Punjab Journal of Politics* 5 (Jan.–June 1981): 1–32; Harish K. Puri, "Akali Politics: Emerging Compulsions," *Punjab Journal of Politics* 5 (Jan.–June 1981): 33–51.

50. See Pedro González Blasco, "Modern Nationalism in Old Nations as a Consequence of Earlier State-Building: The Case of Basque-Spain," in Wendell Bell and Walter Freeman, eds., *Ethnicity and Nation-Building* (Beverly Hills: Sage, 1974), 347.

true for the Basques—or for other, similarly situated advanced groups in advanced regions—even if all group members were to return at once to the home region. The prosperity of advanced groups in advanced regions typically depends, not merely on the contributions of migrant sons located in other regions, but on a web of interregional economic relations that may include dependence on other regions for materials and markets, sometimes specially protected markets.[51] Like advanced groups in backward regions, advanced groups in advanced regions will secede only if the economic costs of secession are low, but the reduction of such costs is far less likely in the case of advanced groups in advanced regions.

This circumstance is reflected in the Basque ambivalence toward secession. The Basque movement is strong but far from unanimous on its goals. Businessmen and others with far-flung interests, or with doubts about the ability of the region to survive an end to protection, have tended to oppose a separate state.[52] Noting that Basque industry has always thought in terms of the broader Spanish economy, Stanley Payne has opined that Basque separatism is "shrill and fanatical" partly "because of its minority position" in the Basque country.[53]

Nevertheless, the Basques have experienced some special conditions conducive to separatism. The Basques have relatively fewer group members outside their region than most other similarly situated advanced groups do, though exact figures are not available. In the past, many who left the Basque country became Castilianized. The Basques have also faced an enormous influx of immigrants from other areas of Spain. Both of these conditions I shall comment on in dealing with forces that foster separatism regardless of the backward or advanced character of the region or group. For the moment, it is enough to note that these conditions are especially acute among the Basques. So, too, was the repression of the Franco regime, a regime that had remarkably few Basques in its public service and that carried out its repression largely through the medium of the *Guardia Civil*, a military body composed of ethnic strangers to the Basque country.

---

51. So far as tariff protection is concerned, much is likely to depend on whether the prosperity of the region is based on production of finished goods for the domestic market or on production of primary products or extraction of minerals for export. For elaboration, see page 257, below.
52. González Blasco, "Modern Nationalism in Old Nations as a Consequence of Earlier State-Building," 366.
53. "Catalan and Basque Nationalism," *Journal of Contemporary History* 6 (1971): 15–51, at 50. The reference to Spanish industry appears at p. 38.

What the Basque case shows is that a powerful secessionist movement is not impossible among advanced groups in advanced regions but that it takes some extraordinary conditions to bring it about. Most of the time, the lure of interests and opportunities throughout the undivided state is enough to ward off the possibility.

The point is well illustrated by what might at first appear to be the exceptional case of Eritrea. With about 8 percent of the total population of Ethiopia, Eritreans have had, by some estimates, as much as one-fourth of the opportunities in higher education and government service all over the country. Their literacy rate is estimated to be considerably higher than the Ethiopian average.[54] Under Italian rule, Eritrea experienced industrial development that more than compensated overall for the region's soil erosion and unreliable rainfall, leaving it with a per capita income higher than the Ethiopian average. Moreover, as Ethiopia's only access to the sea, Eritrea benefited from the transit trade and from priority in government investment.[55] Yet, practically from the moment of federation with Ethiopia in 1952, there was Eritrean resistance, culminating in a full-fledged secessionist war by the 1970s. Is this a case, then, of an advanced group in an advanced region willing to forgo the advantages of the undivided state, including numerous opportunities outside the home region, on scarcely a moment's reflection?

To answer this question, it is necessary to restore some of the complexity that our simplified framework has deliberately omitted. Eritrea is a heterogeneous region, composed of nearly equal numbers of Christians and Muslims. The advanced group that has had opportunities in education and employment, and has migrated out of the region, has been disproportionately Christian.[56] For example, nineteen of one hundred and thirty-eight senior central government officials between 1941 and

54. John Franklin Campbell, "Background to the Eritrean Conflict," *Africa Report*, May 1971, pp. 19–20. Campbell's estimate is three to four times the Ethiopian average. Asmara, the Eritrean capital, had a literacy rate of 50 percent in the early 1970s, higher than any other area of Ethiopia, including Addis Ababa, which had a 43 percent rate. Provisional Military Government of Ethiopia, Central Statistical Office, *Population and Housing Characteristics of Asmara* (Addis Ababa: Central Statistical Office, Statistical Bulletin no. 12, Dec. 1974), 5.

55. Ethiopiawi (pseud.), "The Eritrean-Ethiopian Conflict," in Astri Suhrke and Lela Garner Noble, eds., *Ethnic Conflict in International Relations* (New York: Praeger, 1977), 131.

56. There are many indirect indications of this. Asmara, by far the largest city of the region, is 85 percent Christian. Literacy in those districts of Asmara with the heaviest Muslim concentration (Akria and Geza Berhano) was below the average for the city, and housing in those districts was also of less than average quality. Provisional Military Government, Central Statistical Office, *Population and Housing Characteristics of Asmara*, 68–69, 76–78.

1966 were Eritreans—a total second only to the Emperor's own Shoan Amhara—but, of the nineteen, only three were Muslims.[57] The secessionist movement, although not totally lacking in Christian support, has been disproportionately Muslim. The ties of Christians in the Eritrean highlands have historically been closer to other Ethiopian groups than to the Muslims in the Eritrean lowlands.[58] Around the time of federation, many Christians supported full integration with Ethiopia—witness the growth of a Unionist Party composed of Christians.

When these Muslim-Christian qualifications are introduced, the profile of the Eritrean secessionists no longer resembles that of an advanced group from an advanced region. Rather, it is largely a movement of a backward group from an advanced region. Groups so positioned have, as I shall show very shortly, little reason to equivocate on secession once they detect signs of domination. (In Eritrea, one strong sign that we have observed elsewhere was the frequent appointment of Shoans, rather than Eritreans, to key positions in Eritrea.) Advanced groups from advanced regions, however, are more often inclined to participate actively in the undivided state—and even, if possible, to dominate it—than they are to withdraw from it.

BACKWARD GROUPS IN ADVANCED REGIONS

There is a different reason for the infrequency of secessionist claims made by backward groups in advanced regions. Such groups are quite likely separatists, but they are rarely in a numerically predominant position in such a region.

Economically advanced regions tend to be the home of advanced ethnic groups who have benefited from the economic institutions that bring prosperity to the region. Over and over again, fortuitous location in or near a center of investment has given local ethnic groups opportunities for education and employment denied to those less well situated. Like the Basques, the Yoruba, the Kikuyu, and the Baganda are all advanced groups indigenous to economically advanced regions. But this is not invariably the case. Sometimes opportunities of this kind are taken up by migrants to the area, typically by advanced groups from backward, population-exporting regions. This has been largely the case in the Sind province of Pakistan, the prosperous urban centers of which are

57. Christopher Clapham, *Haile Selassie's Government* (New York: Praeger, 1969), 75–76, 83.
58. Ibid., 81.

controlled by Urdu-speaking migrants from North India, rather than by Sindhis. Where this occurs, the indigenous population becomes a backward group in an advanced region.

Katanga (later renamed Shaba) in Zaire was such a case. Mineral-rich,

> Katanga was sparsely populated . . . with the result that by the 1920s labor recruiters began going farther afield, notably to what became Kasai Province. The new mining towns, Elisabethville, Jadotville, Kolwezi, and others, began filling up with "strangers" from outside Katanga, predominantly Luba from Kasai, who were particularly receptive to European influences and social change . . . . In both commercial and clerical jobs in Katanga towns, the Luba/Kasai were markedly more numerous than the Katangans.[59]

By the late 1950s, Lunda and other indigenous groups were greatly outnumbered by migrants in the towns, especially by Kasai Baluba. In Elisabethville, for example, more than half of those employed came from outside Katanga, and Kasai Baluba outnumbered Lunda by more than four to one, a fact quickly reflected in election results.[60]

Political organization in Katanga responded to this situation. Moise Tshombe's party, the Conakat, described itself as a movement of "authentic Katangans," which was another way of saying it was organized by indigenous Lunda and Bayeke of Southern Katanga and directed against the Kasai Baluba. Conakat had originally had some support from the Baluba of Northern Katanga (a different group from the Kasai Baluba), but this proved short-lived. The key reason for the split was Conakat's hostility to the Kasai Baluba, with whom the Katanga Baluba feel at least some affinity.

It took very little beyond the double threat of immigrant Kasai Baluba power in Southern Katanga and Katanga Baluba power in the Northern part of the province to persuade Conakat of the desirability of a separate state. As Zaire neared independence, the Baluba of Northern Katanga seemed to have greater influence in the central government, and this was

---

59. Turner, "Congo-Kinshasa," 224.
60. Ibid., 226; Jules Gérard-Libois, *Katanga Secession*, trans. Rebecca Young (Madison: Univ. of Wisconsin Press, 1966), 12–13, 27–28; René Lemarchand, *Political Awakening in the Belgian Congo* (Berkeley and Los Angeles: Univ. of California Press, 1964), 235–36, 241; Crawford Young, "The Politics of Separatism: Katanga, 1960–63," in Gwendolen M. Carter, ed., *Politics in Africa: 7 Cases* (New York: Harcourt, Brace & World, 1966), 172–74; René Lemarchand, "Congo (Leopoldville)," in James S. Coleman and Carl G. Rosberg, Jr., eds., *Political Parties and National Integration in Tropical Africa* (Berkeley and Los Angeles: Univ. of California Press, 1964), 581.

enough to push Tshombe over the brink.[61] Within the first fortnight of independence, the secession of Katanga was underway. But the secession was effective only in the South of Katanga, where the Lunda and Bayeke are concentrated. In the North of the province, a separate movement developed among the Katanga Baluba.

The sentiments and claims expressed by backward groups in advanced regions are a hybrid of those put forward by backward groups in backward regions and by advanced groups in advanced regions. They are compounded of a substantial dose of collective anxiety and a desire to end revenue-expenditure imbalances.

Like backward groups in backward regions, those in advanced regions are fearful of competing with advanced groups and keenly sensitive to threats of domination. Their fears are magnified by the large number of advanced group members in their midst. Backward groups in backward regions can escape disagreeable competition by withdrawing from the undivided state. A backward group in an advanced region—such as the Lunda—must also cope with the advanced group within its own regional borders. To do so, it proposes various discriminatory measures. Secession foreshadows yet more severe and xenophobic action.[62]

As noted earlier, backward groups in backward regions typically attempt secession despite economic costs. For backward groups in advanced regions, however, secession appears to promise economic benefits. The region typically contributes more to the income of the undivided state than it receives. The contribution of Katanga to Zaire's total income was close to 50 percent just before independence. But Katanga's share of Zaire's budgetary expenditure was only 20 percent, more than its per capita share but less, obviously, than its share based on productivity.[63] Just as Basques likened Spain to a cow being fed by the Basques but

61. In the 1960 Katanga provincial elections, Conakat did well. It also did better than Balubakat, the party of the Katanga Baluba in the North of the province, in the national elections, but the Balubakat leader, Jason Sendwe, was nonetheless named by the central government to be High Commissioner for Katanga. This appointment triggered the Katanga secession. Turner, "Congo-Kinshasa," 227.

I leave aside the role of Katanga's European settlers in supporting the secession. For the settlers' role, see Gérard-Libois, *Katanga Secession.* Lemarchand's judgment, which seems well supported by the evidence, is that the settlers' secessionist "dispositions could not have led to the secession of the province unless they were shared and abetted by a substantial segment of the African population." *Political Awakening in the Belgian Congo,* 233.

62. In Katanga, this meant, concretely, the exclusion of Kasai Baluba from political and administrative positions and the expulsion of many from the province. Lemarchand, *Political Awakening in the Belgian Congo,* 239; Gérard-Libois, *Katanga Secession,* 28.

63. Gérard-Libois, *Katanga Secession,* 3–5.

milked in Madrid, so in Katanga there was a long-standing slogan, "Katanga, milk cow for the whole Congo."[64] Before independence, Tshombe demanded that "the resources of each province be properly its own."[65] These are claims characteristic of advanced regions, even expressed in the same bovine imagery.

Against the anticipated benefits of secession, backward groups in advanced regions do not need to balance certain costs that trouble the calculations of advanced groups in advanced regions. Unlike advanced groups, backward groups generally do not have widespread interests throughout the undivided state. Unless other regions of the state are industrialized, backward groups are less likely to export population or capital.[66] Tariff protection for the products of an advanced region may be another matter, but three factors are apt to limit or cancel its inhibiting effect on secession. First, there is a difference between industrialized and developing countries. In less developed countries, the prosperity of advanced regions is less likely to be based on production of finished goods for a protected domestic market than on exports of minerals or primary agricultural products. The latter are very often taxed, rather than subsidized. As tariff protection is a disincentive to secession, so tax levies are an incentive. Second, this is particularly so for advanced regions dominated by backward groups, who are likely to be located in areas where primary agricultural products are cultivated or minerals are extracted. Third, even if the economy of the advanced region depends on tariff protection or other benefits derived from membership in the undivided state, the loss of these benefits that accompanies secession, though it hurts the region as a whole, may still be offset by gains that inure to the backward group that controls the region and opts for secession. A regional loss may still be an ethnic gain.

Altogether the incentives are heavily weighted toward separatism in such a case. Backward groups would like simultaneously to have a free hand to deal with the advanced groups in their midst and to retain the

64. Ibid., 51.
65. Ibid., 41.
66. See note 37, above. If anything, a backward group in an advanced region may have the opposite problem: a population so compact it does not cover the whole region. If so, the secession will be of a limited area, as were the Katanga secession and the Rwenzururu movement of Western Uganda, the latter confined to the areas inhabited by Baamba and Bakonjo. Doornbos, "Protest Movements in Western Uganda"; Kasfir, "Cultural Sub-Nationalism in Uganda," 99. In both cases, these happened to be areas within which major mineral resources were also located. As noted earlier, Eritrean Muslims are also confined largely to lowland areas.

TABLE 3   THE DISPOSITION TO SECEDE

Group and Region	Political Claims	Precipitants	Calcu-lations	Timing, Relative Frequency
Backward Group in Backward Region	Proportionality in civil service, occasionally also in revenues	Denial of proportionality in civil service; symbolic issues like language and religion; influx of advanced civil servants	Secede despite economic costs	Early, Frequent
Advanced Group in Backward Region	Nondiscrimination; no revenue issue	Severe discrimination; repeated violence; migration back to home region	Secede only if economic costs are low	Late, Somewhat Frequent
Advanced Group in Advanced Region	Nondiscrimination; spend revenue where generated	Severe discrimination; violence and migration back to home region if population exporter	Secede only if economic costs are low	Late, Rare
Backward Group in Advanced Region	Proportionality in civil service; spend revenue where generated	Denial of proportionality; political claims made by immigrant strangers in the region	Secede regardless of economic benefits or costs	Early, Rare

revenues of economic enterprises located in their region. But, as I have indicated, it is rare that a backward group finds itself in political control of an advanced region. Katanga, once the specter haunting all of Africa, turns out to be an exceptional case.

THE DIFFERENTIAL DISPOSITION TO SECEDE

Table 3 summarizes much of the discussion so far. It makes clear just how much can be deduced from group and regional position. Backward groups tend to measure disadvantage in terms of deviation from some concept of proportionality in relation to population. Advanced groups gauge deprivation by discrimination, utilizing a standard of proportionality in relation to merit. Advanced regions tend to complain of revenue-expenditure imbalances. Backward regions may also complain of inadequate expenditure if they receive from the center less than their per capita share, albeit more than their contribution to revenue. Backward regions that are the home of advanced groups, however, tend not to complain of revenue imbalances, probably because they receive remittances from outside the region and certainly because they eschew claims based on numbers. Here, too, there is more than one criterion of proportionality.

The four categories of political claims are, as the table shows, a combined function of group and regional characteristics. These claims do not, however, invariably ripen into secession. The columns headed "Precipitants" and "Calculations" indicate when dispositions to secede are likely to emerge. Precipitants tend to be events that have the effect of rejecting unequivocally claims put forward by ethnic groups. In the case of backward groups, as we have seen, precipitants foreshadow political domination. In the case of advanced groups, precipitants tend to reduce the advantages of remaining in the undivided state. In short, precipitants may act either to raise the costs or to reduce the benefits of remaining in the state—provided, of course, that benefits and costs are understood to embrace nonmaterial as well as material values.

Indeed, the table makes clear that separatism results from varying mixes of sheer economic interest and group apprehension. Economic interest may act either as an accelerator or a brake on separatism. Yet, among the most frequent and precocious secessionists—backward groups in backward regions—economic loss or gain plays the smallest role, ethnic anxiety the largest.

The precipitating events and the calculations that follow them are not inexorable. Claims need not be denied. Advanced civil servants need not be posted to backward regions. Advanced groups from population-exporting regions can be protected from discrimination and violence; they need not migrate home. Much depends on the reception accorded group claims. The conditions that promote a disposition to secede, though derived from group and regional position, are subject to intervention and deflection.[67] The list of potential candidates for secession is much longer than the list of actual secessionists. Some Basques in Spain want independence; but Nigerian Yoruba, who might have chosen to secede, chose not to; and Baganda, who threatened secession, did not follow through. The Ibo fought a war of secession; but the Lozi, not treated like the Ibo, did not secede; and the Tamils of Sri Lanka might still go either way. Backward groups are frequent secessionists, but the Northerners in Ghana, every bit as backward as Northerners in Nigeria[68]—and far less powerful—have not even mooted secession. Likewise, the backward Batéké in Southeast Gabon, a region rich in uranium and manganese, have evidenced no serious inclination toward a Katanga-like secession.[69] Every category of regional group has its negative cases.

Moreover, as I have suggested all along, there are varying thresholds of secession and therefore differential frequency of secession among the various categories of groups. Clearly, backward groups in backward regions are easily persuaded that it is in their interest to leave. So are backward groups in advanced regions, but there are many fewer such groups in a position to secede. Despite their generally greater reluctance to secede, there are differences among advanced groups. Advanced groups from advanced regions often receive extraregional benefits that are not confined to remittances from migrant sons and therefore not terminated precipitously if back-migration should occur. They are less likely to secede. As the last column in the table shows, the four paths to secession are not equally well-trodden.

The much greater frequency of secessionist movements in backward

67. It would be a mistake, however, to minimize the policy dilemmas created by the coexistence in a single state of various kinds of regional groups. Occasionally, the claims are in direct opposition to each other, so that what can salve the apprehensions of one group will simultaneously precipitate secessionist action by another. I deal with this issue in Chapter 16, below.

68. See Philip J. Foster, "Ethnicity and the Schools in Ghana," *Comparative Education Review* 6 (Oct. 1962): 127–35.

69. Brian Weinstein, *Gabon: Nation-Building on the Ogooué* (Cambridge: M.I.T. Press, 1966), 220–25. The Batéké case, however, may fall within a caveat stated earlier regarding Pakistani Baluch and Pathan reluctance to do anything that might link them with Afghanistan. There is a similar reluctance among Batéké to do anything that might result in their annexation by neighboring Congo (Brazzaville).

regions has a number of important implications. Many regions that choose secession are likely to be economically least capable of sustaining themselves. This applies particularly to the secession of backward groups in backward regions. They may also be short on administrative capacity and personnel. However, the position of advanced groups in backward regions is at least equivocal. They will have no shortage of administrative talent, once their migrant sons return to the region. But this surfeit of talent may quickly become a drain on the budget. The experience of Biafra and Benin's difficulties in reabsorbing civil servants it had exported to other West African states both attest to this.

No doubt many countries once proclaimed "unviable" have survived. It is all too easy to exaggerate the economic problems a secessionist region will face. Yet there is no gainsaying the fact that a great many regions that do manage to secede can be expected to have post-secession economic difficulties.

The distinction between early and late seceders—which, as the table makes clear, is largely coterminous with the distinction between backward and advanced groups—also has important consequences. In general, late secessions are more cohesive, better organized, and more often conducted under the auspices of a political party than are early secessions. Early secessions in countries like Chad, the Sudan, and Burma consisted of more than one movement. The secessionist regions were heterogeneous, and the secessions occurred so soon after independence that no political party had a chance to capture the support of the entire region. Because it was not centrally organized, the warfare was sporadic, and—except in the Sudan—there was no single organization in a position to make peace. In Chad, for example, an amnesty was accepted by members of one ethnic group fighting in one region but ignored by other groups fighting elsewhere. In all the cases, the fighting lingered on for many years; in Burma, it still does. In the late secessions of Biafra and Bangladesh, by contrast, the movements were under much tighter control. The fighting was more intense, widespread, and simultaneous in all areas; and victory for one side or the other was quicker and more decisive.[70]

In the case of groups likely to become late seceders, if seceders at all,

---

70. All else being equal, there will also be more subgroup amalgamation among advanced groups than among backward groups (see Chapter 2, above). On these grounds, too, late seceders will be more cohesive, their fighting forces less likely to fight with each other than with the forces of the rump state.

there is more time to work on policies averting secession and, because of their reluctance to secede, more latitude regarding the actual substance of policies that might prove sufficient to avert secession. There is also, however, more time for both sides to prepare for the battle when it comes: to cement foreign alliances, procure sophisticated weapons, and organize the secessionist region and the rump region for war. This extra time, preparation, and organization are likely to insure that the resolution of the fighting, when it eventually occurs, will be clear-cut.

WHEN PATHS CROSS:
RECURRENT THEMES IN SECESSION

There are times in the development of knowledge when classification is more important than the identification of common elements. Secession, a phenomenon that has been discussed in unduly homogeneous terms, is a case in point. I have been at pains, therefore, to emphasize the existence of different paths to secession. Nevertheless, there are also elements common to all the paths, elements submerged in taxonomy.

Many such conditions could be singled out as contributing to the emergence of separatist sentiment regardless of the character of the separatist group or region. For example, Crawford Young has rightly noted that three major wars of secession—Biafra, Bangladesh, the Southern Sudan—were fought against military regimes inaccessible to the political influence of the secessionist region.[71] The development of a wholly ethnically-based party system may have the same effect of producing inaccessibility—especially if the majority groups that control the center are themselves divided by intraethnic party competition. Such divisions, we shall soon see, frequently encourage intransigence *vis-à-vis* potential secessionists. One can identify this pattern in Sri Lanka, the Sudan, Burma, and Chad. Then, too, the occurrence of violence, particularly in the form of ethnic riots, seems to abet the growth of separatist inclinations. Riots, polarizing elections, or military coups can serve as signs that alternatives to secession are unpromising or that negotiations would be futile. Such events catalyze separatism.

There is another class of common conditions that seems to have a more direct causal relation to the emergence of separatist inclinations in the first instance. Two such conditions are especially powerful: the loss

71. *The Politics of Cultural Pluralism,* 502.

of group members through assimilation and the migration of ethnic strangers into the potentially separatist region.

The separatism of the Kurds, the Basques, and tribal groups in the Indian state of Assam, among others, owes much of its impetus to the erosion of group boundaries. Migrants from all of these groups to towns in the territory of neighboring ethnic groups often became, respectively, Arabized, Castilianized, or Assamized. In the Indian Punjab, too, Sikhs felt their distinctive identity threatened by the prospect of absorption in the much larger Hindu community. In Sri Lanka, untouchables among the Ceylon Tamils have recurrently been targets for conversion to Buddhism and to the Sinhalese language, to the alarm of the Tamil community. In each case, separatism is linked to boundary maintenance.[72]

Even more prominent is the question of in-migration. Over and over again, ethnically differentiated settlers provoke a separatist response. The influx of Franco-Algerians in Corsica, German-speakers in the Swiss Jura, Coastal Andhras in Telangana, Punjabis in Pathan areas of Pakistan, Christians in the Southern Philippines, and Buddhist Thais in Southern Thailand are among many instances. How seriously in-migration is taken is indicated by the case of Mizoram in Northeast India. Periodically, the Mizos issued ultimata that all non-Mizos leave their territory by specified deadlines; when a deadline was ignored, the Mizo National Front proceeded to kill high officials who came from other states.[73]

Government-supported colonization schemes that bring ethnic strangers into the region are uniformly regarded as plots to overwhelm the existing majority in the region by weight of numbers. In Sri Lanka, the quest for agricultural land led governments to place Sinhalese settlers from the South in the Gal Oya Valley, a no-man's-land between traditional Tamil and Sinhalese homelands. Sinhalese have also been moving into the heavily Tamil Eastern Province, creating fears that Tamil majorities and pluralities will become minorities.[74] Nefarious motives are often attributed to governments that promote ethnically differentiated

72. See Urmila Phadnis, "Neo-Buddhists in India and Ceylon," *Economic and Political Weekly*, Dec. 6, 1969, pp. 1897–98.
73. *Far Eastern Economic Review*, Feb. 7, 1975, p. 36; ibid., Sept. 14, 1979, p. 30; *Indian Express* (Madras), June 23, 1975. The same thing happened subsequently in neighboring Manipur, where Meiti separatism grew as the number of Bengali and Nepalese immigrants grew. *Far Eastern Economic Review*, Nov. 30, 1979, p. 22.
74. For some figures, see Schwarz, *The Tamils of Sri Lanka*, 14.

colonization schemes. The Kurds, for example, accused the Iraqi government of attempting to Arabize Kurdish areas in the 1970s by evicting
Kurds and replacing them with Arab settlers.[75] Whatever the motives,
an end to such settlement is both a goal of separatism and a common
negotiating demand of separatists.[76] "Swamping" is, again, a word frequently invoked.[77] And since the relations of groups to regions are an
integral part of separatism, disputed territories are a common accompa-
niment of separatist movements: the Kurds claim the Kirkuk area, which
the Arabs say has an Arab majority; the Basques demand the inclusion
of Navarre province within their territory, though it is the least Basque
province; Muslims have claimed sovereignty over some Christian-major-
ity areas of the Southern Philippines; and Muslims in Southern Thailand
seek a state that will embrace a large part of the Thai-majority Songkhla
province.

Some groups have had to worry simultaneously about out-migration
and assimilation, on the one hand, and colonization and territory, on the
other. Prominent among such groups have been the Basques, whose language is spoken by only a minority within the Basque country, whose
concern, beginning in the nineteenth century, has been with the "*inva-
sión de maketos*," the invasion of Spanish in-migrants, and who speak
of the "process of Basque extinction."[78] The Kurds of Iraq have also
been concerned about both issues. They have demanded double restrictions: an end to Arab colonization and a prohibition on posting Kurdish
civil servants outside of Kurdish areas.[79] They wish to keep Kurdish
elites at home—and keep them Kurdish—and to keep others out. In
point of fact, these two issues are part of the same underlying ethnic
drive to render group boundaries secure. In this drive, relative group size
is a major area of anxiety. Hence the central place accorded related issues
of intermarriage, relative birth rates, and who will speak what language.
Relative group size in the undivided state as a whole is threatened by

75. Martin Short and Anthony McDermott, *The Kurds* (London: Minority Rights
Group, Report no. 23, 1975), 12.
76. See, e.g., Peter G. Gowing, "Muslim Filipinos Between Integration and Secession"
(unpublished paper presented at the 1973 annual meeting of the Association for Asian
Studies), 14; Astri Suhrke, "Loyalists and Separatists: The Muslims in Southern Thailand,"
Asian Survey 17 (Mar. 1977): 237–50, at 241; *Far Eastern Economic Review*, May 2,
1980, p. 30 (Bangladesh hill areas).
77. "Our province has been swamped by the Punjabis." Abdul Ghaffar Khan, quoted
in Sayeed, "Pathan Regionalism," 499.
78. Silva, "Modernization and Ethnic Conflict," 230.
79. Raoof, "Kurdish Ethnic Nationalism and Political Development in Republican
Iraq," 10.

assimilation, and it is equally threatened for the region by in-migration. It is easy to see why such concerns are rapidly converted into separatism, for separatism allows the use of territorial boundaries to control—and to shore up—endangered ethnic group boundaries.

SECESSION AND SUCCESS: THE STRENGTH AND OUTCOMES OF SEPARATIST MOVEMENTS

Many groups have fought separatist wars in the last thirty years, but few have succeeded. The Southern Sudanese were able to negotiate a measure of regional autonomy after years of fighting. By a combination of protracted warfare in the field and surprise operations in the capital, Chadian Muslims managed to overwhelm the Chad government and secure most of the country, but their ascendancy was soon challenged again on the battlefield. Muslims in the Philippines and Kurds in Iraq have periodically been offered regional autonomy schemes, the genuineness of which they doubt or the generosity of which they think can be enhanced by fighting. Various groups in Burma, especially the Shans and the Karens, have long had control of large stretches of territory. Baluch and Pathans in Pakistan have occasionally been able to deny the government full access to their regions, and this has been true of Iranian peripheral groups as well. Yet, despite all of these successes attributable to force or the threat of it, it remains remarkable that only one country—Bangladesh—owes its independence to a war of secession fought since the Second World War.

The infrequency of successful secessions, despite the ubiquity of secessionist movements, cannot be attributed to the legitimacy accorded existing state boundaries or to the efficacy of the international system in promoting conciliation. Many states have been willing to meddle in the affairs of their neighbors by supporting secessionists in border areas. Rather, the inadequacy of this help, together with the internal strains present in many separatist movements and the determination of central governments to secure international aid to subdue them, result in defeat or a willingness to settle for less than the original secessionist aims.

The strength of a secessionist movement is a function of several domestic and international elements, some of which are easy to identify. If, for example, the events preceding the secession are dramatic enough to induce the wholesale defection of forces formerly committed to the government side, a powerful movement is assured. The desertion of Southern Sudanese soldiers, the return of Ibo officers to the Eastern Region of Nigeria, the mutiny of Bengali police, and comparable defections among Kurds and Eritreans all helped produce protracted struggles. Similarly, if separatist aspirations coincide with traditional banditry, a fusion of criminal and separatist violence is likely. The Karen, Shan, and Kachin movements in Burma have thrived on smuggling and theft; the same was true in Northern Chad; some gangsters have been incorporated by secessionist organizations in Southern Thailand; and the first phases of the Moro movement in the Southern Philippines involved extortion and violent enforcement of payments from Christian settlers by Muslim gangs. In areas where martial traditions are strong and weapons are common, separatist organizations will probably be able to harness these military assets. But these are idiosyncratic conditions, present in relatively few cases.

A more general condition affecting the strength of the separatist movement and the strength of the resistance to its demands is the structure of the separatist region and of the rump region. Heterogeneity has opposite effects on the two regions, weakening the separatists but generally strengthening the resolve of the central government.

HETEROGENEITY OF THE RUMP REGION

The more deeply divided a state is on more than one front, the more likely it is to be faced with secessionist movements—and the more likely it is to resist them, no matter what the cost. Countries like Nigeria, Ethiopia, and Pakistan all feared the demonstration effect of a successful secession, and all were willing to combat separatism with force and to invoke the aid of outside powers. Other countries with somewhat less to fear on this score have also been willing to fight to keep the state intact, but it is noteworthy that serious discussions of regional autonomy have occurred in Iraq, the Philippines, and the Sudan (in the latter two, plans were actually implemented). These are all heterogeneous states, but the Kurds, the Moros, and the Southern Sudanese, respectively, are the only major secessionists they need be concerned about.

Heterogeneity of the rump region also has other effects. If that diversity includes even members of the potential secessionists—as the South of Sri Lanka contains some Ceylon Tamils—this, as I suggested earlier, is likely to retard enthusiasm for secession. A geographically divided group may well settle short of complete control of its own regional affairs.

Only in one way does the heterogeneity of the rump region work to the advantage of separatists. An ethnically divided army, called to suppress a secession, may have less than universal eagerness for the job. In the war for the independence of Bangladesh, it was said that Bengali units were able to buy some arms from Baluch in the Pakistan army. Like the Bengalis, Baluch resent Punjabi domination. Much depends on the precise direction of antipathies, for very often the secessionist group will be sufficiently disliked by all groups fighting against it; but, as the Bengali-Baluch transactions indicate, it is possible that covert alliances between nominal opponents will emerge.

HETEROGENEITY OF THE SECESSIONIST REGION

The strength of a secessionist movement and the heterogeneity of its region are inversely related. Since most secessionist regions are ethnically or subethnically heterogeneous, most secessionist movements end up divided, and quite a few begin that way. Asked why the many ethnic groups opposed to the Burmese government do not form an alliance, a Karenni secessionist replied straightforwardly: "Because most of us don't get on well together. That's why we want independence in the first place."[80]

Ethnic diversity within the secessionist region will not prevent the emergence of a secessionist movement, unless groups opposed to the secession of their region are armed.[81] What inhibited a Northern secession in Nigeria in 1966 was not only the opposition of Middle Belters to a movement that would put Hausa in a dominant position but the fact that those Middle Belters were heavily represented in the army. If opponents of the movement are not armed, the secession will be concentrated in some parts of the region and perhaps completely ineffective elsewhere. If opponents are armed, the choice of secessionists is to accede to their wishes and abandon the movement, as Northern Nigerians did, or to fight them.

Kurdish separatists in Iraq chose to fight their Kurdish opponents.

---

80. Quoted in the *Far Eastern Economic Review*, Apr. 1, 1974, p. 23.

81. For the view that heterogeneity inhibits secession, see Josef Silverstein, "Politics in the Shan State: The Question of Secession from the Union of Burma," *Journal of Asian Studies* 18 (Nov. 1958): 43–48.

The Kurdish rebellion of the 1960s was preceded by extensive hostilities between the separatist Barzanis and their rivals, the Baradost and Zibaris, who had cooperated with the Iraqi government. By 1961, there was large-scale fighting among the Kurds, for Mulla Mustafa Barzani had apparently decided that suppression of his Kurdish opponents was a prerequisite to a strong separatist movement. The Iraqi regime supplied and incited Barzani's opponents, whereupon he drove most of them into Iran and Turkey. Barzani thus gained control of the whole Kurdish region, clearing the way for warfare against the regime. Periodically, however, the Barzanis had to attend to their Kurdish opponents, especially the Talabanis, who cooperated with the Iraqi government. Indeed, a major point in the abortive 1970 settlement of the decade-long war was the withdrawal of government support for the Talabanis. Subethnicity among the Kurds meant a divided military effort among Kurdish separatists.[82]

More often than not, opponents of the movement within the secessionist region are not armed—at least initially—and so the movement can begin without the prior need to fight the opposition. Differential enthusiasm for separatism is, nonetheless, not long in manifesting itself. The Moro National Liberation Front has been led disproportionately by Tausug, who populate the Sulu archipelago of the Southern Philippines; the Thai Muslim movement has been strong in some provinces and weak in others; Tamils from the North of Sri Lanka have been more disposed to separatism than Tamils from the East; and Protestants from Ankole and Toro in Uganda were more militantly secessionist than Catholics.[83] Differential enthusiasm for separatism is an aspect of the geography of ethnic extremism mentioned in Chapter 5 and partakes of all the complexity of that issue.

82. See Derk Kinnane, *The Kurds and Kurdistan* (London: Oxford Univ. Press, 1964), 64–67; George S. Harris, "The Kurdish Conflict in Iraq," in Suhrke and Noble, eds., *Ethnic Conflict in International Relations*, 68–92; *Middle East Record* (Jerusalem) 2 (1961): 280–84; J. C. Hurewitz, *Middle East Politics: The Military Dimension* (New York: Praeger, 1969), 156–58; *Violence and Dialogue in the Middle East: The Palestine Entity and Other Case Studies* (Washington, D.C.: Middle East Institute, 24th annual conference, mimeo., Oct. 2–3, 1970), 35–37. For similar clashes in the Chittagong hills of Bangladesh, see *Far Eastern Economic Review*, May 2, 1980, p. 30.

83. *Far Eastern Economic Review*, Feb. 10, 1978, pp. 21–23; ibid., Aug. 17, 1979, pp. 28–30; Astri Suhrke, "The Muslims in Southern Thailand: An Analysis of Political Developments 1968–78" (unpublished paper, Washington, D.C., Dec. 1978), 13; Kearney, "Language and the Rise of Separatism in Sri Lanka," 533; Doornbos, "Protest Movements in Western Uganda," 267–72, 282. For the end of the Rwenzururu movement, see Martin R. Doornbos, *Not All the King's Men: Inequality as a Political Instrument in Ankole, Uganda* (The Hague: Mouton, 1978).

What matters for present purposes is not the correlates of differential enthusiasm but its widespread character and its important consequences—indeed, consequences that grow more important as secessionist warfare proceeds. These consequences are both organizational and military.

Consider the Southern Sudanese movement, which in the late 1960s and early 1970s had the usual array of military and civilian organizations, exiles and in-country leaders, politicians still operating in the capital and those confined to the secessionist region.[84] Permeating all of these divisions were ethnic differences. At first the rebellion was concentrated in Equatoria; like the Sulu archipelago in the Philippines, Equatoria was the southernmost province, furthest removed from the people being fought. Concentration of the fighting in Equatoria signified participation of the Zande and Madi ethnic groups. Less involved were the Dinka and Nuer, located in other provinces. The Dinka, by far the largest of the Southern groups, were generally more moderate than others toward the North and were disproportionately represented among those seeking a parliamentary rather than military solution. The Dinka dominated the Sudan African National Union, which was strongly represented in Khartoum even after fighting was raging in Equatoria. A rival party, the Southern Front, was largely based on ethnic groups in Equatoria that feared Dinka domination.

Equally split were the military units. The guerrilla organization, Anyanya, had Dinka units in Bahr al-Ghazal province, but these had little contact with Anyanya units operating elsewhere. Beginning in 1969, Anyanya began to train ethnically mixed units to bridge such differences. But the differences persisted. Indeed, even Western and Eastern Dinka were divided, and a specifically Zande movement sprung up in 1969 as well.

Efforts to form umbrella organizations repeatedly fell apart, usually over the issue of "Dinka domination." In 1967, a Southern Sudan Provisional Government (SSPG) was formed, but it soon had a rival organization. In 1969–70, a civilian-military Anyidi Revolutionary Council appeared, but the Nile Provisional Government (successor to the SSPG) was convinced the Anyidi, heavily Equatorial in leadership, was anti-

---

84. Some of the complexity of the Southern Sudanese movement is reflected in Godfrey Morrison, *The Southern Sudan and Eritrea* (London: Minority Rights Group, Report no. 5, 1971), as well as in Morrison's newsletter, *Africa Confidential* (London), and in various issues of *The Grass Curtain*.

Dinka. The Anyidi attacked NPG headquarters in 1970 and eventually was defeated. Differences over objectives, strategies, and resources thus tended to overlap ethnic differences, producing multiple organizations that ended up fighting each other. It took years before the Anyanya was able to establish enough authority to conclude a binding peace.

The Southern Sudan was unusually complex but not different in kind from other separatist areas. In the Biafra war, the lack of enthusiasm of the Rivers people for a cause they viewed as Ibo turned to violence between the two as Ibo forces retreated. The separatist Shans in Burma are divided into four movements, and non-Shan minorities in the Shan States have created their own armed forces to insure that the Shans do not take over the entire territory. Sporadic Baluch separatist rebellions in Pakistan have been confined to particular Baluch subgroups, especially the Mengals and the Marris, both of whom have been at least as much engaged in warfare against other Baluch subgroups as against the central government. The Eritrean movement has had Christian and Muslim units that have fought pitched battles with each other. The several movements that operated in the North and East of Chad in the 1960s and '70s also clashed with each other; when the Tombalbaye regime declared an amnesty, only Easterners responded. Muslims in the Philippines have been divided between a Tausug-led organization and a Maranao-led organization, the latter more amenable to compromise with the central government. It is well known that Biharis in Bangladesh identified with the Pakistani regime and fought against the Bengalis. So, too, did the Bazzia, a hill people in the West of Eritrea, fight with the Ethiopian government. The Brong in Ghana reacted to Ashanti demands for federation by supporting the central government and demanding that their own area be carved out of Ashanti. Likewise, Moors in the East of Sri Lanka, though Tamil-speaking, have opposed a separate Tamil state, in which they would be vulnerable to Tamil domination. The appearance of separatism by one group in a region is quite often enough to provoke another group, fearful of the outcome, to support the central government or to demand its own state.

Central governments, of course, attempt to exploit this tendency. They play on group differences, arm one group against another, imply that the more moderate organization will have a leg up in bargaining, attempt to create a Fifth Column in the secessionist region—or all of these things. We have already seen how the Iraqi government was able to take advantage of Kurdish subgroup differences. The Nigerian, Philippine, Pakistani, Ethiopian, Burmese, and Sudanese governments have tried to do the same.[85] Such tactics by themselves are usually not enough to destroy the movement; but, as separatist violence progresses, other things may happen that undermine it.

If the secessionists seek external aid, as they must, the source of the support may drive even those on the same side further apart, either because of ethnic affinities between one of the groups and groups in the foreign state or because of a tendency for states to sponsor one or another separatist organization but rarely all. This may have been a factor in the Southern Sudanese schisms, as supplies came through Equatoria, often from groups related to those who lived in Equatoria. It was important in Chad, for Libyan aid long went to rebels in the East, rather than the North, where the Libyans had their own territorial ambitions and fought the Northern secessionists. It has been decisive in Eritrea, for foreign help came from Arab states: the Sudan, Iraq, Syria, Libya. As the movement gained firepower, it espoused pan-Arab ideals and lost Christian support.[86] Depending on the relations of groups across borders, there may well be a tradeoff between two resources needed for success: internal cohesion and external support.

As the movement gains in military strength, groups united in their opposition to those who control the government at the center begin to appraise each other's intentions more carefully. Some become wary of the independence for which they have fought. "If we did secede," said a Philippine Muslim, "we would only fight among ourselves." Under "a federation," he concluded, "the top government [in Manila] could still exert some control," in order to foster harmony among the Muslims themselves.[87] Heterogeneity can induce a willingness to compromise with the central government.

There is a resemblance between this and the process that occurred at the end of colonial rule: as success approaches, the political context—and with it the focus of effective loyalty—shifts downward. Paradoxi-

85. For a few examples, see R. J. A. R. Rathbone, "Opposition in Ghana: The National Liberation Movement," in *Collected Seminar Papers on Opposition in the New African States, October 1967–March 1968* (London: Univ. of London, Institute of Commonwealth Studies, mimeo., n.d.), 35; von der Mehden, *Religion and Nationalism in Southeast Asia*, 190; *Far Eastern Economic Review*, Feb. 10, 1978, pp. 21–23; ibid., Dec. 22, 1983, p. 26; Nabo B. Graham-Douglas, *Ojukwu's Rebellion and World Opinion* (Apapa, Nigeria: Nigerian National Press, 1968).

86. Morrison, *The Southern Sudan and Eritrea*, 32; Barbara A. Alpert, "The Ethiopian Perplex," *Current History* 70 (Mar. 1971): 151–56, 179, at 153.

87. Quoted in the *Far Eastern Economic Review*, Mar. 18, 1974, p. 28.

cally, the very thing that earlier weakened the states against which secessionists rebel—heterogeneity—weakens the rebels, too. In the concise words of an Eritrean Liberation Front leader, "The nearer we get to independence, the less chance there is for unity."[88]

EXTERNAL FORCES

International relations play a prominent role in explaining the outcome of secessionist movements, including why so few succeed.[89] Virtually all of the strong post-war secessionist movements have been supported by powerful international connections, and so have many regimes fighting against secessionists. At various times, Eritrean rebels have had training in Syria, bases in the Sudan, Soviet and Chinese weapons sent through Libya and South Yemen, and financial aid from Saudi Arabia and Kuwait. The Ethiopians have had training aid from a number of countries, including Israel; they were able to turn the tide of battle against Eritrean forces by enlisting the support of Cuban combat troops. Biafra existed as long as it did because of its formidable international supply network. It was defeated because the Nigerian government arrayed against it an even more powerful, internationally constructed arsenal. Philippine Muslims have had diplomatic support from the Islamic Conference and military aid from Libya, from the Malaysian state of Sabah during the chief ministership of Tun Mustapha, and occasionally from Indonesian provincial officials in Sulawesi. Bangladesh, of course, achieved its independence because India was willing to fight a war with Pakistan and invade East Bengal. The Kurds in Iraq failed to achieve their goals precisely because Iran was not then willing to fight a war with the Iraqis.

The singular case of Bangladesh's success suggests that external support is difficult for separatists to obtain and, once obtained, difficult to keep. There is a certain circularity involved in securing foreign support in the first place. No foreign state will risk committing itself to a movement that appears weak. This is one reason why, as suggested earlier, the *emergence* of separatism is not generally a function of international relations. Yet, to grow in strength, a movement may require outside help. Hence, the very strength that attracts foreign support is also hard to build without foreign support to begin with.

88. Quoted in the *Washington Post*, Apr. 30, 1977.
89. In writing this section, I have benefited particularly from Suhrke and Noble, eds., *Ethnic Conflict in International Relations*, especially chap. 9. See also Joseph Rothschild, *Ethnopolitics: A Conceptual Framework* (New York: Columbia Univ. Press, 1981), chap. 6.

Once secured, foreign support for secessionists is undependable. It is vulnerable at several levels of politics.

First, foreign states usually have more limited motives for supporting separatists than the separatists themselves have for fighting. (This is not true of irredentist states, but they are another matter.) Foreign states are therefore more easily induced to end their support than separatists are induced to abandon their movement. Foreign support tends to come and go, and, in the life of any secessionist movement, there may be periods of no support, multiple sources of support, or dramatically shifting sources of support. To some extent, foreign support is also variable for states fighting against secessionists.

Second, foreign states have multiple international objectives. This opens the way to the *quid pro quo*. States combatting secession can offer states supporting it various inducements in exchange for their forbearance. The multiplicity of objectives works, of course, both ways. It gives states otherwise unsympathetic to separatism reasons to aid separatists despite lack of sympathy, just as it subjects that support to precipitous termination.

Third, the vicissitudes of domestic politics in the assisting states can also produce an abrupt end to their support for secessionists. One strategy of combatting foreign support, then, is to raise the domestic costs for the assisting state, if the international costs are still acceptable.

For all of these reasons, foreign commitments to separatists are likely to be less complete and less enduring than the separatists may require for success in what are often long, drawn-out wars. But what, concretely, are the reasons external actors become involved in secessionist warfare, on one side or the other, or refrain from such involvement?

Diffuse strategic objectives, having little to do with relations between the states that happen to be involved, account for some such decisions. The clearest case of this is Libya's support for separatists in Corsica, Sicily, and the Southern Philippines. These are efforts that do not originate in interstate quarrels but in the desire to expand Libyan influence and ideology. American, Soviet, Chinese, and Cuban involvement in Ethiopia-Eritrea, Nigeria-Biafra, Iraq-Kurdistan, or Pakistan-Bangladesh has the same kind of motive.

Similar to this is intervention that derives from the common propensity to regard the enemies of one's enemies as friends. Israel took the Southern Sudanese side against the North and the Ethiopian side against the Eritreans for these reasons, while Arab states were especially helpful to the Eritreans because of Ethiopia's Israeli connections. Pakistan and China have helped Mizos and Nagas against India. The opportunity to dismember Pakistan was irresistible for India in Bangladesh. Regional rivalries are a natural source of assistance for and against separatism.

Specific interstate disputes also provide occasions for support, because the support becomes leverage for bargaining and concessions. An interesting case of this was the limited Malaysian support for Philippine Muslim separatists. The Philippines had earlier asserted a claim to the Malaysian state of Sabah and had trained guerrillas for an invasion. The Malaysians had ample reason to inflict revenge on the Philippine government and to contemplate that additional pressure might induce the Philippines to abandon the Sabah claim.[90] With Philippine vulnerability demonstrated, the Sabah claim was finally abandoned. Revenge, deterrence, and leverage were equally Iranian motives in Pakistan and Iraq. In 1973 and after, the Iranians supported Pakistan in suppressing Baluch separatism, not only because the Baluch span the Iranian border, but also because the Baluch had support from Iraq. Iran and Iraq had a number of important disputes between them, including Iraqi support for Arab separatists in Southwest Iran and Iraqi claims in the Shatt al-Arab estuary that divides the two countries. For this reason, Iran involved itself deeply in Kurdish separatist warfare in Iraq in 1965–66, 1969, and again in 1974–75. The Iranians helped suppress separatism in one case and abetted it in the other, but they consistently opposed Iraq.

Irredentism aside, ethnic affinities are only occasionally and weakly a motive for intervention in separatist warfare. Trans-border Bengali kinship may have marginally affected Indian willingness to intervene in Bangladesh, and felt kinship with the Ceylon Tamils may yet do the same in Sri Lanka. Groups such as the Madi and Kakwa span the Sudan-Uganda boundary, and Idi Amin, a Kakwa, may have been moved to aid the Southern Sudanese in part on these grounds. But more important was his then-cordial relationship with Israel.

Trans-border ethnic affinities more often promote restraint in supporting separatists or intervention in behalf of a central government fighting to suppress separatism. Fear of contagion and domino effects is widespread. Among separatists, this creates a fear that the failure of a movement in one state will hurt movements in others—hence the ties among them. Among states, fear of the success of separatism works in

90. Astri Suhrke and Lela Garner Noble, "Muslims in the Philippines and Thailand," in Suhrke and Noble, eds., *Ethnic Conflict in International Relations*, 183–84.

the opposite direction. Iran has been apprehensive that Baluch separatism in Pakistan might embrace Baluch in Iran as well. Malaysia, though it modestly took advantage of the Philippine Muslim rebellion, was extremely careful to keep its involvement limited, lest it encourage separatism among related groups in the state of Sabah.[91] For similar reasons, Indonesia has consistently taken the Philippine government side against Muslim separatists. And, unlike the Iranians, who had a tight rein on their own Kurds as they helped the Kurds in Iraq, the Turks took no such risks, preferring instead "a pro-Iraqi neutrality."[92]

Even where ethnic affinities relate, not to peripheral minorities in the external state, but to centrally influential groups, support is by no means automatic. Despite the fact that Thai Muslim separatists are Malays closely related to Malays in the North of Peninsular Malaysia, the Malaysians have eschewed support. Limited Thai cooperation in suppressing Communist guerrillas operating in Malaysia from Thai territory is highly valued and could not be preserved if the Malaysian government aided Malay separatists. Various considerations, some pointing to aid for the separatists, some to aid for the regime fighting them, some to restraint from all involvement, can coexist, and regimes must weigh one against the other.

Now it becomes possible to see exactly why separatists rarely obtain the aid they need or, if they do, rarely retain it for as long as they need it. As the Thai Muslim case suggests, states suppressing separatists may be able to offer potential foreign supporters things they value, in exchange for their forbearance. Sometimes they offer too little, or nothing at all, until external aid to the separatists raises the stakes. It will not necessarily be too late then. Iran's aid to the Kurds in Iraq reached formidable proportions in 1974–75, but Iran was abruptly dissuaded from all-out war when the Iraqis agreed to settle the unrelated dispute over the Shatt al-Arab estuary. In a matter of days, this doomed the Kurdish insurrection. Iran ended its support because of a *quid pro quo*, and Turkey refused to let retreating Kurds cross into its territory because of the fear of infecting Turkey's Kurds with separatism. To be sure, the Iran-Iraq agreement came apart in 1979, but by then Kurds in Iran were on the verge of a separatist revolt that made Iranian aid to Kurds in Iraq un-

91. See Lela Garner Noble, "Ethnicity and Philippine-Malaysian Relations" (unpublished paper presented at the 1974 annual meeting of the American Political Science Association).
92. Astri Suhrke and Lela Garner Noble, "Spread or Containment: The Ethnic Factor," in Suhrke and Noble, eds., *Ethnic Conflict in International Relations*, 219.

thinkable. The chances that domestic and external conditions will simultaneously be conducive to sustained intervention are not great.

To the extent that larger alliances and enemy perceptions are involved in decisions to aid separatists, these alliances can change, either because international conditions change or because regimes change. When Idi Amin's friendship with Israel ended, so did his aid to Southern Sudanese separatists. When East Pakistan became Bangladesh, the Nagas and Mizos of Northeast India lost supplies and bases. Later, Indian and Bangladesh forces mounted joint operations against Mizo fighters in the Chittagong hills. Of course, conditions can change in the opposite direction as well—as when French influence with Libya waned to the point where it could no longer induce nonintervention in Chad.[93] But, overall, the fluidity of international relationships, the availability of bargaining to induce restraint (a matter in which the government side has a clear advantage over the separatists), and the increasing possibility of contagion or other domestic consequences as assistance to separatists increases in scale and duration all point to the ephemeral quality of external forces.

All of this is quite apart from the ability of regimes threatened with separatism to inflict direct harm or indirect revenge on states that offer aid to the separatists. The government of Chad was able to take countermeasures that stopped Sudanese aid to Chadian Muslim separatists; and Sudanese aid to Eritreans fighting an Ethiopian regime that was aiding Southern Sudanese finally induced moderation on the Ethiopian side. Few states, in short, will be willing to go to war for secessionists in another state, as India did in Bangladesh. A willingness to meddle and weaken one's enemies is common enough. But sufficient staying power is a rare thing.

Interestingly enough, external aid seems longest-lived when it comes, not from strong, established states with clear-cut interests, but from irregular forces across porous, remote borders. The long duration of several Burmese separatist insurrections owes much to the uncontrolled Thai-Burmese border, to arms supplied by smugglers, to revenue from opium exports, and to military assistance provided since 1952 by units of the Kuomintang army that escaped from China into Burma. The same is true in Northeast India. Thai gunrunners there have transported American weapons left from the Vietnam war across Burma to Mizo secessionists, Mizos have cooperated with Arakanese secessionists in Burma, and Bihari "Razakers" left over from the Bangladesh war have

93. See Andrew Lycett, "Chad's Disastrous Civil War," *Africa Report*, Sept. 1978, pp. 4–6.

linked up with both Mizos and Nagas. In such cases, external ties make it difficult to end a separatist movement, but the external aid is never enough to allow the movement to succeed either. Where external assistance is plentiful, it may also be ephemeral; where it is enduring, it may be insufficient.

Finally, even strong external support may not achieve the goals for which the separatists aim. Sometimes it provokes the central government to secure its own, overwhelming outside aid. At other times, external help to separatists produces moderation on the part of the regime they are fighting. Cease-fires, amnesties, and concessions far short of autonomy or secession are all recurrent effects of international involvement on the side of the separatists. Indeed, the state supporting them may insist on a drastic scaling down of their goals, as the Libyans did with the Moro National Liberation Front.[94] By opting for foreign help, secessionists risk losing control over their destiny to states that have different, usually more limited, objectives. Even if this does not happen, after protracted warfare any conciliatory gesture may look appealing to some of the separatists, and this may be enough to split or demoralize them, especially if, as is commonly the case, there is more than one group fighting. External support, necessary to the success of the separatist movement, can just as easily end up undermining it.

THE IMPACT OF SECESSIONIST MOVEMENTS

The impact of a secessionist movement will vary with the degree of success the movement encounters. A movement that achieves independence will obviously have different effects from one that meets defeat, but even an unsuccessful war can transform the structure of politics and group relations dramatically.

The extent to which secessionist warfare can alter ethnic alignments and antipathies is illustrated by the Nigeria-Biafra war. When Ibo military officers and civil servants returned to the East, the positions they vacated tended to be filled by Yoruba and smaller, well-educated groups. After the war, much resentment of the sort earlier directed against the Ibo was directed against Yoruba. When civilian rule returned in 1979, Ibo and Hausa found themselves political allies, with the Yoruba opposition isolated. The creation of new states also strengthened the position

94. See the *Far Eastern Economic Review*, Jan. 28, 1977, p. 14.

of Middle Belters and weakened their ties to Hausa, just as the ties between Ibo and other Easterners had been weakened by the war. The secessionist war and its aftermath reshuffled the structure of ethnic conflict without obliterating it.[95]

RECIPROCAL SEPARATISM

The separatism of one region can lead to the separatism of others. Indeed, there are identifiable sequences of separatism in the same state. Some of these have already been noted. In Nigeria, a Northern secession was mooted before the Ibo secession.[96] The Katanga secession, with its center of gravity in the South, quickly produced an equal and opposite secession among the Baluba of North Katanga.[97] In Chad, when it looked as if the Muslim North and East might take control of the newly independent state, the Sara of the South demanded division of the country.[98] Eventually, the Sara took power and excluded Muslims from influence. Then it was the turn of the North and East to pursue a separatist course for more than a decade. When the Chadian government was defeated and Sara fled southward in large numbers, a new Sara secession was proclaimed in 1979. The country settled into a *de facto* partition, albeit one that did not preclude further fighting. In a sense, everyone had seceded.

The key to these sequences is the escalation of mutually exclusive claims to power. When the Bakongo gained political ascendancy in Congo (Brazzaville), Northerners spoke of detaching their region from the state; after a coup brought Northerners to power, the Bakongo spoke in the same terms.[99] When the Sindhis in post-Bangladesh Pakistan spoke of following the Bengalis out, Urdu speakers in the Sind were moved to similar claims. Though the Urdu speakers were proposing, so to speak, secession from secession, the idea was the same: one group's independence is another's servitude.

95. I leave for later treatment the creative political impulses that were also released by the Nigerian and Sudanese wars. Especially in Nigeria, these later produced a new set of institutions to cope with ethnic conflict. See Chapter 15, below.
96. Olorunsola, "Nigeria," 35; Schwarz, *Nigeria*, 206, 210, 215; First, *Power in Africa*, 313–25.
97. Young, "The Politics of Separatism," 190–91; Gérard-Libois, *Katanga Secession*, 123–27, 156.
98. Ballard, "Four Equatorial States," 267–74.
99. René Gauze, *The Politics of Congo-Brazzaville*, trans., ed., and supplemented by Virginia Thompson and Richard Adloff (Stanford: Hoover Institution Press, 1973), 67–69.

The policy response to separatism is complicated by these considerations. What will placate one group may be precisely what is required to inflame another. The satisfactions are seen as zero-sum. In such cases, it is appropriate to speak of reciprocal separatism. Because these effects bear so heavily on policy, I shall defer consideration of reciprocal secession to Chapter 16.

DEMONSTRATION EFFECTS

There is another way in which one separatist movement can lead to another: by demonstration effect. The example of one movement cannot create separatist sentiment where it does not exist; this is not a question of contagion.[100] But the strength of a movement, particularly one supported by external aid, can propel other separatists into action by convincing them of the plausibility of success or of concessions short of success.

The extent to which movements increase their overtly separatist activity in response to such considerations is a function of the strength and proximity of the demonstration movement. Biafra catalyzed a few movements in Africa. In the first stages, there was a possibility the Yoruba in Nigeria might follow suit. This was perhaps not so much demonstration effect as anticipation of an unfavorable Yoruba position *vis-à-vis* the North if the Ibo made good their exit from Nigeria. The Ivory Coast government was one of two African regimes to recognize Biafra. The Ivory Coast was in turn confronted with a resurgence of separatism among the Agni of the former Sanwi kingdom who had earlier fought the Ivorian government. Threatening a Biafran-type conflagration and citing Houphouët-Boigny's recognition of Biafra, the Sanwi movement turned again to armed warfare.[101] Some months after this was suppressed, the Bété around Gagnoa, who had mooted an independent republic, went on the march. The Ivory Coast government had little difficulty putting these insurrections down. The Eritreans and Chadian Muslims also cast more than a sideways glance at Biafra, but their movements continued even after the Nigerian victory; and the Southern Sudanese, who ended their war, did so on the basis of more directly relevant

100. It should also be underscored that demonstration effects are different from reciprocal secession, where two antagonists alternatively opt for separatism. Demonstration effects do not involve antagonists with opposing claims but groups that learn something from the example of an earlier seceder. For reciprocal secession, see Chapter 16, below.

101. *West Africa*, Jan. 3, 1970, p. 10; Colin Legum, ed., *Africa Contemporary Record, 1969–70* (New York: Africana, 1970), p. B498.

considerations of waning foreign support. The emergence and defeat of Biafra were not without external impact, but it was a strictly limited impact.

The success of Bangladesh had a stronger effect than the unsuccessful war in Biafra. The main effect was to unglue relations in West Pakistan, giving a fillip particularly to Pathan and Baluch separatism. The example of Bangladesh was cited by separatists in Sri Lanka and Tamil Nadu in India,[102] but neither of these movements was propelled to concrete action as a result. It was no doubt a factor in encouraging Mizos and Nagas, Philippine and Thai Muslims, the perennial secessionists in Burma, and perhaps even the Kurds. But all of these movements antedated Bangladesh, and each had to consider its own peculiar circumstances before making decisions about warfare.

A secession can have a significant demonstration effect within the state of which the secessionist region is a part. Even the Telangana movement in Andhra Pradesh created a momentary flurry next door in Karnataka, where politicians in the former princely state of Mysore demanded a separate "old Mysore."[103] The creation of Pakistan in 1947 gave great impetus to the demand for Sikhistan, a Sikh state in the truncated Indian Punjab. If the Punjab could be divided once, why not twice? The same was true in post-Biafra Nigeria. Once twelve states had been created, a flood of movements sprung up to demand still more ethnically based states. One movement in Burma also led to another, until there were nearly a dozen. The long-standing Basque and Catalan movements in Spain have been demonstration movements for other Spanish regions, such as Andalusia, the Canary Islands, Galicia, and the Balearic Islands. The Eritreans have inspired the Galla in Bale, Christian groups in the Gojjan, and the Tigreans; some of these have also fought the Ethiopian government. Perhaps the ultimate in demonstration effects has been Assam.[104] First it was the Nagas and the Mizos, then the Khasi and other hill tribes, that demanded separate states, some of which were conceded after protracted warfare. Then it was the plains tribes and the Ahom who demanded territorial recognition. And finally the idea of a separate

102. Urmila Phadnis, "Keeping the Tamils Internal," Far Eastern Economic Review, Mar. 25, 1972, pp. 21–22; New York Times, Mar. 3, 1972.
103. Glynn Wood and Robert Hammond, "The 'Indira Wave' in Mysore—An Extreme Case" (unpublished paper, American Univ., Washington, D.C., Jan. 1972), 7. For a similar example in Uganda, see Doornbos, "Protest Movements in Western Uganda," 275.
104. See the excellent report by Mohan Ram, Far Eastern Economic Review, Nov. 30, 1979, pp. 21–22. See also C. P. Cook, "India: The Crisis in Assam," The World Today 24 (Oct. 1968): 444–48.

state spread to the core group, the Assamese themselves, who began to scrawl "Indians go home" on walls—though, to the tribals, it is the Assamese who are "Indians."

Neighboring states have some modest cause for concern if a powerful secessionist movement takes root. Malaysia, for example, stopped calling its two wings "East" and "West" Malaysia after East Pakistan separated from West Pakistan. And no doubt a wave of successful movements would have wider demonstration effects. Yet the limitations on external aid make such waves improbable. The principal impact of single powerful movements is bound to be in the rump state itself, for the one thing a powerful movement does demonstrate is the vulnerability of that state's central government. *Ceteris paribus*, states experiencing one strong secessionist movement are likely to experience more than one. They are right to be concerned about fragmentation.

IRREDENTISM:
PREROGATIVE OF THE FEW

The potential for irredentism in Asia and Africa is enormous. A quick *tour d'horizon* reveals the rich range of possibilities. The Ghana-Togo border divides the Ewe, as the Nigeria-Benin border divides the Yoruba. There are Hausa in Nigeria and Hausa in Niger. There are Fulani across a wide belt of West and Central Africa, Batéké in Gabon and Congo (Brazzaville), and Fang in Cameroon, Gabon, and Equatorial Guinea. The Bakongo are divided among Zaire, Congo (Brazzaville), and Angola; the Lunda among Zaire, Zambia, and Angola. There are Somalis in Somalia, Ethiopia, Kenya, and Djibouti. There are Wolof in Mauritania, in Gambia, and in Senegal, Kakwa in the Sudan and in Uganda. Various Berber groups are distributed among more than one North African state. There are Malays in Malaysia, Thailand, Brunei, Indonesia, and Singapore. There are Tamils in Sri Lanka, as well as in India; Bengalis in Bangladesh and India; Baluch in Pakistan, Afghanistan, and Iran; Pathans in Afghanistan and Pakistan; Turkomens in Iraq and Iran. If irredentism is conceived as a movement to retrieve ethnic kinsmen and their territory across borders, the common disjunction of group boundaries and territorial boundaries affords scope for irredentas aplenty.[105]

105. Although I have listed only certain African and Asian boundary disjunctions, Europe has abundant examples: Irish in Eire and Ulster, Basques in France and Spain, Albanians in Yugoslavia and Albania, Hungarians in Hungary and Rumania, Tyroleans in Austria and Italy, Croats in Austria and Yugoslavia, Macedonians in Greece, Bulgaria, and Yugoslavia, and so on.

Given these opportunities in an ethnic conflict–prone world, why is it that this particular version of ethnic conflict has not contributed its share of discord? Why, when examples are sought, are the Somalis nearly the only consistent irredentists in the developing world? Clearly, the presence of an ethnic group divided by one or more territorial boundaries is a necessary but not a sufficient condition for a serious movement to unite the group.

The decision to retrieve group members across a territorial border by forcibly altering the border is a governmental decision. In this respect, it differs from the decision to initiate a secessionist movement, which is an ethnic group decision.[106] Group leaders may agitate for a new boundary that embraces group members not within the present boundary, but the irredentist decision, as a matter of state policy, is not simply the product of group sentiment. It is susceptible to all the forces and constraints that impinge upon policy decisions in general. And, because irredentism aims at permanent alterations in the population and territory of the state choosing to pursue it, it differs also from the decision merely to aid a secessionist movement in another country; the latter decision tends to have consequences more ephemeral and less centrally important to the assisting state.

The decision to embark upon an irredentist course is freighted with elements that counsel restraint. Unlike aid to secessionists, it probably means direct involvement in actual warfare. It is, however, the domestic rather than the international consequences that constitute the principal disincentive to irredentism.

The propensity to irredentism is greatly enhanced as the ethnic homogeneity of the retrieving state increases. Indeed, it is tempting to say that irredentism is the prerogative of homogeneous states.[107] In heterogeneous states, irredentism is bound to be a divisive ethnic issue.

If the retrieving group does not have a strong position in the putative irredentist state, its claims will be ignored or suppressed. It frequently happens, in fact, that such groups are themselves participants in domestic ethnic conflict; this acts to discourage the governments to which they

106. As I shall suggest below, the irredentism of groups like the Kurds, spread among several states and in control of none, really requires multiple secessionist movements, rather than retrieval and incorporation of group members and territory in a preexisting state.

107. See Ravi L. Kapil, "On the Conflict Potential of Inherited Boundaries in Africa," *World Politics* 18 (July 1966): 656–73, at 670: "The cultural heterogeneity of most African states is responsible for preventing boundaries issues from coming to the forefront of their domestic and foreign policies."

are subject from considering claims in behalf of their kinsmen across borders. The Ewe, for example, are a minority in Ghana and Togo, and in both countries there are significant tensions between Ewe and others. In Ghana, certain Akan groups would hardly be pleased at the prospect of an accession of yet more Ewe, who are regarded as clannish, shrewd, and nepotistic. The same holds on the other side of the border, where an Ewe regime actually held power until it was overthrown in a coup. No Northern Togolese would like to augment the ranks of Togo's Ewe population by a border adjustment. When the Togolese government is inclined to make a certain amount of trouble for the Ghanaian government, it goes only so far as to tolerate Ghanaian Ewe secessionist organizations on its soil. Likewise, no Ghanaian Ewe, sensing the anti-Ewe character of the Togolese regime, would like to join Togo under present conditions. And so those Ewe who care about unification are consigned to plotting something other than incorporation in one or the other existing regime, thus risking suppression by both.

The situation is much the same elsewhere. The Northerners who control Congo (Brazzaville), but who in the past have been subject to Bakongo control, would not consider for a moment the prospect of adding still more Bakongo to the population of the Congo; and neither would Angola or Zaire. The Lunda, split among three countries, find themselves in the same position.[108] Nor, of course, would any of the countries with Kurdish minorities consider accommodating the Kurdish desire for unity within its borders. All of this practically goes without saying. Groups in this position are much more likely simply to become secessionists—or secessionists who hope ultimately to carve out a new Kurdistan, a greater Eweland, or a resurgent, Bakongo-based San Salvador Empire—than they are to attempt absorption of their kinsmen in unfriendly existing states.

But suppose the putative irredentist state is not unfriendly but merely heterogeneous. Suppose, for example, that the Bakongo are in a controlling position in Congo (Brazzaville), as they were under Fulbert Youlou in the early 1960s. One might expect the regime to support irredentism under such circumstances. This expectation would be misplaced. René Gauze cogently explains why:

... it was improbable that the 350,000 politically divided Bakongo in Youlou's republic could absorb and control the 470,000 Kongo in the former Belgian

---

108. See Brian Weinstein, "Zaire's Shaba Is a Spark That Never Goes Out," *Baltimore Sun*, May 28, 1978.

colony who, moreover, were far from being politically united. . . . If through exaggerated ambition the [Bakongo] "nationalists" actually tried to carry out their expansionist aspirations . . . they in all probability would awaken a strong defensive tribal reaction that could disrupt the precarious unity of Youlou's republic. Already that unity had been undermined by Opangault's efforts to promote a secession of the north.[109]

Gauze, speaking in particulars, has put his finger on three general points. First, within the putative irredentist state, heterogeneity may restrain irredentism even when the retrieving group is in power and enthusiastic. Second, even within the putative irredentist group, enthusiasm for retrieval is not automatic. Third, it is not clear whether the group to be retrieved across a border will in fact wish to be retrieved. Each of these points, as I shall show, is a serious obstacle to irredentism.

If an ethnic group in power attempts to shore up its position in a heterogeneous state by retrieval of group members across a border, it invites disaffection on the part of those groups that would be disadvantaged by a successful irredenta. As Gauze notes, the fear of Bakongo irredentism induced Northern Congolese to contemplate secession from the Brazzaville regime. In Afghanistan, the Hazara, Tadjik, and Uzbek minorities look with disfavor on periodic Pathan appeals to Pathans across the border in Pakistan.[110] Malaysia's espousal of an irredentist claim regarding Malays in Thailand would bring a strong and dangerous reaction from non-Malays in Malaysia. The principle is the same as that which governs ethnic opposition to international regional integration: if such schemes threaten to alter domestic ethnic balances, groups disadvantaged by them will oppose them.[111]

Even if in power, putative irredentists will not necessarily become irredentists in action. The determining variables are to be found in domestic politics and group structure. More often than not, these retard

109. *The Politics of Congo-Brazzaville*, 120.
110. This is a point used by Pakistani governments to counter Pathan irredentism. See, e.g., *Far Eastern Economic Review*, Aug. 2, 1974, p. 12.
111. See also William Petersen, "Upward Mobility and Ethnic Identity: The Case of the Flemish" (unpublished paper presented at the VIIIth World Congress of the International Sociological Association, Aug. 23, 1974), 9: "Holland's political and social institutions have long been divided along religious lines, with the Catholics controlling a plurality of votes and influence. If the Flemish Catholics were to be absorbed into the Dutch state, this plurality would become a majority. Thus, the prime advocates of cultural unity . . . have generally been Catholic partisans. Because of this very fact, however, every non-Catholic in the Netherlands would be dubious about any proposed unity, for it would upset the sometimes delicate balance that has been achieved in Dutch social life."

enthusiasm for retrieval. Suppose the Malaysian government sought to retrieve Malays across the border in Thailand. Apart from adverse non-Malay reaction, what would it get for its trouble? The accession of a group of heavily religious Malays with relatives in the Malaysian states of Kelantan and Kedah—or, to put it more directly, a group of Malays likely to be supporters of the opposition Parti Islam, in numbers sufficient to tip the political balance.[112] What would Albania get if it succeeded in absorbing the Albanians across the border in Yugoslavia? Albanian politics has revolved around the rivalry of Ghegs and Tosks. For several decades, the regime has been overwhelmingly Tosk. To absorb the Albanians in Yugoslavia, who are predominantly Ghegs (and nearly as numerous as all the Albanians in Albania) might doom the Tosk regime.[113] What would the Irish Republic get if it seriously attempted to embrace Northern Ireland? It would get a Protestant majority in the North that would form a recalcitrant minority in Ireland as a whole. The Malaysian and Albanian examples show once again that seemingly cohesive groups are not as solidary as they look from afar—and that subgroup cleavages have a prominent bearing on irredentist decisions. The Irish example shows that the heterogeneity of the group and territory to be retrieved is equally pertinent, for retrieval will import this heterogeneity into the expanded state.

This brings us right up to the third of the issues touched on by Gauze: will the group across the frontier wish to be retrieved? Clearly, Ulster Protestants and other differentiated groups do not. But even groups with ethnic affinities may be averse to being retrieved. Especially where the putative irredentist state is heterogeneous, members of the group to be retrieved may prefer secession to absorption in yet another state they may not wholly control. For some time, this was the response of the Toubou in Northern Chad to the irredentist blandishments of Libya, which has its own Toubou population; in the mid-1970s, the secessionists fought their Libyan liberators. Alternatively, the group to be retrieved may prefer remaining where it is, particularly if there are clear economic advantages to doing so and if it can use the prospect of irreden-

112. Cf. Astri Suhrke, "Irredentism Contained: The Thai Muslim Case," *Comparative Politics* 7 (Jan. 1975): 187–203.
113. Cf. Dennison I. Rusinow, "The Other Albanians: Some Notes on the Yugoslav Kosmet Today," American Universities Field Staff *Reports*, Southeast Europe Series, 12 (Nov. 1965): 1–24. I am also indebted to Melvin Croan for a helpful discussion of this issue.

tism as a bargaining lever to improve its current position, as the Pathans in Pakistan have.[114] Finally, as in secession, the distribution of population can impede the willingness to be retrieved. The overwhelmingly Bengali population of Cachar in Assam might prefer to attach Cachar to West Bengal, but that would abandon the Bengali minority in the Assam Valley. The composition of the territory to be retrieved and the distribution of the group to be retrieved, as well as the composition of the irredentist territory, affect the willingness of a group to be retrieved.

In such decisions, the relative economic condition of the two countries—and their relative prestige—will be aggravating factors. It matters, as I have just indicated, that Afghanistan is poorer than Pakistan and, before the coup of 1978, that it was viewed as a "feudal" country. It apparently mattered, too, to the Sudeten Germans that Nazi Germany had become a major power, for in the mid-1930s they became Hitler's staunchest supporters, abandoning the ethnically conciliatory parties to which they formerly adhered.[115] But these are not necessarily dispositive considerations. It is generally more attractive to be retrieved by a rich rather than a poor neighbor, but rich neighbors like Libya do not invariably attract, and poor neighbors like Somalia do not invariably repel. The same is true for the attractiveness of the region to be retrieved.

The desire to pursue irredentism and the desire to be retrieved by an irredentist power are thus independently variable. Where enthusiasm is present among the retrievers, it may be absent among those to be retrieved, or vice versa. Unrequited irredentism is common.

Given the significant risks and the dubious rewards of irredentism, states that ardently pursue strategies of retrieval probably have some specially compelling reasons for doing so. The irredenta may form part of a generally adventurous, expansionist foreign policy, as it did for Nazi Germany and Fascist Italy and does on a smaller scale for Libya. Beyond this, however, there are some striking common elements in the irredentism of Libya for Northern Chad, Somalia for the Ogaden, and Afghanistan for Pakistan's Northwest Frontier Province.

First of all, though a claim is asserted on the basis of ethnic affinity in general, the source of the affinity is much more particularized. In each

114. The Croats in Austria are yet another group uninterested in joining the large number of Croats in Yugoslavia, in part, no doubt, because of economic disparities. See William T. Bluhm, *Building an Austrian Nation* (New Haven: Yale Univ. Press, 1973), 208–18.

115. Walter B. Simon, "A Comparative Study of the Problem of Multilingualism," *Mens en Maatschappij* (Amsterdam) 42 (Mar.–Apr. 1967): 89–101.

case, traditional trans-border ethnic affinities can be identified, but in each case there is something more: personal links between rulers of the irredentist state and the group or territory to be retrieved. Qaddafi's own family has roots in Northern Chad. Siad Barre is not just a Somali but a Somali Darood; it is the Darood who inhabit the Ogaden across the border in Ethiopia. The last king of Afghanistan and his leading ministers were "direct descendants of the Peshawar Sardars. 'The lure of Peshawar is a passion, deep in their hearts.' "[116] Peshawar is on the Pakistani side of the border. The king's successors have had similar family ties. The first two Marxist rulers of Afghanistan, Nur Mohammed Taraki and Hafizullah Amin, were both Pathans of the Ghilzai subgroup, deeply rooted in Pakistan.[117] Marxism and irredentism have coexisted in Afghanistan since 1978. Tun Mustapha, the Malaysian state politician who aided Philippine Muslim rebels and probably entertained irredentist aspirations in the Southern Philippines, was a Suluk with family ties in the Philippines. In each case, irredentism has been sustained, not merely by ethnicity, but by kinship in a more direct and narrow sense. And it is worth noting that each of these irredentist states was governed by a patrimonial regime in a traditional society where kinship could operate largely unfettered.[118]

If the unswerving pursuit of irredentism is, unlike separatism, an unusual phenomenon, the passion for retrieval has produced results no more impressive than has the passion for secession. No groups have been retrieved across territorial borders in the post-colonial period. The pursuit of irredentism encourages the formation of defensive alliances and other countermeasures. Ethiopia has had Cuban and Soviet help against a Somali invasion. When Iraq contemplated retrieval of Arabs in Southwestern Iran, Iran was able to counter by aiding the Kurds in Iraq. Although irredentism, unlike secession, involves state action to realign borders, this does not weight the scales more heavily in favor of success. Indeed, as I have suggested, the more calculative quality of state decisions probably makes deterrence more effective. But where irredentism

116. Sayeed, "Pathan Regionalism," 503, quoting Olaf Caroe, *The Pathans* (London: Macmillan, 1958), 435.
117. Selig Harrison, "Tribal Pawns in a Superpower Match," *Far Eastern Economic Review*, Dec. 22, 1978, pp. 24–26.
118. In some cases, even these special conditions might not have been enough. The Somali regime that preceded Siad's had reached an agreement for détente with Ethiopia, and the Afghan regime that preceded Taraki's had done the same with respect to Pakistan. The successor governments used these decisions to shore up their own position and in the process became committed to pursuing the irredentas.

does break into violence, the state-to-state character of the conflict makes escalation a more dangerous possibility.

If irredentism should succeed, the results are unlikely to be much different from the consequences of secession: probably a general unglueing of ethnic relations in the rump state and new tensions in the irredentist state as well. For what we know is already sufficient to deflate the myth of homogeneity in the retrieving states. Even in Somalia, so often described as monoethnic, it takes little imagination to forecast the reaction of powerful groups like the Hawiye to the gain in Darood strength that the inclusion of the Ogaden would produce. To be sure, the Hawiye and the Darood are both Somalis, but it is a much more particularized conception of ethnic identity that will prevail in the new, wholly internal context. Ethnic generalities do not determine the impact of a boundary change.

PART THREE

Party Politics
and Ethnic Conflict

CHAPTER SEVEN

Ethnic Parties
and Party Systems

Political parties, Giovanni Sartori reminds us, both "presuppose" and "produce,"[1] reflect and affect. Two-party systems, for example, depend on and in turn nurture a moderate level of ideological difference. Extreme multipartyism thrives on ideological distance and entrenches the polarization of opinion. Party and society act on each other.

Nowhere is the reciprocal relation between party and society more evident than in ethnic politics. Societies in which ethnic conflict is at moderate levels or in which ethnic divisions must compete for attention with other sources of tension produce party systems that sometimes foster and sometimes moderate ethnic conflict. This is the case in some countries of the West, where ethnic cleavages coexist with other historic sources of conflict. However, societies that are deeply riven along a preponderant ethnic cleavage—as in many Asian and African states—tend to throw up party systems that exacerbate ethnic conflict. By appealing to electorates in ethnic terms, by making ethnic demands on government, and by bolstering the influence of ethnically chauvinist elements within each group, parties that begin by merely mirroring ethnic divisions help to deepen and extend them. Hence the oft-heard remark in such states that the politicians have created ethnic conflict.

The main element that ethnic conflict introduces into party politics is the ethnically based party. An ethnically based party derives its support overwhelmingly from an identifiable ethnic group (or cluster of ethnic groups) and serves the interests of that group. In practice, a party will serve the interests of the group comprising its overwhelming support or quickly forfeit that support, so the test of an ethnic party is simply the

1. Giovanni Sartori, *Parties and Party Systems*, vol. 1 (Cambridge: Cambridge Univ. Press, 1976), 192.

distribution of support. In some countries, ethnic parties emerged early, as the anti-colonial movement divided along ethnic lines long before independence—usually over the desirability, nature, or timing of independence. Such splits occurred in India, so far as Hindus and Muslims were concerned, as well as in Sri Lanka and Nigeria. In many other countries, the onset of elections at or after independence brought with it the formation of ethnically based parties. The creation of parallel, exclusive political organizations is the first propensity of a divided polity.

Of course, it is just a propensity and not an iron law. Furthermore, at the margins there are some ambiguities of classification. Formal requirements for party membership are a starting point. The Shiromani Akali Dal of the Indian Punjab is clearly a Sikh party, its membership open only to Sikhs, just as the United Malays National Organization is a Malay party, with similarly restricted membership.[2] Before the January 1966 coup in Nigeria and the abolition of political parties that followed, the Northern People's Congress was open only to people of Northern origin.[3] Despite the difficulty of discerning who qualified as a "Northerner," that party, too, had an ethnically exclusive character. But membership clauses alone are not the test of an ethnic party, and neither are the original intentions of the party's founders. The National Convention of Nigerian Citizens became an Ibo party, however much it aspired to retain pan-ethnic support. Even some limited heterogeneity of membership and support is not the measure. The Jan Sangh became a Hindu party even though it was not formally restricted to Hindus and even though it did, on the rarest occasions, allocate tickets to Sikh candidates in the Punjab.[4] The Sri Lanka Freedom Party is a Sinhalese party even though it has gained some support from the Muslim minority. A small fraction of support from another ethnic group can provide at best a bit of leaven, insufficient to divert a party from the interests of the group that provides its overwhelming support. Party leadership will pursue such minority support only insofar as it is low cost and does not threaten the more valuable principal source of support. This is a major reason

2. Baldev Raj Nayar, "Sikh Separatism in the Punjab," in Donald Eugene Smith, ed., *South Asian Politics and Religion* (Princeton: Princeton Univ. Press, 1966), 170. See J. M. Gullick, *Malaya* (New York: Praeger, 1963), 114, for one of many accounts of the unsuccessful attempt of the first leader of UMNO to persuade the party to accept non-Malays as full members.

3. Richard L. Sklar, *Nigerian Political Parties* (Princeton: Princeton Univ. Press, 1963), 382.

4. Paul R. Brass, "Ethnic Cleavages and the Punjab Party System" (unpublished paper presented at the 1972 annual meeting of the Association for Asian Studies), 20.

why it is so difficult for an ethnic party, once established, to become multiethnic.

To be an ethnic party, a party does not have to command an exclusive hold on the allegiance of group members. It is how the *party's* support is distributed, and not how the *ethnic group's* support is distributed, that is decisive. There are two major Sinhalese parties in Sri Lanka, not one, and several essentially Chinese parties in Malaysia. The leadership of the Akali Dal attempted to put forward the doctrine that a Sikh could not join another party,[5] but many Sikhs and Hindus in the Punjab were members of the Congress Party. This division of Sikh support made the Punjab Congress a multiethnic party flanked by ethnic parties; it did not alter the character of the Akali Dal as a Sikh party. In Trinidad in the 1960s, it was said that Indian Muslims were less faithful to the Democratic Labor Party than were Indian Hindus. This did not prevent the DLP from being an Indian party any more than caste differences in party support in Sri Lanka or the Punjab prevented the SLFP from claiming plausibly to speak for the Sinhalese or the Akali Dal to speak for the Sikhs. Rough edges in a party's support do not undermine its status as an ethnic party.

Yet, as these illustrations show, the shape of the party *system* is determined by the distribution of group support as well as by the distribution of party support. Whether ethnic parties emerge—and when—how many of them, their relative strength, and their interactions all have much to do with group division and cohesion. And the contours of the party system in an ethnically divided society have a profound effect on the ethnic outcomes of party politics.

THE RATIONALE OF ETHNIC PARTIES AND THE CONCEPT OF PARTY

Where ethnic loyalties are strong, parties tend to organize along ethnic lines for much the same reasons that other organizations, such as trade unions, social clubs, chambers of commerce, and neighborhood associations, tend to be ethnically exclusive. The features of an ethnically divided society conspire to impede the development of the full range of social relations among ethnic groups, and this affects its organizational structure in and out of politics. Occupational specialization, residential

5. Nayar, "Sikh Separatism in the Punjab," 163.

segregation, habits of endogamy, dietary customs, religious differences, and all the other things that mark the boundaries between groups tend to foster affinity and a sense of common interest within groups. Centripetal ties of this kind are often expressed in party allegiances. "In electoral politics," as John Dunn remarks, "voters may long for those who will represent them perfectly as individuals; but in practice they must put up with those who are attempting to represent them as components of rather blearily perceived potential action groups."[6] The communitarian aspect of ethnicity propels group members toward concentrated party loyalties.[7]

This is the minimal basis for ethnic party allegiance, recognizable to some extent even in societies that are not deeply divided. In any society, members of various ethnic groups rarely distribute themselves randomly among competing parties. Where conflict levels are high, however, ethnic parties reflect something more than mere affinity and a vague sense of common interest. That something is the mutual incompatibility of ethnic claims to power. Since the party aspires to control the state, and in conflict-prone polities ethnic groups also attempt to exclude others from state power, the emergence of ethnic parties is an integral part of this political struggle.[8]

Ethnic parties thus derive from two sources: the internal imperatives of the ethnic group as a community and the external imperatives of the ethnic group, in relation to others, as the incipient whole community. Ethnically based parties are also cemented by the incentives politicians have to organize along those lines where ethnic groups are a prominent part of the social landscape.[9] Because of the ascriptive character of ethnic identity, attachment to an ongoing ethnic party may not be as susceptible to change at the level of the individual voter as attachment to a party that has the flavor of a voluntary association. Ethnicity offers political

6. John Dunn, "Hoc Signo Victor Eris: Representation, Allegiance, and Obligation in the Politics of Ghana and Sri Lanka" (unpublished paper, Cambridge, England, Sept. 1975), 8.

7. Cf. Sklar, *Nigerian Political Parties*, 474–80.

8. In addition to attempts to exclude others from state power, I include here the defensive side: attempts to resist exclusion, demands for equal treatment and for an inclusive polity.

9. Among such incentives must be counted the greater ethnic homogeneity of individual constituencies than of whole states—a point that has been made by Robert H. Bates, "Ethnic Competition and Modernization in Contemporary Africa," *Comparative Political Studies* 6 (Jan. 1974): 457–84.

leaders the promise of secure support. Politicians who can count have something they can count on.

To be sure, most political parties in most countries have a core of solid supporters, whose fathers and mothers were also supporters of the same party. In the United States, party allegiance has historically been transmitted from generation to generation for perhaps 70 to 80 percent of all voters.[10] In recent years, this has declined to between 50 and 65 percent.[11] Party identification is, furthermore, a powerful predictor of voting behavior.[12] And, of course, ethnic affiliations are also associated with party preference and electoral choice in such countries as the United States, Canada, and Switzerland.[13] Yet there is a difference between the ability of a broadly based party to count on the votes of a majority of a given ethnic group and the dependence of a party solely on the support of a single ethnic group to the exclusion of others.

In both cases, party allegiance may be largely ascriptive. In fact, ethnic affiliation may sometimes be a more reliable predictor of party support where parties are not ethnically based than where they are. As I have indicated, it is perfectly possible for a single ethnic group in a deeply divided society to split its support equally among two or more ethnically based parties. Merely knowing ethnic affiliation in such a setting gives no clue to party support. By the same token, it is possible for an ethnic group to give virtually its undivided support to a single nonethnic party operating in a society with a moderate level of ethnic conflict. So the difference between the two types of party does not derive from the degree to which party allegiance is based on ethnicity.[14]

10. See Angus Campbell et al., *The American Voter* (New York: John Wiley, 1960), 147. For older studies, see V. O. Key, Jr., *Politics, Parties, and Pressure Groups*, 3rd ed. (New York: Crowell, 1956), 585–87.

11. M. Kent Jennings and Richard G. Niemi, *Generations and Politics: A Panel Study of Young Adults and Their Parents* (Princeton: Princeton Univ. Press, 1981), 91; Jennings and Niemi, *The Political Character of Adolescence: The Influence of Family and Schools* (Princeton: Princeton Univ. Press, 1974), 41.

12. Campbell, *The American Voter*, passim.

13. Raymond E. Wolfinger, "The Development and Persistence of Ethnic Voting," *American Political Science Review* 59 (Dec. 1965): 896–908; Michael Parenti, "Ethnic Politics and the Persistence of Ethnic Identification," *American Political Science Review* 61 (Sept. 1967): 717–26; Peter M. Leslie, "The Role of Political Parties in Promoting the Interests of Ethnic Minorities," *Canadian Journal of Political Science* 2 (Dec. 1969): 419–33; Henry H. Kerr, Jr., *Switzerland: Social Cleavages and Partisan Conflict* (Beverly Hills: Sage Professional Papers, Contemporary Political Sociology Series, no. 06-002, 1974).

14. Again, it is necessary to emphasize that whether a party is ethnically based depends on the distribution of party support, not group support.

The difference lies, rather, in the relative independence of the two parties from group claims and demands. Ethnic demands are made through and often espoused by the broadly based party, but not automatically, not without consideration of competing demands, not without adjustment. That the broadly based party can remain broadly based in spite of this is typically evidence of a moderate level of ethnic conflict and the existence of nonethnic issues that also animate its supporters. The ethnic party, on the other hand, embraces ethnic demands as a matter of course, even when these have far-reaching consequences for other groups. An ethnic party is identified with the cause of the ethnic group it represents. Its *raison d'être* is to "unite the Sinhalese," to "fight for the Malay race," to "weld [the Yoruba] together," to work for "the protection of Sikh rights," or the like.[15] No doubt, an ethnic party may need to moderate ethnic demands on occasion, in anticipation of the reaction of other groups outside the party or of practical difficulties in translating the demands into policy. But its overall mission is to foster the interests of the group it represents. There are no countervailing competitive incentives.

The very concept of party is challenged by a political party that is both ascriptive and exclusive. The prevailing concept of party emphasizes the conversion of segmental interests into public interests. On this basis, sharp distinctions are made between parties and pressure groups. "The leaders of pressure groups," according to V. O. Key, "thrive by playing to group interest, by arousing anxieties and fears among their followers, by encouraging class and group cleavages. Political parties, on the other hand, must play down group interest by conciliating conflict, by compromising issues, by seeking formulas for the combination of many groups into a bloc strong enough to win. . . . The pressure group," Key concludes, "must appeal to the partial interest; the political party, to the common interest."[16] The main characteristic of the political party is its quality of mediating, of comprising a "combination of interests."[17]

Key was writing about American political parties, which are broadly based. But cross-national conceptions of the political party make it equally difficult to fit the ethnic party within their bounds. As soon as these conceptions move beyond minimal definitions of the party as an

15. Marvin L. Rogers, "The Politicization of Malay Villagers," *Comparative Politics* 7 (Jan. 1975): 205–25, at 217; Sklar, *Nigerian Political Parties*, 104 n.40; Nayar, "Sikh Separatism in the Punjab," 170.
16. *Politics, Parties, and Pressure Groups*, 177.
17. Ibid., 216.

organization that seeks to place its personnel in public office[18] and move toward analysis of the functions of parties, they stress the generalizing, broadening, and aggregative tendency of the political party. As they grow in strength, Samuel P. Huntington argues, "parties become the buckle which binds one social force to another and which creates a basis for loyalty and identity transcending more parochial groupings."[19] The party, says Sigmund Neumann, is "the great intermediary which links social forces and ideologies to official governmental institutions and relates them to political action within the larger political community."[20] To be a party, Sartori suggests, in terms reminiscent of Key, a political organization must be "capable of governing for the whole," and this means it "must take a *non-partial* approach to the whole."[21] By this he means the party must attempt to serve the "public interest" or the "common good" and " 'organize the chaotic public will.' "[22]

The association of the political party with the quest for public rather than particularistic interests is inimical to the very basis of an ethnic party. As I have already suggested, the ethnic party identifies narrow group interests with the totality of the common interest. The ethnic party does combine intraethnic interests, often very effectively. But it neither combines nor buckles nor takes a non-partial approach to the interests of various ethnic groups in a society. Its rationale is the incompatibility of those interests—and quite often their fundamental incompatibility.

Although, like all parties, ethnic parties seek power, distribute offices, and mobilize support, in some ways they behave differently from political parties that are not ethnically based. Gabriel Almond has pointed out that "particularistic parties" behave much like interest groups.[23] This may be a clue to the character and consequences of ethnic parties, for Key notes that as pressure groups monopolize the loyalty of their members, "intergroup cleavages are widened and deepened. . . . [T]he growth

18. See, e.g., Kenneth Janda, *A Conceptual Framework for the Comparative Analysis of Political Parties* (Beverly Hills: Sage Professional Papers, Comparative Politics Series, no. 01-002, 1970), 83.

19. Samuel P. Huntington, *Political Order in Changing Societies* (New Haven: Yale Univ. Press, 1968), 405.

20. Sigmund Neumann, *Modern Political Parties* (Chicago: Univ. of Chicago Press, 1956), 397.

21. Sartori, *Parties and Party Systems*, vol. 1, p. 26 (emphasis in the original).

22. Ibid., 28, quoting Neumann, *Modern Political Parties*, 397.

23. Gabriel A. Almond, "Introduction: A Functional Approach to Comparative Politics," in Gabriel A. Almond and James S. Coleman, eds., *The Politics of the Developing Areas* (Princeton: Princeton Univ. Press, 1960), 44. Key's description of pressure groups also fits ethnic parties. *Politics, Parties, and Pressure Groups*, 179–80, 216.

of stronger and stronger groups dedicated to the promotion of narrow group claims places greater strain on the social mechanisms for the settlement of group and class conflict."[24] Ethnic parties make the mediation of group interests difficult, and this helps explain why ethnic party systems are so often conflict prone.

There is, however, another reason why ethnic party systems produce conflict, one we shall encounter repeatedly. Conventionally conceived, parties are a vehicle for choice by voters. This view of party tends to exclude the possibility that the support of any political party will be coterminous with the boundaries of any single social group, especially a group in which membership is determined by birth. Such a coincidence of party and group boundaries militates against the exercise of choice by voters. There is thus a certain fixity that sets in where parties are ethnically based that is conducive either to stalemate or to fears of permanent domination. The ascriptive predictability of party outcomes fosters conflict.

This predictability is not absolute. There are variations that derive from differences in how groups choose to spread their support. Some groups cohere around one party, others divide themselves between two, and still others fragment their support in several directions. Furthermore, the existence of ethnic parties does not rule out arrangements across ethnic and party lines: there are variations in the incidence of multiethnic parties and coalitions. Fixity there surely is, but there is also fluidity that affects the propensity of party systems to deepen divisions and their capacity to develop mechanisms of ethnic conciliation. Before we get to these variations in the interplay of party and ethnic conflict, it is necessary to canvass briefly the possible permutations.

PARTIES: ETHNIC, MULTIETHNIC, NONETHNIC

Where party boundaries stop at group boundaries, it is appropriate to speak of ethnic parties, regardless of whether any group is represented by more than one party. Where party boundaries are more inclusive than group boundaries, more information is required before deciding whether parties are ethnic, multiethnic, or nonethnic.

Before dealing with nonethnic parties, it is necessary to explain what

24. *Politics, Parties, and Pressure Groups*, 179–80.

distinguishes ethnic from multiethnic parties. Surely, a party that brings together two or more groups under its organizational aegis is, by literal definition, multiethnic. But suppose, as in Mali in the 1960s, two main parties form, each of them supported by a different combination of ethnic groups gathered around an important core group.[25] Or suppose, as in Upper Volta during the same period, the powerful Mossi, who comprise about 40 percent of the population, support a single political party, thereby inducing smaller ethnic groups to coalesce into two other parties.[26] Internally, the Malian and the non-Mossi Voltaic parties were multiethnic, but externally—in relation to other parties—they reflected ethnic polarization. Here political context is more important than the literal meaning of words in determining the character of parties. If we ask *whose* party the Voltaic parties were, the answer is clear: one was the party of the Mossi, the others were the parties of the non-Mossi, and each party aimed to advance the interests of that group as against the interests of the other. For this reason, I would count the Malian and Voltaic parties as ethnically based, even though some comprised members of more than one ethnic group. For present purposes, a party is multiethnic only if it spans the major groups in conflict. If, for example, the Voltaic parties had Mossi as well as non-Mossi support, they would be multiethnic, even if all groups were not perfectly represented. What is required is that the parties not break clearly along the very ethnic cleavage that rends the society.[27]

This usage differs sharply from the rhetoric of parties themselves, which is often more aspirational and more literal. In Malaysia, for example, there have long been several parties catering to a predominantly Chinese and (to a lesser extent) Indian clientele. Periodically, these parties make heroic efforts to enlist Malays, usually run a few Malay candidates, and elect a few Malays to party office. They proudly call themselves multiethnic on account of these efforts, but the conception of a multiethnic party outlined here makes it clear that these are non-Malay or, to smooth off the rough edges, essentially Chinese parties. And this is

25. Aristide R. Zolberg, "Patterns of National Integration," *Journal of Modern African Studies* 5 (Dec. 1967): 449–67, at 459–60. Cf. Virginia Thompson and Richard Adloff, *French West Africa* (Stanford: Stanford Univ. Press, 1957), 146–55.

26. Thompson and Adloff, *French West Africa*, 177–79. See also Victor D. DuBois, "The Struggle for Stability in the Upper Volta," American Universities Field Staff *Reports*, West Africa Series, vol. 12, nos. 1–5 (1969).

27. No doubt, this is a subjective criterion, but it is less difficult to operationalize in deeply divided societies than might be imagined. Moreover, it is not very much more subjective than deciding where ethnic boundaries themselves lie.

a good example of how wrong one would be to call such parties multiethnic by virtue of their ability to include Chinese and Indians when differences between those two groups are negligible compared to the political differences between Chinese and Indians, on one side, and Malays, on the other.

The distinction between nonethnic and multiethnic parties is also difficult to draw. It depends on whether group members participate in the party on a group basis, whether, in other words, the party comprises a coalition of ethnic groups. A clear example of a multiethnic party is the Parti Démocratique de Côte d'Ivoire around the time of independence. The PDCI was built heavily on local ethnic associations and organized around ethnically based party units. Leaders who were propelled upward considered themselves "ambassadors of the ethnic groups to which they owed their selection."[28] A proposed reorganization of party units along nonethnic lines had to be abandoned because of resistance from local party leaders, who understood that this would alter the very basis of party allegiance.[29]

If the PDCI was a clear case of a multiethnic party, it is more difficult to categorize other parties as multiethnic or nonethnic. If avowed intention is the test, many parties ostensibly aim to turn politics in a nonethnic direction, organizing political conflict around what are thought to be the "real issues" of ideology, development, or economic interest. Few succeed. The criterion, therefore, must be more complex than one that rests on manifest intentions. As the PDCI suggests, party organization affords a clue to the multiethnic character of a party. Where parties are not organized explicitly around ethnically based branches or sections, then the nature of the issues dividing parties, the ethnic demarcation of factions within the party, or the movement of ethnic blocs in and out of the party often testifies to the nature of a party as an internal coalition of ethnic groups. In Senegal, the Lebou and the Fulani, among other groups, acted as "autonomous blocs," moving in and out of the ruling party as it suited their interests.[30] In Zambia, when the United National Independence Party held party elections in 1967, Bemba and Tonga delegates joined hands to defeat candidates of the Lozi and Nyanja groups. After the party conference, the two ethnically based factions formed

28. Aristide R. Zolberg, "Mass Parties and National Integration: The Case of the Ivory Coast," *Journal of Politics* 25 (Feb. 1963): 36–48, at 43.

29. Ibid., 44–45.

30. Aristide R. Zolberg, *Creating Political Order: The Party States of West Africa* (Chicago: Rand McNally, 1966), 26.

separate committees to work for their interests within the party.[31] Clearly, UNIP was a fragile coalition of ethnic groups.

Multiethnic parties like PDCI and UNIP seem to move toward the single-party format, outlawing or pressuring opposition parties out of business. I shall return to this tendency later. For the moment, it suffices to note that the intolerance of competition renders the multiethnic span of such parties suspect as coerced or somehow contrary to "natural" political forces in an environment of ethnic conflict, since it prevents the realignment of ethnic groups and parties. In severely divided societies, multiethnic parties are strongly susceptible to centrifugal stresses.

Parties organized nonethnically are rare or nonexistent in such societies.[32] They may, however, be found in countries where divisions do not run deep or where ethnic groups are so dispersed that it hardly makes sense to organize along ethnic lines for national-level politics. The Congress Party of India and its successor parties are fundamentally nonethnic at the national level. The same, however, cannot be said of the Congress Party in all the Indian states. In Kerala, the four major ethnic cum religious and caste groups have tended to divide along party lines, with Congress often deriving its support from Nairs and Christians.[33] In Bombay, at the height of a Maharashtrian ethnic movement (the Shiv Sena), the Congress Party was largely confined to the support of immigrant ethnic groups.[34]

India is not alone in this respect. The ethnic basis of support of nonethnic parties is often apparent at the local level. As Congress was the party of non-Maharashtrians in Bombay, Nkrumah's Convention People's Party was the party of Southern, non-Ashanti immigrants in Kumasi.[35] Much the same was true of Indonesian parties during the period of free elections in the 1950s. The Nationalists and the Communists,

31. Robert I. Rotberg, "Tribalism and Politics in Zambia," *Africa Report*, Dec. 1967, pp. 29–35; Ruth Weiss, "Mulungushi and Zambia's Tribalism," *Venture*, July 1971, pp. 14–16.

32. It should be clear that the term *nonethnic parties* is used here purely as shorthand for a residual category of parties arranged along a Left-Right, traditional-modern, urban-rural, aristocrat-commoner, secular-religious, or, for that matter, any other axis except ethnic differences.

33. Lloyd I. Rudolph and Susanne Hoeber Rudolph, *The Modernity of Tradition: Political Development in India* (Chicago: Univ. of Chicago Press, 1967), 71–76; V. K. S. Nayar, "Communal Interest Groups in Kerala," in Smith, ed., *South Asian Politics and Religion*, chap. 8; Selig Harrison, *India: The Dangerous Decades* (Princeton: Princeton Univ. Press, 1960), 196–99.

34. *Statesman Weekly* (Calcutta), Mar. 30, 1968; ibid., Apr. 6, 1968.

35. D. G. Austin and W. Tordoff, "Kumasi Votes Again: 3," *West Africa*, May 9, 1959, p. 449.

both major parties nationwide, obtained in 1955 four times as many votes in Javanese areas as in Minangkabau areas.[36] In particular localities, ethnic distinctions among parties were even more finespun, as R. William Liddle has skillfully shown. To take one of many examples, Lower Simalungun in East Sumatra, the Protestant party was the exclusive preserve of the North Tapanuli Batak, Masjumi (a Muslim party) was identified solely with the South Tapanuli Batak, and the Nationalists and Communists were confined to Javanese support.[37] Yet the Ghanaian CPP and the Indonesian parties could accurately be described as nonethnic at the national level. Ethnic issues were not the driving force of party politics, but what was true nationally was not necessarily true locally.

THE VARIETY OF PARTY SYSTEMS

Parties, then, can be ethnic, multiethnic, or nonethnic. Party systems, however, may combine various types of parties.

The first possibility is a party system in which all parties are ethnically based. Zanzibar until 1964, the Sudan, Sri Lanka, Chad, Benin, Kenya, Nigeria, and Congo (Brazzaville) at various times, and Guyana and Trinidad since about 1960 are all countries that have had party systems based clearly on ethnic parties. Other countries have had variations on this theme: two parties representing two clusters of ethnic groups in Sierra Leone in the 1960s (the Mali pattern) and splits in Kenya and Mauritius between a party representing one or two powerful ethnic groups and a party representing a combination of smaller groups (the Upper Volta pattern).

Moving to the opposite extreme, a wholly nonethnic party system is possible but unusual. Perhaps the outstanding case of a nonethnic party system in an ethnically divided society is the two-party system in the Philippines during the period before martial law was imposed in 1972. Built on pyramids of competing factions extending down to the local level, the Philippine system was inhospitable to the monopolization of any ethnic clientele by either party. There were, to be sure, marked propensities toward ethnic voting (on a candidate basis), and the shifting of ethnic loyalties from one party to another, but these were ephemeral and

36. Herbert Feith, *The Indonesian Elections of 1955* (Ithaca: Cornell Univ. Modern Indonesia Project, 1957), 78.
37. R. William Liddle, "Ethnicity and Party Organization: Three East Sumatran Cases," in Claire Holt, ed., *Culture and Politics in Indonesia* (Ithaca: Cornell Univ. Press, 1972), 149–61.

were determined by the ethnic identity of major national candidates in any election.[38] At any given moment, the support of one or another ethnic group may have been concentrated in one party or another, but the parties simply did not divide along ethnic group lines.

Why Filipino parties developed nonethnically remains difficult to say. Filipino parties were not, after all, unique in their clientelistic organization.[39] Perhaps the relative mildness of ethnic conflict in the Philippines is part of the answer, but even the Muslim groups, whose conflicts with the Christians were anything but mild, were tied into the nonethnic parties. Another possible explanation is the dispersion of groups, which is generally a disincentive to ethnic organization at the national level, but this alone is not always enough. In Zaire, where ethnic groups are at least equally numerous and dispersed, parties quickly began to form along ethnic lines.[40] What is clear is that the Philippine system of non-ethnically based parties is well-nigh unique in ethnically divided societies in the developing world. Where parties divide exclusively along Left-Right lines or along nonideological lines determined by patronage patterns, that is an excellent indication that ethnic divisions are not salient.

For similar reasons, party systems involving a combination of ethnic and nonethnic parties (or multiethnic and nonethnic parties) are unlikely in Asia and Africa. Such a system presupposes the prevalence of more than one issue dimension. This is characteristic of ethnically divided societies in Western Europe, where parties simultaneously reflect a Left-Right and a clerical-secular dimension as well as an ethnic one.[41] Religion, class, and language are all strong predictors of party preference in Switzerland.[42] In Belgium, religious and class issues, each well repre-

38. See Crawford Young, *The Politics of Cultural Pluralism* (Madison: Univ. of Wisconsin Press, 1976), 365; Hirofumi Ando, "A Study of Voting Patterns in the Philippine Presidential and Senatorial Elections, 1945–1965," *Midwest Journal of Political Science* 13 (Nov. 1969): 567–86; Nobleza Asuncion-Landé, "Multilingualism, Politics, and 'Filipinism,'" *Asian Survey* 11 (July 1977): 677–92.

39. For the integrative possibilities of clientelistic organization, see René Lemarchand, "Political Clientelism and Ethnicity in Tropical Africa: Competing Solidarities in Nation-Building," *American Political Science Review* 66 (Mar. 1972): 68–90, esp. 69–72, 84.

40. Crawford Young, *Politics in the Congo* (Princeton: Princeton Univ. Press, 1965); René Lemarchand, "Congo (Leopoldville)," in James S. Coleman and Carl G. Rosberg, Jr., eds., *Political Parties and National Integration in Tropical Africa* (Berkeley and Los Angeles: Univ. of California Press, 1964), chap. 15.

41. See Seymour Martin Lipset, "Political Cleavages in 'Developed' and 'Emerging' Polities," in Erik Allardt and Yrjö Littunen, eds., *Cleavages, Ideologies and Party Systems* (Helsinki: Academic Bookstore, 1964), 25–38. Cf. Arend Lijphart, *The Politics of Accommodation: Pluralism and Democracy in the Netherlands* (Berkeley and Los Angeles: Univ. of California Press, 1968), chap. 2.

42. Kerr, *Switzerland*, 7–20.

sented in the party system, for a long time impeded the growth of strong, ethnically based parties.[43] When these did emerge, they had to compete for support with the older Catholic, Liberal, and Socialist parties, which in varying degrees spanned ethnic groups. This mixed party system reflects the existence of strong cross-cutting cleavages arising out of longstanding historical conflicts not strongly reflected in the party systems of developing countries. Consequently, when ethnic parties arise in deeply divided societies in Asia and Africa, they tend to displace rather than coexist with nonethnic parties. Party positioning in such countries quickly becomes unidimensional—along an ethnic axis. I shall say more about this when I consider the fate of Left parties in ethnically divided societies.

If nonethnic parties do not fare well under such conditions, the same is not necessarily true of multiethnic parties or coalitions of ethnic parties. These are not *ipso facto* precluded by the pervasiveness of ethnic issues, and they may form for a variety of electoral or governmental reasons.

Systems involving multiethnic parties are generally of two types. The multiethnic party either competes with ethnic parties on one or more flanks, as in the case of the Congress Party in the Punjab, mentioned earlier; or else the multiethnic party moves to a single-party position, as the PDCI and a number of other multiethnic parties in Africa have. The difference is important, since it involves something central to party politics: the existence or absence of competition.

Coalitions of ethnic parties differ from multiethnic parties in several respects. The multiethnic party is, at least in principle, permanent; the coalition, though it may become permanent, embodies no such necessary assumption. Organizationally, the two also differ. At some level, even if only at the top, the multiethnic party must integrate its ethnic wings. The coalition of ethnic parties need not do so, and indeed the parties may meet only within the framework of government. Electorally, ethnic parties in coalition may or may not contest the same seats, depending in large measure on whether the parties have reached their agreement before or after the election. Multiethnic parties, however, put forward one candidate per single-member constituency or one list in multimember

43. George Armstrong Kelly, "Belgium: New Nationalism in an Old World" (unpublished paper, mimeo., 1969). See also Val R. Lorwin, "Conflict and Compromise in Belgian Politics" (unpublished paper presented at the 1965 annual meeting of the American Political Science Association).

constituencies. As these differences suggest, the process of bargaining and conciliation must be more elaborate and regularized in a multiethnic party than in a coalition where the partners remain organizationally separate. This is also likely to be true because the existence of the multiethnic party reflects some commitment to ethnic accommodation, even though the commitment may be only imperfectly shared among the ethnic participants or among leaders and followers. No such commitment can necessarily be inferred from the existence of a multiethnic coalition. The motivation for its formation may run the gamut from the desire to reduce ethnic conflict to the necessity of joining together simply to form a government.

The burden of what I have been saying so far is that parties and party systems can make a difference in ethnic politics. This position may seem a bit odd in a period that has witnessed the decline of political parties in Asia and Africa, first because the state bureaucracies afforded greater opportunity for advancement and influence than party organizations and then because so many parties were destroyed by the rise of authoritarian personalities or by military coups, or both. Free elections are now a rarity in the developing world.[44] But none of this proves that party is unimportant, either in the states that still enjoy party politics or in those that do not. In the latter, as I shall show in Chapter 12, the growth of ethnic parties has had a profound impact on the incidence of military coups. And, of course, the alleged inability to handle ethnic problems through the existing party system was a reason frequently invoked by civilian authoritarian rulers who smashed the party system. In short, where party politics has declined, ethnic party systems have been a major reason for that decline.

More than this, party systems are not merely established or destroyed. They can be reestablished, and military regimes occasionally move or are pushed in this direction. Uppermost in the minds of some military leaders as they contemplate restoration of civilian rule are concerns about whether the parties that emerge will be ethnically based.[45] That

44. Only a small minority of African states held so much as one free election after independence. John Cartwright, "Party Competition in a Developing Nation: The Basis of Support for an Opposition in Sierra Leone" (unpublished paper presented at the 1971 annual meeting of the Canadian Political Science Association), p. 1. The Asian record—despite major exceptions—is not very much better.

45. In the case of Nigeria, I have described some of these developments in Donald L. Horowitz, "About-Face in Africa: The Return to Civilian Rule in Nigeria," *Yale Review* 68 (Winter 1979): 192–206. For a different perspective, see Republic of Ghana, *Report of the Ad Hoc Committee on Union Government* (Accra: Ghana Pub. Corp., 1977).

this is no fanciful concern is shown clearly by the military turnover to civilians in Ghana in 1969. This was quickly followed by the establishment of a party system largely along ethnic lines, partly because of alignments and rivalries that grew up during military rule. Party systems are a key policy problem of severely divided societies.

If party systems do matter, then it is time to show what difference they make by examining the four most common party systems, those composed of: (1) ethnic parties, (2) ethnic parties and coalitions of ethnic parties, (3) ethnic parties and multiethnic parties, and (4) multiethnic single parties. Ethnic party systems will be dealt with in this and the next chapter. The three remaining systems, which all involve party contact or organization across ethnic lines, form the subject of the two following chapters. For each system, I intend to depict, through the use of case illustrations, the evolution of the party system, its main characteristics and consequences for ethnic conflict, and the sources and directions of change in such systems. Although these four systems have different properties, they are by no means unrelated: one of them can evolve from another. In particular, ethnic party systems often give way to one of the other three party arrangements. Ethnic parties and ethnic party systems are thus the building blocks of party politics in ethnically divided societies.

THE GROWTH OF
ETHNIC PARTY SYSTEMS

The tendency to organize parties along ethnic lines is very strong in most deeply divided societies, particularly those in which a few major ethnic groups meet at the national level of politics. It is a tendency that is cumulative: once one party organizes along ethnic lines, others are inclined to follow suit. The strength of the tendency is illustrated by its ability to overcome the preferences of political leaders in two important respects.

First, ethnic party systems can and do emerge contrary to the convictions of the principal party leaders. Party leaders may genuinely believe that ethnic divisions are not very important, that they only obscure the issues that ought to concern (and unify) a nationalist party. A wholly ethnic party system may come into being despite such ideological convictions.

Second, party leaders oriented toward the electoral process typically have a strong preference for strategies calculated to produce electoral victory. (Revolutionary parties are another matter.) To be sure, they may need to make compromises with their own beliefs or the beliefs of key supporters along the way. These compromises may require them to espouse positions that impair their chances of attaining the majority they seek.[46] By the same token, party leaders may have to settle for mere legislative representation, though they desire outright victory. Especially in multiparty systems, they may realize that the best they can hope for at the polls is a marginal improvement on their minority position.[47] For such parties, "victory" is determined by their share of votes or seats relative to earlier elections and relative to parties specifically competing for the same clientele, rather than relative to a majority or plurality. But none of these qualifications impeaches the general validity of vote maximizing as an electoral strategy.

How, then, to account for the party leader who intentionally pursues a course foreseeably leading to a permanent minority position for his party? Rational models of electoral politics make no provision for such a strategy in an electorally oriented party. Yet that is the situation of the politician who organizes a party around the ethnic sentiment of a demographic minority, especially the politician who leaves a majority party to do so. Many organizers of parties that turn out to have a limited ethnic base believe, with undue optimism, that they are creating a party that will span ethnic divisions. But unrealistic optimism alone cannot explain the conduct of those politicians who choose to break up a broader party for narrower ethnic horizons. Ethnic politics is filled with decisions of this kind.

To some considerable extent, such decisions reflect irresistible voter pressures. "An elderly Ashanti man in Swedru was . . . emphatic" in explaining why he rejected the party led by the Ewe, K. A. Gbedemah, in the 1969 Ghana election: " 'Have you ever heard of an Ewe chief ruling over Ashanti? No, Busia is our man.' "[48] (Busia came from a group related to the Ashanti.) This bit of reasoning, parsimoniously linking

---

46. In the United States, for example, it has been shown that the extreme views of party activists relative to voters have sometimes jeopardized a party's electoral chances. Cases in point include the Democrats' nomination of George McGovern in 1972 and the Republicans' nomination of Barry Goldwater in 1964. David Nexon, "Asymmetry in the Party System," *American Political Science Review* 65 (Sept. 1971): 716–30.

47. Sartori, *Parties and Party Systems*, vol. 1, p. 346.

48. Quoted in Maxwell Owusu, "Politics in Swedru," in Dennis Austin and Robin Luckham, eds., *Politicians and Soldiers in Ghana, 1966–1972* (London: Frank Cass, 1975), 255. See also David Goldsworthy, "Ethnicity and Leadership in Africa: The 'Untypical' Case of Tom Mboya," *Journal of Modern African Studies* 20 (Mar. 1982): 107–26, at 111.

traditional conceptions of chieftaincy and fears of ethnic domination with party allegiance, illustrates the centrifugal currents that underlie the growth of ethnically based party systems.

Sentiment from below, of course, does not exclude the influence of rivalry at the top—in fact, may spur it. The differences between a Kaunda and a Kapwepwe in Zambia, a Tengku Abdul Rahman and a Lim Chong Eu in Malaysia, a Kenyatta and an Odinga in Kenya, a Jagan and a Burnham in Guyana, or a Margai and a Stevens in Sierra Leone—all of which led to ethnic party formation—are no doubt fed by the knowledge that there is a ready-made clientele outside the multiethnic party waiting to be led.[49] This following cannot be captured fully while its potential leader remains tied to a party whose multiethnic composition requires precisely the kinds of concessions to which the waiting ethnic clientele strongly objects. There is thus the anticipation that, in some important ways, the leader will be stronger as the leader of a single ethnic following outside the multiethnic party than he was as the leader of one among several ethnic groups inside. Occasionally, there is also a conviction that the political cause of the ethnic group is so just that it is worth risking permanent opposition for its sake.

A variety of calculations and rationalizations may be indulged by leaders about to secede from a party to form an ethnic minority party. A leader can demonstrate his ethnic drawing power by fighting an election at the head of an ethnic party slate. A return to the multiethnic party at a later point, on better terms, is not foreclosed: Lim Chong Eu and Oginga Odinga did return to the fold years later. Then, too, prospective leaders of an incipient ethnic minority party may calculate that they can broaden their support or make multiethnic alliances with other parties later, especially if they diagnose the multiethnic party they are leaving to be in a process of fragmentation on more than one front. This is generally a dubious calculation—for multiethnic alliances are not easy to form at any time—but if the other elements for a split are in place, it is a gamble likely to be taken.

This is a matter of push as well as pull. Ethnic leaders not only leave multiethnic parties, but are also forced out. Sometimes their expulsion is contrary to the apparent interests of the politicians who force them out,

49. Kapwepwe left UNIP to form his own Bemba party in 1971. Lim Chong Eu left the Alliance Party and formed his own essentially Chinese party in 1962. Odinga resigned from the Kenya African National Union and formed a Luo party in 1966. Burnham split with the People's Progressive Party and formed a Creole party in 1955, as we shall see in more detail below. Stevens abandoned the SLPP to form a Northern party in 1962.

for those who remain in the party may be left in a minority position with the electorate. Again, it is necessary to account for such decisions.

Many parties in Asia and Africa developed in the terminal period of colonial rule, shortly before ethnic issues became paramount, and many therefore began with at least some multiethnic support. As the claims of two ethnic groups begin to appear incompatible, both groups represented in unequal numbers within the party, a kind of lesser-evil or "satisficing" logic may emerge. Party leaders would undoubtedly prefer to keep the strong, multiethnic party intact, but they may sense that it is increasingly risky to attempt to retain the support of both groups. Fearing that if they try to retain the support of both, they will probably lose out to new parties catering solely to ethnic interests, party leaders take action to avoid being left with nothing. Faced with such a choice, those with the ability to retain the support of the larger ethnic group within the party will be willing to forfeit the support of the smaller group within the party, even at the risk of being consigned to only minority ethnic support in the country as a whole.[50] Leaders of the smaller group in the party may likewise be willing to forgo the augmented strength their association with larger groups in the party gives them, when they contemplate that the alternative is the possible loss of all support. As centrifugation is manifested in party organization, then, it rests on assessments of relative risk, specifically on anticipation of the likelihood that, unless action is taken, new, ethnically based political competitors will enter the market. Thus it happens that a party leader, fearing the potential loss of all support, may actually choose to preside over a party representing only a minority ethnic group. This is still electoral logic.

These assessments of risk may or may not be accurate. No doubt they are typically intermingled with other disintegrative forces: uneasy personal relations within the party between leaders from different ethnic groups, mixed feelings about ethnic outcomes in party policymaking, feedback from ethnic supporters along the lines of the Ashanti man in Swedru, and cold calculation about prospects for improving one's political position by moving at least temporarily into an ethnically exclusivist position. Whether the assessment of risk is accurate, the seriousness of the feared consequences, should they occur, cannot be denied. That is why action of this kind is typically taken in an anticipatory way, before

50. This possibility occurs, needless to say, because the larger group in the party may be the smaller group in the country, and vice versa. For the sake of simplicity, I speak of only two groups—larger and smaller—but there may, of course, be more.

the polarization of sentiment is complete. Consequently, the formation of ethnic parties generally does not await the development of a substantive ethnic issue that might split a multiethnic party apart. Such a break comes over intraparty affairs, usually leadership relations. For this reason, the break often appears to result solely from the politicians' own narrow ambitions.

These pressures help explain why the emergence of ethnic parties seems to defy the personal preference of politicians for multiethnic organization as well as their preference for strategies that maximize the chance of electoral victory. This is not, of course, an ineluctable process. There are points of decision along the way. A party leader may feel personally so secure in his support among his ethnic group that he is willing to chance keeping the multiethnic party intact even in the face of ethnic pressure. Alternatively, a party leader may seek the agreement of leaders of the smaller group within the party to scale down its ethnic claims so as to make it clear that the larger group within the party is preeminent. In Malaysia, Tengku Abdul Rahman followed both of these courses to preserve his Alliance Party from succumbing to centrifugal forces. He took sides, and he also sought a demonstrably unequal relationship among groups within the Alliance. Even so, strong competitor ethnic parties emerged to challenge his. A much more frequent response, however, is to end party competition and move to the single-party format before complete centrifugation takes hold. This was Kenneth Kaunda's response in Zambia. Assuming, however, that parties are free to organize and elections are freely conducted on a party basis, parties in a deeply divided society will tend to follow the lines of the major ethnic cleavages.

I intend to say more about the logic of ethnic party systems as we proceed. Now, however, it is best to turn to some concrete examples of this process. The examples are the party systems that developed in Guyana and Trinidad in the 1950s and '60s. These are archetypical cases of ethnic party systems, especially useful because they represent well-documented examples of what happened in many other ex-colonies.[51] To

51. The analysis that follows is based on my own work in Guyana and Trinidad in 1965 and the following accounts of party activity in those two countries: Morley Ayearst, *The British West Indies: The Search for Self-Government* (New York: New York Univ. Press, 1960); Peter Newman, *British Guiana: Problems of Cohesion in an Immigrant Society* (London: Oxford Univ. Press, 1964); Raymond T. Smith, *British Guiana* (London: Oxford Univ. Press, 1962); Leo A. Despres, *Cultural Pluralism and Nationalist Politics in British Guiana* (Chicago: Rand McNally, 1967); Cheddi Jagan, *Forbidden Freedom: The Story of British Guiana* (London: Lawrence & Wishart, 1954); Jagan, *The West on Trial: My Fight for Guyana's Freedom* (London: Michael Joseph, 1966); Peter Simms, *Trouble in Guyana* (London: Allen & Unwin, 1966); Anthony McCowan, "British Guiana," in

illustrate the evolution of ethnic party systems, the Nigerian, the Mauritian, the Congolese, or any of a dozen other cases would have done just as well, and I shall refer to a number of these in the course of the discussion. The data for Guyana and Trinidad, however, happen to show with special clarity the process by which parties crystallized along ethnic lines despite leadership intentions; the patterns of electoral behavior that underlay the party realignment; and the specific properties and effects of an ethnic party system on ethnic politics. Consequently, these two small Caribbean countries, laboratories of ethnic politics, are worthy of sustained attention.

GUYANA AND TRINIDAD: NATIONALIST BEGINNINGS, ETHNIC ENDINGS

Long-standing differences between Creoles and East Indians thwarted attempts to organize parties across ethnic lines in Guyana and Trinidad.[52] Eventually, two major parties developed in each country. Through a process of ethnic alignment and realignment, each party came to represent one or the other major ethnic group. This was not the preferred outcome of any major political leader, and it was contrary to the Marxist ideology of Cheddi Jagan in Guyana and the strongly nationalist aspirations of Eric Williams in Trinidad. It happened in spite of their intentions. Moreover, the growth of an ethnic party system put the leaders of

---

Race and Power: Studies of Leadership in Five British Dependencies (London: The Bow Group, 1956), 17–36; Percy C. Hintzen and Ralph R. Premdas, "Guyana: Coercion and Control in Political Change," *Journal of Interamerican Studies and World Affairs* 24 (Aug. 1982): 337–54; B. A. N. Collins, "The End of a Colony, II: British Guiana 1965," *Political Quarterly* 36 (Oct. 1965): 406–16; C. Paul Bradley, "The Party System in British Guiana and the Election of 1961," *Caribbean Studies* 1 (Oct. 1961): 1–26; Bradley, "Party Politics in British Guiana," *Western Political Quarterly* 16 (June 1963): 353–70; Stephen Cumberbatch, "State and Society in Guyana" (unpublished paper, Cambridge, England, Dec. 1981); Charles Henry Kunsman, Jr., "The Origins and Development of Political Parties in the British West Indies" (Ph.D. diss., Univ. of California, Berkeley, 1963), chaps. 7–9; Ivar Oxaal, *Black Intellectuals Come to Power: The Rise of Creole Nationalism in Trinidad and Tobago* (Cambridge: Schenkman, 1968); Yogendra K. Malik, *East Indians in Trinidad: A Study in Minority Politics* (London: Oxford Univ. Press, 1971); Selwyn D. Ryan, *Race and Nationalism in Trinidad and Tobago: A Study of Decolonization in a Multiracial Society* (Toronto: Univ. of Toronto Press, 1972).

52. *Creoles* refers here to those portions of the Guyanese and Trinidadian populations that had some ancestral contact with Africa. The reason for this term is twofold: to use one word that would include both brown and black Guyanese and Trinidadians (these color groups having a history of some separateness) and that would span differences between Guyana and Trinidad (Guyanese parlance referring to "Africans," Trinidadian in the past to "Negroes"). *East Indians*, or simply *Indians*, refers to the descendants of laborers imported from India. *Amerindians*, by contrast, refers to indigenous American Indians. The term *Trinidad* here is used to include Trinidad and Tobago, both islands politically united, but I do not focus on Tobago politics. *Guyana*, of course, refers, for the colonial period, to British Guiana.

the parties representing minority ethnic party groups in the position of pursuing a party-building strategy that guaranteed their parties' electoral defeat. Nevertheless, the structure of the situation was such that this was the course they felt constrained to pursue.

In the post–World War II period, Guyana and Trinidad were colonies with weak party systems. Such parties as there were tended to be electoral alliances that dissolved after the balloting. Independent candidates were numerous. In the 1956 elections in Trinidad, there were eight parties and 127 candidates, including thirty-eight independents, contesting twenty-four seats. In Guyana, in 1953, there were five parties and 130 candidates, seventy-nine of whom were independents, for twenty-four seats. These elections marked the end of the old order. There were clearly opportunities for new party structures. With independence on the agenda, these opportunities were taken.

In Guyana, Cheddi Jagan, an East Indian, had formed the People's Progressive Party in 1950. The Jagans (Cheddi and Janet) had surrounded themselves with a number of left-wing intellectuals, both Creole and Indian, including the Creole barrister L. F. S. Burnham. The PPP had campaigned on a reformist platform, demanding social welfare programs, tax reform, and attention to the interests of labor. In the 1953 elections, the PPP won eighteen out of twenty-four seats. Marxist in leadership, it had what the main opposition party did not: working-class identification, strong organization, and a clear nationalist program.

The same was true of Eric Williams and the People's National Movement in Trinidad. Formed in 1956, the PNM publicized itself as an instrument of socioeconomic and political reform. It was most emphatic about substituting for the old political "individualism" a strong party able to effect the changes it envisioned. In the 1956 elections, the PNM won thirteen out of twenty-four seats in the legislature.

Trinidad: Merger and Split

The opposition in both colonies was galvanized into action by the maiden elections of the PPP and the PNM. In Trinidad, there were substantial opportunities for alternative parties, for the PNM legislative majority had been won on a base of only 38.7 percent of the total vote. The multitude of parties and candidates had fragmented the remainder.

The opposition remedy was clear—consolidation—and so was its direction. The PNM had gained most of its support from Creole voters in and around urban areas. The strongest centers of opposition were in the predominantly East Indian sugar belt and in the rural, mostly Creole

Eastern districts, where the PNM had won less than half the vote. An alliance of rural Creoles and Indians was unquestionably the way to build a strong alternative to the PNM.

The occasion for consolidation was the formation of pan–West Indian parties to prepare for politics in the ill-fated West Indian Federation.[53] In 1957, the People's Democratic Party, led by an Indian notable, merged with two other opposition parties into a new Democratic Labor Party. An amalgam of Indian politicians reacting to Williams' ability to mobilize the Creole vote and of old-style Creole conservatives from the days of pre-party politics, the DLP's sole basis for unity was the potential antagonism of many rural voters to the PNM's apparent urban bias.

The merger produced handsome returns. The DLP won the 1958 elections for the Federation Parliament, six seats to the PNM's four. Each party received half the total popular vote, but the DLP won the South, with its large Indian vote, and the East. Three of the four PNM seats were located in or around the capital, Port-of-Spain. In the county council elections of the following year, the DLP repeated its performance, capturing thirty-five of the seventy-two seats, one more than the PNM, and securing a majority or plurality in every Southern or Eastern county council except one.

To all appearances, a strong rural-urban, two-party system had emerged in Trinidad. The appearances, however, were illusory. While the DLP was winning at the polls, it was falling apart internally. The party had been more dependent on Indian than Creole votes to begin with, and in the 1958 election had mobilized Indian support on a bloc basis. At least two-thirds of the DLP's votes had come from East Indians. This put the Indian leaders of the party in a dilemma. Creole votes were the marginal increment necessary for victory, but they were a clear-cut minority in the party's overall support. To hold the votes of its Creole supporters, the party would have to concede leadership positions to members of the Creole faction, and such positions were in fact demanded.[54] To have accorded such recognition to the Creole elements in the DLP might have jeopardized the party's standing with East Indians,

53. Williams and the PNM had joined with Norman Manley and his Jamaican People's National Party to form the Federal Labor Party. Manley's opponent, Sir Alexander Bustamante, and his Jamaican Labor Party then created the Democratic Labor Party of the West Indies. Bustamante's party was heavily rural, and it quite naturally turned to the rural Trinidad opposition for support. This was the catalyst for the Trinidadian opposition parties to unite. See Kunsman, "The Origins and Development of Political Parties," 418–25.

54. Personal communication, Oct. 25, 1969. See also Albert Gomes, *Through a Maze of Colour* (Port-of-Spain: Key Caribbean, 1974), 181.

whose support had been attracted by contrasting the DLP with the Creole-dominated PNM. The Indian leaders were unwilling to risk this, and so the *mariage de convenance* dissolved at the height of its electoral success.

The dissolution of the multiethnic party was in the interest of neither component and desired by neither. The results of the split were disastrous for the DLP. The party never again achieved the strength it had in 1958–59. The strong party system inaugurated by the PNM had convinced most voters that their loyalties had to rest with one or the other of the two major parties. When the DLP became an Indian party, rural Creole voters were denied any alternative to the PNM. The former DLP Creole politicians were consigned to obscurity, and the ethnic party system was solidified.

As the DLP became a minority party, it was confined strictly by the number of Indian voters—about a third of the electorate. Its losses were the PNM's gains. Whereas in the 1958 federal elections the two parties had divided the vote evenly, in 1961 the PNM secured 57 percent; the DLP, 42 percent. In 1958, the DLP had won six of the ten federal seats; in 1961, it won only ten of the thirty seats in the Trinidad House of Representatives. By 1961, the Eastern constituencies that had formerly been carried by non-Indian DLP leaders went to the PNM, where they remained from then on. The 1961 results were essentially repeated in 1966, with the PNM winning twenty-four of the thirty-six seats in an expanded House and the DLP taking the rest. Party alignments were ascriptive, and election results were predictable. In 1970, the DLP made yet another attempt to link up with Creole politicians, this time led by defectors from the PNM. This encountered many of the same problems as the DLP merger of 1957, and by the time of the 1971 election the alliance had dissolved in distrust.[55]

The 1971 election was boycotted by the DLP, for the party would again have been confined to the Indian strongholds. The PNM won all thirty-six seats with less than half the electorate voting. So secure was the PNM majority—and hence Creole power—that, in the years after 1966, intra-Creole divisions began to emerge with much greater force than at any time in the preceding decades. Trinidad experienced black-power disturbances in 1970 that would have been unthinkable while the outcome of the Creole-Indian party rivalry remained uncertain.

New parties came and went, but in the 1976 election the PNM again

55. Ryan, *Race and Nationalism in Trinidad and Tobago*, 475–77.

took two-thirds of the seats with a majority of the vote, while a successor party to the DLP captured the East Indian constituencies with 27 percent of the vote. In 1981, an alliance of the Indian party with some left-wing Creoles proved counterproductive; the party won fewer seats than it had five years earlier. A split in the ranks of the PNM produced a new Creole party, which gained no seats. For all the flux in party labels and alliances, the shape of party politics remained the same: Creole majority, Indian minority.

Guyana: Split and Merger

In Guyana, as in Trinidad, there was an opening for an opposition. The PPP had won its two-thirds legislative majority in 1953 with only 51 percent of the vote, and the opposing elements were badly divided. As in Trinidad, externally generated incentives crystallized the opposition. The occasion was different: the suspension of the colonial constitution. And the opposing party was not formed from without the PPP but from within.

Following the 1953 election, the PPP formed a government. Nonetheless, pursuing a strategy Jagan later characterized as "all struggle and no unity,"[56] the PPP government also considered itself the "opposition." This dialectical strategy was designed to protest the limited powers under which the PPP held office and to oppose the "real" government, namely, British colonial officials. In the course of this opposition, the PPP managed to convince the British of its general bad faith, its desire to disrupt the economy by threats of confiscation, its ideological extremism, and its commitment to undemocratic methods.

The British, in response, suspended the constitution and replaced the Jagan regime with an appointed legislature and cabinet. A "period of marking time in the advance to self-government" was declared, and the British made clear their desire for moderate forces to emerge.[57] During this interregnum, a Burnham faction of the PPP appeared.

As early as 1950, Burnham's ambitions had surfaced inside the PPP, when the party's founders yielded to his demand to become its first party chairman—an appointment made to solidify Creole support behind the PPP.[58] Thereafter, Burnham became an intraparty critic of the Jagans.

Rivalries within the PPP leadership were not ethnically based, but the

56. Cheddi Jagan, Speech to the 1956 PPP Congress, *Daily Chronicle* (Georgetown, British Guiana), Dec. 22, 1956.
57. *Report of the British Guiana Constitutional Commission, 1954* (Bel Air Park, British Guiana: Argosy, 1954), 76.
58. Simms, *Trouble in Guyana*, chap. 13; Jagan, *The West on Trial*, 137–39.

need for a prominent Creole in the forefront of the party's leadership testified to the character of the ethnic environment in which the PPP was operating. In fact, party officers, the general council, and party candidates were all carefully balanced between Creoles and Indians. The British provided the occasion and the inducement for a split, but other forces might have sufficed on a later occasion. In Guyana, a two-headed party stood a good chance of becoming two parties.

Both factions retained their interethnic character at the top. Burnham initially also resisted the temptation to merge with the United Democratic Party, a conservative, urban, Creole party. But despite the adherence of the Indian politician who had led the PPP sugar union, Burnham had no organization in the countryside; and that not only meant no Indian support, but not full rural Creole support either. When the electoral process was restored in 1957, the Jaganites took nine of the fourteen seats, the Burnhamites only three seats in the heavily Creole capital, Georgetown. The remaining two seats were divided between the UDP and another minor party.

This election was a way station on the path to complete ethnic realignment. Indian support was heavily with Jagan, but Creole support was divided. There were incentives to realignment, and it occurred.

In 1956, three of the most prominent members of the left wing of the PPP leadership abandoned the party because of disillusionment brought on by Khrushchev's denunciation of Stalin in February 1956 and the Soviet suppression of the Hungarian revolt later that year. The three had been opponents of Burnham before the PPP split, but they all happened to be Creoles. Their resignations left the PPP without a Creole leader of stature.

As the Jagan faction was losing its Creole component, the Burnham faction was solidifying its own Creole foundation and losing its Indian component. Shortly after the 1957 election, the Burnhamites became the People's National Congress and a Creole ethnic party. One of its prominent Indian supporters was expelled in 1958, and another died. One of the ex-Marxist defectors from the PPP joined the PNC, where he became an outspoken black nationalist. Finally, the PNC absorbed the UDP and inherited its Creole clientele.[59] With Indian support so solidly with Jagan, it made no sense to continue to leave Creole support divided. Like the Trinidadian DLP, but by an inverted process of fission and then

59. *Newday* (Kingston, Jamaica), Aug. 1958, pp. 28–29.

fusion, the PNC had become a minority party. Split and merger were the concrete expressions of ethnic forces in politics.

The electoral results of this process were similar. In Guyana, as in Trinidad, close correspondence between ethnic composition and the respective parties' share of the vote was evident. In Guyana, however, East Indians were about half the population (though only a plurality of voters), and this was sufficient initially to put their party in power. In the 1961 election, the PPP received 43 percent of the vote, the PNC obtained 41 percent, and a third party, the United Force, which represented a number of minorities, drew 16 percent.[60] The PPP won twenty seats; the PNC, eleven; and the UF, four. By 1964, the Colonial Office had revised the electoral system to provide for proportional representation. Electors voted for party lists rather than for individual candidates. Notwithstanding this change, voting patterns were not very different (for reasons to be discussed in Chapter 15). The PPP list received 46 percent of the vote— an increase probably accounted for by its failure to run candidates in all constituencies in 1961. The PNC again was left with 41 percent, and the UF was reduced to 12 percent.[61] While the PPP had the largest number of votes, it was short of a majority. Burnham became premier in a PNC-UF coalition government.

The 1961 and 1964 elections were accurate reflections of the parties' support. The constancy of the figures, adjusted for the PPP's nonparticipation in some constituencies in 1961, indicates the extent to which the

60. The United Force appealed to several small and generally privileged minorities: whites, Chinese, and Portuguese. The UF also did very well among Amerindians, who comprised nearly 5 percent of the Guyanese population. (Such a group does not exist in Trinidad.) Survey data gathered by me in 1965 indicate that those of mixed origin—which means, effectively, Afro-Europeans or "mulattoes" (12 percent in Guyana, 16 percent in Trinidad)—divided their vote evenly between the PNC and the UF in the 1964 election, whereas in Trinidad they voted overwhelmingly for the PNM. The existence of the UF, in short, appears to have been attributable to a *potpourri* of minorities. Perhaps the critical mass of support for the UF was provided by the Amerindians, for only they were sufficiently concentrated (in the interior) to elect candidates under the single-member constituency system that prevailed in the 1961 election. The absence of an Amerindian group in Trinidad probably helps explain the absence of a comparable third party there. The 16 percent of the vote won by the UF was, in addition, inflated by the fact that the PPP did not run candidates in some strongly Creole constituencies in 1961. In those constituencies, some normally PPP voters probably did not vote, but many who did no doubt voted for the UF rather than for the PNC.

61. I shall explain the reasons for the adoption of proportional representation and analyze its impact in Guyana in more detail below. Despite the conventional view that PR should enhance the position of third parties, the UF share of the vote declined in 1964, largely because those PPP voters who had voted for the UF in preference to the PNC in 1961 could vote for a PPP slate in 1964. See note 60, above.

parties were drawing on clienteles that were stable because they were ethnically determined.

In subsequent elections, the PNC share of votes and seats increased, permitting it to govern alone. But these elections were conducted in a dubious manner,[62] and the results were unreliable. As in Trinidad, interest in the electoral process declined as ethnic and party outcomes became utterly foreseeable.

THE ETHNIC PARTY DYNAMIC

Once ethnic politics begins in earnest, each party, recognizing that it cannot count on defections from members of the other ethnic group, has the incentive to solidify the support of its own group. As Burnham's experience shows, there is no point in holding back from consolidating the party on an ethnic basis; Burnham's delay in this cost him votes and seats in 1957. Even parties that are initially organized on a multiethnic basis, as the DLP was, are vulnerable to ethnic splits when confronted with a strong, ethnically based opponent like the PNM. (The DLP leaders may have been maladroit in permitting their multiethnic party to break apart so easily, but even if the East Indian leaders had not acted as they did, Creole support might later have eroded under the strong magnetic pull of the PNM.) What Guyana and Trinidad illustrate, therefore, is a dynamic process of ethnic realignment: once past a certain threshold, the realignment proceeds on its own momentum, whatever the real wishes of party leaders.

As I have suggested, leadership decisions in the course of party realignment tend to be made on an anticipatory basis, before substantive ethnic issues emerge to divide the whole country. This, I shall point out later, is quite different from the nature of pivotal events that produce a proliferation of parties serving a single ethnic group. Splits that break up multiethnic parties are designed precisely to avert the growth of ethnic parties competing for the same clientele. Pivotal events in the Guyanese and Trinidadian sequences of party mergers and splits were confined to party leadership disputes and did not involve policy positions. Since party leaders of any consequence have followings that are ethnically differentiated, a leader's decision to leave one party for another—particularly if the latter is clearly identified with that leader's own ethnic group—results in shifts of ethnic followings. The cumulative effect of

62. See Alvin Rabushka and Kenneth A. Shepsle, *Politics in Plural Societies: A Theory of Democratic Instability* (Columbus, Ohio: Merrill, 1972), 103–04; Hintzen and Premdas, "Guyana: Coercion and Control in Political Change," 348, 351.

such shifts is to provide voters with a set of cues about the ethnic identity of the parties based on their leadership composition.

There is, of course, a close interplay between leadership decisions and voter decisions. Voters choose among the parties provided by the leaders; they also choose on the basis of how other voters appear to be voting. Leaders provide party choices in accordance with their sense of how voters are voting, as well as in response to the party-organizing actions of other leaders. In Guyana and Trinidad, both sets of decisions pushed, spiral-fashion, toward an ethnic party system, which is why the term *dynamic* is appropriate. So far, though, our attention has been riveted largely at the leadership level. It is instructive to look a bit more closely at the voter level. Four underlying electoral phenomena are worth special scrutiny: (1) ethnic voting; (2) the sanctions applied to deviant voters; (3) increasingly high voter turnouts as the ethnic party system crystallizes, leading to a crucial, polarizing election, followed by declines in turnout; and (4) the relationship between high voter participation rates and ethnic tension.

Ethnic Voting

A growing polarization of voting patterns is implicit in the rough overall correspondence of party support with ethnic demography. Surveys of voting intentions and voting behavior in Guyana and Trinidad in the critical years of the 1960s all reveal extraordinarily high rates of ethnic voting.

Here it is necessary to explain what ethnic voting means. The term has two possible meanings.[63] Members of an ethnic group may vote heavily for one party over another. Alternatively, members of a given group may vote for candidates belonging to the same ethnic group, irrespective of party affiliation. Where parties are not organized along ethnic lines, ethnic voting takes either or both of these forms. In the Philippines, for example, voters customarily crossed party lines to support candidates of their own ethnic origin.[64]

The organization of parties along ethnic lines changes this. No longer is it advantageous to cross party lines to vote for a *candidate* of the same

---

63. Wolfinger, "The Development and Persistence of Ethnic Voting."
64. Ando, "A Study of Voting Patterns in the Philippine Presidential and Senatorial Elections." For a case where voters were subjected to conflicting pulls, between voting for the party that tended to represent their caste interest and voting for an independent candidate of their caste origin, see F. G. Bailey, *Politics and Social Change: Orissa in 1959* (Berkeley and Los Angeles: Univ. of California Press, 1963), 44. This is a sure sign that parties are not clearly demarcated along ethnic (here caste) lines.

ethnic background as that of the voter if this requires voting for a *party* identified with the opposing ethnic group. Ethnic voting means simply voting for the party identified with the voter's own ethnic group, no matter who the individual candidates happen to be. Hereafter I use the term in this way.

The matter is important, because ethnically based parties commonly feel the need to preserve a facade of multiethnicity by including members of various groups in their leadership and in their list of candidates. Quite often the party chairmanship and, in the case of a ruling party, at least one ministerial portfolio are reserved for members of other ethnic groups.[65] Safe seats are provided. (In this case, safe seats are those located in party strongholds ethnically akin to the party's identification, not the candidate's.) In Guyana and Trinidad, Creole candidates ran on PPP or DLP tickets in the Indian sugar belt, and Indian candidates ran on PNC or PNM tickets in Creole-populated urban areas.[66]

There are many reasons for parties to reserve seats and other positions in this way: the tactical usefulness of having an ethnically mixed parliamentary delegation;[67] the desire to maintain party legitimacy where influential opinion or ideology holds that parties ought not to be organized around ethnic interests; the wish of party leaders to avoid being identified abroad as mere ethnic leaders;[68] the desire to convince members of the opposing group that, even though the party does not represent them,

---

65. There are many examples of reserved places of this kind, especially places reserved for indigenes in parties representing immigrant groups. Chinese parties in Malaysia do this routinely. In Mauritius, the Labor Party, predominantly Hindu, recurrently chose Creoles to be party leader. Adele Smith Simmons, "Politics in Mauritius Since 1934: A Study of Decolonization in a Plural Society" (Ph.D. diss., Oxford Univ., 1969), 354–55, 375.

66. In Guyana, the electoral system was changed for the 1964 election to proportional representation, with the whole country one constituency and each party putting up a single list of candidates. Candidates were declared elected in order of their priority on the lists, the cutoff depending on the proportion of votes received by each party. Guyanese parties took care to place members of the ethnic group with which their party was *not* identified high on the list, so as to insure the election of such candidates. This is the functional equivalent of the safe seat.

67. In Guyana and Trinidad, for example, Creole MPs representing East Indian parties acted as spokesmen for the rights of Indians—a role they could obviously assume without being accused of favoritism toward their own ethnic group.

68. Cheddi Jagan was the most obvious case of a leader with international pretensions, but he was not the only one. For an example of the effectiveness of multiethnic composition in dispelling impressions of ethnically circumscribed support, see *Report of a Commission of Inquiry into Disturbances in British Guiana in February 1962* (Colon. No. 354; London: H.M.S.O., 1962), 17: ". . . it seems to us that whatever racial differences existed were brought about by political propaganda. These differences do not go very deep and it is to be remarked that there are two African Ministers in Dr. Jagan's Cabinet. The counsel of the PPP at the Inquiry was an African barrister and some of Dr. Jagan's strongest opposition in the proceedings before us came from East Indians."

it has no malevolent intentions that they need fear; and, finally, the aim of keeping alive the multiethnic aspirations of the party against the day when its ethnic base may actually be broadened. In Guyana and Trinidad, minority representatives in each party served all of these purposes.[69] The prevalence of the practice elsewhere suggests that similar purposes also exist elsewhere.

Where parties are ethnically based but minority candidates are given party tickets, ethnic voting occurs even if, as commonly happens, a Creole voter votes for an East Indian candidate of a Creole party, or vice versa. Ethnically aware voters have understood that presenting a multiethnic slate is an exigency of political life, even for an ethnic party, and have accordingly voted for the ethnic party rather than for or against the ethnic identity of the individual candidates. When voters elect minority members of their ethnic party, it is wrong to regard this as nonethnic voting.[70] Quite the contrary: it is party and not candidate ethnic identification that counts. No doubt an occasional voter will cross party lines to vote for a member of his ethnic group running on the ticket of the party identified with the opposing ethnic group. But a crossover of this type, away from one's own ethnic party just to support a candidate of one's own group, is a rare case: that is why safe seats provided to minority candidates are in fact safe.

If ethnic voting is defined solely in party terms, the evidence from Guyana and Trinidad is compelling. A survey of Guyanese voting intentions in 1961 found 87 percent of East Indian villagers aligned with the PPP and 81 percent of African villagers aligned with the PNC.[71] Since this sample included nonvoters, who were probably least strongly committed to the ethnic parties, these figures probably understate the incidence of ethnic voting. More to the point are the data on ethnic crossover intentions: only 2 percent of the East Indians and only 6 percent of the Africans indicated an intention to vote for the PNC and the PPP, respec-

---

69. The term *minority representatives*, used in this context, denotes minority in the party, not in the society (e.g., East Indian in a Creole party, and vice versa).

70. Compare K. J. Ratnam and R. S. Milne, *The Malayan Parliamentary Election of 1964* (Singapore: Univ. of Malaya Press, 1967), 13; George Bennett and Carl G. Rosberg *The Kenyatta Election: Kenya 1960–1961* (London: Oxford Univ. Press, 1961), 180; Irene Tinker, "Malayan Elections: Electoral Pattern for Plural Societies," *Western Political Quarterly* 9 (June 1956): 258–82; Owusu, "Politics in Swedru," 256. But see Adele Smith Simmons, *Modern Mauritius: The Politics of Decolonization* (Bloomington: Indiana Univ. Press, 1982), 185. Simmons notes that Mauritian Hindus "voted exclusively for Labour, knowing that if there was a Muslim or Creole candidate on the list, still it was the party of the Hindus."

71. Despres, *Cultural Pluralism and Nationalist Politics in British Guiana*, 172–73. *African* here is synonymous with *black*. See note 52, above.

tively. My own data on those actually voting in the 1964 Guyanese election, drawn the following year from an urban and rural sample (n = 186), also show a very low crossover rate. Not a single Creole reported having voted for the PPP. The few non-PNC votes cast by Creole respondents went to the small third party (the UF). Of those Indians who said they did not vote for the PPP, almost none voted PNC; the overwhelming majority of avowed Indian crossover votes went to the conservative UF—which suggests that these Indian voters refrained from supporting the PPP out of fear of Jagan's Marxism. Thus, even where support for ethnic parties is not unanimous, nonethnic voters are still not likely to vote for the party of the opposite ethnic group.

In any case, my Guyanese data point to high rates of ethnic voting: 96 percent for Africans and 77 percent for East Indians. The latter figure, however, is likely to be understated because of fear of disclosing support for the Indian party, which was in opposition. In Trinidad, the same disparity is manifest in my data (n = 158), with 94 percent of black respondents indicating support for the PNM in the 1961 election and only 78 percent of East Indians professing support for the DLP. The same explanation is, I believe, responsible for the low Indian figure.[72] Another voting study of the same election turned up ethnic voting rates of 92 percent for black respondents and 96 percent for Indian respondents.[73] That study, however, utilized interviewers of the same ethnic background as the respondents. Just as it might be dangerous to admit voting for the DLP to a non-Indian stranger, so it might be equally dangerous to admit not voting for the DLP to a Trinidadian Indian interviewer, who might report the deviance. The 96 percent figure may therefore be a shade too high.

Whatever the exact figure, it is clear that overwhelming numbers of Guyanese and Trinidadians—surely more than 90 percent—voted ethnically in the 1960s. What set this in motion, above all, was the initial identification of one of the major parties—in both cases, the largest party—with a single ethnic group. Since the Trinidad PNM never gained large-scale Indian support, it was early identified as a Creole party. Following Burnham's resignation, the Guyana PPP likewise came to be seen as an East Indian party. Each such identification triggered a reaction in members of the other group. When, for example, the East Indian slogan

72. In neither Guyana nor Trinidad was there any statistically significant correlation between nonethnic voting and the education, age, occupation, or residence of respondents.
73. Krishna Bahadoorsingh, "Trinidad Electoral Politics: The Persistence of the Race Factor" (Ph.D. diss., Indiana Univ., 1966), chap. 3.

apan jaht (Hindi for "vote for your own") became known among Guyanese Creoles, it became a perverse rallying cry for Creole voting solidarity—a felt necessity in the face of the larger Indian population. "The Indians," said a PNC leader, "will support the PPP. If the PPP is to be beaten the bulk of African people will have to vote as a bloc together with minorities and dissident Indians."[74] Indian ethnic voting in Guyana made it easy to organize Creole ethnic voting, and vice versa for Trinidad.

The incentives toward reactive ethnic voting are strong. When voters of one group choose, in effect, not to choose but to give their vote predictably on an ethnic basis to an ethnically defined party, they put voters of the other group who do choose among parties at a collective disadvantage. All else being equal, such voters will seek to reduce their disadvantage by concentrating their votes in a comparable ethnic party. In such a situation, ethnic votes tend to drive out nonethnic votes.

The data on ethnic voting in Guyana and Trinidad are consistent with other kinds of data on party support where parties appeal along ethnic lines. In countries such as Ghana and Congo (Brazzaville), placing the ethnic map over the electoral map reveals clear patterns of party support.[75]

Ghana held one national election between the overthrow of Nkrumah in 1966 and the overthrow of Busia in 1972. In that election, conducted in 1969, parties came to be identified with ethnic groups—the Progress Party with the Brong, Ashanti, Akim, and other Akan-speakers; the National Alliance of Liberals, with the Ewe and Krobo.[76] The allegiance of Northerners was split between the two parties. The PP obtained 85 percent or more of the popular vote in the Akan heartland; much of the NAL vote there was accounted for by the presence of Ewe or Northerners resident in Akan areas. The NAL, for its part, received overwhelming majorities in Ewe areas.[77]

The Congo Republic was polarized even more completely in the

---

74. Quoted in Despres, *Cultural Pluralism and Nationalist Politics in British Guiana*, 261.

75. There is support for this even in Western countries, where religious and linguistic cleavages explain more about voting patterns than does class. Arend Lijphart, "Religious vs. Linguistic vs. Class Voting: The 'Crucial Experiment' of Comparing Belgium, Canada, South Africa, and Switzerland," *American Political Science Review* 73 (June 1979): 442–58.

76. For evidence, see Austin and Luckham, eds., *Politicians and Soldiers in Ghana*, 226, 228, 255, 283, 286.

77. See Emily Card and Barbara Callaway, "Ghanaian Politics: The Elections and After," *Africa Report*, Mar. 1970, pp. 10–15.

1950s. By 1959, each of the two major ethnic parties obtained well over 90 percent of the vote in most of the area inhabited by members of its ethnic group and more than 99 percent in its large core area.[78]

Similarly, Paul R. Brass has shown that correlations between party voting and the ethnic composition of constituencies in the Indian Punjab have been extremely high. In the Punjab, it will be recalled, the Akali Dal has been identified as a party of the Sikhs, while the Jan Sangh was regarded as a Hindu party. For 1969, there was a correlation of 0.73 between Akali Dal votes and the percentage of the constituency that is composed of Sikhs; there was also a −0.76 correlation between Akali votes and the Hindu percentage of the constituency. In the same election, needless to say, Jan Sangh votes were highly correlated with the Hindu proportions of a constituency (0.71) and just about as negatively correlated with the Sikh proportions (−0.68).[79] These unusually strong correlations existed despite the fact that no group in the Punjab voted solidly for any single party: Congress, for example, drew votes from Sikhs and Hindus.

It is not necessary to belabor the point that ethnic parties depend on ethnic voting. Guyana and Trinidad are not at all atypical in this respect.

Sanctions for Deviants

Once it begins, ethnic voting for ethnically defined parties tends to push toward unanimity. As I have said before, a group may divide its support among two or more ethnic parties or between an ethnic party and a multiethnic party, as in the Punjab. What group members will not do, however, is countenance voting for the party of the opposing ethnic group. As one of Brass' respondents commented, "No sensible Hindu will vote for an Akali . . . ."[80] This is not merely because of the incentives, mentioned earlier, to solidify support in the face of tendencies toward ethnic voting by members of the opposing ethnic group, but also because sanctions tend to be applied to deviants. An assumption begins to grow that each group has its own party and that loyal group members will line

78. Jean-Michel Wagret, *Histoire et sociologie politiques de la République du Congo (Brazzaville)* (Paris: Librairie Générale de Droit et de Jurisprudence, 1963), 124, 161, 167, 180, 192.

79. Paul R. Brass, "Ethnic Cleavages and the Punjab Party System" (unpublished paper presented at the 1972 annual meeting of the Association for Asian Studies), pp. 19–21 and Tables 7–8. A revised version appears as Chapter 8 of Brass, *Language, Religion and Politics in North India* (London: Cambridge Univ. Press, 1974). Both Akali Dal correlations were significant at the 0.001 level; both Jan Sangh, at the 0.01 level.

80. Quoted in Brass, "Ethnic Cleavages and the Punjab Party System," 19.

up behind it. In Guyana and Trinidad, each group supported only one party, and it came to be seen as only natural that a group member would cleave to his group's party. "The PPP fights for the Indians," said one of my respondents tersely. "He [Jagan] is Indian, and I am Indian," answered another who was asked to explain his vote. Or simply: "I am a black man." In the colorful expression of an Indian canefield worker who supported the DLP, "That's we own party."

A result of such conceptions is that deviation is not tolerated. In Guyana, East Indians who opposed the PPP were ostracized or beaten.[81] Indeed, as the close identification of party with ethnic group grows, group members on both sides of the ethnic boundary firmly expect widespread ethnic voting. A letter to the editor of the *Trinidad Guardian*, written shortly after the 1958 federal elections and signed "Lame Victim," illustrates the point. The letter was written by an Indian businessman who had supported an unsuccessful PNM candidate and had been beaten by several (presumably Creole) PNM supporters, notwithstanding his profuse professions of PNM sympathy:

It was stated openly and vehemently that no Indians voted PNM and if one said he did, they usually said: "You lie; you only saying so now because PNM in power."

Indians who said they voted PNM were often abused, maligned, and discredited.

I like the policy and principles of PNM. But unfortunately many of its adherents fail to practice it. In trying to explain this to people I come in contact with I am accused of being anti-DLP or anti-Indian, and for that I am not only abused, but my trade has fallen off badly. To boot I am denied entrance to our village theatre.

Here is the big joke, Mr. Editor: I am afraid to be seen in San Fernando [a Creole-majority town] at night for fear of being assaulted, and being called anti-PNM, and in my own district I am being despised for being anti-DLP.[82]

Deviance thus becomes unprofitable, and—so strong are the expectations of ethnic voting—the deviance can even go unrecognized. Again, Guyana and Trinidad are not unique. In the 1969 Ghanaian election, Akans who were affiliated with the NAL soon found themselves stamped

81. Leo A. Despres, "The Implications of Nationalist Politics in British Guiana for the Development of Cultural Theory," in Reinhard Bendix, ed., *State and Society* (Boston: Little, Brown, 1968), 519.

82. *Trinidad Guardian* (Port-of-Spain), Apr. 3, 1958. For the story of a candidate who tried unsuccessfully to keep ethnicity out of his campaign, see Arthur Niehoff and Juanita Niehoff, *East Indians in the West Indies* (Milwaukee: Milwaukee Public Museum Publications in Anthropology, 1960), 68.

as "Ewe sympathizers."[83] Richard L. Sklar sums up a number of violent incidents in Nigeria, where ethnic parties grew up in every region, with the remark that "the supporters of a communal membership party are apt to view opposition to that party by a member of the community with moral indignation and to punish it as antisocial conduct."[84]

The Election as Census

A member of a Commonwealth team sent to observe the 1964 Guyanese election described it as a "a racial census," in which a person's vote was "predetermined by the demands of [his] security" in an "atmosphere charged with fear."[85] What makes this depiction apt is not ethnic voting alone, but also exceptionally high rates of voter turnout. With the crystallization of the ethnic party system in Guyana and Trinidad, the electoral contest became more intense. At the same time, ethnic voting made it easier for ethnic parties to mobilize the vote. Identifying the voters of each party is a simple matter when ethnic and party identifications are synonymous. As Table 4 shows, in the post-war period both Guyana and Trinidad had steadily rising rates of voter participation. (The temporary exception of Guyana in 1957 is undoubtedly explained by the suspension of the constitution from 1953 to 1957.) Voting rates reached a peak in 1964 in Guyana and 1961 in Trinidad. As participation began to approach 100 percent, these elections assumed more and more the quality of a census. The Guyanese election of 1964, which took place in a context of acute conflict and closely balanced party support, brought out nearly all the registered voters.

In both cases, the high point of voter participation produced an unusually large turnout by world standards for free elections, which these were. Exact figures for subsequent elections in Guyana are unreliable, but it is clear that voter participation declined after 1964, as it did in Trinidad after 1961.[86]

The reason for the peak and decline is not hard to discern. The 1961

83. Card and Callaway, "Ghanaian Politics: The Elections and After," 14.
84. *Nigerian Political Parties*, 476. It should be noted that Sklar's conception of "communal participation" and "communal membership" would not necessarily include all ethnic parties.
85. Memorandum of Bakar Ali Mirza, in *British Guiana: Report by the Commonwealth Team of Observers on the Election in December 1964* (Colon. No. 359; London: H.M.S.O., 1965), 14.
86. The Trinidad figure for 1971, however, is unusually low because of a DLP boycott. But the boycott is itself significant: adoption of the boycott strategy reflected the foreseeability of the election results. The DLP, with its East Indian base, would inevitably lose.

TABLE 4   VOTER PARTICIPATION,
GUYANA AND TRINIDAD
(number voting as a percentage of number registered;
elections to colonial or national legislative bodies)

Guyana		Trinidad	
1947	70.0[a]	1946	52.9
1953	74.8	1950	70.1
1957	55.8	1956	80.3
1961	89.4	1961	88.4
1964	96.9	1966	65.8
1968	b	1971	32.9[c]
1973	b	1976	54.0
1979	b	1981	56.3

SOURCES: Official reports.
[a]Approximate.
[b]Participation figures for Guyana after 1964 are unreliable.
[c]The exceedingly low figure in the 1971 Trinidad election resulted from an opposition boycott of the election.

and 1964 Guyanese elections and the 1961 Trinidadian election were crucial tests of the political power of the respective ethnic groups. They occurred after parties had been reordered along clear ethnic lines and the number of ethnic contestants reduced essentially to two.[87] Since voting was known to be largely ascriptive, each party's electoral performance could be expected to be repeated in subsequent elections. Consequently, once party strength was tested and confirmed in a polarizing election, participation rates declined. (Guyana went through such an election

87. This is true in Guyana as well as Trinidad, even though there was a third party in Guyana (the United Force) that had an ethnically differentiated base of support. See note 60, above. The UF's support was best reflected in the 1964 election: 12 percent of the total vote, hardly enough to detract from the overriding Creole–East Indian division. Moreover, the UF was clearly aligned with the PNC. This is because its electoral base shared certain ethnic points of contact with the PNC (particularly the "mixed" population) and because the conservative supporters of the UF saw themselves as being far closer to Burnham's views than to Jagan's avowed Marxism. The UF-PNC alliance was manifested not merely in the two-party coalition formed after the 1964 election. It also took the form of street demonstrations begun as early as 1962 to bring the Jagan government down, as well as serious but unsuccessful negotiations to merge the two parties in 1960 (before the formation of the UF was officially announced). For all these reasons, the existence of the UF as a third party does not detract from the essentially bifurcated character of the struggle in Guyana in the 1960s.

twice because the voting system changed to proportional representation for the 1964 election; although the 1964 results closely paralleled the 1961 results, no one was sure in advance that this would occur.) A kind of census had indeed been conducted.

Voter turnout statistics are thus clearly related to the emergence of the ethnic party system. They vary with its stage of development, peaking at the time when it is most important that all ethnic-group members be counted.

The distinctive character of the electoral process where parties are ethnically based is underscored by contrasting peaks and declines in voter turnout in such a system with the same phenomena in a system without ethnically based parties.[88] The differences that emerge from such a comparison are striking and fundamental.

It has long been observed that upsurges in voter turnout in the United States produce a strong increase in the vote for one of the major parties but little change in the vote for the other.[89] This is because sharp increases in turnout are the result of unusual interest in particular issues or the unusual attractiveness of particular candidates. These events and personalities of the moment bring people to the polls who often do not vote. The issues and candidates that have the power to bring such voters to the polls are not neutral in their effects on the parties. The Depression produced a large turnout in 1932 that inured to the advantage of the Democrats; the Eisenhower candidacy in 1952 brought out masses of voters specifically to vote for the party on whose ticket he ran. "The circumstances which create a high-stimulus election," in other words, "may be expected to create simultaneously a strong differential in the attractiveness of the vote alternatives perceived by the electorate." Thus, concludes Angus Campbell, the very conditions that increase turnout also "swing the partisan division of the vote toward the party which happens to be advantaged by the circumstances of the moment."[90] This is why surges in voter turnout benefit one party more than the other.

Declines in voter participation following such surges in the United

88. Angus Campbell, "Surge and Decline: A Study of Electoral Change," *Public Opinion Quarterly* 24 (Fall 1960): 397–418. I have relied heavily on this article for the analysis of changing turnout in the United States. There are also interesting contrasts here to what V. O. Key identifies as "critical" or "realigning" elections in the United States. See his "A Theory of Critical Elections," *Journal of Politics* 17 (Feb. 1955): 3–18.

89. V. O. Key, *Politics, Parties, and Pressure Groups*, 4th ed. (New York: Crowell, 1958), 638.

90. Campbell, "Surge and Decline: A Study of Electoral Change," 397–418.

States also affect one party more than the other. Marginal voters, whose interest in voting in the preceding election was stimulated by the existence of important issues or attractive candidates, tend not to vote once those ephemeral circumstances have passed. Likewise, voters who switched parties to vote for the party "advantaged by the circumstances of the moment" tend to move back to their former position. Consequently, in the United States, a sharp decline in turnout generally also results in a decline in the share of the vote taken by the party that had benefited disproportionately from the previous surge in turnout.

The contrast with the surge and decline in Guyana and Trinidad could not be clearer. The surge in both of these countries benefited the party with the demographic majority, but only because one ethnic group happened to be larger than the other. The surge was not associated with any transfer of votes from one party to another, either by newly participant marginal voters or by regular voters. In contrast to the situation in the United States, both major parties increased their votes markedly. The surge was associated with strong propensities toward ethnic voting, and rates of participation were very high among members of both of the main ethnic groups. In Guyana (1964), 96 percent of my black respondents and 89 percent of my East Indian respondents voted. In Trinidad (1961), 81 percent of my black respondents and 82 percent of my Indian respondents voted. (These figures are somewhat lower than official voting figures, based on voters as a percentage of those registered, because my samples included respondents who were not registered to vote.)

In the United States, in short, turnouts go up because people go to the polls to register a choice, often a different one from the one they would ordinarily make. In Guyana and Trinidad, on the other hand, turnouts went up because people went to the polls to register their affiliation with the same party they would ordinarily be affiliated with, given the ethnic basis of party politics. High turnouts were not associated with changes in party preference.

The same is true of subsequent declines. Here we are confined to the Trinidad data. From these it is clear that the decline of 22.6 percent in voter participation from 1961 to 1966 did not benefit one party significantly more than the other. The parties split the seats in exactly the same proportions—two to one—in both elections. Both parties lost votes. To be sure, the PNM's share of the vote declined by only 5 percent, whereas the DLP's declined by 7 percent; but this was probably only a function of the differential distribution of third-party and independent candidates in the 1966 election.[91] Whereas declines in voter participation in American elections change the result, declines following a polarizing ethnic party election are unlikely to change anything. They occur, in fact, because results are so foreseeable that the same results can and will be replicated in any given constituency with a lower turnout. In the one case, changes in voter participation are closely related to changes in voter choice; in the other, choice is preempted by birth.

Voter Participation and Ethnic Tension

Not only were voter participation levels high in Guyana and Trinidad, but apprehensions about the outcome made these elections tense and sometimes violent occasions. The 1961–64 period was a time of unparalleled violence in Guyana. In Trinidad, Creole uncertainties were greatest in 1956, when the PNM entered its first election. As indicated earlier, the parties that preceded the PNM had all been weakly organized, but one of them, the People's Democratic Party, was clearly an East Indian Party. Some PNM leaders feared that the Creole vote would be so badly split in 1956 that the PDP might win.[92] The campaign was interspersed with acts of violence and threats to the safety of leading politicians. In the event, the PNM drew enough Creole support to form a government. Then, in 1961, it was time for Indian apprehensions. Outnumbered, the DLP leadership stirred Indian feelings to the brink of violence,[93] in part, no doubt, to maximize the East Indian turnout. By 1966, past the critical test, calm had returned to the electoral process.

There is no guarantee, of course, that ethnic demography will produce closely balanced contests that can only be resolved by a crucial, polarizing election. In Benin (then Dahomey), there were three main groups and three corresponding parties contending for power in the 1960s. Various coalitions of two against one were formed, all of them unstable. But the three contenders were never really reduced to two, and so permanent exclusion was never a foreordained result of the electoral process. Togo did have two main ethnic clusters, but the more numerous Southerners, led by the Ewe, early gained ascendancy, capturing nearly

91. Several ex-DLP independent candidates account in the aggregate for that 2 percent difference.
92. The fear was based not only on the PNM's failure to penetrate the rural areas, but also on the Roman Catholic hierarchy's publicly expressed opposition to the PNM. In later elections, this opposition was moderated.
93. Oxaal, *Black Intellectuals Come to Power*, 172.

two-thirds of the vote in the 1958 election.[94] Both of these countries had ethnic party systems, with the accompanying instability, but they did not have the kind of balanced bipolar ethnic division that lent itself to a tense and crucial electoral test. Benin lacked the bipolarity, and Togo lacked the balanced strengths.

Yet the polarizing election occurs often enough so that a number of such elections can be identified rather easily: Sierra Leone (1967), Nigeria (1964), Congo (Brazzaville) (1959), and Zanzibar (1961). The first three of these elections split the country along North-South lines, between two closely balanced parties. Each of them resulted, sooner or later, in a military coup. I shall therefore discuss them when I deal with military politics and ethnic conflict. For the moment, it is sufficient to point out that the development of this kind of bipolar ethnic party system was typically accompanied by violence and very high voter turnouts, as ethnic followings were mobilized for the crucial electoral count. In Nigeria, the Southern party boycotted the 1964 election to protest questionable electoral practices; but even in 1959, when polarization was incomplete and tension was lower, the turnout was 80 percent nationwide and was over 89 percent in the North, which feared Southern hegemony.[95] In the Congolese election of 1959, voter participation in many areas exceeded 90 percent. The overall rate was 79.2 percent.[96] In Zanzibar, party and ethnic lines were not perfectly matched, but they were close enough so that each party had a commonly accepted ethnic identification. By the 1961 election, 96.2 percent of the electorate voted; and violent disturbances followed.[97]

A central feature of the polarizing election—and to a lesser extent of all elections where parties are ethnically aligned—is the devotion of party efforts to mobilizing known supporters to turn out for the vote. Of course, all electoral parties concern themselves with voter turnout, but there are differences. Here "known supporters" are known by their ethnicity. Since that is their distinguishing feature, they are most readily mobilized by appeals to ethnic interests, threats, and hatreds. The

94. Samuel Decalo, *Coups and Army Rule in Africa* (New Haven: Yale Univ. Press, 1976), 51, 96.
95. Sklar, *Nigerian Political Parties*, 32–33.
96. Wagret, *Histoire et sociologie politiques de la République du Congo (Brazzaville)*, 93, 192.
97. *Report of a Commission of Inquiry into Disturbances in Zanzibar During June 1961* (Colon. No. 353; London: H.M.S.O., 1961), 6.

greater the collective danger, the greater the likelihood that politically apathetic group members will go to the polls.

Attention to turnout can be single-minded. Elsewhere, nonethnic parties divide their electoral energies between two tasks: mobilizing known supporters and appealing for uncommitted votes. These two are not necessarily the same thing. In fact, there is often a tradeoff between whipping up party loyalists to get them to the polls and soliciting the support of those whose loyalty is uncertain. Pandering exclusively to the concerns and prejudices of loyal supporters may well drive away uncommitted or potential crossover voters; sweet reasonableness and moderation may be required to convert the uncommitted to the party cause.

All this is different in an ethnic party system. In such a system, mobilizing known supporters and appealing to marginal voters are effectively the same thing, for there are virtually no uncommitted votes to be had on the other side of the ethnic boundary. What is uncertain is not *how* a voter will vote if he votes—a Creole will vote for the Creole party, an Ibo for the Ibo party, and so on. In such a party system, all that is uncertain is *whether* a potential voter will vote. Accordingly, turnout becomes all-important, and there is no electoral reason to be moderate about ethnic appeals.

As the mobilization of all group members to vote imparts a census-like quality to the electoral count, so the ethnic appeals that push voting rates up also raise the pitch of ethnic conflict and increase the danger of violence. No doubt politicians will later find that it is easier to kindle a fire than to quench one, but in the census-type election ignition takes untrammeled priority. Hence, *apan jaht* becomes the order of the day— or, in the more direct Creole lyric of a Trinidad calypso: "We don't want no coolie [East Indian] premier. We don't want no *roti* government."[98]

98. *Coolie*, originally a Tamil word, was the early pejorative term for the East Indians who came to work the sugar estates as indentured laborers. *Roti*, which means bread in several Asian languages, refers in Trinidad to a widely sold snack food, stuffed with curried potatoes. Its Indian origins make it a convenient vehicle for a disparaging quip at the expense of the DLP.

CHAPTER EIGHT

Competition and Change in Ethnic Party Systems

The realignment process we have just observed for Guyana and Trinidad is reminiscent of two hypotheses advanced by Sartori.[1] The first states that the appearance of one or two mass parties undermines party atomization in the rest of the party system. To compete with the mass party, other organizations need to merge into more solid parties. The second hypothesis, framed with Europe in mind, states that when a religious party becomes a mass party with an outspokenly pro-clerical orientation, this sets in motion a chain reaction in party formation. Parties form to take sides on the secular-religious dimension. The chain reaction, Sartori asserts, is likely to have a centrifugal impact.

There are echoes of these hypotheses, suitably modified for ethnicity rather than religion, in Guyana and Trinidad. Certainly, the consolidation process was quite visible, and it occurred hand in hand with the formation of parties that lined up along ethnic boundaries as soon as the ethnic character of one of the parties was established. The appearance of the first mass parties quickly undermined the position of the former personalistic parties and locally influential independents, forcing them to join together. In this respect, their reaction was no different from the behavior of other organizations in adversary relationships. These typically imitate each other's structural innovations, the better to engage in struggle.[2]

---

1. Giovanni Sartori, "Political Development and Political Engineering," *Public Policy* 17 (1968): 261–98, at 293–98.
2. See James Q. Wilson, *Political Organizations* (New York: Basic Books, 1973), 135. The point goes back to Georg Simmel and has been elaborated upon for governmental organizations by Daniel P. Moynihan, "Imperial Government," *Commentary*, June 1978, pp. 25–32.

As I have shown, a realignment of this sort does have a centrifugal result. In some ways, moreover, it is likely to go beyond the consequences forecast by Sartori. In Afro-Asian societies, an ethnic realignment will exclude other bases of party cleavage, and it will therefore produce a party system with at best a very limited sort of competitiveness. These characteristics and consequences of ethnic party systems, together with the possibilities for further change in the party system, form the subjects of this chapter.

ETHNIC PARTIES AND
THE PREMISES OF THE LEFT

Perhaps the most notable characteristic of ethnic parties is the extent to which they preempt the organizational field, crowding out parties founded on other bases. Left parties have been particularly affected by this. Over and over again, socialist intellectuals in the developing world have organized parties intending to do battle on class lines, only to find that their potential followings had rather different ideas about the identity of the enemy.

The plight of the Guyanese People's Progressive Party in this respect is quite typical of many other Left parties. Led by Marxists, the PPP was initially conceived as a party of "progressive elements"[3] aiming simultaneously at independence and socialism. The party's strong ideological commitments resulted, as we have seen, in the suspension of the constitution by the British in 1953, as well as in the loss of what Jagan called "native capital support for the party."[4]

The defection of Burnham and the resumption of elections made it imperative for the PPP to consider what compromises were required for success at the polls. As parties were being reordered along ethnic lines, it became more important than previously to insure that the PPP did not drive East Indians away by overemphasizing its socialist commitments. In a secret speech to a party congress in 1956, paralleling Khrushchev's famous secret speech of the same year, Jagan reminded his party that it must not "overestimate the political understanding of the people or underestimate the emotional appeal of racialism."[5] At the same time, he

3. Cheddi Jagan, *Forbidden Freedom: The Story of British Guiana* (London: Lawrence & Wishart, 1954), 44.
4. Cheddi Jagan, Speech to the 1956 PPP Congress, *Daily Chronicle* (Georgetown), Dec. 22, 1956.
5. Ibid.

referred to party leaders who openly favored schemes to which the East Indian population was opposed (notably, the West Indian Federation) as being "utopian." The 1956 speech provided, in short, the doctrinal underpinning for reliance on the Indian vote.

Jagan later rationalized this reliance by emphasizing the "progressive role" played by the Indians in Guyana:

The Indians and the Negroes play diametrically different roles in British Guiana and East Africa. In East Africa, Indians and other Asians were used as the middle-class buffers by the British ruling class against the African national movement. In British Guiana, on the other hand, the Indians, because of economic and cultural suppression, have by and large played a progressive role in spite of communal tendencies.[6]

The effect of the policy adopted by the PPP in 1956 was enormous. Indian religious leaders, as well as businessmen, teachers, and rice farmers, affiliated with the PPP. When the PPP returned to office in 1957, its agricultural and commercial policy reflected the dependence of the party on its Indian constituency.[7] From time to time, the PPP was torn between those cadres who saw the party as an instrument of revolutionary change and those who saw it as a vehicle for East Indian interests.[8] But the choice Jagan had made in 1956 was not reversed.

Jagan was neither the first nor the last Marxist politician to compromise a universalistic ideology for the sake of needed ethnic support. Nor was Jagan's doctrinal rationalization unique. Quite independently, the same compromise and the same doctrinal adjustments have been made by Left parties in other ethnically divided societies.

Sri Lanka provides a very clear example, because its Left parties were among the strongest of the electorally oriented Marxist parties of Asia. It was the language issue that tested their ethnic neutrality. At indepen-

6. Cheddi Jagan, *The West on Trial: My Fight for Guyana's Freedom* (London: Michael Joseph, 1966), 342.

7. For examples, see Leo Despres, *Cultural Pluralism and Nationalist Politics in British Guiana* (Chicago: Rand McNally, 1967), 232–38. Cf. Adele Smith Simmons, "Politics in Mauritius Since 1934: A Study of Decolonization in a Plural Society" (Ph.D. diss., Oxford Univ., 1969), 354: "As the Indian intellectuals moved into leadership positions within the Labour Party, it became less a party of the workers and more a party of the Indians."

8. There were many battles fought in the party over this. Jagan repeatedly was forced to defend the Creole party chairman, Brindley Benn, a fanatical Marxist, against attempts to replace him with an East Indian. Young ideologues of the party's Progressive Youth Organization were also unhappy with the PPP's surrender to Indian interests; they periodically challenged the party's "communal elements." *Sunday Graphic* (Georgetown), July 4, 1965. But Jagan viewed such challenges as "Left deviations" that he was not prepared to countenance.

dence, English was the official language of Ceylon, but many politicians favored replacing English with Sinhala and Tamil, the two main languages of the island. Both the Communists and the Trotskyites had espoused a policy of equal treatment for the Sinhalese and Tamil languages. This policy came under great pressure with the surge of Sinhalese ethnic sentiment that brought to power a government led by S.W.R.D. Bandaranaike in 1956. A central concern of the movement that propelled Bandaranaike to power was the demand to make Sinhala the sole official language of Ceylon, to the detriment of Tamil. When the Trotskyites and Communists reaffirmed their support for linguistic parity, they began to lose supporters, and their public meetings were broken up by mobs of "Sinhala Only" proponents.[9]

In the face of this pressure, the Communists gave way relatively early. Shortly before the 1956 election, the Ceylon Communist Party, increasingly isolated in the surge of Sinhalese sentiment, abandoned its policy of linguistic parity. The policy of parity had, the party concluded, "caused a temporary separation between the [Sinhalese] nationalist and working-class movements . . . ."[10] Correcting this "mistake" involved the recognition that there was no real working-class movement in the Tamil areas and that the Sinhalese were more "anti-imperialist" than the Tamils. Accordingly, it was "progressive" to adopt Sinhala as the language of administration and to compel non-Sinhalese to learn it.[11] This conclusion was no doubt fortified by the fact that, though a single Communist candidate had won a seat in the Tamil area in 1956, the support of the Communist Party lay heavily in the Sinhalese South.

The Trotskyites (the Lanka Sama Samaj Party) arrived at a similar position more slowly. In 1963, a "United Left Front" was formed, consisting of all the Marxist parties. A condition of admission to the Front was that the LSSP switch to a policy of Sinhala Only. This it did with little dissent and few defections. Although its leaders conceded that, "in the abstract," linguistic parity is the correct position for a Marxist party, the LSSP, too, suddenly discovered that there was an element of "class struggle" in the quest of the Sinhala-educated to secure official recognition for their language. "The Sinhalese petite bourgeoisie is radical—it

---

9. Robert N. Kearney, *Communalism and Language in the Politics of Ceylon* (Durham: Duke Univ. Press, 1967), 74.
   10. *25 Years of the Ceylon Communist Party, 1943–1968* (Colombo: People's Pub. House, 1968), 67–68, 72.
   11. Interview, Colombo, Aug. 3, 1968.

wants a change," said an LSSP leader,[12] whereas the allegedly more prosperous Tamil petite bourgeoisie was conservative. The Tamils were less involved in the class struggle than the Sinhalese, who were more keenly interested in displacing the English language and the English-educated class from power. Consequently, the struggle for Sinhala Only was "progressive with some reactionary aspects."[13] Predictably, the little Tamil support for the LSSP had withered when its language policy changed. The Trotskyites became an exclusively Sinhalese party.

There is a striking coincidence between Jagan's formulation that the East Indian position is "progressive in spite of communal tendencies" and the Sri Lanka Marxist conclusion that the Sinhalese struggle is "progressive with some reactionary aspects." Progressive and reactionary are, of course, characterizations initially employed in Marxist analysis with respect to the positions of social classes in the historical process. Needless to say, the ethnic groups being compared—Creoles and Indians, Sinhalese and Tamils—spanned social classes. In conventional Marxist thinking, whole ethnic groups, at least unranked ones, could scarcely be said to occupy a class position at all. By redefining ethnic interests in terms used to characterize class positions, it became ideologically permissible to justify the reliance of a left-wing party on the support of a single ethnic group—even if some doctrinal gymnastics were involved in the redefinition.

Such a redefiniton of ethnic positions in para-class terms reflects a fundamental alteration of the strategy favored by the Left in ethnically divided societies. So long as ethnic tensions remained in the background of politics, it was possible for left-wing parties to advocate bridging ethnic divisions by building alliances across ethnic lines. These alliances were to be based on the common class interests and allegiances of workers and peasants of the respective ethnic groups. No matter that it was much easier to plan these class-based alliances than it was to construct them: it was at least possible to speak of their desirability without incurring serious political costs.

An increase in ethnic conflict changes this. Attempts by the Left to span group boundaries become electorally costly. Potential supporters

12. Interview, Colombo, July 29, 1968. The SLFP was likewise characterized by another LSSP leader as "a radical petit bourgeois party," and on these grounds it was permissible for a revolutionary party to align with the SLFP, as Lenin had not hesitated to align with the Social Revolutionaries, who were also petit bourgeois. Interview, Colombo, Aug. 10, 1968.

13. Interview, Colombo, July 29, 1968.

of a left-wing party want to know on which side of the ethnic conflict the party stands. This demands an abandonment of the former Left strategy if the parties are to survive. The labeling of entire ethnic groups as progressive or reactionary may be a travesty of Marxist thinking, but it is a method of avoiding the electoral costs of strict ethnic neutrality in a political system in which all parties have come to be identified with the claims and aspirations of particular ethnic groups.

The Guyanese and Ceylonese Marxists have not been alone in adapting to ethnic pressures successfully. Wherever parties have been ethnically based, Left parties that have retained a substantial measure of electoral support have also been rooted in one or another ethnic group—with or without the benefit of doctrinal rationalization. In Malaysia, the Labor Party, which began as a reformist party modeled on the British Labor Party but became Communist-dominated by the late 1960s, was able to gain electoral success only by espousing specifically Chinese causes; its membership, too, was virtually entirely Chinese.[14] The Communist Party of India in the Punjab was largely a Sikh party—indeed, largely a party of the prosperous Sikh peasantry of the Jat caste—and it accordingly supported the Sikh demand for a separate state within India.[15] In Kerala in the 1950s, the CPI was dependent on the votes of the Ezhava caste. The Ezhava are officially defined as "backward," a legal status that enables them to secure a variety of government benefits. When the Kerala CPI supported a change in the definition of backwardness that would have made income, rather than caste, the criterion, the Ezhava protested. The party quickly gave in.[16] In an ethnic party system, the choice for a Left party is to adapt and become essentially an ethnic party or to wither and die.

Nonetheless, there have been parties operating in such an environment that have made concerted efforts to retain class as their organizing principle and to develop interethnic support. Their experience is not encouraging.

In the period following World War II, the Malay Nationalist Party sought to define Malay politics in class terms. It opposed the privileges of the traditional Malay rulers and of the aristocratic class, and it advocated cooperation across ethnic lines, seeking alignments with Chinese

14. R. K. Vasil, *Politics in a Plural Society* (Kuala Lumpur: Oxford Univ. Press, 1971), 162.

15. Brass, "Ethnic Cleavages and the Punjab Party System" (unpublished paper presented at the 1972 annual meeting of the Association for Asian Studies), 21–22.

16. Lloyd I. Rudolph and Susanne Hoeber Rudolph, *The Modernity of Tradition: Political Development in India* (Chicago: Univ. of Chicago Press, 1967), 72 n.14.

political parties. By 1950, the MNP was quite discredited in Malay opinion, eclipsed by the United Malays National Organization. UMNO drew its leadership from the aristocracy, its sustenance from solid roots in Malay society, and its political advantage from its readiness to define politics in ethnic rather than class terms.[17]

In Northern Nigeria, a comparable contest was fought in the 1950s and '60s between a conservative and a radical party, with much the same results, for much the same reasons. The Northern People's Congress was a party controlled by Hausa-Fulani emirs and aristocrats. It advocated the Northern cause against Yoruba and Ibo aspirations. By contrast, the Northern Elements Progressive Union aligned with the Ibo-dominated National Convention of Nigerian Citizens in the country as a whole. In the North, NEPU advocated fundamental change in traditional social relations. It even spoke of "class struggle." Like the Malay Nationalist Party, NEPU proved less able than its competitor to rely on ties of traditional deference for political support, and its perception of the main lines of social conflict was sharply at variance with that of the Northern electorate. It suffered recurrent electoral defeat.[18]

Although NEPU and the MNP were both ethnically based parties that sought interethnic cooperation, there have also been attempts to found explicitly interethnic parties based on class ties. These have fared poorly in ethnically divided societies.

The Workers' and Farmers' Party of Trinidad, founded in 1965, is as good an example as any. The WFP was led by politicians drawn from the ranks of the DLP and the PNM. One leader was East Indian, the other Creole. They were joined by a third founding member, the president-general of the Oilfield Workers Trade Union. The party's strategy was to secure the votes of the mainly Creole oil workers and to use the influence of the East Indian leader in his community, as well as the success of the oil workers' union in gaining labor concessions, to attract the support of the predominantly East Indian sugar workers. The objective was a strong, labor-based, multiethnic party.[19]

The strategy failed completely. The PNM's prediction that the Trini-

17. Gordon P. Means, *Malaysian Politics* (New York: New York Univ. Press, 1970), 92–93.
18. See, e.g., Richard L. Sklar, *Nigerian Political Parties* (Princeton: Princeton Univ. Press, 1963), 338.
19. I am drawing here on interviews with WFP leaders in Trinidad in 1965. The party also published a weekly paper called *We the People*, in which its strategy was spelled out. See, e.g., "Weekes and CLR: A Conversation," *We the People* (Port-of-Spain), July 23, 1965, p. 2.

dad Treasury would be swelled by the lost deposits of a plethora of unsuccessful candidates in the 1966 elections was fulfilled by the WFP in every constituency. Not only did the WFP fail to win the votes of the sugar workers, but it did not make any showing even in the oil districts. The union leader ran fourth of four candidates in his home constituency, polling exactly 4.9 percent of the vote. The East Indian leader lost the constituency he had won for the DLP by two-to-one in 1961, this time attracting only 5.6 percent of the vote. Other party leaders did even worse. Clearly, the voters believed that Creole political power and Indian political power were mutually exclusive alternatives. Once ethnic interests were organized into ethnic parties, there was no room for a party founded on completely different assumptions about the appropriate lines of social conflict.

ETHNIC PARTY SYSTEMS, NONETHNIC PARTIES, AND INDEPENDENTS

I have highlighted the dilemma faced by left-wing parties operating in an ethnic party system, because the argument has sometimes been made— and it is grounded solidly in Marxist doctrine—that the "real" lines of social cleavage are not ethnic lines at all. More often than not, therefore, the impetus to ignore or to cross ethnic lines in party organization emanates from the Left. The electoral survival of socialist parties only when they espouse ethnic causes, and their conspicuous electoral failure when they do not do so, attests to the preemptive power of ethnic party systems when they emerge in Asia and Africa.

Yet, if left-wing parties provide the clearest examples of the inability of parties that are not ethnically based to break into an ethnic party system, they do not provide the only such examples. Nonethnic parties of the nonsocialist variety have had the same experience. In Trinidad, not only did the left-wing WFP fail at its maiden election in 1966; a conservative nonethnic party, the Liberal Party, also polled an insignificant share of the vote. The Liberals were composed mainly of former DLP leaders, both Creole and Indian. They won not a single seat. Ethnic party systems are as inhospitable to right-wing parties that attempt to ignore or surmount ethnic lines as they are to left-wing parties that do so.

The rise of an ethnic party system also precludes a significant role for independent candidates or for popular personalities who have defected from ethnic parties to run on other tickets. With ethnic groups polarized, it is a risky course for voters to register a preference for even a popular candidate of their own ethnic group if that candidate is not affiliated with the party of that group. Ethnic representation is channeled through ethnic parties. Victorious independents or members of minor parties, however popular they are locally, dilute ethnic party strength and thus also dilute ethnic group strength.

This point could be demonstrated by tracing the electoral fortunes of independents and defectors in a number of countries, but again the Trinidad election of 1966 serves very well as a laboratory for the electoral manifestations of an ethnic party system. There were many contests involving recently resigned party leaders and local notables. The results were dramatic. Independent and maverick candidates were uniformly defeated.

Prominent Indian leaders who ran without DLP endorsement included Bhadase Maraj, president-general of the sugar workers' union, head of the Hindu Maha Sabha, former leader of the DLP, wealthy benefactor and ward heeler of the Indian community. Maraj ran as the only candidate of the virtually defunct People's Democratic Party and won only 10 percent of the votes cast in his constituency. Three other well-known East Indians, all defectors from the DLP, were defeated in their own former constituencies. One received under 5 percent of the vote; another, only 217 out of 8,584 votes cast; and the third attracted fewer votes than even the PNM candidate in an overwhelmingly Indian constituency.

Creole politicians who were unaffiliated with the PNM fared equally poorly. T.U.B. Butler, who had led the oilfield strikes of 1937 that constituted the first stirrings of Trinidad nationalism, still had a following in the oil refinery region in the 1950s. He had been elected to the legislature in 1950 and 1956. As soon as strong ethnic parties emerged, he and his Butler Party were consigned to oblivion. Most of the party's following went to the PNM. In 1961 and 1966, Butler himself was overwhelmingly defeated by PNM candidates. So, for that matter, were other Creole notables running on Liberal tickets.

No doubt there are exceptions. In some countries with ethnic party systems, party mavericks have on rare occasions been able to hold their own seats, at least where the basis of their earlier support was the firm grip of family influence on a rural constituency. Yet the general point remains. As ethnic party systems grow, the stakes become too high and

342	Ethnic Groups in Conflict

the pressures toward the census-type election too strong to permit the luxury of representation outside the ethnic parties. That is not to say that each group must have one and only one party. As we shall see, there are sometimes forces that work toward the emergence of more than one ethnic party per group. Whatever the number of parties, ethnic party systems leave little room for parties organized without regard to the preeminence of ethnic issues in a severely divided society or for politicians aiming to struggle for ethnic interests outside the ethnic party. In such a system, there is a single axis of political conflict and a single way of pursuing that conflict: through the ethnic parties.

THE COMPETITIVE CONFIGURATION: SEGMENTED ELECTORATES

Ethnic parties function in a segmented electoral market. If party competition is taken to mean competition for support from the electorate, rather than all forms of interparty rivalry, then party competition in an ethnic party system occurs within ethnic groups but not across ethnic group lines. Nothing is as responsible for the conflict-promoting character of ethnic party systems as this configuration of competition. Let us look first at party competition within groups and then at the absence of party competition between groups.

Within-group party competition can be intense, and it can result in the replacement of one ethnic party by another party representing the same group. In Sri Lanka at the 1956 election, the Sri Lanka Freedom Party of S.W.R.D. Bandaranaike won a resounding victory over the United National Party that had brought the country to independence. Both were Sinhalese parties, but the SLFP had made a convincing case with the Sinhalese electorate that the UNP had been neglecting Sinhalese interests.[20]

Competitive concerns can influence the behavior of an ethnic party even when it effectively dominates the scene. It is fatuous to assume that followers follow wherever leaders lead. Rather, they follow only if they are being led in a direction they believe is preferable to the available alternatives. The existence of lively intraethnic party competition, as I shall show, attests to the rise of alternatives when followers begin to

20. W. Howard Wriggins, *Ceylon: Dilemmas of a New Nation* (Princeton: Princeton Univ. Press, 1960), 326–69.

disapprove of the direction in which ethnic parties are taking them. Ethnic party leaders, including leaders of dominant ethnic parties, often entertain understandable apprehensions that an intraethnic competitor party will steal their clientele from them. Many of the actions taken by seemingly secure ethnic parties can be understood in this light—as measures to prevent competition from emerging and to defeat it if it does emerge.[21] Consequently, it is possible for a party to adopt a competitive posture even without active party competition.

That posture explains much about the preemptive way ethnic parties treat non-party organizations that also aim to promote ethnic group interests. In the developing world, these organizations run the gamut from so-called "tribal unions" in Africa to associations of "vernacular-medium" teachers, of Buddhist or Muslim clergy, and of language activists in Asia, not to mention ethnically differentiated chambers of commerce and trade unions. In their infancy, ethnic parties required the active support of such organizations.[22] As the parties grew strong, however, they became the chief spokesmen for ethnic interests, often displacing those ethnic associations that had previously served as all-purpose ethnic interest groups. The League of Coloured Peoples in Guyana, for example, atrophied as the PNC assumed the role of advancing Creole interests across the board. More specialized organizations could not be dispensed with so easily. Ethnic parties usually attempted to convert these organizations into transmission belts for party policy and instruments of electoral mobilization.

One thing ethnic parties did not readily countenance was the survival of politically autonomous ethnic associations. If, for example, a Malay language organization could formulate its own set of linguistic policy priorities, it could also accuse a Malay party of doing too little for the language of the Malays. Politically powerful ethnic interest groups pose a danger to an ethnic party, because they may transfer their organizational allegiance and abet the rise of a competitor party within the same ethnic group. Accordingly, it is prudent for an ethnic party to control the activity of ethnic interest groups, while at the same time taking over their functions of ethnic interest representation. Against this background, Almond's earlier quoted remark that particularistic parties resemble inter-

---

21. On the possibility of new entrants into party competition, see Giovanni Sartori, *Parties and Party Systems*, vol. 1 (Cambridge: Cambridge Univ. Press, 1976), 220–21.
22. See, e.g., Sklar, *Nigerian Political Parties*, 463, 465; Wriggins, *Ceylon*, 342–48; Means, *Malaysian Politics*, 104, 196, 203.

est groups takes on heightened meaning. The ethnic party *is* the interest group.

The desire to prevent the emergence of party competition is perfectly familiar in party systems that do not center on ethnic conflict. But there is a difference. If a nonethnic party loses the support of an ethnic group that previously voted heavily for the party, it becomes weaker; but the party may pick up compensatory support, perhaps from other groups not favorably disposed to the party's former ethnic supporters. Loss of the support of an ethnic group does not necessarily threaten to put a nonethnic party out of business. An ethnic party, on the other hand, is exclusively dependent upon the support of its group. It has little ability to diversify its electoral support. If an ethnic party is discredited and loses the support of the group it represents, for failing to protect the interests of that group, recouping the loss will be difficult. This is partly because the ethnic cause has an element of sacredness to it. The charge of neglecting it may carry an indelible stigma. It is also because group members will usually hesitate to divide their support between more than one ethnic party if that will benefit the ethnic enemy—as it often will. Competititve comebacks for ethnic parties cannot be counted on.

The likely inability of an ethnic party either to defray competitive losses by diversifying its clientele or to recoup them means that competitive threats tend to look like genuine matters of survival to party leaders. If the competition succeeds, the party may actually die. The desire to control ethnic interest-group activity is just one part of these competitive apprehensions.

The competitive behavior of an ethnic party is limited to its own ethnic group. That is the very meaning of segmented electorates. But how does this differ from limitations on party competition that are common to all party systems? Surely, in other systems, left-wing parties do not compete for right-wing voters, and vice versa. Yet there are differences, and they are important differences for the impact an ethnic party system has on ethnic politics.

Sartori has pointed out that there are two systemic reasons why parties may fail to compete with each other. The parties may not be positioned along the same issue axis; for example, one may be a religious party, another a working-class party. These two parties arose out of different sets of conflicts, and their followings, oriented toward different issues, respond to different electoral stimuli. Alternatively, the parties may be positioned along the same issue axis, but at such disparate points that there is no transferability of votes between them. This is illustrated by the case of the left-wing and right-wing parties mentioned a moment ago. Their voters may well be moved by common issues, but their positions may be literally poles apart. The ideological distance between the parties, in other words, may be so great that no appeal made by one of the parties could induce followers of the other to support it. Parties may thus fail to compete either because they are not in the same issue space or because, although they are in the same space, the distance between them precludes the transfer of votes.[23]

Either of these reasons may prevent party competition in Western Europe, where there is typically more than one issue axis. In the ethnic party systems of Asia and Africa, where parties are in the same issue space, typically only the second reason for lack of party competition exists. Nonetheless, it operates to limit party competition sharply. As we shall see, it is the element of ascription that makes the difference.

Using European data, Sartori suggests that the transferability of votes from one party to another is a matter of party distance. Voters locate themselves roughly at some point along the party spectrum. Parties are then perceived by given voters as being more or less compatible with their preferences. Parties located close to a voter's location on the spectrum are regarded by the voter as plausible competitors for his vote. Of course, even here there are some voters who are irrevocably committed to support one party and one party alone. Still, other voters are more open to competition for their vote. But, among these, each voter will only move along the party spectrum up to a certain point, after which he will not consider transferring his vote.[24] Obviously, what is postulated here is a graduated relationship between vote transferability and party distance.

The case of ethnic parties is different, because that relationship is not graduated: it is either-or, not more-and-less. There is a qualitative distinction between the parties, depending on their ethnic identity and that of the voter; it is not a matter of degrees of distance. A voter is either Creole or Indian, Sinhalese or Tamil, Bakongo or Mbochi—and the same is true of the parties. Consequently, where parties are ethnically

23. Sartori, *Parties and Party Systems*, vol. 1, chap. 10. In a later paper, however, Sani and Sartori point out that, in practice, there may well be some overlap of issue axes. Giacomo Sani and Giovanni Sartori, "Polarization, Fragmentation and Competition in Western Democracies" (unpublished paper presented at the 1978 World Congress of the International Sociological Association, Uppsala), 13–15.

24. Sartori, *Parties and Party Systems*, vol. 1, p. 343.

based, the competitive cutoff is a sharp precipice, not a gradual slope. Ethnic voting means exactly this: no vote transferability across ethnic lines. Observed a PNM cabinet minister at a party rally in the early 1960s, "I do not see any DLP faces around." By this, of course, he meant he saw no Indian faces.

We are now in a position to see exactly why ethnic party systems tend to foster rather than to moderate ethnic conflict. The competitive configuration is crucial in this. From the standpoint of competition, ethnic party systems are characterized by three main features that bear on conflict.

First, there is one principal issue axis—the ethnic conflict axis— which preempts others. All parties are positioned on it. This means that there is little relief from the ethnic character of politics in the form of alternating issues. Hence, divisive issues can cumulate in the party system, and all voters are identified with parties that have taken a stand on the main divisive issues.

Second, there is party competition, or the possibility of it, within ethnic groups. The possibility of intragroup party competition creates strong incentives for parties to be diligent in asserting ethnic demands, the more so when they consider the life-or-death implications of that competition for the party's fortunes. Outbidding for ethnic support is a constant possibility.

Third, because ethnicity is a largely ascriptive affiliation, the boundaries of party support stop at the boundaries of ethnic groups. There are many working-class Tories,[25] but there are very few Hindu Akalis—to take an example from among the least rigidly ascriptive ethnic groups and parties. In an ascriptive system, it is far more important to take effective steps to reassure ethnic supporters than to pursue will-o'-the-wisps by courting imaginary voters across ethnic lines. The near-impossibility of party competition for clientele across ethnic lines means an absence of countervailing electoral incentives encouraging party moderation on ethnic issues.[26]

25. Eric A. Nordlinger, *The Working-Class Tories: Authority, Deference, and Stable Democracy* (Berkeley and Los Angeles: Univ. of California Press, 1967).

26. Again, the contrast with nonethnic parties—even those with heavy doses of ethnic voting—is instructive, for small infusions of competition across ethnic lines can make a significant difference. In New Brunswick, Canada, for example, the Conservatives have had little support from French-speaking Acadians. Yet that minimal support can be the difference between forming a government and not forming one, and this has encouraged the Conservatives not to oppose programs the Acadians demanded. Concludes P. M. Leslie from this experience: ". . . if a party is even marginally dependent upon support from an

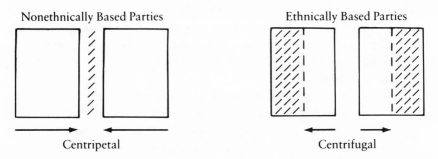

FIGURE 2. The Direction of Competition
in Nonethnic and Ethnic Two-Party Systems

Nonethnically Based Parties   Ethnically Based Parties

Centripetal   Centrifugal

KEY: Each rectangle represents a party.
  Dotted lines indicate the potential location of new competitor parties in ethnic party systems.
  Hatched lines indicate the probable location of floating voters (defined below).
  Arrows indicate the direction of competitive appeals, convergent or divergent.
NOTE: From the figure, it is clear that the two nonethnically based parties form part of a single competitive system. Floating voters, potentially available to support either party, tend to be located between the parties. Competition, and thus the nature of competitive appeals, brings the positions of the parties closer together. By contrast, the two ethnically based parties are not in the same competitive system. Since the parties are ascriptively defined, no significant number of floating voters is located between them. Competition, if it comes, will be located on the flanks in the form of new parties appealing for support within each ethnic group. Voters who may shift party allegiances are located at the extremes. The threat of such competition drives both parties to protect their flanks, thus pushing their positions apart.

In fact, ethnic two-party systems, such as those described for Guyana and Trinidad, are anything but moderate. It is a fundamental mistake to view such a two-party system as being similar to the two-party systems of, for example, Britain, the United States, or New Zealand. The critical differences between them lie in the realm of party competition, as Figure 2 shows. In the nonethnic two-party systems, competition makes the parties converge; they compete for undecided or shifting voters whose views lie between the positions of the two parties. This creates a pull toward moderation. The competition of the two parties is centripetal.

ethnic minority, ostentatious rejection of its demands will incur an electoral penalty." "The Role of Political Parties in Promoting the Interests of Ethnic Minorities," *Canadian Journal of Political Science* 2 (Dec. 1969): 419–33, at 426. If, however, a party is not even marginally dependent on the support of such a minority, then the more ostentation in rejecting its demands, the more security the party gains with its own supporters, and indeed the greater the electoral turnout of its ethnic supporters may be.

This is not true, as Sartori has noted, for parties perceived "as being alien and extraneous,"[27] for they do not gain votes by strategies of convergence. Floating voters are not situated between the parties. The party system becomes bifurcated. The position of one party is the negation of the other: one party stands for Creole power, another for Indian power. Here, then, is a two-party system founded on antagonism and, in general, furthering it.

There may be extrinsic reasons for ethnic parties to exercise caution in the untrammeled pursuit of ethnic advantage. Depending on each party's share of votes and legislative seats, there may be a need to cooperate or coalesce with other parties across ethnic boundaries in order to form a government. Once in power, an ethnic party may likewise temper its response to ethnic constituency demands because the responsibilities of governing seem to require that such demands be balanced against other goals with which they may be in conflict. Economic development objectives are often in this category; their attainment may require concessions to ethnic groups heavily represented in particular sectors of the economy. The fear of civil disorder may also induce moderation on the part of an ethnic party. (Immoderation by ethnic parties has frequently helped provoke disorder—in Nigeria in 1964–65, in Sri Lanka in 1977, in Congo [Brazzaville] in 1958–59, and in Guyana in 1962–64.) These and other concerns may indeed provide counterweights to the immoderate thrust of electoral politics in ethnic party systems. The point here, however, is that nothing in the competitive equation requires moderation. Moderation is dependent upon the vagaries of forces extrinsic to competition.

The main features of the ethnic party system are readily summarized: stable parties, unstable politics. Support of parties in such a system is heavily ascriptive. The parties act as the organizational expression of the ethnic groups they represent. As the groups advance mutually exclusive claims to power, so, too, do the parties. The ultimate issue in every election is, starkly put, ethnic inclusion or exclusion. The census quality imparted to elections, as well as the high stakes involved, raises electoral turnouts until there is a decisive test and tends to make more people more actively partisan than would otherwise be the case. Where there are two parties representing two ethnic groups of unequal numbers, as described for Guyana and Trinidad, only demographic change, drastic

27. Sartori, *Parties and Party Systems*, vol. 1, p. 344.

electoral revision, *coup d'état*, or all-out ethnic warfare can convert the opposition into the government. To the excluded, exclusion from power appears permanent.

CHANGE IN ETHNIC PARTY SYSTEMS

Ethnic party systems are unstable not only in their tendency to aggravate ethnic conflict. They are unstable also because, as just indicated, they produce powerful impulses to change. Two types of change are worthy of consideration at this point. The first involves the number of contending parties within an ethnic party system. The second entails change from an ethnic party system to some other type of party system or to some completely different way of ordering the polity.

CHANGE WITHIN ETHNIC PARTY SYSTEMS

The most important changes that occur within the framework of ethnic party systems involve expansion or contraction in the number of parties. The possibilities of competition and coalition are affected by the number of parties per ethnic group and how they divide the total vote. I propose here to treat two common and profoundly important changes in the number of ethnic parties: first, from intraethnic monopoly to intraethnic competition; second, from tripolar to bipolar party systems.

The Emergence of Intraethnic Competition

Quite often each major ethnic group enters the electoral process represented by only one ethnic party or, at all events, by a party that has an overwhelmingly dominant hold on the group's support. In many cases, however, sharp party competition later emerges for the adherence of group members. Usually, this is preceded by a split in the dominant party, though it can also take the form of entirely new parties with entirely new leaders.

Whether more than one party per group emerges depends on five main conditions. The first is the existence of pronounced social divisions within the ethnic group. Usually, these are ascriptive divisions, based on caste, clan, religion, or region of origin. The second is the collective sense of how many parties an ethnic group can afford without weakening itself in ethnic conflict. The third is the existence of strong differences of opinion regarding the appropriate group posture *vis-à-vis* the other ethnic groups in conflict relations. The fourth relates to leadership rivalries within the ethnic group. The fifth condition is the effect of the formal incentive structure on party proliferation.

Here I intend to deal only with the first three of these. I shall touch on the leadership question in passing and reserve the incentive structure for fuller consideration when we consider devices to reduce ethnic tensions in Chapter 15. In any event, subethnic divisions, differences regarding conflict relations, and the calculation of how many parties a group can afford are by far the most important determinants of intraethnic party proliferation or its absence.

The apparent cohesion of ethnic groups in times of tension should not be mistaken for social homogeneity. Within an ethnic group, there are nearly always ascriptive subdivisions based on differences of caste, clan, language, religion, or region. These subdivisions I refer to as "subethnic," because they are present at a level below the principal lines of politically relevant group boundaries. Of course, what is only "subethnic" now can become the main politically relevant affiliation later, depending on changes in political context.

The importance of subethnic divisions for party politics is easily demonstrated by use of a few examples. In Sri Lanka, the Sinhalese are divided into a number of castes. The defection of a particularly cohesive Sinhalese caste faction (the Salagama) from the ruling United National Party in the 1950s played a considerable role in the opposition landslide of 1956. Eight years later, the Salagama leader C. P. de Silva and a bloc of fourteen members of parliament, most of them also Salagama, crossed the aisle again, bringing down the government of the Sri Lanka Freedom Party on a vote of no confidence.[28] In Malay parties, state of origin plays a significant role. The fortunes of politicians and their supporters are scrutinized to see if Malays from the state of Johore are ascendant over Malays from Kedah, or vice versa. Among the Sikhs, both caste and region of origin have been important. Sikh Harijans, fearful of domination by the powerful Sikh Jat community, often preferred Congress to the Akali Dal, while in the 1960s the Akali Dal itself split into two, the support of each rump based largely on one or another region of the Punjab.[29]

28. For these events, see H. B. W. Abeynaike, *The Parliament of Ceylon, 1965* (Colombo: Associated Newspapers, 1965), 9–14.

29. Baldev Raj Nayar, *Minority Politics in the Punjab* (Princeton: Princeton Univ. Press, 1966), 181, 194–95; Balraj Puri, "Hindu Backlash Caused Akali Rout," *Economic and Political Weekly* (Bombay), Mar. 27, 1971, pp. 709–10; J. C. Anand, "Punjab Politics: A Survey (1947–65)," in Iqbal Narain, ed., *State Politics in India* (Meerut: Meenakshi Prakashan, 1967), 242–43.

Subethnic divisions fit easily into accepted conceptions of party factions, one basis for which is often said to be "affinity based on . . . common origins."[30] When parties are ethnically based, subethnicity also makes a major contribution to the creation of new ethnic parties. It is possible to postulate a continuum of intragroup homogeneity-heterogeneity. The more cohesive an ethnic group is, the more likely it is that there will be only one ethnic party; the more fragmented, the more likely it is that more than one ethnic party will emerge.

At the more cohesive end of the continuum, groups may even resist party proliferation in the face of electoral incentives. The adoption of proportional representation in Guyana had, as we shall see in Chapter 15, no significant effect on the existing East Indian and Creole parties. It had been hoped by the British (who imposed PR) that the new electoral system might weaken Jagan's Indian support, perhaps by splitting Muslims off from Hindus. However, the migration of Indians to the West Indies long antedated the upsurge of Hindu-Muslim rivalries in India. Consequently, with the partition of India in 1947, Indian Muslims in Guyana did not become "Pakistanis," as overseas Indian Muslims elsewhere did. By the 1960s, Hindu-Muslim divisions among Guyanese Indians were no longer very prominent; Hinduism and Islam merely represented "alternative ways of being Indian."[31]

It might be said that submerging these residual differences was required because neither Indians nor Creoles could afford a party split while the other group remained solidly committed to only one party. This is true as far as it goes. Political interest and the overriding Creole-Indian cleavage reinforced the insignificance of the Hindu-Muslim division. Yet it is also true that, at the fragmented end of the continuum, ethnic groups have split into two or more parties, based in large part on subethnicity. Such splits have occurred even when it was manifestly contrary to the political interest of the group to do so. In 1977, for example, there was a party split among Indians in Fiji right after their party had won the largest number of seats in parliament.[32]

The Yoruba represent a conspicuous case of subethnic schism. A composite people, the Yoruba fought a number of internecine wars in the nineteenth century, and their divisions along lines of ancestral city con-

30. Raphael Zariski, "Party Factions and Comparative Politics: Some Preliminary Observations," *Midwest Journal of Political Science* 4 (Feb. 1960): 27–51, at 35.
31. Chandra Jayawardena, *Conflict and Solidarity in a Guianese Plantation* (London: Athlone Press, 1963), 23.
32. R. S. Milne, *Politics in Ethnically Bipolar States* (Vancouver: Univ. of British Columbia Press, 1981), 73–74.

tinued into the twentieth. The Action Group was a Yoruba party, but it was riven by differences between its leader, Obafemi Awolowo, a member of the prosperous Ijebu subgroup, and Samuel L. Akintola, an Ogbomosho. The differences did not concern merely subethnic rivalries, though the Ijebu are an especially dynamic and often disliked Yoruba subgroup. When the Action Group split in 1962, there were strong elements of subethnicity in the lines along which the party broke.[33] The effect of this split was greatly to diminish Yoruba power, for each of the two successor parties became a junior partner in alliance with parties of other ethnic groups. Indeed, a minor theme in the split was whether the Yoruba should line up with the North or the East. Here overall ethnic interest took a back seat because the Yoruba were at the fragmented end of the cohesion continuum.

So, for that matter, are the Malaysian Chinese, divided since independence into a variety of parties. The fragmentation has reduced their political effectiveness. The divisions relate to province of origin in China, education in English or Chinese, social class, and state of origin in Malaysia. For example, Hakkas and Hainanese, the latter often treated badly in Malaysia, have been disproportionately affiliated with left-wing Chinese parties.[34] Differences of this sort are fortified by radically different views among Chinese about how legitimate Malay preeminence is and how overtly a Chinese party should pursue Chinese ethnic interests. Periodically, there have been calls for demonstrations of "Chinese unity," but the prominence of subethnic cleavages among the Malaysian Chinese insures that their party support is more fractionated than that of the Malays, whatever their political interests may dictate.

In the middle range of the continuum of intragroup homogeneity-heterogeneity, there is perhaps more consistency between the interests of an ethnic group and its proclivity to produce one or more than one ethnic party. Where subethnic fissures exist but do not run very deep, those who begin to play on them to form separate ethnic parties may find

33. For a concise view of the split, see Walter Schwarz, *Nigeria* (New York: Praeger, 1968), 130–31, 273–75. See also Richard L. Sklar and C. S. Whitaker, Jr., "The Federal Republic of Nigeria," in Gwendolen M. Carter, ed., *National Unity and Regionalism in Eight African States* (Ithaca: Cornell Univ. Press, 1966), 71. For the importance of subethnicity among the Yoruba, see David D. Laitin, "Religion and Ancestral City Among the Yoruba: A Study in the Rise and Persistence of Ethnicity" (unpublished paper, Univ. of California, San Diego, Oct. 1978).

34. Michael Stenson, "The Urban Bases of Communist Revolt in Malaya" (unpublished paper presented at American Council on Learned Societies Research Conference on Communist Revolution, St. Croix, V.I., Jan. 24–28, 1973), 6–7.

themselves subjected to sharp accusations of splitting the ethnic group, contrary to its interest. Where modest subethnic divisions exist but where, on the other hand, a split would not necessarily weaken the political position of the group, intraethnic party competition often emerges.

A considerable number of cases is consistent with these generalizations. Divisions among the Ibo ran less deep than those among the Yoruba. Neither could "afford" a party split, but whereas the Yoruba party split anyway, the Ibo in the 1960s never did.[35] On the other side, groups with significant majorities can afford a second party, and often they produce one. The Sinhalese, the Burmans and Northern Sudanese before military rule, and the Hindus in Mauritius all have had lively intraethnic party competition.[36] In Mauritius, it was largely caste that divided the Hindu parties. In the Sudan, sectarian and regional differences, coupled with divergent views toward Egypt, formed the basis of party proliferation. In Burma, policy differences were more important. A variety of overlapping cleavages spurred the competition in Sri Lanka. But in each case the luxury of more than one ethnic party could be indulged because, despite conflict with other groups, these groups formed strong electoral majorities. As Simmons notes for Mauritius, party competition among the Hindus emerged as soon as it was clear that a Hindu party would win a safe majority in any event. Then the question became "which Hindus?"[37] and caste differences surfaced.

When ethnic parties split off from multiethnic parties, they often proceed (as I noted earlier) in an anticipatory way, before the development of a contentious ethnic issue. This is not usually true when intragroup party competition begins. Ethnic parties that split off from multiethnic parties fear that if they fail to do so, new, ethnically based competitors will preempt their position. Hence, they must move early. The emergence of more than one party per group, however, encounters the opposite danger, that group members will accuse leaders of the new party of needlessly dividing the group. Breach of unity is a particularly potent

35. For a discussion of the relation of Ibo group structure to Ibo politics, see Howard Wolpe, "Port Harcourt: Ibo Politics in Microcosm," *Journal of Modern African Studies* 7 (Apr. 1969): 469–93, at 487.

36. Adele Smith Simmons, *Modern Mauritius: The Politics of Decolonization* (Bloomington: Indiana Univ. Press, 1982), 141, 149, 160, 175; Robert O. Collins and Robert L. Tignor, *Egypt and the Sudan* (Englewood Cliffs, N.J.: Prentice-Hall, 1967), 147–64; Donald Eugene Smith, *Religion and Politics in Burma* (Princeton: Princeton Univ. Press, 1966), 235–43; Wriggins, *Ceylon,* 106–24.

37. "Politics in Mauritius Since 1934," 361–62.

charge when it applies to a backward group that already feels itself to be weak in those attributes that are necessary for intergroup competition. Consequently, intragroup party proliferation usually awaits the emergence of an ethnic issue that spurs party formation and assures the new party some following.

Such an issue generally relates to intergroup relations. Unless party proliferation is practically ordained by the existence of sharp subethnic divisions, the pivotal event at the point of intraethnic party formation is usually an accusation that the existing ethnic party has sold out group interests by its excessive moderation toward other ethnic groups.

The history of Sri Lanka contains vivid examples of intragroup party proliferation that show the interplay of ethnic issues and subethnic cleavages. At independence in 1948, the country was ruled by the United National Party (UNP), mainly Sinhalese in support but containing a few Tamil members. In addition to the Left parties, there was also a small Tamil Congress and a Ceylon Indian Congress representing, respectively, Ceylon Tamils and Indian Tamils.[38]

The Tamil Congress split first, over the question of citizenship for the Indian Tamils. Shortly after independence, the UNP introduced legislation to deprive the Indian Tamils of citizenship and the right to vote. Although the Ceylon Tamils had little contact with the immigrant Indian Tamil community (the two reside in quite separate areas), the citizenship and franchise laws were viewed as foreshadowing second-class citizenship for all non-Sinhalese. Despite these apprehensions, the Tamil Congress leader, G. G. Ponnambalam, joined the cabinet. Another group in his party remained in opposition and became the nucleus of the Federal Party, a party that advocated a federal state to maximize Tamil interests in the North and East, where Tamils are concentrated. For many years, the Tamil Congress consistently opposed a federal solution to Sri Lanka's ethnic problems, arguing that the Tamils could achieve more by applying pressure at the center.

The belief that the Tamil Congress had sold out the interests of the Indian Tamils spurred the formation of the Federal Party. But many other forces were also at work. Before independence, there had been differences within the party over the exact shape of the proposals made by the

38. Wriggins, *Ceylon*, 105. The Ceylon Tamils are descendants of migrants from South India hundreds and even thousands of years ago. So-called Indian Tamils migrated much more recently. Here, however, our concern is with the Ceylon Tamils. This account of party competition among the Sinhalese and the Ceylon Tamils is based both on the Wriggins book and on interviews I conducted in Sri Lanka in 1968.

party to the Soulbury Commission that drafted the independence constitution. Intertwined with these differences were resentments about Ponnambalam's peremptory style of leadership. Then, too, the Christian minority among the Ceylon Tamils divided, Catholics tending to support Ponnambalam, whose brother was a priest, Protestants tending to support the Federal Party leader, S. J. V. Chelvanayakam, a Protestant.

For a time, the Tamil Congress remained ascendant. But in 1956 the UNP shifted its position on the language issue and began to advocate that Sinhala alone should become the official language. The Tamils who had previously cooperated with the UNP were discredited, and the balance of power in the Tamil community shifted from the Tamil Congress to the Federal Party. In the 1956 election, Ponnambalam alone, of all the Tamil Congress candidates, retained his seat. The Federal Party emerged with a substantial majority in Tamil areas, including the Tamil portions of the Eastern Province, which the Congress had failed to penetrate. From then on, the same pattern of Federal Party ascendancy prevailed until the Congress and the Federalists finally merged in the early 1970s.

The emergence of party competition among the Ceylon Tamils illustrates very well the mutually reinforcing character of policy differences regarding the appropriate Tamil response to Sinhalese demands, differences of leadership style, and differences of religious and regional—subethnic—affiliation. The precipitating issues were discrimination against the Indian Tamils and the advisability of joining the UNP government, but the split was sustained by all of these conditions.[39]

On the Sinhalese side, there was a comparable split, fostered by a comparable set of converging conditions. The UNP had embraced a variety of organizations, one of which was the Sinhala Maha Sabha, an association representing Sinhalese Buddhist interests. Its leader was S.W.R.D. Bandaranaike, scion of an illustrious family that apparently regarded itself as superior in status to the family of D. S. Senanayake, leader of the UNP and prime minister at independence. When it became

39. It should be noted that the Ceylon Tamils are a minority of only 11 percent—though they sought the support of the largely Tamil-speaking Ceylon Moors (another 5 percent). Yet, if the Tamil community could ill afford division, inhibitions on splitting the Tamil vote could be overcome by the strength of personal animosity toward Ponnambalam, the sense that the Tamil Congress really had sold out the birthright of the Tamils, and the fact that the Ceylon Tamils were, for the most part, territorially concentrated. Under a first-past-the-post electoral system, territorial concentration meant that a slight but consistent edge in competition for the Tamil vote would give the Federal Party a disproportionately large parliamentary delegation and so free it from any real responsibility for having weakened the power of the Tamils by dividing their vote.

clear that Senanayake was grooming a member of his own family to be his successor, Bandaranaike joined the opposition and formed his own Sri Lanka Freedom Party. This was in 1951.

As leader of the Maha Sabha, Bandaranaike had associated himself with the claims of segments of the Sinhalese community that had grievances against both the English-speaking, disproportionately Christian elite and the Tamil minority.[40] Language issues were part of his differences with the UNP leadership, committed as it was to a gradual transition to Sinhala and Tamil for official purposes. Nevertheless, these issues were not prominent at the time of the split, and Bandaranaike's party, the SLFP, did not gain broad support until language issues became prominent. In the 1952 election, the SLFP won nine seats to the UNP's majority of fifty-four.

In the years following, however, Bandaranaike dropped his support for parity between Sinhala and Tamil, and he espoused the Buddhist cause with increasing fervor. Ultimately, the UNP was forced to declare its support for a policy of official status for Sinhala, to the exclusion of Tamil, and to welcome the new Buddhist political activism. The UNP shift cost it all of its Tamil support, but without offsetting Sinhalese gains. In 1956, the SLFP, in coalition with a number of Left parties, rode to power on a landslide of Sinhalese ethnic sentiment.

Clearly, divisive ethnic issues were entangled with family rivalries and leadership aspirations. So, too, were Sinhalese subethnic cleavages. As indicated earlier, the UNP command had offended leaders of the Salagama community, who transferred their loyalty to the SLFP. Bandaranaike was also able to tap low-caste resentment at Goyigama domination of the UNP; on the whole, non-Goyigama Buddhist priests lent their support to the SLFP, while Goyigama priests tended to favor the UNP. There were other factors as well, such as Bandaranaike's astute cultivation of locally influential Sinhalese elites: *ayurvedic* physicians, Sinhala-educated teachers, and village headmen.

In both the Sinhalese and Tamil cases, the ethnic issues that formed the cutting edge of intragroup party competition involved the accusation of a basic sacrifice of group interests by the established ethnic party. In both, the new ethnic party took a more extreme stand on divisive inter-ethnic issues. This gave the established ethnic party a choice. It could

40. On the movement against the English-speaking elite, see Donald L. Horowitz, *Coup Theories and Officers' Motives: Sri Lanka in Comparative Perspective* (Princeton: Princeton Univ. Press, 1980), chap. 2.

adhere to its former, moderate position, at the risk of losing considerable support, or it could cover its flank by adjusting its position to meet the competition. The Tamil Congress did the former and never regained its previous ascendancy. The UNP, however, saw quickly that Sinhalese Buddhist feeling was strong, and it changed its position on ethnic issues dramatically. In the first years after 1956, segments of the UNP became quite anti-Tamil. This in turn solidified the position of the Federal Party on the other flank, for it gave evidence that both major Sinhalese parties stood for an unyielding policy of Sinhalese exclusivism. However, the shift in UNP position also gave rise to a lively and enduring intra-Sinhalese party competition. Beginning with the 1956 election, the UNP and SLFP, sometimes in coalition with smaller parties, have alternated in office no fewer than six times.

The Sri Lanka materials show very clearly the centrifugal character of intraethnic party competition. They also, of course, tend to confirm the apprehensions of ethnic party leaders that their moderation in interethnic relations will be rewarded by members of their own group with the formation of a competing party that takes a more unyielding position. Apprehensions, however, are one thing—a competing party already in existence is another. If the formation of a competing party is merely apprehended, party leaders can still take risks for the sake of interethnic harmony. Statesmanship is not precluded. But if party competition is already keen, the obstacles to interethnic accommodation may prove insurmountable.

This certainly seemed true in Sri Lanka. The 1956 election polarized Sinhalese and Tamil opinion. For nearly a decade thereafter, no Tamil entered the government. Sinhala Only legislation was passed by the Bandaranaike government shortly after it took office, with few safeguards for the Tamils. Tamil protests were met with Sinhalese violence in 1956 and again in 1958, when most of the island was subjected to a wave of killing. An attempt by Bandaranaike to compromise Sinhalese-Tamil differences with the Federal Party leader in 1957 was thwarted by an onslaught from the formerly conciliatory UNP, from Buddhist monks, and from Sinhalese activists. As the Tamils were increasingly excluded from the public life of the country, the Federal Party turned to tactics of peaceful noncooperation, culminating in a two-year state of emergency in Tamil areas. On both sides, intraethnic party competition had produced a politics of outbidding on ethnic demands that made reconciliation difficult.

Much the same process could be traced for intragroup competition (particularly of the two-party variety) in other countries, such as the Sudan and Burma, where the results were even more disastrous.[41] The 1960 election in Burma was rather like the 1956 election in Sri Lanka, resulting in a victory for Burmese ethnic sentiment that spurred secessionist insurrections among the various non-Burman groups. Sudanese party competition also gave a fillip to secessionist warfare. In the early 1950s, the two main Northern Sudanese parties had begun to compete for Southern votes. The Liberal Party, a Southern party, sought an alliance with one of the Northern parties. All of this was quickly undone in the first flush of divisive demands. Neither of the major Northern parties proved willing or able to respond to Southern fears of domination. As in Sri Lanka, a policy of ethnic exclusion gave rise to a Federal Party, which captured nearly all the Southern parliamentary seats in the 1958 election. The ultimate result of centrifugal competition was the civil war that began in 1963 and lasted nearly a decade.

In short, if there are two groups, each represented by one party, stalemate results, with all the consequences described for Guyana and Trinidad. But if intraethnic competition provides each ethnic group with its own two-party system, the centrifugal character of the competition may so increase the distance between the positions of the groups as to propel them toward violent outcomes, including secession.

Figure 3 depicts the tendency of intragroup competition to widen the gap between the positions of the groups. Here is another reason for the opinion, commonly expressed in deeply divided societies, that ethnic differences were relatively mild until the politicians went to work on them. In a sense, this popular impression is quite correct, for this is one of the points at which it can be seen just how big a difference party politics does make in ethnic conflict.

Party competition, however, can cut both ways. In Sri Lanka, the outcome so far has been more moderate than in Burma or the Sudan, stopping short of a full Tamil attempt at secession. This, too, can be explained by intense competition. At times, the Sinhalese parties, having

41. For Burma, see Smith, *Religion and Politics in Burma*, 235–43. For the Sudan in the 1950s and '60s, see Mohamed Omer Beshir, *The Southern Sudan: Background to Conflict* (London: C. Hurst, 1968); Collins and Tignor, *Egypt and the Sudan*, 147–64; Keith Kyle, "The Southern Problem in the Sudan," *The World Today* 22 (Dec. 1966): 512–20; George W. Shepard, Jr., "National Integration and the Southern Sudan," *Journal of Modern African Studies* 4 (Oct. 1966): 193–212; Joseph Oduho and William Deng, *The Problem of the Southern Sudan* (London: Oxford Univ. Press, 1963); I. William Zartman, *Government and Politics in Northern Africa* (New York: Praeger, 1963), chap. 7.

FIGURE 3.   Party Distances under Conditions of
Intraethnic Competition and No Competition

Ethnically Based Parties, One Per Group

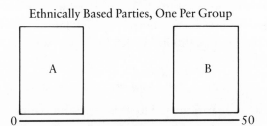

Ethnically Based Parties, Two Per Group

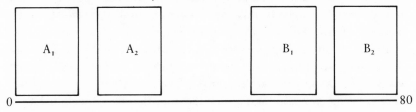

divided the Sinhalese vote, have had to bid for Tamil support—or anticipated they might have to do so. For a long period, this kept the Tamil
parties closely attuned to the parliamentary system and served to counter
the centrifugal force of intragroup electoral competition. The possibility
remained open that Tamil demands might be met within the framework
of a government based on interethnic coalition.

This is the other side of proliferating parties. Where there is more
than one party per group, it may become difficult for any one party to
gain power alone. If so, interethnic coalitions may be necessary, just as
they might if there were several main groups, each represented by one
ethnic party. Moreover, fluidity is introduced by the unpredictability of
electoral outcomes. When an ethnic group is represented by two or more
parties competing for its votes, election results need not be a straight
reflection of ethnic demography. There is the possibility of three- or four-
way contests, plurality victories, and perhaps disproportionate minority
representation. All of this can mitigate the census quality of elections.

Intraethnic party competition can thus be ambivalent in its consequences. Where there are two main parties per group, competition is
conducive to a politics of intraethnic outbidding.[42] Alternatively, the

42. I emphasize here the two-party character of the competition, which is very common, because the splintering of a group's support in many different directions has rather
different effects, as I shall show in Chapter 10 with respect to the Malaysian Chinese.

allegiances of the electorate may be distributed in such a way as to foster a politics of interethnic bargaining. Both tendencies, in fact, can coexist—the one manifested primarily before elections, the other after. This, however, puts us a bit ahead of ourselves, for it launches us into a consideration of interethnic coalitions, which forms the next chapter.

From Tripolar to Bipolar:
Reducing the Number of Contestants

I have intimated at various points that a system with only two ethnic parties, one per group, is especially conflict prone. Now I want to make this more explicit by pursuing the notion of fluidity of outcome introduced a moment ago. In this case, however, fluidity derives from the existence of three rather than two main groups.

The implications of tripolarity should by now be apparent. The sense of clear-cut exclusion and inclusion is likely to be less absolute than where there are only two ethnic parties. Three parties create the possibility of rotating coalitions and with it the hope that being excluded today does not necessarily mean being excluded indefinitely. Bifurcation, however, provides good reason for the excluded minority party to depart from the electoral road to power—since that road in fact does not lead to power. Such a party may turn to extreme strategies, as indeed the Guyanese opposition did in the period between Jagan's reelection in 1961 and his defeat in 1964.

On this score, it is instructive to compare the experience of Guyana with that of its neighbor, Surinam, similarly composed ethnically except that Surinam has a 15 percent Javanese population and some smaller minorities in addition to its Creoles (more than 30 percent) and East Indians (about 37 percent).[43] From 1966 to 1973, the Javanese, represented by two parties, provided a degree of flexibility in the party system by alternately aligning with Creole or Indian parties to form governments. From 1966 to 1969, the major East Indian party found itself in opposition, but it then displaced the major Creole party in power from 1969 to 1973. While this fluidity prevailed, Surinam had none of Guyana's ethnic violence and instability.

In 1973, however, a serious change occurred. The various parties united into two clear-cut ethnic clusters, one of them embracing the Creole parties and a Javanese party, the other comprising the East Indian

43. See Edward Dew, "Surinam's Balance of Power Politics" (unpublished paper presented at the 1977 annual meeting of the International Studies Association).

parties and another Javanese party. Between them, these two clusters won all the seats in the 1973 election, resulting for the first time in clear-cut bifurcation: with the Javanese split, there were no Creoles on the opposition benches and no Indians on the government benches. The result was a dramatic increase in conflict and the use of violence by the excluded Indian party. When Surinam's politics was tripolar, it was more moderate than when it turned bipolar.

In point of fact, there seems to be a strong tendency for three-group ethnic party systems to reduce themselves to two. Where this occurs, the two parties are organized along the broadest line that cuts through the whole polity. Typically, this is North versus South, but there is no reason why it might not be Muslim versus Christian or indigene versus immi-grant. The main impetus for this development is the need to aggregate support, as predictably as possible, in order to form a government under conditions of majoritarian democracy.

There are two elements here: the requirement of a majority and the desire that the majority be stable and dependable. The former leads to the formation of coalitions among the parties—if there are three main parties, then probably two-against-one. A coalition will produce the needed majority. But that is no guarantee that the same coalition will be formed next time. The *ad hoc* coalitions that are likely under a tripolar system tend to prove ephemeral. Hence, the desire for a predictable, stable majority leads to attempts to reduce the number of parties so one party can form a government and coalitions will not be necessary. Need-less to say, the reduction does not always occur—it did not, for example, in Benin—but quite often it does.

The reduction to two also signifies something more important than the search for a stable parliamentary majority. It generally reflects the emergence of a specially strong antipathy between two of the three main groups: Hausa and Ibo in Nigeria, Bakongo and Mbochi in the Congo, Creole and Indian in Surinam. The third group, often politically weaker or less cohesive to begin with, increasingly becomes a marginal partici-pant in the struggle and is ultimately pressed to take sides. This is pre-cisely what happened to the Yoruba in Nigeria, the Vili in the Congo, and the Javanese in Surinam. When this occurs, the reduction to two parties greatly solidifies the emerging sense of bipolarity and the ineluc-tability of the lines of tension.

Sometimes the first step in the reductive process is actually an *increase* in the number of parties. This happens if one of the three main groups is less cohesive than the others, as the Javanese proved to be in Surinam and as the Yoruba did in Nigeria. As the other two groups solidify their support behind their two ethnic parties, the less cohesive group continues to spread its support among two or more parties (Surinam), or it may actually split into two parties where formerly it was represented by one (Nigeria). Either way, the two competing parties of the less cohesive group are likely to be mutually hostile, and so it is natural that each of them will link up with the party of one of the other two groups. Hence, the third group ends up on both sides. This process is depicted in the following diagram, in which the letters stand for the respective ethnic groups:

Parties: A Party, B Party, C_1 Party, C_2 Party

Alignments: A Party + C_1 Party versus B Party + C_2 Party

At this point, the stage is set for bifurcation. With the less cohesive Group C split, the other two groups become the only significant antagonists.

An alternative route to the same result begins with three ethnic parties and has the two largest groups competing for the adherence of the third. One of these contestants ultimately succeeds, absorbs the third party, and reduces the number of parties to two. This was the course followed in Congo (Brazzaville).[44]

However it occurs, the reduction of the contesting parties to two saps party maneuvering of all flexibility. From then on, the sights of each ethnic party are fixed, not on a quest for coalition partners but on the struggle to defeat, and even destroy, the other ethnic party. This, then, is a most important change within ethnic party systems. For this reason, change from three to two ethnic parties is likely to be the harbinger of even more drastic change. Ethnic party systems often give way to something else, especially once the number of ethnic parties is reduced to two. Avoiding bifurcation may well be an important goal of ethnic policy.

CHANGE TO OTHER SYSTEMS

Ethnic parties and party systems are often building blocks of other regimes. It is easy to see why, once the character of two-party ethnic party

44. On the common tendency for three to become two in a conflict situation, see Coral Bell, *The Conventions of Crisis* (London: Oxford Univ. Press, 1971), 64.

systems is clear and the likely direction of changes within ethnic party systems is known.

Since two-party ethnic party systems consign the minority party to perennial minority status, they generate keen dissatisfaction among members of the excluded group. Since such systems are usually suffused with tension and violence, the satisfaction of leaders of even the majority party is tempered by the threat of instability. By and large, the initiative for change inheres in these two sets of sentiments, and they also suggest the respective directions the change will probably take.

If leaders of the ruling party genuinely aim to reduce tension, or if they use ethnic instability as a pretext to limit party rivalry, they are likely to move toward a one-party system. Sometimes one-party systems emerge as a result of rigged elections under the guise of continuing democratic party rivalry (Guyana and Sierra Leone after 1968). Sometimes the electoral process is abruptly terminated, with the losing party dissolved or merged in the interest of "national unity" (Congo [Brazzaville], 1959–63; Togo, 1958–63). One-party systems are a common outgrowth of ethnic party systems, as I shall explain in Chapter 10.

The same result—an authoritarian regime that reflects the interests of ethnic groups previously represented by one of the ethnic parties—can also be achieved by military intervention. Coups have indeed demolished ethnic party systems, again typically after tense, polarizing elections. This is a subject that will receive full-dress consideration in Chapter 12.

One thing is already clear at this point. Regardless of whether an ethnic party system falls victim to civilian or military authoritarianism, whether party rivalry is suppressed by those who have already captured power through the party or by those who have been shut out of power, an ethnic party system is highly vulnerable to being transformed into an authoritarian but no less ethnically partial regime.

There is, however, another possible transformation for an ethnic party system—to a regime at once less authoritarian and less ethnically exclusive than military and single-party regimes are apt to be. I am referring here to a party system composed of both ethnic parties and multiethnic coalitions.

These, then, are the three principal directions in which ethnic party systems seem likely to move: toward single-party regimes that conceal their limited ethnic base, toward military regimes that do the same, and toward more fluid party arrangements that encourage the formation of multiethnic parties and coalitions even while ethnic parties remain. Only the last of these possibilities is really deserving of the name "party system." It stands at least a chance of breaking the stalemate that ethnic party systems produce. Not surprisingly, multiethnic parties are the strongly preferred option of political leaders who value both ethnic harmony and democratic party competition. But it remains to be seen whether, in a deeply divided society, multiethnic parties and coalitions can put back together what ethnic party systems have helped pull apart.

CHAPTER NINE

Multiethnic Coalitions

On the face of it, there is much to commend the commonsense view that parties and coalitions that reach across ethnic lines, embracing the various groups in conflict, will somehow have the capacity to bridge ethnic differences. There are, to begin with, the deep failings of ethnic party systems, the centrifugal character of competition within them, and the feelings of exclusion that are fostered when the party of one group is in power indefinitely and the party of another is in opposition indefinitely. Violence in Guyana, Congo (Brazzaville), Zanzibar, Pakistan, Sierra Leone, and Guinea, among others, can be traced to the ascendancy of one ethnic party over another. Secessionist movements in Nigeria, the Sudan, Burma, and Chad owed much of their impetus to the changing fortunes of ethnic parties, to intraethnic party competition (with its customary ethnic outbidding) pushed to extremes, or to the dissolution of party ties that extended across ethnic lines.

Multiethnicity is the term I shall apply to ties across ethnic lines, even if there are only two ethnic groups involved. Multiethnicity in party organization presumably requires mutual restraint and reciprocal concessions. It may be accompanied by the sobering responsibility for governing a divided society. Compromise policies may emerge; feelings of exclusion may give way to a sense of power sharing. The apparent decline of a multiethnic party or coalition is typically received with popular expressions of deep foreboding and has been the occasion for outbreaks of ethnic rioting in Malaysia, the Sudan, Zaire, and various Indian states. If ethnic parties frequently exacerbate conflict, perhaps parties built on multiethnic foundations will have the incentive and the power to alleviate ethnic tensions. That, at all events, is the promise of multiethnic organization.

These expectations are not necessarily misplaced, but they are too sweeping. Multiethnic arrangements come in several packages. Their properties vary with such central features as how and why they are formed, whether they are intended to be permanent, whether the component parties are fused or remain organizationally separate, and whether the multiethnic party is also a single party or faces electoral competition.

Group relations in multiethnic party settings can be placed readily along a spectrum, according to the nature and duration of the parties' commitments and the organizational form appropriate to each arrangement. First of all, there is the *coalition of convenience*, fostered by little or nothing beyond the necessity for ethnic parties to form a government. Next, there is the coalition of mixed convenience and commitment, hereafter called *coalition of commitment*, again catalyzed by the need to form a government but also by some hope of having a beneficial impact on ethnic conflict. Beyond this, there is the *permanent coalition of ethnic parties*, also a blend of conviction and convenience. It is formed before elections, runs a single slate of candidates, and, in principle, survives even electoral defeats. Hereafter, I shall also call permanent multiethnic coalitions *alliances*, to distinguish them from post-election coalitions. Finally, there is the *multiethnic party*, lacking organizationally separate ethnic components, though ethnic factions can generally be identified and ethnic blocs may move in and out of the party. In addition to them, but not properly placed along the same spectrum, there is the *multiethnic single party*. Its existence implies nothing about its commitments regarding ethnic problems.

Leaving multiethnic parties for later consideration, what separates the various forms of multiethnic coalition is their approach to the electoral process. In terms of the coherence of their effort to link the electoral fortunes of their component parties, there is a gradation from coalitions of convenience to coalitions of commitment to single-slate alliances. The gradation corresponds roughly to three levels of involvement: the pooling of seats alone, the pooling of seats and of some votes, and the complete pooling of seats and votes that is implied by the single slate. These three levels of involvement are produced by different conditions and tend to produce different effects. The import of these differences can be appreciated in a preliminary way by a glimpse first at the polar types and then at the intermediate type. The basic characteristics are presented graphically in Table 5.

Partners in coalitions of convenience have fought the election separately and have usually taken separate, often mutually inconsistent, po-

TABLE 5   TYPES OF MULTIETHNIC COALITIONS

Type	Goal	Timing	Electoral Method	Parties' Ethnic Policy Positions
Convenience	Form government only	Formed after election	Separate slates: Pool seats	Independent, often incompatible
Commitment	Form government and reduce conflict	Negotiated before but formed after election	Separate slates: Pool seats and some votes	Independent, some compromise
Alliance	Form government, reduce conflict, and contest elections	Formed before election; in principle, permanent	Single slate: Pool seats and all votes	Coordinated, more extensive compromise and adjustment

sitions on ethnic issues, even if they reached some form of no-contest agreement or put forward a number of joint candidacies.[1] They enter the coalition as independent entities, their relations governed by reciprocity, by the bargain they strike. They leave when reciprocity fails or when the benefits of the association begin to decline or the costs rise. The transitory character of such coalitions affects the positioning of parties not embraced in the coalition. These do not, in general, freeze themselves into a posture of permanent opposition, for they quite often must regard themselves as plausible candidates for inclusion in some similar coalition in the future.

Permanent multiethnic coalitions—alliances—fight elections as a unit, with a single slate and a single program. To be sure, the program

1. This is common among prospective coalition partners. See Sven Groennings, "Patterns, Strategies, and Payoffs in Norwegian Coalition Formation," in Sven Groennings, E. W. Kelley, and Michael Leiserson, eds., *The Study of Coalition Behavior* (New York: Holt, Rinehart & Winston, 1970), 74.

Unless otherwise specified, the electoral system assumed in the remainder of this chapter is a first-past-the-post (non-proportional representation, non-runoff) parliamentary system.

may leave room for disagreement on the main ethnic issues, and candidates may depart from it quietly as ethnic constituency requirements dictate. In the nature of things, agreement in advance of election, especially on a recurrent basis, must be more thoroughgoing and more centrally directed than agreement achieved afresh after each election. Relationships between politicians of the respective groups will presumably vary, depending on whether permanent arrangements are intended. If they are, the ethnic policy positions of the partners may have to be more compatible than if the coalition is not intended to be permanent. Likewise, the scope of matters touched on in those relations will have to be broader in an alliance; it may be necessary to devise mechanisms for handling ethnically contentious issues. By the same token, parties outside an alliance may react differently from parties outside a temporary coalition, positioning themselves in clear-cut opposition to the alliance rather than leaving the way open for their own participation in a coalition that may succeed the present one.

It is easy to see where the coalition of commitment fits in here. Like the coalition of convenience, it is temporary. The parties run candidates on their own tickets and retain their separate organizational identity. Like the alliance, however, the coalition of commitment is formed with a view to moderating conflict. It is formed afer an election in which the parties have helped each other's candidates in multiethnic constituencies. They do this, in part, because they have agreed on at least some policy compromises. Still, the linchpin of the coalition is reciprocity, and the arrangement lasts only as long as it serves the transitory interests of the parties.

As this sketch suggests, coalitions of convenience, coalitions of commitment, and alliances are likely to have some fundamentally different properties. Variations may extend to the inducements necessary to form each type of coalition, the choice of coalition partners, the dynamics of interethnic bargaining, the likely durability of the coalition, the events that precipitate a dissolution, and the probable impact of the coalition on ethnic policy and conflict.

The task here is to explore these variations and identify the conditions that underpin the various possible arrangements. In this chapter, the focus is on coalitions—of convenience and commitment—in which the partners retain their separate electoral identities. The next chapter deals with multiethnic alliances and multiethnic parties (including single parties), in which the partners submerge their separate electoral identities in a single slate.

In examining the conditions underlying the various coalition arrangements, one circumstance that does not appear to be decisive is the severity of the underlying ethnic conflict. Severely divided societies are present in all the coalitional categories. This suggests a potential for coalition to mitigate conflict. The question then becomes whether the conditions fostering the various forms of coalition are subject to manipulation or whether they are simply givens, happenstance features of the political environment that no farsighted policymaker can affect by deliberate action. As we examine the emergence and durability of multiethnic coalitions, we shall certainly want to bear that question in mind.

COALITIONS OF CONVENIENCE

The tension between the electoral process and the governing process, familiar in so many political settings, affects multiethnic coalitions as well. As the need to build majorities of seats for governing pushes ethnic parties toward coalitions across ethnic lines, so the desire to win elections drives the coalition partners apart. In a divided society, votes are often best won on an ethnic basis, but governments cannot always be formed by ethnic parties alone.

The contradictory tendencies of these two imperatives are manifested in coalition behavior. Coalitions of convenience are easy to form but hard to sustain. They crumble readily under pressure. As we shall see, some of the pressure derives from the prospect of having to face elections, some from the desire of one partner to dominate the coalition.

PARTNERS IN CONFLICT:
NIGERIA, UGANDA, BENIN, PUNJAB

With this tension in mind, we shall consider four sets of multiethnic coalitions of convenience: Nigeria (1959–64), Uganda (1962–64), Benin (then Dahomey) (1957–65), and the Indian Punjab (1967–70). For each, it is possible to identify criteria for the choice of partners and sources of stress leading to dissolution. Since these were coalitions of convenience—each founded merely to gain the requisite majority to form a government—the basis of agreement on matters of ethnic substance was in each case very thin. It took little to break them up. Table 6,

TABLE 6   MULTIETHNIC COALITIONS
OF CONVENIENCE IN FOUR STATES
(minor parties omitted)

State, Period	Major Parties	Main Electoral Competitors	Main Coalition Partners	Coalition Duration (months)
Nigeria, 1959–64	NPC, AG, NCNC	NCNC vs. AG, NPC vs. AG	NPC + NCNC	54[a]
Uganda, 1962–64	UPC, KY, DP	UPC vs. DP, KY vs. DP	UPC + KY	22
Benin, 1957–65	Regional, under various names	Southwest vs. Southeast	North + 1 of South	9[b]
Punjab, 1967	Congress, Akali, Jan Sangh	Congress vs. Akali, Congress vs. Jan Sangh	Akali + Jan Sangh	8
Punjab, 1969–70	Congress, Akali, Jan Sangh	Congress vs. Akali, Congress vs. Jan Sangh	Akali + Jan Sangh	16

[a] From official inception to official dissolution. Actual dissolution occurred earlier.
[b] Average.

which provides a simplified basis for the discussion that follows, shows coalition alignments and durations.

The Nigerian coalition formed just before independence illustrates the slim basis of such coalitions.[2] The sharp differences between Hausa and Ibo that were to tear Nigeria apart within a few years were already visible. In 1945 and again in 1953, there had been anti-Ibo riots in the North. Yet, in 1959 a coalition was formed between the Northern People's Congress, in which the Hausa-Fulani were especially powerful, and the mainly-Ibo National Convention of Nigerian Citizens. This left the

2. Richard L. Sklar, *Nigerian Political Parties* (Princeton: Princeton Univ. Press, 1963), 505–12; Richard L. Sklar and C. S. Whitaker, Jr., "The Federal Republic of Nigeria," in Gwendolen M. Carter, ed., *National Unity and Regionalism in Eight African States* (Ithaca: Cornell Univ. Press, 1966), 120; Robin Luckham, *The Nigerian Military: A Sociological Analysis of Authority and Revolt, 1960–67* (Cambridge: Cambridge Univ. Press, 1971), 211–15.

predominantly-Yoruba Action Group in opposition. It was not overall group affinity or antipathy that drew the NPC and NCNC together or kept the NPC and AG apart, though there were initially good personal relations at the summit of the NPC and NCNC.

It was the competitive situation, above all, that dictated the choice of partners. Both the AG and NCNC had campaigned against the NPC in the North. The NCNC was aligned with the Northern Elements Progressive Union, a radical party whose support was circumscribed by its class-based ideology and its alignment with the NCNC, considered alien to the North. The Action Group, on the other hand, supported the United Middle Belt Congress, a non-Muslim party that sought to detach the heavily-Christian Middle Belt from the Northern Region, thereby gravely threatening the power of the North and of the NPC in the country as a whole. Whereas NEPU was seen merely as an ineffective opposition party, the UMBC was viewed by the NPC as secessionist and dangerous. Aligned with the UMBC, the Action Group naturally favored the creation of a new region for the Middle Belt, as well as a transfer of certain Yoruba areas from the North to the West. The NCNC took a more conciliatory position on these issues. In the North, the NCNC was a less serious competitor for the NPC than was the Action Group.

As between the NCNC and the Action Group, then, it was easy for the NPC to choose, and the choice was largely made before the election. Serious competitive rivalries between the NCNC and AG in the South also impeded coalition prospects between the two of them. There was a further fear that leaving the NPC out of government would mean leaving out the largest party (142 seats to the NCNC/NEPU's 89 and the AG's 73) and risking feelings of alienation all over the North.

Here, clearly, was a coalition formed on the basis of avoiding less attractive alternatives. Even at this, the formation of the government marked the high point of NPC-NCNC agreement and cooperation. The coalition took barely two years to begin crumbling.

The sources of stress in the coalition were several. A census conducted in 1962 was rigged to put the North in a minority position.[3] The regional apportionment of parliamentary seats turned on the census results. The figures were challenged, but NCNC leaders, determined to hold on to population increases reported in the East, endorsed them, touching off a dispute within the coalition. The results were then annulled, and a new

3. A good account of the census controversies is contained in Walter Schwarz, *Nigeria* (New York: Praeger, 1968), 157–64.

census was conducted in 1963. The reenumeration seemed designed to favor the North. Now the figures were rejected by NCNC leaders, but to no avail. The dispute produced tension between the coalition partners and growing anti-Ibo sentiment in the North and West.

In the meantime, the NPC had managed to consolidate its hold over the North. With defections from members of other parties, the NPC could now command an outright parliamentary majority, rather than just the plurality with which it had begun. No longer was the NPC the senior partner in the coalition—it was the only partner that counted. With the opposition Action Group split,[4] the NPC had its choice of partners from the South. There was hardly any point in propitiating a strong and intractable coalition partner like the NCNC when a weak and subservient one was available and would do just as well. Eventually the NPC chose the Akintola faction of the former Action Group to join it in a new alliance for the 1964 election.

The Nigerian coalition of convenience thus dissolved at practically the first signs of ethnic tension. When the arrangement was no longer strictly necessary to the NPC, nothing held it together. Far from moderating ethnic conflict, the Nigerian coalition provided an echo chamber for divisive issues. The coalition exaggerated the conflict and was itself vulnerable to it.

The Uganda coalition did no better.[5] Its formation bore resemblances to the formation of the Nigerian coalition of three years earlier, and its equally rapid demise also had points in common with the dissolution of the NPC-NCNC coalition.

Ugandan politics at the time of independence centered largely on the efforts of other groups to prevent the emergence of Baganda hegemony over the country. The Baganda, located in the South, overwhelmingly supported a party known as Kabaka Yekka. The Kabaka was the traditional ruler of Buganda, and Kabaka Yekka—which means "the Kabaka only"—was not merely royalist; it also stood for Baganda claims to ethnic preeminence. Outside of Buganda, especially in the North and East, the Uganda People's Congress of A. Milton Obote was built largely

---

4. See Chapter 8, above.
5. Crawford Young, *The Politics of Cultural Pluralism* (Madison: Univ. of Wisconsin Press, 1976), 247–62; Nelson Kasfir, *The Shrinking Political Arena: Participation and Ethnicity in African Politics* (Berkeley and Los Angeles: Univ. of California Press, 1976), 195–204; Cherry Gertzel, *Party and Locality in Northern Uganda, 1945–62* (London: Athlone Press, 1974); Hugh Dinwiddy, "The Search for Unity in Uganda: Early Days to 1966," *African Affairs* 80 (Oct. 1981): 501–18.

on anti-Baganda sentiment, but its support was mainly limited to Protestants. Catholics were organized into the Democratic Party.

Since many Baganda were Catholic (whereas the royal establishment of the Kabaka was Protestant), the Democratic Party was the only party to span the lines separating Baganda from non-Baganda. But just barely: in the 1962 elections, the Democratic Party won less than 10 percent of the vote in Buganda. So intense was Baganda sentiment that Kabaka Yekka won more than 80 percent of the vote and virtually all the seats in Buganda. Outside of Buganda, the UPC won more than half the seats on just over half the vote, while the DP won practically all the remainder.

As in Nigeria, there were three main parties, none with a majority nationwide. Again, the structure of electoral competition dictated the choice of partners. Again, it was clear even before the election. Although the DP had done poorly in the election in Buganda, it had nonetheless competed against KY there and against the UPC in the rest of the country. Both Kabaka Yekka and the UPC regarded the Democratic Party as their rival. Only the UPC and KY had not been competitors for votes, because neither competed in the territory of the other. These two then became partners in the coalition that took power at independence.

As in Nigeria, again, the choice of partners implied nothing about affinities between them. Quite the contrary: the UPC and KY had not competed against each other precisely because each of the two parties was the negation of the other. One stood for Baganda aspirations; the other stood against them. Since lack of competition defined the more desirable—more accurately, the less objectionable—coalition partner, this meant that the coalition would necessarily be composed of the two parties whose positions were most opposed to each other.

The consummation of the UPC-KY coalition was widely viewed as a master stroke on Obote's part, because it showed his apparent ability to bridge serious ethnic differences. When Obote made the Kabaka president of Uganda in 1963, Obote's genius for accommodation seemed confirmed.

This was all wishful thinking, for Obote was doing other things as well. Most important, he was encouraging defections from both the DP and KY to his own party. These tactics succeeded. Within a year of independence, he had an absolute majority of seats and, like the Nigerian NPC, his interest in the coalition declined precipitously thereafter. Obote also insisted on a referendum on the so-called "lost counties," parts of Buganda populated by Banyoro people who wished their territory to be returned to the jurisdiction of Bunyoro. This was a most contentious issue, and the Kabaka's prestige was implicated. Since the lost counties were populated by non-Baganda, the outcome of the vote was not really in doubt; but Obote helped it along. When the Kabaka lost the referendum, the UPC-KY coalition was at an end. Nonetheless, Obote managed to keep almost half of the KY legislators with the government when most of the Kabaka's party crossed the floor into opposition in 1964. By then Obote had nearly a two-thirds majority.

The sequel was not long in coming. Within the cabinet, a clique of Southern (Baganda and non-Baganda) ministers plotted against the Northern inner circle of Obote's confidants. Obote arrested the plotters early in 1966. He then had enacted a new constitution, which at a stroke created a new and powerful presidency for Obote and sharply reduced the special status of Buganda. The Baganda rebelled, and Obote responded with a military attack on the Kabaka's palace, routing the defenders and forcing the Kabaka into exile. In less than four years, Kabaka Yekka was a spent force, Obote and his UPC were supreme, and all coalitions were superfluous.

It was a very limited convenience that the Nigerian and Ugandan coalitions fostered. To be sure, the need for a parliamentary majority created the coalition situation. But, in both cases, electoral considerations preempted governing considerations in the choice of partners. In both, the electorally less threatening party was chosen as partner. In neither case was there a commitment to anything other than to forming the government on what seemed then to be equitable terms, given the respective strength of the parties at the moment of coalition. In both, the leading party then set out to secure an outright majority, through defections, so as to be able to dispense with the coalition. The coalition was not expected to be a durable mode of governing—it was to be undone at the earliest opportunity.

In both cases, too, the weakening of the coalition partner entailed an attempt to undermine its ethnic strength (via the census and the "lost counties" disputes), unrestrained by any conflict management procedures in the cabinet or elsewhere. Consequently, the dynamics of the coalition relationship—especially the desire to be free of it—fostered the very ethnic conflict that was at the root of the electoral cleavage that had made the coalition necessary in the first place. These two coalitions were thus not just coalitions of convenience, but of momentary convenience only.

Against the Nigerian and Ugandan backgrounds, the welter of coalitions in Benin (then Dahomey) is more easily understood.[6] As in Nigeria, three main, ethnically based parties emerged even before independence. Although their names changed frequently, their leaders remained constant: Hubert Maga in the North, Sourou Migan Apithy in the Southeast, and Justin Ahomadegbé in the Southwest.

Because of the three-way split, no one could be sure of a parliamentary majority in advance. Just as they did in Nigeria, therefore, each of the two Southern parties made efforts to compete outside of its own area. In the 1957 elections, Apithy, whose support was based on the Goun people, put up a slate to rival Maga's in the North. It did not compete effectively with Maga in his core area, consisting of the Somba people in the Northwest, but it did well among the Bariba of the Northeast. Ahomadegbé, however, tried unsuccessfully to challenge Apithy in his home area, and in later elections Apithy reciprocated by running candidates in Ahomadegbé's core area—with greater success. In 1959, Apithy's party actually outpolled Ahomadegbé's in the Southwest, though the results were later challenged. In short, the three-way split gave rise to two different kinds of party competition: intense competition in the South, with the two Southern parties invading each other's core areas; marginal competition in the North, with no invasion of Maga's core area but an occasional effort to detach his peripheral support.

These competitive patterns predict most of the coalitions that were formed. The details are intricate, but the main thrust of the interactions is familiar. A plethora of coalitions involving two of the three major parties was formed and re-formed from 1957 to 1965, all but the last of them between the Northern party and one or the other Southern party. As in Nigeria and Uganda, noncompetitors or less threatening competitors were preferred coalition partners.[7]

The Nigerian and Ugandan experience was also replicated in the relations of the coalition partners. In each case, one of the two partners sought to subordinate or eliminate the other. Recurrently, the leaders

6. Dov Ronen, *Dahomey: Between Tradition and Modernity* (Ithaca: Cornell Univ. Press, 1975), 107–30; Samuel Decalo, *Coups and Army Rule in Africa* (New Haven: Yale Univ. Press, 1976), 47–53; Decalo, "Regionalism, Politics, and the Military in Dahomey," *Journal of Developing Areas* 7 (Apr. 1973): 449–77; W. A. E. Skurnik, "The Military and Politics: Dahomey and Upper Volta," in Claude E. Welch, Jr., ed., *Soldier and State in Africa* (Evanston: Northwestern Univ. Press, 1970), 71–79.

7. For the competitive patterns, see Decalo, "Regionalism, Politics, and the Military in Dahomey," Table 1, p. 454.

discovered that it was impossible to form a government without the support of at least two of the ethnic blocs (variously organized into separate parties but occasionally under the formal umbrella of a single party). With equal regularity, however, the power of one partner was neutralized, often as the party in opposition was being brought into power to fill the position of the ousted party. The three-way split was conducive not only to coalitions of two-versus-one but to the process of squeezing out the weaker partner of the two. As in Nigeria, the availability of the third party in Benin to take the place of the undesired coalition partner catalyzed the struggle for supremacy inside the coalition. Twice, in 1963 and again in 1965, such efforts of one of the coalition partners to gain ascendancy brought on severe conflict and militiary intervention. The second time marked the beginning of a round of coups and counter-coups and the end of ethnic party coalitions.

Finally, there is the case of the Indian Punjab, divided since 1966 almost evenly between Sikhs and Hindus.[8] In the 1967 election, the Congress Party, drawing support from Sikhs and Hindus, gained only a plurality of 48 out of 104 seats in the state legislature. Like the Democratic Party in Uganda—but more effectively—Congress was the only major party spanning both ethnic groups, competing with the Akali Dal for Sikh votes and with the Jan Sangh for Hindu votes. Predictably, the parties chose not to align with their main electoral competitors. Consequently, Congress was not a participant in the coalition.[9] Instead, the Sikh Akali Dal and the Hindu Jan Sangh—their aims and programs utterly opposed—joined with the small, overwhelmingly-Sikh, Communist Party to form a coalition government.

This coalition of ethnic opposites lasted only eight months. Then, in 1969, after new elections were held, the Jan Sangh and the Akali Dal formed another coalition. Previously, the Akalis had only twenty-six seats. Now, however, they had won forty-three, and the Jan Sangh had only eight. This new plurality the Akalis promptly began to parlay into

8. Paul R. Brass, *Language, Religion and Politics in North India* (London: Cambridge Univ. Press, 1974), 357–64. See also Brass, "Coalition Politics in North India," *American Political Science Review* 62 (Dec. 1968): 1174–91.

9. It is striking that, despite the "openness, fluidity and inclusiveness" Brass found in North Indian party systems ("Coalition Politics in North India," 1189), Congress was excluded as a coalition partner. In the Punjab and other North Indian states, there was a strong Congress/non-Congress duality. The duality, which affected the choice of coalition partners, may be explained in part by Congress' electoral breadth and hence its competitive position with other parties.

an outright majority, mainly through defections from Congress.[10] This had the by-now familiar effect: it rendered the Jan Sangh superfluous as a coalition partner. In June 1970, the Jan Sangh left the government when the Akalis took an uncompromising line on an ethnic issue—namely, the control of a Punjabi-language university over certain Hindi-medium colleges.

COALITIONS WITHOUT COMPROMISE

The brittleness of coalitions of convenience in Nigeria, Uganda, Benin, and the Punjab illustrates the rather strong impetus toward ethnic exclusiveness. No sooner were the coalitions formed than efforts were afoot to undo them, even when these entailed high-risk and high-conflict strategies leading often to violence and military intervention.[11] Certainly these coalitions did not result in very much interethnic power sharing. The effects of coalitions of convenience on ethnic conflict were not much different from the effects of the ethnic parties into which the coalitions tended to decompose—except that the events leading to the dissolution of the coalition were themselves often disruptive.

A major reason for the brittleness of coalitions of convenience is the choice of partners by patterns of avoidance of electoral competition. To some extent, this reflects the fact that the parties, especially in three-way competition, readily foresee that no party will receive a majority in a forthcoming election. They then set out to arrive at tentative coalition understandings in advance of the election. This happened in Nigeria, Uganda, and sometimes in Benin and Punjab. Insofar as coalitions reflect such preelectoral understandings, the natural lines of partnership run between those parties that will not oppose each other at the polls. Preelectoral negotiations between parties in strong competition with each other are difficult. Even when coalitions are freshly formed after the elections, direct competitors have more difficulty reaching agreement than noncompetitors do—the more so when the competitors have both been striving for the privilege of exclusively representing a single ethnic group.

Because the motives for coalition formation were so minimal—any majority of seats would suffice—no attention was given to compatibility

10. *The Statesman Weekly* (Calcutta), June 7, 1969.
11. In the Indian Punjab, the central government could act as a brake on conflict, and of course no military coup was possible at the state level.

of objectives or position on the ethno-political spectrum. Since electoral-competitive concerns dominated the choice of partners, party distance could actually be a virtue. The most likely coalition partners—parties that stood the least chance of competing for the same clientele—were also those with programs completely antithetical to each other. This point is illustrated by all four cases, but perhaps most graphically by the UPC-Kabaka Yekka coalition in Uganda, which had a competitive overlap of zero.

The inevitably stormy relations produced by combining opposites in a single government were made stormier by the persistent—and related—desire of the stronger partner to rid itself of the weaker. Wherever there was a strong plurality—in Nigeria, Uganda, Punjab—the quest for a majority through defections from other parties began. Not surprisingly, the coalitions tended to be short-lived, averaging little more than a year (counting the Nigerian coalition as lasting four-and-a-half years, though it was moribund long before that). Only the Nigerian coalition endured more than two years. In no case did a coalition last through so much as a single election. This is understandable. None of these coalitions could have agreed on a program for an election, and none of the partners would have enjoyed facing its ethnic electorate while allied with ethnic antagonists. No-contest agreements before the coalition is formed are one thing; facing election as coalition partners is another.

This brings me to a crucial point, which derives from the positions of the partners. These were not coalitions of parties located at or near the center of an ethnic spectrum. On the contrary, they were coalitions of parties far apart and not interested in moving together. The whole dynamic of their relationship was to drive them toward a rapid dissolution of the coalition amidst heightening tension. The issues on which they split were various, but always reflected disagreement on basic issues of ethnic politics: the Nigerian census, the Ugandan lost counties, the Punjabi language of education. These, then, were coalitions without compromise, coalitions of convenience that rapidly turned inconvenient.

COALITIONS OF COMMITMENT

Several features distinguish the coalition of commitment from the coalition of convenience. Like the coalition of convenience, the coalition of commitment is formed because of the need to build a majority of parliamentary seats. But it also entails a measure of agreement on the terms of amicable ethnic relations—agreement absent in coalitions of convenience alone. This means that the guiding principle in the choice of partners is not solely lack of electoral competition. Party distance and party position on the ethno-political spectrum are therefore important in a way that they are not in the coalition of convenience. In this respect, the coalition of commitment resembles those European coalitions which are usually thought to reflect some minimal meeting of the minds ("Center-Left" or "Center-Right," for example) as well as of the seats.

In order to be multiethnic at all, the coalition of commitment necessarily consists of a converging ethnic Center, whereas the coalition of convenience is composed of diverging ethnic extremes. But where is the Center to be found in a society so divided? Where there is only one party per ethnic group in a deeply divided society, there is no real Center. Moreover, as we have seen, party proliferation involving intragroup competition (and the fear of it before it happens) frequently tends to have centrifugal consequences. What is required is a form of intraethnic competition that is not wholly centrifugal, so that ethnic parties can find rewards in taking moderate positions on matters of interethnic relations, hence making themselves available for coalitions of commitment.

There are times when the dynamics of party competition encourage ethnic parties to stake out differing positions along the ethnic spectrum, placing some closer to the Center than others. When this occurs and parliamentary arithmetic also encourages coalition across ethnic lines, prospects for a coalition of commitment are propitious. When do such occasions arise? Rather than answer this abstractly, it is preferable to examine in depth the formation, functioning, and dissolution of an actual coalition of commitment.

FORMING A COALITION OF COMMITMENT: SRI LANKA

The coalition that took office in Sri Lanka (then Ceylon) in 1965 called itself a "National Government." The term signified the participation of both Sinhalese and Tamils. The government was composed of the overwhelmingly dominant United National Party of Dudley Senanayake and six smaller parties, three of them also Sinhalese, two Ceylon Tamil, and one Indian Tamil. The cabinet contained a Ceylon Tamil, a member of the Federal Party, for the first time in almost a decade, and the government committed itself to find ways of healing the breach that had grown up between the two major ethnic groups of the island. This is what sets it apart from coalitions of mere convenience.[12]

The background to the coalition lay in the growing exclusion of Tamils from the public life of the country during the previous decade. In 1956, the Sri Lanka Freedom Party of S.W.R.D. Bandaranaike (in coalition with other Sinhalese parties) came to power on a promise to make Sinhala the sole official language. The Tamil response was an overwhelming electoral shift to the Federal Party, with its demands for a federal state. These developments have been described in Chapter 8.

The Federalists at first refused to confer with the Bandaranaike regime, but in 1957 Bandaranaike and the Federal Party leader, S. J. V. Chelvanayakam, negotiated a far-reaching agreement, called the B-C Pact, designed to settle outstanding Sinhalese-Tamil differences.[13] The Pact was, however, quickly abrogated by Bandaranaike under pressure from Sinhalese extremists and the opposition United National Party. In 1958, the country was engulfed in Sinhalese-Tamil rioting, and no settlement seemed possible after that.

Bandaranaike was assassinated in 1959. Elections the following year brought to power a short-lived UNP minority government, followed by new elections and an SLFP government headed by Bandaranaike's widow. Despite Federal Party support in the election, Mrs. Bandaranaike's regime was even more uncompromising with the Tamils. There was considerable favoritism in appointments of Sinhalese Buddhists.[14] Exemptions from language requirements for Tamil civil servants recruited before 1956 were ignored; those who did not demonstrate proficiency in Sinhala were denied salary increments and sometimes forced to retire. By default, these measures gave the UNP an advantage in dealing with the Federalists thereafter.

The impetus to form the coalition of 1965 arose in the first instance from conditions of party fragmentation, particularly on the Sinhalese side. Out of a total of 151 elected parliamentary seats in the 1965 elec-

12. The Sri Lanka data are derived from a series of twenty-five interviews with politicians conducted by me in Colombo in 1968. See also Robert N. Kearney, *Communalism and Language in the Politics of Ceylon* (Durham: Duke Univ. Press, 1967); Kearney, *The Politics of Ceylon (Sri Lanka)* (Ithaca: Cornell Univ. Press, 1973); H. B. W. Abeynaike, ed., *Parliament of Ceylon, 1965* (Colombo: Associated Newspapers of Ceylon, 1965).

13. The text of the B-C Pact is contained in Kearney, *Communalism and Language in the Politics of Ceylon*, 144–46.

14. For evidence, see Donald L. Horowitz, *Coup Theories and Officers' Motives: Sri Lanka in Comparative Perspective* (Princeton: Princeton Univ. Press, 1980), chaps. 2, 9.

TABLE 7   PARTIES AND SEATS AFTER
THE 1965 ELECTION IN SRI LANKA

Governing Coalition		Opposition	
United National Party[a]	66	Sri Lanka Freedom Party[a]	41
Federal Party[b]	14	Lanka Sama Samaj Party[a]	10
Sri Lanka Freedom		Communist Party[a]	4
Socialist Party[a]	5	Independents	3
Tamil Congress[b]	3		
Mahajana Eksath			
Peramuna[a]	1		
Jathika Vimukthi			
Peramuna[a]	1		
Independents	3		
Total	93[c]		58

SOURCE: Adapted from Robert N. Kearney, *The Politics of Ceylon (Sri Lanka)* (Ithaca: Cornell University Press, 1973), 42.
[a]Sinhalese parties.
[b]Tamil parties.
[c]There were, in addition, six appointed members.

tion, the UNP won 66, while the SLFP won 41. The Sinhalese Left parties captured 14 seats between them, and smaller Sinhalese parties won a total of 7. Despite the more than two-thirds Sinhalese majority in the population, no Sinhalese party approached a majority of seats, as Table 7 shows. Neither the UNP, nor the SLFP alone, nor the SLFP and the Left parties together, could form a government.

It was reasonable for the UNP to look across ethnic lines for coalition partners. The major Sinhalese parties were not plausible partners. Long-standing electoral enemies, the UNP and SLFP were unlikely allies. To this extent, just as in the coalitions of convenience we have examined, electoral-competitive considerations account for patterns of avoidance. For their part, the Left parties considered the UNP a reactionary, capitalist party, and the UNP reciprocated the hostility. The Tamil parties, by contrast, were not in significant electoral competition with the UNP, and the parties had no ideological antipathies. By itself, the Federal Party controlled a larger bloc of seats than any other party except the UNP and SLFP. The seventeen Tamil seats were attractive to the UNP as it contemplated the prospect of forming a government.

Nonetheless, the UNP was not obliged to coalesce with the Tamil

parties. With the support of three small Sinhalese parties, a few independents, and the six appointed members of the House, the UNP could have
formed a coalition government without Tamil participation. Such a government, however, would have had a very narrow majority. Since the
previous SLFP-led government had fallen on a vote of no confidence
resulting from defections, the UNP might well have feared a repetition of
the same phenomenon, had it proceeded to form a government on so
thin a majority.

From the Federal Party standpoint, the key to the coalition was the
contrasting positions of the SLFP and the UNP on matters of Sinhalese-
Tamil relations. As I suggested earlier, intragroup competition, especially of the two-party variety, tends to be centrifugal in character. So it
was as SLFP-UNP competition for the Sinhalese vote developed in the
mid-1950s. In the years following the SLFP victory of 1956, the UNP
moved to regain its Sinhalese clientele, becoming in the process extremely anti-Tamil. This posture the UNP maintained through the election of July 1960. Subsequently, however, the UNP moved away from
the extreme Sinhalese position and became generally more moderate on
ethnic issues than the SLFP.

Electoral demography played the most significant role in differentiating the ethnic positions of the two major Sinhalese parties. The proliferation of Sinhalese parties meant that neither of the two major parties
could necessarily count on a parliamentary majority even in an election
that it clearly won. The 1965 election was thus a foreseeable example of
a situation inherent in party fragmentation on the Sinhalese side. In the
election of March 1960, a somewhat similar situation had arisen. At that
time, the UNP had the largest bloc of seats, but was far short of a majority. Federal Party support was sought by the UNP, but the discussions
came to an abrupt end when the UNP rejected the Federalists' demand
for the considerable measure of local autonomy provided by the B-C
Pact. The Federalists then turned to the SLFP, which had no difficulty
renewing its commitment to the B-C pact.[15] The UNP had formed a
government, but the Federal Party voted against the UNP's Speech from
the Throne, thus insuring the downfall of that government. In the July
1960 election that followed, the Federal Party supported the SLFP, which
won a majority and formed a government by itself.

15. Both sets of negotiations in 1960 have been recounted for me in a series of interviews with UNP, Federal Party, and SLFP leaders. See also *Parliamentary Debates* (Han-
sard), House of Representatives, vol. 45, 1961–62, col. 1802–1817 (Colombo: Government Printer, 1962).

The aid of the Federal Party in the July 1960 election was a boon to the SLFP, for the Federalists had campaigned among Tamils living in Sinhalese-majority constituencies. In perhaps fifteen of these, Tamil voters were in a position to tip the scales in favor of the SLFP or the UNP, where competition between them was close. Shortly after the July 1960 election, a UNP committee suggested that greater sensitivity to Tamil interests might yield electoral benefits in such marginal constituencies.[16]

After 1960, the UNP recalculated electoral costs and benefits. The lesson of March 1960 was that, confronted with a coalition situation, the Federal Party would entertain bids on the substance of Tamil demands from the two largest Sinhalese parties. The lesson of July was that the aid of the Federal Party could be decisive, not only in putting together a coalition government after elections, but in winning seats for the UNP during the elections. The two elections together showed that single-minded devotion to the Sinhalese cause might not yield enough support to form a government. According to a leading party strategist of the time, the UNP calculated that the Tamil parties together might control as many as twenty-two seats in the North and East, which, combined with pivotal Tamil minorities in Southern constituencies, would bring the number of Tamil-controlled seats to nearly forty. If the UNP won fifty additional seats, a UNP-Tamil Congress-Federal Party coalition could count on about ninety seats, a clear majority. The UNP was determined to secure Federalist support among Tamil voters in the South and to commit the Federalists to a coalition with the UNP, preferably on a permanent basis.[17] Taken together, these two considerations—votes as well as seats—were powerful influences pushing the UNP toward the Center of the ethnic party spectrum.

The growing moderation of the UNP on ethnic issues was also fostered by the behavior of the SLFP government from 1960 to 1965. Less chastened by the punitive electoral power of the Federal Party, the SLFP regime had taken a hard line on ethnic issues, advancing the claims of Sinhalese Buddhists at the expense of Tamils, Christians of all ethnic groups, and other minorities. The fruit of this policy was an unprecedented period of unrest: strikes, protests, and civil disobedience campaigns. Unyielding implementation of Sinhala as the official language was met with a massive Tamil noncooperation movement in the North

16. Kearney, *Communalism and Language in the Politics of Ceylon*, 120–21. After the 1965 election, the SLFP likewise attributed the UNP victory to a swing of ethnic and religious minorities away from the SLFP.

17. Interview, Colombo, Aug. 20, 1968.

and East. Army and navy units occupied the Tamil areas under a state of emergency. When the Federal Party began to issue its own postage stamps, Federalist leaders were arrested. The extreme policies of the SLFP made it easier for the UNP to be at once more moderate than the SLFP and still pro-Sinhalese.[18]

The ability of the Federal Party to make moderation electorally profitable for the UNP depended on an asymmetry in intragroup competition. The Sinhalese side was fragmented, whereas the Ceylon Tamils overwhelmingly supported the Federal Party. In a Sinhalese-majority constituency, the Sinhalese vote would probably be split, but the Tamil vote could be delivered to one of the Sinhalese contestants more or less intact—provided that Sinhalese party were willing to be accommodating on Tamil issues. This magnified the influence of the Federalists beyond the small numbers of Tamils in most Sinhalese-majority constituencies. Thus, it was not ethnic demography alone, but in tandem with divergent patterns of ethnic cohesion and fragmentation, that induced UNP moderation and made the difference between what might have been a mere coalition of convenience and what turned out to be a coalition of commitment.

The Federal Party might have struck a bargain instead with the SLFP, which also needed a coalition with the Federalists in order to form a government in 1965. During the election campaign, the Federalists, although favorable to the UNP, made no final commitments about post-election coalition partners. Because it left open the possibility of coalition with the SLFP, the Federal Party reportedly lost some votes to its rival, the Tamil Congress. Among others, Catholic Tamils, who wanted the Federalists to have nothing to do with the SLFP, voted for the Tamil Congress, which was solidly committed to the UNP. Intra-Tamil compet-

18. The task of the UNP was eased even further in 1964, when the Trotskyite Lanka Sama Samaj Party joined the government and the pro-Moscow Communists offered their parliamentary support without formally joining. This made it easier for the UNP to appeal to the overwhelmingly Buddhist Sinhalese on grounds of the Marxist hostility to religion and also introduced some new, nonethnic issues into public debate. The participation of the Left parties in government made some people fearful for democracy, and the first steps the government took to nationalize the traditionally free press in 1964 temporarily submerged ethnic issues.

The potential cost of moderation was also reduced for the UNP. In the early 1960s, as a result of SLFP policy, the Christian minority among the Sinhalese attached itself firmly to the UNP. The same was true for the Salagama caste following the defection of its best-known leader, C. P. de Silva, from the SLFP in 1964. De Silva formed his own party, clearly aligned with the UNP from the outset. The more an ethnic party's support is based upon such ascriptively defined subgroups, the greater its latitude to adjust its position on interethnic relations.

itive considerations thus counseled against another bargain with the SLFP.

So, too, did Federal Party experience with the SLFP in 1960 and after. As the Federalists saw it, Mrs. Bandaranaike had dishonored the commitment she had made to them. The SLFP's anti-Tamil policies were clear as early as 1961, and parliamentarians of the UNP and FP had begun to talk. Belatedly, in 1964, Mrs. Bandaranaike had proposed the establishment of district councils, a measure long sought by the Federalists. But it was too late, and the Federal Party voted to bring down the SLFP government:

How could we support her just for the district councils when they'd acted the way they had for nine years before? They arrested us, starved our area of development funds—roads and bridges in the North came to a standstill—and tried to step on us. And then they were getting dictatorial—they wanted to take over the press. Compared to all that, the district councils were nothing. And it was just a mention in a Throne Speech—nothing concrete. We'd been waiting for the chance to throw her out, so we took it.[19]

Clearly, the Federal Party was by then more favorably disposed to dealing with the UNP, for it had staked a better claim to moderation.

Still, after the 1965 election, two sets of talks were held by the FP: one with the SLFP and its allies, one with the UNP. There is some evidence that the SLFP was prepared to concede more to the Federalists than the UNP was. Despite the temptation, there was lingering distrust of the SLFP,[20] and the fact that the Tamil Congress was bound to be aligned with the UNP government meant that a Federal Party-SLFP coalition would constantly be under Tamil Congress attack.[21] A coalition of the Federalists, the SLFP, and its Left allies would have had only a bare majority. In a likely new election, the Federal Party would have had to face the Tamil electorate as the full partner of a formerly anti-Tamil party before that party had had a chance to demonstrate its repentance for past acts of ethnic oppression.

Once the choice of dealing with the UNP was made, agreement was easily reached, largely on the basis of earlier discussions. Essentially, it

19. Interview, Colombo, July 29, 1968.
20. One view was that the Federal Party, not being "enamoured of either Sinhalese party," should deal with the party from which we can get the most." Interview, Colombo, Aug. 11, 1968. But the prevailing view was that it was "better to take less from Dudley [Senanayake], who is honest." Interview, Colombo, July 29, 1968.
21. This was a consideration heavily influential with some Federal Party leaders. Interview, Colombo, Sept. 1–2, 1968.

provided that, despite the status of Sinhala as the official language—a status conceded by the Federalists for the first time—the Tamil language would continue to be used in the Tamil North and East, and would also be acceptable for use in the courts. The Federal Party's long-standing demand for the creation of district councils was conceded by the UNP, as was a system of preferences for Tamils in land colonization schemes in Tamil areas threatened by an influx of Sinhalese settlers. For its part, the Federal Party conceded, contrary to its previous policy, that Tamil civil servants would have to be proficient in Sinhala, but those recruited before passage of the Official Language Act of 1956 would be exempt from this requirement. This was a comprehensive set of compromises on contentious ethnic issues, compromises that stamp the arrangement clearly as a coalition of commitment.

CAUSES OF COALITIONS OF COMMITMENT

It is sometimes said that elite ethnic attitudes are the major factor in interethnic accommodation. If leaders are more temperate than those they lead, they will seek ways of putting a brake on ethnic conflict. Leadership was not unimportant in Sri Lanka, but leadership alone was not decisive. The National Government was not brought into being by leaders willing to take major risks but by leaders who saw gains in the coalition.

The electoral character of the anticipated gains provides the key to ethnic compromise. Coalitions of convenience, which merely pool parliamentary seats, require no appeal to the electorate on an interethnic basis. They therefore induce no moderation of ethnic party positions, which are always geared to electoral demand. In addition to pooling parliamentary seats, the Sri Lanka coalition was based on a prior agreement to pool votes in those constituencies that had Tamil minorities. Vote pooling required the Federal Party to appeal actively to Tamil voters in behalf of the UNP, an appeal possible only if there were evidence of UNP moderation. The pooling of votes makes a fundamental difference in the nature of the coalition.

Two other catalysts of the coalition of commitment can be identified. While they can be stated in general terms, they are the kinds of conditions that are highly variable from country to country. The first has to do with group legitimacy; the second, with elite political culture in general.

Although the Indian Tamils in Sri Lanka were largely disfranchised after independence, the Ceylon Tamils had a far more secure position. Many Sinhalese, no doubt, view the Ceylon Tamils as a traditional enemy,[22] but few politicians view them as illegitimate participants in Sri Lankan government. Where, however, there are disparities in group legitimacy, particularly deriving from relatively recent immigration, it is not as easy to bring all parties into government.

The way party politics is played in Sri Lanka also facilitates arrangements like the National Government. No coalition is automatically foreclosed, except perhaps a UNP-Left coalition. In 1968, when the coalition showed signs of breaking down, partly because of SLFP opposition on a policy matter, an SLFP leader approached an influential Federalist in parliament with an offer to negotiate a new arrangement between the Federal Party and the SLFP.[23] Sri Lankan politicians sometimes underestimate the prodigious ability of their opponents to change position, but it is taken for granted that party politics is characterized by a good deal of flexibility in positions and alignments—certainly far more flexibility than characterizes the politics of ethnic parties in many severely divided societies. Both of the main Sinhalese parties had alternately taken conciliatory and unyielding positions on Tamil issues. Both were willing to talk with the Federalists, and they with both of them. There is no question about the propriety of interethnic bargaining in Sri Lanka. The phrase "What are your terms?" has been uttered on more than one occasion, without a trace of hesitation, by UNP and SLFP leaders dealing with the Federal Party[24] and later with its successor, the Tamil United Liberation Front.

No doubt, this flexibility fosters a certain cynicism in party politics:

22. The myth that best expresses this traditional ethnic opposition is the legend of Duttugemunu and Elara, folk heroes of the Sinhalese and Tamils, respectively, who fought a great battle resulting in the restoration of Sinhalese sovereignty. For the significance of the legend, see S. Arasaratnam, *Ceylon* (Englewood Cliffs, N.J.: Prentice-Hall, 1964), 52.

23. Interview, Colombo, Sept. 1–2,1968.

24. For example, a Federal Party politician stated: "The UNP leaders said, 'Reduce your terms to writing.' We did, and they said, 'Okay, we can sign them.'" Interview, Colombo, Aug. 14, 1968. Likewise, an SLFP former cabinet minister: " . . . I told Mrs. Bandaranaike we can't let this [tension] go on. I want to speak to Chelvanayakam [then the leader of the Federal Party]. So I sent for Tiruchelvam [a Federalist often involved in interparty negotiations] and arranged a meeting with Chelvanayakam. I told him we wanted a settlement; would he please state his minimum demands . . . ." Interview, Colombo, Sept. 4, 1968. The assumption that bargains can be struck has, of course, two sides. While it is conducive to dealing on the basis of strict reciprocity, it also encourages a Sinhalese party to take an anti-Tamil line when it is advantageous to do so, for it may still be possible to deal with the Tamil parties later anyway.

" . . . all parties are so opportunistic that for the sake of power they'll abandon anything," remarked an experienced politician.[25] Yet, in Sri Lankan politics, the word *opportunist* is more often used in a humorously cynical than in a moralistic vein. Flexibility of this sort means that parties will grasp coalition opportunities that are presented more readily than will ethnic parties that are expected to espouse the sacred cause of their group without any deviation.[26] In the nature of things, coalitions of commitment will be rare, but electoral and party systems can bring them into being nonetheless.

THE COALITION IN OPERATION AND DISSOLUTION

Although the UNP had a substantial plurality in the 1965 parliament, it did not attempt to gain an outright majority and push its Tamil and other partners aside. In this respect, its behavior differed from that of plurality parties in coalitions of convenience. Rather than seek opposition defectors, the government began to implement its agreement with the Federalists, thus rendering itself vulnerable to defections.[27] Early in 1966, the government promulgated regulations that made it permissible to transact official business in the Tamil language in the North and East and to correspond with the central government in Tamil.[28] Deadlines for Tamil civil servants to learn Sinhala were also relaxed. Civil servants who had lost salary increments under the previous regime because they did not pass Sinhala proficiency examinations had their increments restored, and those recruited before 1956 were exempted from the exami-

25. Interview, Colombo, Sept. 1–2, 1968. The theme recurs in interviews with politicians of all parties. Interestingly enough, the *Far Eastern Economic Review* (Hong Kong), May 18, 1979, p. 34, reported that close relations were developing between the UNP and the Janatha Vimukthi Peramuna, the leftist organization that had launched the 1971 insurrection, and that a meeting had taken place between leaders of the Communist Party and the Tamil United Liberation Front, successor to the Federal Party. Both turnabouts, albeit short-lived, underscore the flexible character of the Sri Lanka party system.

26. The roots of Ceylonese political flexibility are not easy to identify. They may lie deep in the rather open and absorptive cultures of the island, notably the Sinhalese (see particularly Bryce Ryan, *Caste in Modern Ceylon* [New Brunswick: Rutgers Univ. Press, 1953]), or they may be imbedded in the elite political culture. Perhaps long parliamentary experience and continuity (since 1931) have contributed to the light cynicism that derives from political seasoning, or perhaps party fragmentation has forced pragmatic adaptation on the politicians. The sources of Ceylonese flexibility are important because they indicate whether it is *sui generis* or likely to be found elsewhere.

27. A good account of the early phases of the coalition is contained in Kearney, *Communalism and Language in the Politics of Ceylon*, 128–36.

28. The text of the regulations and the act under which they were made is contained in ibid., 147–50.

nation requirements.[29] Tamil government servants' unions were not entirely happy with these concessions, which still required post-1956 civil servants to learn Sinhala, but they went as far as the UNP could be expected to go on language issues. Other concessions required less visible action. Settlement of Sinhalese in Tamil areas was reduced. The Federal Party was also able to reap its fair share of patronage opportunities: jobs, schools, and other benefits for the Tamil areas. All of these concessions left the UNP open to the charge that the Federal Party, by taking "bids" from the SLFP and UNP and aligning with the highest bidder, had succeeded in "auctioning the rights of the Sinhalese."[30]

The linchpin of the Federal Party program was the proposal to establish district councils. The Federalists were committed ultimately to a federal state. In the meantime, they would be content with a measure of local autonomy for the Tamil areas. If the Tamils were deprived of linguistic parity by a policy of Sinhala Only in the South, then at least they could return to the North and East, protected against demographic change by restrictions on Sinhalese settlement. There the district councils would assure the Tamils first-class citizenship, denied them in the South, as well as government employment to substitute for jobs lost as a result of linguistic discrimination in Colombo.

The district councils proposal was not put forward immediately.[31] Only in 1968 did the bill finally emerge from the cabinet. The proposed district councils had fewer powers than Federal Party draftsmen had first contemplated, and these were to be exercised "under the direction and control of the central government."[32] It was a weaker decentralization than Bandaranaike had been willing to grant in 1957. Even so, the proposal met with resistance.

Opposition within the UNP to the Tamil language regulations had

29. In addition to interviews with UNP and Federal Party leaders, I am drawing here on an interview (Colombo, Aug. 19, 1968) with a well-placed Tamil civil servant, whose own earlier-forfeited increments were restored after 1965.

30. The statement is that of a Sinhalese extremist politician. Interview, Colombo, July 31, 1968.

31. The FP leader, Chelvanayakam, apparently felt that his mistake at the time of the B-C Pact was in trying to achieve language concessions and district councils simultaneously, so now he held back on district councils. As it happened, this fit the UNP timetable well. After the language regulations were promulgated, the UNP faced a series of by-elections. The government also had other unpopular measures to put forward, and it did not want to have them all on the table simultaneously. Interviews, Colombo, Aug. 12 and 30, 1968.

32. Government of Ceylon, *Proposals for the Establishment of District Councils Under the Direction and Control of the Central Government* (Colombo: Government Press, 1968).

been overridden by Dudley Senanayake.[33] The district councils issue was taken far more seriously. The UNP feared the Left parties might take control of some localities if councils were set up. Members of parliament feared the district council chairman would become a rival local power. The Ceylon Moors, an important Muslim minority in the East, feared that local councils there would be Tamil-dominated. The Tamil Congress remained wedded to a unitary state and argued that district councils could be used to oppress the Tamil minority in the South.

Most important were UNP electoral concerns. Following the 1965 election, the SLFP had moved back to an anti-Tamil line, portraying the UNP as a party manipulated by the Federalists. The district councils issue provided a focus for such attacks, spurred by Buddhist monks. Some UNP back-benchers, fearful of the electoral consequences—for the government would have to go to the polls by 1970—were on the verge of revolt. In the end, the UNP leadership withdrew the bill because, as a very close observer noted, the party had not yet faced election "with the Federal Party millstone around its neck and doesn't know how much it weighs."[34]

This was a turning point in the coalition. Federal Party leaders suspected the UNP was less genuinely enthusiastic than the SLFP for local councils, and some began to regret that SLFP coalition proposals had not been entertained more receptively in 1965.[35] After the district councils fiasco, it was in the best interests of the Federal Party and the UNP that the two parties contest the next elections separately. After a period of measured drifting apart, the FP withdrew from the coalition but continued to vote with the government on non-Tamil issues.[36] The final

33. The language issue had a rather abstract quality to it. English was still indispensable for certain official purposes, as a UNP parliamentarian noted pointedly: "It will be one hundred years before Sinhala becomes the language of the courts and two hundred years before Tamil becomes the language of the courts." Interview, Colombo, Aug. 3, 1968.

34. Interview, Colombo, Aug. 20, 1968.

35. Interviews, Colombo, Aug. 12 and Sept. 1–2, 1968. Their suspicions of UNP lack of enthusiasm were not wholly amiss. Top UNP leaders tended to be centralists, unenthused about creating additional local bodies in a country as small as Ceylon. Interviews, Colombo, Aug. 14, 20, and 30, 1968. S. W. R. D. Bandaranaike, who had first proposed decentralization as a way to resolve Tamil grievances, had, by contrast, been Minister of Local Government and genuinely favored devolution of authority. Nevertheless, there is no real evidence that the UNP entered into the coalition agreement in bad faith.

36. See Ralph E. Fretty, "Ceylon: Election-Oriented Politics," *Asian Survey* 9 (Jan. 1969): 99–103. Despite the district councils setback and criticism of the way the UNP leaders had handled the proposal, Federal Party leaders were still remarkably favorably disposed toward the UNP. Most still believed the SLFP to be a party much less well-intentioned toward the Tamils.

break came in 1969. The stage was set for the elections of 1970, elections the SLFP and its Left allies won by an overwhelming majority.

ELECTORAL CYCLES AND
THE LIMITS OF COMMITMENT

As the coalition had been forged by electoral calculations, so it was undermined by them. By 1968, it began to appear to the UNP leaders that further concessions to the Tamils might cost the party more seats and votes than the Tamil parties controlled. If this was true in 1968, why did it not impede formation of the coalition in 1965? Because the shape of Sinhalese party competition looked different then. The fragmentation of electoral support among the Sinhalese parties—with no party gaining a majority of seats—as in the 1965 election and the March 1960 election, is one model of Sinhalese politics. This is a model conducive to centripetal positioning that facilitates interethnic coalitions of commitment. However, the elections of 1956, of July 1960, and of 1970, in which SLFP majority governments came to power, provide another model of Sinhalese party competition. This model, in which one of the two Sinhalese parties is able to consolidate enough support to form a government without Tamil support, is far less conducive to forming or maintaining interethnic coalitions of commitment.

Oscillation between the models is largely a function of concessions to minority demands. The SLFP landslide of 1956 had been produced in large part by UNP moderation toward the Tamils. By 1968, it seemed to UNP leaders that a repetition of the 1956 election results might be in the offing. This forecast proved correct. In short, a convincing case can be made that Sinhalese electoral support will be fragmented only when neither of the two main parties seems to be yielding unduly to the Tamils.[37] When Sinhalese support is fragmented, Tamil support is sought. When the price for that support begins to be paid, competitive opportunities open up for the other main Sinhalese party, and the system moves toward the consolidated model.[38] Once the impact of the earlier concessions is dissipated, fragmentation can be expected again. Even as their coalition was dissolving, Federal Party leaders recognized that with subsequent fragmentation of the Sinhalese vote, there would be renewed

37. That is not to say that concessions to the Tamils are the only cause of oscillation in the support of the Sinhalese parties, only that such concessions do produce consolidation.

38. In advancing the district council proposal, the coalition partners apparently misjudged the SLFP's willingness to reverse its previously favorable position on the issue. Interview, Colombo, Sept. 1–2, 1968 (with a major Federal Party leader).

opportunities to bargain for their demands. The parties were caught in a competitive cycle.

Cycles of this kind are likely to be endemic to coalitions of commitment. Such coalitions depend for their formation on electoral uncertainty resulting from fragmentation of party support within the majority ethnic group and are undermined by changes in that pattern of fragmentation. The dynamics of intraethnic competition thus sets limits to the likely durability and accomplishments of such coalitions. Vulnerable as they are to competitive pressure, the coalitions necessarily function intermittently and incrementally. Overall settlements of all outstanding ethnic issues at a stroke are unlikely, but partial settlements are not. Long-term survival of the coalition through competitive elections is doubtful.

All of this, however, presupposes an electoral system in which fairly modest changes in the number of votes won are reflected in significant shifts in the number of seats won. This is common in first-past-the-post electoral systems of the sort that prevailed in Sri Lanka during the time of the coalition. It makes leaders of parties in the coalition highly vulnerable to competitive pressures and consequent changes in the intraethnic pattern of party support. Ethnic moderation and concessions produce these cyclical changes and thereby undermine the coalition. The Sri Lankan electoral system was changed in 1978. This raises the intriguing question, which I attempt to answer in Chapter 15, whether electoral policy can be used to foster coalitions of commitment by limiting the impact of swings in the competitive cycle, thereby reducing the sensitivity of conciliatory coalition leaders to changing patterns of party support.

CONSEQUENCES OF THE COALITION

Facility at striking bargains is no indication of how a bargain will turn out. The National Government brought the parties closer together on the language issue. The Federalists, who had formerly discouraged Tamil civil servants from learning Sinhala, acknowledged its special status in the South, while the prime minister relaxed language requirements for Tamil civil servants and accorded Tamil official status in Tamil areas. The compromise was aptly described by a Federalist leader as "Sinhala Only, but Tamil also."

The coalition also succeeded in allaying certain other Tamil anxieties, but it did not satisfy the most keenly felt demand it had agreed to—local autonomy. The UNP needed to meet the minimal demands of the Federal

Party, lest it drive the Federalists reluctantly into the waiting arms of the SLFP. But to meet all the Tamils' demands, district councils included, would have risked a major loss of Sinhalese support. There is no escaping the fact that two-party competition for the Sinhalese vote has made Sri Lanka's moderately serious ethnic conflict far more severe than it would otherwise have been.

The competition of the UNP and SLFP for the favor of the Federal Party had important effects on the party system. For some years, it put a brake on the most extreme ethnic incitements among Sinhalese politicians. Neither the turmoil of the late 1950s and early 1960s nor the blatant hostility of the major parties toward the Tamils was manifest from 1965 to 1970. The SLFP accused the UNP of selling out to the Federalists, but tactics comparable to the shrill UNP opposition to the B-C Pact or the SLFP military occupation of the Tamil North during the Federalists' civil disobedience movement were not utilized. In the 1970 election campaign, the SLFP and its coalition partners, the Sinhalese Left parties, took a generally conciliatory line toward Tamil language issues. The SLFP contemplated the possibility that the election results might make Tamil support indispensable for forming a government. With that in mind, a few quiet meetings were held with Federalists leaders, meetings made possible by the SLFP's new moderation on Tamil issues.[39] In the event, Federal Party support proved unnecessary, but the regime of Mrs. Bandaranaike which came to power in 1970 had a Tamil minister, the first time any SLFP-led government did. In that same 1970 election, a Sinhalese extremist party, led by a maverick cousin of Dudley Senanayake, attracted no significant following and elected no one.[40] In 1977, when the UNP returned to power, the Federal Party did not formally join the government. But, aided by some constitutional changes that made ethnic moderation somewhat less risky, the UNP government reinstituted a process of compromise with the Federal Party.

The coalition also had its effect on the Federal Party. Most obviously, it retarded the development of separatist sentiment. When the district councils bill was withdrawn, Federal Party leaders disagreed on what course to take, but no Federalist leader of the late 1960s proposed tactics of civil disobedience or all-out struggle for separatism. The Federal

39. For the deliberately murky terms of the manifesto of the SLFP and the Left parties on language issues, see *Ceylon Daily News* (Colombo), May 15, 1970.

40. See James Jupp, "Five Sinhalese Nationalist Politicians," in W. H. Morris-Jones, ed., *The Making of Politicians: Studies from Africa and Asia* (London: Athlone Press, 1976), 191–92.

Party, which had begun as a party of protest, threatening and occasionally performing acts of civil disobedience, had become a more or less professionalized parliamentary party. It made concessions on language and on participation in government it had sworn not to make, in exchange for only pieces of its program. Later events, particularly the adoption of a new constitution, discrimination in university admissions, and backtracking on certain language concessions by the SLFP-led government that came to power in 1970, tested this parliamentary commitment severely. In 1976, when the Tamil position had been badly eroded, the Tamil United Liberation Front (composed of the Federal Party and the Tamil Congress) finally demanded the independent Tamil state that had never previously been a serious part of Sri Lankan political discourse.[41] By then, Tamil grievances had grown dramatically, and Tamil terrorists were able to polarize opinion on the ground even as politicians were working out new compromises after 1977. But these developments should not obscure the consequences of the 1965 coalition, which encouraged the Federalists to seek the best bargains they could get for their constituents. By discouraging the most extreme Sinhalese appeals and moving the Federal Party toward acceptance of partial satisfactions, the coalition tended temporarily to pull both ends of the spectrum a bit further toward the Center. In an environment of conflict often viewed by the participants as zero-sum, small centripetal movements are significant.

THE ELECTORAL LOGIC
OF TEMPORARY COALITIONS

Before moving on to an examination of permanent coalitions of ethnic parties, I want to highlight the distinctions between coalitions of convenience and coalitions of commitment. This will make clearer the extent to which the logic of the electoral situation governs their dynamics.

Coalitions of convenience come into existence solely to pool parliamentary seats to form a majority. Partners are chosen on the basis of electoral noncompetition, often producing a marriage of implacable eth-

41. In 1972, the main Tamil parties, long-standing rivals, formed a Tamil United Front after a republican constitution was adopted that made no gesture of recognition of the Tamil minority. W. A. Wiswa Warnapala, "Sri Lanka in 1972: Tension and Change," *Asian Survey* 13 (Feb. 1973): 217–30; *Far Eastern Economic Review*, Aug. 19, 1972, p. 20. The Indian Tamil component dropped out when the Front added "Liberation" to its name and a separate Tamil state to its aims.

nic opponents. Such coalitions make no progress on policies of accommodation. Rather, they tend to dissolve in violent disagreement over basic ethnic issues. This disagreement usually goes hand in hand with attempts by the plurality party in the coalition to secure an outright majority, by defections or otherwise, or at least to find a more acquiescent partner. When coalitions of convenience break up, they reinforce preexisting ethnic party systems. A common aftermath of their dissolution has been widespread violence and military intervention.

Coalitions of commitment are brought into being by an agreement to pool both parliamentary seats and at least some votes in the antecedent election. Because the pooling of votes entails a transfer across ethnic lines, the price of such a transfer is a commitment to moderation on the part of the vote-receiving party. Not electoral avoidance but electoral cooperation cements this coalition. Although negotiations may be held with a number of parties, the terms of the bargain are set by concessions required to seal the vote transfer. Partners are thus chosen by the congeniality of their positions on ethnic policy matters, and the term of the coalition is characterized by some limited policy compromise. If, however, intraethnic party competition is lively, this may raise the electoral cost of the concessions beyond the gains resulting from vote pooling. Dissolution, then, stems not from struggles for dominance within the coalition, but from competitive pressures arising outside of it.

In one respect, however, coalitions of convenience and of commitment are alike. Both are characterized by relatively short duration. The parties are linked only for as long as it seems mutually beneficial. There is no effort to make the arrangement permanent or to join the parties organizationally. Negotiations are conducted at arm's length, on a basis of strict reciprocity. In Sri Lanka, there was a preference on the Federal Party side for dealing with the UNP, but no intention to coalesce with the UNP irrespective of the terms of the bargain or to support it through thick and thin. Although the conditions and consequences of dissolution were quite different, the Sri Lankan coalition of commitment, like the coalitions of convenience in Nigeria, Uganda, Benin, and Punjab, did not last through even a single election.

CHAPTER TEN

Multiethnic Alliances and Parties

In a severely divided society, a multiethnic party or coalition is a fragile institution. Some multiethnic coalitions and parties, however, manage to survive despite fissiparous pressures. The permanent multiethnic coalition is an alliance of ethnic parties, each of which can still profess to be working for the interests of its own ethnic group even while participating in the alliance. Alliances, I shall suggest in this chapter, are the product of some rather unusual formative conditions. Nonetheless, they can have a substantial impact on ethnic conflict. Multiethnic parties, on the other hand, tend to take one of two courses. They either split into ethnic parties or they move to the single-party format, in which case they are likely to be less genuinely multiethnic than they appear.

MULTIETHNIC ALLIANCES

In principle, there is a bright line between temporary coalitions, whether of convenience or commitment, and permanent coalitions. Of course, the test is not whether they in fact last forever or even for a long time. The criterion is whether the partners intend to create a relationship of indefinite duration and follow through with arrangements that commit them to it. By far the most important of these arrangements is the single slate of candidates.

The single slate reflects a decision of the parties to pool all votes in an electoral arena.[1] I have already indicated that vote pooling promotes

1. It is easy in principle to distinguish single-slate alliances from coalitions of ethnic parties, but sometimes not so easy in practice. An example of how the two types can blur into each other occurred before the 1978 elections in Malaysia, a country that had had a permanent multiethnic coalition for more than a quarter of a century. In the state of Sarawak, the Sarawak United People's Party, a Chinese party affiliated with the governing

moderation on ethnic issues. The nationwide single slate should go even further in this direction. To elect candidates of the various groups in conflict under a single banner across the country will require mutual concessions on divisive issues. Such concessions could not be made by parties at opposite ends of the issue spectrum. The contrast with coalitions of convenience could not be sharper.

Coalitions that put forward in each constituency a single candidate or a single list are, says Maurice Duverger, more difficult to form than other electoral arrangements between parties "but more binding."[2] And, he adds, single-slate coalitions are also "more unequal" in relations among the partners than separate-slate coalitions are. These cryptic statements conveniently suggest three inquiries pertinent to single-slate multiethnic coalitions. The first is *formation*: under what conditions can the obstacles to permanent coalitions be overcome? The second is *duration*: what keeps them going in the face of disintegrative forces that, we have seen, jeopardize even coalitions of commitment elsewhere? The third is the quality of *relations*: how do permanent coalitions differ in internal dynamics from temporary coalitions? These lead in turn to other questions, involving the relationship of the coalition partners to the rest of the party system, the nature of ethnic policies produced by such alliances, and their capacity for change.

All of these matters are of enormous importance for ethnic conflict. Although there are a number of resemblances between temporary and permanent multiethnic coalitions, especially in their formation, there are also differences that are clear-cut and consequential. Whatever the actual intentions of the parties at the moment of inception, the single slate implies permanence and a mutual commitment to ethnic compromise that will not expire the moment the costs of reciprocity seem to outweigh the benefits.

The outstanding example of such an arrangement is the Malaysian Alliance (later National Front). A permanent coalition of three ethnic

---

multiethnic coalition but formerly in opposition, asked permission from the coalition to contest the elections under its own party banner, presumably without jeopardizing the party's status in the coalition. This request, made to enhance the party's competitive position *vis-à-vis* a Chinese opposition party, was a major deviation from the prevailing assumption that the coalition partners had to choose between their separate electoral identity and their good standing in the coalition. See *Far Eastern Economic Review* (Hong Kong), Oct. 27, 1978, p. 26.

2. Maurice Duverger, *Political Parties*, trans. Barbara North and Robert North (London: Methuen, 1954), 344. Duverger is speaking of alliances for single-ballot electoral systems, and I shall be doing the same.

parties, the Alliance began during a tense and uncertain period in ethnic relations in what was then the Federation of Malaya. Despite this difficult environment, it got off to a remarkably successful start in 1952. Going back this far, the Malaysian experience is rich in illustration of all the major problems likely to be encountered by permanent multiethnic coalitions in severely divided societies.[3]

FOUNDING AN ALLIANCE

World War II worsened ethnic relations in Malaya.[4] The Japanese occupation forces treated the Chinese in Malaya as enemies, for the Japanese were also fighting in China. The Malayan Chinese reciprocated the sentiment, and many joined Communist-led guerrilla bands in the jungle. These came into frequent conflict with Malay villagers, from whom they sought food. Malays organized to counterattack. Toward the end of the war, whole areas of the peninsula were the scene of large-scale massacres. In the interregnum before the British reoccupied the country, the guerrillas emerged from the jungle, took over some towns, proclaimed the abolition of Malay sultanates, and declared that Malaya might thereafter become part of China. Malay reaction was swift and violent. The

3. Data from Malaysia are derived from a voluminous set of interviews conducted by me in 1967–68 and in 1975, as well as from documentary sources. See also Gordon P. Means, *Malaysian Politics* (New York: New York Univ. Press, 1970); R. S. Milne, *Government and Politics in Malaysia* (Boston: Houghton Mifflin, 1967); K. J. Ratnam, *Communalism and the Political Process in Malaya* (Kuala Lumpur: Univ. of Malaya Press, 1965); Karl von Vorys, *Democracy without Consensus: Communalism and Political Stability in Malaysia* (Princeton: Princeton Univ. Press, 1975).

Several points of nomenclature and scope need to be mentioned at the outset. The Federation of Malaya became independent in 1957. Joined by the Borneo states of Sarawak and Sabah and by Singapore, Malaya became Malaysia in 1963. (Singapore left Malaysia in 1965.) I shall generally speak of Malaya when referring to the period before 1963, Malaysia after; but, in any case, I do not include in this treatment politics in Sabah and Sarawak. I also refer to the Alliance when dealing with the Alliance that was formed in 1952; the term *alliance* without the capital *A* is reserved for the species of permanent multiethnic coalitions. The term *non-Malays* includes the Chinese and Indians who together comprise nearly half of the population of peninsular Malaysia. Occasionally, I speak simply of the Chinese, but for most political purposes Chinese and Indian can be grouped under the same "non-Malay" rubric. I use the term Pan-Malayan Islamic Party, rather than the more common Malay names for this party, for the sake of simplicity and consistency. For the same reasons, I have retained Malay spellings of parties and titles as of the time of the events to which they refer.

4. The definitive study of this period is Halinah Bamadhaj, "The Impact of the Japanese Occupation of Malaya on Malay Society and Politics" (M.A. thesis, Univ. of Auckland, 1975). See also Cheah Boon Kheng, *Red Star Over Malaya: Resistance and Social Conflict During and After the Japanese Occupation, 1941–1946* (Singapore: Singapore Univ. Press, 1983).

claims of the guerrillas were a portent of what unchecked Chinese power might mean.

Hardly had the country recovered from these episodes when the British, in 1945, proposed the so-called Malayan Union, a scheme for direct and centralized rule, with reduced powers for the Malay sultans and provision for easy acquisition of citizenship by Chinese and Indians. The result was a protest movement of the Malay masses, in concert with the Malay royalty and aristocracy. This resulted in the formation of the United Malays National Organization, first merely as a vehicle of protest, later as a full-fledged Malay political party.

The protest succeeded. The Union plan was withdrawn by 1947, replaced by the Federation of Malaya. Under the Federation, the decentralized structure of government was preserved; the sultans' powers and symbolic role were left more or less intact; and stringent requirements for citizenship were imposed on non-Malays.

Now it was the non-Malays' time to protest. A variety of mainly Chinese organizations formed an All-Malayan Council of Joint Action (AMCJA). The AMCJA linked up with several left-wing Malay organizations, led by the Malay Nationalist Party (MNP) and joined together in the *Pusat Tenaga Ra'ayat* (People's Power Center, abbreviated PUTERA). Whereas the Chinese saw the Federation as an obvious threat to their aspiration for equal treatment, the MNP, inspired by the radical current of Indonesian nationalism, had early broken with UMNO, which it regarded as controlled by Malay feudalists. The MNP fought the Federation, because it feared the Federation would entrench the Malay aristocracy and the British so as to preclude the growth of an egalitarian nationalist movement of the sort that was fighting the Dutch—and deposing the sultans—in Indonesia.[5]

In the end, AMCJA-PUTERA failed. The Federation was imposed. But the short history of this multiethnic organization had profound effects.

First, it accelerated the demise of the Malay Nationalist Party. By joining the Chinese and Indians who opposed the Federation, which most Malays saw as being in their interest, the MNP isolated itself from Malay mass support and so solidified UMNO's base. Ironically, it was

---

5. The MNP was also infiltrated by the Malayan Communist Party. This is certainly one reason why the MNP opposed the British proposals for the Federation, but the non-Communist MNP leadership independently rejected the assumptions of the Federation. The MNP was banned by the British in 1950.

UMNO's monopoly position among the Malays that later provided it with the freedom of action to align itself with a Chinese organization.

Second, AMCJA-PUTERA shaped Chinese calculations as well. The failure of the campaign to defeat the Federation convinced Tan Cheng Lock, its leading Chinese participant, of the need for a strong Chinese organization and of the potential utility of aligning with Malays. In 1952, the Malayan Chinese Association that Tan Cheng Lock created pursued this strategy and allied with UMNO.

But we are a bit ahead of ourselves. The short-run effects of the two campaigns, first against the Malayan Union and then against the Federation, were greatly to widen the gulf between the Malays and Chinese. The differences were widened much further when Communist guerrillas, nearly all Chinese, began a full-fledged insurrection in 1948. This immediately raised doubts about Chinese loyalty to Malaya. The police, troops, and home guards who hunted the insurgents were mainly Malay, and so the battles had the quality of ethnic warfare. The atmosphere was not conducive to ethnic accommodation. When elite members of all ethnic groups gathered together for meetings of a newly formed Communities Liaison Committee in 1949, the sessions were acrimonious. Nevertheless, the idea of reciprocal concessions by the ethnic communities gained ground in the CLC. Outside, segments of the Malay press urged the colonial government to send the Chinese back to China.[6]

The Communist insurgency had major effects on the Chinese side. With the British prodding Chinese business leadership to provide an alternative to communism, the Malayan Chinese Association was initially a combination of many things: a welfare organization and benefactor of the Chinese community, providing financial aid to rural Chinese resettled in "New Villages"; an interest group petitioning the government in behalf of the Chinese; and an intermediary for the government with the Chinese community. At the outset, Tan Cheng Lock was unsure whether the MCA would evolve into a political party or whether parties would be organized along ideological rather than ethnic lines.[7]

In UMNO, there was the same uncertainty. As the Communist insurrection continued, the British felt the need for bringing the Chinese more effectively into the polity. The leader of UMNO, Dato' Onn bin Ja'afar, agreed. In 1951, he proposed that UMNO open its doors to non-Malays.

6. *Majlis* (Kuala Lumpur), Oct. 19, 1948.
7. Memorandum by Tan Cheng Lock (mimeo., 1951), 2 (copy in the Malaysian National Archives).

Reaction from the branches was overwhelmingly unfavorable. Dato' Onn eventually resigned, founding instead an explicitly multiethnic Independence of Malaya Party (IMP). The IMP had the encouragement of the British.[8]

The MCA national leadership was favorably disposed to the IMP, but the municipal elections to be held in all the major towns of Malaya in 1952–53 reversed these inclinations. The towns and cities were overwhelmingly Chinese. Even with restricted citizenship opportunities, most municipal voters would surely be non-Malays, despite the Malay majority in the country as a whole. Preeminent among the Malays, UMNO nonetheless stood to lose out to Dato' Onn if it contested the municipal elections alone. Instead it made a local alliance with the MCA for the Kuala Lumpur election, which came first. The alliance was made possible by the fortuitous circumstance that the influential Kuala Lumpur leader of the MCA, H. S. Lee, happened not to favor Onn's IMP.

Running an ethnically mixed slate, the UMNO-MCA Alliance defeated the IMP first in Kuala Lumpur and then in other towns. By the end of 1952, the Alliance had won twenty-six of the thirty-four seats it had contested in seven towns, including several major ones.

Drained of Chinese support, defeated at the polls, the IMP was consigned to oblivion. By contrast, UMNO and MCA moved to formalize the Alliance as a permanent body.[9] The Alliance was to be constituted neither as a mere coalition of separate ethnic parties nor as a multiethnic party like IMP, but, in the words of the UMNO leader, Tengku Abdul Rahman, as "a united party" based on its ethnic components.[10]

The Alliance went from one success to another. Eventually joined by a small third partner representing Indians, the Alliance captured fifty-one of the fifty-two seats in the first Legislative Council elections ever conducted in Malaya, in 1955, and went on to negotiate independence

8. The preference for multiethnic organizations in the colonies became something of a British policy in the 1950s as the British came to grips with emerging nationalist movements. See, e.g., R. J. A. R. Rathbone, "Opposition in Ghana: The National Liberation Movement," in Collected Seminar Papers on Opposition in the New African States, October 1967–March 1968 (London: Univ. of London, Institute of Commonwealth Studies, mimeo., n.d.), 51–52.

9. The MCA leadership had for a time envisioned triangular cooperation between the IMP, UMNO, and the MCA. Tan Cheng Lock to Edna D. Lee, Aug. 8, 1952. I am indebted to Agnes Tan for making this and other papers available to me.

10. Minutes of an informal meeting between representatives of the UMNO-MCA Alliance, Kuala Lumpur, and representatives of the Malayan Indian Congress, Oct. 11, 1954 (typescript), 3. The context was the Tengku's rejection of a claim by the MIC, then considering joining the Alliance, to a fixed number of seats.

from the British in 1957. In six subsequent national elections, the Alliance or its successor, the National Front, has always won at least a plurality of votes and a majority of seats and has ruled the country continuously.

In the formation of the Alliance, the precise sequence of events was a decisive force. It happened that the municipal elections, in which Malays were in a minority, preceded the national elections, in which the reverse was true. In the 1955 national elections, before most Chinese and Indians were given citizenship, 84 percent of the electorate was Malay; in the 1959 elections, after the citizenship issue was resolved, 56 percent of the electorate was Malay. It is inconceivable that UMNO would have acceded to an alliance with the MCA had the 1955 national elections come first. UMNO could easily have won a decisive majority alone. Links with a Chinese party could only have spurred the growth of a competing Malay party to contest the elections. The prior scheduling of elections in which non-Malay votes were decisive prompted formation of the Alliance.

Sequencing was important in other ways, too. The Alliance was formed early in relation to the issues that still had to be resolved. The divisive questions of citizenship, language, the "special position" of the Malays, and the other matters to be negotiated before independence were still years away. Relationships could be formed before these issues had to be faced. Nevertheless, there had been earlier attempts to thrash out some of these questions, particularly in the CLC and in AMCJA-PUTERA. Although these attempts were far from successful, they established precedents for interethnic cooperation without loss of organizational distinctiveness and for discussions marked by candor, reciprocal concessions, and the development of close personal relations. These forerunners made the Alliance seem more natural than it would have, had they not preceded it.

The ongoing Communist insurrection also played a role. Without any doubt, the Emergency and the anti-Chinese reaction it produced gave rise to an urge to moderation on the part of the MCA. As one MCA leader expressed it, "as most of the terrorists happen to be Chinese, our community just now is under a cloud and the more we clamour for our rights the more will we incite the Malays to take advantage of this emergency to undermine our position in Malaya."[11] The MCA was seeking

11. Tan Chin Tuan to Tan Cheng Lock, Nov. 9, 1948 (copy in Malaysian National Archives).

opportunities to link up with Malay parties. When one came up, it was grasped. The British, too, had made it known as early as 1952 that interethnic unity was a prerequisite to independence.[12] Since Dato' Onn had already linked ethnic groups in the IMP, it behooved UMNO, if it were to lead Malaya to independence, to find a format in which to do the same.[13]

Either of two faces can be put on the formation of the Alliance. It can fairly be said that the Alliance was produced by chance, by a curious and irreplicable combination of circumstances: the fortuitous order in which events occurred; the political environment (including the Emergency and the British response) that pushed the two parties together; the lack of strong competing Malay and Chinese parties; the demography that put the Chinese in the urban and the Malays in the rural areas; the decision to hold town council elections first; and the fact that H. S. Lee was not on good terms with the IMP leaders. Had any of these chance conditions not been present, the Alliance might never have materialized.

There is another way of interpreting these events, a way more pertinent to our concerns and equally valid. When elections were held in which non-Malay votes were decisive, the leading Malay party was willing, in spite of an atmosphere fraught with Sino-Malay tension, to reach across ethnic lines and conclude an arrangement that promised electoral victory. The response to formal electoral incentives is no random factor. It is something that can be built on by constitutional engineers.

The electoral roots of the Alliance also constitute a clear link between it and the Sri Lanka coalition of commitment formed in 1965. Equally, their electoral roots separate these two from coalitions of convenience. In both countries, the strongest ethnic party (UNP in Sri Lanka, UMNO in Malaysia) was induced to seek a partner representing the other ethnic group because of an electoral configuration that magnified the bargaining power of that partner. In Sri Lanka, it will be recalled, fragmentation of support among the Sinhalese parties, coupled with the concentration

12. Ratnam, *Communalism and the Political Process in Malaya*, 22.
13. R. K. Vasil, *Politics in a Plural Society* (London: Oxford Univ. Press, 1971), 10, 20, is therefore off the mark in likening the UMNO-MCA Alliance to a hypothetical arrangement between "the Hindu Mahasabha and the All India Muslim League, the communal organizations of the Hindus and Muslims respectively, joining hands in the pre-Independence period to fight against the non-communal Indian National Congress." The analogy fails for a fundamental reason: the Mahasabha and the Muslim League were flank organizations at odds with the ethnic compromises of the Center; the MCA and UMNO were deliberately joining together to displace IMP at the Center, and we shall soon see that an effect of the Alliance was to produce reactions on the flanks.

of Tamil support in the Federal Party, enhanced the Federalists' ability to deliver marginal votes. In Malaysia, MCA power was magnified by the large non-Malay majorities in the town council electorates. This enabled the MCA to deal initially with UMNO on an equal footing. In both cases, the marginal utility of minority support was far greater than minority numbers in the national electorates would have suggested.

The form of the interethnic arrangement was, however, different in the two countries. This is because the nature of the competition was different. The UNP and the Federal Party faced no multiethnic competitors. Only electoral costs would have accrued from a decision to link up organizationally before the election or to put forward a single slate. UMNO and the MCA, by contrast, did face a multiethnic IMP, and they had no significant ethnically based competitors. No competitive costs attached to running a single slate; short of a single slate, a mere no-contest or informal vote-pooling agreement might not have been enough. From the beginning, therefore, the Alliance was more than a coalition of completely independent parties and yet less than one, unified party. When competitive ethnic parties did arise to challenge the Alliance, each of its components—and especially UMNO—could claim to be an ethnic party.[14]

DURABILITY: THE SINGLE SLATE AND THE WEB OF RELATIONS

Unlike the Sri Lanka coalition, the Malaysian Alliance did not dissolve when electoral circumstances changed. It survived even elections in which the ratio of Malay to Chinese voters was dramatically reversed, and it endured the tense period between the 1955 election and the attainment of independence in 1957. During this time, crucial compromises were necessary. The MCA was under pressure from the Chinese community to achieve complete equality of collective status. Among the Malays, there were demands for "no diplomacy with the Chinese" and fears

14. In one Malay village in 1966, Marvin Rogers found that only half of the men and none of the women were able to differentiate between UMNO and the Alliance. For local leaders, Rogers comments, working in election campaigns for the Alliance provides "a sense of participation in the promotion of Malay interests," while for ordinary villagers voting constitutes "an expression of communal solidarity in which they reaffirm loyalty for the Malay community, UMNO, and prominent Malay politicians." The survival of such beliefs despite the UMNO-MCA linkage is testimony to the utility of the Alliance format. "The Politicization of Malay Villagers," *Comparative Politics* 7 (Jan. 1975): 205–25, at 221.

that Malay "sovereignty" was about to be lost.[15] Under these conditions, it was one thing to declare the Alliance permanent and quite another to keep it so.

The ability of the Alliance to forge a permanent arrangement is to be found in the nature of relations between the partners and their position *vis-à-vis* the evolving party system. The basic elements of durability can be reduced to seven, which I shall list and then describe briefly in turn. First, there was the speed with which commitments were made to establishing the Alliance on a permanent basis. This was done while the first benefits of the arrangement were fresh and while more were in the offing. Second, steps were taken to cope with changes in power relations between the partners. These steps cushioned potentially disruptive events. Third, the less prominent partner in these power relations had good reason to accept its changed position. Fourth, the emergence of an arbitrator at the helm of the Alliance provided a focal point for ethnic advocacy, a court of last resort whose decisions could be accepted. Fifth, the parties found themselves locked in a growing net of non-electoral entanglements that made rational calculations about whether to leave the Alliance and go it alone very difficult. Sixth, a mystique came to surround the successful UMNO-MCA negotiations of 1956–57. This enduring memory of a watershed achievement solidified relations inside the Alliance. Seventh, as the parties cemented their relations, parties outside the Alliance took up positions in opposition to it. The Alliance partners began to be hemmed in by parties on their flanks and to discount the attractiveness of alternatives to the Alliance.

Immediately after the first municipal election in 1952, Tengku Abdul Rahman wired his congratulations: "Alliance great achievement profiting Malaya. May it be everlasting and may it spread." In early 1953, an Alliance organization was formally established. It was not too late for either party to withdraw, but the stakes had already been raised. The early and firm commitment of the Tengku in particular helped the Alliance over the first of many divisive disputes, those in late 1952 and 1953 over the status of the Chinese and of Chinese schools.[16]

The Tengku's commitment led him to take steps to ease the transition to a new set of relations. For the 1955 federal election, he allocated to

15. *Utusan Melayu* (Singapore), Sept. 2, 1955; *Warta Negara* (Penang), Feb. 27, 1957.
16. See Means, *Malaysian Politics*, 135, 138. It has become customary to see the Alliance, even after the first Kuala Lumpur elections, as being temporary and fragile. However, although Tan Cheng Lock's position was not entirely clear for some time, the Tengku's commitment was firm.

the MCA nearly three times as many candidacies as the proportion of Chinese voters would have warranted—a liberality not equalled thereafter. This allocation probably reflected the likelihood that the Chinese share of the vote would rise dramatically as soon as the citizenship issue was settled; UMNO would then need the MCA. Even so, the Tengku's decision in 1955 was taken over strong objections from within UMNO. Along the way, he secured a vote of confidence in himself and in the Alliance from the UMNO general assembly. A drastic reversal of power that might otherwise have broken the Alliance was cushioned.[17] The results of the election put the Tengku—and the Alliance—in an unrivaled position in the country.

The 1955 election was a major turning point in Alliance relations. Before 1955, parity was the governing principle of Alliance relationships. The chair of the Alliance Council was to alternate between the UMNO and MCA presidents. It was even thought that an equal number of Malay and Chinese candidates might be presented to the electorate. Before the election, MCA leaders spoke openly of widespread use of all the "vernacular" languages, including Chinese. The election changed all of this. It left the Tengku (and his successors at the head of UMNO) indisputably at the head of the Alliance. Candidacies were carefully apportioned on an ethnic basis. Thereafter the Chinese were told by the MCA to hold back on delicate ethnic demands like official recognition of the Chinese language. After 1955, UMNO was recognized as the predominant partner.

For the MCA, this was not a desirable position, but it was not wholly unbearable. The Emergency had weakened the overall Chinese position, undermining Chinese legitimacy in a way that Ceylon Tamil legitimacy, for example, has never been challenged. Not only did this point the way to a course of moderation, but at the same time a significant reward lay in store for an MCA practicing moderation. That reward was the attainment of citizenship for the vast majority of Chinese. For this, the MCA was prepared to make many concessions. Leaders of the Chinese community were so vexed by the earlier British rebuff to their citizenship

17. The Tengku's liberality can easily be explained by the transitory character of the ethnic proportions of voters in the 1955 election. This election preceded settlement of the citizenship question that would inevitably bring flocks of new Chinese voters to the polls in 1959. Indeed, the MCA had previously expressed its desire to hold the first federal election in 1956 or 1957, so that a large number of new Chinese voters could participate. So, in some ways, the Tengku was simply anticipating the proportions ultimately arrived at.

claims that they put great efforts into the drive for citizenship, the more so as extreme Malays demanded repatriation of Chinese to China. Because of the dangers of non-citizenship in such an environment and the stronger Chinese position that would presumably flow from the grant of citizenship, many MCA leaders were willing to play junior partner to an UMNO that was prepared to accede to Chinese citizenship demands.

They were particularly willing to do this while Tengku Abdul Rahman was at the helm of UMNO. In 1955, as noted, the Tengku had claimed and received authority to allocate candidacies among the Alliance partners, a claim he later renewed. A recurrent theme in his political discourse was the demand that UMNO and MCA should trust him to be fair to both of them. The Alliance increasingly became a system of interethnic bargaining and arbitration, and the Tengku established a reputation for justice and generosity for the Chinese.

Before very long, the network of relations binding the parties transcended mere electoral advantage—or at least transcended tangible, easily calculable reciprocal advantage. For a considerable time, the financial burden of the Alliance, including electoral and administrative expenses, fell upon the MCA. The MCA also administered a "Malay Welfare Fund." The party provided money for scholarships, land resettlement, and a host of other financial gestures of good will toward the Malays, often calculated to solidify Alliance relationships.[18] From 1955 onward, both parties benefited from all the patronage rewards that participation in government brings. MCA candidates also benefited disproportionately from Malay votes; some MCA leaders were accorded Malay-majority safe seats. But, even here, the benefits were not all one-way. In close contests, some UMNO candidates were also elected on margins provided by the MCA. Although the MCA benefited more, the net vote exchange was not easily calculated.

In a variety of small ways, the parties and their leaders were bound up with each other. When the electoral costs of the Alliance did threaten to become intolerable for one or the other party—as they did in 1959 for the MCA and in 1969 for the UMNO—there were strong voices in the respective parties urging dissolution of the Alliance, just as the Sri Lanka coalition dissolved under such circumstances. But in Malaysia clear-cut electoral calculations were never the exclusive touchstone of the rela-

18. See, e.g., Minutes of the 8th Meeting of the MCA Cabinet, Mar. 31, 1953 (mimeo.), 10, reporting a recommendation that "the Malays should be assisted as much as possible, especially at this time when a bid was being made to undermine UMNO-MCA alliance."

tionship. As Duverger notes, single-slate alliances are characterized by relationships of "intimacy" and "fusion."[19]

Intimacy was enhanced at the national leadership level by the negotiation of the ethnic terms of independence. By these terms, the vast majority of Chinese and Indians became citizens. The "special position" of the Malays was recognized, but so were the "legitimate interests" of the non-Malays. In practice, this created a system of preferences for Malays in the public service, scholarships, and certain licenses. It was understood, however, that Chinese and Indian businesses would not be expropriated. The symbols of state authority were to be heavily Malay, and Malay was ultimately to become the sole official language, displacing English. It was a complex set of trades, made in a difficult political environment. Embattled on both sides—for some Chinese pressed for official recognition of the Chinese language, and many Malays were apprehensive about liberal citizenship for the non-Malays—the negotiators were drawn close together. From this lengthy bargaining process, UMNO and MCA leaders drew the lesson that many of their differences could be resolved in a spirit of reciprocity and good will. That sense of achievement was not entirely shared by younger leaders who had not participated in the independence negotiations. But it certainly solidified the Alliance at the leadership level.

As the Alliance got going, it quickly preempted the ethnic Center. This, too, drove the partners together. The demise of the IMP left the MCA without practical alternatives to UMNO. All the other Malay parties drew what electoral strength they had from opposing UMNO's accommodation with the MCA. From time to time, there were those who urged the MCA to proceed without a Malay ally. But, given the Chinese electoral minority and the fact that a separate MCA would mobilize only a fraction of the Chinese vote, this course never appealed to the MCA leadership. Equally, on the UMNO side, a more moderate Chinese partner was not available. Malay parties emerged as rivals to UMNO rather than as potential allies. The formation of the Alliance helped create the very ethnic opposition whose absence had facilitated formation of an alliance in the first place. This most significant phenomenon—flanking—I shall discuss shortly. Here the point is that UMNO and the MCA leaders felt drawn together by the forces that surrounded them. Moreover, those forces consisted, in considerable measure, of seg-

19. Duverger, *Political Parties*, 344.

ments of their communities which the UMNO and MCA leaders respected least: Chinese schoolteachers and Malay *ulama* (theologians), both regarded as intolerably parochial and chauvinistic.

As in the case of formative conditions, this enumeration of seven survival-enhancing elements in the early Alliance experience can be regarded as consisting of somewhat random and eclectic factors. Certainly, the UMNO leadership might just as easily have adopted a cautious, wait-and-see attitude after the municipal elections, especially since the first national elections were likely to make MCA help look much less indispensable than it was in 1952. Can the decisiveness, even impetuousness, of UMNO leaders in embracing the Alliance be codified into a condition of systemic importance? Can the willingness of the MCA to subordinate other goals to the attainment of citizenship be denominated anything other than a *sui generis* structure of preferences? Surely, these are nonrecurring ingredients of the Alliance arrangement. But, just as I emphasized the electoral and competitive configuration in explaining the formation of the Alliance, here I want to underscore the exigencies of the single slate as a prime source of its durability.

The single slate required a central allocation of candidacies. Assumption of this responsibility permitted the Tengku to apportion seats so as to take account of the likely ethnic composition of the electorate. This role formed a principal support for the Tengku's more general position as arbitrator of ethnic claims. Such a position was also buttressed by the need for a common program that went hand in hand with the single slate. The common program extended also to the independence negotiations that cemented the *esprit de corps* of the Alliance elite. It was agreed that UMNO and MCA would submit a single memorandum to the commission appointed by the British to draft the independence constitution. Likewise, the single slate implied at least some common organization. While the Alliance organization was never as strong as that of either UMNO or the MCA, still both the organization and the Alliance campaigns had to be funded. This permitted the MCA to compensate for electoral weakness with financial strength, thereby muddying the calculus of reciprocity, as I have suggested. And, finally, the single slate affected the behavior of parties outside the Alliance. The single slate is an earnest of permanence. As the partners take the first steps to commit themselves to a permanent alliance, they encourage others to harden their own positions in opposition to it. What this did in Malaysia was further to diminish prospects for alternative coalitions. In short, then,

most of the key elements that sustained the Alliance during its first trials
were the logical product of the initial decision to pool all votes and put
forward a single slate. The same would seem to be true of multiethnic
alliances elsewhere.[20]

THE CENTER AND THE FLANKS

In an environment of ethnic conflict, there is room for only one multiethnic party or alliance. After one such party establishes itself, all the electoral opportunities are located on the ethnic flanks. Attempts to form
competing multiethnic parties typically end by recognizing that the party
really represents one or another of the ethnic groups in conflict. Malaysia
is rich in such abortive attempts. After the Alliance defeated the IMP, the
IMP dissolved, and Dato' Onn formed a new party, which was strongly
pro-Malay. In the mid-1950s, a Left alliance, the Socialist Front, was
founded by a Malay party and a Chinese party; but its support was
almost entirely Chinese, and it eventually separated into its component
ethnic parties. In 1968, a moderate, multiethnic party, the Gerakan
Ra'ayat, was founded. It, too, had no appreciable Malay support. If
there were real two-party competition between multiethnic parties or
alliances, that would be a sure sign that ethnic divisions were declining
in importance, for it would indicate the presence of broad sectors of
moderate opinion.

By the same token, the establishment of a multiethnic party or alliance
will inevitably be followed by the formation of parties on the ethnic
flanks, provided that democratic norms of permissible party activity are
observed.[21] The reason for this is straightforward. In a severely divided
society, consorting and compromising with ethnic opponents are bound
to be viewed with disapproval by members of the various groups. The
sense of betrayal and the disagreement with the substance of the compromise give rise to electoral opportunities on the ethnic flanks, opportunities to which politicians will respond.

The same opportunities exist on the flanks even where temporary

20. That this is indeed true can be demonstrated by the emergence of basically similar
features in multiethnic alliances operating under comparable conditions. Among the bet-
ter-documented cases is the Alliance Party of Fiji. See R. S. Milne, " 'The Pacific Way'—
Consociational Politics in Fiji," *Pacific Affairs* 48 (Fall 1975): 413–31.
21. For other examples, see R. S. Milne, *Politics in Ethnically Bipolar States* (Vancouver: Univ. of British Columbia Press, 1981), 66–82; Brass, "Ethnic Cleavages and the
Punjab Party System" (unpublished paper presented at the 1972 annual meeting of the
Association for Asian Studies).

multiethnic coalitions have been formed. This is why they have such difficulty staying together through the next election. But the permanence of an alliance makes the flank opportunities unequivocal and irresistible. In such a situation, an ethnic party has everything to gain and nothing to lose by taking a firm position on ethnic issues.

This point can be made clearer by contrasting the situation of ethnic parties during the time of the coalition in Sri Lanka with their situation in Malaysia. In Sri Lanka, the temporary character of the coalition and the precarious balance among the Sinhalese parties made it unwise for any such party to take a position that would preclude it from joining in future interethnic coalitions. For Sinhalese parties, John Dunn aptly remarks, the central problem was "how to present themselves to the Sinhalese electorates as authentically bigoted against the Tamils (and hence dependably unyielding in their hostility towards Tamil interests), while at the same time (if hardly on the same occasions) presenting themselves to the Tamil political parties, with whom they might well need to ally immediately after the election in order to form a government, as honest and trustworthy political partners."[22] The very temporariness of the coalition tended to induce modest centripetal movements, as I explained earlier. In Malaysia, the permanence of the Alliance induced a centrifugal reaction, a flowering of ethnic parties, each claiming that the Alliance had sold out the interests of its group. There was no expectation that the situation was fluid or that today's opponents might have to be tomorrow's partners.

The flanking of a multiethnic alliance by ethnic parties is merely a special case of intragroup party proliferation discussed in Chapter 8. All the same rules apply. The flanks are populated by parties that differ from the alliance at least somewhat in their subethnic composition and fundamentally in their posture regarding interethnic relations.

On the Malay side, for example, the main party to challenge the Alliance was the Pan-Malayan Islamic Party, also called Parti Islam. Its electoral support has been concentrated heavily in two East Coast states. In 1959, the PMIP captured about one-fifth of the vote nationwide, but more than two-thirds in Kelantan and nearly half in Trengganu. Chinese flank parties have been, if anything, more regionalized. The Labor Party was strong in the states of Penang and Selangor, but hardly anywhere

22. Dunn, "Hoc Signo Victor Eris: Representation, Allegiance and Obligation in the Politics of Ghana and Sri Lanka" (unpublished paper, Cambridge, England, Sept. 1975), 16–17.

else, whereas the People's Progressive Party drew virtually all of its support from Perak. On both the Malay and Chinese sides, other forms of subethnic division, such as religion, language, and ancestral place of origin, play important roles in party affiliation.[23]

Subethnic differences among the parties are matters of degree, not always noticeable. The differences between the Center and the flanks in orientations toward the ethnic problem are, however, obvious, deep, and abiding. The success of the Malaysian flank parties is attributable to the formation of the Alliance or to the major policy compromises that followed from it. Some flank parties, such as the PMIP, antedate the Alliance, but their ability to gain significant support was a product of UMNO's linkage with a Chinese party.[24] In the 1955 election, the PMIP won the sole parliamentary seat not captured by the Alliance. But, by 1959, after the Alliance constitutional compromise, the PMIP became the second largest party, with 13 out of 104 seats, won on a platform of Malay sovereignty and the reservation of major positions for Malays only, as well as an Islamic state. UMNO, led by secularists, had been built on a base of village schoolteachers; village religious functionaries, often in rivalry with the teachers, were sometimes slighted. But the accession of many of the PMIP's most influential leaders is traceable to the formation of the Alliance.

Several Chinese parties drew their sustenance from the compromises of 1956–57. The electoral success of the Labor Party and the People's Progressive Party dates to this period. Still another Chinese party (the United Democratic Party) arose out of a dispute within the Alliance in 1959. In each case, segments of an ethnic group aggrieved by the results of interethnic bargaining appealed to the electoral process. The vitality

23. By way of illustration, I have previously mentioned the propensity of Hakkas and Hailams to support Chinese parties with left-wing pretensions. Likewise, in the state of Johore, Malays of Javanese origin tended to support UMNO, which had a prominent Johore Javanese in its leadership; while, in Lower Perak, Malays of Banjarese origin often supported PMIP, which had a prominent Banjarese from the area in its leadership. Among Chinese, the cleavage between those educated in English and those educated in Mandarin has been important in politics. In the Labor Party, for instance, a second generation of Chinese-educated leaders ousted the founding generation of English-educated leaders in the 1960s.

24. For a careful account of the founding of the PMIP, see N. J. Funston, "The Origins of Parti Islam Sa-Malaysia, With Special Reference to Ideology" (unpublished paper presented at the Sixth Congress of the International Association of Historians of Asia, Yogyakarta, Indonesia, Aug. 1974). See also John Funston, *Malay Politics in Malaysia* (Kuala Lumpur: Heinemann, 1980).

of the flank parties was directly attributable to their opposition to the Alliance.

The programs of the flank parties are mirror images. Where the PMIP claimed that "This country is a Malay country," justifying "absolute sovereignty" for the Malays and an exclusive position for the Malay language, the Chinese opposition parties demanded multilingualism and ethnic equality.[25]

The names and precise number of parties on the flanks may change, and the distribution of support between the Center and the respective flanks may fluctuate, but the condition of flanking is a permanent feature of an ethnically divided polity with an alliance at the Center. The Center and its compromise policies produce reactions on the flanks. The flank parties take extreme positions. These positions are the luxury of parties with neither the responsibility for governing nor the expectation of forming their own interethnic coalition—the ethnic Center is already occupied. The extreme positions thus taken further disqualify the flank parties for participation in coalitions of commitment. At most, there is an off chance of forming a coalition of convenience in the event the Center weakens. In Malaysia, even no-contest agreements between the Malay and Chinese flank parties have been difficult to reach.

Not that the flanks are unimportant; they are among the most important features of the system. The function of the flank parties—at times their conscious intention—was to erode the strength of the Alliance on the Malay or Chinese side and, in so doing, put pressure on the Alliance to bend in one ethnic direction or the other, to pay more attention to the needs of the Malays or to the aspirations of the Chinese and Indians. Whether the Alliance did bend, and in what direction, was in significant measure a function of the electoral balance between UMNO and the PMIP and between the MCA and the Chinese flank parties. To insure its continued ability to govern, the Alliance adjusted. It then regained its strength, and the flank parties were confirmed in their expectation that, except perhaps in the distant future, they would not have to govern. This reinforced their proclivity to express unmitigated ethnic claims, thus renewing the pressure.

The flank parties helped the Alliance calculate the electoral price of

25. The PMIP quotations are taken from the party's "General Policy Statement" (mimeo., 1965), 2. The Chinese opposition position is drawn illustratively from the 1969 PPP election manifesto, "Malaysia for Malaysians" (mimeo., 1969), 1.

various ethnic policy mixes. The price could be gauged by observing the waxing and waning of support on the edges of the Alliance. The aggregate strength of the parties on either flank was determined largely by the sense that UMNO had gone too far in yielding the Malay patrimony to the Chinese or that the MCA had abandoned the quest for Chinese equality. The shape of the party system on each flank, however, was determined by the structure and culture of the particular ethnic groups involved. For a number of reasons, the Chinese are a more heterogeneous ethnic group than the Malays, prone to scatter their support among several parties. The Chinese flank always had between two and four major parties, and at one point it also had a significant number of independent candidates with vote-drawing power. In sharp contrast, the Malay flank consisted, for all practical purposes, of the PMIP alone.[26] The two sides were not symmetrical or equally influential.

Consider the election of 1959, which is a good baseline from which to gauge the relation of the Center and the flanks, because it followed the constitutional compromises of 1956–57. The Alliance polled 51.5 percent of the total vote. The Malay flank parties polled 23.4 percent of the vote; the Chinese flank parties and independents, roughly the same. But the Chinese parties and independents split the anti-Alliance Chinese vote several ways, whereas the PMIP took 91 percent of the Malay flank vote. In 1964, fragmentation on the Chinese flank was more extreme, because more Chinese parties had entered the contest. The Chinese flank vote of 25.8 percent was fought over by four Chinese parties. On more than a quarter of the total vote, they managed to elect only 6 out of 104 members of parliament. The PMIP, virtually alone on the Malay flank, took nearly all of the Malay opposition vote, capturing 9 parliamentary seats.

What matters, then, is not just the existence or size of the flanks, but how they are composed. The practical effect of Chinese fragmentation, coupled with a frequent inability to reach electoral understandings, was to produce a large number of three- and even four-way contests in Chinese-majority parliamentary constituencies. MCA candidates frequently won election on less than half the vote in their constituencies. In short, fragmentation weakened the electoral power of the Chinese flank

26. In making these statements, I arbitrarily disregard parties like Negara and the Malayan Party, which in 1959 polled, respectively, 2.2 and 0.9 percent of the electorate; each elected one candidate. I also count the Socialist Front (Labor Party and Party Ra'ayat) as a Chinese party, because, with the exception of one area in Trengganu, virtually all of its voters were Chinese and Indians.

parties by splitting their Chinese vote. Small wonder that Chinese politics is punctuated by periodic movements to achieve "Chinese unity." Disunity and its consequences are acutely felt.

In terms of competition, plural polities have plural party systems. Segmented electorates can produce ethnically divergent patterns of competition for the vote. The Chinese electorate was faced with a multiparty system, exhibiting many of the traits associated with such systems. The impulse to expand clienteles often took a back seat to the drive to mobilize existing clienteles; the incentive to be inclusive was less attractive than the desire to be distinctive.[27] Thus, the PPP was content to represent the Chinese of Perak; the UDP hardly broadened out from its base in Penang; and the Labor Party, the most potent of the Chinese parties, purged its English-educated leadership and became a doctrinaire, Communist party, contracting its electoral appeal, in the late 1960s.

The Malay flank was quite different. The Malay party system tended toward two-party competition. In 1959, the PMIP received about 37 percent of all Malay votes, with the Alliance gaining most of the remainder. By 1969, the shares were much closer to even: about 40 percent to 54 percent.[28] The PMIP followed the textbook model of a competitor in a two-party system. Distinctions between *ulama* and secular Malay nationalists were papered over; a diverse following was sought on the basis of a vague platform; and special efforts were made to recruit English-educated professionals and intellectuals and to win seats in the West Coast states. These tactics were the antithesis of the course pursued by the Chinese parties. All of this made the Malay flank far more dangerous for the Alliance than the Chinese flank—again despite the roughly equal initial size of the flanks.

The flanks do more than provide electoral guidelines for the Center. Though the flank parties flourish as a reaction to the Center, their existence in turn reinforces the Center. By splitting both the Malay vote and the Chinese vote, the flank parties insured that neither UMNO nor MCA could govern alone: they drove the Alliance partners together and committed each to the survival of the other—save for those few people in UMNO who were prepared to think the unthinkable thought of lining

27. See Samuel P. Huntington, *Political Order in Changing Societies* (New Haven: Yale Univ. Press, 1968), 428–29; Giovanni Sartori, "European Political Parties: The Case of Polarized Pluralism," in Joseph LaPalombara and Myron Weiner, eds., *Political Parties and Political Development* (Princeton: Princeton Univ. Press, 1966), 159.
28. K. J. Ratnam and R. S. Milne, "The 1969 Parliamentary Election in West Malaysia," *Pacific Affairs* 43 (Summer 1970): 203–26, at 220.

up alone with the disdained competitor, the PMIP (run, it was said, by obscurantist *hajis* and religious teachers) to form an all-Malay government. What the flanks do to Center participants is to make them feel embattled by their respective competitors. At the same time, the flanks put competitive pressure on the alliance partners to make ethnic demands that are bound to test and strain the alliance relationship at many points.

RULES OF THE ALLIANCE GAME

The permanence of the commitments to the Alliance led to precisely that intimacy that Duverger claims is characteristic of single-slate coalitions. Relations between UMNO and MCA were thus never dependent on a single policy measure, such as the district councils proposal that disrupted the UNP-Federal Party coalition. Moreover, because of the continuing nature of the UMNO-MCA relationship, no issue was ever finally resolved.

The language issue is a good example. The constitution envisioned that English would continue to be an official language for ten years after independence. As that period drew to a close, a language bill was enacted that, in an extremely skillful compromise, made Malay the sole official language but permitted the continued use of English for many official purposes, as well as the "liberal" but unofficial use of Chinese and Tamil. Non-Malays, whose fluency rates in English were higher than those of the Malays, were not severely disadvantaged. The Chinese-educated, however, were disaffected. After the language act was passed, pressure grew on the flank for a Chinese-medium university, which immediately raised the inconceivable prospect of government recognition of its degrees and employment of its graduates. The MCA did not embrace the proposal, but did manage to achieve the opening of a vocationally oriented college to train graduates of Chinese-medium secondary schools, including preparation for possible university admission of students with facility in English and Malay. On the Malay side, the riots of 1969 were followed by an accelerated schedule to make Malay the medium of instruction in primary and secondary schools. Language issues provide many other illustrations of the process of continual readjustment of ethnic interests within the Alliance framework.

If the relationship was a continuing one, the terms of which were not settled by the original coalition agreement, this does not mean that reciprocity was unimportant. The Alliance style was suffused with elements of contractualism. Bargaining, employed so successfully in achieving a united front before independence, was a hallmark of the Alliance relationship, and its utility for ethnic harmony was often proclaimed. But the intimacy that the partners achieved led also to an emphasis on trust and mutual support to insure joint survival.[29] Relations among the partners were in fact governed by a series of unspoken and half-spoken rules that defined what was permissible and, in so doing, cushioned otherwise tense and difficult interactions.

The rules of Alliance bargaining extended to matters of substance and process. During the 1950s, UMNO and MCA leaders developed a core of consensus on principles. The MCA, for example, was to forgo claims to official multilingualism, but the UMNO leaders demonstrated considerable flexibility on language issues apart from official status. UMNO leaders agreed that certain opportunities, such as civil service positions, previously open only to Malays, should be more widely available, though not always on a freely competitive basis. The net effect of these and other areas of agreement was to rule extreme claims out of bounds and to solidify the Center. This fed ammunition to the flank parties as its implications for policy became clear, but it kept the partners together.[30]

It was understood that the MCA's position would be secondary. The Malay preponderance in the electorate and the ever-present danger on the Malay flank insured such a position. It was clear to the Tengku that the MCA might be able to broaden its support among the Chinese by espousing Chinese causes with less restraint, but this could not be done if the Alliance were to retain the support of the majority of Malays; on these grounds, it was discouraged.[31] In Alliance policy discussions, it was pointed out by UMNO leaders that some MCA candidates had to rely on Malay votes that would be harder to guarantee if the UMNO-MCA balance were altered, and the Tengku himself frequently re-

29. For example, the Chinese Unity Movement of 1971 was discussed at its inception in the UMNO Executive Council. The MCA's stock in the Chinese community was low, and top UMNO leaders supported the Unity Movement to help the MCA recruit members—though they certainly did not always approve of the turns the Movement took at later points.

30. Examples of actions taken in pursuit of the Alliance consensus are legion. Two of the better-known examples concern the Chinese language and Chinese middlemen. When some Chinese schoolteachers vociferously pressed for multilingualism in the 1950s, certain of their China-born leaders later found their citizenship withdrawn. When in 1962 the minister of agriculture failed to renew the licenses of Chinese rice millers in the state of Perak, the Tengku ordered the licenses restored. For this and other reasons, the minister eventually left the cabinet and UMNO.

31. Minutes of Alliance Executive Committee, Dec. 29, 1958 (mimeo.).

sponded to Chinese demands by indicating their unacceptability to the UMNO rank and file and to the Malay electorate. He perceived, in short, that where claims are incompatible, the breadth of the Center has very clear limits.

Competitive considerations on the Malay flank were much on the minds of the UMNO leaders as they bargained with the MCA. In the 1959 elections, large numbers of new Chinese citizens voted for the first time. The MCA leadership attempted to capture their vote. Conspicuous concessions on Chinese education and the number of MCA parliamentary candidates were sought from the Tengku, who, with equal conspicuity, denied the concessions. The state elections had already been held, and the PMIP had seized control of two states from the Alliance. Yielding to Chinese demands would jeopardize the fate of UMNO candidates. One faction in the MCA left the party over this issue, and large numbers of urban Chinese voters were permanently consigned to the opposition as a result.[32]

The MCA was not without its own bargaining levers. Outright alienation of the Chinese could lead to accelerated Communist guerrilla activity. Then, too, close personal relations had been built up between a few top MCA leaders and a few top UMNO leaders. On matters of keen importance to the MCA, these ties assured the party a sympathetic hearing (particularly from the Tengku in his capacity as arbitrator) and very often a favorable outcome.

Electoral dynamics thus slanted the Alliance toward UMNO and the Malays, and—given the strong sense of Malay priority—any other slant might have threatened public tranquility. But the outcome on any issue was not always predictable. Outside the core consensus, all issues were negotiable. The style of negotiation was deeply affected by the permanence envisioned for the coalition. The emphasis was on "open-hearted discussions in the spirit of give-and-take,"[33] a formulation that neatly illustrates the close intertwining of reciprocity with mutual trust and good will. The linkage of exchange with personal relations is quite characteristic of Malay culture. For the Malays, as noted earlier, work rela-

---

32. This brief depiction of the 1959 crisis does not do justice to its many interesting facets. The competitive dimension, albeit very important, is only one side of what was involved. Moreover, the Tengku did accede to some of the education policy demands made in 1959, but quietly and without the publicity MCA leaders sought.

33. Notes of a discussion at a meeting between Alliance representatives and M.I.C. representatives, Kuala Lumpur, Sept. 3, 1953 (mimeo.), 2. I am indebted to Tun Tan Siew Sin for permission to consult this and other documents in the MCA files in 1968.

tions are also personal relations, not merely matters of reciprocal advantage or convenience.[34] The Alliance functioned within the framework of the Malay cultural system, hospitable as it is to such enduring relationships.

Another element in the Alliance mix was the strong belief that contentious issues had to be resolved privately and quietly: "All Chinese and Indian leaders in the Alliance should be aware that complicated problems cannot be solved by holding demonstrations or emergency meetings or by headlines in the Press. It is only through mutual discussion and goodwill that amicable settlement can be reached."[35] It was not uncommon in the Alliance style for issues to be taken from the noisy, semipublic forums to which they were ostensibly committed and removed to the more tranquil meetings of the six or eight top MCA and UMNO leaders, to surface again only when an irrevocable decision had been reached. An example was the Alliance Action Committee on Language, which found itself divested of jurisdiction over the shape of the 1967 language bill as soon as its proceedings showed the depth of ethnic feelings on the issue. Nothing more was heard of the language bill until the finished product was presented to UMNO and the MCA on the eve of its introduction in parliament.[36]

How seriously these rules of procedure were taken can be shown by the way breaches of them were treated. The clearest of many cases is the 1959 UMNO-MCA dispute. When the then MCA president, Lim Chong Eu, released to the press a letter he had sent to the Tengku, a crisis was precipitated. The Tengku, reported a very reliable go-between, Cheah Toon Lok, "said the release of the letter was a bad mistake and it was tantamount to an ultimatum. It would have been much better if we had talked with him privately."[37] The Tengku demanded "trust," and he used the occasion to solidify his role as neutral arbitrator above all disputes. But the showdown was precipitated by the MCA breach of precepts of appropriate interpersonal behavior. The MCA leadership of the time had invoked public pressure in the midst of a process of private negotiations

34. See, e.g., Peter Wilson, *A Malay Village and Malaysia* (New Haven: HRAF Press, 1967), 106–07, 132, 146–48. See Chapter 3, above.
35. *Malaya Merdeka* (Kuala Lumpur), Apr. 19, 1956. This advice from the UMNO newspaper was dispensed in the midst of a serious dispute over citizenship rights for the non-Malays that threatened a breach in the Alliance. The advice was taken, and the issue was resolved.
36. Interview, Kuala Lumpur, Apr. 5, 1968.
37. Minutes, MCA Central Working Committee, Kuala Lumpur, July 11, 1959 (mimeo.), 3.

among people who should have been on intimate terms. The UMNO
leadership refused to play on these terms and forced the MCA—narrowly—to back down.[38] The Alliance process was thus a combination of
pressure outside and inside the component parties and of tightly regulated palace decision-making, a process open at some points, closed at
others.

The operational code was sufficiently elaborate that it could only have
emerged in a permanent coalition. Concepts of obligation, authority,
reciprocity, and friendship all came into play. Parties in only short-run
contact could not have mastered it in time to make the requisite adaptations. Indeed, it took the MCA quite some time to adjust to playing by
these rules. No comparable rules emerged to govern interaction in the
Sri Lanka coalition—it was governed entirely by contract, by the arm's
length agreement between the parties. For matters beyond the terms of
the agreement, there was no established conciliatory process. And when
the agreement could not be fulfilled without incurring intolerable costs,
the Sri Lanka coalition dissolved.

The Malaysian rules were in key respects the outgrowth of the decision to attempt a permanent coalition. They went hand in hand with the
need to apportion candidacies on a centralized basis, made necessary by
the decision to put forth a single slate, and they evolved further in the
lengthy process of hammering out the common program that was implied by a single slate. This could not have been forged unless a code
emerged to smooth the inevitable stresses, for outside the Alliance walls
the flank politicians and leaders of opinion were stating in no uncertain
terms what the Malays required and what the Chinese must insist on.
Inside, the participants created a rarified atmosphere that made continuing relations possible. This particular code was, of course, culturally
determined. The point is that some governing code is likely to emerge in
a permanent coalition, and the rules it embodies signify that the alliance
is more than just an arrangement between political buyers and sellers.

SIMPLIFYING THE FLANKS

In some ways, the closeness of relations among the Alliance partners
helped create a reaction that forced a fundamental change in relationships. Within UMNO and the PMIP, it was said in the late 1960s that

38. These norms were also invoked against UMNO leaders who sought to fashion a
different style of politics. The point here is that the norms governed both interethnic and
intraethnic relations.

the Tengku in particular was too generous to his Chinese friends and too ready to yield to Chinese demands in general. Many compromise outcomes provided the context for such assertions. Simultaneously, the appeal of a "Malaysian Malaysia" continued to be strong among many Chinese long after Singapore left the federation in 1965. In the 1969 election, the Chinese opposition parties capitalized on this, while the PMIP pressed its campaign for untrammeled Malay primacy. Differences among the Chinese parties were less pronounced than in the past—the Labor Party, by then Communist-dominated, boycotted the election—and no-contest agreements were reached by the three main Chinese opposition parties. The electoral effect of the no-contest agreements and of mutual discontent on the flanks was to reduce the Alliance majority in parliament and in state assemblies. For the first time, the Alliance polled less than half the vote nationwide (48 percent), though it still had a strong majority of parliamentary and state seats. The PMIP increased its share of the vote to 24 percent, while the three Chinese flank parties together won 26 percent. Clearly, the Center had contracted on both sides. The MCA, whose number of parliamentary seats was cut in half, announced that, in view of its repudiation by the electorate, it would not accept cabinet positions in the new government.

The Alliance position in some state assemblies was precarious. In Selangor, where Kuala Lumpur was located, the Alliance and the opposition had equal numbers of seats. Nevertheless, the opposition celebrated as if it had won a victory, and the Alliance responded as if it had lost. Opposition processions insulted Malay bystanders, and some Malays organized counterprocessions, which quickly turned to violence. The result was widespread disorder in Kuala Lumpur, a twenty-one-month period of emergency rule, and some basic changes in the Alliance format.

The apparent decline of a multiethnic coalition is often received with foreboding and violence. Both characterized Malaysia in May 1969. A consensus began to emerge among UMNO leaders that something had to be done about the flanks. Some advocated an UMNO-PMIP coalition, but the solution that emerged was at once more ingenious and far less favorable to the PMIP. "Sensitive issues"—citizenship, language, the special position of the Malays, and so on—were, by constitutional amendment, put beyond the reach of lawful debate. Impediments were thus placed in the way of the flank parties, for the appeal of those parties was premised on the unfairness of the ethnic equilibrium sanctioned by the constitutional compromises. New policies were also adopted to aid the Malays. Tengku Abdul Rahman was succeeded by his deputy, Tun Abdul Razak. Finally, soon after the resumption of parliamentary rule, the old Alliance coalition was broadened to absorb large segments of both flanks: the PMIP on the Malay side and the PPP and the Gerakan Ra'ayat on the Chinese side, as well as certain parties in East Malaysia. The new, broader coalition was eventually called the National Front. It was premised on the desirability of sharing the benefits of government more widely in order to obtain protection against electoral competition. The non-Malay Democratic Action Party was the only major party to resist the lure of office.[39]

What the creation of the National Front did, in the first instance, was to take the flank pressure off the government. On the Malay side, no significant force remained outside the government. On the Chinese side, the DAP might grow stronger, but it could no longer contribute to the possible downfall of the government. Indeed, the DAP did grow stronger, because the Chinese parties that joined the governing coalition disqualified themselves as spokesmen for alienated Chinese voters. In 1974, in 1978, and again in 1982, the DAP won about 20 percent of the total parliamentary vote.[40] When Chinese opposition parties like the PPP joined the governing coalition, much of the support they formerly derived from alienated Chinese voters was displaced to the DAP. It is striking that, regardless of the number of parties competing on the Chinese flank, the percentage of support that goes to the Chinese opposition holds steadily between 20 and 25 percent.

The PMIP was compromised from the inception of the Front. There was opposition within the party to joining the government, and this produced a split. The apportionment of candidates in the next election confined the PMIP to roughly its former share of parliamentary seats, thus insulating UMNO from continued erosion. More than this, the coalition itself produced conflicting strains inside the PMIP, for some leaders were more inclined than others to cooperate with UMNO. Fi-

39. Discussions were held between DAP and MCA leaders on the possibility of merging their two parties. These proved abortive.

40. On the electoral decline of the Chinese opposition that joined the Front, as well as for a cogent explanation of an apparent exception in Penang, see Chandrasekeran Pillay, *The 1974 General Elections in Malaysia* (Singapore: Institute of Southeast Asian Studies, Occasional Paper no. 24, 1974), 8–11. In Penang, the Gerakan Ra'ayat had captured the state government in 1969. No Chinese opposition party, the DAP included, was prepared to compete with Gerakan there, and the alternative in that Chinese-majority state would have been an UMNO-led government.

nally, in 1977, the PMIP split again, and the party was expelled from the National Front. So weakened was the rump PMIP that in 1978 it won only 17 percent of the total vote. By 1982, it was down to 14 percent, and it then split yet again.

Every prime minister of Malaysia has handled the Malay flank in his own way. The Tengku attempted to insure that UMNO was competitive—witness the part played by the PMIP electoral threat in the 1959 crisis with the MCA. Tun Razak neutralized the PMIP by bringing it inside the ruling coalition. His successor, Tun Hussein Onn, finished the job by splitting the party and then expelling it from the Front, weaker than when it had joined.

The results were equally comforting for UMNO on the Chinese side. Two things happened simultaneously to undermine the MCA's exclusive claim to speak for the Chinese inside the government. One was a passage of power, in UMNO and MCA, to a new generation of leaders who were neither privy to the formative Alliance experience nor on intimate terms with each other. The second was the admission of other Chinese parties to the government. The Gerakan Ra'ayat and the MCA, nominal allies, found themselves competitors in representing the Chinese. Mutual support in elections could not always be taken for granted,[41] and in governing councils UMNO leaders could often choose among conflicting Chinese views on given issues. The effect of these developments was to reduce Chinese influence.

Broadening the Alliance by creating the National Front was motivated by the desire to neutralize threats on the flanks.[42] The Alliance showed itself in 1969, as in 1959, to be especially sensitive to simultaneous erosion on both flanks. The result is a more complex coalition but a simplified party system, with a weakened party on the Malay flank and a strengthened one on the non-Malay flank.

Some major changes in conflict behavior have been wrought by the newer, much looser coalition. With Chinese interests no longer so strongly represented, cleavages within the Malay community have become more important. There has been a noticeable increase in factional divisions within UMNO, among the newly created Malay business class, and even among Malays of various state and subethnic origins. There are more political and economic benefits for Malays to compete for,

41. In certain constituencies, the organization of one party might drag its feet in mobilizing support for the candidate of the other, even though they are nominal allies.
42. Cf. von Vorys, Democracy without Consensus, 294–95, 308.

sometimes on an exclusive basis. To this extent, staving off the Chinese by unified action is less vital.

For the same reasons, there has been an increase in Chinese and Indian alienation, especially regarding the middle-class educational and employment opportunities increasingly reserved for Malays after 1969. With the competitive pressure off, the government can respond to non-Malay grievances as it perceives them to be reaching the point of serious discontent. Motives other than electoral-competitive ones always played some part in the Alliance accommodation of Chinese demands. The desire to maintain productivity, discourage support for the Communists, and preserve peace and harmony were important sources of conciliation. But, unaccompanied by strong electoral incentives, these motives are not sufficient to provide more than minimal protection of ethnic interests.

When multiethnic coalitions falter, they commonly dissolve into their component ethnic parties. The Alliance, too, faltered in 1969, but it did not break up into ethnic parties. Instead, it gave way to a broader coalition with a looser set of commitments, both of the various partners to each other and of the partners to a particular set of ethnic compromises. The Alliance habit, so to speak, produced a dramatic change in response to altered circumstances, but a change that fell far short of abandoning the coalition altogether.

CONFLICT AND COALITION: TEMPORARY AND PERMANENT

Several rather striking conclusions emerge from a comparison of the Sri Lankan coalition and the Malaysian Alliance and National Front. Perhaps the most striking is the absence of a linear relationship between the conflict situation and the political devices forged to deal with it.

By any reckoning, ethnic conflict was more acute in Malaysia. The Chinese and Indian population was substantial and yet precariously placed in the polity: a very large number of non-Malays became citizens only at independence. Malaysian politicians were also less inclined to deal with opposing political parties than Sri Lankan politicians,[43] who were geared to expect interparty negotiations. Even electoral no-contest agreements were difficult to reach in Malaysia. The conflict situation, the fluidity of party alignments, and elite attitudes all were more favora-

---

43. Early in the history of the Alliance, the partners turned aside overtures from smaller parties on the flanks, typically on grounds of programmatic incompatibility.

ble to prospects for interethnic coalition and conciliation in Sri Lanka than in Malaysia.

Yet, in the end, these proved to be mere background factors. Although the elite political culture and the potentially manageable level of conflict may have helped the Sri Lankan coalition along, less propitious conditions did not preclude a more complete and enduring Malaysian coalition. Coalition behavior was governed, not by any such general conditions, but by the particular structure of incentives at given moments of decision. Because of these incentives, the Malaysians developed a relationship that was more extensive in the number of matters that fell within its purview than was the coalition in Sri Lanka. And the Malaysians, who were far more discriminating about whom they would deal with in the opposition, even included their enemies on the flanks within the coalition when particular circumstances seemed to demand it. Clearly, the country with the less hospitable general conditions produced both a more tightly bonded arrangement and an arrangement capable of stretching and adapting.

Small differences at the moment of formation had large consequences later. Crucially important was the centrifugal or centripetal character of competition at the outset. In Malaysia, UMNO and the MCA happened to be opposed by a multiethnic party (the IMP). This fleeting moment of exclusively centripetal competition pushed them to a single slate, the form appropriate to a permanent coalition. In turn, this generated the inevitably sharp reaction on the ethnic flanks that always played a significant part in Alliance deliberations. In Sri Lanka, the UNP and the Federal Party were opposed by Sinhalese ethnic parties. These centrifugal pressures precluded a permanent arrangement. The coalition put forward no single slate, no common program, and it kept relationships among the parties indeterminate. This indeterminacy staved off the most extreme ethnic reactions by parties outside the coalition, because they could not tell when they in turn might need to form a multiethnic coalition. The permanent arrangement propelled by centripetal competition generated extreme reactions but accomplished more in ethnic compromise. The temporary arrangement constrained by centrifugal competition held extreme reactions temporarily in check but was confined to a brief period of incremental measures.

Equally important was the extent of vote pooling. Tamil votes transferred to the UNP constituted a marginal increment that could rapidly be offset by Sinhalese disaffection with the coalition. The more equal numbers of Malays and Chinese and the larger number of significantly heterogeneous constituencies in Malaysia provided a considerable exchange of Malay and Chinese votes between the MCA and UMNO that was not as easily outweighed by threats on the flanks.[44]

Vote pooling also affected the long-term durability of the Malaysian arrangements. In Sri Lanka, it was possible for a Sinhalese party to gain an absolute majority of seats. Both the UNP and SLFP have, at various times, done so. But, so long as there was significant competition from the PMIP, the large number of Chinese voters plus the division of Malay votes meant that no Malay party could count on securing a majority of seats by itself. In the early 1970s, it was possible for UMNO and PMIP to have formed a coalition to govern alone. But, from UMNO's perspective, it was useful to include other parties—and all other potential partners were non-Malay parties—as a counterweight to the PMIP. Moreover, by then the long history of non-Malay participation in the Alliance had made "one-race government" something of a bogey, a great step into the unknown, quite different from the all-Sinhalese governments familiar to Sri Lanka. Arrangements perpetuated by the long practice of vote pooling had the effect of making drastically different options seem unattractive and risky.

None of this is to deny, of course, the role of leadership commitments, the development of mechanisms within the coalition to handle contentious issues, or personal relations among coalition leaders. All of these were important in Malaysia and were less well developed in Sri Lanka. But, at the same time, there is no reducing coalition-maintenance practices to a few formulae focused solely on internal relationships or mechanisms, such as the exclusion of divisive issues from debate or the insistence on unanimity before decisions are taken.[45] The Malaysian coalition had its internal practices and rules, but it also functioned in an external electoral environment that conditioned its behavior at every point. In the Malaysia of 1969, that external electoral environment exerted the most powerful, disruptive effect on internal Alliance relations, just as it had earlier driven the partners together and kept them together.

44. For some estimates of vote transfers in 1969, see von Vorys, *Democracy without Consensus*, 302–03, 305.

45. See, e.g., John E. Schwarz, "Maintaining Coalitions: An Analysis of the EEC with Supporting Evidence from the Austrian Grand Coalition and the CDU/CSU," in Sven Groennings, E. W. Kelly, and Michael Leiserson, eds., *The Study of Coalition Behavior* (New York: Holt, Rinehart & Winston, 1970), 235–49. Cf. William T. Bluhm, *Building an Austrian Nation* (New Haven: Yale Univ. Press, 1973), 115–16.

If the electoral system is functioning, leaders in developing countries will respond to electoral incentives.

MULTIETHNIC PARTIES

If multiethnic coalitions are difficult to sustain in severely divided societies, unitary parties organized across ethnic lines are far more vulnerable to schism. The incompatibility of ethnic claims to power; the propensity for demands to be made at the expense of other groups; the taint that often attaches to working in political concert with members of opposing ethnic groups; and the incentives politicians have to organize their clienteles along ethnic lines before someone else does so—these are among the forces that undermine multiethnic parties.

Yet multiethnic parties are not always impossible. There is, for example, the Punjab Congress in India, which operated as a consolidated multiethnic party, flanked by ethnic parties, in an environment of conflict between Sikhs and Hindus. "All lines of conflict were reflected within the Punjab Congress, which contained sub-groups whose leaders articulated the major viewpoints expressed outside the Congress."[46] Moreover, the Punjab Congress was able to absorb certain stresses that multiethnic alliances would find it very difficult to cope with. As the strength of the flank parties fluctuated, Congress experienced considerable alternations in the basis of its support.[47] Sometimes it was more Sikh than Hindu, sometimes the reverse; but the party survived these oscillations. Such pendular movements would be destabilizing for an alliance organized around existing ethnic parties, for each component party has an organizational interest in maintaining its own strength within the coalition. Duverger's point that inequality is inherent in the alliance relationship means that major swings of ethnic support will threaten that relationship.

Paul Brass attributes Congress' success in maintaining Sikh and Hindu support during the 1950s and '60s to three factors: "it was able to evolve a minimally successful compromise on the language issues"; it overrepresented in state cabinets the group with the stronger flank party (the Sikhs); and a Sikh led the party between 1956 and 1964.[48] No doubt

46. Paul R. Brass, *Language, Religion and Politics in North India* (London: Cambridge Univ. Press, 1974), 348.
47. Brass, "Ethnic Cleavages and the Punjab Party System," 15–16.
48. *Language, Religion and Politics in North India*, 358.

the various decisions to show solicitude for the group advancing "special claims" to the Punjab had much to do with maintaining the multiethnic character of the state Congress.[49] A party not slanted toward the group with pretensions to legitimacy would be unlikely to keep that group's support. But, as the movement for a separate, Sikh-majority state grew, Congress might not have kept Sikh support—after all, Hindus were attached to Congress as the party *resisting* the Sikh claim to statehood[50]— were it not for the fact that the Congress Party also ruled at the national level of politics.[51] Congress in New Delhi had the power to confer what the Sikhs wanted and eventually received in 1966: a Sikh-majority state. While that demand was pending, there was good reason for both Sikhs and Hindus to maintain their presence in the Punjab Congress. The Punjab was part of a larger political system, and the Punjab Congress had influence with the Congress Party in New Delhi.

All of this goes simply to show that the Punjab Congress was a special case, in which the pressures likely to tear a unitary multiethnic party asunder were countered by strong incentives for both sides to remain attached. In most independent countries, there is no higher level of political authority, no New Delhi. In such countries, the Guyanese People's Progressive Party of the 1950s provides a more reliable guide to the schismatic fate of multiethnic parties where divisions are sharp and elections are free.[52]

49. See Baldev Raj Nayar, *Minority Politics in the Punjab* (Princeton: Princeton Univ. Press, 1966), 264.

50. See generally ibid., 305–21.

51. Nayar comments: "Even if some group is disaffected with the Congress party at the state level it feels it has a chance to be heard by the Congress party at the center and to have its grievances redressed." Ibid., 283.

52. Some multiethnic parties fought hard to resist the pressures. One that did was the Somali Youth League (SYL), dominant party of the Somali Republic until the military coup of 1969. At various times, the SYL represented more strongly one or another of the various Somali groups (usually called clans, but for political purposes tantamount to ethnic groups). At the core of the SYL were two of the largest groups, Darood and Hawiye, uneasily linked together, though subject to the defection of subgroups from time to time. The cultivator groups, the Rahanwein and Digil, and the Northern Isaq tended to support their own ethnic parties, from which the SYL repeatedly tried to lure them. Groups and subgroups moved in and out of the SYL with bewildering rapidity as the party sought to stitch together multiethnic majorities. But "the more effectively the League widened its base, and the greater its electoral success, the more profound became its internal divisions." I. M. Lewis, *The Modern History of Somaliland* (New York: Praeger, 1965), 147. In 1969, the SYL gained a majority of seats, but with only 40 percent of the vote, in an election filled with violence, much of it interethnic. The main ethnic opposition parties also lost support, while small parties, primarily representing local subgroups, gained. The SYL put together yet another carefully balanced government, reportedly at a very high price. When the assembly met, all the opposition members crossed the floor to the SYL, effectively ending

FROM COMPETITIVE PARTY
SYSTEMS TO SINGLE-PARTY SYSTEMS

The ethnic divisions cannot be willed away, but the free elections can be. Where multiethnic parties have survived, they have done so by outlawing electoral competition, dissolving opposition, and coercively recreating their threatened multiethnic base. Single-party systems, says Samuel P. Huntington, are typically found in societies rent by a social-class or an ethnic cleavage.[53] To be sure, they may also arise from other circumstances. In Ghana, for example, the one-party state was created by Nkrumah after the worst period of ethnic conflict had ended. Nkrumah's personal fears and suspicions, some of them well-founded, played a role over and above the ethnic element.[54] But, in one country after another, and particularly in Africa, single-party regimes have been a response to the inability of multiethnic parties, typically forged to oppose colonial rule, to keep their multiethnic support intact in the face of elections.

Most often the move to a one-party state occurs as a reaction to flanking. A ruling multiethnic party is confronted with the growth of ethnic parties that threaten to erode its constituency or to make it difficult to rule. In the name of national unity, the electoral contest is ended by decree. There are two variants of this process. In one, typified by Zambia, ethnic parties grow on both flanks and hold out the prospect that the multiethnic party, unable to satisfy either side, will be left with a drastically shrunken base. In the other, exemplified by Kenya, an ethnic party grows on only one flank, but the cleavage it represents is sharp and intense.

Zambia is an archetype of bilateral flanking.[55] Zambia became a one-

---

the Somali experiment in multiethnic parties with free elections. Some months later, a coup confirmed the end of the multiethnic party. See I. M. Lewis, "The Politics of the 1969 Somali Coup," *Journal of Modern African Studies* 10 (July 1972): 383–408; Lewis, "Nationalism and Particularism in Somalia," in P. H. Gulliver, ed., *Tradition and Transition in East Africa* (Berkeley and Los Angeles: Univ. of California Press, 1969), 339–61; E. A. Bayne, "Somalia's Myths Are Tested," American Universities Field Staff *Reports*, Northeast Africa Series, vol. 16, no. 1 (1969); Al Castagno, "Somalia Goes Military," *Africa Report*, Feb. 1970, pp. 25–27; A. A. Castagno, "Somali Republic," in James S. Coleman and Carl G. Rosberg, Jr., eds., *Political Parties and National Integration in Tropical Africa* (Berkeley and Los Angeles: Univ. of California Press, 1964), 512–59.

53. "Social and Institutional Dynamics of One-Party Systems," in Samuel P. Huntington and Clement H. Moore, eds., *Authoritarian Politics in Modern Society: The Dynamics of Established One-Party Systems* (New York: Basic Books, 1970), 11.

54. Martin L. Kilson, "Authoritarian and Single-Party Tendencies in Africa," *World Politics* 15 (Jan. 1963): 262–94.

55. See Thomas Rasmussen, "Political Competition and One-Party Dominance in Zambia," *Journal of Modern African Studies* 7 (Oct. 1969): 407–24; Margaret Rouse

party state by fiat in 1972 despite repeated pronouncements by President Kenneth Kaunda that this would only happen if the electorate willed it. What changed Kaunda's mind was the challenge to his multiethnic party from parties representing three of the major ethnic groups in the country.

Kaunda's United National Independence Party (UNIP) is the product of several splits in the first Zambian nationalist party, the African National Congress (ANC), led by Harry Nkumbula. Of the two parties, UNIP was determined to wage a more militant struggle against the British. Though Bemba were in the forefront, UNIP attracted a multiethnic following—with a major exception. In the South, Nkumbula, an Ila, managed to keep the allegiance of the Ila and Tonga groups with the ANC. UNIP led the country to independence, and in the first national elections in 1964 won 85 percent of the parliamentary seats on 70 percent of the vote. Only then did severe ethnic problems manifest themselves within the party.[56]

Participants framed the issue in terms of Bemba power. The Bemba, a large group (perhaps a third of the population if all Bemba-speakers are counted, close to a fifth if not), were strongly represented in government positions and in UNIP. So, too, were Nyanja and other Easterners. The Lozi of the Western Province, wary of Bemba domination, were much less active; some Lozi leaders sought British protection from what they saw as premature independence. Tonga voters remained loyal to the ANC. Nonetheless, all groups were represented on UNIP's central com-

---

Bates, "UNIP in Postindependence Zambia: The Development of an Organizational Role" (Ph.D. diss., Harvard Univ., 1971); Robert I. Rotberg, "Tribalism and Politics in Zambia," *Africa Report*, Dec. 1967, pp. 29–35; Ruth Weiss, "Mulungushi and Zambia's Tribalism," *Venture*, July 1971, pp. 14–16; Richard Hall, *The High Price of Principles: Kaunda and the White South* (New York: Africana, 1970), 190–204; Robert H. Bates, "Approaches to the Study of Ethnicity," *Cahiers d'Etudes africaines* 10 (1970): 546–61; Ian Scott and Robert Molteno, "The Zambian General Elections," *Africa Report*, Jan. 1969, pp. 42–47; Dennis L. Dresang, "Ethnic Representation and Development Administration: A Comparative Study of Kenya and Zambia" (unpublished paper presented at the 1974 annual meeting of the American Political Science Association), 8–9; William Tordoff, ed., *Politics in Zambia* (Manchester, England: Manchester Univ. Press, 1974); *Africa Report*, May 1970, pp. 5–6; ibid., Oct. 1970, p. 5.

56. Perhaps because of the suddenness with which they struck, ethnic problems in Zambia have been regarded, even more than elsewhere in Africa, as an epiphenomenon, an artifact of something else, or a creation of politicians. See Rotberg, "Tribalism and Politics in Zambia," 30; Robert Molteno, "Cleavage and Conflict in Zambian Politics," in Tordoff, ed., *Politics in Zambia*, 62–106; Rasmussen, "Political Competition and One-Party Dominance in Zambia," 419. Although writers might argue that ethnic conflict had no pre-colonial roots and little reality beneath elite levels, nonetheless in 1968 there was Bemba-Lozi violence on the Copperbelt. See *Africa Report*, Oct. 1968, p. 35. Bemba hegemony and Lozi separatism proved to be major issues in the post-independence period.

mittee. Kaunda had to balance the composition of his cabinet and his party leadership. "From its very inception, UNIP has had to convince Zambians that it was not a Bemba-dominated party."[57]

One result of the balancing process was that Bemba felt underrepresented in the party apparatus, both in proportion to their numbers and to their role in the party's fight for independence. In 1967, Bemba leaders linked up with Tonga leaders in UNIP to gain a larger share of seats in the party central committee. They won a decisive victory over Lozi and Easterners, capturing the offices of party vice-president, secretary-general, and treasurer. In the most dramatic contest, a Bemba, Simon Kapwepwe, defeated an Easterner, Reuben Kamanga, for the party vice-presidency and automatically became Vice-President of Zambia.

The effects of this victory were immediate. All groups took measures of political self-protection. Two committees sprung up inside the party. Bemba were at the core of one; the other was designed to fight Bemba domination. A "Unity in the East" movement also developed. A dormant Lozi party, the United Party, came to life, but it was banned before the 1968 general election. Lozi opposition leaders thereupon took their following into the ANC, which swept the Tonga areas of the South and the Lozi areas of the West. UNIP won the election overwhelmingly, but the swing of Lozi away from the ruling party was decisive: the two highest-ranking Lozi in UNIP and three Lozi ministers all lost their seats.

Within months of the party elections, the strong position of Bemba in government departments and commissions appeared to grow even stronger.[58] Kapwepwe, lionized in the Bemba North, became an object of hostility elsewhere. With the growth of a strong ANC, united on the issue of Bemba hegemony, Kaunda took action to reduce the influence of the Bemba, and to do so visibly. On the eve of a 1969 party central committee meeting at which a strong majority of provincial party units was prepared to vote no-confidence in Kapwepwe, Kaunda dissolved the central committee. Over the next two years, Kaunda scaled down Kapwepwe's power and in general placated non-Bemba, so much so that Bemba began to complain of persecution. When Kaunda dismissed four Bemba ministers in 1971, Kapwepwe formed a new party, the United Progressive Party, catering to Bemba interests. The response to grievances expressed through parties on one flank had produced an equal and opposite reaction on the other.

57. Rasmussen, "Political Competition and One-Party Dominance in Zambia," 421.
58. See Dresang, "Ethnic Representation and Development Administration," 8.

The UPP pulled a significant segment of Bemba support away from UNIP, but its virtually all-Bemba composition did not prevent the party from reaching a no-contest agreement with the ANC for by-elections held at the end of 1971. It was an agreement that might later have ripened into a coalition of convenience. The by-election results were mixed. Kapwepwe won a seat, four other UPP candidates lost, and the ANC won four of its six contests with UNIP. But the threat on the flanks was enough to induce Kaunda to ban the UPP and later the ANC, detain Kapwepwe and some two hundred of his followers, and announce that Zambia would have a one-party state. Kaunda had found it impossible to harmonize Bemba and non-Bemba claims, each made relative to the other.

Kenya's party history replicates the merger and split pattern examined in Chapter 7.[59] The Kenya African National Union (KANU), formed in 1959, embraced the two largest groups, Kikuyu and Luo. Most of the other major groups were at first organized in separate ethnic parties: one for the Kalenjin, one for the Kamba, one for the Coastal groups, and one for the Masai. As fear of Kikuyu and Luo domination grew, several of the other groups merged into a Kenya African Democratic Union (KADU). Of the major groups, only the Kamba joined KANU, but in 1964 KADU was finally merged into the ruling party, leaving Kenya for a time without any opposition. The opposition soon came, however, when Oginga Odinga, a leading Luo in KANU, was edged out in the struggle to succeed Kenya's President Jomo Kenyatta. Odinga formed his own party, the Kenya People's Union, which contested the 1966 election and won the support of most Luo. Still, ethnic alignments were not perfect: some Kikuyu had joined the KPU, and some Luo, including another contender for the succession, Tom Mboya, had remained in KANU.

When Mboya was assassinated in 1969, all this changed. Luo closed ranks, and so did Kikuyu. The KPU took the killing up as a Luo cause. A Kikuyu vice-president of the KPU left the party and rejoined KANU.

59. George Bennett and Carl G. Rosberg, *The Kenyatta Election: Kenya, 1960–1961* (London: Oxford Univ. Press, 1961); Cherry Gertzel, *The Politics of Independent Kenya, 1963–8* (Evanston: Northwestern Univ. Press, 1970); Stuart H. Schaar, "A Note on Kenya," American Universities Field Staff *Reports*, East Africa Series, vol. 7, no. 3 (1968); Norman N. Miller, "Assassination and Political Unity: Kenya," ibid., vol. 8, no. 5 (1969); Stanley Meisler, "Tribal Politics Harass Kenya," *Foreign Affairs* 49 (Oct. 1970): 111–21; Richard Stren, "Factional Politics and Central Control in Mombasa, 1960–1969," *Canadian Journal of African Studies* 4 (Winter 1970): 33–56; *Africa Report*, Apr. 1970, pp. 8–11.

Party and ethnic boundaries had become coterminous. At that point, as Luo unrest developed, the KPU was banned, and its leaders were arrested. Many of them later rejoined KANU, now irreversibly in the single-party mold.

In both Zambia and Kenya, the one-party state was a response to the growth of ethnic parties that challenged the multiethnic inclusiveness of the ruling party and threatened to produce an ethnic party system. Both the Zambian and Kenyan variants can be found elsewhere in Africa. In Mauritania, for example, ethnic parties appeared on both the Moorish and black-African flanks before all opposition parties were outlawed in 1959.[60] In Chad, the consolidation of Muslim opposition in 1960 left the regime entirely Southern and Christian. Soon thereafter, there was only one legal party.[61]

THE ETHNIC EFFECTS OF ONE-PARTYISM

It is often said that the creation of a single-party system does not end bickering and disputation but merely shifts its venue. The assertion of group claims no longer takes place between parties but rather within parties. Sometimes provision is made for competition among candidates, all belonging to the single party and seeking public office. More usually, control of the party and the cabinet are the objects of competition between factions, including those based on ethnic groups. This is all true as far as it goes, but it does not go far enough. The end of party competition in elections means the end of the most important form of public accountability. It opens opportunities for ethnic and even subethnic cliques and factions to attain hegemonic influence that would probably be checked in openly democratic systems, where failure to pay careful attention to ethnic distribution and representation risks loss of power.[62]

60. Alfred G. Gerteiny, *Mauritania* (New York: Praeger, 1967), chaps. 11–12.
61. John A. Ballard, "Four Equatorial States," in Gwendolen M. Carter, ed., *National Unity and Regionalism in Eight African States* (Ithaca: Cornell Univ. Press, 1966), 270–72. See also Virginia Thompson and Richard Adloff, *The Emerging States of French Equatorial Africa* (Stanford: Stanford Univ. Press, 1960), 427–41.
62. Huntington, "Social and Institutional Dynamics of One-Party Systems," 15–16, suggests that one-party systems arising out of ethnic bifurcation are usually "exclusionary" in that they perpetuate "the indefinite exclusion of the subordinate group from politics." He cites the cases of South Africa, Liberia, and the United States South under Jim Crow, but the point holds in general even for unranked groups, as we shall see. And the enormous exclusionary power of single-party regimes exists despite the general withering of the party in favor of the state bureaucracy in many developing countries. However rusty its machinery, the party, among other things, can still control recruitment to key state positions.

Examples of strong ethnic and subethnic hegemony in single-party systems are easy to come by. In the Ivory Coast, Houphouët-Boigny's Baoulé group has consistently been overrepresented in the ruling inner circle.[63] In Mauritania before the 1978 coup, not only did the Moors have a preeminent position, but supreme power was far more narrowly held: both Moktar Ould Daddah and his early rival, Souleymane Ould Cheikh Sidya, belonged to the Ould Biri subgroup, and so did other influential politicians.[64] In Guinea, the single-party regime of Sékou Touré provided a facade for the dominance of the Malinké, who comprise a third of the population.[65]

In determining which groups achieve hegemony, the precise sequence of events is important. Groups outside the ruling party at the time of conversion to a single-party state will tend to be left outside, whatever their earlier position. Why this is so can be explained by a glance at the ethnic effects of one-party rule in Zambia and Kenya.

When Kaunda took measures to reduce the influence of Bemba in UNIP between 1969 and 1971, the unintended beneficiaries were Nyanja and other Easterners.[66] The other major groups, Lozi and Tonga, tended not to support UNIP. The Eastern Province remained solidly pro-UNIP; it had always furnished a significant number of party functionaries. It was, in fact, the Nyanja-speaker, Reuben Kamanga, whom Kapwepwe had ousted as party vice-president in 1967. When the one-party system was installed, "the political pattern in the country indicated a heavy swing in Government toward the Eastern Province. The Southern

---

63. See Aristide R. Zolberg, *One-Party Government in the Ivory Coast*, rev. ed. (Princeton: Princeton Univ. Press, 1969), 13, 275, 278. Zolberg also reports that some important groups like the Bété were not integrated into the single party at local levels; the Bété, like another major group, the Agni, were organized early on into separate flank parties. Ibid., 129–30. Documentation for later periods is lacking. But see *Africa Confidential*, May 11, 1983, p. 7.

64. Clement H. Moore, "One-partyism in Mauritania," *Journal of Modern African Studies* 3 (Oct. 1965): 402–20; William Eagleton, Jr., "The Islamic Republic of Mauritania," *Middle East Journal* 19 (Winter 1965): 45–53.

65. 'Ladipo Adamolekun, *Sékou Touré's Guinea* (London: Methuen, 1976), 173–74, in an otherwise glowing treatment of the Guinean regime, notes that, of seven members of the politburo as of 1972, there were five Malinké, only one Foulah ("a political lightweight" brought in "as the representative of the Foulahs"), and only one Soussou (of dubious political reliability). Adamolekun puts the Malinké share of the population at 34 percent, the Foulah at 29 percent, and the Soussou at 18 percent. Ibid., 131. For discussions of the ethnic politics of the Guinean regime, I am also indebted to conversations with certain Guinean exiles.

66. William Tordoff and Ian Scott, "Political Parties: Structures and Policies," in Tordoff, ed., *Politics in Zambia*, 118–19.

Province carried little political weight in the center, the Western Province not very much more . . . . The North and Copperbelt, with its UPP supporters, had lost ground, too, leaving the field in Lusaka to leaders from the Eastern Province."[67] Kamanga became party secretary-general.

To be sure, the newly banned parties were to be integrated into UNIP. The ANC voted to merge with the single party in 1973. Kapwepwe and other top UPP leaders rejoined UNIP in 1977. But UNIP branches put obstacles in the way of former ANC members, while Kamanga helped prevent Kapwepwe from running for the UNIP presidency.[68] Although important positions were later given to Lozi, they never recovered the influence they sacrificed by defecting to the ANC.[69] The Tonga had no influence to recover. Above all, the Bemba had made everyone else so wary of their ambitions that party members were quite ready to block their return to UNIP. Although the Easterners had at first obtained their preeminence by default, later, as the support of other groups began to fall away from UNIP, the Easterners were able to consolidate their position by deliberate action. The hegemony of Easterners may not continue forever, but its existence for over a decade despite Kaunda's intentions is impressive testimony to the difficulty of achieving an ethnic balance of power under a single-party system.

The end of opposition in Kenya had the same effect. When KPU leaders rejoined KANU, that did not signify the return of Kikuyu-Luo dominance. In the interim, the Kikuyu had solidified their hold on the party and the state. The Mboya assassination and the violent Luo reaction had precipitated a wave of Kikuyu ceremonial oaths not to let power pass from Kikuyu hands. As the UNIP apparatus prevented Kapwepwe from making a comeback within the Zambian party, so the KANU machinery was twice used to prevent Odinga from running for party vice-

---

67. Colin Legum, ed., *Africa Contemporary Record, 1973–1974* (New York: Africana, 1974), p. B331.

68. Kapwepwe was barred from running in 1978 by a hastily passed amendment to the party constitution. It was said that his former party opponent, Kamanga, had pushed the amendment. For the obstacles earlier placed in the way of ex-ANC members, see Colin Legum, ed., *Africa Contemporary Record, 1974–1975* (New York: Africana, 1975), p. B330.

69. For the decline of the Lozi within UNIP, see Colin Legum, ed., *Africa Contemporary Record, 1975–1976* (New York: Africana, 1976), p. B383. Many Lozi leaders had been arrested in 1973. Legum, ed., *Africa Contemporary Record, 1973–1974*, p. B328. For later gestures, see Legum, ed., *Africa Contemporary Record, 1980–1981* (New York: Africana, 1981), p. B898; *Africa Confidential*, Nov. 25, 1981, p. 7.

president and for parliament,[70] and in 1982 he was expelled from the party. The Luo were no longer partners.

So securely were the Kikuyu in control during Kenyatta's last years that the cleavage that mattered most was within the Kikuyu group, between those from Kiambu and those from Nyeri and Muranga. Kenyatta was a Kiambu and so were nearly all of his Kikuyu cabinet ministers and others in his inner circle. The assassination in 1975 of J. M. Kariuki, a popular Nyeri leader, was widely interpreted as evidence of the bitterness of the Kiambu-Nyeri struggle. This conflict between subgroups was made possible by the unchallenged primacy of the Kikuyu in the single-party state.

When Kenyatta died in 1978, the succession struggle revolved around two groups, both mainly Kiambu Kikuyu. Each of them struck alliances with non-Kikuyu. One clique had the allegiance of Luo leaders; the other had aid from some Kamba politicians. But in both cases this backing did not bespeak any real ability of non-Kikuyu to affect the outcome—the links were as much gestures of fealty as offers of support. No one thought it possible to prevent a Kikuyu-controlled succession.[71] A Kalenjin, Daniel arap Moi, became president, with the backing of the stronger of the two Kikuyu factions. The ability of Kikuyu leaders, even when divided among themselves, to determine the outcome without any challenge to their power speaks eloquently for the conclusiveness of Kikuyu control. Despite episodic conciliatory gestures toward the Luo and toward groups well represented in the armed forces, intra-Kikuyu rivalry continued to be the mainspring of Kenyan politics.[72]

The single party, then, is not a likely vehicle for the preservation of an imperiled multiethnicity. Groups that left the multiethnic party in favor of a flank party do usually return once opposition is prohibited. But the absence of interparty electoral competition weakens their hand in negotiating the terms of their return. More to the point, those ethnic groups that stayed continuously in the party that is now the only legal party

70. Magina Magina, "Kenya: Election Hurdles," *Africa*, Nov. 1979, pp. 20–21; Colin Legum, ed., *Africa Contemporary Record, 1977–1978* (New York: Africana, 1979), p. B264.
71. See ibid., pp. B263–65; *Africa Confidential*, Aug. 25, 1978, pp. 1–4; ibid., Oct. 20, 1978, pp. 6–7.
72. For early assessments, see M. Tamarkin, "From Kenyatta to Moi—The Anatomy of a Peaceful Transition of Power," *Africa Today* 26 (Nov. 1979): 21–37; Godfrey Muriuki, "Central Kenya in the Nyayo Era," ibid., 39–42; Vincent B. Khapoya, "Kenya Under Moi: Continuity or Change?" *Africa Today* 27 (May 1980): 17–32. See also *Africa Confidential*, June 8, 1983, pp. 1–3.

were consolidating their hold while others were off playing competitive politics on the flanks. They do not accept the reentry on equal terms of those (like the Luo or Bemba) who had earlier left the party or (like the Tonga) never been part of it. The inclusiveness of the single party in principle is thus belied in fact.

The single party can afford to favor some groups and subgroups because elections between parties are at an end. It is no longer necessary to build a majority. While elections continued, the opposition may have been ethnically defined, and so may the ruling party. The electoral process and ethnically based party antagonisms may have sharpened ethnic divisions. But, while they lasted, the exigencies of elections required at least enough ethnic spread to win. With this necessity obviated, the single party paves the way for minority rule, while providing a multiethnic cover for those groups and subgroups that are well positioned to exclude the rest. In this respect, the narrow ethnic base of single-party systems resembles the equally narrow ethnic base of other non-electoral systems. These may be civilian, such as the Ethiopian monarchy under Haile Selassie, which grossly favored, not just Amhara, but Amhara of the Shoan subgroup. They may also be military, as we shall see in Part Four. The common element is the absence of electoral brakes on the spiral of ethnic exclusiveness. The peculiar paradox of the single party is that, in ethnic terms, often the party that begins with the broadest base becomes the narrowest.

MULTIETHNIC ORGANIZATIONS IN CONDITIONS OF ADVERSITY

The difficulty of sustaining multiethnic parties and coalitions demonstrates the fidelity with which political organizations in ethnically divided societies reflect underlying tensions. We have observed that unitary multiethnic parties tend to decompose into ethnic parties. We have witnessed the short-lived character of coalitions of convenience, and we have seen that even coalitions of commitment are vulnerable to parties on their flanks. Finally, attempts to preserve or restore a threatened multiethnicity by abolishing flank parties and moving to single-party politics have proved futile. There is abundant evidence on all fronts that durable multiethnic parties and coalitions are rare exceptions where ethnic divisions are sharp.

There is, however, more to be said. I have shown earlier that coalitions of commitment are products of electoral incentives. The difficulty of sustaining multiethnic parties and coalitions is equally the result of electoral-competitive incentives. Even ethnic outcomes of single-party politics are explicable in these terms: the failure of the single party to preserve broad-based multiethnic participation is a function of the withdrawal of electoral-competitive incentives, which would otherwise place limits on narrowing tendencies. The structure of electoral incentives shapes the calculations of politicians who join coalitions and those who destroy them, of those who form ethnic parties and those who control single parties.

It is true that most often the effect of existing electoral incentives on multiethnic parties and coalitions has been disintegrative. It is also true that political leaders who are willing to take the risks entailed can radically alter the structure of electoral incentives in their favor—indeed, can smash the electoral system altogether. But neither of these points detracts from the significance of the formal incentive structure, either in explaining party and coalition development in ethnically divided societies or in pointing the way to accommodative institutions. On the contrary, the ready mutability of electoral systems can be turned to the advantage of statesmen as well as scoundrels. The powerful impact of formal incentives means that multiethnic coalitions and alliances may be possible in countries with otherwise inhospitable conflict conditions and impossible in countries with seemingly more promising and conducive conditions. We shall return to this theme when we consider devices to foster ethnic accommodation.

In the meantime, a distinction needs to be drawn between the formation and durability of multiethnic coalitions. These coalitions are in a dynamic relation with their environment. Their formation and the policies they adopt change the very electoral-competitive conditions that fostered their initial creation, usually making their survival more difficult. It is no accident that the only survivor of the cases we have reviewed, the Malaysian Alliance/National Front, established early in its history a set of relations that were never entirely contractual and never totally constrained by electoral threats. Both reciprocity and competition were major determinants of the partners' behavior, but their effect was mitigated by bonds among the partners traceable ultimately, as I have suggested, to the decision to present a single slate. Indeed, the case can be made that the secret of coalitional durability is the determination to do two things: (1) to surmount the pure contractualism that brings the coalition into being but which can equally jeopardize it the moment there is a failure of reciprocal advantage; and (2) to take effective steps to limit the coalition's vulnerability to centrifugal electoral forces.

The decision to enlarge the Malaysian coalition in the 1970s can be seen as an example of the latter course. There is in general a discernible pattern of early action in response to the possibility of flanking. As mentioned in Chapter 7, decisions to form ethnic parties tend to be made in an anticipatory way, before major ethnic issues emerge. There is an equally clear pattern of early action by the leaders of multiethnic parties and coalitions confronted with growing threats on the flanks. Neither the Alliance in the Malaysia of 1969 nor UNIP in the Zambia of 1972 was in imminent peril of losing its solid parliamentary majority. Yet both—and the same point could be made for multiethnic parties confronted with losses on the flanks elsewhere—took dramatic action aimed at reversing losses on the flanks. The nature of the action was quite different in the two cases, but in each it reflected some expectation of a slide toward loss of all support.

Various combinations of motives can be adduced for such actions. Some might explain these preventive measures, taken so early, as the result of undue apprehension. Some might interpret them as shrewd decisions to seize an opportunity to reduce competition by exaggerating its dangers. It is also plausible that the slope is indeed slippery, that, in a conflict-prone environment, popular anxieties can result in rapid rates of growth in support for parties on the ethnic flanks. If so, a rational response to popular sentiment must necessarily occur early. Alternatively, if the durability of the coalition does depend on a substantial margin of invulnerability to electoral threats on the flanks, then, too, anticipatory action is required.

Whatever the explanation, anticipatory action of this kind is a reminder that the effect of formal incentives is mediated through the eyes and judgment of political decision-makers. What I have said about the powerful impact of electoral incentives should not be stretched into an argument for perfect rationality in the response of politicians to those incentives. To stress the incentive structure is by no means to argue for unmitigated electoral determinism, least of all in the passionate arena of ethnic conflict.

Finally, questions remain about the various forms of multiethnic organization. I have maintained that alliances have certain advantages for survival over temporary coalitions of commitment. Relations among alliance partners are far more likely to transcend narrow conceptions of the *quid pro quo*, and the contentious matters touched by the partnership are likely to be far more extensive. As between alliances and unified multiethnic parties, it is easy to see why the latter seem to dissolve so easily under the impact of centrifugal forces. There are advantages to negotiating in a coalition format, where group interests are explicitly represented by separate organizations within the alliance. There are advantages in competing with flank parties, for the alliance consists of components that at election time are still ethnic parties of a sort. There are advantages in adaptability to flank pressures. Coalitions and alliances can cope with flank threats by expanding the coalition to include flank parties—presumably, it is easier for an existing coalition to form a broader coalition. It comes as no surprise that the Malaysian Alliance responded to its flank threats as it did in the early 1970s, whereas the Zambian UNIP responded to comparable threats as *it* did in the early 1970s. The form of the multiethnic arrangement is likely to point toward alternative strategies for dealing with the flanks.

"England," said Disraeli, "does not love coalitions." Neither does a multiethnic polity, to judge by how difficult it makes things for them. Difficult but, as we have witnessed, not impossible. And they are apparently indispensable. So far, the only escape from regimes of ethnic inclusion and exclusion lies in coalition arrangements. The question we need to confront before too long is how to foster them.

PART FOUR

Military Politics and Ethnic Conflict

CHAPTER ELEVEN

The Militarization
of Ethnic Conflict

The military is both a resource and an object of ethnic conflict. It is a resource in conflict because the ethnic composition of military (and police) units is frequently out of joint with the composition of the societies from which they spring and of the governments to which they owe obedience. Consequently, the military can become a hotbed for ethnic resentment and an instrument for the advancement of ethnic claims to power. Like the civil service, it is an object of ethnic conflict, because military positions, with substantial salaries and perquisites, are coveted,[1] because skewed ethnic composition means that these advantages are unevenly distributed, and because control of the military is a significant symbol of ethnic domination.

The military can play a variety of roles in ethnic conflict. The army may be an integrating institution, as has sometimes been claimed, though in a deeply divided society it is doubtful that any single institution can reverse the cumulative effects of all the others. Instead, bitter experiences in the armed forces often seem to generate ethnic resentments.[2] The use of military force may help control ethnic rioting, but if the army favors one group or another, its intervention may exacerbate the violence. If there is a secessionist movement, an ethnically divided army may help make protracted warfare possible. By the time a civil war starts, the divided army may have become two or more armies, as was the case in Burma, Nigeria, and Lebanon.[3] But, depending on how they

1. See J. M. Lee, *African Armies and Civil Order* (New York: Praeger, 1969), 93–95.
2. For examples of ethnic ridicule within the armed forces that had a profound and lasting effect on some of its victims, see Gustave Morf, *Terror in Quebec: Case Studies of the FLQ* (Toronto: Clarke, Irwin, 1970), 67–68, 74.
3. Hugh Tinker, *The Union of Burma*, 4th ed. (London: Oxford Univ. Press, 1967), 323; A. R. Luckham, "The Nigerian Military: Disintegration or Integration?" in S. K.

are structured, intramilitary ethnic divisions may also discourage attempts at secession. When a Northern secession was mooted among Northern Nigerian officers after the coup of July 1966, officers from the Middle Belt (especially Tiv) were fearful of becoming a minority within the North, and they proved instrumental in preventing the secession.[4]

These possibilities illustrate the point that the military is quite often an active participant in ethnic conflict.[5] Barring civil war, the most powerful form of its participation—and certainly the most recurrent—is intervention or the threat of intervention in civilian politics. In general, the military reflects divisions in the society at large. What makes its political contribution distinctive is that the ethnic composition of most military organizations does not mirror the composition of the existing regime.

Broadly, the action of the army can reverse or reinforce the ethnic outcomes of civilian politics. The military can attempt to bring excluded ethnic groups to power or prevent them from gaining power, and it can act to exclude from power groups that currently enjoy it. Under certain conditions, military rule may perpetuate ethnic affinities and antagonisms that prevailed under the former civilian regime. But, under different conditions, a coup may cause old interethnic links to crack, and may result in a degree of ethnic exclusiveness unlikely in a civilian regime and difficult to reverse once it occurs. Contrary to suggestions that the occurrence of a coup changes essentially nothing in a political system,[6] military intervention may have substantial effects on the ethnic distribution of power. Accordingly, the main focus of this and the next two chapters is on the interplay of military and civilian ethnic politics. I begin with two preconditions to ethnically related military intervention in Asia and Africa: the ethnically skewed composition of armed forces and the close connections between civilian and military affairs. The next chapter specifies recurrent patterns of military intervention in support of ethnic interests. Following this, I consider the enormous impact that such interven-

---

Panter-Brick, ed., *Nigerian Politics and Military Rule: Prelude to the Civil War* (London: Athlone Press, 1970), 60–62; Cynthia Enloe, *Ethnic Soldiers: State Security in Divided Societies* (Athens: Univ. of Georgia Press, 1980), 227–30.

4. Ruth First, *Power in Africa* (Baltimore: Penguin Books, 1972), 313–34.

5. The police are often involved as well, although separate consideration will not be given here to the interplay between ethnicity and the role of the police in politics. Included in the term *military* are all branches of the armed forces, although sometimes the term *army* is substituted.

6. First, *Power in Africa*, 22; Samuel Decalo, *Coups and Army Rule in Africa* (New Haven: Yale Univ. Press, 1976), 27.

tion has had on the ethnic composition of regimes and armed forces alike. Finally, I turn to the techniques utilized to avert military intervention in support of ethnic interests. As elsewhere, the aim is to highlight the role of ethnic forces, although these are commonly bound up with organizational, generational, and other social cleavages.

DIFFERENTIAL RECRUITMENT AND ETHNIC CLEAVAGE

As in many aspects of politics in Asia and Africa, pre-independence policies and patterns set the framework for developments well into the period of independence. Recruitment practices, in particular, have had sustained effects. By definition, recruitment governs composition. Because individual careers may span twenty or thirty years, the composition of a government body is difficult to change without taking drastic, irregular, and sometimes provocative steps. Once heavy recruitment of certain ethnic groups begins, it is likely to continue. Career aspirations and individual educational decisions begin to move in established directions. Stereotypes and self-stereotypes of attributes fitting group members for such occupations and unfitting others may form. Recruiters may favor or be thought to favor members of the group already serving. Hiring criteria may be framed to replicate the attributes of those successfully performing the jobs for which new recruits are sought. The pool of applicants from the group already serving may become larger and better qualified than the pool of applicants from other groups, whose more able members begin to sense better opportunities in other directions.

What began as ethnic favoritism is thus sustained by judgments of objective qualifications, because the qualifications have been tailored to match imputed group attributes and because group aspirations respond to available opportunities. The wisdom of early policy decisions or the good fortune of early accidents is "confirmed." The special difficulties (real or alleged) of bringing new ethnic groups into ongoing organizations, considerations of morale, and the common argument against abandoning the known for the unknown may all operate to perpetuate uneven recruitment. And so, one career span may turn into two or three, and a few basic recruitment decisions may result in skewed composition lasting many decades. This was the case with military recruitment almost everywhere in Asia and Africa.

RECRUITING THE RANKS

In theory, the colonial army had two missions: to maintain order within the colony and to fight at or beyond its borders. In practice, however, the colonial army usually served as an army of occupation, rather than as a fighting force. In most colonies, most of the time, its tasks were pacification and internal security, not the protection of borders or the acquisition of new territory.[7] These differing missions had a great influence on the recruitment of soldiers from within the colony. If the mission is conquest, then fighting qualities are the paramount consideration in recruiting troops. If, however, the mission is to maintain internal control, to put down disorders and threats to the regime, then reliability in times of domestic disturbance becomes paramount. The different qualities required for different missions might point to recruitment from different ethnic groups.

For the British, military recruitment policy was first an issue in India, and the Indian experience colored thinking about the problem in the rest of the Empire. The mutiny of 1857 was a watershed in British policy. The mutiny was begun by the sepoys of the Bengal army, the units of which were ethnically homogeneous. When the Peel Commission investigated the mutiny, it concluded that the way to a secure military force was to create "a counterpoise of natives against natives."[8] The result was a policy of ethnic balance in the armed forces. Units in India, the Sudan, and Burma were composed in a heterogeneous fashion, their component companies proudly bearing their ethnic designations.

In India, the British also developed their well-known concept of the "martial races," drawing on the long military experience or warrior pretensions of a number of groups, especially from the Northwest of the subcontinent. After the decision to annex Burma by force, the British relied heavily on the so-called "fighting classes," imputing distinctive characteristics to each. Some were said to be "relatively independent and calculating (Pathans), others were shy and proud (Dogras), others playful and comical, yet crazed and bloodthirsty in battle (Gurkhas), others prone to scheming and plotting yet tenacious in defense (Sikhs), and still

---

7. The next several paragraphs borrow heavily from Donald L. Horowitz and Valerie P. Bennett, "Civil-Military Relations in a Multiethnic Society: The Case of Sri Lanka (Ceylon)," *Journal of Asian Affairs* 3 (Fall 1978): 157–69.

8. Quoted by Stephen P. Cohen, *The Indian Army: Its Contribution to the Development of a Nation* (Berkeley and Los Angeles: Univ. of California Press, 1971), 38.

others stolid and dense (Jats)."[9] As a result of such preferences in recruitment, Muslims outnumbered Hindus, and the Punjab alone contributed as much as 54 percent of the men of the Indian army in the pre–World War II period.[10]

The "martial races" might or might not be reliable for internal security duty; as indicated, they were initially recruited for foreign warfare. Consequently, an additional criterion of recruitment was invoked: distance of home region from the area of likely civil disorder. Generally, this meant recruiting from around the periphery of local colonial power and interest.[11] It is more than coincidence that martial characteristics were often discerned among groups that resided in mountainous or arid border areas remote from the administrative and economic centers where the colonial impact was most profound—in other words, far from the areas that, as time passed, also became the centers of anti-colonial activity and potential disorder. In a territory as large as India, it was possible to garrison forces in locations far from their home regions, so that local sympathies would not interfere with the performance of duty in the event of unrest. Elsewhere, the functional equivalent was to import troops from other colonies.

The Indian model was applied in recruiting enlisted men in other British Asian and African colonies. "Warrior traditions" were valued, but not at the expense of political reliability. Groups like the Ashanti and the Burmans, whose capacities in warfare might be formidable but whose fealty was suspect, were for some time unwelcome in the ranks of the colonial army. Generally, "backward" ethnic groups, often drawn from the remote hinterland, were overrepresented. In Burma, it was the Arakanese, the Chins, the Kachins, the Shans, and especially the Karens, who served in large numbers.[12] In Iraq, the British employed Kurds, Assyrians, and Yazidis. Northerners were recruited in Nigeria, Ghana, Sierra Leone, and Uganda. Some colonial officials in Nigeria thought that Yoruba made particularly good soldiers,[13] but the Yoruba were

9. Ibid., p. 51.
10. Hugh Tinker, *India and Pakistan: A Political Analysis*, rev. ed. (New York: Praeger, 1968), 154.
11. See, e.g., Hilary B. Ng'weno, "Tribes, Armies and Political Instability in Africa" (unpublished paper, Harvard Univ. Center for International Affairs, Mar. 1969); Edward Luttwak, *Coup d'Etat: A Practical Handbook* (New York: Knopf, 1969), 72.
12. Tinker, *The Union of Burma*, chap. 11; Ba Maw, *Breakthrough in Burma: Memoirs of Revolution* (New Haven: Yale Univ. Press, 1968).
13. See James Willcocks, *From Kabul to Kumasi* (London: John Murray, 1904), 179.

located at the center of colonial activity. So Hausa, Tiv, and Kanuri were recruited instead. Among the conditions which perpetuated Northern entry into the ranks was the use of the Hausa language within the army. Perhaps 75 percent of the riflemen in the Nigerian army were from the North.[14] Northerners, generally Muslims, also swelled the ranks of the Gold Coast forces; as late as 1961, some 80 percent of the Ghanaian N.C.O.s were drawn from the North.[15] Ashanti, more than 13 percent of the population, comprised only 5 percent of the ranks at independence.[16] Some effort was made to balance ethnic groups in Sierra Leone, but Northerners, especially Temne, were much overrepresented. Those recruited in Kenya were principally Kamba and Kalenjin. In Uganda, Acholi, Langi, and other Northern groups were heavily represented, their predominance assured by a height requirement that tended to exclude men of generally shorter stature from other areas.[17]

Although these tendencies derived from quite explicit aspects of British policy, they were not distinctive to the British. The French, the Dutch, the Italians, and the Belgians also sought "martial" qualities, recruited men from the peripheries of their territories, and used troops from other colonies. In Somalia, both Italian and British forces were heavily infused with Darood militiamen and gendarmes. The most numerous group, the nomadic Darood occupied the most arid regions, far from the ports and commercial centers located in the Isaq areas of British Somaliland and the Hawiye areas of Italian Somalia.[18] The Dutch relied heavily on the outlying, usually Christian, Ambonese in Indonesia, and they imported Indonesian troops to serve in Ceylon, where they remained as soldiers after the British took over and continued to play a prominent role in the Ceylon army centuries later.[19] In the Belgian Congo, the colonial power at first attempted to create an ethnically representative and integrated

14. First, *Power in Africa*, 161. Luckham, "The Nigerian Military," 73, estimates that 65 to 70 percent of the Nigerian army ranks were Northerners.

15. First, *Power, in Africa*, 77; Morris Janowitz, *The Military in the Political Development of New Nations* (Chicago: Univ. of Chicago Press, 1964), 52 n.16.

16. J. 'Bayo Adekson, "Army in a Multi-Ethnic Society: The Case of Nkrumah's Ghana, 1957–1966," *Armed Forces and Society* 2 (Feb. 1966): 251–72, at 253.

17. Nelson Kasfir, "Cultural Sub-Nationalism in Uganda," in Victor A. Olorunsola, ed., *The Politics of Cultural Sub-Nationalism in Africa* (Garden City, N.Y.: Anchor Books, 1972), 80.

18. I. M. Lewis, "Nationalism and Particularism in Somalia," in P. H. Gulliver, ed., *Tradition and Transition in East Africa* (Berkeley and Los Angeles: Univ. of California Press, 1969), 343–44.

19. During World War II, these "Malays," though only 3 percent of Ceylon's population, comprised more than one-sixth of all of Ceylon's forces. Marshall Singer, *The Emerging Elite: A Study of Political Leadership in Ceylon* (Cambridge: M.I.T. Press, 1964), 126.

army. But, after the "Batetela mutinies" of the 1890s, the Belgians moved to a deliberate policy of ethnic balancing and recruitment of those groups who were "both fierce and quick to learn . . . ."[20] For their part, the French recruited "warlike" Northerners (especially Kabrai) into the ranks in Togo,[21] Berbers in Morocco,[22] Mbochi and Kouyou in Congo (Brazzaville),[23] Malinké in Guinea,[24] Alawi, Druze, Isma'ilis, Kurds, and Circassians in Syria,[25] and Northerners in Dahomey.[26] These groups were generally from rather remote areas, most of them were uneducated, and all of them had reason to fear, as did the French, the aspirations of other ethnic groups.[27] The French also followed the policy of employing reliable aliens, and so posted troops from one distant colony to another where it was advantageous to do so. As the Gurkhas were employed by the British in far-flung locations, so Senegalese troops left their mark in many French colonies, some of them quite distant from Senegal.

It was, then, not just some curious affectation that led the British to recruit soldiers differentially. That the composition of other colonial armies was skewed, and skewed in roughly similar ethnic directions, suggests that the basic security requirements of the colonial situation were at work.

RECRUITING THE OFFICER CORPS

Officer corps were a different matter. The colonized peoples had contributed soldiers for many decades before consideration was given to commissioning them as officers in the colonial armies. Asian colonies were far ahead of African in this respect. The first King's Commissions were bestowed on Indians in 1918.[28] Only in 1949 were Africans granted

20. Thomas Turner, "Congo-Kinshasa," in Olorunsola, ed., *The Politics of Cultural Sub-Nationalism in Africa*, 200–01.

21. Lee, *African Armies and Civil Order*, 45; Leslie Rubin and Brian Weinstein, *Introduction to African Politics* (New York: Praeger, 1974), 153.

22. Bruce Exstrum, "Ethnicity and the Military in the Middle East" (unpublished paper, Johns Hopkins Univ. School of Advanced International Studies, Apr. 1976), 11.

23. Decalo, *Coups and Army Rule in Africa*, 146.

24. I am indebted to Donald Herdeck for information on Guinea.

25. Tabitha Petran, *Syria* (New York: Praeger, 1972), 62; Stephen Hemsley Longrigg, *Syria and Lebanon Under French Mandate* (London: Oxford Univ. Press, 1958), 160–61.

26. René Lemarchand, "Dahomey: Coup Within a Coup," *Africa Report*, June 1968, pp. 46–54.

27. There were exceptions to the practice of recruiting distant, martial groups to the ranks, for the French as for the British. In Chad, for example, educated, Christianized Southerners formed the backbone of the army the French recruited, because control over the Northern and Eastern regions, with their Muslim populations, was only imperfectly established until quite late in the colonial period.

28. Tinker, *India and Pakistan*, 155.

commissions in the West African Frontier Force.[29] In all the colonies, a significant intake of local officers occurred in the few years immediately preceding or following independence.

Until World War II, the colonial powers presumed that Asian and African territories would remain theirs. But they also knew that not all Asians and Africans shared their expectations. Anti-colonial movements were beginning to grow. The qualities sought in military officers recruited in the pre-war period reflected this situation. A premium was placed on loyalty to the colonial power. By and large, the same groups who had served loyally in the ranks could be counted on to serve loyally in the officer corps. Consequently, in the principal Asian colonies, such as India, Ceylon, Burma, and Malaya, there was considerable congruence between the ethnic composition of the ranks and the early ethnic composition of the officer corps.

When, after the war, the presumption of colonial continuity gave way to policies of preparing colonies for self-government, unswerving loyalty to the colonial power ceased to be the prime value. In principle, this widened the ethnic pool from which officers could be recruited, but countervailing considerations constricted it. A major policy choice was whether to respond to the urgent need to commission many officers quickly or to uphold "standards" even at the expense of slowing down the pace of localization. How this choice was resolved had lasting effects on the ethnic composition of the military and on civil-military relations.

To localize rapidly usually entailed heavy reliance on promoting men from the ranks. Like considerations of loyalty, this meant that those ethnic groups disproportionately represented in the ranks would also be disproportionately represented among the new officers. To uphold "standards," on the other hand, meant sending recruits for officer training at the appropriate colonial military institutions: St. Cyr, Sandhurst, Mons. As this was regarded as a form of higher education, it required educational preparation. Consequently, recruits tended to be selected from groups that were relatively well educated. In general, these were not the "martial," rural groups from distant areas whose men served in the ranks. The groups that were well situated to take advantage of colonial educational opportunities typically resided close to the major centers of colonial power, were at least somewhat urbanized, and were not known to the colonialists for their military traditions. They were, rather,

29. Valerie Plave Bennett and Donald L. Horowitz, "The Military and the Transfer of Power in West Africa and Southern Asia" (unpublished paper, 1976), 8.

the same groups that were usually to be found in the colonial civil service. The British and French were perfectly willing to take a "fierce," "bloodthirsty," "stolid" peasant and turn him into an obedient foot soldier. If need be, they were even prepared to commission him in an officer corps short of experienced manpower. But they would scarcely send such a man to the premier military institutions of the metropole, expecting him to pass out with a commission equal to that of his European fellow-cadets—except in the unlikely event that he had previously distinguished himself by finishing secondary school and passing some appropriate academic examination.

In ethnic terms, therefore, the mode of officer training created a fork in the road. Countries like Kenya, Uganda, and Togo, whose officers were frequently commissioned from the ranks, produced officer corps ethnically akin to the ranks: Northern groups that were generally less educated, more rural, and less "modern." Contrariwise, countries like Nigeria, Dahomey, Ceylon, Ghana, Iraq, and Sierra Leone, whose officers were mainly trained at British or French military academies, developed officer corps drawn from educated, somewhat urban, more "modern" ethnic groups. Of the thirty-six Nigerian officers commissioned before 1960, only seven came from the North. About half of the total were Ibo, for the Ibo were in a good position to take advantage of opportunities requiring education. By 1965, half of the officer corps was still Ibo.[30] The majority of officers in Dahomey were Fon, who benefited from educational advantages and from the French stereotype of them as a "militaristic" group.[31] The Ceylonese officer corps was composed heavily of Westernized, educated members of minorities: Sinhalese Christians, Tamils, and Burghers.[32] Ghana's was drawn disproportionately from the coastal people with access to the best schools. Of the first twenty-eight Gold Coast officers commissioned, only one came from Ashanti and one from the North. Thirteen of the first twenty-two were Ga or Ewe.[33] Officers in Iraq came from the urban, educated, Sunni minority.[34] In Sierra Leone, there were some fluctuations in the early

30. Lee, *African Armies and Civil Order*, 176–77; Luckham, "The Nigerian Military," 72; First, *Power in Africa*, 162.

31. Decalo, *Coups and Army Rule in Africa*, 55.

32. Donald L. Horowitz, *Coup Theories and Officers' Motives: Sri Lanka in Comparative Perspective* (Princeton: Princeton Univ. Press, 1980), 53–63.

33. Bennett and Horowitz, "The Military and the Transfer of Power in West Africa and Southern Asia," 14. See also Adekson, "Army in a Multi-Ethnic Society," 253.

34. Exstrum, "Ethnicity and the Military in the Middle East," 13. Compare J. C. Hurewitz, *Middle East Politics: The Military Dimension* (New York: Praeger, 1969), 155.

1960s, but generally the Mende were somewhat overrepresented, while the Temne, so conspicuous in the ranks, were present only in very small numbers in the officer corps.[35]

The pronounced impact of mode of recruitment on ethnic composition obtains, not only between countries, but also within countries. A shift from one mode to the other marks a shift from one ethnic group to another. In Uganda, as indicated, officers promoted from the ranks tended to be Northerners. When, however, cadets were sent to Sandhurst, they were mainly from the more educated Baganda and other Southern groups—despite the fact that such groups had no real tradition of service in the colonial armed forces.[36] Guinean officers selected for training at St. Cyr were often Fula; the Fula had a strong educational tradition. But the army ranks, including noncommissioned officers, were composed heavily of Malinké. From these men came an increasing number of officers as the Sékou Touré regime consolidated its power and commissioned from the ranks.[37] When the Moroccan government at independence began to recruit officer candidates by competitive examination, there was a large influx of urban, literate, middle-class Arabs, instead of the rural Berbers preferred by the French.[38] The availability of alternative modes of officer recruitment, biased in alternative ethnic directions, provides a regime with a lever to manipulate the ethnic composition of its officer corps.

Some refinements are required to round out this picture of officer corps composition at about the time of independence. For the most part, the refinements have to do with groups that were disqualified or essentially disqualified themselves from serving in the new officer corps.

Some immigrant groups, such as the Indians in Burma and the Chinese in Malaya, might have fared very well in competition for military training at British academies, but their position in their adopted lands was regarded as insufficiently legitimate to permit their recruitment. The Kikuyu, Kenya's most educated and centrally located ethnic group, would also have claimed many such places, but their participa-

35. Thomas S. Cox, *Civil-Military Relations in Sierra Leone* (Cambridge: Harvard Univ. Press, 1976), 53–54.
36. A Special Correspondent, "The Uganda Army: Nexus of Power," *Africa Report*, Dec. 1966, p. 38.
37. Cf. Victor D. Du Bois, "The Role of the Army in Guinea," *Africa Report*, Jan. 1963, pp. 3–5, at p. 5.
38. John Waterbury, "The Coup Manqué," in Ernest Gellner and Charles Micaud, eds., *Arabs and Berbers: From Tribe to Nation in North Africa* (Lexington, Mass.: Lexington Books, 1972), 406.

tion in the "Mau Mau" revolt resulted in a British decision to exclude them from serving in the officer corps.

Certain ethnic groups that had served loyally in the colonial army proved to be so faithful to the colonial power that they entertained reservations about the benefits of independence. Other groups, more strongly anti-colonial, entertained, in turn, reservations about them. As the anti-colonial movement progressed, these mutual suspicions sometimes turned to violence. Assyrians in Iraq had early demanded regional autonomy, and shortly before independence there had been a Muslim massacre of the Christian Assyrians.[39] This hostility ended any chance of prominence for Assyrians in the Iraqi officer corps, as similar hostility also did for the Kurds. The Karens had fought loyally alongside the British during the Japanese invasion of Burma. Burman nationalists, on the other hand, had sought to use the Japanese occupation as a means to independence. The two sides clashed violently, during the course of the war and after. When independence came in 1948, the Karens, apprehensive about trusting their fortunes to the Burmans, rebelled. All the regular Karen battalions mutinied, and thereafter all Karen officers were relieved of their posts.[40] The same fate befell the Ambonese in Indonesia. Loyal to the Dutch, suspicious of the Javanese and Sumatran nationalists, the Ambonese chose a futile secession in 1950, forfeiting any prospect of continued military prominence and paving the way for the Javanese and Batak officers who now command the Indonesian army.[41] For some groups, membership in the colonial army was one of the elements that tainted their claim to full inclusion in the emerging polity. Groups that tried to opt out of the new political system also opted out of the new officer corps.[42] I shall have more to say later about the consequences of these movements.

39. Ernest Main, *Iraq from Mandate to Independence* (London: Allen & Unwin, 1935), 139–55.

40. Tinker, *The Union of Burma*, 323.

41. For the post-war events relating to the Ambonese, see Virginia Thompson and Richard Adloff, *Minority Problems in Southeast Asia* (Stanford: Stanford Univ. Press, 1955), 165–69; Willard A. Hanna, "Molukkan Retrospect: Part IV, Molukkan Decline," *American Universities Field Staff Reports*, Southeast Asia Series, vol. 21, no. 12 (1973): 6–8.

42. Something of the same thing might have happened in India had a civil war been fought over Muslim aspirations for Pakistan (or, for that matter, Sikh aspirations for "Sikhistan"). Had a rebellion been put down, Muslim (or Sikh) officers would no doubt have been uprooted from the Indian Army. As events developed, however, the Indian and Pakistani armies have enjoyed a considerable measure of ethnic continuity in their officer corps, often to the displeasure of unrepresented groups, such as the Bengali Muslims in the pre-Bangladesh period of Pakistan.

Finally, it would seem that the presence of a local military academy affected the ethnic composition of those selected for officer training.[43] Whereas the colonialists insisted on sending only acculturated, educated men to metropolitan military academies, adherence to such standards was likely to have been far less strict in selections for academies located in the colony or newly independent territory. Druze and Alawi, for example, often attended the Homs Military Academy in Syria, though many of those who were admitted might not have been eligible to receive comparable training in France. A military academy was opened in Libya in 1957. The academy "enrolled students without the general education certificate" and, as a result, drew cadets who "did not qualify for university entrance." Often its graduates were from the "oases and the interior," rather than from the dominant Cyrenaican groups.[44] Barring manipulation of admission requirements, local military training is more likely to produce an officer corps comparable to the officer corps produced by promotion from the ranks—that is, an officer corps whose ethnic composition is generally congruent with the ethnic composition of the soldiery as a whole.

ALTERATIONS UPON INDEPENDENCE

At independence, then, the ranks of most ex-colonial armies tended to be drawn from backward ethnic groups. Such groups were not infrequently two to three times as numerous in the military ranks as in the general population. The officer corps might be skewed in the same direction or in the opposite direction—toward educated, advanced groups— but the manner of officer selection virtually guaranteed skewing in one direction or the other.

For the most part, the ethnic composition of the ranks changed little after independence. There was scant demand for such change, and it would have been difficult to effect it without either massive military expansion or upheaval in the ranks. Occasionally, as in Zambia, there were efforts to set maximum percentages for each province—a policy with obvious ethnic implications—but nowhere were these percentages rigidly enforced; in Zambia, as elsewhere, skewed composition persisted.[45] Nor was there much tampering with colonial routines that affected the ethnic composition of the ranks. Formal requirements, dietary

43. I owe this point to Bruce Exstrum.
44. Ruth First, *Libya: The Elusive Revolution* (Baltimore: Penguin Books, 1974), 115.
45. Ng'weno, "Tribes, Armies and Political Instability in Africa," 40.

practices in the mess, and in some cases explicitly homogeneous units were generally retained.

The composition of the officer corps was less firmly fixed. Military officers received salaries and perquisites that placed them rather clearly in the elite category. Competition for such posts was keen. As European military officers departed during the first years of independence, positions were made available; no one had to be displaced to create new openings. Furthermore, military command positions were regarded—quite correctly, as it turned out—as politically sensitive, and so there was concern expressed about the ethnic identity of incumbents in those positions.

The composition of the officer corps thus became a matter for concern in a number of post-colonial governments, and several set out to do something about it. The direction of the changes, however, varied with the composition of the civilian government.

Where the politicians and officers were mainly from the same ethnic group, efforts were sometimes made to reinforce the dominance of that group in the army. This was most dramatically the case in Sierra Leone. There a Mende-dominated government increased the proportion of Mende officers from 26 percent of the African officers in mid-1964 to 52 percent by mid-1967. Thirteen of the seventeen cadets who passed out of a new Sierra Leone military academy in June 1967 were Mende, which is suggestive of the trend.[46] The same skewing occurred in Uganda under the first regime of A. Milton Obote. A Northerner, Obote strengthened the role of the Acholi and of his own ethnic group, the Langi, within the officer corps.[47] In Jordan, an experiment in raising an infantry brigade of Palestinian officers and men was abandoned when the brigade seemed bent on overthrowing the king. Subsequent purges of Palestinians in the 1950s and '60s strengthened Beduin control of the officer corps and simultaneously strengthened the position of the ruling elite, drawn heavily from Southern, nomadic groups.[48]

Where, on the other hand, the civilian politicians either had reason to doubt the loyalty of an officer corps disproportionately composed of ethnic strangers or were genuinely concerned to rectify "ethnic imbalances," efforts were made to diversify recruitment. The Nigerian leader-

46. Cox, *Civil-Military Relations in Sierra Leone*, 75.
47. Grace Stuart Ibingira, "The Principal Causes of Instability in Post-Independence Sub-Sahara Africa and Some Lessons" (unpublished paper, Woodrow Wilson International Center for Scholars, Oct. 12, 1976), 28; *Washington Post*, Sept. 12, 1971.
48. Hurewitz, *Middle East Politics*, 320–23.

ship formalized this in a system of quotas for the intake of officers: 50 percent Northerners, 25 percent Westerners, and 25 percent Easterners.[49] The early regime of the Northerner, Hubert Maga, in Benin (Dahomey) brought with it an influx of Northern officers.[50] Uneasy about the loyalty of his Ga and Ewe officers at the time of Ga and Ewe unrest, Nkrumah sought to balance the Ghanaian officer corps by a shift in recruitment. Between 1957 and 1960, about thirty officers were recruited,[51] of whom only four were Ga and one was Ewe. This was a marked departure from the pre-independence period, when most of the first twenty-two officers commissioned had been either Ga or Ewe. By the time of the coup against Nkrumah in 1966, only a third of the officers above the rank of captain were Ga or Ewe.[52] In Kenya, a Kikuyu-led regime took power in a country from whose army Kikuyu had generally been excluded. Measures were taken to redress this imbalance. By 1967, there were about as many Kikuyu officers as there were Kamba, formerly dominant in the officer corps.[53]

Not all civilian governments made conscious efforts to alter the ethnic direction of officer recruitment. Some, such as Sri Lanka, were content for quite some time to let the commissions fall where they might. The point is that those regimes which succeeded in modifying the colonial inheritance in this respect also had the effect of modifying the lines of cleavage. Where the officer corps was ethnically differentiated from the ranks, as in Sierra Leone, reinforcement of the already preponderant group in the officer corps sharpened that cleavage. Where, however, the policy was to broaden the ethnic base of the officer corps, the effect was to weaken its cohesion by superimposing ethnic and generational conflicts upon it.[54] For the new ethnic groups entered as junior officers, and if the mode of officer training shifted simultaneously, tension developed between the rough-hewn officers drawn from the ranks and the polished officers trained at the academies—these two sets of officers differing not merely in age, experience, and training, but also in ethnic origin. Precisely such tensions have been reported, at various times, from several

49. First, *Power in Africa*, 161.
50. Lemarchand, "Dahomey: Coup Within a Coup."
51. Bennett and Horowitz, "The Military and the Transfer of Power in West Africa and Southern Asia."
52. Lee, *African Armies and Civil Order*, 112.
53. Ibid., 110.
54. There were also organizational tensions, for new officers were sometimes assigned to newly created units.

countries.[55] As J. M. Lee has rightly said, "the more a government has striven to make its officer corps representative of the new nation, the more it makes its army vulnerable to complete collapse if the coalition of interests in the civilian order also breaks down."[56]

COMPOSITION AND CLEAVAGE:
THE FIRST LINES OF STRESS

In an ethnically divided society, domination of any powerful institution by a single ethnic group constitutes a danger that that institution will be used for ethnic purposes. Split domination—an arrangement in which the key institutions of the society are dominated by different ethnic groups—may provide the basis for a bargain to stabilize this balance of power by recognizing ethnic spheres of influence. More often, however, split domination is unstable, particularly when one ethnic group controls the armed forces and another dominates the civilian regime. Each of these institutions is a potential master of the other. In the absence of highly skillful bargaining or preventive arrangements, the civilian regime stands in danger of military overthrow. *doesn't fit India!*

Split domination is made likely in many states by recruitment practices shaped by such pervasive fears of revolt that the colonial authorities went far afield in their search for loyal officers and men. When the colonialists departed, their civilian inheritors were likely to be the very groups against whom such precautions were taken. Consequently, unfriendly military and civilian leaderships are left poised against each other. Equally, the enforcement of strict educational prerequisites for officer training in countries with relatively large ethnic hinterlands is likely to leave the military in the hands of advanced ethnic groups, confronting a government dominated by more numerous backward groups. In some countries, both of these juxtapositions may be at work. The *①* extent to which skewed recruitment really means unrepresentative armed forces may thus be brought home for the first time after elections have been held.

A second possibility is that the composition of military and civilian *②* leadership is ethnically congruent. This fortuitous situation in a divided

---

55. See Tinker, *The Union of Burma*, chap. 11; A. R. Luckham, "The Nigerian Military," 72–73; A Special Correspondent, "The Uganda Army," 38; W. A. E. Skurnik, "The Military and Politics: Dahomey and Upper Volta," in Claude E. Welch, Jr., ed., *Soldier and State in Africa* (Evanston: Northwestern Univ. Press, 1970), 105; J. D. Legge, *Sukarno: A Political Biography* (New York: Praeger, 1972), 376.

56. Lee, *African Armies and Civil Order*, 111.

society is likely where advanced groups, dominant in the officer corps, are also electorally powerful. It may also occur where a backward group gains electoral power and where an advanced group had been effectively disqualified from officer training by virtue of the kinds of ethnic disloyalty or illegitimacy noted earlier, or where officers have been commissioned from the ranks, generally consisting of backward groups.

A third possibility is that an unrepresentative officer corps confronts a government more broadly representative of the spectrum of ethnic groups. This is likely wherever cross-ethnic coalitions must be shaped if elected government is to function. This is not quite split domination, but neither is it congruence between civilian and military composition.

Congruence between civilian and military composition may help perpetuate civilian rule. It rules out ethnically motivated intervention, provided the civilian regime does not go out of its way to accommodate unrepresented ethnic groups. Especially where ethnic tensions are high and where the civilian government is regarded as guardian of the interests of the ethnic group or groups it represents, a similarly composed military may be disposed to let the civilians continue in that role. It is exactly such tolerance on which civilian elites count when they alter the composition of the officer corps in the direction of ethnic congruence. Civilian regimes that have survived under such circumstances include post-1964 Guyana, post-1971 Sierra Leone, Malaysia, Jordan, and post-1962 Sri Lanka.[57]

Ethnically motivated interventions are, however, a distinct possibility in countries where there is a divergence between civilian and military ethnic composition.[58] In such countries, however, civilian regimes have been prone to alter the composition of the officer corps, in order to increase ethnic balance. Those attempts may well bring on the very coups they are designed to avert. They also create two cleavages where before there may have been only one, as efforts to broaden or balance the officer corps divide it between senior and junior officers. Regimes and analysts must thus reckon with intramilitary as well as civil-military divisions. A coup with ethnic overtones by senior officers might then prompt subsequent action against them by junior officers sympathetic to the displaced regime or to the ethnic group it represented. Presumably, some ethnically

---

57. For two cases of congruence, see Cynthia H. Enloe, "Civilian Control of the Military: Implications in the Plural Societies of Guyana and Malaysia," in Claude E. Welch, Jr., ed., *Civilian Control of the Military* (Albany: State Univ. of New York Press, 1976), 65–98. For Sri Lanka, see Horowitz, *Coup Theories and Officers' Motives*, 211–13.

58. For a somewhat similar analysis, see Ng'weno, "Tribes, Armies and Political Instability in Africa," 44–45.

motivated coups have been deterred by the existence of this intramilitary cleavage or thwarted by accidental leaks of action plans from senior officers to unsympathetic junior ones. The survival of civilian government in Kenya was, for some time, attributable to such a cleavage in the officer corps.

Even if efforts to broaden or balance the officer corps are not undertaken, an intramilitary ethnic cleavage may already be present. Because the officer corps and the ranks were not infrequently recruited from quite different ethnic groups, an officers' coup that was ethnically motivated, in whole or in part, might then bring on a countercoup by N.C.O.s, though the N.C.O.s' position in the military hierarchy makes this less probable than an officers' coup.

Examples of the interaction of these cleavages and the groups they divide are readily available. Togo and Syria began at independence with civilian regimes dominated by advanced ethnic groups and officer corps dominated by backward groups. The civilian regimes were displaced by the army within a few years. Nigeria went in the opposite direction with the so-called "Ibo coup" in January 1966, and Sierra Leone had elected a government dominated by backward groups when the army commander from the advanced ethnic group intervened to prevent it from taking office. The Nigerian and Sierra Leonean armies were, however, ethnically divided, and in both cases these internal divisions provided the foundation for countercoups soon after.[59]

This is about as far as an analysis based solely on composition can go. Its limitations are apparent. It can identify cleavages and groups likely to engage in political activity, but compositional analysis holds civilian politics constant—altogether too constant. It can suggest some standard repertoires of ethno-military intervention, but without explaining when or why they occur. For this, the interactions of military and civilian ethnic politics become indispensable.

ETHNIC COUPS AND THE CIVIL-MILITARY ORDER

To understand ethnically based military coups, civilian and military ethnic politics must be viewed in tandem. Perhaps the two spheres are not quite a seamless web, but they are at least a single web. If this is so, it is

59. Cox, *Civil-Military Relations in Sierra Leone*, 198–99. See also Lee, *African Armies and Civil Order*, 169–71; Christopher Allen, "Sierra Leone Politics Since Independence," *African Affairs* 67 (Oct. 1968): 305–29.

because the political systems in which ethnic coups occur permit or encourage the interweaving of the two spheres.

The very idea that armed forces might faithfully reflect divisions in the society at large or that military action might proceed in response to events in civilian politics contradicts some commonly held conceptions of what a professional army is and ought to be. Armed forces, after all, are supposed to be impervious to entreaties from civilian factions. The professional soldier is supposed to be deaf in rather the same way that justice is supposed to be blind.[60] As the army is expected to be impervious to political implorations, so also is it supposed to be immune to the worst intrusions of the politicians. Hence, the conditions of service in the armed forces resemble those in the civil service; these protect both sets of bureaucrats from interference as they pursue their calling and do their duty. In the civil-military division of labor, there is an element of reciprocity. Though the bounds are not always clear, neither side is to impinge on the prerogatives of the other. Membership in the army, moreover, is supposed to give rise to loyalty transcending obligations to ethnic collectivities, at least within the realm of military duty. The military emphasis on duty and the untrammeled obligation to obey presuppose at least the soldier's ability to compartmentalize his ethnic affiliation.

The men who organized colonial armies did not share all of these assumptions. They were not at all sure that soldiers recruited in the colonies could be expected to marshal the requisite indifference to civilian politics, and so they were careful about who was recruited. As I have shown, they had little confidence in the ability of soldiers to put their affiliations aside as they pursued their military duty. Ethnic affiliations mattered both in recruitment and in the organization of military units. I have suggested that this heritage had its impact after the colonial departure, but it may be fanciful, whatever the heritage, to expect soldiers to compartmentalize their ethnic ties completely.

Ethnically motivated intervention does not proceed from the organizational separateness of Asian and African armed forces or from a distinctively military outlook or interests.[61] When officers move to change the ethnic base of a regime, the only thing that is distinctively military is the methods. What stands out is not the separateness of military and

60. See Samuel P. Huntington, *The Soldier and the State* (Cambridge: Harvard Univ. Press, 1957), 16.
61. Compare William R. Thompson, *The Grievances of Military Coup Makers* (Beverly Hills: Sage Professional Papers, Comparative Politics Series, no. 01-047, 1973).

civilian ethnic politics, but their essential continuity. This continuity is made possible by the weakly developed organizational structure of the armed forces. Contrary to the theory of the ideal-type army, the boundaries between civilian and military structures are permeable, the ethnic loyalties of military officers are not compartmentalized or contained, and the reciprocal nonintervention of civilians in matters of military administration is not well established. All of these conditions are conducive to an active military role in ethnic politics.

POROUS CIVIL-MILITARY BOUNDARIES

Speaking to assembled military officers in 1974, President Omar Bongo of Gabon warned them "to stop approaching Ministers and Deputies" instead of discussing their problems with the commander-in-chief. There was danger, he said, in these contacts, because civilian politicians "will incite you to resort to coups" for their own purposes.[62] There is often a propensity among officers to develop close ties with civilian politicians. The basis for these ties may be sheer reciprocity, as the Bongo statement intimates. Officers seek to resolve problems they encounter by appealing to cabinet ministers or to members of parliament. Politicians seek to secure or advance their own position by making known their alignments with well-placed commanders or by invoking military aid to execute a coup. Ethnic and family relationships usually cement these ties based on mutual interest, the more so in states with a small and socially restricted elite.

The most coup-prone of the ethnically divided polities afford ample evidence of such civil-military connections. The close ties of Northern Nigerian officers like Murtala Mohammed and Hassan Katsina to Northern party politicians and ruling emirs were well known. When they spoke, they were often understood to be speaking for the Northern People's Congress or for the rulers. It has likewise been asserted that the planning of the January 1966 coup in Nigeria "owed something to radical figures in the UPGA [the Southern coalition formed to contest the 1964 parliamentary elections] and perhaps among Ibo politicians."[63] Northerners certainly interpreted the coup in this way.[64]

What has been said of Nigeria also holds for Benin, Sri Lanka, Ghana,

62. Quoted by Colin Legum, ed., *Africa Contemporary Record, 1974–75* (New York: Africana, 1975), p. B589.
63. M. J. Dent, "The Military and the Politicians," in S. K. Panter-Brick, ed., *Nigerian Politics and Military Rule: Prelude to the Civil War* (London: Athlone Press, 1970), 81.
64. Ibid., 85.

and Uganda. The same army officers who ordered elections to be held in Benin in 1970 then proceeded to campaign for their favorite civilian candidates.[65] The attempted coup in Sri Lanka in 1962 occurred after social acquaintances of many of the officers had asked them repeatedly whether something could not be done about the excesses of the Bandaranaike regime.[66] In Ghana, only a year after independence, as Nkrumah's Convention People's Party began to bend the constitution out of shape, a distraught opposition, based heavily on disaffected ethnic groups, turned to army officers of two of those groups (Ga and Ewe) for help.[67] This conspiracy did not go very far,[68] but it foreshadowed the close relations between officers and their favorite politicians of similar ethnic background that characterized the latter part of the National Liberation Council period, following the overthrow of Nkrumah. And, as Ghana's officers in power had their favorite politicians, Uganda's politicians had their favorite officers. In 1966, the Southern politicians who challenged Milton Obote's position in his own party had made contact with officers from their home region and apparently attempted to rally troops against Obote.[69] For their part, the Baganda were linked to the then-chief of staff, an Iteso favorably disposed to the Buganda ruler and uneasy with the growing number of Northern officers under his command. Fearful of a coup, Obote removed the chief of staff and his "Teso group" before embarking on an attack against the Buganda ruler.[70] This left Idi Amin in command of the army. As tension grew between Obote and Amin, Obote himself sought allies in the officer corps, particularly among his Langi kinsmen.[71] All major political contenders felt the need for military protection.

Informal arrangements between military officers and civilian politicians reached their apogee in Sierra Leone and Syria, where a realistic

65. Samuel Decalo, "Regionalism, Politics, and the Military in Dahomey," *Journal of Developing Areas* 7 (Apr. 1973): 447–77, at 470.

66. Horowitz, *Coup Theories and Officers' Motives*, 186–90.

67. For extracts from the proceedings of a commission of inquiry into this plot, see Dennis Austin, *Politics in Ghana, 1948–1960* (London: Oxford Univ. Press, 1964), 424–29.

68. However, it was followed by other plots involving Ga. See Adekson, "Army in a Multi-Ethnic Society," 264.

69. Decalo, *Coups and Army Rule in Africa*, 194–95, 205; A Special Correspondent, "The Uganda Army: Nexus of Power," 39; Kasfir, "Cultural Sub-Nationalism in Uganda," 110–11.

70. Decalo, *Coups and Army Rule in Africa*, 205–06.

71. Ibid., 209.

organization chart would have to include, in addition to the formal chain of command, the network of close alliances that crisscrossed military units and civil-military boundaries. In Sierra Leone and in Kenya, civil-military links included carefully planned marriages between members of the elites.[72] In Syria, the principal pattern was for party politicians to use their army allies against their party enemies. The end result was the triumph of army over party, as well as of one army subgroup over the others. In Sierra Leone, politicians asked soldiers to save them from the results of the elections. The elections ultimately vanished, but the soldiers were brought under control.

Beginning in the mid-1950s, when leaders of the Arab Socialist Party (later to merge with the Ba'th) drew army officers into a plot to overthrow the regime of Adib Shishakli, party intrigue in Syria involved the frequent use of army sympathizers to execute coups. At first the coups were to restore civilian rule, at a later stage to support or defeat Nasserist designs on Syria, and then, after Ba'th officers had gained ascendancy inside the army, to support one side or the other in the increasingly bitter struggles within the civilian wing of the Ba'th Party. As all this was going on, officers came to control the party apparatus, displacing the original civilian leadership and even displacing army officers who made their base in the party.[73]

Similar civil-military ties were formed in Sierra Leone in advance of the first coup. They fell along predictable ethnic and subethnic lines. David Lansana had been made army commander by Albert Margai in 1964. Lansana had close ties to Margai's faction of the Sierra Leone People's Party through Lansana's sister-in-law, a cabinet minister and Mende paramount chief in Margai's own Moyamba district. Lansana became Margai's protégé and, in return, identified himself with Margai's wing of the party. His second-in-command, John Bangura, was a Temne-Loko, distrusted because of his connections with the All People's Congress, which had Temne support. When Bangura was arrested for allegedly plotting a coup in early 1967, the assumption of civilians and officers alike was that Bangura had been counting on APC support; participants in later coups were also linked to one or another SLPP

72. Cox, *Civil-Military Relations in Sierra Leone*, 67; Henry Bienen, *Armies and Parties in Africa* (New York: Africana, 1978), 185.
73. Petran, *Syria*; Itamar Rabinovich, *Syria Under the Ba'th, 1963–66: The Army-Party Symbiosis* (Jerusalem: Israel Universities Press, 1972).

faction, to the APC, or to organizations formed by discontented APC leaders.[74] Party factions and military cliques tended to be based on ethnic and subethnic ties extending across civil-military boundaries. Every attempted coup was a joint venture of soldiers and politicians.

Syria and Sierra Leone are extreme cases, but porous civil-military boundaries are a common phenomenon throughout much of the developing world. This porosity seems capable of coexisting even with the disdain which military officers typically have for politicians.[75] The disdain can be overcome, or at least forced into the background, by the discovery of common ethnic interests among soldiers and civilians and by the discovery of reciprocal career interests that can be advanced by cooperation. These two are often mutually reinforcing.

The existence of such links across civil-military frontiers is fostered by factionalism within the armed forces and within civilian regimes. That intramilitary factionalism could proceed to the point at which alliances with politicians seem necessary or attractive is evidence of incompletely developed organizational loyalties.

THE ETHNIC LOYALTIES OF OFFICERS

The persistence of ascriptive loyalties among officers and men is not in doubt. The reliability of predecessor colonial armies was founded on the willingness of troops to do their duty, not in spite of ethnic loyalties, but because of them. In some unreconstructed armies, this tradition survives. A particularly brutal example was the West Pakistani suppression of the Bengali resistance in 1971. In other armies, the reconstruction of the ex-colonial officer corps to align its composition with that of the civilian regime was equally inimical to the development of ethnically detached professionalism.

The ability of ethnic loyalties to supersede professional loyalties is naturally greatest in times of ethnic crisis. The ease with which the Lebanese army splintered in four or five different directions at the time of the civil war in 1975–76 provides rather dramatic evidence. Not a single reliable interethnic unit remained intact.[76] The Lebanese army split

74. Cox, *Civil-Military Relations in Sierra Leone*, 52, 57–71, 102–03, 109–11, 130–31, 199, 213–14, 227–28.
75. See, e.g., Dent, "The Military and the Politicians," 78.
76. When the new regime of Elias Sarkis wanted a unit to patrol the South of Lebanon and separate Palestinians and Christians fighting there, the regime had to set about organizing the unit from scratch. *Washington Post*, Apr. 25, 1977. For the early stages of the Lebanese mutinies, see Joseph Fitchett, ibid., Mar. 11, 1976.

again in 1984, even after it had been carefully "reconstructed." Perhaps 10,000 Kurds had defected from the Iraqi army by 1965, the time of an attempted Kurdish secession.[77] The Nigerian and Burmese armies were likewise split by the wholesale departure of Ibo and Karen officers and men as those civil wars began. But, even in less violent and polarized settings, ethnic affiliations can compete with professional conceptions of military duty.

The mechanisms by which ethnic affiliations begin to crowd out occupational loyalties are easily specified. Officers who attempt to put their ethnic loyalties aside may miss opportunities for career advancement. They may find themselves at a disadvantage when their colleagues are aligning on an ethnic basis. In Sri Lanka, the formation of a Buddhist Association within the officer corps was one of the events that provoked a reaction among Christian and Hindu officers who thought of themselves as being noncommunally oriented. In a fashion reminiscent of Gresham's Law, the more ethnically committed officers tend to set the pace for the rest.

For all their efforts, the most correct and professional officers may still find themselves suspect in the eyes of the civilian regime they serve. When a Tamil commander and his Tamil deputy were ordered not to accompany their unit on emergency duty in a Tamil area of Sri Lanka, they received a blunt reminder of the importance of their origins. A regime's suspicion of officers in certain ethnic categories is likely to provoke their solidarity in spite of themselves.

The persistence of ethnic ties is also fed by regime efforts, however gradual, to undo the colonial legacy and realign armed forces with regime ethnic composition. These efforts necessarily entail favoritism, generate resentment, and make it plain that the civilian leadership itself is thinking along ethnic lines.

The course of ethnic events, both inside and outside the army, may thus cause officers to reconsider their professional assumptions and may overcome heroic efforts to control their private ethnic feelings. The compartmentalization of ethnic affiliations depends, in short, on the insulation of the armed forces. In a great many countries, that insulation is full of holes that permit ethnic conflicts originating outside the army to leak into it.

Officers who are unable to compartmentalize their ethnic affiliations

77. Hurewitz, *Middle East Politics*, 158.

are usually sensitive to the flow of ethnic politics in the civilian sector. Ethnic loyalties provide much of the cement for the civil-military alliances made possible by the porous boundaries dividing the two spheres. Together, ethnic loyalties and civil-military alliances render the officers vulnerable to involvement in civilian ethnic struggles.

The forging of factional links is facilitated by the strength, not merely of ethnic, but of subethnic ties, based typically on district or clan origins. In Pakistan, a significant cleavage in an officer corps dominated by Punjabis revolves around region of origin. Officers from East Punjab (now part of India) appear to control most high command positions, although West Punjabis comprise some 80 percent of the armed forces. A coup was attempted in 1980 by a score of officers, virtually all West Punjabis.[78] In Sierra Leone, the cleavage between Moyamba Mende and Kenema Mende played a major role in civilian politics even at the height of a wider North-South and APC-SLPP conflict. In a hotly contested election in 1967, some Kenema Mende had left Albert Margai's cabinet and run as independents. These rivalries reverberated in the army command. All this intra-Mende competition coincided with what was perceived as a threat from the Temne and the North—which raises some interesting questions about the cliché that people invariably unite in the face of a common enemy. Members of the different subgroups, of course, did not simply originate in different regions. They also tended to have different family and marriage connections, and sometimes a different outlook on interethnic questions. This was as true on the Temne side as it was on the Mende.

It is easy to document the importance of subethnic affiliation in military politics in other states. In Uganda, Obote's General Service Unit recruited heavily from his own Akororo district.[79] Local rivalries between the Darood Marehan and the Hawiye Habr Gidr, each a subgroup of a wider group, were expressed first in civilian disorders and then in a 1969 coup in Somalia. Among the ruling Sunni officers in Iraq, a small group from the town of Takrit wields supreme power.[80] Particularly where overarching ethnic identities are relatively new and have taken a

78. *Asiaweek* (Hong Kong), Mar. 28, 1980, p. 9.
79. Decalo, *Coups and Army Rule in Africa*, 207.
80. Cf. Phebe Marr, "The Political Elite in Iraq," in George Lenczowski, ed., *Political Elites in the Middle East* (Washington, D.C.: American Enterprise Institute, 1975), 134; *Washington Post*, Nov. 28, 1971.

composite form as a result of amalgamation,[81] subethnic allegiances will make themselves felt in military politics.

These loyalties and relationships, ethnic and subethnic, are as various as they are in civilian politics. In fact, what is striking about the activation of ethnic and subethnic affinities is that the officers pursue the interests of ascriptive groups just as civilian politicians might. Only their weapons are different. In most severely divided societies, the compartmentalization of ethnic ties by army officers is a chimera.

BREACHES OF MILITARY AUTONOMY

Divisions of authority typically depend on mutual noninterference, and they are quickly eroded by breaches of this reciprocity. The *coup de grâce* to military indifference to civilian ethnic politics has frequently been provided by blatant regime intrusion into the conditions of service in the armed forces. This intrusion goes much beyond the ordinary matters of budgets, equipment, and remuneration that concern armies everywhere. It has generally taken the form of drastic attempts to alter the composition or command structure of the armed forces.

Typically, the purpose of these actions has been to protect the regime from anticipated military intervention or resistance to its ethnic policies. Virtually always, such protective actions have had ethnic implications, usually because they aim in some way to redress or circumvent the effect of ethnic imbalances. They have taken two main forms, neither necessarily inconsistent with the other. Feeling endangered, some regimes have tried both.

First, the chain of command has been short-circuited, so as to bypass ethnically unsympathetic or dangerous commanders. This was done twice in Uganda. On the latter occasion, Obote shunted Amin to the post of chief of defense staff to remove him from troop command. The effect was to incite Amin to activate his network of contacts with Kakwa and Nubians in the army.[82] The same was done in Sierra Leone, when Siaka Stevens arrested or pensioned off a number of Temne officers and bypassed his commander, John Bangura, in favor of Bangura's deputy, who was, like Stevens, a Limba.[83] Within a matter of months, Bangura at-

81. See Chapter 2, above.
82. David Martin, *General Amin* (London: Faber & Faber, 1974); Decalo, *Coups and Army Rule in Africa*, 209–10.
83. Cox, *Civil-Military Relations in Sierra Leone*, 211–12.

tempted a coup. The same moves were made in Ghana by Nkrumah, who retired chief of defense staff S. J. A. Otu and army commander J. A. Ankrah when they protested the removal of the presidential guard from their command. The retirement of Ankrah angered other officers, especially inasmuch as the dismissed officers were succeeded by more pliable men who collaborated in Nkrumah's schemes to control the army.[84] Though Kofi A. Busia, who came to power some years later, might have learned from Nkrumah's mistakes, he, too, felt obliged to manipulate personnel for his own security. When the chief of staff was retired in 1971, Busia refused to appoint his second-in-command, an Ewe, to succeed him. The Ewe air force commander was also "hurriedly assigned to a one-year course at the Indian Defense College, and Lt. Col. Kattah (also an Ewe), having been posted as Military Attaché in the Indian capital, was brought back to face charges of theft arising after the 1966 coup, and put before a civilian court."[85] These departures from orderly military assignments, intended to safeguard Busia's position, rather clearly undermined it.[86] I mentioned earlier the less drastic but still portentous order to two senior Tamil officers in Sri Lanka that they were not to accompany the unit they commanded. Other officers took this as a deplorable sign of the growing role of ethnic considerations in civil-military relations, and it contributed to their determination to act against the regime responsible for it.[87]

Civilian circumvention of the chain of command for manifestly ethno-political purposes uniformly arouses military disquiet. The very idea of the chain of command (as indeed of the uniform itself) is that rank and office, rather than any individual incumbent, are to be determinative of status and role. Interference with the chain of command suggests the vulnerability of every officer and the fragility of his seniority. That ethnic reasons are important enough to motivate violations of the chain of command implies that more far-reaching manipulation may be in the offing. Such interference brings home to the officers in a most concrete way the permeability of civil-military boundaries.

84. First, *Power in Africa*, 198; W. F. Gutteridge, *Military Regimes in Africa* (London: Methuen, 1975), 68–69; Anton Bebler, *Military Rule in Africa* (New York: Praeger, 1973), 34; Jon Kraus, "Arms and Politics in Ghana," in Welch, ed., *Soldier and State in Africa*, 185–86.
85. Valerie Plave Bennett, "Malcontents in Uniform—The 1972 Coup d'Etat," in D. Austin and R. Luckham, eds., *Politicians and Soldiers in Ghana* (London: Frank Cass, 1975), 304.
86. See ibid., 308.
87. Horowitz, *Coup Theories and Officers' Motives*, 113–14.

The second type of protective action to call forth a preemptive reaction involves not just one or two commanders but whole forces. In country after country, attempts to homogenize the armed forces by packing them with members of ethnic groups friendly to the regime (and sometimes packing off members of other groups) or to neutralize them by creating rival paramilitary organizations have brought about the very coups these actions were designed to avert.[88] The roster of ethnically divided countries in this position includes, among others, Ghana, Uganda, Zanzibar, Libya, Mali, and Benin.

Perhaps this merely reflects the correctness of the regime's forecast that what I have called split domination is a dangerous state of affairs: coups might have occurred no matter what preventive action the regime attempted. The evidence indicates, however, that these preventive measures, unless carried out with great delicacy, are themselves provocative. They figure prominently and passionately in the litany of post-coup grievances.[89] The paramilitary forces are typically less professional than the regulars; any resources allocated to them are bitterly resented, even when, as in Nkrumah's Ghana, the budget of the regular armed forces remains generous. They are sometimes ideologically committed, morally fervent, and given to a variety of excesses, all of them at odds with the cautious spirit of a regular army.[90] Their commanders are often selected with primary regard to ethnic affiliation and personal loyalty and little or no regard to military seniority. Their favored position and access to civilian rulers are enduring sources of friction. Establishing new, ethnically differentiated irregular forces, bolstering existing ones, or tinkering with the command structure of regular units for reasons having nothing to do with ostensible military objectives constitutes the kind of civilian political involvement in military affairs that amounts to a major breach in boundaries.

Above all, the growing power of ethnically differentiated paramilitary units or the changing ethnic composition of regular forces at the instance of politicians is resisted because it portends, at best, misfortune and, at worst, disaster for soldiers and civilians belonging to the ethnic group whose strength is being diluted. To denominate interventions that follow civilian attempts to tamper with the military structure as deriving from

88. For a full discussion of coup-prevention measures, see Chapter 13, below.
89. Cf. First, *Power in Africa*, 429.
90. For an example, see Francis G. Snyder, "An Era Ends in Mali," *Africa Report*, Mar.–Apr. 1969, pp. 16–22.

mere "corporate interests" is to miss their survival—often their ethnic survival—aspects.

These breaches in boundaries might well have been accepted with greater equanimity by the regular officers, had other events not also undermined the ideal structure of civil-military relations. Ethnic conflict in the civilian arena had often shown the politicians to be petty-minded partisans of their own ethnic group interests, rather than national leaders who commanded the confidence of the whole people. Moreover, there had also been strikes, riots, and disturbances (many of them ethnically related) that required the cooperation of the army to insure public order. In fact, if not in theory, internal security is the primary mission of armed forces in Asia and Africa, as it was in the colonial period. It is a mission fraught with ambiguity about where civilian authority ends and military authority begins, and it requires close cooperation with political leaders. Civil disorder occasioned civil-military contact that was eye-opening for some officers. For the first time, they could glimpse at close range the patent inadequacies of civilian leaders in the actual handling of crises.[91] Occasionally, military judgment was overruled for political reasons. The disorders themselves sometimes made the officers feel the army was being used to save the politicians from the results of their own misguided policies. How, under these conditions, would it be possible to defer to civilian expertise? Once invited in to quell civil disorder, officers may later write their own invitations.

For many armies, therefore, the conditions underlying the maintenance of clear civil-military boundaries had ceased to exist. With civilian ineptitude exposed and encroachments abounding, precious little stood between the armed forces and their deployment in the ethnic struggles that suffused their political systems.

COMPARTMENTS AND BOUNDARIES, MILITARY AND ETHNIC

It should be clear that the three elements just discussed—the connections between soldiers and politicians, the difficulty officers experience in putting ethnic affiliations aside, and civilian intrusion into military affairs—are mutually reinforcing conditions. The ties of officers to politicians are usually based on common ethnic background. The soldiers' tolerance for civilian manipulation might be greater if civil-military boundaries were

91. There is direct evidence of this in the case of Sri Lanka and a strong likelihood in many other cases, among them Congo (Brazzaville), Somalia, Upper Volta, Benin, and perhaps Nigeria.

firmer to begin with and if ethnic loyalties were weaker or more adequately compartmentalized. Likewise, the temptation of politicians to restructure the army might be reduced if the politicians did not fear the connections of some officers with opposing politicians or suspect the intentions of officers of different ethnic backgrounds. Any chance of compartmentalizing the private feelings of officers is also effectively destroyed by regimes that intrude blatantly into army affairs and by the preexisting factional connections of some officers based on ethnic affiliation. The interlocking character of these conditions makes it very difficult to brake the entry of armies into the center of the ethnic conflicts of their societies, once a slide begins.

ETHNIC POLITICS
BY MILITARY MEANS

Taken together, ethnically skewed composition and the close connections between civilian and military affairs lay the foundation for ethnically motivated military intervention. The skewed composition of regimes and officer corps reinforces the apparent importance of ethnicity, facilitates the interactions of officers (including conspiratorial interactions) on an ethnic basis, and may also increase the tendency for politicians and officers to view each others' actions as ethnically motivated. The intersection and occasional collision of civilian and military spheres make it natural for cross-boundary ethnic networks to form. Prudent officers may find it impossible to rely solely on formally correct behavior. In the apprehensive environment created by civilian intrusion into military affairs, they often feel it necessary to take measures of self-defense, including measures based on ethnic linkages.

In ethnically divided societies, then, the military *coup d'état* is not so much a substitute for civilian politics as an extension of it. In many Asian and African states, the connection between military and civilian politics has been close and direct, with the military responding to events in the civilian sphere. Given the different directions in which the ethnic composition of armed forces and civilian regimes tends to be skewed, there are frequent occasions for response. Those occasions, I shall argue in the next chapter, are highly patterned. The strength of the military and its constant proximity to power accord it a kind of counterpoint status to political parties and civilian regimes in struggles for ethnic inclusion and exclusion.

CHAPTER TWELVE

Paradigms of
Military Ethnicity

For a coup to have profound ethnic consequences, every conspirator need not think in unequivocally ethnic terms. Soldiers who displace existing regimes may entertain the panoply of political motives, singly or in combination. Coalitions of conspirators are more readily built if a spectrum of grievances exists, but not every coup requires a coalition. Some have been made by notably narrow cliques of officers. But neither ambivalence in individual motivation nor plurality in collective motivation vitiates the significance of ethnicity in coup behavior. The ethnic import of a coup is a joint function of the intentions of officers at the time and the intentions imputed to them after the event.

The reactive character of military politics being what it is, the relative prominence of ethnic motives among coup plotters is more often than not determined by the prominence of ethnic motives in the conduct of the regime the coup seeks to displace. Yet even coups that derive from mixed motives are sometimes interpreted as deriving heavily from ethnic motives. Such interpretations are likely to shape political responses to the coups. Inferences are drawn from ethnic composition—of both plotters and victims of plots—and from the conduct of regimes before and after the event. These, after all, are the most tangible pieces of evidence from which conclusions can be drawn.

Two examples suffice to make the point. The so-called "Ibo coup" of January 1966 may well have proceeded from a combination of motives. But the plotters were mainly Ibo; some had apparently been in touch with Ibo politicians; the politicians murdered during the coup were non-Ibo; an Ibo officer came to power after the coup; his most prominent advisers were Ibo; and he promulgated a number of decrees that had long been sought by Ibo and resisted by Northerners. Under the circumstances, is it surprising that the coup came to be seen as an Ibo plot that installed an Ibo government? In Morocco, the coup attempt of 1971 could scarcely be described as an explicitly Berber plot. But the composition of the military was such that any conspiracy had to involve key Berber officers. When the plot was defeated, many Berber officers were executed. Afterward, members of the Moroccan elite asserted "that it was the fruit of Berber duplicity, savagery and madness," while Berbers in turn were deeply resentful of the execution of so many Berber officers.[1] Events have a way of purifying motives retroactively.

An analysis of ethnically related coup behavior, therefore, need not be confined to the subjective motivation of the coupmakers. Basic distinctions among coups and the major characteristics of each type can be derived as well from the structure of behavior and relationships. Two main types of ethnic coup will be analyzed. The first is the "seesaw coup," so called because it effects a sudden drastic shift in the balance of ethnic power between the main contestants. The second is the coup of attrition, which results in the progressive narrowing of the ethnic base of a regime until only one or two small ethnic groups come to dominate the rest. A variant of the seesaw coup is the coup to retrieve a lost position of ethnic preeminence, and a variant of the attritional coup entails a narrowing process in ethnically divided countries that gained their independence through the use of force. Finally, there is a less prevalent type, the coup to pursue traditional ethnic enmities by military means.

As I shall explain, these distinctions are enormously important in their consequences for ethnic groups that live under the resulting regimes. In particular, it matters whether a narrow ethnocracy emerges from a series of coups and purges. At their most extreme, ethnocracies are brutal, difficult to dislodge, and, once dislodged, probably unlikely to give way to an ethnically inclusive polity.

In elucidating these distinctions, I shall make liberal use of paradigm cases. The presentation of detailed data from a number of countries will make clear just how striking the similarities are among them and just what determines the evolution from one form of coup to another.

ETHNIC DIALECTICS: SIERRA LEONE

Sierra Leone is the pristine case of military action to avert or reverse ethnic exclusion. There have been several coups and coup attempts in

1. Octave Marais, "Berbers and the Moroccan Political System After the Coup," in Ernest Gellner and Charles Micaud, eds., *Arabs and Berbers* (Lexington, Mass.: Lexington Books, 1972), 431–32. See also A. Coram, "The Berbers and the Coup," in ibid., 429.

Sierra Leone, all with this effect, and it therefore becomes possible to track an ethnic coup progression. The tracking is made possible because of an abundance of detailed data and profitable because of the intimate connections between party and military politics.

To be sure, ethnicity has not been everything in Sierra Leone politics: family relationships, intraethnic regional differences, school ties, and sheer personal animosities have all been entangled with ethnic conflict, as they often are elsewhere. Yet ethnicity has been so prominent in military and civilian politics that an analysis that sorts out ethnic variables is warranted. In 1966, for example, a group of non-Mende officers complained to the prime minister of the "nepotism" and "tribalism" being practiced by their commander; and a year later, facing election, the same prime minister opined less elegantly that the opposition consisted of a "Temne-Creole axis" that would "cut the Mende man's throat" if it came to power.[2]

After independence, Sierra Leone party politics polarized around the issue of Mende domination. In 1960, Siaka Stevens, a Limba, had formed an opposition party that appealed to Northern interests, and it had been joined by the Temne, most numerous among Northern groups, as well as by Susu, Loko, and Mandingo. By 1962, Stevens' All People's Congress had captured the majority of Northern constituencies. Creoles (putative descendants of resettled slaves) also supported the All People's Congress, probably because, after 1964, the government of Albert Margai had tended to be opposed to Creole domination of the civil service. Margai's Mende constituents were increasingly well educated, and many of them chafed under their Creole superiors in government. Margai promoted many Mende to important civil service positions. As the 1967 general elections approached, the APC, with its broad Northern support, posed a formidable threat to Margai's Sierra Leone People's Party. The SLPP government had become more and more synonymous with Mende interests, and the election took on the aspect of a contest of Temne and other Northerners against Mende and their allies, the Sherbro and Fula.[3]

2. Quoted by John R. Cartwright, *Politics in Sierra Leone, 1947–1967* (Toronto: Univ. of Toronto Press, 1970), 248.

3. See John R. Cartwright, *Political Leadership in Sierra Leone* (Toronto: Univ. of Toronto Press, 1978), 189–202; Gershon Collier, *Sierra Leone: Experiment in Democracy in an African Nation* (New York: New York Univ. Press, 1970), 71–75; Christopher Allen, "Sierra Leone Politics Since Independence," *African Affairs* 67 (Oct. 1968): 305–29; John Cartwright, "Shifting Forces in Sierra Leone," *Africa Report*, Dec. 1968, pp. 26–30.

Boundaries between party and army were not always clear-cut. The army commander, David Lansana, a Mende, was a close confidant of Albert Margai, and a relative of one of Margai's Mende cabinet ministers. Such civil-military relationships by marriage were not uncommon. The SLPP regime also took pains to recruit Mende officers into the army. A new military academy was established in 1966, and most of the cadets who passed out of it were Mende. The first coups in Ghana and Nigeria had already occurred, and the regime seemed to be preparing for the inevitable involvement of the military in Sierra Leone's political life. As its civilian base grew narrower, the SLPP's military support grew stronger.

Military intervention came soon enough. Early in 1967, the army's second-in-command, John Bangura, a Temne-Loko, and eight other officers, also mainly Temne, were arrested on charges of plotting a coup that would have brought the APC to power. Whether the officers were acting preemptively in response to the packing of the officer corps with Mende or whether the alleged coup was merely a pretext for Margai to homogenize the army command further is uncertain,[4] but it had the latter effect. By the time of the election in March 1967, the army command was overwhelmingly Mende. The election itself was close, but the APC held a lead, and the governor-general chose to ask Stevens and the APC to form a government. No sooner had Stevens been sworn in than he was arrested by Brigadier Lansana, who quite plainly was prepared to turn power back to Albert Margai.

This coup, however, was not uniformly popular, especially with Mende officers aligned with other factions of the SLPP. Within two days, Lansana himself had been overthrown by Mende and other Southern officers determined to hold rather than hand back power. They established a "National Reformation Council" that perpetuated Mende rule.[5]

The 1967 coup effected a reversal of the election results. The majors

4. See Allen, "Sierra Leone Politics Since Independence," 315–16. But see Thomas S. Cox, *Civil-Military Relations in Sierra Leone* (Cambridge: Harvard Univ. Press, 1976), 100–03.

5. For details, see Humphrey J. Fisher, "Elections and Coups in Sierra Leone, 1967," *Journal of Modern African Studies* 7 (Dec. 1969): 611–36; Government of Sierra Leone, *Report of the Dove-Edwin Commission of Inquiry into the Conduct of the 1967 General Elections in Sierra Leone* (Freetown: Government Printer, 1967). The core of Albert Margai's support was the Moyamba area; the Mende majors who overthrew Lansana were more closely tied to the Kenema area of Mendeland, as we shall see later. Cox, *Civil-Military Relations in Sierra Leone*, 129–31. Though the NRC's policies sometimes embarrassed the SLPP, SLPP supporters continued to hold key posts during the NRC period, and it is fair to say that the NRC perpetuated Mende power. See ibid., 144, 148, 153, 164.

who displaced Lansana "still wished for a Southern-based SLPP-like government, which would not enquire into the actions of the Margai administration, nor divert funds from the South, both of which the APC intended to do."[6] Not only was the NRC dominated by Mende officers, but its civilian advisory committee was also "biased towards the South and East," containing as it did many supporters of Margai.[7] The officers had saved Mendeland from Northern domination.

But only temporarily. In April 1968, a group of enlisted men arrested their officers, recalled John Bangura from exile, and restored Stevens to power in the guise of an APC-SLPP coalition. In Sierra Leone, the other ranks are composed heavily of Northerners, and the conspirators had surely been in touch with Bangura.[8] As the officers had reversed the election results, the other ranks had reversed the officers, and the wheel of power turned to the North.

The ethnic significance of each of the events of 1967–68 is clear. At the time of the alleged Bangura coup attempt in early 1967, there were units in which only Mende troops received arms; during the Lansana coup, ammunition was also distributed along ethnic lines.[9] Shortly after his return to power, Stevens, in a drive to "eliminate as many Mendes as possible" from the army, removed even the Mende colonel and three Mende warrant officers who had cooperated in bringing him back.[10]

Stevens was as quick as Margai to sense the close connection of military and civilian politics, but more thorough. He simultaneously harassed the opposition and purged the army. Some SLPP leaders were detained while formally serving as junior partners in Stevens' nominal coalition government. Within months, the SLPP was excluded from the government and forced to contest a series of by-elections required by the judicial unseating of victorious SLPP candidates accused of electoral malpractice in 1967. By the liberal use of incentives and coercion, the APC won half of the vacant seats. The SLPP was reduced to a shadow of its former self, and in Mende areas violence broke out between Mende and Northern migrants.[11]

6. Allen, "Sierra Leone Politics Since Independence," 324.
7. Ibid., 326. See also Hilary Ng'weno, "Tribes, Armies and Political Instability in Africa" (unpublished paper, Harvard Univ. Center for International Affairs, Mar. 1969), 36.
8. Cox, *Civil-Military Relations in Sierra Leone*, 199.
9. Ibid., 106, 131.
10. Ibid., 206, 209.
11. For these developments, see Cartwright, "Shifting Forces in Sierra Leone," 30; Christopher Clapham, "Sierra Leone: Civilian Rule and the New Republic," *The World Today* 28 (Feb. 1972): 82–91, at 84–85.

Having been arrested by the coupmakers of April 1968, army officers were released selectively and reinstated in the army even more selectively. Bangura, who had been detained for plotting against Margai and whose pro-Stevens sympathies had prevented his release by the NRC, became army commander. The leaders of the 1967 coups were tried for treason and then detained even after their convictions were quashed. A substantial number of noncommissioned officers who had demonstrated loyalty to Stevens received commissions.[12] The result of these changes was a vast increase in Northern representation in the officer corps. With many Mende officers in jail, in exile, in retirement, or in private employment, by 1970 only one of the top ten officers and less than a third of the whole officer corps was Mende, more than a third was Temne, and nearly 30 percent consisted of Koranko and Yalunka, Northerners who had earlier formed an insignificant fraction of the officer corps.[13] Given the position of Mende officers in 1967, when they outnumbered Temne by 4 to 1 and when the new military academy was turning out overwhelming numbers of Mende graduates, the ethnic reconstruction of the officer corps in the first two years of the Stevens regime was drastic.

With the Mende under control, fissures quickly opened up inside the APC government.[14] The most important were those between Temne, on the one hand, and other Northerners and Creoles, on the other. Unlike Stevens and some of his other colleagues, the leading APC Temne were educated men from prominent families. There seemed to be a claim to preeminence for them and for the Temne as the largest Northern group. Instead, Temne leaders were being slighted in favor of Creoles, the Limba (Stevens' own group), and even a few prominent Koranko. In addition, Stevens had been cultivating ties with Guinea. This was an issue with an ethnic component. Several leading APC Temne came from the Tonkolili district, an area isolated from contact with Guinea, whereas a number of their colleagues felt more affinity with groups across the border. Indeed, one intra-Temne dividing line was between those in the elite who saw themselves as "purer" Temne than those who were of mixed Temne-Sherbro, Temne-Susu, or Temne-Loko origin.

Prominent Temne began to take action in 1970, capturing the Provincials Organization, which had begun the previous year as an anti-Creole, Mende association in Freetown. By mid-1970, the Provincials was be-

12. Clapham, "Sierra Leone," 86; Cox, *Civil-Military Relations in Sierra Leone*, 207.
13. Cox, *Civil-Military Relations in Sierra Leone*, 209.
14. The following account of the 1970–71 conflict is drawn from several sources: conversations with Thomas Cox; Cox, ibid., 210–16; Colin Legum, ed., *Africa Contemporary Record, 1970–71* (London: Rex Collings, 1971), pp. B444–46.

coming a largely Temne organization; its Mende founders and a prominent Limba leader had been pushed aside. Important Temne ministers—
all of them from the Tonkolili district—left the Stevens cabinet and the
APC. Then, joined by a Temne-Loko from Tonkolili, John Karefa-Smart,
they founded a new party, the United Democratic Party. Its leadership
was almost entirely Temne.

Stevens' reaction was prompt and decisive. Confronted "with a potentially lethal threat to his northern base,"[15] he banned the party, detained its leaders, and arrested or cashiered a number of army officers
and N.C.O.s, mainly Temne. According to some sources, Stevens chose
Limba, Yalunka, and Koranko troops to make the arrests, thus under-
scoring the cleavage between Temne and other Northern groups.[16] At
about the same time, Stevens had begun to bypass his army commander,
Bangura, the man who had helped restore Stevens to power in 1968.
Stevens began to rely heavily on Bangura's deputies, a Creole and a
Limba. Bangura, closely associated with Karefa-Smart and, like him, a
Temne-Loko from Tonkolili, had become a mere figurehead. Presumably
kept on as commander because of his popularity with the heavily Temne
army ranks, Bangura was increasingly isolated within the officer corps
as his Temne subordinates were arrested.

The military sequel to the civilian ethnic conflict was not long in
coming.[17] Bangura made his move in March 1971, after an attempt on
Stevens' life had failed. This coup, however, was promptly disavowed by
Bangura's Creole and Limba subordinates, who restored Stevens to
power. The aid of Guinean troops was invoked, and they stayed on for
quite some time to guard Stevens' residence. Bangura himself was later
shot; he had claimed that his coup had been instigated by Karefa-Smart.

For a time, the Stevens regime, no longer able to count on significant
Mende or Temne support, was left mainly in the hands of Limba, Creoles, and Northern minorities such as the Koranko. The leaders of the
state, the party, and the army were all Limba. A further purge of the
army decimated the Temne component of the officer corps. Though there
might be unrest among the Mende and Temne, who together comprise
60 percent of the Sierra Leone population, thereafter Siaka Stevens was
far less likely to be deposed in a *coup d'état.*

15. Clapham, "Sierra Leone," 89.
16. Cox, *Civil-Military Relations in Sierra Leone*, 211.
17. See *Manchester Guardian*, July 7, 1971; ibid., Jan. 22, 1971; *New York Times*,
Mar. 24, 1971; *Washington Post*, Mar. 24 and 29, 1971.

TABLE 8   ETHNIC CHRONOLOGY OF ELECTIONS
AND COUPS IN SIERRA LEONE, 1967–74

February 8, 1967:	Arrest of Col. John Bangura and eight other officers, mainly Temne, by predominantly Mende SLPP regime, on charges of plotting a pro-APC coup.
March 17, 1967:	After a close election, Stevens is sworn in at the head of an APC government, with the support of Temne and other Northerners.
March 21, 1967:	Mende army commander, Brig. David Lansana, arrests Stevens, with apparent intention to restore Mende regime under Albert Margai.
March 23, 1967:	Three majors overthrow Lansana and establish a Mende-dominated military regime.
April 17, 1968:	Other ranks overthrow military regime and restore Stevens to power. Purges of Mende officers follow. They are replaced by Northerners.
March 23, 1971:	Brig. John Bangura attempts an unsuccessful coup after Stevens' suppression of a predominantly Temne party with which Bangura had been linked and Stevens' arrests of Temne officers.
July 30, 1974:	A group of Mende and Temne civilians and soldiers join together for futile action against the regime.

A subsequent conspiracy illustrates these points. In 1974, a group of soldiers and civilians was arrested for plotting a coup.[18] Eight of them were later hanged. The civilians were mainly Temne, two of them prominently associated with the UDP. The soldiers were mainly Mende, none of them an officer. The plot was poorly organized and easily thwarted; it got only as far as a single explosion at a politician's home. Ethnic grievances against Stevens abound, but the means of expressing them through the officer corps are not readily accessible. Later plots were also easily thwarted.

Having cracked down on Temne opposition, Stevens later moved to broaden his regime somewhat, appointing, for example, a Temne vice-president. In 1978, he proclaimed a one-party state and invited remnants of the Mende SLPP to join the ruling party. They were formally admitted but with the reluctance reserved for ethnic party enemies that we have witnessed in other single-party regimes. This Mende window dressing

18. Cox, *Civil-Military Relations in Sierra Leone*, 227–28; Colin Legum, ed., *Africa Contemporary Record, 1974–75* (New York: Africana, 1975), pp. B764–65.

did not alter the ethnic basis of the regime, which was principally Limba and only secondarily Temne. By 1983, commanders of the army, the paramilitary State Security Division, and the police were all, like Stevens, Limba. Comprising less than 10 percent of the population, Limba were nonetheless preeminent.

The Sierra Leone coups and coup attempts show very clearly the reactive nature of ethnically motivated coups. In each instance, soldiers representing an ethnic group that had been or was about to be excluded from political power moved to vitiate the exclusion. Lansana made a Mende coup against the new Northern government, the privates made what amounted to a Northern countercoup against the Mende military regime that succeeded Lansana, and Bangura attempted a Temne coup against what had become essentially a Limba-Creole regime upon the arrest and exclusion of prominent Temne. The pattern of action and reaction is both clear and striking, and so is the continuity between civilian and military politics.

While ethnic motives were sharply defined, ethnic alignments were not constant. They shifted as groups were eliminated and others arose. Most dramatic was the breakdown of the APC's solid Northern support soon after the Mende had effectively been eliminated from electoral and military competition.

This shift in alignments marks the distinction between seesaw and attritional coups. Both aim at inclusion of excluded groups. The first, represented by the 1967–68 situation in Sierra Leone, arises in a democratic, electoral phase of ethnic politics, when ethnic parties are nearly evenly balanced. In a polarized ethnic equilibrium, the military acts to reverse the results of the elections (1967) or to reaffirm them (1968). The second type, which in Sierra Leone occurred in 1970–71, arises after this equilibrium has broken down and the democratic, electoral phase of politics is over. Then an attritional struggle begins among the survivors of the first phase. In this phase, ethnic majorities do not necessarily win. Both patterns are common enough to permit comparative analysis in order, moving outward from the Sierra Leone paradigm.

ELECTORAL POLARIZATION
AND THE SEESAW COUP

The balance of forces in Sierra Leone as of the 1967 election was similar to that which obtained in a number of other African states within a few years of independence. Party politics had settled down to competition between two main parties, each of which represented a cluster of opposed ethnic groups. Often the core of each cluster was one relatively large ethnic group, around which smaller groups, generally from the same region, gravitated. Party differences generally corresponded with the distinction between backward and advanced groups. In Sierra Leone, the core groups in the respective parties were the Mende and Temne. This pattern of sharp, two-party confrontation gave the appearance of democratic, competitive politics, but, as we have seen, the competition for clientele occurred, if at all, only at the margins. Party alignments had crystallized on the basis of ethnic antagonisms, and cross-ethnic electoral competition scarcely occurred. These were census-type elections of the sort we have witnessed previously. When the results were in, they portended a permanent opposition status for the losing ethnic party, since it usually could not expect to improve its share of the vote by competitive methods in future elections. A number of serious ethnic riots occurred following such elections. So, too, did a number of ethnic coups where the officer corps and the victorious party were drawn in the main from different ethnic groups. The Lansana coup of 1967 is merely one of this class of coups by groups excluded from power by the electoral process in a bipolar ethnic situation.

The so-called Ibo coup of January 1966 in Nigeria had also been preceded by a party polarization along ethnic lines.[19] When Nigeria attained independence, each of three major groups—Hausa-Fulani, Ibo, and Yoruba—was represented by one of three major political parties. When, however, the Yoruba fell out along subethnic lines in the early 1960s, the Yoruba party split, one faction aligning with the North and the Hausa-Fulani, the other with the East and the Ibo. With the possibility of shifting coalitions gone, the fluidity went out of the Nigerian arrangements. The Northern coalition proved stronger than the Eastern, and appeared bent on a vindictive form of domination. This polarization, a test of strength at the polls, and a taste of the prospect of permanent exclusion were some of the main ingredients of the Ibo coup.

Togo and Congo (Brazzaville) experienced similar polarizations. In each case, two ethnic blocs confronted each other; in each, one emerged victorious in elections, but the other emerged victorious in a subsequent coup.

19. For a review of events leading up to the January 1966 coup, see Walter Schwarz, *Nigeria* (New York: Praeger, 1968), 152–90.

Togo's independence government, headed by Sylvanus Olympio, was supported by the Ewe, who comprise some 44 percent of the population.[20] Southerners who had been favored by the German colonialists, the Ewe had also benefited from missionary education and from their favorable location in the colony. Under French rule, the Ewe areas of Togo, like the Fon areas of Dahomey, supplied administrators for the colonial apparatus throughout French Africa. By the time of independence, the Ewe were strongly represented in the Togolese civil service.

Olympio had a less than generous attitude toward the North, which was represented by an opposition party. Like the Northern regions of many coastal West African states, the Togolese North was characterized by economic backwardness, illiteracy, and a lack of educational facilities and urban amenities. Members of the Northern Kabrai and related groups (23 percent of the population) had, however, been recruited for service in the French colonial forces, and the small Togolese army at independence was largely a Kabrai force.

Olympio's neglect of the North was resented in the army. When, in 1963, he refused to incorporate demobilized Togolese soldiers—principally Kabrai—of the French army into the Togolese armed forces, "Olympio did not hide his contempt for the 'petits nordists'. . . ."[21] Leaders of the demobilized veterans, with the support of their Kabrai army allies, responded by assassinating Olympio and turning power over to his electoral opponent, Nicholas Grunitsky.

For several years, Grunitsky ruled with the assent of the army, which had become about 80 percent Northern. Grunitsky attempted to propitiate the Ewe, but with little success. At the same time, Grunitsky's failure to establish a Northern-based regime and his demotion of a popular Northern rival weakened his support in the army, officered by Kabrai ex-privates and N.C.O.s who had commissioned themselves after the coup. In 1967, Olympio's assassins assumed power for themselves.

With this coup, the regime became unequivocally Northern in support and composition. Ewe comprised just over two-thirds of the cabinets of Olympio and Grunitsky; Kabrai formed about one-fifth of each. Under the military regime, these proportions were more than reversed.

20. Samuel Decalo, *Coups and Army Rule in Africa* (New Haven: Yale Univ. Press, 1976), 87–121; Ruth First, *Power in Africa* (Harmondsworth, England: Penguin, 1972), 89, 208–09, 435; J. M. Lee, *African Armies and Civil Order* (New York: Praeger, 1969), 163–64; Russell Warren Howe, "Togo: Four Years of Military Rule," *Africa Report*, May 1967, pp. 6–12; ibid., Nov. 1970, pp. 8, 11.
21. Decalo, *Coups and Army Rule in Africa*, 98.

The cabinet was only one-fourth Ewe, barely more than half the Ewe proportionate share; Northerners comprised two-thirds; and the Kabrai alone represented 42 percent of the cabinet, almost twice their proportionate share.[22] Here is a graphic indication of the meaning of a seesaw coup.

Congo (Brazzaville) was much more complex, but there, too, the coup served to provide an ethnic group with relief from the unfavorable results of an election. As in the other cases, the background to military intervention lay in the gradual polarization of politics around two parties, each of them representing a regional cluster of several ethnic groups. As in the other cases, too, each party rested on the core support of an important ethnic group bitterly opposed to the group at the core of the other party. As in Nigeria, the military confrontation was brought on after a third political party had proved ineffective and left the field to the other two. As in Togo, the transition to full military rule occurred after an interval of several years. And, as in Sierra Leone, the ethnic group in whose interest the coup was made was not in total control of the armed forces, and so the coup was followed by military purges and reorganizations.

The heart of politics in the Congo Republic had long been the rivalry of the Northern Mbochi with the Southern Bakongo, especially its Lari subgroup.[23] Each of these groups was associated with its own party, and a third group, the Vili, was represented by a third party that withered with a change to proportional representation in 1957. By the time of the 1957 elections, the Mbochi and Bakongo parties had each captured twenty-one of the total of forty-five seats. Three independents who had also been elected divided their allegiances, thus completing the polarization. A coalition of convenience was formed, but it proved unstable. Among the divisive forces was the fierce rivalry of the two parties for the allegiance of the now-partyless Vili population.

As a result of defections, the Bakongo party, under Fulbert Youlou, emerged in a majority position. Youlou did everything he could to solidify his precarious advantage over his Mbochi opponents, bringing on in

---

22. Ibid., 112.
23. See René Gauze, *The Politics of Congo-Brazzaville*, trans., ed., and supplemented by Virginia Thompson and Richard Adloff (Stanford: Hoover Institution Press, 1973); John A. Ballard, "Four Equatorial States," in Gwendolen M. Carter, ed., *National Unity and Regionalism in Eight African States* (Ithaca: Cornell Univ. Press, 1966), 244–53, 313–19; Arthur H. House, "Brazzaville: Revolution or Rhetoric?" *Africa Report*, Apr. 1971, pp. 18–21; J. M. Lee, "Clan Loyalties and Socialist Doctrine in the People's Republic of the Congo," *The World Today* 27 (Jan. 1971): 40–46; Decalo, *Coups and Army Rule in Africa*, 123–72.

the process several serious episodes of rioting. The Mbochi party was gradually eclipsed, and later outlawed, but Mbochi feelings had by no means been assuaged.

In 1963, Youlou fell from power in a confrontation with trade unions. He was succeeded by Alphonse Massamba-Débat, a Bakongo but not a Lari. The Lari had fallen from power with Youlou.

It took several years, however, before the Mbochi completely filled the vacuum. During this time, there were Lari demonstrations in Brazzaville, some of them violent, in support of Youlou. Only in 1968 was Massamba-Débat finally dislodged. Massamba-Débat had resorted to the use of force against potential opponents. In the course of this, he made the mistake of arresting a popular Northern paratroop commander, Captain Marien Ngouabi, and he compounded the mistake by using the predominantly Lari gendarmerie to make the arrest. Thereupon, Ngouabi's angry Northern troops moved into Brazzaville and released their commander. By stages, army officers under Ngouabi's leadership established a Northern-dominated regime. By 1980, the Bakongo, some 30 percent of the population, had been reduced to one member of the politburo.

Coups that follow the destruction of an electoral equilibrium perform a seesaw function. Thwarted by electoral demography, the plotters proceed to do what an election cannot do: tip the balance. But a seesaw has two seats, and is capable of going up and down. Consequently, the coup made in such conditions is likely to be followed by a countercoup, the more so as ethnic followers of the displaced regime may feel cheated out of the legitimate fruits of electoral victory. In each of these cases, countercoups occurred, two of them successful. In Sierra Leone, as we have seen, Northern enlisted men restored Stevens to power in 1968. Northern officers and other ranks ended the Ibo regime in Nigeria in July 1966. The Ewe in Togo attempted to displace the Northern regime in 1966, but so complete was Kabrai control of the army that the effort was easily defeated.[24] In Brazzaville, Mbochi control of the armed forces was much more tenuous. Hence the repeated reorganization of military units to bring centers of Lari support under Northern command. In the first several years of the Ngouabi regime, there were repeated Lari plots, countercoups, and invasions by exiles from across the Congo River in Kinshasa.[25] As in Sierra Leone, the process of ethnic purging was extensive.

24. First, *Power in Africa*, 208–09, 435.
25. See, e.g., Gauze, *The Politics of Congo-Brazzaville*, 173–76.

Significantly, the Nigerian and Sierra Leonean countercoups succeeded, whereas the others failed. The armies of Nigeria and Sierra Leone were rent by pronounced intramilitary ethnic cleavages. Military rank and ethnicity tended to coincide. This made possible concerted counteraction against military superiors who were also ethnic opponents. In Togo, where such a cleavage was not really present, the attempted counteraction was feeble. In Congo (Brazzaville), where the army was heterogeneous, units important to the defense of the regime were not. Consequently, Lari raids against the military regime were consistently repelled. From the standpoint of the relations of ethnic groups to party, elections, and army, these four cases are virtually identical except for the structure of intra-army cleavages. Also in the seesaw category are coups that occurred in Surinam (1980), where Creole armed forces prevented an East Indian government from coming to power; in Rwanda (1973), where Northern army officers overthrew a Southern civilian regime; and arguably in Madagascar (1972), Mali (1968), the Sudan (1958), and Libya (1969).[26]

The coups we have been considering are not so much a negation of the electoral process as an extension of it. Ethnic groups have an array

26. On Surinam, see Edward Dew, "The Year of the Sergeants," *Caribbean Review* 9 (Spring 1980): 5–7, 46–47. On Rwanda, see Stanley Meisler, "Rwanda and Burundi," *Atlantic*, Sept. 1973, pp. 6–16. On Mali, cf. Anton Bebler, *Military Rule in Africa* (New York: Praeger, 1973), 90–91; F. G. Snyder, *One-Party Government in Mali* (New Haven: Yale Univ. Press, 1965), 57–58.

The Sudan coup of 1958 developed into something very much in the category of a seesaw coup. Rivalry between the two predominant Sufi sects in the Sudan, the Mahdists and the Khatmiyyah, was sufficiently ascriptive to be tantamount to ethnic rivalry. Each group was represented by a separate party, and the army was divided along sectarian lines. The Khatmiyyah—and especially the Shaigia tribe, with its reputation for military prowess—was strongly represented in the army and its high command. When the coup appeared to strengthen rather than displace the Mahdist civilian government it nominally overthrew, a number of Khatmiyyah officers deflected its course and turned the military regime in an anti-Mahdist direction. The 1969 coup had much the same effect; shortly thereafter the Mahdists' own private army made a last stand against the military regime on Aba Island in the White Nile. In 1976, a countercoup, with Mahdist overtones, was put down after two days of heavy fighting. See First, *Power in Africa*, 130–36, 144, 233–35, 244, 272–77; J. C. Hurewitz, *Middle East Politics: The Military Dimension* (New York: Praeger, 1969), 165–76.

Perhaps Colonel Qaddafi's 1969 coup against King Idris of Libya was a seesaw coup, even though Idris' was a traditional monarchy rather than an elective regime. Idris' base was in Cyrenaica, and he favored Cyrenaicans in the army. The conspirators who overthrew him were, however, overwhelmingly non-Cyrenaicans, many of them from the backward Fezzan region. It is not wholly fatuous to regard the coup as a movement of the "oases and the interior against the established society of the large families and dominant tribes." Ruth First, *Libya: The Elusive Revolution* (Baltimore: Penguin, 1974), 115. See generally Hurewitz, *Middle East Politics*, 231–40. Nonetheless, electoral politics is more likely to bring on a seesaw coup because of the visible, clear-cut ethnic cleavage that accompanies electoral equilibrium.

of political resources. Parties may be one resource; an officer corps may be another. Where parties are aligned with ethnic boundaries, where electoral victory and loss are foreordained by demography, the tendency to move from party to army is strong. Paradoxically, the hotly contested elections that were followed by coups were often regarded as evidence that a democratic, competitive tradition was taking hold; the coups were viewed as breaking the democratic circuit. In fact, as we have seen, the elections were not mechanisms of choice, and the coups were not really discontinuous with them at all. The coups did not bring on a failure of democracy, but merely confirmed the inadequacy of the electoral process in a situation of polarized ethnic equilibrium. They were a natural outgrowth of ascriptive party allegiance.

ETHNIC NARROWING
AND THE COUP OF ATTRITION

Whether or not the officers who make the first coup truly intend to turn power back to the civilians, the prospects for a return to democratic rule soon after such a coup has occurred are remote. The seesaw character of polarized equilibrium insures countercoups and the purges that either follow them or are necessary to avert or defeat them. The ethnic equilibrium is upset, and a new period of authoritarian rule begins. In this period, one tendency is toward rule by a smaller ethnic segment of the population. This narrowing tendency is very well illustrated by the role of the Limba in the Stevens regime in Sierra Leone.

In this later stage, military intervention again plays a role. By this time, in fact, prior military intervention has loosened the restraints on military involvement in politics, and the armed forces typically play an important part in fostering the ethnic narrowing process or in challenging that process. For, once the cycle of elections is broken, it is possible for ethnic minority regimes to rule. Then ethnic splits in the ruling party may develop, as they did in the Sierra Leone APC in 1970, or ethnic divisions may split a politically involved officer corps.

Either way, power cannot be concentrated in the hands of minority ethnic groups without the connivance or decimation of the army. Stevens, though elected in 1967, had to be restored to power by the 1968 coup and had to reconstruct the officer corps in order to defeat Karefa-Smart and Bangura when they later moved against him. In Uganda and Syria, even more prominent roles were played by the army. In both, civilian rulers needed at least the tacit assent of military men, and, in both, minority military regimes ultimately emerged.

UGANDA: FROM MAJORITY TO MINORITY RULE

Uganda's ethnic politics in the early and mid-1960s was dominated by a single issue: the place to be occupied by the Baganda and their home-land, the Kingdom of Buganda, situated in the South of Uganda.[27] Political parties crystallized along these lines. We have already seen that when A. Milton Obote came to power in 1962, he sat at the head of an odd coalition between his Uganda People's Congress and the royalist Baganda Kabaka Yekka movement. Obote's UPC was essentially a party of Northerners and Easterners, many of whom were hostile to the Baganda, with their strong positions in the civil service and in educational institutions. Obote took the first opportunity to end the coalition with Kabaka Yekka in 1964. Thereafter, the influential Baganda population was alienated from his government. With Obote's defeat of a challenge by Southerners inside his own party in 1966 and the arrest of five Southern cabinet ministers, the government became a largely Northern regime, at odds with the majority of the population.

Such a minority regime had to have an unusually sympathetic army and police. To insure this, Obote placed a loyal Northerner in the position of Inspector General of Police. The overwhelming majority of the police had long consisted of Northerners. A Lango himself, Obote packed the army with Langi and Acholi officers and men, and expanded its budget rapidly in the early years of independence.[28] Conservative estimates gave the Acholi, less than 5 percent of the population, at least one-third of the army.[29] Northern N.C.O.s were frequently commissioned, particularly after the East African army pay strikes of 1964 and the repatriation of British officers that followed. The paramilitary General Service Unit, composed heavily of Langi, was strengthened. Like the army, the GSU was distinctly hostile to the Baganda and clashed with

---

27. See Hugh Dinwiddy, "The Search for Unity in Uganda: Early Days to 1966," *African Affairs* 80 (Oct. 1981): 501–18.

28. A Special Correspondent, "The Uganda Army: Nexus of Power," *Africa Report*, Dec. 1966, p. 39; cf. Michael Lofchie, "The Uganda Coup: Class Action by the Military," *Journal of Modern African Studies* 10 (1972): 19–25, at 21–23.

29. Ali A. Mazrui, *Soldiers and Kinsmen in Uganda* (Beverly Hills: Sage, 1975), 113. David Martin, *General Amin* (London: Faber & Faber, 1974), 105, says the Acholi share may have been closer to three-fourths. Later, Martin claimed the army was only about half Langi and Acholi. *Boston Globe*, Aug. 15, 1976.

them from time to time.[30] Both the army and the GSU got their chance when Obote's forces attacked the palace of the Kabaka of Buganda in 1966, driving him into exile. At that point, many of the remaining Baganda officers fled the army. When Obote further suppressed the Baganda and banned all opposition parties after an unsuccessful attempt on his life in 1969,[31] there were no further Southern threats, electoral or military, to his control. The equilibrium had been destroyed.

Instead, the locus of conflict moved to the North. The Northerners who supported Obote were far from homogeneous, and there is evidence that in the end he trusted only Langi, preferably relatives. He placed his cousin at the head of the GSU and the secret service.[32] General Amin, formerly army commander, was given a staff posting, a sure sign of Amin's loss of favor with Obote. From that point on, Amin's position was precarious. Suspicion had been aroused that he was involved in the murder of a senior Ugandan officer, and Amin's public behavior seemed increasingly questionable.[33]

A Northerner, Amin was neither an Acholi nor a Lango, but a Kakwa.[34] In the army, he seemed to command the special loyalty of members of the Kakwa, Lugbara, and Alur ethnic groups from his own West Nile district and of the Madi next door. Amin was also in contact with Southern Sudanese rebel groups, and it is said that he supplied them with arms to be used against the Khartoum government.[35] The Kakwa straddle the Uganda-Sudan-Zaire border.

Himself a former N.C.O., Amin maintained contact with N.C.O.s after losing favor with Obote.[36] In the months preceding the coup, Amin

30. A Special Correspondent, "The Uganda Army," 38.

31. After the shooting, twenty-six people were arrested, twenty-one of them Baganda. The total number of people detained, according to an official list, was sixty-six. Of these, fifty-one were Baganda, fifteen other Southerners. No Northerners were on the list. These were signs of the extent to which conflict had polarized along North-South lines. *Africa Report*, Mar. 1970, pp. 6–8.

32. Another cousin headed one of two Muslim organizations, the one friendly to the regime. A younger brother served in the Ministry of Home Affairs. Other Langi headed the Public Service Commission, with its important power over appointment and promotion, and the Immigration Department.

33. Amin boasted that he feared no one but God, and he joined a Muslim organization that rivaled the one supported by the regime.

34. Martin, *General Amin*, 14, says Amin's father was a Kakwa who lived many years in the Southern Sudan. According to Martin, Amin's mother was a Lugbara.

35. Ibid., 138–39; Henry Kyemba, *A State of Blood: The Inside Story of Idi Amin* (New York: Ace Books, 1977), 28.

36. A Correspondent, "Uganda After the Coup," *Swiss Review of World Affairs* 20 (Mar. 1971): 9–10.

also manipulated the ethnic composition of certain army units. He relied particularly on West Nilers and "Nubians," the latter an elastic category that includes descendants of Muslim Sudanese brought to Uganda as soldiers in the nineteenth century, certain groups of West Nile Muslims, and apparently even some recent converts to Islam.[37] Amin packed one unit with Nubians, only to have Obote break it up in late 1970.[38] By then, however, Amin had transferred some twenty-two Nubian and West Nile officers to another unit, the Malire Mechanized Battalion. By the time of the coup in 1971, thirty-two of the Malire unit's forty-three officers were Nubian, Kakwa, or Lugbara; only five were Acholi, and three were Langi.[39] When the coup came, the loyalty of this unit to Amin was a key factor. When Obote threatened to move against Amin in January 1971, troops from Malire surprised Obote's forces and seized power.[40]

Amin's coup depended on ethnic loyalties. Its perpetrators were principally West Nilers and Nubians, as well as some Southern Sudanese recently recruited into the Uganda army.[41] The results were visible soon after the coup. The General Service Unit was abolished, and Acholi and Langi soldiers were massacred to the point where virtually no officers from either group were left in the army.[42] (Most of Obote's guerrillas who later invaded Uganda from Tanzania were Acholi and Langi who had fled the army in 1971.) Much of the killing was done by the Malire unit. Punitive expeditions were launched into the Lango district, where AWOL soldiers were hunted down, there to be killed with their families.[43]

West Nile men were promoted to take the places of Acholi and Langi officers and soldiers. The army was expanded. Many of the new recruits were also West Nilers. Of the twenty-four top military posts in 1973, only three were not held by West Nilers; some of the new commanders

37. Nelson Kasfir, *The Shrinking Political Arena: Participation and Ethnicity in African Politics* (Berkeley and Los Angeles: Univ. of California Press, 1976), 220.
38. Martin, *General Amin*, 89.
39. Ibid., 59.
40. Ibid., 25–61.
41. See ibid., 59–61.
42. Amin said later that he had moved against Obote only after Obote had ordered Acholi and Langi troops to disarm the rest of the army and kill Amin. Whether intended as such or not, this statement proved to be a signal to Amin's own supporters to take violent action against Acholi and Langi soldiers. A final purge and slaughter of all remaining Acholi and Langi soldiers was reported six years later. *Washington Post*, Mar. 3, 1977.
43. Martin, *General Amin*, 137.

had formerly been N.C.O.s.[44] Among West Nile groups, the Lugbara in particular assumed a new prominence in the army.

If "Northerner" is not a homogeneous category, neither is "West Niler." With the Acholi and Langi decimated, fissures developed among their military successors. Madi and Alur officers were rather quickly purged; they were gone by 1973. The Lugbara proved more persistent. Beginning in May 1972, and extending over the next two years, Lugbara officers planned a series of at least seven coup plots, assassination attempts, and confrontations with Amin, all of which miscarried.[45] Amin had begun to rely increasingly on Muslim officers, particularly Kakwa. In 1972, for example, the armories were placed securely in Muslim hands. Whether these steps provoked disquiet among Lugbara in the army or resulted from it, the reliance on Muslims and the Lugbara unrest were certainly related. No longer certain of their loyalty, Amin transferred a number of prominent Lugbara officers. Finally, in March 1974, Lugbara troops, from a unit whose Lugbara commander had been replaced by a Kakwa, staged an unsuccessful revolt.[46] No senior Lugbara officer remained in the army thereafter.

While this sorting out was taking place among West Nile groups, the very few remaining Southern sources of power were also being eliminated. Prominent civil servants, among them many Baganda, were dismissed or murdered in 1972–73. West Nilers, and especially Muslims, succeeded to many of these positions, as they also did to many of the businesses left by the Asians Amin expelled from Uganda at about the same time.[47] Then, in 1974 and again in 1977, there were attempts by air force officers to kill Amin. There were still some Baganda officers in the air force—as might be expected, given the difficulty of replacing highly trained personnel in a short time. These plots "had a definite 'Buganda flavor,' "[48] and they led to more bloody purges of Baganda in the armed forces and civil service.

---

44. Ibid., 240. Of the twenty-three top officers in army service at the time of the coup, only four were still on duty three years later; at least thirteen of them had been murdered. Ibid., 154. See also Holger Bernt Hansen, *Ethnicity and Military Rule in Uganda* (Uppsala: Scandinavian Institute of African Studies, 1977), 108.

45. See Martin, *General Amin*, 182, 230, 238–39; Colin Legum, ed., *Africa Contemporary Record, 1973–74* (New York: Africana, 1974), pp. B293–96.

46. Hansen, *Ethnicity and Military Rule in Uganda*, 113–16; Legum, ed., *Africa Contemporary Record, 1974–75*, p. B310. Compare Kyemba, *A State of Blood*, 134–36.

47. Martin, *General Amin*, 168, 213, 234–35; Legum, ed., *Africa Contemporary Record, 1973–74*, pp. B294–95.

48. Legum, ed., *Africa Contemporary Record, 1974–75*, p. B311.

TABLE 9   UGANDA'S DESCENT
INTO ETHNOCRACY

Scope of Contest	Year	Event	Alignment	Outcome
National	1962	Election	North-South	Northern plurality
National	1966	Arrest of ministers	North-South	Northern regime
National	1964–69	Packing of army	North-South	Northern-dominated forces
Intra-Northern	1971	Coup	West Nile vs. Acholi, Langi	West Nile regime
Intra-Northern	1971–72	Army killings	West Nile vs. Acholi, Langi	West Nile-dominated forces
Intra-West Nile	1972	Purges	Lugbara, Kakwa vs. Madi, Alur	Lugbara-Kakwa-dominated regime and forces
Intra-West Nile	1972–74	Plots, revolts	Lugbara vs. Kakwa, Nubians	Kakwa-dominated regime and forces

In the four years following the anti-Obote coup in 1971, all of the most sensitive positions—including defense minister, armed forces chief of staff, and air force squadron commander—came to be occupied by Muslim Kakwa, Nubians, and certain increasingly prominent groups of foreigners. The various secret police and terror units were commanded and staffed by Nubians. There was an increase of Southern Sudanese, some of them ex-Anyanya rebels, in the army, as well as some ex-Simba rebels from Zaire. The military police was commanded by a Southern Sudanese. Most of the young cadets and officers sent abroad for military training were Kakwa, Nubians, Sudanese, or Zaireans. The presidential bodyguard was composed of some 400 Palestinians.[49]

49. Ibid., p. B309. On the various terror units and their commanders, see Kyemba, *A State of Blood*, 111–14.

At each stage of this narrowing process, ethnic rivals were eliminated, and then the previous successful alliance disintegrated. First the North-South conflict was resolved on terms unequivocally favorable to the Northerners, who were left in control of the government and the army; then the Northern groups supporting Obote, the Langi and Acholi, were eliminated by the West Nile groups; and then the Alur, Madi, and Lugbara were eliminated by the Kakwa and Nubians. In an abbreviated way, the narrowing process is depicted by Table 9. Ultimately, Amin ended up ruling with the active support of ethnic groups comprising well under 10 percent of Uganda's population.[50]

SYRIA'S MARCH TO MINORITY RULE

In post-war Syria, ethnicity was not originally the major political cleavage. Gradually, ethnic affiliation became the servant of ideological, organizational, and personal rivalries. Once deployed in these struggles, however, ethnicity itself became the struggle. When the guns were laid down, one small ethnic group emerged in power, just as in Uganda. Once politics had become both military and ethnic, the ethnic group most favorably placed in the armed forces found itself able to defeat all other contenders. In the process, the ethnic "complexion of the officer corps"[51] and of the regime was transformed.

In Syria, as in Lebanon and Iraq, ethnic politics is defined in confessional terms. Ethnic groups are heavily demarcated by religion, religion that denotes not just a certain stream of belief but a certain version of peoplehood. A majority of the population is orthodox Sunni Muslim, but several dissenting sects rooted themselves many centuries ago among mountain people. The most prominent are the Alawi (comprising at most 11 percent of the population), the Druze (about 3 percent), and the Isma'ili (perhaps 1 percent). There are also significant Christian and Kurdish communities. All of these minorities had been disproportionately represented in the army from the time of French rule and onward into independence. The ethnic history of the post-war period is the story of how some of these groups, powerful in the army, gradually displaced the Sunni civilian political elite and then were themselves eliminated

---

50. Some estimates put the Kakwa at less than 1 percent of the Uganda population. See Kasfir, *The Shrinking Political Arena*, 110. Muslims, all told, are probably 10 percent or less of the population. See also Legum, ed., *Africa Contemporary Record, 1973–74*, pp. B294–97.

51. Hurewitz, *Middle East Politics*, 152.

from military leadership, one at a time: first the Kurds, then the Sunni, and then the Druze, until only the Alawi remained.

The story is as complicated as it is fascinating. In the 1940s and intermittently in the 1950s, Syria had a lively and relatively free parliamentary political life. Elections for the most part brought to power regimes dominated by prosperous Sunni landowners, the traditionally important families, and the rising bourgeoisie.[52] Party politics was heavily sectionalist, the National Party representing mainly the Damascus region and leaning toward Egypt and Saudi Arabia, the People's Party based in the Northern areas of Homs and Aleppo and inclining toward Iraq. Civilian politics was, however, Sunni politics.

Coups marked the debut of minorities in politics. From 1949 to 1970, there were at least eighteen coup attempts in Syria, about half of them successful. As in some other countries, the first military intervention in Syria was more or less in response to a civilian call for help,[53] but the army soon learned that it did not need an invitation. The most prominent leaders of the first coup were Kurds, and the regime of Colonel Husni Za'im displayed a partiality to Kurdish and Circassian army units that alienated other officers. In August 1949, Za'im was killed by, among others, Druze officers who had earlier supported him.[54] The civilian regime they established, dominated by the pro-Iraqi People's Party, also had strong civilian and military opposition. In December 1949, a Kurdish officer, Adib Shishakli, overthrew the regime, thwarted plans for unification with Iraq, and turned the government back to civilians. Two years later, Shishakli took power back and ruled autocratically. Once again, however, a Kurdish ruler offended the Druze, and they took action against Shishakli's assimilative and anti-Iraq policies.[55] In 1954, a mutiny led by a Druze officer but supported by a wide-ranging group of civilian politicians resulted in the overthrow of Shishakli.[56]

The 1954 coup, the purges that followed it, and the elections that took place reorganized the Syrian political-military establishment. Kurdish officers were removed and never regained a prominent place in the

52. Tabitha Petran, *Syria* (New York: Praeger, 1972), 93.
53. Hurewitz, *Middle East Politics*, 152.
54. Petran, *Syria*, 98.
55. In 1956, Druze leaders again cooperated with Iraq in an unsuccessful attempt to overthrow a Syrian government. Ibid., 115–17.
56. Ibid., 99–105; Itamar Rabinovich, *Syria Under the Ba'th, 1963–66: The Army-Party Symbiosis* (Jerusalem: Israel Universities Press, 1972), 11–12.

army.[57] Beyond this, a firm tendency had been established for military officers to plot with politicians in bringing down and setting up governments. Among the most active participants in this process was Akram Hourani, long the leader of the Arab Socialist Party and then a major leader of the Ba'th Party, with which his ASP had merged. As time went on, the Ba'th gained a strong military following with which it plotted and schemed but which eventually came to dominate the party itself.

Ba'th was particularly in need of military support, for it was a small party at the polls. With a considerable following of rural Druze and Alawi and with a secular ideology, Ba'th had difficulty expanding its Sunni, urban constituency. "Most of the Sunni *petite bourgeoisie*, even in Damascus, was influenced by the Muslim Brotherhood and later also by President Nasser. The Ba'th, however, won a following among students and military cadets—future intellectuals and army officers."[58] The very disabilities that limited Ba'th support to a small number of parliamentary seats were the source of its impact on army officers, who were disproportionately members of minority groups. When the army was involved in politics, the Ba'th was generally close behind.

In principle, Ba'thists favored the merger of Arab states, and in the mid-1950s they were attracted toward union with Egypt. But experience of partnership with Nasser, beginning in 1958, and the special reservations Druze and Alawi officers had about smothering Syria in a Sunni Egyptian embrace soon led these officers to conspire against the union.[59] In the event, this proved unnecessary: separation of Syria from Egypt was accomplished in 1961 without them, but from their cabal a stronger Ba'th Military Committee emerged.

Ba'thist officers played a major role in the coups of the following year. But these were only the prelude to the coup of 1963, from which the Ba'th emerged triumphant. The Ba'th Military Committee, at first only one of several groups of officers in the plot, eliminated the other factions one after another until, a "minority among minorities, the Ba'th officers became masters of Syria."[60]

The 1963 coup was followed by purges of Sunni officers.

To fill the vacancies, the Military Committee recalled to active service all Ba'thist reserve officers and all officers with whom it was connected by family, clan, or

57. Hurewitz, *Middle East Politics*, 153.
58. Petran, *Syria*, 92. See Rabinovich, *Syria Under the Ba'th*, 6–11.
59. Petran, *Syria*, 146; Rabinovich, *Syria Under the Ba'th*, 24–25.
60. Petran, *Syria*, 167.

sectarian relations. This brought an influx of Alawi, Druze, and Isma'ili officers, since both traditional army recruitment and Ba'th party membership drew largely on the rural areas where these minorities live. The committee's enemies inevitably accused it of sectarian discrimination in promotions and transfers, and in acceptance of students in the Military Academy and of officers and NCOs in the party.[61]

Thus, nine years later, the Sunni officers went the way of the Kurds. The Sunni also lost their dominance in the civil service, which, like the army, experienced an influx of Alawi.

Reaction among the Sunni community to Druze and Alawi dominance was hostile and sometimes violent. Contemptuous toward the Alawi as backward rustics, urged on by a bitter Nasser, who depicted the Druze and Alawi as less than genuine Arabs, the Sunni clashed with the minorities in a half-dozen Syrian cities during 1964 and 1965.[62] The violence was suppressed by the now-reliable army, and still more Sunni officers were dismissed and replaced by Alawi and Druze.[63]

Much of the purging had to do with factional struggles among the Ba'th officers themselves. The first of these pitted a Sunni, Amin Hafez, against an Alawi, Muhammad Umran. Umran packed units of the army with Alawi by manipulating the active-duty tours of reserve officers, selecting out candidates for the party and the military academy, and posting friends near Damascus and others far away.[64] But Umran was becoming dangerous, and two other leading Alawi generals, Salah Jadid and Hafez Assad, shrewdly backed his Sunni rival, Amin Hafez, instead. When Umran was defeated, Jadid inherited his Alawi support, which he then proceeded to turn against Amin Hafez, using many of the same techniques of manipulating the army as Umran had used earlier. Jadid also had the backing of Druze and Isma'ili officers. Hafez in his turn was defeated.[65]

Umran and Hafez, the two enemies, both allied after their defeat with what remained of the civilian wing of the Ba'th Party, by then gravely weakened by the Military Committee's increasing control. When they attempted to transfer officers loyal to Jadid, he and his ally, Assad, struck. In 1966, in a bloody coup, they ended at a stroke the party-army

61. Ibid., 171.
62. Ibid., 175–76; Rabinovich, *Syria Under the Ba'th*, 109–15. For Nasserite incitements, see Petran, *Syria*, 175–76; Rabinovich, *Syria Under the Ba'th*, 72.
63. Petran, *Syria*, 179.
64. For Umran's techniques, see Rabinovich, *Syria Under the Ba'th*, 180–81.
65. Ibid., 135–39, 159–60, 180–85; Petran, *Syria*, 180–81.

competition, the Hafez-Umran-Jadid triangle, and the Sunni-Alawi rivalry.[66] "The voice was the voice of the Ba'th, but the hand was the hand of the Alawi officers."[67]

No sooner was it victorious than the Jadid coalition began to crack along ethnic lines. The Druze commander of an elite commando battalion sought an expanded role for himself and for his efforts was excluded from an influential policymaking body. When Jadid dismissed a number of Druze officers, the Druze commandos attempted a coup, which the Jadid-Assad forces put down.[68] This marked the end of Druze prominence in the regime. With the suicide of an influential Isma'ili officer in 1969, the Alawi were left in control virtually by themselves.

Intra-Alawi rivalries then emerged. Jadid had been left in charge of the party, Assad in charge of the army. Eventually, Assad's superior position was converted into effective power, and Jadid was dislodged in 1970.[69] The narrowing process had moved inside ethnic boundaries until Assad began to depend on his own family for protection. A key guard division is under the command of his brother.

THE NATURAL HISTORY OF ETHNIC ATTRITION

Developments after 1968 in Sierra Leone, from 1966 to 1979 in Uganda, and after 1963 in Syria ran along remarkably similar tracks. In each case, a major ethnic contestant—Mende, Baganda, Sunni—was defeated by force, and the country then moved at an accelerating pace toward more and more narrowly based regimes. Former ethnic allies—even very strong ones—fell from power in stages with a rapidity that made the process of ethnic attrition appear frighteningly inexorable. Ultimately, the regimes became military ethnocracies, as if, once the contest of arms begins, the tendency for each ethnic group to seek control of its own state moves quickly toward fulfillment.[70] Similar narrowing tendencies were displayed in Iraq after the Qassim coup of 1958 and in Burundi after the Micombero coup of 1966.[71] Indeed, in Iraq, not merely did the

66. Petran, *Syria*, 181–82; Rabinovich, *Syria Under the Ba'th*, 180–203.

67. Hurewitz, *Middle East Politics*, 155.

68. Rabinovich, *Syria Under the Ba'th*, 215–16; Petran, *Syria*, 185.

69. Rabinovich, *Syria Under the Ba'th*, 216–17; Petran, *Syria*, 242–44, 248–49; Nikolaos Van Dam, *The Struggle for Power in Syria: Sectarianism, Regionalism and Tribalism in Politics, 1961–1978* (London: Croom Helm, 1979), 90.

70. I use the term *ethnocracy* in a somewhat different sense from its use by Ali Mazrui, *Soldiers and Kinsmen in Uganda.*

71. Of the fourteen officers in Qassim's conspiracy, only two were Shiites, although Shiites comprise more than half the Iraqi population; there were no Kurdish officers in the

Sunni minority eventually take power, but the regime became essentially the property of Saddam Hussein's family and a small clique drawn from his home village of Takrit.

The process speeds up as it nears its conclusion, and it grows increasingly violent. Throughout the 1970s in Syria, this proved to be the case; in Uganda, violence reached a fearful pitch; and there were executions by the far milder Sierra Leone regime beginning in 1971. The first coups usually require a minimum of force, partly because they benefit from a maximum of surprise and a minimum of defensive precautions. As coups recur, distrust and precautions against coups both increase. Yet the stakes of a coup are higher, for with fewer ethnic participants each coup yields a proportionately larger share of power. Having been through so much, the groups that have survived the first stages also have a greater investment in the outcome than was the case earlier on. The precautions taken against coups also generate animosity, since they often take the form of excluding formal ethnic allies from sharing in authority. And so, at a later stage, there are scores to settle.

Toward the end of the narrowing process, anticipatory coups occur. Suspicion rises to the point where the remaining ethnic contestants in the armed forces sense the need to strike preemptively, for fear that delay will find them on the receiving end of military action. Such fears are generally well founded. Amin's own coup might be placed in this category, for it appeared that Obote was moving toward a reliance on Acholi and Langi so exclusive that it would mean the end of West Nile power in

---

coup group, though the Kurds comprise 15–20 percent of the Iraqi population and were not then in revolt. What little Shiite and Kurdish support Qassim had he gradually lost, and his government became essentially a Sunni regime. Successor regimes were even more narrowly identified with segments of the Sunni population. Hurewitz, *Middle East Politics*, 155–58, 161, 429; Majid Khadduri, "Iraq, 1958 and 1963," in William G. Andrews and Uri Ra'anan, eds., *The Politics of the Coup d'Etat* (New York: Van Nostrand Reinhold, 1969), 71, 73.

Micombero's coup established Tutsi hegemony over the Hutu population, which comprised some 80 percent of the total. Each succeeding Hutu attempt to overthrow the regime brought a new round of reprisals against the Hutu, culminating in the massive atrocities of 1972. With the Hutu effectively eliminated from military contention, Tutsi rivalries grew increasingly prominent and at each stage increasingly narrow. At first, Micombero, who had overthrown the monarchy, favored his Hima subgroup and his Bururi district, located in the South. He thereby provoked conspiracies among non-Southerners (Ruguru). Thereafter, the Bururi Tutsi themselves were subregionally divided into Matana and Rutovu groups. Micombero is from Rutovu, and he installed his brothers-in-law, his wife's uncles, and various other relatives in key positions. In November 1976, a number of these relatives put an end to the rivalry by arresting Micombero, ousting the leading Matana from power, and guaranteeing the longevity of the Rutovu "family corporation." Warren Weinstein, "The Burundi Coup," *Africa Report*, Jan.–Feb. 1977, pp. 52–56.

the army. The unsuccessful Lugbara revolt against Amin surely does fall in the anticipatory category, because it responded to Amin's preliminary efforts to purge Lugbara officers. The same is true of Bangura's move against Stevens in 1971, easily thwarted because Temne power, among both officers and politicians, was already under control. The Druze coup attempt of September 1966 likewise was a response to the new situation that found Alawi and Druze finally in unchallenged control of Syria. What this meant was that the aid of the Druze officers could be dispensed with, and that is exactly what Jadid had begun to do when the Druze, sensing impending doom, hastened it by striking first. Had the Druze coup succeeded, it might have been followed by widespread killing of Alawi, much as Amin's coup was followed by the slaughter of Acholi and Langi. All of these coups were last-ditch efforts by those groups that had become junior but no longer essential partners to remain in power.

Attritional politics becomes much more sharply and overtly ethnic as it proceeds. It is no longer sufficient to be broadly categorized as a "Northerner" or a "Nilotic," or at a later stage a "West Niler." Narrowing progressively diminishes the significance of overarching identifications of this kind and demands greater ethnic precision. If one is a West Niler, it may make a critical difference whether he is an Alur or a Lugbara. Indeed, the distinction may be worth his life. At a still later stage, it may matter a great deal whether a person is a Christian Kakwa or a Muslim Kakwa.

Furthermore, the political significance of membership other than ethnic membership begins to fade. Observers noted Amin's tendency in public statements "to discuss people as if their ethnic identity were the most salient feature of their personality"[72] and to treat entire ethnic groups as units, more often than not potentially disloyal units.[73] Amin was no doubt extreme on this score, but attrition had also gone to extreme lengths in Uganda. Parallel developments occurred in Sierra Leone[74] and even in Syria, where virtually the only characteristic about an officer that counted was his ethnic affiliation. Before attrition begins, a modicum of bureaucratic regularity insures that individuals are often treated on the basis of other than ethnic characteristics, and most political activists can generally feel secure about their lives. After attrition

---

72. Kasfir, *The Shrinking Political Arena*, 219.
73. Legum, ed., *Africa Contemporary Record, 1973–74*, p. B299.
74. See Stevens' accusations against the UDP. Clapham, "Sierra Leone," 90.

begins, force alone comes to dominate, ethnic membership becomes the crucial affiliation, and physical security cannot be taken for granted. Attritional regimes have an important effect on ethnic politics that is likely to outlast them. They transform the role of ethnicity from one among several important affiliations to a preeminent position. This tendency is difficult to reverse once it occurs, since whole populations have come to see the transcendent importance ethnicity assumed over the years. After such experiences, few will think it safe to ignore ethnicity again. Furthermore, such regimes build up hatreds and desires for revenge. Their demise is likely to result in a settling of ethnic scores. Ugandan politics after Amin returned to the former struggles, peaceful and violent—now including guerrilla warfare and massacres—between North and South, Langi and Baganda, and among Northern groups aligned, respectively, with Obote and Amin.[75] Even overthrown, ethnocracy reasserted itself.

Once an ethnocratic regime is in power, opposition is not likely to make its will felt through further coups. Amin was finally overthrown not by a coup but by a full-scale invasion. The regimes of Stevens and Assad have both set records in their countries for their longevity. Internal military threats to their regimes became increasingly ineffective. The 1974 conspiracy against Stevens and the various plots against Amin in the post-1974 period[76] were impotent—really assassination attempts more than coup plots. A campaign of selective killings of Alawi civilian and military leaders in Syria began in 1977 and went on for several years, triggering mass reprisals by the regime against the Sunni population in a number of Syrian cities between 1980 and 1982. There were also further purges and executions of Sunni military officers. Assassination is the weapon of the weak and the outsider. Recourse to assassination means that the military coup is no longer a feasible mode of ethnic opposition. Only an escalation of the violence to the dimensions of civil war or invasion—and both require external assistance—is likely to dislodge an ethnocratic regime that has gone through a series of coups and purges.

When we consider the question of coup prevention, we shall examine more precisely the actions taken by these narrowly based regimes that

75. *Uganda* (London: Minority Rights Group, Report no. 66, 1984); Cherry Gertzel, "Uganda After Amin: The Continuing Search for Leadership and Control," *African Affairs* 79 (Oct. 1980): 461–90; *Africa Confidential*, June 8, 1983, pp. 3–7. Restored to power, Obote in the early 1980s relied heavily on the Langi in the armed forces once again.

76. See, e.g., Colin Legum, ed., *Africa Contemporary Record, 1975–76* (New York: Africana, 1976), p. B352; *Washington Post*, Feb. 24, 1977; ibid., June 23, 1977.

have made their longevity possible. This much is clear: regimes that rest on the support of small minority groups are not likely to be lulled into a false sense of security. They have every reason to take the most effective precautions against coups, not only because they are so unrepresentative, but also because, during the earlier succession of coups, they have made more enemies than most other regimes have. Moreover, their minority status, as we shall see, happens to propel them toward some rather effective preventive measures.

One thing they seem to do is expand the armed forces, probably to a greater degree than do other military regimes.[77] As in other matters, Amin's proclivities in this direction were particularly extreme. Already profligate under Obote, military spending was increased, and the size of the armed forces was approximately doubled in a period of two to three years.[78] Partly, this is to create overwhelming force to combat the combination of their enemies that minority regimes fear. Partly, too, it is to enable the regime to pack the ranks, as well as the officer corps, with its ethnic following. As I suggested earlier, it is far more difficult and dangerous to pack the ranks than to pack the officer corps simply by purging. Packing the ranks requires expanding them unless the regime is prepared to risk mutiny. An alternative, adopted in Sierra Leone, is to expand paramilitary forces, again packing them with supporters.

Such expansions of the instruments of force make ethnocratic regimes not merely military but militarized and highly oppressive. In these respects, Assad's Syria resembles Amin's Uganda. Privacy becomes difficult to secure, informers abound, secret police units flourish (Uganda's was called the "State Research Unit"), torture is practiced, and people regularly disappear. Ethnic solidarity and military and police penetration of the society render internal conspiracies difficult to create, but the majority disaffection and the many exiles such regimes produce provide raw material for other forms of violent opposition. These take longer to develop and require more military force to succeed than do coups. Ethnic attrition may thus ultimately end the cycle of coup and countercoup,

---

77. Cf. Eric A. Nordlinger, "Soldiers in Mufti," *American Political Science Review* 64 (Dec. 1970): 1131–48, at 1135. But see R. D. McKinlay and A. S. Cohan, "A Comparative Analysis of the Political and Economic Performance of Military and Civilian Regimes: A Cross-National Aggregate Study," *Comparative Politics* 8 (Oct. 1975): 1–30, at 13.

78. See Legum, ed., *Africa Contemporary Record, 1970–71*, p. B193; Legum, ed., *Africa Contemporary Record, 1973–74*, p. B298. See also A Special Correspondent, "The Uganda Army," 39; Lofchie, "The Uganda Coup," 22–26; *Washington Post*, Mar. 26, 1972; ibid., Nov. 15, 1972.

thereby imparting a measure of durability to the ethnocratic regime that emerges. But when ethnocracies ultimately fall, they will likely fall in bloody warfare, not in palace conspiracy.

EQUILIBRIUM, ATTRITION, AND ETHNOCRACY

We have been looking at two different patterns of coups, occurring at different stages of ethnic politics. It is important to be careful about what is and what is not meant by stages in this sense. Countries need not pass ineluctably from ethnic equilibrium and seesaw coups to coups of attrition that end in the establishment of ethnocracies. However, if both patterns do occur in any given country, the first is logically prior to the second, because polarized ethnic balances and electoral systems must be destroyed before attrition can begin. Diagrammatically, the path of countries passing through either or both of these phases is represented by Table 10.

COUP SEQUENCES AND THE AVOIDANCE OF ATTRITION

Several countries that experienced seesaw coups—among them Congo (Brazzaville), Togo, and Nigeria—did not move into the progressive narrowing of the ethnic base of the regime that Sierra Leone did. On the other hand, Uganda moved from electoral politics to ethnic attrition without quite experiencing seesaw coups. What, exactly, are the conditions that underlie the two patterns and determine whether the full Sierra Leone syndrome occurs?

If we recall the conditions associated with seesaw coups, we shall be able to see why Uganda did not experience them. Such coups occur in countries with an ethnically based party system and an officer corps ethnically at odds with the winning party. Uganda had an ethnically based party system, for no party was able to accommodate Baganda and non-Baganda aspirations simultaneously. But a Northern-led regime was installed from the beginning, and it excluded Baganda and other Southerners early on. As the regime and the officer corps were both Northern-dominated, a coup to reverse the ethnic results of the elections was unnecessary. Later, with the Southerners defeated and the electoral process at an end, attrition began.

Why, then, do some countries that clearly experience seesaw coups

TABLE 10   THE EQUILIBRIAL AND ATTRITIONAL
PHASES OF MILITARY ETHNICITY

Phase	Event	Ethnic Alignments	Outcome
Equilibrial	Election	A + B + C vs. D + E + F	A + B + C win
	Coup	A + B + C vs. D + E + F	D + E + F win
	Countercoup	A + B + C vs. D + E + F	A + B + C win[a]
	Purge	A + B + C vs. D + E + F	A + B + C win
Attritional	Party Split	A + B vs. C	A + B win
	Purge	A + B vs. C	A + B win
	Coup	A + B vs. C	A + B win
	Purge or Coup	A vs. B	A wins

[a] If the countercoup succeeds.

not move into attritional coups? Attritional coups require a decisive break with the electoral process and with ethnic equilibrium. So decisive must this break be that the ethno-political field sharply contracts. Groups victorious at each successive coup stage can then safely regard those groups defeated at earlier stages as if they were no longer effective political actors. Stevens could ignore the Mende after 1968, for both their party and their strength in the officer corps had been brought under control. Obote could ignore the Baganda and other Southerners after 1969, and Jadid could ignore the Sunni after 1966. But both conditions must be present for attrition to begin. The electoral process must be at an end, and the power of former ethnic opponents must be decisively broken. If elections continue or if the power of former ethnic opponents remains, then the former alliances will hold and a narrow ethnocracy will be impossible.

Both conditions were not present in Togo or Congo (Brazzaville). Elections were at an end in both countries, but the power of former ethnic opponents was not finally broken in the way Mende or Baganda power had been.

In the Congo, Lari coup attempts and raids continued long after the Northerners had seized power, and the regime was plainly fearful of them. Throughout the early 1970s, armed Lari attacks were launched from Zaire, with some cooperation from the Lari population in Brazzaville.[79] Under the circumstances, it would hardly have been prudent for any Northern government to count the Lari out as contenders for power and proceed to sort matters out on the basis of ethnic affinity within the Northern cluster. This point was driven home again by the assassination of Ngouabi in 1977. The official account attributed the killing to Bakongo, and Massamba-Débat was executed for it. Another version suggested the assassination was a response by Ngouabi's Northern colleagues to his effort to seek a rapprochement with the Bakongo.[80] Both versions emphasize the incompleteness of the Northern victory over the Bakongo.

The same situation prevailed in Togo. The Northern regime was not free of Ewe plots for several years.[81] In Togo, the army was more clearly Northern than in Congo (Brazzaville). Coup plots were less threatening and more easily handled, but could not be ruled out altogether.

In both countries, Northern regimes made a key decision that kept Southern power alive and helped prevent an attritional phase from beginning. This was the decision not to reconstruct the civil service. Syria had displaced its Sunni bureaucrats and packed the ministries with Alawi. In stages, Uganda had purged the Baganda from their preeminent place in the bureaucracy. Sierra Leone had taken care to reduce the number of Mende civil servants. Such moves are costly in terms of lost expertise and run the risk of creating a popular movement of ethnic opposition. The weaker military regimes in Togo and Congo (Brazzaville) did not choose to purge their civil services, which were veritable bastions of, respectively, Ewe and Lari supremacy. The effect of this was to retain important centers of Southern opposition within government, which, in turn, made it necessary for the Northern groups to remain together. Attrition was impossible.

The flavor of this situation is conveyed by Russell Warren Howe's description of the Togolese government:

The ministries and other services were being operated largely by Ewe title-holders or Ewe assistants to northern title-holders. These men who made the bureaucracy and services function rarely met the junta leaders themselves; they dealt

79. Legum, *Africa Contemporary Record, 1973–74*, pp. B583–84.
80. *Le Monde*, Apr. 19, 1977; *Le Monde Diplomatique*, May 1977, p. 12.
81. See, e.g., Legum, ed., *Africa Contemporary Record, 1970–71*, pp. B452–53.

instead with a group of mostly northern civilian ministers. These ministers lacked the popular authority to deal with the [Ewe] mandarins' obvious contempt for the regime they served, yet feared for their jobs if they admitted to the military rulers that they could not arrest the disaffection. . . .

. . . Short of wholesale arrests—which would have caused, among other things, a virtual collapse of the bureaucracy—there was nothing the army could do but glower forcefully and rattle its sabres. The Ewe mandarins lived lives of quiet, if sometimes truculent, desperation, waiting for a chance to act.[82]

In the Congo, too, the regime's decision to stop short of eliminating Lari dominance in the civil service had given Lari opposition a base from which to express the feeling "that their superior education and abilities entitle them to political preeminence, and they are not reconciled to its loss, though they . . . no longer dare to offer overt resistance to the government."[83]

In both countries, therefore, the seesaw coup led ultimately, not to attrition, but to something like a new ethnic equilibrium. Now, however, it was without ethnic parties. Instead, Northern power was expressed through the army, Southern power through a subordinate but still dangerous bureaucracy.[84]

Finally, there is the case of Nigeria, which experienced seesaw coups in 1966. Did it move into attritional politics once Northern power was established in July 1966? Certainly not in the way Sierra Leone did, with relatively small groups emerging in control of army and state. Full Northern control could not be established while the civil war against the Ibo secession went on. The Ibo hoped for, and the North feared, a Western (that is, Yoruba) secession that would split the country completely along North-South lines and increase the chances for Biafra to win the war. But, in 1967, Yoruba leaders finally turned against secession. While the war went on, the North had ample reason to conciliate rather than suppress the Yoruba, particularly as some Yoruba officers had defected to the Biafran side. When the war ended, Yoruba found themselves in important positions in the army and especially in the civil service, which their Ibo colleagues had effectively abandoned. The effect of the events

82. Howe, "Togo," 10. See also *Africa Report*, Nov. 1970, pp. 8, 11.
83. Gauze, *The Politics of Congo-Brazzaville*, 211, 236.
84. Two other factors impeded coups of ethnic attrition. In Brazzaville, Southerners were also influential in the "revolutionary" party sponsored by the military regime. In Togo, the army was already rather firmly in the hands of Kabrai officers, owing to Kabrai recruitment by the French. Consequently, the prospect of intra-Northern attrition was rather less to begin with, and the continuing Ewe discontent was enough to thwart what rivalries might have emerged.

of 1966 was, therefore, to tip power toward the North, but not to exclude all of the South. Only the Ibo were politically excluded: more than
five years after the civil war ended, only one Ibo officer sat on the 23-
member Supreme Military Council. As in Togo and Congo (Brazzaville),
suppression of the South was incomplete.

This meant that there were significant constraints on intra-Northern
attrition in Nigeria. Despite those constraints, from the first days of the
July 1966 coup a major rivalry developed within the Northern components of the army, between the Muslim Hausa-Fulani and the Christian
Middle Belters, especially the Tiv, who were heavily overrepresented in
the army. With Ibo power removed from the army at the time of the July
coup, these conflicts emerged clearly.

The first divisive issue was whether the North should stay in the fed-
eration at all. The July coup had Northern-secessionist overtones, but
the Middle Belters, who stood to become a permanent minority in a
Northern state dominated by Hausa-Fulani, quelled these sentiments.
Indeed, they succeeded in extracting a concession long desired by Middle
Belters: the division of the North into separate states within a united
Nigeria.[85]

A second question was leadership. Colonel Murtala Mohammed, a
man close to the civilian leaders of the main Northern political party,
was at the center of the July coup. He was a logical candidate to assume
power. But again the Middle Belters, fearful of Hausa-Fulani dominance,
objected. Lieutenant-Colonel Yakubu Gowon, a Middle Belter (an
Anga) and a Christian, was the candidate of the strong group of Middle
Belt N.C.O.s, who found themselves able to make their will felt on this
issue as well.[86]

The Gowon-Mohammed rivalry lingered, and with it the intra-Northern competition. At points, it threatened to break out into violence
within the army.[87] After the civil war, it emerged again. The coup that
deposed Gowon in 1975 was made by many of the same Northern officers who had overthrown the Ironsi regime in 1966. Hausa-Fulani were
prominent in the conspiracy, which at last brought Murtala Mohammed
to power. The coup had been preceded by the fall from the cabinet of the
powerful Tiv leader J. S. Tarka. (Mohammed was, in fact, Tarka's cabi-

---

85. M. J. Dent, "The Military and the Politicians," in Panter-Brick, ed., *Nigerian Politics and Military Rule*, 90.
86. See First, *Power in Africa*, 313–25.
87. Dent, "The Military and the Politicians," 89, 148 n.19. See also First, *Power in
Africa*, 360.

net successor.) The Mohammed coup was announced on the radio by
Colonel Joseph Garba, an Anga like Gowon, in order to avert anticipated violence between Hausa and Middle Belters. The foiled countercoup of less than a year later, in which Mohammed was nonetheless
assassinated, was followed by arrests and executions of military men
from Gowon's home area. The killing of Mohammed and the bloody
retribution exacted for it both renewed the intra-Northern tension.

The increasingly prominent position of the Yoruba, however, helped
to brake the Hausa–Middle Belt conflict. Even in the army, where they
had earlier not enjoyed a strong position, Yoruba officers had advanced
to senior ranks and important postings. Following the Mohammed
coup, a third of the new Executive Council was Yoruba.[88] Two of the
three divisional commanders, as well as the navy commander, were also
Yoruba. Mohammed's successor, himself a Yoruba, went out of his way
to allay Northern fears of Yoruba hegemony by promoting a young
Northern officer to be chief of staff. Middle-Belt and Hausa-Fulani officers appear alternately to have feared Yoruba power and to have used
Yoruba allies against each other's ambitions. The effect was to prevent
full-fledged attrition, on the Sierra Leone–Syria–Uganda model, from
setting in.

Whether a regime passes through an attritional process, in which
power is held by more and more narrowly defined ethnic groups, makes
several important differences. First, as we have seen, ethnocratic regimes
are oppressive. They impose quiescence on society and execute their
enemies. Second, equilibrial regimes necessarily embrace a significant
fraction of the population, though rarely much more than half if the
regime is elected, and often less if it is not. Ethnocratic military regimes
are commonly ruled by ethnic groups comprising a small minority of the
population. Third, if equilibrium can be maintained over a significant
period of time, rough norms of ethnic inclusion may develop. In Nigeria,
such norms may well have played a role in the development of new
institutions to avoid a recurrence of severe ethnic conflict when the military announced preparations for a return to civilian rule in 1979. I shall
describe these institutions in Chapter 15. They are unlikely to have
emerged from a background of attrition and ethnocracy. In this respect,
the contrast between post-1979 Nigeria and post-1979 Uganda, still
riven by ethnic violence, could hardly be sharper. Fourth, as already

88. See the list of commissioners in *Africa Research Bulletin*, Aug. 1–31, 1975, p.
3725.

noted, regimes that have experienced the attritional process seem able to discourage or defeat ethnically based countercoups, because they have rooted out ethnically unreliable sources of military power. However, their oppressiveness, their narrow composition, and the completeness of their ethnic domination all make them fit targets for longer-term insurgencies and for external intervention in behalf of excluded groups. The Tanzanian-supported Acholi-Langi invasion of Uganda in 1972, as well as the Tanzanian invasion of 1979, which brought the Amin regime down, and the Iranian-supported Shiite dissidence in Iraq, before and after the overthrow of the Shah, illustrate the possibilities.

THE BROADENING IMPACT OF ELECTIONS

It is necessary to underscore the role of the electoral process in forging bonds among ethnic groups, even as it divides them from others. The exigencies of elections, with their incentives for obtaining support wide enough to win, provided the cement that bonded Mende to Sherbro and Fula, on one side, and Temne to Limba, on the other. To be sure, these incentives built on earlier affinities. The categories "Northerner" and "Southerner" came to have some significance in Sierra Leone, as they did in Nigeria, Togo, and Congo (Brazzaville). In all of these countries, these categories demarcate, in a rough way, backward groups from advanced groups. The emergence of a democratic process requiring a majority of seats to rule created incentives to build on these vague regional-ethnic affinities and weld them into powerful bases for party support. Parties pursued strategies of regional solidarity sufficient to make them credible contestants to win a majority of seats. In the electoral phase, ethnic groups in all countries except Syria acted as if they were aiming at something approximating William Riker's "minimum winning coalition"[89]— not exactly 50 percent of the individuals plus one, but 50 percent of the ethnic groups plus one. This, of course, is the meaning of the fierce contest that occurred in Congo (Brazzaville) for the allegiance of the Vili; their loyalty would (and did) tip the scale.

As long as the electoral process reigns, ethnic groups sharing a sense of commonality must link up. An end to elections is a precondition of the reductive process here designated as attrition. Two things then happen: there is a change in the structure of political incentives and a change in the context within which affinities are judged.

89. William H. Riker, *The Theory of Political Coalitions* (New Haven: Yale Univ. Press, 1962).

If a coup removes from competition those groups that were successful in the elections, the effective field of political competition is constricted; it embraces only ethnic groups powerful in the armed forces. From that point on, the minimum winning coalition need no longer have majority voting strength; it need only be stronger than the opposing groups within the armed forces. With successive stages of the contest, the elimination of opponents means that less and less breadth of support is required to win. With the Sunni gone, the Alawi need defeat only the Druze. With the Baganda gone, the West Nilers need only defeat the Acholi and Langi, and then the Kakwa need only defeat the Alur and Madi and then the Lugbara. What was a minimum winning coalition of ethnic groups becomes simply one ethnic group. The ethnic incentives of the electoral process are far more inclusive than those that typically prevail when politics embraces just the armed forces. To put the point in its simplest terms, even if there is ethnic polarization, elected regimes will generally represent ethnic groups comprising about 50 percent of the population, whereas regimes that follow attrition may represent 10 percent or less.

As the scope of the competition narrows, so does the structure of affinities. Interethnic affinities that seemed firm during the wider, electoral phase may prove to be surprisingly transitory. The several Syrian minorities who chafed under patronizing Sunni domination soon forgot their common predicament, as did the Sierra Leone Northerners who feared Mende hegemony. Some formerly weak cleavages, such as those dividing Lugbara from Kakwa, grow in importance, and fine distinctions, as, for example, between Christian and Muslim Kakwa, begin to be made. Ascription still matters, but, as distrust grows, there is a tendency for the leader to rely only on members of his own ethnic group and ultimately to rely most on members of his own family. This is another reminder of the extent to which ethnicity is closely tied to kinship.

ETHNIC EXCLUSION
AND COUPS OF RETRIEVAL

I shall deal only briefly with an important variant of the seesaw coup. This is a coup made by members of a group formerly well represented in the state apparatus in order to retrieve their advantageous but declining position.

Rare is the regime in Asia or Africa that is able to accord position and influence to various ethnic groups in proportions generally acceptable across group lines. Most governments are ethnically unbalanced. They slight some groups; they lean toward others. Many such governments, moreover, ride to power on promises to curtail the influence or privilege of particular ethnic groups.

A group so excluded from its former position is unlikely to accept the exclusion equanimously. Where such a group is heavily represented in the officer corps, the regime is confronted with a difficult choice. To purge these officers is to increase ethnic discontent, perhaps to bring on a coup before the purging is complete, and to risk spreading discontent among other officers who sense that careers abruptly ended today for one reason can be equally abruptly ended tomorrow for other reasons. On the other hand, to permit a potential focus of military discontent to remain unchecked is also to risk a coup.

A coup to retrieve the lost or declining position of an ethnic group is not inevitable. Such a coup depends on a particular configuration of circumstances.

In the first place, groups that have recently been excluded from a position of preeminence are more likely to be advanced ethnic groups: disproportionately educated, urban, willing to migrate from their home area, and stereotyped as diligent, industrious, energetic, and intelligent. Typically, these groups are disproportionately represented in educational institutions, in commerce and the professions, and in the civil service. But such groups are not necessarily significantly represented in the officer corps—unless educational prerequisites for entry into military academies have been enforced and the military has been a career affording salary and status at least roughly comparable to civilian government service. Where these conditions are met, representation of an excluded group in the officer corps may be sufficient to make a retrieval coup possible.

Moreover, retrieval coups are mixed-motive coups, because a declining or excluded group is unlikely to be able to bring off a coup all by itself. For a retrieval coup to occur, officers who are not members of that ethnic group must also be convinced that the exclusion threatens to affect their own interests, or they must have their own reasons for turning against the regime.

Two coups in Ghana illustrate these points. Both involved a complex mix of motives, in which ethnicity played an important but not overriding role.

As we have seen, the Ghanaian officer corps was drawn from the well-educated Ewe, Ga, and Fanti groups. Nkrumah's electoral support was also somewhat skewed. His Convention People's Party had been outpolled in 1956 by the National Liberation Movement in Ashanti and by the Northern People's Party in the North. The Ewe areas of the Trans Volta were divided between the CPP and the Togoland Congress. No sooner had independence been achieved than the regime was also confronted with an Ewe separatist movement in the Trans Volta region and a militant Ga movement in Accra.[90] Nkrumah moved to suppress the dissidents, and the suppression increased after he learned of conspiratorial approaches from opposition politicians to army officers, principally of Ga and Ewe origin, in 1958. A shift in officer recruitment away from Ga and Ewe was the result of these events.

Nkrumah offended his officers by tampering with their prerogatives. He introduced party cells in the army, established a President's Own Guard Regiment as a counterweight to the regular army, then favored the Regiment in budgetary allocations, and played favorites in certain conspicuous appointments and dismissals of officers.[91]

Nkrumah's policy of using his emergency powers against opposition ethnic leaders only increased ethnic grievances. The Ashanti did not forget their humiliation at Nkrumah's hand. They complained of the domination of Ashanti by the CPP's Southern leaders.[92] An advanced group from an unusually poor region, the Ewe were particularly dependent on government largess for their survival. Bitter at Nkrumah's punitive policy and the force with which he put down their rebellion, the Ewe never accommodated themselves to CPP rule. Nor did Nkrumah trust them; not a single Ewe was appointed to his cabinet after 1961. The three men who first plotted Nkrumah's overthrow in 1966 were all Ewe. Of the eight members of the National Liberation Council (NLC) established after the coup, three were Ewe and two were Ga.

The prominent role of Ewe in the coup and in the NLC gave rise to fears of Ewe favoritism. During the NLC period, 1966–69, various Akan groups—including some, such as the Ashanti and Fanti, that earlier had been mutually suspicious—began to forge close links. What gave them a new sense of cohesion was the alleged threat from the Ewe. Akans tended to see the NLC as dominated by the Ewe and Ga.[93] When a countercoup

90. See David R. Smock and Audrey C. Smock, *The Politics of Pluralism: A Comparative Study of Lebanon and Ghana* (New York: Elsevier, 1975), 70.

91. First, *Power in Africa*, 197–200; Robert E. Dowse, "The Military and Political Development," in Colin Leys, ed., *Politics and Change in Developing Countries* (Cambridge: Cambridge Univ. Press, 1969), 235.

92. Jon Kraus, "Arms and Politics in Ghana," in Claude E. Welch, ed., *Soldier and State in Africa* (Evanston: Northwestern Univ. Press, 1970), 165.

93. Smock and Smock, *The Politics of Pluralism*, 203–05, 240–41.

failed in 1967, taking the lives of three officers, all of them Ewe, the NLC felt obliged to deny the "wicked rumor" that the move had been "planned by Ashantis and Fantis against Gas and Ewes."[94]

The prospect of a return to civilian rule only deepened cleavages. Some of the principal NLC members had ties to civilian politicians of the same ethnic group. The leading NLC Ewe, John Harlley and A. K. Deku, were close to the prominent Ewe leader K. Gbedemah. General J. A. Ankrah and police commissioner John Nunoo, both Ga, were involved in efforts to form a political party based on Ga support. Brigadier A. A. Afrifa, an Ashanti, was closely linked to the Ashanti politician K. A. Busia. As the end of military rule grew nearer, the Akan-Ewe rivalry, epitomized by the antipathy between Afrifa and Harlley, was expressed in official actions impinging on the political interests of the respective groups. Ewe officers obtained, under threat of force, revocation of a decree issued by Afrifa that would have banned from partisan activity a large number of former CPP politicians, including Gbedemah.[95] The removal of the ban on Gbedemah fanned anti-Ewe sentiment. Shortly before the 1969 election, the NLC removed two Ewe brigadiers from troop commands.

When civilian politics was restored in 1969, parties quickly crystallized along ethnic lines. The rivalry of Harlley and Afrifa was supplanted by the rivalry of their respective civilian ethnic kinsmen, Gbedemah and Busia. Gbedemah's party appealed principally to the Ewe. Nearly every other area voted for Busia's Progress Party, in large part due to "fears of Ewe domination of national government . . . ."[96]

Busia in office proved distinctly unfriendly to the Ewe. No Ewe served in his cabinet, and legal action was even taken to unseat Gbedemah. The list of 568 civil servants and policemen dismissed in 1970 contained more than a fair share of Ewe names, and Ewe were pushed out of command positions in the armed forces. By the end of 1971, only one Ewe was still serving in a senior army position.[97]

Once again, Ewe officers moved to retrieve their position. This they did, as before, in conjunction with others acting (as no doubt they them-

94. Quoted in Dowse, "The Military and Political Development," 243; First, *Power in Africa*, 403.
95. First, *Power in Africa*, 405; Kraus, "Arms and Politics in Ghana," 200.
96. Kraus, "Arms and Politics in Ghana," 220.
97. Smock and Smock, *The Politics of Pluralism*, 246–47; Valerie Plave Bennett, "Malcontents in Uniform—The 1972 Coup d'Etat," in Dennis Austin and Robin Luckham, eds., *Politicians and Soldiers in Ghana* (London: Frank Cass, 1975), 304; Philippe Decraene, "Ghana Coup," *Le Monde* (English ed.), Jan. 22, 1972.

selves were) out of diverse motives. Two of the four organizers of the 1972 coup were Ewe majors. Reduced military budgets, inequity in promotions due to participation or nonparticipation in the coup against Nkrumah, and civilian interference in army affairs—including punitive action taken against Ewe officers—all appear to have had a part in the decision to depose Busia's government. Most conspicuously overrepresented in the new government's National Redemption Council (NRC) were two identifiable groups: officers whose careers had stagnated in the post-Nkrumah period and Ewe officers. At the outset, almost half of the council was Ewe.[98]

A somewhat similar case could be made for the attempted coup in Sri Lanka in 1962, which followed discriminatory action against Tamils and Christians.[99] Both followed expansions of political participation unaccompanied by drastic change in the composition of the officer corps. Both regimes threatened the officer corps on ethnic, social class, and organizational fronts simultaneously. The concatenation of these threats linked officers who had otherwise disparate interests, causing them to see the regimes' actions as part of a coherent pattern of malevolent conduct. The essential ingredient of a retrieval coup is simultaneous regime action that facilitates the creation of the interethnic military coalition. For this purpose, the combination of ethnic discrimination and tampering with military careers is particularly likely to incite officers. Both can be subsumed under the rubric of "favoritism," which offends the conceptions of merit, order, and regularity that are thought to underlie military recruitment, tenure, and promotion.

Whereas a full seesaw coup is preceded by polarization of the polity into two antagonistic ethnic clusters, which make mutually exclusive claims on power, the retrieval coup aims merely to restore the former position of a recently excluded group. The retrieval coup occurs in an ethnically less explosive atmosphere, and the coupmakers are typically multiethnic in composition. Ethnic retrieval is the goal for only some of them. In the absence of polarized ethnic equilibrium, then, exclusion of a single ethnic group need not split the army. In fact, it may increase the cohesion of the army and make possible military intervention based on a coalescence of differing motives.

Cohesion sufficient to make a coup, however, does not assure enough cohesion to maintain interethnic alliances once the coup is made. After both Ghanaian coups, reinclusion of the Ewe was aborted. Shortly after

98. Bennett, "Malcontents in Uniform," 308–09, 312 n.18.
99. Cf. Horowitz, *Coup Theories and Officers' Motives.*

the 1966 coup, Brigadier Afrifa propounded the historically dubious proposition that the Ashanti and the Ewe were traditional allies.[100] As we have seen, it was not long before Ewe and Ashanti members of the NLC fell out among themselves. By 1969, the Ewe were left to contest the elections practically alone in their own party, and they were decisively defeated. A more serious split followed the 1972 coup. Reflecting widespread distaste for the anti-Ewe policy of the Busia regime, Colonel Acheampong said the coup was made partly to combat "the politics of tribalism."[101] Again, however, the military council divided along Akan-Ewe lines, Akan expressing discontent at what they felt was inordinate Ewe influence in the NRC. This coincided with the reemergence of Ewe separatism, which ultimately received some support from Togo. By 1975, the pressures on Acheampong to push the Ewe out were apparently quite strong—some sources speak of an ultimatum from senior Akan officers—and Acheampong purged the leading Ewe officers who had conspired with him in 1972. Some months later, a number of Ewe former officers and N.C.O.s were arrested and convicted of plotting a coup.[102] This was followed by another unsuccessful Ewe plot in 1976. By this time, the Ewe were right back where they were under the Busia regime: politically excluded despite their significant representation in the officer corps.

In the three and a half years from July 1978 through December 1981, Ghana experienced four more changes of government, three of them through coups. In these kaleidoscopic events, the position of the Ewe was not the principal issue, but the issue did not go away either. Jerry Rawlings, who led coups in 1979 and 1981, is an Ewe. The first of his regimes was disproportionately composed of Ga and Ewe, and it seemed to engender resistance on these grounds among Akans. The elected government that succeeded it embarked on a campaign against Rawlings and the leading Ewe members of his council, "fueling Ewe discontents to new heights."[103] After Rawlings' second coup, in 1981, he cut back on the prominence of the Ewe, but, by some accounts, Akan-Ewe conflicts nonetheless proceeded apace.[104]

100. A. A. Afrifa, *The Ghana Coup* (London: Frank Cass, 1966), 40.

101. Quoted in Smock and Smock, *The Politics of Pluralism*, 249.

102. For these events, see Legum, ed., *Africa Contemporary Record, 1975–76*, p. B694; *West Africa*, Oct. 20, 1975, p. 1257; ibid., Oct. 27, 1975, p. 1287; ibid., Dec. 1, 1975, p. 1460; ibid., Jan. 5, 1976, p. 21; ibid., July 12, 1976, p. 981.

103. Naomi Chazan, "Ethnicity and Politics in Ghana," *Political Science Quarterly* 97 (Fall 1982): 461–85, at 483.

104. Ibid.

The Ewe thus tend to find themselves sharing power when the military takes power and excluded soon after. Periods of civilian rule generally leave the Ewe unrepresented, while periods of military rule serve to sharpen political differences between the Ewe and the various Akan groups. Ghanaian governments seem chronically unable to keep both Ewe and Akans included on a stable basis.

THE REVOLUTIONARY
ROAD TO ETHNOCRACY

Most ex-colonial countries gained their independence without warfare. But a minority of countries did fight for their independence, and the armed struggle sometimes had profound consequences for the ethnic composition of their armies and the ethnic character of the resulting regimes. Here, as in attritional coups, narrowing occurred, and a single ethnic group was left in control of the state. But this variant of attrition was not the product of successive coups so much as it was a direct offshoot of the alignment of military forces in the anti-colonial war.

The difference is attributable to the plurality of military forces created by the war of liberation. Countries that did not fight for their independence typically inherited the local component of the colonial army and made it their own. As we have seen, the military side of ethnic conflict occurred within that army and between it and the civilian regime. Countries that fought for independence, however, did not inherit a single army. They inherited more than one force, either because of the division between the ex-colonial forces and the anti-colonial forces, as in Burma and Indonesia, or because of the split between different units of the anti-colonial forces, as in Algeria and Angola. Due to their divergent sympathies and wartime experiences, these various units may have had different perspectives on independence; they incurred mutual enmity along the way; and they tended to be ethnically differentiated. In the confluence of these differences lay the basis for ethnic attrition once independence was won. In each case, one side won out.

EX-COLONIAL VERSUS ANTI-COLONIAL
FORCES: BURMA AND INDONESIA

At independence, the Burmese and Indonesian armies consisted, on the one hand, of forces trained by the Japanese to fight the British and Dutch and, on the other, forces trained by the British and Dutch to control the nationalists and fight the Japanese.[105] In Burma, the British forces included practically no Burmans; they were composed mostly of Karens, Kachins, Chins, and Shans. But the Burma Independence Army, subsequently organized by the Japanese, was dominated by Burmans. The Dutch forces in Indonesia had few Javanese; they recruited heavily among Outer Islanders (especially Ambonese, but also Minahassians and some groups of Sumatrans). The Japanese, however, trained nationalist forces that were predominantly Javanese. Although there were also Japanese-trained units in Sumatra, the eastern islands that contributed so heavily to the Dutch forces contributed virtually no manpower at all to the units raised by the Japanese. By stages, these two sets of forces came into conflict, and in both countries the anti-colonialist soldiers—hence Burmans and Javanese—prevailed.

In Burma, there was bitter warfare in 1942 between Karen troops and pro-Japanese Burmans who tried to disarm them.[106] When insurrections broke out after the war, the uneasily-put-together Burmese Army came apart. Whole Karen battalions disappeared from the government side, and the same was true to a lesser extent of the other groups whose home areas became centers of ethnic resistance to Burman domination. Steadily, Burmans came wholly to control the armed forces. As they did, the remaining Karen officers were purged. Following the Ne Win coup of 1962, these trends accelerated. Some Chins, whose area was not in revolt, remained in the ranks, but the officer corps became heavily Burman.

The Indonesian army came apart equally palpably. Like the Karens, the Ambonese opted out quickly, but other non-Javanese did not. In the period that followed independence, there was rivalry between the Dutch-trained officers, mostly non-Javanese, and the Japanese-trained officers, mostly Javanese. The influence of the Dutch-trained officers was buttressed by the then-powerful position of non-Javanese, especially certain Sumatrans, in the first civilian independence governments. But as the influence of the non-Javanese civilians waned, so, too, did that of their military counterparts, to whom they were sometimes related.[107]

105. On Burma, see James F. Guyot, "Efficiency, Responsibility, and Equality in Military Staffing: The Ethnic Dimension in Comparative Perspective," *Armed Forces and Society* 2 (Feb. 1976): 291–304; Tinker, *The Union of Burma*, chap. 11. On Indonesia, see Ann Gregory, "The Influences of Ethnicity in the Evolution of the Indonesian Military Elite," *Journal of Asian Affairs* 3 (Fall 1978): 140–56.

106. See Ba Maw, *Breakthrough in Burma: Memoirs of a Revolution, 1939–1946* (New Haven: Yale Univ. Press, 1968).

107. See Harold Crouch, *The Army and Politics in Indonesia* (Ithaca: Cornell Univ. Press, 1978), 26.

At the same time, unrest grew in the Outer Islands, culminating in a series of anti-Jakarta revolts in the 1950s, these joined or led by territorial commanders who had usually been posted to areas where they had ethnic ties. When the major revolts of 1958 had been crushed, Javanese commanders generally replaced these regional commanders. The retirement of many non-Javanese officers after 1958 gave the officer corps a distinctly Javanese complexion. By the time the army took power in 1965, Javanese were far overrepresented in the elites of all the armed services.[108]

As in Burma, these trends accelerated after the coup. Although Javanese are only about half the population, by 1969 some 68 percent of the army leadership, 89 percent of the navy leadership, 81 percent of the air force leadership, and 76 percent of the students in the army general staff and command college were Javanese.[109] Central Javanese, who comprise the core of Gen. Suharto's loyalists, were especially overrepresented in the military elite. Impressionistic evidence suggests that many of the remaining elite positions are held by Batak officers.[110] The share held by members of other ethnic groups at senior levels is thus quite limited.

MULTIPLE ANTI-COLONIAL FORCES: ALGERIA

Two armies confronted each other after independence in Algeria, too, but both were anti-colonial forces. In the end, this distinction did not matter. The two tended to be ethnically differentiated, to be linked up with different civilian politicians, and to be mutually hostile.

The two forces arose out of the circumstances of the Algerian war against France.[111] While guerrilla groups were formed to fight the French army within Algeria, a regular force was raised to invade the colony from Tunisia and Morocco. Especially effective were those guerrilla forces that could use mountain retreats inhabited by Berbers. Berbers

108. There have, of course, been exceptions, such as General Mohammad Jusuf, a Bugis who helped suppress the revolt of the late 1950s in the Celebes and who became armed forces commander in 1979. See Far Eastern Economic Review, Mar. 2, 1979, pp. 18–22.
109. Gregory, "The Influences of Ethnicity in the Evolution of the Indonesian Military Elite," 146, 156b.
110. I am drawing here on my interviews in Jakarta in 1975. See Ulf Sundhaussen, The Road to Power: Indonesian Military Politics, 1945–1967 (Kuala Lumpur: Oxford Univ. Press, 1982), 15. There has been, however, a tendency to commission junior officers on a more proportionate basis.
111. Hurewitz, Middle East Politics, 187–99; William B. Quandt, "The Berbers in the Algerian Political Elite," in Gellner and Micaud, eds., Arabs and Berbers, 288–301.

were accordingly predominant among the so-called internal, or guerrilla, forces. Arabs, however, predominated in the external, or regular, forces, which were unable to breach French defenses and operate inside Algeria.

At independence, the external army entered Algeria, and a three-way struggle began among the externals, the guerrillas, and the civilian provisional government. Some guerrillas linked up with the external forces, but some of the most independent Berber guerrilla leaders—especially the Kabyles—were determined to fight. In August 1962, bitter fighting broke out in Algiers, from which the external army and its political leadership emerged victorious. The Kabyles, however, were undaunted. Even after a compromise settlement was reached, the Kabyle deputies in the assembly were generally opposed to the regime of Ahmed Ben Bella. Fighting broke out again in 1963, but the regular army eventually brought it under control. With many guerrillas who had earlier joined the externals now also discharged from the army, the Kabyle threat had been neutralized.

For some time, Berber-Arab problems faded as Ben Bella struggled with his army commander, Houari Boumedienne. Both were Arabs. After Boumedienne's coup in 1965, Berber dissent arose again, this time not among the Kabyle, but among powerful Shawiya Berbers in the cabinet and army, culminating in a coup attempt by the Shawiya chief of staff, Tahar Zbiri, in 1967. Zbiri's support came from other Shawiyas, but it proved insufficient. In the aftermath of the coup, there was a purge of former guerrilla leaders, especially Kabyle and Shawiya. From then on, Berber military power was in eclipse, the victim of the alignment of forces that began in the fight against the French.

THE IMPACT OF ANTI-COLONIAL
STRUGGLE ON MILITARY ETHNICITY

The paradoxical effects of the anti-colonial struggle on ethnic conflict are striking. They are best seen in Indonesia. There it is often asserted that the anti-colonial movement, transcending ethnic lines, helped forge links among disparate ethnic groups.[112] At the same time, the existence of a strong anti-colonial movement sharpened divisions between those groups most active in the movement and those most closely associated with the colonial regime. It sharpened those conflicts to a degree that

112. See Crawford Young, *The Politics of Cultural Pluralism* (Madison: Univ. of Wisconsin Press, 1976), 360–61. Cf. Harsja Bachtiar, *The Indonesian Nation: Some Problems of Integration and Disintegration* (Singapore: Institute of Southeast Asian Studies, Southeast Asian Perspectives, no. 2, 1974).

went much beyond the level of the tensions between equally divergent groups in countries with weaker nationalist movements. So the anti-colonial struggle simultaneously cut both ways, softening ethnic conflict on some fronts, feeding it on others. And, in the end, even the decades-long history of cross-ethnic cooperation was not sufficient to avert the 1958 rebellions. Neither, once the French were gone, was the common cause sufficient to prevent the pitched battles between externals and internals in Algeria, with their clear Berber-Arab aspect. Nor, for that matter, did it do so a dozen years later in Angola, where three ethnically based armies fought each other more intensely than they had fought the Portuguese, until the best-supplied of the three—the one based in the capital—drove the other two back to their own areas. In Burma, the anti-colonial movement, largely Burman, did not have the softening effect on ethnic conflict that the Indonesian movement did, and so the warfare was early and overtly ethnic. In all of these instances, the exigencies of anti-colonial warfare militarized ethnic divisions and brought on armed clashes. However, as I shall suggest shortly, the unifying effects of the Algerian and Indonesian movements were not wholly ephemeral: most paradoxical of all, they seem even to have survived the establishment of ethnocracies.

The militarization of ethnicity was made possible by the heightened value of armed forces. Since independence had to be fought for, armies gained an early importance that they did not have where independence was simply granted or negotiated. The proliferation of military units broadened ethnic participation in the total array of armed forces, ex-colonial and anti-colonial. And here there is still another paradox: once military recruitment opens up, barring radical efforts to integrate units, an ethnically plural society is likely to have a plural system of armed forces, just as such a society is likely to have a plural party system and, indeed, a plural system of public institutions in general.

Had it been possible to demobilize one of the contending forces, thereby reverting to a single army and skewed composition, the warfare might have been avoided. This is what the civilian politicians allied with the external army in Algeria attempted to do with the guerrilla forces, but with only limited success. In Kenya, on the other hand, the Kikuyu "Mau Mau" fighters were effectively demobilized. The ex-colonial army, led by Kamba and Kalenjin officers who had fought the guerrillas in behalf of the British, became the sole independence army; and no warfare ensued. The former guerrilla fighters were predictably aggrieved, but the Kikuyu character of the civilian regime and the patronage possibilities this created were a sufficient salve. Kenya, however, was the exceptional case. In Burma, Indonesia, and Algeria, broadened recruitment, congruence between ethnic affiliation and military unit, and divergent wartime experiences, rivalries, and locations among the respective groups provoked hostilities.

The same elements—broadened recruitment and a plurality of units—explain why ethno-military conflict in these countries took the form of revolts rather than coups. In all three cases, military attrition along ethnic lines, in the form of revolt, preceded coupmaking, but continued in other forms as well after military regimes assumed power.[113] Again, the contrast with regimes that simply inherited the colonial army is instructive. As I have shown, those countries that took over colonial armies typically inherited ethnically unrepresentative ranks. On ethnic grounds, one line unit would scarcely contemplate waging war against another. Not so where there was effectively more than one army and where the ranks of each such force were ethnically skewed in opposing directions. Warfare between them was not inconceivable. The effect of creating one or more anti-colonial armies was to take military ethnicity out of the officers' mess and bring it right into the barracks and onto the battlefield, where it could be played out in the form of hostilities among the former anti-colonial forces or between them and the inherited colonial army.

Moreover, the very factors that made outright warfare likely also made ethnically motivated coups unlikely. The ethnic and territorial basis of units placed the aggrieved forces outside the capital, whereas coups must be made in the capital. Thus, a different kind of military action marked the attrition process where ex-colonial and anti-colonial armies confronted each other: revolts of units generally remote from the center of power, in Sumatra and Sulawesi, in Burma's hill country, and in the Kabylia. This was action more massive than a coup, but less effective. The creation of parallel armies facilitated revolt but impeded capture of the state.

Putting down these revolts nevertheless had to take precedence over

113. In Indonesia and Burma, certain postings, retirements, and admission to advanced courses seem to have accelerated the homogenizing process. In Algeria, there was the Zbiri coup of 1967, which in some ways resembles the preemptive strikes of the Druze in Syria and the Lugbara in Uganda, both of which were last-gasp efforts to avert the emergence of full-fledged ethnocracy and both of which by their failure abetted the very consequence they sought to avert.

coupmaking by officers of the former anti-colonial forces. In each case, the military defeat of ethnic rebels made possible the coups that occurred later. Those coups were intraethnic: by Suharto against Sukarno, both Javanese; by Ne Win against U Nu, both Burman; and by Boumedienne against Ben Bella, both Arab. Yet the two sets of events—the revolts and the coups—were not wholly unrelated. Both proceeded from the militarization of the anti-colonial struggle, which placed military commanders in a strong guardian position vis-à-vis the first civilian regimes. Freedom fighters, with impressive nationalist pedigrees, could scarcely be placed under civilian control in the usual sense of the term. From the first, the military proximity to power made civil-military partnerships precarious, and ultimately all the regimes succumbed to coups.[114]

Despite attritional warfare, the ethnocracies that emerged in Algeria, Indonesia, and even Burma were rather mild by comparative standards. Neither the brutality nor the degree of ethnic exclusiveness of the Amin or Assad regime is present in Algeria or Indonesia. For while the militarization of the anti-colonial struggle also militarized the ethnic struggle, the breadth and success of the independence movement seem to have imparted a certain legitimacy to its product which makes even ethnically unrepresentative governments more bearable, their use of force more restrained.

Burma is, on this score, in a somewhat different category. The Burmese movement had to fight less. Furthermore, unlike the Algerian or Indonesian movements (both of which were cross-ethnic), Burmese nationalism was a Burman phenomenon from the beginning, and it provoked revolt among other groups early on. If Burman domination is less severe and complete than, say, Alawi domination, that may simply be a reflection of the fact that the Burmese regime has never controlled all of its territory; and its control has been least effective where ethnic antipathies are strongest, most notably in the Karen, Kachin, and Shan areas.

Another reason for the comparative mildness of these regimes is the size of the predominant group. If Alawi and Kakwa are small, utterly unrepresentative minorities, the same cannot be said for Burmans, Javanese, and Algerian Arabs. The strength of these groups may be one reason why they were able to mount powerful anti-colonial movements in the first place. Nationalist resistance might have been more difficult, even if organized on a cross-ethnic basis, in societies that had no such

114. Hurewitz, Middle East Politics, 187–99, describes the rise and disintegration of the Algerian civil-military partnership and explains the instability of such arrangements.

large groups at the center of colonial activity. Although careful analysis would no doubt reveal that certain ascriptive segments of Arab and Burman society have a particularly strong grip on power, as has already been shown for the Central Javanese,[115] the regimes are not readily identified as being dominated by numerically insignificant ethnic groups. Nor have they experienced the full sequence of coups and countercoups that characterizes the process of narrowing down to very small ethnic segments identified in the cases of Sierra Leone, Syria, and Uganda. In this sense, they almost resemble the kinds of military regimes that come to power after a seesaw coup. Full-scale attrition is braked by the fact that the nationalist armies derived, at their core, from large groups.

Equally important, the regimes in Syria, Uganda, and Sierra Leone could be viewed as the preserve of groups that previously were politically unimportant and socially contemptible.[116] By mere force of arms, these backwoodsmen stole the state from those who asserted a rightful claim to it. The root illegitimacy of such regimes, as well as the bloody road to their entrenchment, requires their continuing resort to force and fear. The same characteristics simply cannot be attributed to the anti-colonial successor regimes in Burma, Algeria, or Indonesia. They are controlled by groups whose size, centrality, and nationalist record impart a certain legitimacy to their ethnocracy. Though they came to power by force, force is less necessary to sustain them.

COUPS TO PURSUE
TRADITIONAL ENMITIES

I have argued in Chapter 3 that ethnic conflict cannot be understood solely in terms of a recrudescence of traditional rivalries. The military materials are not the most appropriate evidence to prove or disprove this thesis in the large. From what is already well known about the recruitment and training of most colonial and post-colonial officer corps, it is clear that educated, "modern" army officers, though by no means free of ethnic concerns, are among the least likely political actors to be infused with a longing to return to traditional ethnic glories or to settle centuries-old scores.

Yet traditional rivalries sometimes survive the colonial experience.

115. Gregory, "The Influences of Ethnicity in the Evolution of the Indonesian Military Elite," 144.
116. See, e.g., Rabinovich, *Syria Under the Ba'th*, 212 n.2.

Even army officers can be affected by dreams of reversion to glories enjoyed or revenge for indignities suffered. It has been argued, for example, that the long-standing enmity between the Yoruba and Fon kingdoms of Southern Benin has "diminished little over the years." These kingdoms, at Porto Novo and Abomey, "had been locked in a state of semipermanent warfare that only ended with the final invasion of French troops in 1892."[117] Civilian politicians have enjoyed success in Benin only when they could establish clear links to traditional royal houses, and within the armed forces "traditional status or royal descent has played an important role, interfering with the impersonal bureaucratic hierarchy of rank."[118]

It is more difficult, however, to establish close connections between repeated coups in Benin and traditional warfare between the two Southern kingdoms. The officer corps at independence was disproportionately composed of Fon. Efforts at balancing it after independence were directed at increasing Northern, not Yoruba, membership. Subsequent military interventions had far more to do with previously insignificant North-South rivalries than with reenactment of Fon-Yoruba warfare. Nonetheless, it seems probable that a number of senior Fon officers, descended from the Abomey kings, Glélé and Ghézo, entertained visions of Fon hegemony in the new state, while officers connected to less powerful Northern royal houses were partly actuated by a desire to prevent the rise of a new Fon kingdom with the trappings of a modern state.

In muted form, similar memories have probably been present in the minds of some of the officers who made or attempted coups in Nigeria, Congo (Brazzaville), or Ghana—in fact, wherever expansionary or hegemonical kingdoms had been disrupted by the arrival of the Europeans. But this seems to have been no more than a background factor at best. After all, the Northern Nigerians who overthrew Ironsi in July 1966 were not merely Hausa-Fulani who might have been fired by the example of Dan Fodio's *jihad*; they included Middle-Belt Christians. Whatever their faith or ethnic affiliation, Northern soldiers had much more urgent, contemporary reasons to intervene against what they saw as the Ibo regime than the desire to resume a holy war. Ashanti officers, too, may have been proud of their kingdom, but the control of Ashanti by Nkrumah and the Southern Ghanaian functionaries of the CPP was quite enough to move them to action in 1966; and the Ewe who joined them

117. Decalo, *Coups and Army Rule in Africa*, 40.
118. Ibid., 49.

had no great kingdom to look back to. The Bakongo, of course, did have the powerful Kongo kingdom, and perhaps it contributed to their indefatigable efforts to overthrow Ngouabi and restore a Bakongo regime in Brazzaville. But polarized ethnic equilibrium seems sufficient to account for their efforts, if not entirely for their zeal. Most of the time, traditionalist forces are not readily identifiable in coup behavior.

Nonetheless, there are occasions when military intervention can be traced in some measure—but probably never entirely—to the persistence of traditional rivalries. In Libya, for example, a key role in the coup that deposed King Idris was played by Lt. Col. Musa Ahmed, "a member of the Hassa tribe, which had a longstanding history of friction with the dominant Barassa tribe, itself a pillar of [Idris'] Sanusi regime."[119] When Musa Ahmed led a party of conspirators to an army camp at Gurnada, he was able to persuade the officer in charge of a guard company that had been alerted to call off the alert and disarm the company. That officer was also a Hassa. The traditional tension between Barassa and Hassa appears to have helped move these crucial Hassa officers into the conspirators' camp.

The Somali coup of 1969 was also related to complex, traditional ethnic and subethnic rivalries. The unusually violent 1969 parliamentary election campaign sorely tested the Somali tradition of clan balancing and shifting alliances. It was followed, some months later, by the assassination of President Abdirashid Ali Shermarke. As a deadlocked parliament debated the succession, the coup occurred. The coup can be traced, in conventional terms, to army resentment at the efforts of the civilian regime to achieve détente with Ethiopia and Kenya, shifts from military to development spending, and police resentment at their deployment for partisan purposes and at the dismissal of the police commandant who had tried to prevent this.[120] Like Idi Amin, the army commander had covertly continued to supply rebels whom his civilian superiors were no longer supporting. The army, heavily Darood in composition and led by a Darood officer, could be expected to react unfavorably to the détente policy of an Isaq prime minister. The Darood community spills across the Ethiopian and Kenyan borders, and so the Darood have a special stake in Somali irredentism.

Over and above these considerations, developments in the Somali party system had increased the political importance of subethnic alle-

119. First, *Libya*, 108.
120. See Al Castagno, "Somalia Goes Military," *Africa Report*, Feb. 1970, pp. 25–27.

giance. The most significant development in this direction was the growing split among Darood within the dominant Somali Youth League in
the years following 1964. As this occurred, the extended lineage groups
that had previously been the basis of party alignments and combinations
"temporarily lost their significance in party politics, and effective allegiance had fallen back to the smaller constituent lineages which were
now combining *across* their parent divisions."[121] By the time of the 1969
election, political loyalties had reverted so powerfully to traditional lineage segments that some sixty-two parties, principally representing these
lower levels of identity, fielded more than a thousand candidates for 105
assembly seats.

To a considerable extent, the larger blocs of Darood, Hawiye, Isaq,
and so on, are artifacts of the modern political system. Certainly, traditional animosities reside at lower—and therefore local—levels of identification. Hence, a political reversion to these levels is likely to give renewed importance to such rivalries. Close analysis of the composition of
the pre-coup and post-coup regimes suggests that this is what happened,
though such a conclusion would be obscured by the efforts of both
Somali regimes to achieve overall ethnic balance.

During the election campaign, disorders had broken out between the
traditionally hostile Darood Marehan and Hawiye Habr Gidr subgroups
when the minister of justice, a Marehan, was accused of ballot-stuffing.
It happens that the army commander, Siad Barre, is also a Darood Marehan, one who looked out for the interests of his ethnic compatriots in
the army. In the 25-member Supreme Revolutionary Council established
after the coup, the formerly influential Habr Gidr were eclipsed by their
traditional rivals. Only one of seven Hawiye SRC members was Habr
Gidr. Of the ten Darood members, however, three (including Siad and
his nephew) came from the previously uninfluential Marehan subgroup,
a fourth was Siad's son-in-law, and nearly all the Darood members were
staunchly loyal to Siad.

As in Libya, the coup appears in part to have been a way of pursuing
traditional ethnic enmities by military means. Nonetheless, in both
countries, the traditional rivalry cannot be described as the sole factor.
These coups, like retrieval coups, involved mixed motives.

The extent to which traditional ethnic rivalries were instrumental in
bringing on the Somali coup derived from the fact that Somali politics

121. I. M. Lewis, "The Politics of the 1969 Somalia Coup," *Journal of Modern African
Studies* 10 (Oct. 1972): 381–408, at 396 (emphasis in the original).

"is not something separate and distinct from local traditional politics but rather a direct extension of it . . . ."[122] This fact is of central importance. Coups that reflect traditional ethnic antagonisms are likely to occur only in the least modernized countries of the developing world, where traditional allegiances are not just dimly recalled but played out daily by nomads and subsistence farmers.

In the remainder of Asia and Africa, where contemporary politics is not a mere extension of the traditional political system, ancient glories and battles are not likely to be the stuff of ethno-military politics. What shows through the welter of coups, countercoups, and purges are the same themes that pervade ethnic conflict in its civilian manifestations. Above all, perhaps, there is the dichotomy between backward and advanced groups. This polarity is reflected in the structure of North-South and similar alignments that shape seesaw coups and countercoups, as well as coups of retrieval. The relationship between the respective ethnic groups and the colonial power, which has an impact on civilian ethnic relations, also extends into the ethno-military sphere, typically by means of competing armed forces. For the most part, then, the sources of alerts and mobilization orders reside, not in vestiges of bygone events, but in juxtapositions and irritants that have more recent origins, in anti-colonial movements and post-colonial politics.

122. Lewis, "Nationalism and Particularism in Somalia," 354. See also David D. Laitin, "The Political Economy of Military Rule in Somalia," *Journal of Modern African Studies* 14 (Sept. 1976): 449–68, at 456, 458.

CHAPTER THIRTEEN

The Effects of Intervention and the Art of Prevention

Military intervention does not leave ethnic conflict where it finds it. However faithfully ethnic coups reflect the existing structure of civilian ethnic conflict, they also affect that conflict in powerful and dramatic ways. I intend in this chapter to venture some general conclusions about the impact of ethnic coupmaking on the composition of regimes and on armed forces. I shall then turn to the matter of coup prevention. In view of the profound changes in regimes and armies wrought by military intervention, the enumeration and evaluation of techniques of coup-proofing in severely divided societies assume heightened importance.

THE CONSEQUENCES
OF MILITARY ETHNICITY

Some standardized patterns of interaction between armed forces and regimes were considered in the last chapter. The accent was on classification, on understanding the characteristics of several types of intervention. Now I want to put back together what I have taken apart—that is, shift the emphasis to the larger subject of military ethnicity in general by analyzing the ethnic consequences of coups in ways that crosscut the several types just enumerated. When this is done, three themes stand out. The first is that the ethnic consequences of coups were traceable in large measure to the colonial inheritance, both military and electoral. The second is that, in overcoming that inheritance, the extent of ethnic turnover was enormous. The third is that there is a general propensity among military regimes in severely divided societies to be limited in the breadth of their ethnic base.

THE INFLUENCE OF THE
COLONIAL INHERITANCE

The starting point for the militarization of ethnic conflict in the post-colonial period was the colonial inheritance, especially as reflected in recruitment patterns. Its impact was formidable, even though in some countries the colonizer had only succeeded in commissioning a few dozen officers by the time of independence. There are several reasons for the magnitude of the colonial legacy.

Colonial military recruitment was initially not merely an aspect of the running of a politically neutral bureaucratic machine. Rather, recruitment was heavily imbued with ethnic stereotypes and was one of the most important arenas for the working out of colonial ethnic policy. At the broadest level, therefore, the transfer of military institutions to new states bequeathed to them instruments of force that were very much a part of ethnic politics.

Later, when preparations for independence were being made, early officer recruitment decisions tended to entrench some groups at the expense of others and, equally important, to establish standard methods and qualifications for recruitment. Whether educational qualifications or examinations were required, or whether commissioning from the ranks was practiced, the initial mode of recruitment had ethnic effects, created expectations, and acquired a certain life of its own. Changing the method of recruitment, since such changes inevitably had ethnic consequences, raised suspicions, sometimes, of course, well-justified suspicions.

Many of the possible relationships between military and civilian leaders were fraught with tension. I have referred in general terms to split domination to describe ethnically differentiated—and often polarized—control of military and civilian political institutions. Three forms of split domination were especially precarious. First, if the military were left in the hands of those groups that had faithfully carried out the colonialists' policy of preserving the colonies, whereas the civilian regime were controlled by the very groups against whom military precautions had been directed, this was an unstable situation. Second, the probability of a civil-military clash was great if the electoral process threw up a civilian government of backward groups determined to "catch up" by reducing the representation of advanced groups in the civil service, educational institutions, and commerce, but those latter groups were also well positioned in an officer corps selected by educational qualifications. Third, when the electoral process polarized ethnic positions so that the vanquished ethnic party was identical in composition with the officer corps, the demise of the electoral process was generally not long in coming— though sometimes the demise was accelerated by crude efforts to reconstruct the officer corps in the regime's own ethnic image. In each case, skewed recruitment put military leadership at odds with elected leadership.

The alternative was sometimes better, but not always. Where there was congruence between the ethnic composition of the civilian regime and the officer corps, sometimes this perpetuated civilian rule. But sometimes, if that congruence facilitated the defeat of a large group of ethnic antagonists (as it did in Sierra Leone and in Uganda), it merely paved the way for a new struggle, narrower in its ethnic scope, between the civilians and the military.

The skewed recruitment of the officer corps, an integral part of the colonial inheritance, contributed heavily to the incidence of military coups in many of the successor states. And skewed recruitment did this by the fortuitous ways it interacted with the ethnically divisive properties of elections in severely divided societies. Electoral institutions were also part of the colonial inheritance, but a quite different part, founded on clashing assumptions. Military institutions were based on limited conceptions of reliability or capacity; electoral institutions, on broader conceptions of participation. Skewed recruitment also guaranteed the ethnically unrepresentative character of practically any regime that resulted from a coup. The colonial inheritance thus had long-term effects.

ETHNIC RESHUFFLING

If the colonial military inheritance was powerfully important in shaping what was to come, part of what was to come was the overthrow of that very inheritance. The instability fostered by skewed recruitment paved the way for the remolding, and in some cases obliteration, of the established ethnic contours of the ex-colonial army.

In one country after another, the materials at hand indicate a drastic reshuffling of officer corps composition. This may seem strange, given the incidence of coups related to the skewed composition of the ex-colonial army, for the occurrence of such coups should put the new military rulers in a position to perpetuate the ethnic composition of the officer corps in its original form. But some such coups were made by mere segments of the officer corps, and these then expanded their share of the whole. Then, too, the first coup was by no means necessarily the last. There were also countercoups, purges, sequences of attritional coups, struggles between anti-colonial and ex-colonial forces as well as among the anti-colonial forces themselves, and army schisms in countries where secessionist movements or civil wars emerged. In countries that avoided coups, there were also efforts by civilian regimes to alter officer corps composition in directions ethnically favorable to the regimes' own longevity. The result of all these upheavals was wholesale ethnic turnover.

The dimensions of this turnover are difficult to overestimate. In some countries, certain ethnic groups heavily represented in the officer corps were largely eliminated from it. In some, they made way for the participation of formerly unrepresented groups; in others, they were pushed aside by groups with whom they had shared officers' billets.

The magnitude of these changes can be appreciated by reflecting on the respective fates of several formerly preeminent and formerly unrepresented groups. The Acholi and Langi in Uganda, the Druze, Kurds, and Isma'ilis in Syria, and the Mende in Sierra Leone were purged and driven out of officer corps in which they were solidly entrenched. The Ambonese in Indonesia and the Karens in Burma lost their military leadership positions through secessionist warfare. In Nigeria, the Ibo lost theirs through a combination of coups and the Biafran war. The Fon in Benin, the Ewe in Ghana, and the Tamils, Burghers, and Sinhalese Christians in Sri Lanka were all dislodged from their favorable positions following coups or coup attempts, though none of these groups was purged entirely. The Berbers in the Algerian forces suffered a decline as a result of internecine warfare, as did many non-Javanese in Indonesia and Lari in Congo (Brazzaville). The Berbers, favorably situated in Morocco, were gravely weakened by their participation in two attempts on the king's life, as well as by examination requirements for admission to the military academy. By contrast, groups like the Alawi in Syria and the Kabrai in Togo built on their initial advantages to enhance their domination inside the army, while the Kikuyu in Kenya, the Burmans, and certain groups of Northerners in Sierra Leone all found their way into the officer corps from the outside.

One of the most important long-term consequences of coups and countercoups in ethnically divided societies is, then, to effect radical ethnic transformations in the officer corps. These transformations sometimes come in successive waves. In Uganda and Sierra Leone, ethnic groups represented in the first generation of officers after independence were replaced by an ethnically differentiated new generation, which was swept aside in its turn by the next wave of newly commissioned officers. Where there is less complete purging, there may be oscillations of ethnic power. The Fon military establishment, temporarily eclipsed by the Benin coup of 1967, proceeded to make a comeback in 1970, but was retired after the 1972 coup. Younger Fon officers were included in the mainly Northern leadership circle after the 1972 putsch; but, when they attempted their own plot in 1975, the Fon officers were forcibly ousted. As in other countries, perhaps the most enduring effect of the long string of coups in Benin has been compositional: replacement of the Fon military elite by a Northern military elite. In various sequences, upheaval in the ethnic composition of the officer corps is a major trend in postcolonial armed forces.

The same is true for the ethnic transformation of regimes, as I said earlier. Many Asian and African regimes no longer have the same ethnic base as the regimes that assumed power at independence. This is especially the case in countries that have experienced coups. Many initially powerful ethnic groups—Mende in Sierra Leone, Baganda in Uganda, Sunni in Syria, Ewe in Togo, Lari in Congo (Brazzaville), Cyrenaicans in Libya—have lost their influence to other groups able to bring their military, or military and civilian, power to bear. In these struggles, bureaucratic position counted in the end for little. In addition to their political power, most of these groups started with a strong position in the civil service. Some groups even managed to retain their disproportionate bureaucratic representation; the ranks of others in government offices were decimated. Either way, the striking thing is that the strong bureaucratic position of an ethnic group might ward off the most extreme forms of ethnocracy but could not be translated into effective political power in the face of a military controlled by others.

The radical ethnic transformation of armies and regimes in the postcolonial period provides some justification for the fears that underlie the intensity of ethnic conflict. The worst fear—extinction—does not materialize, at least not in the short run, although some ethnocratic military regimes do practice indiscriminate killings of members of antagonistic ethnic groups. But the political fortunes of various ethnic groups, and all that goes with them, are subject to enormous fluctuation. Whether it was just a reasonable forecast or a self-fulfilling prophecy, the apprehension that ethnic groups felt about their precarious political position on the brink of independence was confirmed by events in the military politics of the post-colonial period.

ETHNIC INCLUSION: THE LIMITS OF MILITARY REGIMES

This brings me to the last of the themes to be underscored here: the propensity of military regimes to be at best only partially inclusive of the full range of ethnic groups and at worst to be narrowly exclusive. Whatever the ethnic direction of the regime changes effected by military intervention, no military regime seems to have broadened the range of ethnic groups included in its embrace, and a number have moved to contract the range of included groups.

If the evidence for this conclusion were merely the incidence of seesaw coups, an argument might be made that the seesaw coup is an artifact of the colonial military and electoral legacy. As such, it might have no general bearing on the capacity of military regimes to be broadly inclusive. Attritional coups, however, cannot be described as the product of such parochial conditions. On the contrary, they are made possible by a decisive break with the colonial military and electoral inheritance. What such coups seem to signify is that, when restraints are removed, there is a strong tendency toward narrowing the base of the regime. In fact, there seem to be some such homogenizing propensities at work even in Indonesia and Algeria, where ethnic tensions are not especially pronounced by world standards.

From this standpoint, coups of retrieval have a special significance, for they aim to reinclude excluded groups. Yet, in Ghana the effort has several times come to naught—and this despite military revulsion at the discriminatory practices of the former civilian regime. The incompatibility of group claims is brought home by the difficulty of identifying in the coup materials a successful case of retrieval or broadening.

All of this should make us properly skeptical of the capacity of military regimes to become broadly inclusive. As a matter of fact, the ethnocracies that have emerged from lethiferous sequences of attritional coups and purges appear to be significantly narrower and more brutal than could have been produced by civilian regimes alone, at least by elected civilian regimes. Like the experience of single parties, the experience of military regimes underscores the disincentives to ethnic narrowing that are provided by free elections. The ethnic politics of military intervention exhibits the same proclivity as civilian ethnic politics for a part of a diverse society to claim control of a whole state—only sometimes a smaller and more oppressive part.

COUP-PROOFING:
THE ART OF PREVENTION

If, as I have indicated, coups are sometimes provoked by regime attempts to alter the ethnic structure of the armed forces, measures taken to thwart conspiracies may actually help to produce them. In the prevention of coups, as in other policy matters, doing nothing is sometimes preferable to doing something, even when the stakes are high.

Nonetheless, civilian regimes have generally not been content with laissez-faire as a strategy for coup protection. On the contrary, many regimes have taken pains to structure their armed forces so as to reduce the likelihood of coups. With the urgency of the matter felt keenly, activism, rather than restraint, has been the prevailing thrust of preventive strategies.

THE RANGE OF COMPOSITIONAL STRATEGIES

The signal importance of ethno-military composition has already been stressed. It was a necessary, although not a sufficient, condition of all the coups we have considered that the ethnic composition of the armed forces diverge in some significant way from that of other government bodies. In view of this, it is perhaps not startling that compositional techniques are overwhelmingly the most widely used strategies for coup-proofing.

Often the measures taken are cumulative. In Kenya, for example, "President Kenyatta proceeded to appoint fellow Kikuyus to the posts of Defense Minister, Chief of Police, chief of intelligence, chief of criminal investigations; he has also granted fast promotions to Kikuyu officers in the army and the police. In addition he retained many British advisers and officers within these bodies." On top of this, Kenyatta "sacked most Luo officers in key security jobs" and "moved to strengthen the highly mobile para-military force of the police, the General Service Unit, which is now almost entirely Kikuyu-dominated."[1] Especially for those regimes confronted, as Kenya was, with what I have referred to as split domination, extensive tinkering with the composition of the armed forces seems a natural way of averting military action against the regime.

Interestingly, compositional strategies have traditional analogues in multiethnic polities. In seventeenth-century Ceylon, commanders and soldiers were "dispersed all over the Land; so that one scarcely knows the other, the King not suffering many Neighbours and Townsmen to be in one Company; which hath always heretofore been so ordered for fear of Conspiracies."[2] The spatial ordering of the capitals of traditional societies in Southern Africa was geared to coup prevention, with the wards carefully laid out to place the chief's retainers between him and "potentially hostile elements," notably men of other tribes and nobles of other lineages.[3] In the modern state, the spatial dimension of coup prevention is not entirely obsolete, but it is no longer adequate merely to insure that the precincts of the ruler are surrounded by friendly forces. Now the manipulation of composition reaches much further afield, into the armed forces as a whole. Nonetheless, prevalent coup-prevention techniques in contemporary and traditional society share common assumptions: it is the identity of personnel deployed in physically threatening positions that counts, and in the end there is no substitute for ethnic affinity among such personnel. Compositional strategies are the time-honored way of averting coups.

As we have seen, however, tinkering with the structure of the armed forces poses grave risks, for it can backfire and provoke officers to move against the politicians who jeopardize their positions. Why regimes persist in utilizing such measures, in the face of these risks, is a significant question, the answer to which, I believe, sheds light on coup motives attributed to the officers by the politicians. If political leaders believed that officers were actuated by motives of sheer personal gain or corporate military interest, they have available far less risky means of averting coups. To be sure, some regimes have essentially struck deals with their officers by adopting profligate policies regarding pay, perquisites, pensions, and promotions, or by pandering to officers' ambitions for new

1. Hilary Ng'weno, "Tribes, Armies and Political Instability in Africa" (unpublished paper, Harvard Univ. Center for International Affairs, Mar. 1969), 38.

2. Robert Knox, *An Historical Relation of Ceylon* (Dehiwala, Ceylon: Tisara Prakasakayo, 1966; originally published in London, 1681), 104.

3. I. Schapera, *Government and Politics in Tribal Societies* (New York: Schocken Books, 1967; originally published in 1956), 172.

weapons, better postings, or greater influence in the political process.[4] But, withal, what stands out in ethnically divided societies is not attempts to placate the military by alleviating organizational grievances and satisfying individual ambitions—or even to devise elaborate civilian control schemes—but far riskier attempts to insure that ethnically kindred incumbents are placed in sensitive positions and sensitive units or that ethnically antipathetic officers are removed from them.

It may be, of course, that this simply bespeaks the discomfort and distrust that often pervade relations between elites of different ethnic groups—feelings that certainly do lead to thrusts toward homogenization of elites, as attritional coups illustrate. It may also be that straightforward efforts to rectify ethnic composition, rather than resort to more subtle control techniques, signify a lack of political imagination. But I suspect that the prevalence of compositional strategies reflects as well the implicit belief of the politicians that army officers who intervene in the politics of multiethnic societies do not generally do so merely out of personal or corporate ambitions that can be placated, but out of a desire to advance or defend the wider political interests of the ethnic group to which they belong. If this is so, then it may be reasonable for politicians to believe that nothing short of ethnic realignment of the military will protect them.

As the variety of methods adopted in Kenya indicates, several compositional techniques can be used together, but they are not all of a piece. Some measures involve appointing trusted officers to key commands or according preferential treatment to one ethnic group in recruitment and promotion, whether or not this is accompanied by purges of ethnically disfavored officers. Other steps entail creation of new armed units that can be appropriately composed and equipped. Not all of these measures are necessarily equally effective or equally risky.

Five main compositional strategies have been employed:

1. *Homogenization of the army.* This technique involves altering the internal composition of the main regular units of the armed forces, especially, of course, the officer corps. The aim is to achieve ethnic congruence between the officer corps and the regime.

4. For surveys of techniques, see David Goldsworthy, "Civilian Control of the Military in Black Africa," *African Affairs* 80 (Jan. 1981): 49–74; Elise Forbes Pachter, "Contra-Coup: Civilian Control of the Military in Guinea, Tanzania, and Mozambique," *Journal of Modern African Studies* 20 (Dec. 1982): 595–612.

2. *Balance inside the army.* Here the objective is to redress unfavorable ethnic ratios within the officer corps. Officers of divergent ethnic memberships are placed in close proximity, so that they not only counterbalance each other but also form a single communications network. The intended result is that conspiracies are deterred in the first instance, detected if they do form, and defeated by quick response if they reach the point of action.

3. *Balance outside the army.* This involves creating wholly new units outside the main regular army units, often outside the army itself, or greatly bolstering such units of this kind as already exist. Since such special units are to be constructed from scratch or radically upgraded, there is considerable opportunity to structure their ethnic composition and command to favor the regime. These units can also be garrisoned and equipped in ways that specially suit them for internal security missions, emphasize mobility, and accord them a weapons advantage over ethnically less reliable units. Potential coupmakers within the army are on notice that they would probably have to fight superior forces ethnically aligned with the regime.

4. *Foreign forces.* Foreign forces can be employed inside or outside the regular army. Foreign commanders can be positioned at sensitive points ranging from chief of staff to service commander, chief of intelligence, and even commander of field units. Alternatively, foreign troops can provide personnel for units outside the regular army that serve as a counterpoise to regular forces. Often these are praetorian guard units. Whether used in force or only in key command and staff positions, foreign personnel afford dual protection. They are unlikely to enter into or support conspiracies against the regime they have been employed to defend, and if for some reason foreign officers should conspire against the regime, it is most unlikely that anyone else would follow them. To serve these functions, the "foreigners" involved need not always come from foreign states. It is enough, for these purposes, that they come from ethnic groups uninvolved in the major ethnic conflicts in the state.

5. *Kinship control.* Leaders of some states have learned very well that perfect trust is rarely justified and that even elaborate prevention arrangements can go awry if the loyalty or vigilance of commanders is eroded. Consequently, it is tempting to supplement the restructuring of the armed forces by placing close relatives in command of key units, especially those units already packed with troops ethnically akin to the

rulers of the regime. It is risky for potential conspirators to approach close relatives of political leaders for support in plotting a coup. Similarly, since close relatives are likely candidates for punitive action or execution in the event of a successful coup, they have every incentive to be vigilant in coup prevention. In situations fraught with danger, the intention of the leadership is to use kinsmen as military alter egos.

Underlying these approaches are a few commonly accepted, if rarely stated, principles of coup-proofing:

1.   Make questionable units heterogeneous to reduce their capacity to unite against the regime.

2.   Make loyal units homogeneous to increase their capacity to defend the regime.

3.   Position supporters in mobile, heavily armed, elite units near the capital.

In summary: integrate opponents, segregate supporters, and deploy them accordingly.

It is remarkable just how closely these coup-prevention techniques resemble measures adopted by the colonial powers to insure the reliability of their armies. Although they feared mutiny and revolt rather than conspiracy and coup, and they generally kept most of the commissions in their own hands, colonial rulers, we have seen, resorted to policies of ethnic balance within units and balance among units, as well as dependence on foreign troops or troops drawn from areas far from the center of colonial interest and conflict. Ethnic congruence, balance, and alienage were the reigning principles of colonial protection. Only kinship control has no analogue in colonial practice, partly because colonial rulers could at least trust each other and had no need of blood ties among themselves and perhaps partly because kinship is generally far more important in Asia and Africa than in the West. Kinship control aside, the similarity of compositional strategies is striking.

The similarity is not accidental. Once practiced by the colonialists, some of these techniques became embedded in military policy and tradition. Successor regimes thus inherited certain of the colonial arrangements, whether they wanted them or not. Contrary to its predilections, the independent government of India, for example, took over an army that had developed out of the preference for "martial races" and the "counterpoise of natives against natives."[5] At a time of external threat (from Pakistan), there was an understandable reluctance to destroy the structure and regimental pride of the army in order to refashion it along nationalist lines. Consequently, ethnic change in the Indian army has been slow. Long after independence, the Gurkha and Sikh regiments still contained only Gurkhas and Sikhs. The Rajput Regiment contained some Bengali battalions, and the Madras Regiment recruited from all over the South, but still these units survived.[6] The "counterpoise" persisted even though the civilians had no great enthusiasm for the protective arrangements devised by their British predecessors.

Many other regimes, aware of the received tradition, learned from it and sensed its general utility for their own purposes. Sometimes under the influence of British and French officers left behind as military advisers and commanders, these regimes moved to expand and refine the colonial techniques. This, of course, did not prevent them from making drastic changes in the specific ethnic composition of the military personnel involved, where that seemed to be required by the situation.

The fact that control strategies adopted to support foreign occupation remain applicable suggests, then, more than just blind acceptance of the colonial inheritance. The continuing use of measures to insure ethnic congruence, balance, and alienage is a commentary, perhaps, on the resemblance of rule by ethnic strangers to foreign rule. Post-colonial governments find that their situation may not always be as different from that of the colonial powers as they had imagined. Continued resort to colonial techniques of military control testifies that there is a long road to political legitimacy in ethnically divided countries. The reversion to colonial techniques implies a resurgence of colonial problems, though, as I shall suggest later, since the specific dangers to be guarded against vary somewhat from the colonial period, the effectiveness of the measures adopted also varies accordingly.

Although variations from country to country have been considerable, there has been a general tendency to move from lighter prevention strategies to heavier ones. Regimes that start out, for example, by placing a few foreigners in command of already constituted units or by favoring a

5. See, e.g., the comments on counterpoise in the colonial army in Jawaharlal Nehru, *The Discovery of India* (Bombay: Asia Pub. House, 1961), 322, 348.

6. Stephen P. Cohen, *The Indian Army: Its Contribution to the Development of a Nation* (Berkeley and Los Angeles: Univ. of California Press, 1971) 187.

few ethnically congruent officers with rapid promotions or key postings tend to move toward reconstituting the entire officer corps, creating and arming wholly new units, or bringing in foreign troops. The trend has been from retail to wholesale coup-proofing.

Ghana under Nkrumah is an archetypical case.[7] At independence, in 1957, the Ghanaian officer corps was, as I have said, skewed toward groups whose attachment to Nkrumah was at best equivocal. The over-represented Ga and Ewe, together a majority of the African officers, were especially suspect. Late Africanization of the officer corps had also left Nkrumah with some 220 British officers, far more than the number of African officers. Despite Nkrumah's vaunted African nationalism, he retained these British officers, at the same time gradually shifting officer recruitment away from the Ga and Ewe without wholly excluding them from receiving commissions. This he did with considerable finesse, and it can be said that, during the first four or five years of Ghanaian independence, Nkrumah pursued a preventive policy of control from above, by retaining foreign officers and trying gingerly to achieve balance within the army.

But Nkrumah's apprehensions grew dramatically in the 1961–62 period, especially after uncovering a plot on his life involving Ga officers. He then proceeded to purge Ga from his cabinet, as well as from the army and police. He exercised great care, too, in the posting of Ewe. He turned in earnest to all-out policies of control from below, using all the major strategies. He sought balance inside the armed forces, promoting and relying heavily on a few influential Northern officers within the army and police. Northerners were outside the main conflicts of Ghana's ethnic politics; with the British presence reduced, Northern officers served essentially in the role of reliable aliens. Nkrumah also tried to achieve balance outside the armed forces, establishing an infamous rival force, the President's Own Guard Regiment. This was largely staffed and led by members of Nkrumah's own ethnic group, the Nzima, who also played the most prominent role in the major intelligence units. By 1965,

---

7. See Valerie P. Bennett and Donald L. Horowitz, "The Military and the Transfer of Power in West Africa and Southern Asia" (unpublished paper, 1976); J. M. Lee, *African Armies and Civil Order* (New York: Praeger, 1969), 67; J. 'Bayo Adekson, "Army in a Multi-Ethnic Society: The Case of Nkrumah's Ghana," *Armed Forces and Society* 2 (Feb. 1976): 251–72, at 258, 264, 266; Anton Bebler, *Military Rule in Africa* (New York: Praeger, 1973), 31–36; Ruth First, *Power in Africa* (Baltimore: Penguin Books, 1972), 197–99; David R. Smock and Audrey C. Smock, *The Politics of Pluralism* (New York: Elsevier, 1975), 238.

Nkrumah's fear had driven him to turn the armed forces topsy-turvy in his relentless efforts to have Northerners and Nzima in every place where a putsch might be uncovered.

COMPOSITIONAL STRATEGIES IN ACTION

Although insecurity drives many political and military leaders to wholesale restructuring of the armed forces, some emphasize one technique more than others. The mix of methods is not foreordained. Moreover, each of the various compositional strategies tends to have its own conditions of adoption, its own specific risks, and its own probable effectiveness under given circumstances. It is time to take a closer look at the compositional strategies, one at a time.

Homogenization of the Army

Almost by definition, homogenization of the officer corps is a very effective strategy of prevention. It is possible, however, only in very unusual circumstances. If the officer corps is already dominated by the ethnic group favoring the regime, then it is generally not difficult to extend that domination to the point where all important military positions are occupied by that group (Creoles in Guyana, Kabrai in Togo, Beduins in Jordan). Alternatively, an opportunity to homogenize may arise out of previous military upheavals. Skillful purging in the wake of coups and countercoups can homogenize even an officer corps that was formerly quite diverse. We have seen these conditions in the attritional regimes of Sierra Leone, Syria, and Uganda. A coup attempt also triggered arrests and retirements in Sri Lanka's heterogeneous officer corps, thereby providing the opportunity—which the regime took—to create a Sinhalese Buddhist officer corps.[8]

Short of such conditions, however, homogenization is highly risky. Its implication for ethnic relations is easily understood, both inside and outside the armed forces. The adoption of such a policy is therefore likely to precipitate preemptive coups before the policy can be implemented. Unless the favored group begins with a substantial nucleus already well-placed within the officer corps, most regimes opt for other strategies. The Arab regime in Zanzibar attempted an extreme form of homogeni-

8. Donald L. Horowitz, *Coup Theories and Officers' Motives: Sri Lanka in Comparative Perspective* (Princeton: Princeton Univ. Press, 1980), 210–13.

zation and paid for it dearly.[9] The regime distrusted the loyalty of the mainland Africans in the principal armed force, the police. It accordingly dismissed many mainlanders, repatriating only some, and replaced them with Arabs, Asians, or Shirazis. The result was to set loose a trained force ripe for rebellion, and in 1964 the Arab regime was overthrown by a force of ex-policemen, largely of mainland origins.

Balance Inside the Army

If homogenization is impossible, balance may still be possible. Obviously, balance is easier to establish where the officer corps is already heterogeneous. A minimum of fiddled promotions and careful postings may be all that is required under the best of circumstances. But the officer corps may be skewed in a direction unfavorable to the regime, or ethnically favorable officers may not possess the requisite seniority, qualifications, or positioning to enable them to be deployed in the regime's own interests. Where this is the case, there are obstacles to be overcome.

The difficulties of establishing control inside the army are easily identified. Recruitment biases tend to be self-perpetuating, for reasons already examined in Chapter 11. Some groups disproportionately possess the established qualifications and the inclination to pursue military careers. To break patterns of skewed recruitment involves securing agreement to a program of quotas or else outright tampering with set requirements (Nigeria after 1960 and Sierra Leone, 1964–67, respectively). Even then, changes in ethnic composition are likely to be so slow and so concentrated at junior levels as to be of little value in gaining immediate control. Furthermore, there is the danger of creating sharp intramilitary ethnic cleavages. These were the stuff of countercoups in countries like Nigeria and Benin. To proceed more rapidly so as to achieve faster and more complete control generally entails grave violations of the chain of command in assignments, promotions, and postings; it may even require ethnic purges. All of these are extremely hazardous actions. In addition to their ethnic implications, these actions constitute major intrusions into the military domain that tend to undermine the army's reciprocal disposition not to intrude into civilian affairs.

The results of balance-within strategies are quite mixed. Once established, they seem to work as intended: various groups inside the officer

9. Michael F. Lofchie, *Zanzibar: Background to Revolution* (Princeton: Princeton Univ. Press, 1965), 267–68; John Okello, *Revolution in Zanzibar* (Nairobi: East African Pub. House, 1967), 17–19, 119, 132.

corps keep an eye on each other to prevent untoward action. An important reason why civilian ethnocracies could survive for long periods in single-party regimes such as Guinea, Kenya, and Zambia is that the officer corps in each case had a large infusion of high-ranking officers from the same ethnic group that dominated the civilian regime: Malinké, Kikuyu, and Nyanja and other Easterners. In none of these armed forces was the command ethnically homogeneous. Kamba and Kalenjin were very well placed in Kenya's army; Zambia had a Lozi armed forces commander; and Guinea had a Fula chief of general staff until he was retired after an ostensibly Fula coup plot in 1976. Nor is the strategy foolproof: Kenya also had a major coup attempt in 1982, and Guinea had a successful coup in 1984. But the strategy works better than these events might suggest, for the 1976 Guinean conspiracy was mainly associated with the popular militia outside the regular army, and the Kenyan plot was the creature of air force officers.[10] The marginality of the units in which both plots took shape is an indication that the prevention system in the army proper was working. Likewise, the military takeover in Guinea was only possible upon the death of Sékou Touré, who was so successful in coup-proofing that he was able to maintain a Malinké-dominated civilian regime for more than a quarter of a century. Vulnerable as all such narrowly composed regimes are to ethnic discontent, their ability to remain in power must be attributable in large measure to armed forces composition that deters and detects conspiracies among groups still represented in the officer corps but holding no effective power in the regime.

That is the situation once the composition of the army is balanced in the desired direction. But the process of bringing such a balance about in the first place may be another matter. Along the way, the infusion of new ethnic groups into the officer corps can bring ethnic conflict into the army and defeat the purpose of the strategy. The introduction of young Northern officers into the Beninese officer corps, formerly dominated by the Fon, certainly had much to do with the long sequence of coups that Benin experienced after 1963. One suspects that the more gingerly the strategy is applied, the greater its chances of success. Large doses are provocative.

I have been speaking of balance within the officer corps as a strategy for gaining control of an army of dubious reliability. But suppose the

---

10. For Guinea, see *Africa Confidential*, Sept. 24, 1976, pp. 4–5; for Kenya, see the informative analysis in ibid., Mar. 2, 1983, pp. 7–8.

opposite situation—that the regular army is ethnically reliable but paramilitary units are not. Here, too, strategies of internal balance may be applicable.

In fact, there are times when internal balance is virtually the only prevention technique available. Regimes that come to power through coups by the regular army often find themselves confronted with hostile paramilitary forces whose ethnic composition is stacked against them. If the governments they overthrew utilized a strategy of balance outside the regular army, the new regimes are then threatened by irregular units loyal to the old regimes. They are thus in a position converse to that of their predecessors, who feared the regular army and relied on the irregulars as a counterforce.

Under these circumstances, if the new regimes do not absorb hostile paramilitary units into the regular army, thereby creating a new deterrent balance within the army, they may not survive. The post-Nkrumah Ghanaian and post-Obote Ugandan military regimes were able simply to dissolve these paramilitary units, but other regimes, notably Francophone ones, have had difficulty doing so. The units may be long-established, and they may perform a variety of essential civil-order functions. They may be too strong or too large to challenge directly at the outset; their force levels may approach or exceed those of the regular army itself. Even if reorganized, they may reappear in a new organizational form.

The new military regimes in Madagascar after 1972 and Congo (Brazzaville) after 1968 both confronted hostile units outside the armed forces. In both cases, these units had been unable to prevent regular-army coups from occurring, though they were able to make the resulting military regimes unstable afterwards. Both regimes took action against the paramilitary units, but the action took different forms and had different results.

In Madagascar, student disorders brought the military to power in 1972, effecting what amounted to a seesaw coup. The civilian government of Philibert Tsirinana had rested heavily on the support of Côtiers and had never really captured the allegiance of the important plateau peoples, particularly the Merina, who had ruled the island before the arrival of the French. In 1970, for example, Tsirinana had created four vice-presidential positions, and all of them went to Côtiers. The army, however, was led by French-trained officers, many of them Merina (for the Merina are educationally advantaged), including the commander, General Gabriel Ramanantsoa. To protect himself, Tsirinana had strengthened the gendarmerie and the presidential bodyguard, the *Force Républicaine de Sécurité*, both overwhelmingly Côtier in composition. Though used against the predominantly Merina students in 1972, these units were unable to avert the assumption of power by General Ramanantsoa, who established a regime of Merina officers. From this new regime, the Côtiers in turn were largely excluded.[11]

After taking power, Ramanantsoa dissolved the *Force Républicaine de Sécurité*. But the action was not thorough: a successor force emerged, the *Groupe Mobile Policier*, and it contained many of the same personnel. Together with the ousted Côtier politicians, the GMP intrigued against the regime. The GMP was apparently implicated in the assassination of Ramanantsoa's Merina successor, Colonel Richard Ratsimandrava, early in 1975, and it then fought a pitched battle against forces loyal to the regime.[12] Though the Côtier paramilitary forces were defeated, the upheaval they caused seems to have forced the military to diversify the ethnic base of the regime and to confer the leadership of the junta on an officer from the East Coast of Madagascar.[13] Clearly, the peril to the regime and its subsequent reorganization resulted from the persistence of separately organized Côtier units.

The Congolese regime inherited a similar problem of ethnically hostile units outside the regular army. At first, Ngouabi's Northern-dominated government proceeded circumspectly, but, when it acted, it did so more decisively. It used its control of key army units to neutralize ethnically hostile irregular units. One by one, the Bakongo-dominated paramilitary units made their move against the regime. First it was the Civil Defense Corps and the *Jeunesse* militia of the post-Youlou governing party (the *Mouvement National de la Révolution*) which showed their hand shortly after Ngouabi had seized power in 1968. Defeated by the army, they were then absorbed into it in 1969.[14] Then Lari officers of the

11. Colin Legum, ed., *Africa Contemporary Record, 1974–75* (New York: Africana, 1975), pp. B217–18.

12. Colin Legum, ed., *Africa Contemporary Record, 1975–76* (New York: Africana, 1976), pp. B235–37. I am indebted to Brian Weinstein for a helpful discussion of Madagascar's ethnic politics.

13. The ethnic impact of the 1975 changes was reflected in subsequent plotting. In 1978, many Merina were in turn arrested for conspiring against the regime, from which by then they felt excluded.

14. Arthur H. House, "Brazzaville: Revolution or Rhetoric?" *Africa Report*, Apr. 1971, pp. 18–21; René Gauze, *The Politics of Congo-Brazzaville*, trans., ed., and supplemented by Virginia Thompson and Richard Adloff (Stanford: Hoover Institution Press, 1973), 226–27; Samuel Decalo, *Coups and Army Rule in Africa* (New Haven: Yale Univ. Press, 1976), 154.

army were found to be plotting against Ngouabi, and this provoked a reorganization of the army.[15] This left a heavily Lari and Vili gendarmerie, cohesive and well-trained. The gendarmes had been employed to arrest Ngouabi in 1968, and they were unreconciled to his assumption of power. Unreconstructed Youlouists, they had been placed under the command of a loyal army officer in 1969. But this was not enough to prevent their involvement in the Lari coup attempt of March 1970. This resulted in the dismantling of the gendarmerie and its integration into the regular army.[16] Finally, after the police (again, heavily composed of Lari) were implicated in yet another coup plot, their turn came: in 1973, the police force was dissolved, its duties assumed by the army, and its personnel only selectively reabsorbed.[17]

The Brazzaville regime thus dealt with its paramilitary enemies one at a time, in each case destroying structures outside the army and bringing their functions and some of their personnel under the aegis of the army or, rather, loyal units of the army, where they could be counterbalanced and controlled. Despite the fact that Northern officers were in a minority in the army, they were so placed as to be able to control the rest. They prevailed in the most effective fighting units, the paracommando battalion and the armored car company, both stationed near Brazzaville. Ngouabi's strategy was to gather the plethora of irregular forces established before he came to power within the structure of the regular army, in which his Mbochi and Kouyou followers occupied the most critical positions. His was the epitome of the balance-inside-the-army approach of coup prevention, utilizing loyal, homogeneous units within a most heterogeneous regular army.

Considering the ethnic structure of the armed forces inherited by Ngouabi, especially the strong initial position of the Bakongo, the strategy was remarkably successful. It is an ironic tribute to Ngouabi's success at coup-proofing that his enemies were eventually forced to turn to assassinating him. The assassination was not accompanied by a coup attempt. Ngouabi could be removed. His regime could not be.

Balance Outside the Army

The strategy of balance outside the regular army is, of course, likely whenever regime ethnic composition and officer corps composition are

15. Gauze, *The Politics of Congo-Brazzaville*, 173; Decalo, *Coups and Army Rule in Africa*, 159.
16. Decalo, *Coups and Army Rule in Africa*, 162–63.
17. Ibid., 167.

sharply divergent and vacancies in officers' billets in the regular army cannot readily be arranged. The strategy of balance-outside became more and more attractive in post-colonial states after officers from the former metropole had departed and regular army positions were all occupied. Such a strategy is especially congenial in Francophone countries and in traditional monarchies, for different reasons.

In former French colonies, military functions are generally not as centralized in the regular army as they are elsewhere. The gendarmerie or paramilitary forces have traditionally had more than a mere policing role, and in some cases have been stronger than the regular army. Different units may have varying ethnic composition, depending on their history, their prior relation to other forces, the role of technical skill and education in the units' missions, and the earlier intake of personnel into certain units to achieve ethnic balance or alleviate resentments. Of course, the ethnic differentiation of various units is not confined to Francophone countries.[18] But there differentiation is often coupled with the traditional dispersion of major internal security functions among several units.

Where such units exist, they are easily augmented and adapted to coup-prevention goals. When the Northerner, Hubert Maga, came to power in Benin in the early 1960s, he was confronted with an 1,800-man army led by Fon and, to a lesser extent, Yoruba officers. But he also had a 1,200-man gendarmerie, which he "packed with Baribas [from the North] who often regarded themselves as Maga's private militia."[19] Likewise, the sûreté and palace guard in the Ivory Coast were placed in the hands of Félix Houphouët-Boigny's own Baoulé, though the army was dominated by Northerners. A presidential guard was created after a coup attempt by ethnic enemies in 1963, and Houphouët was also able to mobilize a party militia, known colloquially as the "Baoulé warriors," in times of crisis.[20] Syria's Republican Companies, "for all intents and purposes another army . . . stationed near Damascus and equipped with

18. In 1969, for example, Chinese comprised half the officers of the Malaysian air force, Malays one-third. Chinese and Indians were also heavily represented in the technical services of the army, but the line units remained overwhelmingly Malay at all levels. Cynthia H. Enloe, "Civilian Control of the Military: Implications in the Plural Societies of Guyana and Malaysia," in Claude E. Welch, Jr., ed., Civilian Control of the Military (Albany: State Univ. of New York Press, 1976), 80, 97 n.30.

19. Samuel Decalo, "Regionalism, Politics, and the Military in Dahomey," Journal of Developing Areas 7 (Apr. 1973): 447–77, at 459.

20. Aristide R. Zolberg, "Political Development in the Ivory Coast Since Independence," in Philip Foster and Aristide R. Zolberg, eds., Ghana and the Ivory Coast (Chicago: Univ. of Chicago Press, 1971), 16–18; Legum, ed., Africa Contemporary Record, 1974–75, p. B687.

its own helicopters, planes, artillery and other modern materiel,"[21] were put under secure Alawi control. The same was true of the General Headquarters Guard units and the elite troops guarding Assad. In Niger, the Presidential Guard, composed of Tuareg, performed its appointed role and resisted, albeit unsuccessfully, the coup made by the regular army in 1974.[22] In all these cases, and in Guinea and Mali as well, the French tradition was conducive to building up, in effect, parallel armies to counterbalance the regular army.

In traditional monarchies, tribal levies or territorial units, ethnically kindred and loyal to the king, typically play a key role in counterbalancing the regular army. They become particularly important because, as we have seen, a modernized army usually draws upon advanced, educated ethnic groups to constitute its officer corps. These groups may be ideologically opposed to the monarchy, and are, more often than not, ethnically differentiated from the monarch. In Saudi Arabia, for instance, the army had great difficulty, as it developed in the 1950s, in finding qualified officer candidates among the king's Najdis, and so it turned for cadets to the more cosmopolitan Hijazis. Reliance on the Hijazis was necessary but dangerous for the king, and so the National Guard, composed of dependable Najdis, was refurbished and strengthened.[23] The king of Jordan had the same problem, exacerbated when he introduced Palestinian units into his armed forces. Having discovered his mistake, he leaned increasingly on the armored and Royal Guards Brigades, both comprised of southern East Bankers, ethnically loyal to the king.[24] King Idris of Libya used basically the same technique, but with less success. Besides favoring his own Cyrenaicans in the army, he bolstered his separate tribal forces and went out of the way to isolate his Eastern Force from contact with the regulars.[25] Equally unavailing were the efforts of Emperor Haile Selassie of Ethiopia, who kept the Shoan Province Territorial Army close to Addis Ababa. Like the territorials and

21. *Washington Post*, Apr. 4, 1976.
22. Legum, ed., *Africa Contemporary Record, 1974–75*, p. B724. Edward Luttwak, *Coup d'Etat: A Practical Handbook* (New York: Knopf, 1969), 93, suggests that paramilitary forces do not defend the regimes that create them against coupmakers. The Tuareg did fight; so did Nkrumah's President's Own Guard Regiment in 1966 and Mohammed Daoud's Republican Guard in Afghanistan in 1978. Moreover, once a coup is made, they may organize countercoups, as in Madagascar and the Congo Republic.
23. J. C. Hurewitz, *Middle East Politics: The Military Dimension* (New York: Praeger, 1969), chap. 13.
24. Ibid., 313, 320–23.
25. Ibid., 231–40; Ruth First, *Libya: The Elusive Revolution* (Baltimore: Penguin Books, 1974), 78–79, 89.

most of his generals, the emperor was a Shoan Amhara. Because traditional monarchies are often based in the less developed areas and ethnic
groups of a country, whereas officer recruitment is often based on education, monarchs, to have a hope of survival, must raise their own back-
woods, irregular forces.[26]

If the strategy of balance outside the regular forces is most natural to
Francophone and monarchical countries, it is not confined to them. Anglophone and elected regimes have borrowed the technique; in Sierra
Leone, such units far outnumber the regular army. The use of counter-
forces outside the regular army is by now virtually universal in Africa
and not uncommon in Asia.[27] Understandably so. The creation of new
units outside the regular armed forces provides greater flexibility for
rapid personnel changes than is usually available within the regular
army, where existing officers' positions are generally filled. That is why
Presidents Kenyatta and Nkrumah created the Kenya General Service
Unit and the Ghana President's Own Guard Regiment, respectively. No
regular units could have been packed with Kikuyu or Nzima so quickly
or completely. That is also why, before the Idi Amin coup, President
Obote established his own General Service Unit, as well as a paramilitary
Special Force, both of them overflowing with Acholi and Langi troops
and officers.[28] One of the first things Amin did after he seized power was
to eliminate these units. In the cases of Uganda and Ghana, it is quite
clear that the creation of separate units, outside the chain of command,
infuriated regular army officers.

What is attractive about such units to political leaders is exactly what
is provocative about them to military officers. They are so easily composed to replicate the ethnic composition of the regime because they are
wholly new or greatly expanded. To be completely reliable, they must be
placed outside the normal chain of command, and, as I have already
noted, this constitutes a grave breach of expectations regarding civil-
military relations. Such units therefore inevitably create frictions among

26. King Hassan of Morocco followed the rule, though he crossed ethnic lines to do it.
Fearing the anti-monarchical sentiments of urban Arabs, he built on the French preference
for Berbers in the officer corps. See Octave Marais, "The Political Evolution of the Berbers
in Independent Morocco," in Ernest Gellner and Charles Micaud, eds., *Arabs and Berbers:
From Tribe to Nation in North Africa* (Lexington, Mass.: Lexington Books, 1972), 277–
83.

27. See the list in Goldsworthy, "Civilian Control of the Military in Black Africa," 70–
71.

28. Decalo, *Coups and Army Rule in Africa*, 205, 207; A Correspondent, "Uganda
After the Coup," *Swiss Review of World Affairs* 20 (Mar. 1971): 9–10.

the services. If they are adequately manned, trained, and equipped to defeat a coup attempt, they are probably also so strong as to be regarded with great hostility by the army. If they are not, they are easily brushed aside or persuaded to stand aside in the event of a coup, as General Gowon's Nigerian Brigade of Guards, headed by a fellow Anga, was in 1975.

The effectiveness of a strategy of balance from without may turn in part on timing. Both Nkrumah and Obote, in his first regime, created their irregular forces after strong ethnic opposition had been manifested within the armed forces. In these tense circumstances, the new units were seen at once as a blatant intrusion into military affairs and a barefaced attempt to insure ethnic supremacy. They were a challenge that seemed to require an answer. Kenyatta, however, moved earlier, before Kenya's pronounced ethnic tensions had found expression in conspiracies among officers. If such units are to be utilized, it helps if there is a preexisting gendarmerie tradition or a practice of using tribal levies. Perhaps one reason the Philippine army was so tolerant of Ferdinand Marcos' pack-ing of the Philippine Constabulary with members of his own Ilocano ethnic group—some eighteen of twenty-two PC generals were reported to be Ilocano as of 1981[29]—is that the constabulary was a long-estab-lished parallel force. There was no question of creating a new, threaten-ing force and packing it ethnically all at once. In the absence of such a tradition, creating such units before ethno-military hostility has devel-oped may be the only way to prevent them from provoking the coup they are designed to avoid.

Another determinant of the effectiveness of balance-outside strategies would seem to be the precise configuration of the unit. One reason for the mixed record of balance-outside strategies employed by traditional monarchies is that they are likely to turn to tribal levies and territorial forces. Unless these are greatly upgraded to enhance firepower and mo-bility and positioned around the capital, they are not likely to be a credi-ble coup deterrent or, for that matter, counterforce when the coup comes. The same may be said for the popular militias that seem to be favored by regimes professing socialist ideology. Their creation builds up jealousy without necessarily increasing protection for the regime. Indeed, Guinea's militia, intended for coup prevention, actually partici-pated in the 1976 coup attempt. The army took great delight in the

29. *Far Eastern Economic Review* (Hong Kong), Jan. 30, 1981, p. 29.

ensuing purge. Elite, highly professional units on the model of the General Service Unit seem likely to be more effective and more reliable.

Even in the best of circumstances, however, the creation of, essentially, two armies is practically a guarantee that one of them will be hostile to the regime that succors the other. That is why strategies of balance from without tend to be accompanied or followed by reshuffling to gain control of the top levels of the regular army as well.

Foreign Forces

Where it exists, the neutrality of foreigners in internal conflicts or, even better, the positive commitment of foreign states to the existing regime commends foreign forces for coup-prevention functions.

Many Asian and African regimes, of course, relied on colonial officers long past the time required for local officers to gain the skills needed to replace them. Clearly, this was done to protect the regime internally. After a certain point, in most Anglophone countries, the political costs of continued dependence on foreign commanders exceeded the coup-proofing benefits, as local officers, resenting career blockages, brought pressure to bear for the indigenization of the coveted top posts. Military positions are, as I have said, a valued object. Even so, as late as 1983, Kenya's General Service Unit was commanded by a European. In some Francophone African countries, however, more than a few French officers stayed on, sometimes in the gendarmerie or *sûreté* rather than the regular army, where they would be more conspicuous. Foreigners fit naturally into balance-outside strategies. In the extreme case, of course, the foreigners drop from the sky to save or restore a favored regime from a coup, as the French did in Gabon in 1964.

The temptation to use alienage as a bar to conspiracy remains great, and ingenious political leaders have found functional equivalents to foreign commanders. Siad Barre chose as Somalia's army commander a member of the despised blacksmith clan.[30] A coup plot could scarcely form around a member of this group. The armed forces of Singapore have been commanded by an Indian. It is unlikely in the extreme that Chinese officers in predominantly Chinese Singapore would follow an Indian officer into a conspiracy against the regime.[31] Yet, overall, such devices are no longer major coup-proofing techniques.

30. Legum, ed., *Africa Contemporary Record, 1974–75*, pp. B266–67.
31. See T. J. S. George, *Lee Kuan Yew's Singapore* (London: André Deutsch, 1973), 204–05.

By and large, where foreigners are used, they are employed *en masse*. A number of palace guard units have been composed of significant numbers of foreign troops: Guineans and Palestinians in Sierra Leone, Cubans in Guinea, Congo (Brazzaville), and Angola, and Palestinians, Southern Sudanese, and Zaireans in Amin's Uganda.[32] These arrangements, however, depend on the vicissitudes of international relations, as some African leaders, relying on French troops for their survival, discovered too late. If the foreign troops are sent by a foreign state, their presence or commitment to the regime is not likely to last indefinitely— unless the sending state has an ulterior motive that carries its own dangers for the receiving regime.

The use of foreign mercenaries, not recruited on a state-to-state basis, is another matter. Appropriate mercenary support is more difficult to locate, but more reliable once obtained. The foreign troops are then utterly dependent on the regime's survival for their lives and livelihood. Idi Amin happened to be well placed to recruit foreigners. His own Kakwa group spills over into the Sudan and Zaire. After 1972, the Southern Sudan had a surplus of unemployed soldiers, ex-members of the Anyanya, rebels who had fought the Sudanese government. Eastern Zaire, too, had rebels for export, in this case ex-Simbas left over from the insurgency of the 1960s. The more amorphous ethnic category of Nubians also spans the Uganda-Sudan border. The core of the Nubian group was originally composed of soldiers recruited from the Sudan in the nineteenth century to fight with the British in Uganda.[33] In each instance, then, there was availability, a military background, and often some affinity with the Kakwa. Amin drew upon these resources in reconstructing his military apparatus, especially his key security units. Much of the killing in Amin's Uganda is reported to have been done by these groups of foreign soldiers, who numbered in the thousands. Together with several hundred Palestinians who formed Amin's bodyguard, these troops were the guarantors of his regime.[34]

32. Cox, *Civil-Military Relations in Sierra Leone*, 216–17; Christopher Clapham, "Sierra Leone: Civilian Rule and the New Republic," *The World Today* 28 (Feb. 1972): 90–91; *Washington Post*, Sept. 20, 1972; ibid., July 5, 1976; Legum, ed., *Africa Contemporary Record, 1974–75*, p. B319; *Africa Confidential*, Sept. 24, 1976, pp. 4–5; Colin Legum, ed., *Africa Contemporary Record, 1979–80* (New York: Africana, 1981), p. B632; Legum, ed., *Africa Contemporary Record, 1981–82* (New York: Africana, 1983), p. B356.

33. See Crawford Young, *The Politics of Cultural Pluralism* (Madison: Univ. of Wisconsin Press, 1976), 233.

34. David Martin, *General Amin* (London: Faber & Faber, 1974), 25, 45, 212, 224, 240; Ali A. Mazrui, *Soldiers and Kinsmen in Uganda: The Making of a Military Ethno-*

There are few regimes so well positioned to gain foreign support of this kind. The domestic equivalent of foreign troops is to utilize members of distant, peripheral groups within the country for coup-proofing missions. Nkrumah's use of Northerners who were largely uninvolved in Ghana's political struggles is one such example. But this particular technique is far less applicable now than it was during the colonial period. Fewer groups remain disinterested outsiders. Many such groups are now involved in calculating their own ethnic interests in the independent states, and some even ponder the possibility of secession.

Except on an idiosyncratic basis, resort to reliable aliens for coup-proofing missions is a less and less attractive option. Rare indeed is the regime that finds foreign troops adequate by themselves to insure its longevity.

Kinship Control

The ultimate compositional strategy is to trust no one but oneself. As this is impossible, the next best thing is to rely on relatives. In fact, compositional strategies run the gamut from utilizing regional groups, ethnic groups, subethnic groups, and actual kinsmen. Analytically, kinship control is not really a distinct method of coup prevention, but an extreme form of some of the other techniques. The use of relatives as military alter egos of the political leadership implies that no other preventive arrangements are fail-safe.

If the army itself is relied on for coup prevention, then that is where kinsmen are likely to be found—as, for example, in Guyana, where the army command was reshuffled in 1979 and a relative of the prime minister became commander.[35] Relatives are also likely to be found in command of regular army units assigned to the capital.[36]

Typically, however, more extensive use of kinship is made in balance-outside strategies. Brothers, cousins, or sons are placed in command of palace guards or paramilitary units. In Togo, Eyadéma's cousin was made director of the police academy, and his half-brother was put in charge of the presidential guard.[37] Hafez Assad's brother took command

cracy (Beverly Hills: Sage, 1975), 49; Decalo, *Coups and Army Rule in Africa,* 213; Legum, ed., *Africa Contemporary Record, 1973–74,* p. B297.

35. Percy C. Hintzen and Ralph R. Premdas, "Guyana: Coercion and Control in Political Change," *Journal of Interamerican Studies and World Affairs* 24 (Aug. 1982): 337–54, at 348.

36. In Togo, Eyadéma placed himself in command of the Lomé garrison. In Iraq, the Baghdad garrison was put under the command of a Takriti.

37. *Africa Confidential,* Sept. 8, 1982, p. 6.

of the parallel army known as the Syrian Republican Companies, his brother-in-law was made deputy commander, his nephew was given control of a 10,000-man bodyguard, and Assad, originally an air force officer, made himself commander of an elite paratroop force. In Iraq, Saddam Hussein appointed a cousin and two half-brothers to supervise internal security and intelligence units. During his first term, Obote's General Service Unit was commanded by his cousin, Akena Adoko. He drew its Langi personnel from his home district, presumably using his own relatives.[38] Obote's brother was carefully positioned in the security apparatus of the Ministry of Home Affairs.[39] When Siad Barre came to power in Somalia in 1969, he packed the new Supreme Revolutionary Council with his supporters. Among them were his nephew, commandant of the air force, and his son-in-law, director of the National Security Service. Already in control of the regular army, Siad unofficially assumed personal command of the police.

Nevertheless, the use of kinship ties need not be confined to either balance-inside or balance-outside strategies. Through the 1970s, President Marcos had been appointing Ilocanos, including several relatives, to some of the most important Philippine army commands.[40] Subsequently, relatives of Marcos and his wife were appointed to command all the likely counterforce groups: the Philippine Constabulary, the Integrated National Police, the Presidential Security Command, the National Intelligence and Security Authority, and the army reserve.[41] And Syria, always near the end of any ethnic spectrum, is extreme here as well: relatives, including five of Assad's brothers, were given high positions in the Ba'th Party, the army, and units outside the regular army.[42] These are good illustrations of the general shift from lighter to heavier strategies of coup-proofing that I mentioned earlier.

A functional equivalent of kinship is origin in the same village or region. Siaka Stevens, who relied increasingly on his family, also began to rely on his home area. Limba in the Internal Security Unit were recruited heavily from Kambia, Stevens' home district. In Togo, Eyadéma

38. Decalo, *Coups and Army Rule in Africa*, 207.
39. Martin, *General Amin*, 152.
40. Nena Vreeland et al., *Area Handbook for the Philippines*, 2d ed. (Washington, D.C.: Government Printing Office, 1976), 227; *Far Eastern Economic Review*, Jan. 7, 1977, p. 29.
41. *Far Eastern Economic Review*, Jan. 30, 1981, pp. 29–30.
42. Nikolaos Van Dam, *The Struggle for Power in Syria: Sectarianism, Regionalism and Tribalism in Politics, 1961–1978* (London: Croom Helm, 1979), 90–91.

drew on his home village of Pya for commanders of the gendarmerie and the security police, the so-called Research Brigade.[43] Like Eyadéma, Assad supplemented family ties with village ties. And virtually everything of importance in Iraq was put in the hands of personnel from Saddam Hussein's home village of Takrit. Given the frequent interchangeability of kinship and village ties in Asia and Africa,[44] for these purposes the two can be considered synonymous.

In the nature of things—even with a large family or a loyal home village—it seems obvious that the uses of kinship in coup-proofing are limited. Reliable as they may be, relatives cannot be everywhere. Kinship control seems especially useful in counterpoise strategies. If a regime is able to augment or create paramilitary units for coup-proofing purposes without provoking the regular army, then entrusting their command to a close relative will probably not be additionally provocative. On the other hand, to place relatives in important regular army commands, in defiance of seniority expectations, is an obvious irregularity, difficult for regular officers to overlook. The use of kinship may then be a sign of insecurity more than a guarantee of security.

THE EFFECTIVENESS OF COMPOSITIONAL STRATEGIES

Most compositional strategies of coup-proofing seem to carry high risks. The measures that promise the highest levels of protection from military intervention seem to increase ethnic grievances and raise the chances of other forms of violent attack against the regime and its rulers. Similarly, the most effective strategies are usually the hardest to implement. Each compositional device breaks the formal rules of civil-military relations; each constitutes a breach of military expectations of reciprocal civil-military noninterference. So tinkering with composition is inherently dangerous.

On all these grounds, the choice of techniques is difficult. Homogenization, for example, is preferable to the rivalries introduced by balance strategies. It is far better to control the regular army than to build up alternative forces able to fight it. As we have seen, regimes that are able to achieve ethnic congruence with their armed forces generally increase their immunity from coups. Even narrowly based attritional regimes seem to be in this position. But, short of upheaval, homogenization is

43. *Africa Confidential*, Sept. 8, 1982, p. 5.
44. See Chapter 2, note 22, above.

highly risky to attempt. Moreover, in a multiethnic setting, homogenization is a technique that entails exclusion. That it may prevent coups in ethnically divided societies does not mean that it forecloses other violent options, ranging from assassination to secession or invasion.

Comparable dilemmas attach to the other methods. Balance outside the regular army is administratively easy to arrange, since it can be done with wholly new units if necessary, but it is very risky to put into effect. On the other hand, balance inside the regular army is usually far more difficult to establish, but, once established, is a more effective method of coup-proofing. Foreign troops are often not difficult to obtain in the first instance, but unreliable over the long term. More dependable are foreign troops not recruited on a state-to-state basis, but the ability of regimes to locate and employ such troops is fortuitous. For every regime that has employed a compositional strategy effectively, there is another that has succumbed to a coup despite—and sometimes partly on account of—its use of such techniques.

It seems very clear that the techniques which served the colonial powers so well are no longer fail-safe. Of course, part of the explanation rests with the dramatically different expectations of ethnic groups in the postcolonial period. Ethnic competition is sharper, and it spreads more rapidly to officers than it once did. It is harder, too, to find a nucleus of foreign, and therefore truly uninvolved, troops to post far from their homes. In this respect, the existence of multi-territory colonial empires facilitated military control by making long-distance troop deployment possible. Part of the difference also relates to the frailty of the postcolonial regimes. The colonial power was vulnerable to mutiny and revolt, not to the *coup d'état*. The seizure of the capital by rebellious troops did not mean the seizure of the colony, if only because the colonialists had reserves available inside and outside the colony with which to retake the capital. In any case, the colony was ultimately ruled, not from its capital, but from the metropole. Today this situation is reversed. Most regimes can cope with mutinies and revolts, but if rulers lose their capital, their regime is at an end. Ironically, colonial measures devised mainly to avert uprisings are sometimes too cumbersome for the lesser—but more lethal—event, the coup.

Despite the mixed record of compositional strategies, a Machiavelli attuned to ethnic concerns might have a few recommendations for his prince. First of all, it is preferable to control the regular army, if that is possible, than to control countervailing paramilitary forces. Whereas gaining control of the army may pose grave but transient dangers, the existence of the paramilitary forces may constitute a continuing irritant to the regulars, especially in an environment of budgetary scarcity. Second, if control over the regular army is impossible to establish, the use of paramilitary forces is much easier if there is some tradition that supports the use of such forces for internal security purposes. Otherwise, the breach of custom, coupled with the ethnic character of the preventive purpose, creates risks that may be greater than the protection it affords. Third, if something irregular must be done, it should probably be done with the irregular forces, so that the irregularity is kept at a distance from the regular officers. Fourth, whatever control strategy is adopted, it must be regarded as axiomatic that provocation, as well as prevention, increases with the number and severity of the measures taken to avert coups. In the middle range of measures, provocation probably outruns the additional increments of protection.

The evidence on the effectiveness of alternative compositional strategies is surely not all in, but what evidence there is seems to favor the extremes—delicacy, on the one hand, thoroughness, on the other—and to discredit temporizing. The attritional regimes are secure from coups because of their ruthlessness. A regime like that of Ahmadou Ahidjo in Cameroon, however, was long able to maintain its authority in the face of split domination, one suspects, because it proceeded gingerly. The army, heavily Ewondo, was commanded by an Ewondo. The Ewondo are concentrated in the southeast of the country. The civilian regime, by contrast, had a distinctly Northern, Muslim cast. The defense portfolio was consistently assigned to a Northerner, often a man from the same district as Ahidjo. Apparently, however, Ahidjo did nothing drastic, save keep a close watch on the armed forces and pay careful attention to the postings of officers. This circumspection probably had a good deal to do with his survival for two decades. Certainly, as I have argued, Kenyatta's early but careful manipulation of military composition in Kenya and Ngouabi's step-by-step but decisive maneuvers in Congo (Brazzaville) suggest that timing and discretion are important. If the steps are gradual, so that no single increment is enough to constitute a provocation but the totality of steps establishes control, that is ideal from the standpoint of the regime. This also explains why Francophone and monarchical states have an advantage in using balance-outside strategies. Not only are the units already in place, but their use for internal security tends to be customary and accepted; their manipulation appears to be only a minor irregularity.

From this perspective, the fruitless machinations of Obote and Nkrumah are more easily understood. Neither was really willing to purge his army in the ruthless way that Jordan's King Hussein was willing to do, for example, but both were willing to sanction blatant breaches of civil-military boundaries. Likewise, the half-measures adopted by Madagascar's military rulers, which soon redounded to their disadvantage, contrast sharply with Ngouabi's prudent blend of watchful waiting alternating with a willingness to dissolve well-established but untrustworthy units once they tipped their hands.

This much is clear: the probable effectiveness of a given strategy may be as much a function of the caution or thoroughness with which it is implemented as a function of its inherent risks and benefits. Light strategies are not discredited. Unless the militarization of ethnic conflict has already proceeded far, placing a few foreigners or close relatives in key command and staff positions in already constituted units may be easier and less risky than reconstituting the officer corps or creating and arming new units. Once ethnic conflict pervades civil-military and intramilitary relations, then it is not clear that any essentially reactive compositional strategy will be effective, except to raise the stakes of ethno-military involvement and to send endangered officers scurrying for their own protection, thus increasing the chances of a preemptive coup.

NON-COMPOSITIONAL STRATEGIES

If compositional strategies are of such problematic effectiveness, why are they so pervasively employed? Several explanations can be advanced for the prevalence of the compositional approach to coup prevention in ethnically divided states.

To begin with, there are the apprehensions and discomfort aroused by split domination or, in less extreme form, by the differential ethnic composition of various bodies influential in the state. All else being equal, this produces an impetus to reconcile composition or at least insure that those bodies are under control. Then, too, the felt danger from the armed forces usually entails an element of urgency, for the military may strike without warning. This biases protective measures in favor of those that are most direct, immediate, and responsive to the specific character of the threat. After all, if the effectiveness of manipulating composition is uncertain, the effectiveness of more general policies to abate underlying ethnic grievances appears even more doubtful. Even if successful, the benign effects of general policies will probably not be felt in the short term, when the danger is presented. By the time they are felt, the coup may already have occurred.

The character of non-compositional strategies that might be pursued also has a bearing on this question. As we shall see shortly, many of these measures are actually nonmeasures. They largely involve adhering to counsels of restraint, avoiding actions likely to give offense to the military. Not only are such negative actions difficult for analysts to detect—hence the emphasis in all policy studies on what is done, rather than what is not done—but they are also difficult courses for policymakers to adopt. It is often easier to start something than to stop something, and it is tempting, when confronted with a genuine danger, to take some action, rather than merely to avoid action that may increase the danger. Few are the politicians who will sit supine when they face a threat to their office.

There is another, more general reason for the overwhelming emphasis on composition. It is a reason that also underlies the important place occupied by ethnic conflict in the public life of most post-colonial states. Coup-proofing by tinkering with the composition of the armed forces exemplifies the extent to which these states are governed by reference to the identity of persons rather than the impersonal occupation of roles or the inexorable workings of institutions. To be sure, the governments of all countries embody a mix of such considerations; the differences are matters of degree. Compositional strategies reflect the assumption that, whatever the institutional arrangements, a person's ethnic identity can easily undermine his established official loyalty. The post-colonial experience contains much evidence to support the assumption.

For all these reasons, compositional strategies dwarf all others. Still, it remains possible to speculate in an informed way on the probable consequences of coup-proofing measures that do not rest mainly on manipulating the composition of the armed forces.

Obviously, the most important of these, and ultimately the most effective, is the use of political ingenuity to prevent ethnic conflict from reaching the point at which it spills across civil-military boundaries. These measures are difficult to devise, difficult to implement, and difficult to control once implemented. The ethno-military position of some regimes, however, seems to afford them relatively little choice. If it is not possible to gain control of an ethnically differentiated regular army and if the use of paramilitary forces for prevention tasks is inadvisable, civilian regimes tend to be propelled toward policies of ethnic accommodation. These policies are intended to reduce the chance of military intervention, just as they are intended to reduce ethnic conflict in general. The military situation may have been one of the motive forces for Ahidjo's efforts to achieve at least a semblance of balanced representation in the political life and public institutions of Cameroon, despite the generally Northern slant of his regime. No doubt, Bamiléké, Ewondo, and Bassa felt discontented, but they may simultaneously have wondered whether the risks of conspiring against Ahidjo were outweighed by the improvement that was anticipated to result from a successful conspiracy. When power finally passed from Ahidjo to a Southern-dominated regime, it did so gradually, through civilian institutions, in 1982–83.[45]

The fear of ethno-military intervention may thus be a motive for accommodationist policies. But the nature of such policies is not distinctively military. Consequently, consideration of these is best left for separate, full-scale treatment in Part Five. More directly relevant to the armed forces are policies designed to reassure officers about their own security, afford them job satisfaction, or avoid actions that provoke conspiracies and cement coup coalitions.

At this level of coup-prevention, some pieces of conventional wisdom seem to hold up fairly well. Keeping the army busy fighting real enemies appears useful. The Malaysian, Cameroonian, and Filipino armed forces all had to combat insurgencies, and all three, despite lapses, have been less involved in ethnic politics than armies elsewhere. Foreign adventures, on the other hand, are likely to be seen as just that—adventures—which is how Nkrumah's efforts to play a major role in Zaire in the early 1960s were regarded by his leading officers.[46] Similarly, the frequent deployment of armed forces in episodic civil disorders poses, as we have seen, dangers that the military will attribute the disorders to the regime that provoked them, will resent being called to make sacrifices to bail out the politicians, and will glimpse the political process at unflatteringly close range. Finally, as retrieval coups suggest, some kinds of military intervention are dependent on the formation of intramilitary coalitions

45. There was a coup attempt in 1984. Significantly, the officers involved consisted of Northern remnants of Ahidjo's regime, conspiring against a successor regime that had become heavily slanted toward the South.
46. First, *Power in Africa*, 194.

across ethnic lines. Governments that do battle on more than one sensitive political front simultaneously invite the formation of such coalitions; regimes that restrain their impulse in this direction enhance their own safety.

Regimes that play favorites within the officer corps, meddle with the chain of command, involve the army repeatedly in the suppression of strikes, riots, and protests with a political flavor, or use the army for what appear to be the fanciful ends of politicians—such regimes risk the involvement of the armed forces in civilian ethnic politics. These actions contribute to the breakdown of civil-military boundaries. The rigorous maintenance of civil-military boundaries is the best general guarantee against ethnically motivated military intervention.

Here, then, is the dilemma of coup-proofing. The compositional and non-compositional strategies are at odds. Compositional strategies all involve breaching civil-military boundaries in order to inculcate loyalty to leaders of the regime, activating the ethnic ties of officers and indeed relying on them, and interfering in matters of military administration to deploy favorably those with affinity for the regime. These, I have argued, are the kinds of action that foster military involvement in ethnic politics. They are undertaken, despite their attendant risks, because boundaries are already permeable, because the ethnic loyalties of officers are not compartmentalized to begin with, and because the army may already have been employed to suit civilian political purposes. Yet there is no blinking the fact that the benefits of regime restraint in the pursuance of political goals—restraint in the service of preserving boundaries, keeping ethnic ties quiescent, and minimizing civilian interference in the military sphere—are readily undone once compositional measures are adopted. A regime cannot meddle with the ethnic composition of its armed forces and hope to salvage their neutrality at the same time.

PART FIVE

Strategies of Conflict Reduction

CHAPTER FOURTEEN

Ethnic Policy:
The Constraints and
the Opportunities

When the Japanese hurriedly evacuated Christmas Island, south of Java, in 1945, they left some small arms behind. The Malays and Chinese who inhabit the island had had enough of fighting, and it is said that they arranged for the Chinese to keep the rifles and the Malays to keep the bolts. The Malays, on the other hand, were to keep the pistols but give the magazines to the Chinese. By these devices a bloodbath was averted.

The tale, perhaps apocryphal, is instructive. It underscores how dangerous the islanders believed ethnic conflict to be. Good will alone, they knew, would not suffice to cope with ethnic conflict, for it is the product of forces independent of individual good will. Deliberate measures were required. The Christmas Islanders seized on a ripe moment to consummate an agreement.

The action the Christmas Islanders took—separating rifles from bolts and pistols from magazines—illustrates the important role that reciprocal concessions can play in conflict reduction even when the parties share little beyond a desire to reduce conflict. Their agreement also shows that useful results can be wrought by structural half-measures that do not reach down to the deep sources of conflict but nevertheless may affect conflict behavior by changing the resources available to, and the calculations made by, the parties.

Compared to the modern state, Christmas Island was a rather simple society. In most places, the regulation of weapons alone will not be enough to have a measurable impact on ethnic conflict. But reciprocal concessions at strategic moments, concessions motivated by fear rather than reflecting deeper consensus—these constitute an approach that has potential applicability far beyond a single speck in the Indian Ocean.

What the Christmas Islanders sensed is that it is not necessary to resolve ethnic conflict in order to do something about it.

OBSTACLES TO INNOVATION

A cardinal assumption of this study has been that efforts to ameliorate ethnic conflict must be preceded by an understanding of the sources and patterns of that conflict. Altogether too many policy prescriptions for ethnic harmony have been dispensed without benefit of careful diagnosis. Accordingly, the evaluation of ameliorative techniques and policies comes last.

To follow this order is to emphasize the constraints on policy innovation, for it is to see in advance just how intractable a force ethnicity can be. The evidence suggests that serious ethnic conflicts are likely to be resistant to sweeping policy change. It is worthwhile recapitulating some of the major obstacles to accommodation.

To begin with, it is necessary for observers to avoid projecting their own good intentions onto policymakers. Not all leaders in ethnically divided states want to promote accommodation. Policymakers are participants in their societies. As such, they may entertain hostile feelings toward members of other groups. If not, they may still have a view of intergroup relations that sees ethnic conflict as necessary to advancement of the interests of their group. Even if political leaders do not hold such views, they may nonetheless benefit, politically or materially, from continuation of the conflict and be loath to pursue policies of amelioration.[1]

Whatever the personal beliefs of policymakers, their hands may be tied by the beliefs and interests of others: group members, voters, party supporters and colleagues, and bureaucrats, all of whom may have their own reasons for pursuing the conflict. Above all, in civilian regimes, the party system and the search for competitive advantage in it constrain accommodative policies. One only needs to be reminded of the fate of conciliatory efforts undertaken by top leaders and undermined by party competitors and lesser leaders—the Bandaranaike-Chelvanayakam Pact in Sri Lanka is a good example—to recognize that more is involved in the process of accommodation than the wishes of those in positions of

---

1. See, e.g., Myron Weiner, "Traditional Role Performance and the Development of Modern Political Parties: The Indian Case," *Journal of Politics* 26 (Nov. 1964): 830–49, at 841–42, explaining that Congress Party mediators proved unsuccessful at mediating an interethnic dispute because no one was neutral—like everyone else, the usual mediators were "a party" to the dispute.

formal authority. Although some form of regularized interethnic bargaining may be essential, this may require precisely the kind of pragmatism that is lacking among ethnic groups that see their vital interests threatened by other groups. From the perspective of a group member, multiethnic bargaining may itself be illegitimate, a form of appeasement or dealing with the Devil. This kind of bargaining requires deference from group members, which may make the possibility of accommodation peculiarly dependent on the internal social structure of the particular ethnic groups involved.

Even if the leadership is committed to accommodation, and party structure and ethnic ideology permit it, the execution is never easy. The ethnic division of labor, and more general cultural differences as well, imply divergent principles of stratification: these tend to produce different types of elites among various ethnic groups. The leadership of one may be composed predominantly of university-educated professionals, while leadership in another may be confided to traditionally oriented aristocrats. This was the situation in Nigeria, where the Hausa-Fulani aristocracy led Northern parties, whereas the Ibo, lacking an aristocracy, relied on Western-educated elites.[2] In Malaysia, the business class, later joined by university-educated professionals, led Chinese parties, while Malay parties were initially led by aristocrats, civil servants, and schoolteachers. Good intentions will not necessarily be enough to establish points of contact and sympathy among elites whose backgrounds do not mesh.

Leadership recruitment aside, cultural differences affect the relations of elites even as they strive for accommodation, as our previous discussion of permanent coalitions makes clear. Notions of propriety in inter-

---

2. Hugh H. Smythe and Mabel M. Smythe, *The New Nigerian Elite* (Stanford: Stanford Univ. Press, 1960), 39–41. In Lower Simalungun in Sumatra, the North Tapanuli Batak threw up civil servants, Christian ministers, and other educated leaders; South Tapanuli Batak (Muslims) threw up Islamic teachers and functionaries, traders, and civil servants; the uneducated Javanese relied on South Tapanuli religious teachers; the Simalungun Batak turned to its traditional aristocracy. R. William Liddle, "Ethnicity and Political Organization: Three East Sumatran Cases," in Claire Holt, ed., *Culture and Politics in Indonesia* (Ithaca: Cornell Univ. Press, 1972), 138–39. In Fiji, trade union leaders have provided most of the leadership for the Indian community, while Fijian leadership has been drawn mainly from traditional chiefs, the latter often hostile to Indian-led strikes of cane-farmers. Adrian C. Mayer, *Indians in Fiji* (London: Oxford Univ. Press, 1963), 108–20. And in India, it has been suggested, the departure of the Muslim leader M. A. Jinnah from the Congress was attributable to his distaste for what he saw as Gandhi's Hindu revivalism, compared to G. K. Gokhale's earlier, more comfortable liberalism. Penderel Moon, *Divide and Quit* (Berkeley and Los Angeles: Univ. of California Press, 1962), 270.

personal relations, of directness and indirectness in negotiation, of cogent argument, and of appropriate solutions may all diverge.[3] The nature of divisive issues also limits the possibility of accommodation. Since group prestige or well-being is relative, many claims will be zero-sum and therefore not susceptible to a strategy of enhancing everyone's rewards. The psychological sources of conflict do not readily lend themselves to modification by the manipulation of material benefits that is so often the stuff of modern policymaking. For similar reasons, symbolic demands seem to be less compromisable than claims that can be quantified. It may be possible to specify the purposes for which a language may be used, but how does a political system cope with a demand for it to "Glorify the National Language!" when that language is the language of only one of the groups in conflict? "Glorification," as I indicated in Chapter 5, would seem to be an indivisible objective.

The whole structure of ethnic politics conspires to make the problem of conflict intractable. But it is not absolutely so. There are, as I shall show, certain times and conditions that are more propitious for policy intervention than others. Still, the obstacles are formidable enough to behoove anyone who is serious about reducing ethnic conflict to consider the full range of reasonable possibilities. This includes those advanced by theorists, as well as those implemented by practitioners.

PERSPECTIVES ON ETHNIC ACCOMMODATION

The problems of "national integration" and "nation-building" began to occupy writers on the new states even before independence.[4] Yet national

3. In a series of conversations with former Quebec cabinet ministers and other political leaders, in Montreal in 1980, it was made clear to me that Francophones and Anglophones had rather different ideas of how to conduct public business; the differences extended to formality of agenda, approaches to achieving agreement, and to some extent "Cartesian" versus "pragmatic" styles of thought.

4. See, e.g., Marjorie Nicholson, *Self-Government and the Communal Problem* (London: Fabian Society and Victor Gollancz, 1948); Karl W. Deutsch, *Nationalism and Social Communication* (Cambridge: M.I.T. Press, 1953); Karl W. Deutsch and William J. Foltz, eds., *Nation-Building* (New York: Atherton Press, 1963); James S. Coleman and Carl G. Rosberg, Jr., eds., *Political Parties and National Integration in Tropical Africa* (Berkeley and Los Angeles: Univ. of California Press, 1964); Philip E. Jacob and James V. Toscano, eds., *The Integration of Political Communities* (Philadelphia and New York: J. B. Lippincott, 1964); J. A. Laponce, "Political Community, Legitimacy and Discrimination," *British Journal of Political Science* 4 (Apr. 1974): 121–37, esp. 134–35. Cf. Charles Tilly, ed., *The Formation of National States in Western Europe* (Princeton: Princeton Univ. Press, 1975).

integration in the sense of this literature is as elusive a goal now as it was at the outset: few, if any, nations have been built, though a number have been repaired. The literature, based largely on the historical experience of certain European countries and colored by optimistic interpretations of the nationalist significance of anti-colonial movements,[5] was part of a general and hopeful fascination with prospects for large-scale change in Asia and Africa. Although the literature was not uniform, it tended to postulate, if not genuine assimilation, at least the growth of interethnic nationalism, conceived in terms of "mutual interests" and "common purposes."[6] At bottom, integration was "dispositional,"[7] a matter of sentiments of community and loyalty to the state. Since nation-building embodied the learning of new sentiments and loyalties, the main paradigms of this line of thought were derived from learning theory.[8]

It was a line of thought unabashedly maximalist in its objectives; it aimed too high. It inquired into the processes by which existing habits might change, but did not ask whether it might be possible to maintain some form of political community even if those habits did not change. It had no answer when events such as the Nigerian civil war made ethnic loyalties seem far more persistent and dangerous than they once did.

Politicians also entertained hopes of attaining nationhood quickly in ethnically divided societies. The stroke-of-the-pen or crack-of-the-whip measures they used proved not only ineffective but counterproductive, tending to exacerbate what they sought to eradicate. We have already seen that several groups that underwent cultural revivals in order to thwart tendencies to assimilation also became strongly separatist, and conscious policies of assimilation have frequently provoked the same response, in the Sudan, Burma, and Iraq, for example. If indeed ethnicity and ethnic organizations provide security to groups in an uncertain en-

5. Hence, it frequently cast the problem of national integration in terms of an elite-mass gap, rather than in terms of differences between whole communities. See, e.g., Leonard Binder, "National Integration and Political Development," *American Political Science Review* 58 (Sept. 1964): 622–31; William J. Foltz, "Building the Newest Nations: Short-Run Strategies and Long-Run Problems," in Deutsch and Foltz, eds., *Nation-Building*, 118–19.

6. Philip E. Jacob and Henry Teune, "The Integrative Process: Guidelines for Analysis of the Bases of Political Community," in Jacob and Toscano, eds., *The Integration of Political Communities*, 5–6.

7. Ibid., 9–10.

8. The most explicit statement of this linkage is Henry Teune, "The Learning of Integrative Habits," in ibid., 247–82, but the relationship between transaction flows and the learning of new habits also pervades Karl Deutsch's work. See, e.g., Deutsch, "Communication Theory and Political Integration," in ibid., 46–74.

vironment, then attempts to replace or outlaw them may have the effect of increasing insecurity. The measures taken against ethnic organizations by regimes such as Nkrumah's in Ghana and Obote's in Uganda were counterproductive in precisely this sense.

The vision of a massive shift of loyalties from the ascriptive group to the state nonetheless continues to exert a powerful pull. It is thus suggested for Cyprus that a new elite should emerge, "freed from the slogans and rhetoric of the past, an elite which will stake its claims to power and reputation on interethnic cooperation, not on rivalry," and for Lebanon that a new "legitimate Lebanese political system be built" on institutions "both effective and respected" and on a "new tacit consensus on the meaning of Lebanese national identity . . . ."[9] If countries so divided could indeed produce such an elite, such a system, or such a consensus, they would not have the problems that they have. Such characteristics might appear as the *effects* of accommodation somewhere down the line, but they are not measures that can be adopted to *cause* ethnic accommodation to occur. States like Cyprus and Lebanon cannot hope just now for beautiful architecture. They will have to settle for sound engineering.

Among the engineers are theorists of "consociational democracy," "conflict regulation," or "conflict management."[10] As the pervasive importance of ethnic conflict and the deficiencies of maximalist conceptions of integration came to be recognized, a fork appeared in the intellectual road, with some writers turning primarily to the study of ethnic conflict[11] and others to the analysis of measures to alleviate it. Divorcing

9. Kyriacos C. Markides, "Ethnicity, Power Politics and the Cyprus Tragedy" (unpublished paper presented at the 1978 annual meeting of the International Studies Association), 22; Michael C. Hudson, *The Precarious Republic Revisited: Reflections on the Collapse of Pluralist Politics in Lebanon* (Washington, D.C.: Georgetown Univ. Center for Contemporary Arab Studies, Seminar Paper no. 2, 1977), 23. As we shall see later, Hudson's careful analysis of the Lebanese system points in a quite different direction.

10. Arend Lijphart, *Democracy in Plural Societies* (New Haven: Yale Univ. Press, 1977); Lijphart, "Consociational Democracy," *World Politics* 21 (Jan. 1969): 207–25; Lijphart, "Typologies of Democratic Systems," *Comparative Political Studies* 1 (Apr. 1968): 3–44; Kenneth D. McRae, ed., *Consociational Democracy: Political Accommodation in Segmented Societies* (Toronto: McClelland & Stewart, 1974); Hans Daalder, "The Consociational Democracy Theme," *World Politics* 26 (July 1974): 604–21.

11. Notably, Crawford Young, *The Politics of Cultural Pluralism* (Madison: Univ. of Wisconsin Press, 1976); Cynthia H. Enloe, *Ethnic Conflict and Political Development* (Boston: Little, Brown, 1973); Alvin Rabushka and Kenneth A. Shepsle, *Politics in Plural Societies: A Theory of Democratic Instability* (Columbus, Ohio: Charles E. Merrill, 1972). Interestingly enough, none of the theorists of ethnic conflict reviewed in Chapter 3 has advanced an explicit theory of ethnic accommodation.

as it did conflict from accommodation, this separation was not an alto-gether fortunate development for the theory of conflict reduction.[12]

Theories of consociationalism or conflict regulation diverge in several important respects from the earlier maximalist theories.[13] They are far more modest about goals. They assume that it is necessary for ethnically divided states to live with ethnic cleavages rather than wish them away. They argue that efforts to contain conflict must begin at the top. Conse-quently, they assume that the agreement of group leaders is an important step toward accommodation, especially because the habits, sentiments, and loyalties of followers are difficult to alter in the short run. The thrust of these theories is that leaders need not wait for inexorable social pro-cesses to do their work, but can have an impact on conflict despite hostile attitudes. These views are premised, not on a hopeful image of some future state, but on the actual experience of certain divided societies. That experience has also made these theorists properly skeptical of the claim that ethnic conflict makes democracy impossible, a claim too read-ily accepted by some of the proponents of nation-building. And, finally, unlike theories of national integration, which emphasized informal so-cial processes to the near-exclusion of formal arrangements, theories of consociation and conflict regulation tend to accord considerable weight to formal institutions, such as federalism or proportional representation. In all of these ways, they are a refreshingly realistic counterpoint to the earlier theories. If they fall short, they are at least pointed in the right direction.

The consociational and conflict management writers all identify promising techniques to deal with ethnic and, in some cases, other forms of severe conflict. There are differences among them, but also much overlap. Arend Lijphart identifies four defining characteristics of conso-ciational democracy: (1) "grand coalition" of all ethnic groups; (2) mu-tual veto in decision-making; (3) ethnic proportionality in the allocation of certain opportunities and offices; and (4) ethnic autonomy, often ex-

12. See the interesting remarks of Maurice Pinard, "The Moderation and Regulation of Communal Conflicts: A Critical Review of Current Theories" (unpublished paper pre-sented at a workshop of the European Consortium for Political Research and the Canadian Political Science Association, Louvain, Belgium, Apr. 8–14, 1976), 34–35.

13. The statements in this paragraph refer to the general thrust of these theories and not to the arguments of any individual proponent of them. Compare, e.g., the position of Milton J. Esman, "The Management of Communal Conflict," *Public Policy* 21 (Winter 1973): 49–78, at 72–75, with that of Eric A. Nordlinger, *Conflict Regulation in Divided Societies* (Cambridge: Harvard Univ. Center for International Affairs, Occasional Paper no. 29, 1972), 73–87.

pressed in federalism.[14] A key element in all of these is the need to mitigate the unfortunate effects of majority rule in ethnically divided societies. A recurring theme in Lijphart's advocacy of consociationalism is the
unsuitability for plural societies of "adversary," Anglo-American democratic institutions. Something of the same spirit pervades Eric A. Nordlinger's attempt to enumerate the six "successful" conflict regulating
practices: (1) stable coalition; (2) proportionality; (3) mutual veto; (4)
"depoliticization," that is, agreement to keep government out of the
most contentious issues or prevent their public discussion; (5) compromise, either on particular issues or on a package of issues; (6) concessions, which differ from compromise in that they are not reciprocated.[15]
Milton J. Esman categorizes four "regime objectives." Some of these,
such as "institutionalized dominance," might not qualify as conflict
managing, and others, such as "induced assimilation" or "syncretic integration," he finds, not surprisingly, to be of dubious utility. This leaves
"balanced pluralism," which is then decomposed into (1) proportionality; (2) territorial autonomy, including federalism; and (3) legal-cultural
autonomy.[16] No two lists are identical, but the resemblances are
striking.[17]

Some of the differences in the lists stem from the different scope and
approach employed. Esman's first cut at inclusion contains no requirement of success; therefore, the scope of what he includes is broader.
Nordlinger includes only devices he judges successful; therefore, he
omits federalism, which he regards as more harmful than helpful. With
this judgment, both Lijphart and Esman disagree.[18]

This example brings to the surface a difficulty with consociational
and conflict-managerial theories as policy analysis: inadequate specification of consequences. Lijphart is aiming at stable democracy: his consistently employed criterion for evaluation is whether something proved
"workable" or "successful" or whether the arrangement "broke down"

14. Lijphart, *Democracy in Plural Societies*, 25–44.
15. Nordlinger, *Conflict Regulation in Divided Societies*, 21–31.
16. Esman, "The Management of Communal Conflict," 60–68.
17. For additional statements, see Robert A. Dahl, *Polyarchy* (New Haven: Yale Univ.
Press, 1971), 114–21; Gerhard Lehmbruch, "A Non-Competitive Pattern of Conflict Management in Liberal Democracies: The Case of Switzerland, Austria and Lebanon," in
McRae, ed., *Consociational Democracy*, 90–97. Cf. John E. Schwarz, "Maintaining Coalitions: An Analysis of the EEC with Supporting Evidence from the Austrian Grand
Coalition and the CDU/CSU," in Sven Groennings, E. W. Kelley, and Michael Leiserson,
eds., *The Study of Coalition Behavior* (New York: Holt, Rinehart & Winston, 1970), 238.
18. Esman, "The Management of Communal Conflict," 64; Nordlinger, *Conflict Regulation in Divided Societies*, 104–110; Lijphart, *Democracy in Plural Societies*, 42–44.

or "fell apart."[19] Nordlinger defines conflict regulation as the "absence of widespread violence and government repression";[20] he judges degrees of "success" in achieving this. Esman describes the "main purposes" of conflict management as "the authoritative allocation of scarce resources and opportunities among competing communal actors"—which may unnecessarily import a potential *technique* of conflict management into its definition—as well as "the prevention or control of overt hostility and violence. A secondary purpose may be to reduce the long-range political salience of communal solidarities."[21] He, too, then makes broad judgments about "effective" or "successful" control or management.[22] A given device, then, may make things better, worse, or the same.

In all of this, there is little recognition that any policy or technique may have an array of consequences—some desired, some undesired, some intended, some unintended—or that a given measure may have varying or opposite consequences under varying environmental conditions, and there is nothing whatever about a phenomenon endemic to policy and policy analysis: the second-order consequences that all policies tend to have. This is by no means to impugn the achievement of these macro-level statements. It is rather to call attention to a feature they have in common: a circumscribed view of consequences that limits their utility for policymakers.

There is another problem of cause and effect that is most serious with those theories that generalize from European models to Asian and African conflict conditions. Lijphart has made the case for this most strongly, noting that Switzerland, Austria, Belgium, and the Netherlands have attained democracy and stability in spite of considerable heterogeneity. Their success he attributes to consociation, "cooperation by the leaders of the different groups which transcends the segmental and subcultural cleavages,"[23] and he advocates the utility of this model for developing countries.

As Val R. Lorwin has cautioned, the "segmented pluralism" of the smaller European democracies differs significantly from politics based on the more rigid "cleavages of caste, communalism, race, or even lan-

19. See, e.g., Lijphart, *Democracy in Plural Societies*, 150, 152, 192, 237–38.
20. Nordlinger, *Conflict Regulation in Divided Societies*, 11.
21. Esman, "The Management of Communal Conflict," 55.
22. See, e.g., ibid., 64, 75.
23. Lijphart, *Democracy in Plural Societies*, 16. Lijphart is keenly sensitive to issues surrounding the applicability of European models to Asian and African conflicts. See ibid., 21–24, 223–38.

guage."[24] Lorwin rightly emphasizes that the "spiritual families" into which these European polities are divided are not as airtight as ascriptive groups are. There are other important differences as well; these we have examined in Chapter 1. Even where differences are ascriptive, as between language groups in Belgium and Switzerland, the main political parties are not organized along ethnic lines, and ethnic differences alternate and compete for attention with class, religious, and (in Switzerland) cantonal differences. Hostility toward members of other groups is less intense than in the severely divided societies of Asia and Africa. There are supra-segmental sentiments that tie group members to the Swiss or the Dutch nation in a way that group members are not tied to an inclusive conception of the Lebanese, Malaysian, or Ugandan nation. The European conflicts are thus less ascriptive in character, less severe in intensity, less exclusive in their command of the loyalty of participants, and less preemptive of other forms of conflict.

The difficulty is in ascertaining whether the moderation and fluidity that characterize the European cleavages have been produced by consociational arrangements or whether, on the contrary, the relatively low intensity and fluidity of the European conflicts are what make consociational relationships possible. Which, in other words, is the dependent and which the independent variable?

In the post–World War II period, particularly in Austria and the Netherlands, there has been a discernible decline in segmental antipathies.[25] Although Lijphart and others do not claim that consociational practices can affect deeply held attitudes, it is possible that such practices have helped soften hostility. Even if so, the problem of causality is not resolved, because it is reasonable to assume that political arrangements made possible by a moderate level of conflict can operate in turn to moderate the conflict even further. So long as it is plausible that the level and character of the European conflicts were such as to facilitate the emergence of consociational practices, there is a circularity of cause and

24. "Segmented Pluralism: Ideological Cleavages and Political Cohesion in the Smaller European Democracies," in McRae, ed., Consociational Democracy, 35.
25. See William T. Bluhm, Building an Austrian Nation (New Haven: Yale Univ. Press, 1973), chap. 8; Arend Lijphart, The Politics of Accommodation: Pluralism and Democracy in the Netherlands (Berkeley and Los Angeles: Univ. of California Press, 1968), chap. 9; Hans Daudt, "Party System and Voters' Influence in the Netherlands" (unpublished paper presented at the Third International Conference on Political Sociology, Berlin, Jan. 16–20, 1968).

effect in consociational theory,[26] and its application to the more severely
divided societies of Asia and Africa remains problematic.

For Asia and Africa, this is not just a matter of epistemology. It bears
on both the opportunities for and the techniques of interethnic conciliation. Consider the constraints under which leadership operates. Much
emphasis is placed by Lijphart on the freedom of leaders to enter consociational arrangements, but little is placed on the structure of incentives
within which leaders work. Consociational democracy "assumes that
political elites enjoy a high degree of freedom of choice, and that they
may resort to consociational methods of decision-making as a result of
the rational recognition of the centrifugal tendencies inherent in plural
societies and a deliberate effort to counteract these dangers."[27] Such
freedom does not generally characterize conditions in severely divided
societies. There has been, for example, much discussion in the consociational literature of the Malaysian Alliance but too little recognition of
what a near and fragile thing it was—how it arose almost accidentally
and how specific electoral and other incentives were responsible for creating and sustaining it. In such ventures, leadership is important, but
leadership often has limited freedom to choose its own path.[28] Moreover,
since elite competition is one of the sources of ethnic conflict, it is a

26. This circularity shows up in the enumeration of conditions favorable for the emergence and maintenance of consociational democracy. In early formulations, Lijphart listed
the following as favorable conditions: favorable popular attitudes toward or "widespread
approval" of consociational arrangements, as well as a moderate degree of nationalism.
"Typologies of Democratic Systems," 25–30; "Consociational Democracy," 221–22. The
presence of such conditions suggests precisely that the cleavages are not so intense. In a
later formulation, these conditions give way to "overarching loyalties" as a facilitator of
consociational arrangements. Overarching loyalties are said to moderate conflict. Thus,
the proposition is that the emergence of consociation is facilitated by moderate levels of
conflict. *Democracy in Plural Societies*, 81–83.
    A perfect circle is drawn by Claude Ake, *A Theory of Political Integration* (Homewood,
Ill.: Dorsey Press, 1967). He conceives of integration in terms of deference and consensus,
suggesting these are more likely where there is a "mature political culture." Mature political culture, in turn, is more likely where there is a high level of social mobilization; but that
mobilization can best be achieved without disruption where a political system is "authoritarian, paternal, 'identific' [the interests of rulers and ruled are identical], and consensual."
Ibid., 101. Consequently, deference and consensus are best achieved in a system where
deference is no problem and consensus already exists: integration is most likely in integrated systems!
    27. Lijphart, *Democracy in Plural Societies*, 165; see also ibid., 53–55.
    28. There are many other examples of formidable constraints on leadership. To cite
just one, even in authoritarian Indonesia it took fifteen years, much backing and filling,
and finally a justification in terms of preventing Chinese subversion in order to arrive at
the point where one million Chinese could be granted rudimentary citizenship rights. *Far
Eastern Economic Review* (Hong Kong), Mar. 14, 1980, pp. 31–33.

mistake to impute good intentions to leaders without good political reasons for thinking they in fact entertain such intentions. What is needed is a theory of timing and incentives for elite cooperation. Leadership intentions and leeway are variables rather than constants.[29] Providing more leadership latitude can be an object of policy, but it is wrong to assume it as given.

Related to this is the working assumption of Lijphart and Nordlinger that each ethnic group is represented by a single set of leaders.[30] Lijphart's firm propositions about the optimal number of groups for consociation are based on the premise that each group is cohesive and has unitary leadership. Likewise, he celebrates the creation and maintenance of ethnic parties as building blocks of coalitions, again assuming that each ethnic group will have only one party and neglecting the conflict potential inherent in ascriptively based party systems.[31] Party monopoly and leadership latitude tend to co-vary: if each group were represented by a single set of leaders, then leaders would indeed have more latitude to cooperate across group lines. But this is not the way groups are consistently organized. Particularly where some group leaders opt for cooperation with leaders of other groups, we have seen that intragroup competition tends to arise, and it is usually based on the argument that group interests have been sold out. Only rarely does any single set of leaders speak for an entire ethnic group, if those leaders speak in conciliatory terms. In short, a principal limitation on interethnic cooperation is the configuration of intraethnic competition, both present and anticipated. Theories of accommodation that rest on elite initiative must include variables related to group structure and competition, for these constrain the opportunities for interethnic elite relations.

These variables also impinge on the specific techniques of accommodation. For Lijphart, the "grand coalition" is the main instrument of consociationalism: "The primary characteristic of consociational de-

29. Of the writers reviewed here, only Nordlinger approaches in detail the problem of "conflict-regulating motivations." *Conflict Regulation in Divided Societies*, 42–53. Significantly, Lijphart argues that elite behavior is an unpredictable variable. *Democracy in Plural Societies*, 53–55. Compare Pinard, "The Moderation of Communal Conflicts," 19.

30. E.g., Lijphart, *Democracy in Plural Societies*, 25, 31: "the leaders of all significant segments"; Nordlinger, *Conflict Regulation in Divided Societies*, 118: "conflict-group leaders." On this point, Esman diverges, rightly noting the common tendency for intraethnic competition to emerge and to challenge interethnic arrangements as a sacrifice of vital group interests. "The Management of Communal Conflict," 73. See also Pinard, "The Moderation of Communal Conflicts," 20.

31. Lijphart, *Democracy in Plural Societies*, 64–65, 169.

mocracy is that the political leaders of all significant segments of the plural society cooperate in a grand coalition to govern the country."[32] Since leaders of all significant segments are included, each with a unitary leadership, the grand coalition has the support of the "overwhelming majority" of the electorate.[33] The rationale is that, "in a political system with clearly separate and potentially hostile population segments, virtually all decisions are perceived as entailing high stakes, and strict majority rule places a strain on the unity and peace of the system."[34] The coverage of the grand coalition, therefore, approaches unanimity.

Four developing countries are identified as having followed consociational practices: Lebanon, Malaysia, Surinam, and the Netherlands Antilles. Of these, Lijphart contends that the Malaysian Alliance and the cooperation of major officeholders in Lebanon constituted grand coalitions.[35] Surinam and the Netherlands Antilles, he notes, were governed by coalitions "of the parties rather than of the segments," since each segment had more than one party; hence, these were "not truly grand coalitions . . . ."[36] In fact, none of the four was a grand coalition, in each case for the same reason. Each group in each country was represented by more than one set of leaders. At the height of its success, in 1964, the Alliance polled only 58.5 percent of the total vote and was opposed by strong parties on the Malay and Chinese flanks. Before and after, it hovered around 50 percent.[37] As we shall see later, the Lebanese arrangements, less tied to party, were nonetheless made possible by factional differences within each group that facilitated intergroup cooperation, extending to the highest offices. The point is not that coalitions are not possible, for they are. It is rather that, in democratic conditions, *grand* coalitions are unlikely, because of the dynamics of intraethnic competition. The very act of forming a multiethnic coalition generates intraethnic competition—flanking—if it does not already exist. What is more, the

32. Ibid., 25.
33. Ibid., 26. A "small and weak opposition" is all that is left, or perhaps none at all. Ibid., 47.
34. Ibid., 28.
35. Ibid., 148, 151, 178.
36. Ibid., 205, 201.
37. I am referring, of course, to the 1955–77 period covered by Lijphart. Even the National Front, successor to the Alliance Party, but embracing some former opposition parties, was opposed in the 1978 election by a Chinese party which captured 20 percent of the vote and a Malay party which gained 17 percent. So the Front had less than two-thirds, and neither it nor the Alliance had a majority of Chinese votes. The same proved true in the 1982 election, despite the substantially improved electoral performance of the Front and its Chinese components.

Asian or African regime which declares that it has a grand coalition probably has, not a consociational democracy, but an ethnically exclusive dictatorship. The *sine qua non* of consociationalism turns out to have little applicability in the severe conflict conditions of Asia and Africa.

To the general theme that what conflict-prone societies need is interethnic cooperation, and that political engineering can help bring this about, there can hardly be any demurrer. Lijphart is eminently correct in taking issue with the academic nihilism which condemns divided societies to fratricide or dictatorship. Yet, to the particular prescriptions of consociational theory, the possible objections are many and frequently decisive. As Peter De Vries would say, the whole of consociation is greater than some of its parts. It is, for example, repeatedly stated by Lijphart that three or four groups, equal in size, provide the most favorable conditions for interethnic accommodation.[38] But the point remains unproved, and a strong case can be made for a larger number of dispersed groups, as in India or Tanzania. Similarly, Lijphart takes a strong stand against the presidential system as incompatible with government by grand coalition, though he then excepts Lebanon's presidential system from this stricture.[39] We shall soon see that the most significant and carefully planned experiment in ethnic accommodation—Nigeria's—involved adoption of a presidential system, as did Sri Lanka's effort to break the cycle of Sinhalese-Tamil conflict.

There is an important point here; it has to do with the whole approach to conflict reduction. Both of these presidential systems were established on the assumption that the freedom of leadership to pursue a conflict-reducing course is a variable that, within limits, is amenable to deliberate intervention. Put more generally, it is possible to alter the structure of incentives that impinge upon political leaders. Coalition may be one way; there may be others. Rather than becoming committed to a single institutional form, it seems wiser to assume that appropriate institutions will vary with, among other things, the structure of cleavages and competition. The search for arrangements to reduce conflict must be premised on the general requirement of a close fit between, on the one hand, constraints and opportunities that derive from the dynamics of the conflict and, on the other, prescriptions to abate the conflict. *A priori* prescriptions will not do.

38. Lijphart, *Democracy in Plural Societies*, 56–57, 170–71. Compare Chapter 8, note 44, above.

39. Lijphart, *Democracy in Plural Societies*, 178, 187, 210.

MOTIVES, TIMING, AND TECHNIQUE

The major determinant of the effectiveness of measures to reduce ethnic conflict is the content of the policies adopted. But we already know that, in severely divided societies, ethnic conflict is pursued more frequently than are policies to abate it. Consequently, before examining what the policies are, how they work, and what results they are likely to bring, there are two matters, prior in time and prior in logic, that warrant consideration. The first relates to the motives of policymakers. The second concerns the timing of policy innovation and a specific technique of ethnic policymaking: the comprehensive settlement achieved by reciprocal concessions.

POLICY MOTIVES AND EVALUATION

Although theorists speak of policies as being intended to effect ameliorative, integrative, conciliatory, or other positive purposes, policy motives are not always so easy to characterize in practice. There is an elusive line between policies adopted out of accommodative intent and those adopted in pursuance of the conflict objectives of particular groups. Were the new states in Nigeria created in order to assuage ethnic tensions, or were they created to break up the Northern Region and permanently reduce the power of the Hausa-Fulani at a time when they were temporarily vulnerable? Were the policies that give preference to Malays adopted to reduce the possibility of conflagration in Malaysia or to enhance the position of the Malays at the expense of the non-Malays? Perhaps, in the end, it comes to the same thing: what was needed to assuage ethnic tensions in Nigeria, it might be argued, was a reduction in the power of the Hausa-Fulani; conceivably, what was needed to dampen the conflict in Malaysia were preferences for the Malays. But, if so, one could not judge that from the motives of the policymakers or the immediate reactions of other participants alone. The best test of ethnic accommodation is an evaluation of consequences, not of intentions.

Because leaders often have so little leeway to embark upon explicitly accommodative policies, it may well be that the arrangements most likely to be adopted are those which seem to favor one of the groups. That may be why policies that impose ethnic preferences and quotas are so frequently adopted in the name of accommodation. The most cogent justification of a policy favoring or disfavoring one of the groups is that it is necessary to avert further conflict. This is certainly the way opposition to the policy is neutralized.[40] But the argument from necessity has another function: it may be the way previously reluctant policymakers convince *themselves* that, by favoring one group, they are really pursuing the common weal. There is strong public and private pressure on political leaders to adopt ethnically slanted policies and label them accommodative.

Of course, many accommodative policies result from genuine efforts to reduce conflict. These efforts typically flow from arrangements, such as coalitions of commitment or alliances, that have built-in incentives for conciliation. Yet it is also true that many policies bearing on ethnic conflict are the result of biased or ambivalent intentions. Much will be lost by focusing solely on policies adopted with a pure heart, even if it were always possible to know which these are. Again, there is no substitute for an evaluation of consequences.[41]

A policy that disadvantages a particular ethnic group may nevertheless contribute to accommodation if it is acceptable as a *quid pro quo* in a larger package. Reciprocity can be a technique of promoting accommodation, particularly insofar as it widens the leeway of leaders to undertake a series of initiatives that, considered separately, would be blocked. There are, therefore, times when the impact of particular policies cannot be evaluated apart from the impact of other policies. In fact, it is sometimes difficult to discern the exact boundary of a "particular" policy, for precisely the reason that its adoption was linked to the adoption of some other "particular" policies. Imprecision in policy boundaries may be a useful device to make group judgments of gains and losses

40. See, e.g., *Washington Post*, June 3, 1980, quoting prominent Chinese in Indonesia to the effect that policies discriminating against the Chinese are "wise" and "necessary," "even though it hurts. It could actually prevent a bigger catastrophe in the future." For the general phenomenon of labeling and promoting policies carefully to maximize consensus and reduce opposition, see Barbara J. Nelson, "Setting the Public Agenda: The Case of Child Abuse," in Judith V. May and Aaron B. Wildavsky, eds., *The Policy Cycle* (Beverly Hills: Sage, 1978), 36.

41. If pure heart is not the test of accommodative policy, two corollaries follow. First, policies with no discernible ethnic intentions can have important ethnic effects. It takes very little imagination, for instance, to realize that the Indonesian policy of transmigration, which disproportionately involves settling Javanese in the Outer Islands, is likely to have profound ethnic effects. But, in the main, nonethnic policies with ethnic effects are too far-flung, their effects too concealed from view, to make tracking them down the first order of business. It makes more sense to attend to the consequences, including the unanticipated and second-order consequences, of policies with manifest ethnic goals. And, second, the relevance of negative (low-conflict) cases comes again to mind, for it may well be that they inadvertently point the way to useful policies.

more difficult, though it should be added that reciprocity as a technique of accommodation has some specific pitfalls, to be examined soon.

If policies that appear unhelpful in conflict reduction sometimes need to be examined in a package, there are also times when too-broad judgments are misleading. Some countries that are regarded as generally "successful" in conflict management may nonetheless have adopted policies that have not contributed to that success and may even have made it harder to attain. The mere presence of a given policy or technique in such a country is no proof of its contribution to ethnic accommodation. Equally, the "failure" of a country in accommodative efforts (such as Lebanon) is no proof that its policies and techniques were poorly designed. Such failures may simply demonstrate that countervailing forces were too strong or that the policies were put in place too late to abate the conflict.

Nor is the frequent adoption of a practice, even by an array of "successful" countries, evidence of the utility of such a practice in promoting accommodation. There are regularities in the claims advanced in ethnic conflict, and some of the claims find their way into policy in one country after another without necessarily having accommodative effects. There are also fashions in policy that sometimes explain the adoption of similar policies from country to country. And there have been explicit transfers of techniques and policies from one country to another. Guyana borrowed the Israeli list system of proportional representation; Fiji adopted the device of the multiethnic alliance directly from Malaysia; and Nigeria's second constitution drew heavily on the American model. The similarity of policy in several countries testifies only to its popularity, not to its effectiveness. Experience with conflict behavior ought to give rise to skepticism regarding the specific effects of policy, as it should regarding policy motives.

It is, however, notoriously difficult to measure the actual consequences of policy in this field, and the more so in Asia and Africa, where data are so often unavailable, fragmentary, noncomparable, or unreliable. That does not mean that we are relegated to an overall evaluation of whether a whole system "works" or not or whether a regime has been "successful" or not in containing conflict. There are intermediate ways of judging the impact of policy—ways that involve analysis of the demonstrated or likely effect of a policy on the political incentive structure. We shall see more of this in examining specific approaches.

TIMING AND TECHNIQUE:
THE GRAND SETTLEMENT

Not every time is equally apt for reevaluating the direction of ethnic policy and charting new courses.[42] A disproportionate number of accommodative policies have been adopted at watershed moments of ethnic conflict, especially on the eve of independence or after serious civil violence. Reevaluations of policy prompted by recent experience painful for all groups probably stand the best chance of producing evenhanded and enduring accommodative policies. Among the "functions of social conflict"[43] is the propensity for outbreaks of severe conflict to demonstrate the need for new rules of conflict prevention. The desire to avert a likely conflagration that has not yet occurred may also yield good results, but not if some groups fear the conflagration less than others or anticipate that they may emerge from it in an improved position. Measures of accommodation adopted when recent developments have affected the various groups unevenly appear least promising of all. Groups whose position has been improved may resist any change. Thus, Sinhalese thwarted the Bandaranaike-Chelvanayakam Pact in Sri Lanka after Sinhala Only legislation had been enacted a year before. By the time accommodative policies were implemented after 1977, a Tamil terrorist movement was already entrenched. All of this suggests a caveat: it may be more difficult to backtrack on ethnically biased policies than policymakers anticipate, or to do so in time to have a favorable impact; and it may be preferable to proceed on a comprehensive basis that provides some gains and some concessions for all groups.

There seems to be a direct relationship between the magnitude of the event (if any) that prompts the policy inquiry and the comprehensiveness of the arrangements that emerge from it. The most inclusive arrangements seem to be produced by the need to reach agreement at independence (the Lebanese "National Pact" of 1943; the Malaysian constitutional "bargain" of 1956–57) or the desire to avert a recurrence of civil war (the Nigerian constitution of 1978). Less disruptive watershed events, such as independence, seem more likely to produce a policy package that is the result of exchange—reciprocal concessions—whereas the more disastrous events make it plausible to think in terms of creating

42. For helpful insights into issues of timing and sequencing, see Samuel P. Huntington, "Reform and Stability in South Africa," *International Security* 6 (Spring 1982): 3–25.
43. Lewis A. Coser, *The Functions of Social Conflict* (Glencoe, Ill.: Free Press, 1956), 125–26.

wholly new structures. The differences between these two approaches, however, should not be exaggerated. Sometimes new structures can be created by a process of bargaining, and reciprocal concessions can have major structural effects, as the Lebanese arrangements certainly did.

For the moment, I intend to focus on ethnic policymaking by reciprocal concession. There are a number of important examples of this device. The Lebanese National Pact and the Malaysian constitutional bargain are among the better known. In the Indian Punjab, the "Regional Formula" of 1956 was designed to compromise the conflicting political claims of Sikhs and Hindus. (The B-C Pact in Sri Lanka is another illustration, but was never put into effect.) In each case, at a propitious moment several basic, divisive issues were laid to rest in a candid spirit of reciprocity. The consequences of specific policies embodied in these contractual settlements I shall treat in the following chapters. Here what is of interest are the advantages, characteristics, and pitfalls of such packages—in other words, the grand settlement *as a technique.*

Paradoxically, these far-reaching arrangements may be most likely in the most severely divided societies. In such societies, perhaps the only way to get off dead center is for each side to make trades that, in the aggregate, produce a comprehensive arrangement. If several issues are embraced in a single bargain, it becomes more likely that each side will see benefits in it.[44] In deeply divided societies, furthermore, the neutrality, representativeness, or legitimacy of central policymakers is typically not conceded by all groups. It may therefore be easier to persuade the groups to make policy by sacrificing some goods in exchange for others than it is to persuade them that centrally formulated policy will satisfy their interests, even when they have some input into the making of central policy. There is an analogy here to another society deeply divided along ethnic lines—international society—where much law and policy are made by a comparable mechanism, the treaty.

Ethnically divided societies commonly possess certain characteristics that make a strategy of exchange particularly feasible. One is the ethnic division of labor; another is the territorial concentration of groups. Each lends itself to a bargain based on spheres of influence.

The ethnic division of labor means that the groups have complementary areas of advantage. If it is necessary to reassure a group that its

44. Roger Fisher, "Fractionating Conflict," in Fisher, ed., *International Conflict and Behavioral Science* (New York: Basic Books, 1964), 97–98; James S. Coleman, "Collective Decisions," *Sociological Inquiry* 34 (Spring 1964): 166–81.

interests will be protected, promises to respect these group advantages can be exchanged. And if one of the groups is aiming to alter some portion of the existing pattern of advantages, the exchange of promises can provide reassurance to the other by including a time frame that makes the changes amenable to anticipation and planning.

These two features characterize the Malaysian constitutional bargain.[45] By its terms, the Chinese essentially recognized Malay predominance in politics and the civil service, in exchange for Chinese citizenship, gradual progress toward political and civil equality, and protection of their economic position against confiscation. There was also a vague understanding that the Malays were to be helped (by certain preferences and by other, unspecified means) gradually to improve their backward economic position. In ten years, Malay was to become the sole official language, replacing English, in which the non-Malays held an advantage; but parliament could provide for the continued official use of English after that date. Here was a bargain steeped in the ethnic division of labor and in the use of time to allay insecurities on both sides.

If the groups are territorially concentrated, rather than intermixed, that, too, can provide a basis for reciprocity. The "Regional Formula" in the Indian Punjab was premised on the concentration of Sikhs in some areas of the state and Hindus in others.[46] The state was divided into two language zones, in which Punjabi or Hindi would operate for certain educational and administrative purposes. The state assembly was also divided into two regional committees. On a number of important subjects, bills had to be approved by the appropriate regional committee. This was a way of using territorial concentration to permit each group to recognize the autonomy of the other in certain fields. Mutual noninterference was the basis of the bargain.

Even without a strong ethnic division of labor or extensive territorial separateness, reciprocal concessions for the sake of mutual security are possible. The Lebanese National Pact entailed a promise on the part of Maronite Christians to recognize the Arab character of Lebanon and to forgo assistance from any European power, in return for which Sunni

45. For a concise summary, see R. S. Milne, *Government and Politics in Malaysia* (Boston: Houghton Mifflin, 1967), 36–41.
46. See Paul R. Brass, *Language, Religion and Politics in North India* (Cambridge: Cambridge Univ. Press, 1974), 291; Baldev Raj Nayar, *Minority Politics in the Punjab* (Princeton: Princeton Univ. Press, 1966), 222; Joan V. Bondurant, *Regionalism versus Provincialism: A Study in Problems of Indian National Unity* (Berkeley: Univ. of California Indian Press Digests-Monograph Series, no. 4, 1958), 116–24.

Muslims forswore allegiance to a "greater Syria," pledging instead their loyalty to Lebanon. The Pact also treated the ethnic communities "almost as the units of a federal state,"[47] leaving each group a considerable measure of autonomy and apportioning political offices and parliamentary seats by ethnic group and government jobs by ethnic quotas based on the population ratios of the 1932 census. Here proportionality served as an arbitrary principle to which both sides could subscribe.

Recognition of existing spheres of influence is a natural result of the contractual mode of ethnic policymaking. Policy process and policy product are frequently related. To choose one mode of policymaking over another may also be to choose one kind of outcome over another. The goal of these grand settlements was to find a minimal basis for living together. That they ended up by pursuing the path of least intrusion into existing areas of group strength is not evidence that such an approach is essential to conflict reduction. It is, rather, evidence that contractual settlements are likely to impinge as little as possible on the interests of the contracting parties and to leave many areas of social life unregulated.

To suggest that such an approach is not essential to conflict control is not to say that these arrangements are doomed to failure. On the contrary, I have argued in Chapter 3 that the ethnic division of labor is generally a shield against conflict. Arrangements to respect the existing division of labor, unless they thwart already existing aspirations to break it down, are likely to help avert conflict.

Grand settlements also have other forces working for them. As certain moments are especially propitious for a settlement, so, too, the historical accomplishment—particularly independence—made possible by the agreement is linked to the agreement and adds to its durability. The Lebanese settlement, which held up for more than thirty years, and the Malaysian bargain, which survived unamended for a dozen years, were both associated with the attainment of independence. The Punjabi settlement, which was not linked to any comparable historical event, was quickly undone by Sikh separatism and Hindu discontent.[48] A grand settlement, moreover, is not possible without the extended participation of political leaders, who must negotiate the agreement and then persuade their followers of its advantages. Although the contracting parties purport to be leaders of whole ethnic groups, they are in fact leaders of ascendant parties or factions. The concessions they make are opposed

47. George E. Kirk, *Contemporary Arab Politics* (New York: Praeger, 1961), 117.
48. Brass, *Language, Religion and Politics in North India*, 321, 329–32.

by other leaders even at the time of the agreement. The Lebanese National Pact was especially opposed by some Christians. The Malaysian bargain was opposed both by some Malays, who saw it as a surrender of Malay sovereignty, and by some Chinese, who wanted equal status for all languages. Such opposition creates among the contracting parties a psychological investment in the arrangements, which must be defended if their historic achievement is to be recognized. The Lebanese and Malaysian leaders responsible for those settlements did indeed defend them, then and later, against charges of sellout.

Although these settlements helped Lebanon and Malaysia survive difficult periods (including the Lebanese civil war of 1958 and the destabilizing incorporation of Singapore into Malaysia from 1963 to 1965), both arrangements finally crumbled. The agreements contained a number of weaknesses that undermined their ability to withstand the pressure that was put on them. The weaknesses derived from pitfalls likely to be built into such settlements. Some of these pitfalls may also attend ethnic policymaking in general.

The Incommensurables Pitfall

One problem of contractual settlements is inherent in the exchange of incommensurables. At the time of agreement, a settlement may look beneficial to all the parties, in the sense that every group emerges with both prospective gains and losses—a *quid* for every *quo*. Years later, however, the agreement is likely to be challenged if, as is probable with incommensurables, the actual ethnic incidence of gains and losses is uneven. This is especially so if one side received the benefits of the agreement early on, while another's benefits, which were longer term, failed to materialize at all. "What the Soviets got," said an American diplomat of an analogous agreement, "they put in their pockets long ago. What we get, we have to collect as we go at every meeting like this one."[49]

The Malaysian bargain provides excellent examples of this risk. One of its most important provisions was to extend citizenship to the Chinese and Indians on generous terms, approximating *jus soli*. Because the conferral of citizenship required only strokes of the pen, this benefit was realized soon after the negotiations. On the other hand, economic advancement for the Malays, inherently more difficult, could not be achieved by a stroke of the pen. As Malay elites became disappointed

49. Quoted in the *Washington Post*, Nov. 14, 1980.

with the economic results of independence, some suggested that there had been a failure to perform the contract and that, therefore, the citizenship of the non-Malays ought to be reconsidered. Some Chinese made much the same argument with respect to non-Malay recognition of the symbolic predominance of the Malays, on the understanding that gradually non-Malays would become equal participants in the political process. As the latter had not materialized, why should the former continue? Eventually, these inflammatory arguments, which went to the heart of the bargain, were handled by a constitutional amendment in 1971, prohibiting challenge to the main elements of the settlement.

The problem, however, is intrinsic to the grand settlement. Packages have a way of unraveling as each group computes its benefit-cost ratio. The items most susceptible to shortfalls in anticipated benefits are those that were vaguest in the original bargain. In the Malaysian case, these were promises to help the Malays economically and to accept gradual non-Malay political equality. That these items were left vague does not mean that the leaders did not agree on them—for they did—but that it was impolitic to spell them out. In the case of Malay economic advancement, the reason is that the commitment was just a hope, involving little in the way of program, and was hedged with restrictions because of promises to the Chinese.[50] In the case of non-Malay political equality, no one really knew at what point that might be feasible, so no promises could be made. In both cases, what were vaguely stated and peripheral parts of the bargain generated expectations greater than had been envisioned by the contracting parties. These unfulfilled expectations were contrasted with promises to the other side that had been fulfilled.

The danger, then, is that the components of the bargain will provide returns at various rates, undermining the sense of reciprocity. Incommensurability makes it easier to achieve a bargain but harder to make one stick.

The Firm Target Pitfall

There is a strong tendency to postpone delivery of some of the more controversial benefits obtained in bargaining. Transition time can allay insecurities and accord policymakers an opportunity to prepare for

---

50. Thus, it was agreed that nothing should be done to aid the Malays at the expense of Chinese economic interests—or, as Tun Abdul Razak expressed it, "no person should be deprived of his existing rights solely for the purposes of reserving rights for the Malays." Minutes of the 4th Meeting of the Alliance Ad Hoc Political Sub-Committee, Apr. 26, 1957 (mimeo.; copy in Tun Leong Yew Koh papers of the Malaysian National Archives).

changes that cannot be accomplished immediately. So implementation at a firm future date is promised. The Malaysian language deadline is a good example.

The original intentions of the parties were clear. As they saw it, it would be impractical to do away with the use of English even after 1967, and so they expected parliament to provide for its continued official use.[51] The expectations of some Malay elites were different. As 1967 drew closer, pressure mounted for a genuine conversion to Malay. The language bill, which perpetuated the use of English and provided for the "liberal use" of Chinese and Tamil, came as a great disappointment.[52]

If a benefit cannot be delivered at the time the bargain is made, the likelihood is that a fixed target date for delivery will simply spotlight the importance of the benefit, inducing interest groups to gather around it, without enhancing the ability of the government to deliver it. Postponement to a fixed date does not do what the Malaysian contracting parties thought it would—bury the issue, making acceptance of yet another postponement easier. Rather, it creates a promissory note on which members of the beneficiary groups will demand payment.

The Frozen Quota Pitfall

Ethnic quotas are not inherent in grand settlements. It is possible to have grand settlements without quotas and quotas without grand settlements. Nevertheless, quotas are appealing to the makers of settlements, because they are one of the few ways of quantifying and compromising claims that are generally difficult to quantify. I am not concerned here with the consequences of quotas in general. It is, rather, the freezing of quotas that creates a problem.

The Lebanese National Pact froze civil service appointments at a 6:5 Christian-to-Muslim ratio based on the 1932 population ratios.[53] Rates of natural increase, however, were uneven, as they often are with ethnic groups. Within a couple of decades, the Muslim proportion of the population was at least half; exact figures are unavailable because the exis-

51. As Tun Ismail said at an Alliance meeting in 1957: "It is a matter of being practical and realistic. India, for example, has had to extend the use of English beyond the period laid down in her constitution." Ibid., Apr. 2, 1957. See also Minutes of a Meeting of the Alliance National Council, Kuala Lumpur, Sept. 2, 1956 (mimeo.); "Political Testament of the Alliance" (mimeo., n.d. [1955?]).

52. See Margaret Roff, "The Politics of Language in Malaya," *Asian Survey* 7 (May 1967): 316–28.

53. Ralph E. Crow, "Religious Sectarianism in the Lebanese Political System," *Journal of Politics* 24 (Aug. 1963): 489–520.

tence of fixed quotas made it politically impossible to conduct any census after 1932. These demographic changes were enormously destabilizing, because they created a perceived gap between entitlement and actual benefit. Tragically, one of the major consequences of the Lebanese civil war of 1975–84 may be the alteration of the 6:5 quota to a 1:1 quota. What appeared to be a reasonable and objective means of distributing opportunities—indeed, what was designed to increase Muslim representation in the civil service—proved to be a rigid standard incapable of keeping up with changes in the underlying facts on which it was based.

It is interesting to contrast the quotas adopted by Malaysia in its constitution. A 4:1 Malay-to-non-Malay quota was approved for the elite Malayan Civil Service (MCS). Although non-Malays considered this unfair, it never proved to be the destabilizing issue the far more equitable Lebanese quota did. The reasons are several. The quota was grounded in the ethnic division of labor, which gave non-Malays outlets in the private sector. The 4:1 quota did not extend to the professional and technical services, in which non-Malays predominated.[54] Consequently, there was more fluctuation in ethnic ratios in government service than the 4:1 figure would suggest—it was not really "frozen." Equally important, the 4:1 quota was not intended as a fair compromise based on some objective and presumably immutable referent (population ratios); it was instead a concession demanded and given in return for other concessions from Malays. That it was part of a package made it more acceptable than it would have been if it had had to be defended on its own. The Lebanese quota, on the other hand, was asserted to be just, not because it was a *quid pro quo*, but because it was tied to an external standard. When that standard later became obsolete, the justice of the quota evaporated.

Reciprocity and Change

From the examination of these pitfalls, it is clear that the items in a settlement do not all have equal standing. Explicit concessions that are reciprocated (the MCS quota) stand the best chance of enduring, even when distasteful on the merits. Concessions that are unreciprocated, either because the *quid pro quo* fails to materialize (Malay economic advancement, Chinese political equality) or because there was no reciprocal concession to which they were tied initially (the Lebanese quotas), stand a good chance of being repudiated. Besides the failure of an antici-

54. Milton J. Esman, *Administration and Development in Malaysia* (Ithaca: Cornell Univ. Press, 1972), 74–78.

pated benefit to appear, a major cause of repudiation is reinterpretation of the bargain by the groups years later. Ironically, the Lebanese National Pact was seen as a victory for the Muslims in 1943. By 1958, it was viewed as the Christians' last line of defense. By 1972, Muslim discontent with the Pact was profound.[55] Various provisions of the Malaysian bargain were also subject to reinterpretation by the groups, generally in the direction of retroactively exaggerating what had been promised.

That the grand settlement tends to become frail with the passage of time is no reason to denigrate its utility. To be sure, it is chimerical to think, whatever the mythology of the settlement, that every issue can be laid to rest permanently by consummating a bargain. Over time, contract is a limited tool for ordering group relations. As the differential accrual of group benefits and costs under the agreement becomes clear, as expectations change and history is rewritten, settlements will need some elastic capacity. The concrete terms of the original settlements, too, need to be designed to reduce incentives to overthrow them—a point we have temporarily neglected in our concern with the grand settlement as a technique. Yet, despite its inevitable deficiencies, the grand settlement by itself is usually a worthwhile achievement. In the absence of a common currency of benefits, barter—and that is what the settlement is— may be the only way to reach an agreement; and an agreement may be the only way to assure harmony in the short run. Retrospective evaluation of the failings of settlements should not obscure the importance of the short run, the dangerous short run, in ethnically divided societies.

RADICAL SURGERY:
PARTITION AS A SOLUTION

If the short run is so problematical, if the constraints on policy innovation are many, if even grand settlements need patchwork readjustment, perhaps it is a mistake to seek accommodation among the antagonists. If it is impossible for groups to live together in a heterogeneous state, perhaps it is better for them to live apart in more than one homogeneous state, even if this necessitates population transfers. Separating the antag-

---

55. Michael C. Hudson, *The Precarious Republic: Political Modernization in Lebanon* (New York: Random House, 1968), 194; David R. Smock and Audrey C. Smock, *The Politics of Pluralism: A Comparative Study of Lebanon and Ghana* (New York: Elsevier, 1975), 137, 162–63, reporting survey data.

onists—partition—is an option increasingly recommended for consideration where groups are territorially concentrated.[56]

Rare, of course, is the regime that will agree to this solution without a fight. This reluctance is not merely because of the contemporary fetish about sovereignty but because willingness to contract state boundaries invites potential foreign enemies to pick at a country's territory in the hope of eventually splitting some of it off. In spite of these difficulties, partitionist solutions deserve full-dress consideration, for the benefits, if they materialized, would be substantial.

The case for partition has been argued on several grounds, only some of which are pertinent to ethnic conflict.[57] So far as ethnicity goes, the linchpin of all the arguments is the assumption that the probable outcome of secession and partition will be more homogeneous states and, concomitantly, a lower ethnic conflict level. If the assumption were correct, the conclusion would follow. But the assumption is wrong: the only thing secession and partition are unlikely to produce is ethnically homogeneous or harmonious states. This is so for at least four reasons, all of them foreshadowed by our exploration of group boundaries in Chapter 2 and of secessionist movements in Chapter 6.

First, the vast majority of secessionist regions are ethnically heterogeneous. More than this, ethnic identity is not static; it changes with the environment and especially with territorial boundaries. Given the contextual character of group identity, the attainment of independence in such a region is likely to increase the significance of ethnic divisions considerably. Subgroup cleavages will also assume heightened importance. Biafra, for example, had great heterogeneity, embracing, as it purported to, a variety of non-Ibo peoples (among them, Efik, Ibibio, and Ijaw), as well as a variety of Ibo subgroups generally at odds with each other in Eastern Region politics. Ethnic conflict would have accel-

---

56. Lijphart, *Democracy in Plural Societies*, 44–47; Dahl, *Polyarchy*, 121; Samuel P. Huntington, *Civil Violence and the Process of Development* (London: International Institute for Strategic Studies, Adelphi Paper no. 83, 1971), 14; Nathaniel H. Leff, "Bengal, Biafra and the Bigness Bias," *Foreign Policy* 3 (Summer 1971): 129–39.

57. Leff, "Bengal, Biafra and the Bigness Bias," for example, suggests that large states do not have an economic development advantage over small states. There are doubts about whether this is true for the existing constellation of states, because the list of small and prosperous states includes a number of entrepôts and financial centers that may skew the results. Assuming it is true, it would probably not continue to be true if secession and partition were increasingly tolerated. Since backward regions are so disproportionately represented among secessionists, the states that would emerge would be, in the main, economically disadvantaged.

erated with the emergence of an independent Biafra, as it surely would in Eritrea, the Southern Sudan, and the Southern Philippines.

Second, ethnic diversity within the secessionist region is what frequently triggers the secession, and secessionist movements make this diversity a major political issue. As noted earlier, an influx of ethnically differentiated settlers helps provoke separatism. Where this is the case, movements to restrict, disfranchise, expel, or exterminate ethnic strangers can be expected after independence. Increased conflict—or much worse—is the likely result.

Third, in focusing on the secessionist region, it is necessary not to forget those the secessionists would leave behind. Would secession render the rump state homogeneous? There is practically no state facing a secessionist movement in Asia or Africa which would become homogeneous if it simply severed the secessionist region. One of the reasons why regimes move with such bloody decisiveness against secessionists is fear of a demonstration effect in the rump region. And again the situation is contextual and dynamic. If the secessionists prevail, the political context will contract in the rump state, as in the secessionist state, marking off new lines of cleavage and deepening old ones. This is precisely what happened in the former West Pakistan; it began to happen in Ethiopia as one secessionist war turned into several; and it would likely have happened had Biafra made good its departure from Nigeria, as the North-South balance and the balance of Hausa-Fulani versus all others would have altered decisively.

Fourth, if it comes to fighting, as it often will, secessionist warfare exacerbates ethnic tensions within the secessionist region. Contending groups within the region may fight each other, as well as fighting the central government, either before the secessionist war breaks out, as the Kurds did, or after, as the Southern Sudanese, Eritreans, and Chadian Muslims did. In some cases, the prospect of independence is so threatening that some groups within the secessionist region reject it outright and side with the central government. Hence the participation of Biharis in the Pakistani Razakers or the reciprocal atrocities between Ibo and Ijaw in Biafra. The dynamics of fighting tend to reduce prospects for post-secession or post-partition harmony.

For most ethnically divided states, then, secession or partition is merely likely to effect a reordering of heterogeneity. The prescriptions that postulate a clean break are heedless of both the complexity of ethnic configurations in such states and the fluidity of ethnic identities at different levels of salience. Pakistan, twice the product of partition, is testimony to the propensity for new cleavages to supplant the old. No simple population transfer can meet these problems. In fact, population transfers increase the resulting heterogeneity by creating a new immigrant population which may soon find itself at odds with indigenous groups, as Urdu-speakers from India did with respect to the Sindhis of Pakistan. Again, the intention to consolidate homogeneity can achieve the opposite.

There is a further question raised by partitionist measures. Is it not likely that, by placing an international boundary between former domestic antagonists, creating two states and two armies where previously there was one, a domestic conflict will be transformed into a more dangerous international conflict? Experience on this score is not encouraging. Under most conditions, relations between the secessionist state and the rump state will be marked by tension and the threat of *revanche*, if not outright warfare. One need only mention the partitions of India and Palestine to recognize the potential for international conflict that inheres in such arrangements.[58]

If the benefits of partition are not likely to materialize but new costs are, partition can hardly be recommended as a generally applicable solution to domestic ethnic conflict. That does not preclude its application in particular cases. There are times when a resulting homogeneity may be envisioned or when, despite all its problems, partition is the least bad of the alternatives. That time was surely reached once the Pakistan army launched its assault on Dacca in March 1971. There are times when the passion for "self-determination" is so strong that it is senseless to thwart it. But even here there are ambiguities. To encourage some groups to determine their own future may also mean allowing them to determine the future of others. This point was most clearly brought home in the Biafran case, in which Ibo seemed to be asserting the right to determine the future of non-Ibo peoples in the Eastern Region of Nigeria.

And there is also the question of the means to be employed in main-

---

58. A further result of the internationalization of the conflict effected by partition is the unfavorable position in which minorities who are left behind are likely to find themselves. After partition, the Muslims of India were often thought to be loyal to Pakistan. If population transfer is incomplete, as it often will be, this will be a common suspicion. If the suspicion should be even modestly well founded, it will produce repressive policies in the successor states, making ethnic accommodation much more difficult.

taining unity. If partition is a bad idea, it does not follow that all available weapons should be brought to bear to avert the undesirable result. Partition is likely to be a bloodier event than it looks on paper. Even those divorces that proceed more or less by consent, such as the partition of India in 1947, may take an enormous toll in lives. "Population transfer" only *sounds* hygienic. Still, protracted civil violence or warfare may be worse, and prudential judgments will have to be made. The point is not that partition is always avoidable, only that, with rare exceptions, it ought to be not the policy of choice but of desperation. Even in the face of formidable constraints, the tools for achieving limited goals of conflict reduction without partition may be more plentiful and realistic than the well-known disasters in ethnic relations would suggest. In ethnic conflict, desperation cannot be ruled out, but most states will find it advantageous to cope with ethnic conflict with their present international boundaries intact.

PLASTIC SURGERY: INTERNATIONAL INTEGRATION AS A SOLUTION

The same conclusion follows for international regional integration. If partition is a policy of desperation, the opposite course—international integration—is a policy founded on more optimistic assumptions. If the partition of states is advocated on the frequently spurious ground that it will create ethnic homogeneity, the unification of independent states can be expected to create greater heterogeneity. The implicit model here is India or Tanzania, both states in which, as we have seen in Chapter 1, the number and dispersion of groups provide some barrier to destructive ethnic conflict at the center.

That dispersed systems seem less prone to severe ethnic conflict can be appreciated by comparing India's politics at the center to Pakistan's or Tanzania's politics to that of its neighbors, Kenya and Uganda, both of which began at independence with one or two large and threatening groups. Pakistan, Kenya, and Uganda have undergone serious conflict at the center, whereas India and Tanzania have in the main managed to confine their ethnic conflict to dispersed, largely watertight compartments.

As I shall argue in the next chapter, there are ways of manipulating territorial boundaries *within* an independent state so as to channel conflict in a localized direction. Here, however, the question is whether the

obliteration of territorial boundaries *between* independent states creates
the possibility of replicating the Indo-Tanzanian model by enlarging territorial scale and the number of ethnic groups.[59]

At the threshold, there is an objection to such a strategy based on the
same contextual character of ethnic identity that was said a moment ago
to limit the utility of partitionist strategies. If contracted territorial
boundaries are conducive to subgroup schism and conflict at lower levels
of ethnic identity, then enlarged territorial boundaries are likely to be
conducive to expanding ethnic boundaries and thus conflict at higher
levels of ethnic identity.

Despite this possibility, international integration remains attractive to
some policymakers and some ethnic groups. In part, perhaps, growing
ethnic conflict in Europe was a catalyst for the European Economic
Community. Groups such as the Basques and Tyroleans, divided between two states, have had more than usual enthusiasm for the EEC.[60] If
the territorial boundary that divides them has less significance, their
opportunities to act in concert will increase. Then, too, separatist minorities find a European Community desirable, because it may be conducive
to substate autonomy all over the continent.

It is, however, no accident that international integration has come to
very little on a world scale. There are many reasons for this, but ethnic
diversity has contributed at least its fair share. The decisive fact is that
for every ethnic group that enthusiastically favors unification with a
neighboring country or countries, there is another group that vehemently and often violently opposes the idea. In ethnically divided societies, international integration becomes a central aspect of ethnic arithmetic, comparable in potency to those divisive issues, the census, the
immigration policy, birth rates, and birth control.

Indeed, it is related to those issues. East Indians in the Caribbean have
been distinctly unfriendly to West Indian integration. In Guyana, East
Indians are a bare majority, and, in Trinidad, they are a large minority.
In both, Indians have higher rates of natural increase than do Creoles.
The Creole-dominated governments of both countries have repeatedly
searched for ways of aligning them with Creole-dominated West Indian
islands, such as Granada.[61] Clearly, the intention is to augment the Cre-

---

59. This possibility is neglected by Lijphart, because he is flatly opposed to "too many
segments." *Democracy in Plural Societies*, 57, 170–71.
60. It was Walker Connor who called this point to my attention.
61. For one of many examples, see *Washington Post*, Nov. 2, 1971.

ole population, an especially urgent priority for Guyana. Each such effort has met with resounding Indian objections, and the Guyanese government resorted instead to a less effective policy of encouraging West
Indian immigration to the unsettled Guyanese interior.

The same themes are sounded over and over again. The Kurds in Iraq
have forced the Arab regime in power to back off efforts to unite with
other Arab states.[62] Alawi in Syria have opposed union with Egypt, and
so have Southern Sudanese.[63] Alawi were bound to be an inconsequen-
tial minority in a United Arab Republic. Some Syrian Sunni military
officers, on the other hand, were enthusiastically Nasserist. In the early
1960s, perhaps half a dozen Syrian coups, countercoups, and purges
were related to this issue. Fear of Arabization and fear of Egypt were
related for Southern Sudanese, and the two together played a considerable role in the long Sudanese civil war. The East African Federation of
Kenya, Tanzania, and Uganda was an explosive issue for the Baganda,
the largest Ugandan ethnic group, which feared submergence in the
wider context.[64] In Upper Volta, the vote in a referendum on the now-
defunct Mali Federation was split bitterly along ethnic lines. The powerful Mossi, like the powerful Baganda, opposed the federation, while non-
Mossi tended to favor it.[65] In each case, group attitudes toward regional
integration were dictated by whether group interests in domestic politics
would be advanced or retarded by the merger.

Not only is international integration ethnically contentious, but the
respective groups often aim their integrative efforts in different directions. In Djibouti, the Afars regard themselves as related to neighboring
Ethiopians; the Issas see themselves as Somalis. When the future of the
British Cameroons was being decided in 1961, Northern Nigerians
wanted the heavily Hausa-Fulani Northern Cameroons to stay with Nigeria. Ibo, on the other hand, cared less about the Cameroons and more
about the island of Fernando Po in then-Portuguese Guinea, for it had a

62. George S. Harris, "The Kurdish Conflict in Iraq," in Astri Suhrke and Lela Garner
Noble, eds., *Ethnic Conflict in International Relations* (New York: Praeger, 1977), 76.
63. Tabitha Petran, *Syria* (New York: Praeger, 1972), 149–70; J. C. Hurewitz, *Middle
East Politics: The Military Dimension* (New York: Praeger, 1969), 155; *Manchester
Guardian Weekly*, Oct. 7, 1972; *The Grass Curtain* (London) 2 (Oct. 1971): 1, 15, 30.
64. R. C. Pratt, "The Politics of Indirect Rule: Uganda, 1900–1955," in D. Anthony
Low and R. Cranford Pratt, eds., *Buganda and British Overrule: Two Studies* (London:
Oxford Univ. Press, 1960).
65. Victor D. DuBois, "The Struggle for Stability in the Upper Volta: Part I," American
Universities Field Staff *Reports*, West Africa Series, vol. 12, no. 1 (1969): 12.

large Ibo minority.[66] In Congo (Brazzaville), as ethnic hostility grew after independence, so did competing proposals for international integration. Among Mbochi, there was support for joining the Central African Republic; among Vili, there was movement toward Gabon; among Bakongo, there was discussion of recreating the fifteenth-century San Salvador Empire that would unite Bakongo from the Congo, Zaire, and Angola.[67] Each group saw the proposals of its antagonists as fundamentally inimical to its interests.

Just as irredentism is an unlikely course for ethnically divided societies,[68] so is international regional integration. As a matter of fact, so strongly do integration proposals derive from ethnic interest that it is difficult to determine just where irredentism leaves off and international integration begins. Both impart reality to the fears of groups that the international regional context is relevant—and often distinctly unfavorable—to their long-term interests.

On occasion, to be sure, a delicately balanced arrangement, offering something for all sides, can be worked out. The Federation of Malaysia, joining Sarawak, Sabah, and Singapore to Malaysia in 1963, is one such example. But the example cuts both ways. There was considerable opposition to the original proposal, from Malays who feared the ethnic impact of including overwhelmingly-Chinese Singapore, and within two years political activity from Singapore had tipped the delicate balance, resulting in the expulsion of Singapore.[69]

As ethnic conflict proceeds, partition can become the least bad of several bad alternatives, and conflicting groups may conceivably choose it on these grounds. But international integration rarely appears in this light, for it seems inevitably to favor one or another of the contestants. Consequently, it seems less and less a policy to reduce conflict and more and more an irritant in ethnic relations. The dispersion model of ethnic conflict, represented by India and Tanzania, remains appealing, but in-

66. Bolaji Akinyemi, "Nigeria and Fernando Poo, 1958–1966," *African Affairs* 69 (July 1970): 236–49.

67. Jean-Michel Wagret, *Histoire et sociologie politiques de la République du Congo (Brazzaville)* (Paris: Librairie Générale de Droit et de Jurisprudence, 1963), 79–80, 176–77; René Gauze, *The Politics of Congo-Brazzaville*, trans., ed., and supplemented by Virginia Thompson and Richard Adloff (Stanford: Hoover Institution Press, 1973), 67–69, 82, 119–20.

68. See Chapter 6, above.

69. Nancy McHenry Fletcher, *The Separation of Singapore from Malaysia* (Ithaca: Cornell Univ. Southeast Asia Program, Data Paper no. 73, 1969).

ternational regional integration does not seem a promising way to get to it. There may be better ways.

STRUCTURAL AND DISTRIBUTIVE APPROACHES

If most ethnically divided societies must find ways for groups to live together within current territorial boundaries, it behooves us to examine the most promising policy approaches to that end. This is what the next two chapters attempt, and it is useful here to relate those approaches to each other.

The most important approaches to dealing with ethnic conflict fall into two more or less determinate classes: distributive or structural. Distributive policies aim to change the ethnic balance of economic opportunities and rewards. Structural techniques aim to change the political framework in which ethnic conflict occurs; they do not necessarily make promises about ethnic outcomes.

Distributive policies generally involve either ethnically skewed investment or preference. A government may concentrate investment disproportionately in geographic areas or functional sectors where members of one or another group are located. Rural development in Malaysia, land colonization in Sri Lanka, and the cooperative movement in Guyana are all examples of ethnically skewed investment for distributive purposes. On the other hand, a government may adopt policies of ethnic preference designed to reduce disparities between ethnic groups. Many countries have experimented with policies to augment ethnic representation or achieve ethnic proportionality in employment, educational enrollment, share ownership, scholarships, business licenses, and contracts. The policies vary in scope and approach. All, however, share the objective of increasing the representation of "backward" groups in activities in which "advanced" groups are found in proportions greater than their share of the population. In Chapter 16, I shall assess preferential policies in detail, but make no attempt to deal with the rather more diffuse subject of ethnically skewed investment.

The main structural techniques, discussed in Chapter 15, involve the reshaping of territorial or electoral arrangements. Federalism and regional autonomy are the most common territorial devices. Electoral devices run the gamut from constituency delimitation to seat allocation by ethnic group to various electoral formulae. Often territorial and electoral arrangements are used together, and for that matter so are structural and distributive policies.[70]

Although convenient, the distinction between structural and distributive policies is inadequate. Each contains components of the other. Some ostensibly distributive policies may have important effects on the structure of conflict. The reservation of specific offices for members of particular ethnic groups, for instance, tends to redirect conflict between contenders for that office who belong to the same ethnic group. Conversely, certain structural policies have distributive aspects. It is sometimes contemplated that regional autonomy will provide an opportunity for an ethnic group disadvantaged at the center to put preferential policies into effect in a limited region. Federalism, too, can have a preferential impact. If, in a federal system, ethnic and state boundaries overlap each other, then any benefit that is distributed by state is also, *ipso facto*, distributed by ethnic group. Frequently, each state in a federation is treated equally for certain purposes, despite variations among states in population. If so, then smaller ethnic groups with their own states or those ethnic groups that are divided among the largest number of states per capita will be preferred for such purposes at the center. (The same principle prefers citizens of less populous states such as Delaware and regions such as New England in representation in the United States Senate.) Likewise, some electoral arrangements have the purpose of augmenting the electoral power of particular ethnic groups or compensating for the adverse effects of particular electoral formulae on geographically dispersed ethnic minorities. Such territorial and electoral arrangements affect ethnic distribution without saying so and sometimes without meaning to. Once their impact is assessed, then, there is a considerable measure of overlap between structural and distributive policies.

FIVE MECHANISMS
OF CONFLICT REDUCTION

Another way to view conflict reduction is to consider how any given technique or policy actually works. More important than any institu-

70. For a survey, see Claire Palley, *Constitutional Law and Minorities* (London: Minority Rights Group, Report no. 36, 1978). I have also surveyed policy approaches in two reports to the Ford Foundation: "Policies to Reduce Ethnic Tensions in Three African Countries" (unpublished paper, Washington, D.C., Feb. 1980); and "Policies to Reduce Ethnic Tensions in South and Southeast Asia" (unpublished paper, Washington, D.C., June 1980).

tional form or policy is whether it brings into play an effective mechanism to reduce conflict. Several common mechanisms of conflict reduction can be identified. The techniques and policies described in the next two chapters utilize, at one point or another, all of these mechanisms, so it is worthwhile enumerating them in advance.

First, interethnic conflict may be reduced by dispersing it, by proliferating the points of power so as to take the heat off of a single focal point. One way to do this is by scattering power among institutions at the center, as the United States system does. If the capture of no single body or office will suffice to gain complete power for any ethnic group, then ethnic conflict may lose some of its urgency and its capacity to inspire fear that the worst is about to come to pass. Politics becomes a much more diffused game. More often the dispersal takes a territorial form, involving the creation of lower-level units with important policy functions. This may make the states, provinces, or regions objects of political competition, so that the struggle to control the whole regime at the center becomes less intense. Conflict in one region is generally less dangerous than conflict that engages a whole country. A corollary is that interethnic conflict may be reduced by arrangements that effectively compartmentalize or quarantine it within substate units.

Second, interethnic conflict may be reduced by arrangements that emphasize intraethnic conflict instead. Intraethnic conflict is usually (though not always) less dangerous and violent than interethnic conflict. If intraethnic conflict becomes more salient, this may reduce the energy available for conflict with other groups. As noted earlier, reserved offices may have this effect, and so may territorial devolution, if it activates subgroup identities that compete for attention with overarching group identities. Some subethnic conflict, however, is conducive to a species of intraethnic party competition that tends to exacerbate interethnic conflict, as Chapter 8 makes clear.

Third, interethnic conflict may be reduced by policies that create incentives for interethnic cooperation. Electoral inducements for coalition may be one way to heighten the incentives for cooperation, but certain preferential and territorial arrangements may also do this. Interethnic cooperation may be more likely where intraethnic divisions are present, since links may be easier to forge between portions of groups than between groups that are cohesive and undivided. Intraethnic monopoly provides the leeway for interethnic cooperation, but often not the incentives. Intraethnic competition provides the incentives, but sometimes not the leeway.

Fourth, interethnic conflict may be reduced by policies that encourage alignments based on interests other than ethnicity. In deeply divided societies, it seems unlikely that nonethnic lines of cleavage, such as those based on social class or territory, can be manipulated so as to displace ethnic cleavages. If they could, ethnic conflict would not be the intractable force that it is. But some measures may provide the impetus for nonethnic lines of cleavage to compete for attention with ethnic cleavages.

Fifth, interethnic conflict may be reduced by reducing disparities between groups so that dissatisfaction declines. Measures to produce such results are based on certain premises about the nature of ethnic conflict. This mechanism cuts deeper than most of the other mechanisms reviewed here, which in the main emphasize restructuring the incentives for conflict behavior, largely on the part of political leaders. To cut deeper takes longer, though of course in the end the deep cut may produce the more enduring result.

If these are the main mechanisms of conflict reduction, merely identifying them implies no *a priori* judgment of relative likelihood of success. Difficulties of implementation and of matching means to ends may vary among policies operating on different mechanisms. Cost-benefit ratios may also vary, and so may the difficulty of anticipating, detecting, and controlling unintended consequences. Sometimes it is not even clear in advance what is a cost and what is a benefit in terms of ethnic conflict reduction. If distributive policies create a new class of ethnic leaders among a formerly underrepresented group, will interethnic tensions necessarily be assuaged or will divisive new demands be voiced? If intraethnic conflict grows among a group that already feels weak, will interethnic conflict grow or decline? There are, after all, intervening variables that make it supremely important to fit the mechanism to the environment it is supposed to change.

Nevertheless, merely to enumerate the various structural and distributive approaches, and the mechanisms through which they might work, begins to suggest something very important. Between the naïveté of those who would abolish ethnic differences in short order through "nation-building," the cynicism of those who would simply suppress those differences, and the pessimism of those who would counsel costly and disruptive partition as the only way out—between these shoals, there lurk passages that are at once less dramatic, less visionary, and more realistic. The approaches we are about to consider are peaceful and compatible with democracy. They entail measures to contain, limit, channel, and manage ethnic conflict, rather than to eradicate it or to aim at either a massive transfer of loyalties or the achievement of some consensus. They involve living with ethnic differences and not moving beyond them. All of these measures fall within the domain of political engineering. Not learning theory, but the theory of political incentives, inspires these more limited measures. What we shall see, above all, is that there is much more scope for constructive policy innovation in the area of ethnic conflict than policymakers in divided societies have generally acknowledged. Ethnic problems are intractable, but they are not altogether without hope.

CHAPTER FIFTEEN

Structural Techniques to Reduce Ethnic Conflict

The time is propitious for a preliminary assessment of structural techniques to reduce ethnic conflict. In recent years, a number of countries have turned to such techniques in the quest for measures to promote accommodation. Some results of innovations in federalism, regional autonomy, and electoral systems are now available. In yet other cases, territorial and electoral arrangements adopted for purposes not related to ethnicity nevertheless have had a significant impact on ethnic conflict. Consequently, there is some accumulated evidence on which to rest judgments of efficacy.

What formal institutions do is to structure incentives for political behavior of one kind or another. But they have a more powerful influence on some incentives than on others. Broad judgments are less helpful here than a searching examination of the precise effects of specific innovations. This examination consists of two parts. The first deals with territorial devolution, beginning with the far-reaching consequences of the new Nigerian federalism. The second considers the impact of an array of electoral innovations.

It has often been said that fundamental conflicts cannot be bridged by constitution-writing. No doubt there is truth in this observation, but it is a half-truth. Where there is some determination to play by the rules, the rules can restructure the system so that the game itself changes.

FEDERALISM, REGIONAL AUTONOMY, AND CONFLICT REDUCTION

In spite of the store of human experience with the relation of territory to ethnicity,[1] few are the practitioners or observers who could give confi-

---

1. See generally Ivo Duchacek, ed., "Federalism and Ethnicity," *Publius* 7 (Fall 1977).

dent advice on the key questions of federalism and regional autonomy: Under what circumstances is the creation of a separate state or region likely to forestall or encourage secession? What is the optimal form and scope such arrangements should take? How many units should there be, and should they be ethnically homogeneous or heterogeneous? What powers should be devolved upon them and what controls retained? The skillful division of authority between regions or states and a center has the potential to reduce conflict, but there is little more than dogma available about the utility of federalism; and even then the dogmas are equally divided between those who assume that territorial boundaries should follow ethnic boundaries and those who counsel that they should cross-cut them.[2] The occasional assumption of policymakers who contemplate federal solutions—in the 1985 Cyprus negotiations, for example—has been that federalism is a lesser version of partition and, as such, requires homogeneous states, one per group. Such assumptions should not be regarded as the last word.

FEDERALISM: THE NIGERIAN EVIDENCE

Every so often, political systems create quasi-experimental conditions in which propositions are inadvertently tested. These conditions are never as controlled as genuine experiments, but the propositions are generally more significant than those that can be tested in experiments. Nigeria

---

2. For the former view, see Ronald L. Watts, *Multicultural Societies and Federalism* (Studies of the Royal Commission on Bilingualism and Biculturalism, no. 8; Ottawa: Information Canada, 1970), 34; Ivo D. Duchacek, "Antagonistic Cooperation: Territorial and Ethnic Communities," *Publius* 7 (Fall 1977): 3–29, at 13; Kenneth C. Wheare, "Federalism and the Making of Nations," in Arthur W. Macmahon, ed., *Federalism, Mature and Emergent* (Garden City, N.Y.: Doubleday, 1955), 32. See also Arend Lijphart, *Democracy in Plural Societies* (New Haven: Yale Univ. Press, 1977), 42–43, 163, 193; Max Beloff, "The 'Federal Solution' in Its Application to Europe, Asia, and Africa," *Political Studies* 1 (June 1953): 114–31. For the latter view, see Seymour Martin Lipset, *Political Man: The Social Bases of Politics* (Garden City, N.Y.: Doubleday, 1960), 91–92.
   For purposes of this discussion, the precise differences between federalism and regional autonomy are not of great moment. In some cases, such as the Sudan, regional autonomy was accorded to particular regions by otherwise unitary governments. In others, such as Sri Lanka, the grant of autonomy to one region would not be feasible unless the same arrangements were made for all regions. The line between federal and unitary states is elusive, but, in substantial measure, the distinction turns on whether the relation between the center and the component units is regarded as having an intrinsically constitutional character, often exemplified by representation based on the units in a separate legislative chamber at the center. Whereas regional autonomy necessitates only devolution, and regional decisions are sometimes subject to a central veto, federalism generally entails some degree of independence on the part of the constituent units. Cf. Claire Palley, *Constitutional Law and Minorities* (London: Minority Rights Group, Report no. 36, 1978), 13–14.

provides a far-reaching test of the impact of federalism on ethnic conflict.[3]

With two quite differently designed federal systems, separated from each other by thirteen years of military rule, Nigerian federalism affords the best evidence available on the varying impact of federalism under civilian rule. The long period of military government produced greater discontinuity between the two sets of federal arrangements than is ordinarily present when federal systems are altered. For this reason, causal relationships between the new federal arrangements and the subsequent behavior of civilian politicians and electorates are fairly clear-cut. These changes in political behavior stand out in especially sharp relief, because some continuities in behavior, harking back to the period before military rule, are also evident. Despite inevitable rough edges in the quasi-experiment, despite the problems inherent in historical comparisons, despite the short duration of the Second Nigerian Republic (1979–83)—despite all of this, the Nigerian evidence shows that federalism can either exacerbate or mitigate ethnic conflict. Much depends on the number of component states in a federation, their boundaries, and their ethnic composition. Particularly important is the relationship of ethnic group distribution to the distribution of states.

The First Nigerian Republic (1960–66) consisted of three main regions, each of them controlled by a single ethnic majority (and a party representing it) which used its control of the region to struggle furiously for power at the center. The dominance of the three major groups in their regions weakened the representation of minorities by opposition parties. Patronage, coercion, and the apportionment of seats worked together to overrepresent the regional majorities. Most overrepresented were the Hausa-Fulani, who, with little more than half of the North's population, held nearly three-quarters of the regional assembly seats from 1961 to 1965.[4] The Northern People's Congress, dominated by Hausa-Fulani and centered in the traditionally ascendant Sokoto emirate, won the vast majority of federal seats in the North and, as we saw in Chapter 9, was soon in a position to control parliament in Lagos. That control was challenged by Yoruba and Ibo parties that had also used their regions as staging areas for the battle at the center. Under this federal system, the

3. For a discussion of such "natural experiments," see Richard A. Brody and Charles N. Brownstein, "Experimentation and Simulation," in Fred I. Greenstein and Nelson W. Polsby, eds., *Handbook of Political Science*, vol. 7 (Reading, Mass.: Addison-Wesley, 1973), 218.
4. C. S. Whitaker, Jr., *The Politics of Tradition: Continuity and Change in Northern Nigeria, 1946–1966* (Princeton: Princeton Univ. Press, 1970), 324.

power of the three main groups, who together comprised less than two-thirds of the total population, was not merely reflected at the center; it was magnified by their control of regions whose boundaries extended somewhat beyond ethnic boundaries.[5]

The advent of military rule and the Biafra war provided the occasion for restructuring the federal system. To counter the Biafran charge that Nigeria was dominated by the large Northern Region, to secure the loyalty of Northern minorities strongly represented in the army, and to wean the Eastern minorities away from Biafra, the regions were carved into twelve states in 1967.[6] The three main groups were relegated to seven states. The dissolution of the old political parties by the military and the creation of new states together liberated the minorities from control of regionally dominant groups and paved the way for new alignments.

The new fluidity was enhanced by the creation of seven more states in 1976, before the return to civilian rule.[7] Now the Hausa were spread among half a dozen states, the Yoruba among five, and the Ibo between two. The proliferation of states produced a lively state politics and a more complex—and therefore less tense—politics at the center. Both of these effects of the new states were visible when civilian politics re-emerged in 1979,[8] and both effects would increase if more new states were created.

The new arrangements transferred a good deal of conflict from the all-Nigeria level to the state level. State-level conflicts have been intraethnic and interethnic. More than half the nineteen states have a substantial measure of ethnic heterogeneity, especially in the former regional minority areas. In such states, there has been tension over the allocation of civil service positions and other benefits to various groups and areas of the state. Disappointed groups have in several cases demanded creation of their own separate states. The Ibo and Yoruba states have much less

5. This was no longer true of the Yoruba after a fourth, largely non-Yoruba region was carved out of the Yoruba Western Region in 1963. Thereafter, the West, save for cosmopolitan Lagos, was nearly all Yoruba.

6. For a succinct analysis, see Crawford Young, *The Politics of Cultural Pluralism* (Madison: Univ. of Wisconsin Press, 1976), 301–08. See also Brian Smith, "Federal-State Relations in Nigeria," *African Affairs* 80 (July 1981): 355–78.

7. The nineteen states were intended, as were the twelve, to respond to the demands of minorities and to subdivide the large ethnic groups further. See Ali D. Yahaya, "The Creation of States," in Keith Panter-Brick, ed., *Soldiers and Oil: The Political Transformation of Nigeria* (London: Frank Cass, 1978), 201–23.

8. The observations that follow are based on interviews I conducted in Nigeria in 1978, supplemented by several additional interviews I conducted in 1980.

ethnic heterogeneity, but they have experienced considerable intraethnic tension. Disputes have arisen in Imo, an Ibo state, between Bende and Owerri administrative divisions over jobs and development projects; the same sort of quarrel has occurred in Yoruba states, such as Oyo, among subgroups clustered in Ife, Ilesha, and Oshogbo. The boundaries of the Ibo and Yoruba states tend to follow—and therefore reinforce—existing lines of subethnic cleavage. The Owerri Ibo in Imo have long been at odds with the Onitsha Ibo of Anambra, while the Oyo and Ogun Yoruba, consigned to states with those names, have disputed the apportionment of resources between their two states. The nineteen states thus created a new, lower layer of conflict-laden issues around which already existing differences crystallized, greatly reducing the previously unchallenged importance of contention at the all-Nigeria level.

This dispersal of conflict was reinforced by a distributive side effect of creating nineteen state bureaucracies. The federal and state bureaucracies are differently composed. Inevitably, the ethnic composition of state civil services tended to reflect the composition of the respective states, albeit not at all proportionately within heterogeneous states. These new bureaucratic opportunities reduced—though they by no means eliminated—the potentially explosive significance of a major ethnic issue at the center: the disproportionate representation of Yoruba, Edo, and a number of smaller groups in the central bureaucracy following the Ibo departure for Biafra.

None of this state-level conflict was sufficient in the South to prevent the recrudescence of essentially Ibo and Yoruba parties at the all-Nigeria level. In the 1979 senatorial, gubernatorial, and presidential elections, these two parties won between 74 and 95 percent of the vote in the solidly Ibo and Yoruba states. With the exception of a minority segment of Ibo who supported one of the parties with a substantial Northern base, at the all-Nigeria level of politics the subgroup loyalties of the two main Southern groups did not effectively compete with overarching group loyalties. Indeed, as the 1979 elections approached, both the Yoruba and Ibo parties grew more cohesive. Opposition to the Yoruba United Party of Nigeria (UPN) in the Yoruba Oyo and Ondo states was overcome, and Ibo flocked from other parties to the banner of the venerable Ibo nationalist Nnamdi Azikiwe when he took command of the Nigerian People's Party (NPP). Despite some changes in group cohesiveness in the 1983 elections, both Ibo and Yoruba parties persisted.

Major changes were wrought in the alignments of minorities in the

East and North. The Biafran hostilities had widened the gap between Ibo and the minorities in the former Eastern Region. Now concentrated in Rivers and Cross River states, the Eastern minorities tended, in the Second Republic, to align with Northern-based parties. Non-Muslim minorities in the North were also free to choose new alignments. The period of military rule had sharpened tensions between groups strongly represented in the armed forces—notably between Hausa and certain Middle Belt groups—particularly after the execution of Middle Belt officers implicated in the 1976 assassination of Murtala Mohammed. Now Plateau state, the heart of the Middle Belt, eschewing Northern alignments, supported the predominantly-Ibo Nigerian People's Party.

Most striking of all the changes was the new political significance accorded by the proliferation of states to cleavages within the Muslim North. These cleavages, always observable, were formerly muted by the undivided regional structure and the overriding struggle between the Muslim-majority North and the South.

The new states breathed new life into former Northern opposition parties based on ethnic and subethnic differences. Previously, it made little sense to support a party that would be consigned to futile and often punishing opposition in the Northern Region as a whole. In the federal election of 1959, the Northern People's Congress (NPC) won all but 6 of the nearly 100 Northern constituencies outside the Middle Belt.[9]

Now, however, electoral incentives were transformed. The pains of opposition in the undivided region became the rewards of power in the states. The creation of ten states in the former Northern Region simultaneously brought into being ten state legislatures, ten governors, and, since each state sent five senators to Lagos, fifty federal senators. A party with only minority support in the old North could now control one or more states, could gain one or more federal senate seats—for these are apportioned by territorial constituencies within states—and could have a respectable voice at the center. There had always been leaders willing to take up the cudgels of opposition in the North, but other leaders and

---

9. Richard L. Sklar, *Nigerian Political Parties* (Princeton: Princeton Univ. Press, 1963), 338. Properly modified for ethnic differences, the situation of Northern Nigeria under the NPC was not far from that described by V. O. Key, Jr., for one-party Virginia under the Byrd machine. For opposing parties to emerge, Key notes, "each party must, almost of necessity, have a territorial stronghold in which it can win legislative election and control local governments. . . . The punitive powers of the organization, through its control of the perquisites of local officials and its ability to obstruct local bills in the legislature, can discourage competing factions territorially segregated." *Southern Politics in State and Nation* (New York: Vintage Books, 1949), 33.

most voters had responded more sensibly to the logic of the situation by supporting the NPC. The new state boundaries turned that logic around, making ethnic and subethnic loyalties at the state, rather than regional, level more important in determining party support. The new federal structure thus facilitiated the expression of Northern heterogeneity more accurately than the earlier regional structure had permitted.

Two parties in the Muslim North benefited from the new structure. One, centered in Borno, was dominated by the Kanuri, a large majority in that state but only about 10 percent of the North as a whole. The other, centered in Kano state, embodied elements of Kano resistance to Sokoto,[10] Hausa resentment of Fulani overlordship, and social-class differences. Both parties had direct antecedents in the First Republic.

The Kanuri had been tied closely to the ruling Northern People's Congress in the First Republic. Some Kanuri, to be sure, had organized the Bornu Youth Movement (BYM), an explicitly Kanuri party. But the NPC carefully nurtured Kanuri support by a combination of rewards and pressure. The Bornu Youth Movement fought back, and interparty conflict, sometimes overlapping Hausa-Kanuri conflict, was often bitter. Nonetheless, the BYM won few elections and was confined largely to urban areas.[11]

In 1976, however, the Kanuri were awarded their own Borno state. They responded by supporting their own Great Nigeria People's Party (GNPP) to govern it.[12] In 1979, the state assembly, the governorship, and four of Borno's five senate seats were won by this party; the fifth was narrowly lost in a triangular race. The GNPP's strength also spilled into adjacent areas in the north of neighboring Gongola state. With some historical ties to the old Bornu empire, Gongola gave the GNPP a plurality of its state assembly seats (enabling it to form a fragile minority government in that state), as well as the governorship and two senate seats.

The Kanuri had fought and repelled Fulani armies in the nineteenth century. It is not surprising that, once it became possible to control their

10. Cf. Whitaker, *The Politics of Tradition*, 279–82; John N. Paden, "Islam, Constitutional Change, and Politics in Nigeria" (unpublished paper, Northwestern Univ., Oct. 1979), 4.
11. Sklar, *Nigerian Political Parties*, 339–44; Whitaker, *The Politics of Tradition*, 386.
12. The GNPP was not intended to be solely a Kanuri party, for it was earlier linked to a party with Ibo support, as explained below. But that does not detract from the fact that it was assuredly not linked to the successor to the NPC.
It should be noted that the spelling of Bornu has now been altered to Borno.

own state government, most Kanuri would leave their ties to a Hausa-Fulani party behind them. The GNPP, which was led, significantly, by a former NPC cabinet minister, Waziri Ibrahim, could easily be viewed as the Bornu Youth Movement writ large.[13] Ibrahim, however, proved maladroit at managing intraparty affairs. By the time of the 1983 elections, the GNPP was badly factionalized. Many of its leaders defected to other parties. In the presidential election, Ibrahim received fewer than half the Borno votes he had received in 1979, and the state fell to the National Party of Nigeria (NPN) in the later gubernatorial and federal legislative rounds as well.

Despite Ibrahim's quixotic quest for national power and his eventual rejection by the Kanuri, the general point remains: carving the old North into ten states created ethno-political opportunities foreclosed by the earlier system. The proof lies in another Northern state, Kano, whose political independence in 1983, as in 1979, survived the death of the founder of its ruling party.

Aminu Kano's People's Redemption Party (PRP) had considerable success in 1979 in the Hausa-Fulani state of Kano and in neighboring Kaduna state. The PRP was the reincarnation of the old, unsuccessful Northern Elements Progressive Union (NEPU), also led by Aminu Kano. In the First Republic, NEPU could be suppressed by the NPC's judicious use of regional patronage, by accusations that NEPU was dividing the North in the great struggle to control Nigeria, and by the taint of its affiliation with the leading Ibo party.[14] In the Second Republic, however, patronage was controlled at the state level, it was more difficult to see the North-South struggle as all-encompassing, and the other Northern parties were the strangers in Kano compared to the PRP. In 1979, Aminu Kano's party captured the Kano state assembly, the governorship, and all five senate seats by overwhelming majorities. In neighboring Kaduna, the PRP won two senate seats, the governorship, and a strong minority position in the state assembly. It was a far cry from the lean years of NEPU's fruitless opposition, during which, in six regional and federal elections between 1956 and 1964, the party had won a grand total of eighteen seats. In the last Northern regional elections, in 1961, NEPU

13. So uncanny, in fact, was the resemblance that the former interparty, interethnic violence has reappeared in Borno; and, in the 1979 election, the traditional ruler of the Bornu emirate, the Shehu, threw his support to the NPN just as he had earlier supported the NPC over the Bornu Youth Movement.

14. Whitaker, *The Politics of Tradition*, 385, 410.

had won one seat to the NPC's 156.[15] While factionalism hurt the PRP in Kaduna in 1983, the party did very well again in Kano, winning the governorship, nearly every federal and state seat, and the presidential vote in the state.

Many of the forces that had supported the NPC in the First Republic were drawn to the NPN in the Second. In 1979, the NPN did well in many traditional areas of NPC strength—indeed, in practically all except those areas where the GNPP and PRP showed the strength denied to their antecedent parties in the First Republic. This limitation, however, was enough to crimp the Northern support of the NPN, so that it won, for example, only half the governorships in states of the former Northern Region. In 1983, however, in an election marred by fraud, the NPN won all the Northern governorships except Kano.

Each of the five major parties of the Second Republic was thus recognizable as a somewhat altered version of one or more of the parties of the First Republic. This was most abundantly clear for the GNPP and the PRP. The Yoruba UPN was a recrudescence of the Action Group but without the Action Group's allies outside Yorubaland. The mainly-Ibo NPP inherited most of the support of the Ibo NCNC, but with the addition of support in Plateau state that would earlier have gone to the old United Middle Belt Congress. In the First Republic, the UMBC had been aligned with the Action Group. The NPN, with the same following the NPC had in many Hausa-Fulani areas of the North, also developed a strong following in the Ibo state of Anambra and in the Eastern minority areas. Much of the latter support had formerly been linked to the Action Group. These elements of party continuity attest to the persistence of ethnic forces in Nigeria, even in the face of certain changed ethnic alignments and of NPN strength outside the Muslim North.

The main impact of the new federal structure on party politics was, then, not to abolish ethnically based parties. To the contrary, as parties formed and re-formed in 1978–79, it was easy to discern the sorts of mergers and splits that are so characteristic of the evolution of ethnic parties in divided societies. The GNPP, for example, was originally part of the now mainly-Ibo NPP. It split off when Azikiwe took the NPP leadership, depriving Waziri Ibrahim of a chance to be the NPP presidential candidate. Originally, Ibrahim took some Ibo leaders with him to the GNPP; but these returned to the NPP camp after the 1979 elections,

15. Ibid., 374.

TABLE 11   FEDERAL ELECTION RESULTS IN NORTHERN NIGERIA, 1959, 1979, AND 1983

(by party; in percentage of Northern seats in federal legislative bodies)

		1959 House (n = 174)	1979 House (n = 240)	1979 Senate (n = 50)	1983 House (n = 240)	1983 Senate (n = 50)
NPC	NPN	77	51	58	75	76
NEPU	PRP	5	21	14	17	10
AG/UMBC	→UPN	14	5	8	2	4
	→NPP		8	8	6	8
BYM and Other	GNPP	4	16	12	0	2
Total		100	101[a]	100	100	100

SOURCES: For 1959, C. S. Whitaker, Jr., *The Politics of Tradition: Continuity and Change in Northern Nigeria, 1946–1966* (Princeton: Princeton Univ. Press, 1970), 374; for 1979, official returns; for 1983, *West Africa*.
[a]Total does not equal 100 because of rounding.

leaving the GNPP with no significant Southern support and the NPP with no support north of the Middle Belt. Not an end to ethnic parties but a rearrangement of the building blocks of such parties, and—in 1979—a less distorted reflection of their underlying strength, particularly in the North: these were the main consequences of the new federal structure.

The results of this in federal legislative elections for Northern constituencies are visible in Table 11, which lists parties competing in the North in the First Republic opposite their nearest successors in the Second. The table shows plainly that the difference in 1979 was the way seats were spread among the Muslim parties of the North: the decreased strength of the NPN *vis-à-vis* its predecessor, the NPC, and the concomitantly increased strength of both the Kano-based PRP *vis-à-vis* its predecessor, NEPU, and the Kanuri-based GNPP *vis-à-vis* the Bornu Youth Movement.

Looking carefully across the first line of the table, depicting NPC and NPN percentages, it appears as if the 1983 results entailed a reversion to the pattern prevailing in the First Republic, whereby the party representing Hausa-Fulani was able to capture support disproportionate to its underlying population in the North. There are, however, two considerations that militate against such a clear-cut interpretation. First, two-thirds of the NPN increase from 1979 to 1983 was due to the collapse of the GNPP. Indeed, despite the GNPP's factionalization and defections, the NPN presidential candidate won both Borno and Gongola states with less than a majority—which is quite different from the overwhelming support the NPC enjoyed there in the First Republic. This rather clearly implies that a revival of Kanuri cohesion, under the aegis of the GNPP or some other party, would restore the 1979 NPN results. Second, there is something more important about the 1979 results. The first election under the new constitution was a watershed event. Since, in that election, the NPN could not count on the undivided support of the North, it proceeded to cement relationships with groups outside the North, as I shall point out very shortly. These relationships survived the change in the Northern balance of power in 1983, so that, while the NPN was a Hausa-Fulani party in the North, it was not just that in the country as a whole. The fortuitous collapse of Kanuri cohesion in 1983, rather than in 1979, is testimony to the capricious but decisive significance of sequences of behavior in determining the impact of institutional innovations.

It may seem odd to lay so much emphasis on the electoral impact of the new states, but it is not wide of the mark. The Nigerian experience shows that federalism can act as a kind of electoral reform, setting off one arena from another, making and unmaking legislative majorities and minorities by adjusting the territory in which their votes are to be counted. As the new states changed electoral incentives, their effect in the North was rather like a change in electoral formula. The new states substituted something akin to proportional representation for the winner-take-the-whole-region formula that had exaggerated the strength of the largest regional party and of the largest ethnic group that comprised the party's support. If additional states are created, and if elections return to Nigeria, this proportionality effect should increase.

The new states reduced the overall power of the Hausa-Fulani, so it was no longer plausible for them to think of dominating the whole country. The reduced strength of the NPN in the North in 1979 gave the party a powerful incentive to do what new electoral requirements also encouraged it to do—appeal to ethnic groups outside the core area of its support and, indeed, outside the North altogether. The NPN had more success in reaching out to groups across the country than any other party did: it won the presidency and the largest number of seats in both federal houses in 1979 and in 1983. That the new states had the secondary effect of reinforcing incentives for interethnic cooperation across North-South lines is evidence of the efficacy of using territorial boundaries as an instrument of conflict reduction. Federalism, in short, can create a new framework for electoral reasoning on the part of voters and party leaders. By heightening the importance of cleavages within the North, the new framework ultimately reduced more dangerous cleavages at the all-Nigeria level.

Finally, the creation of nineteen states ranging in population from less than two million to more than eight million also created incentives for political actors to see at least a few all-Nigeria level issues in terms of competition among states, rather than among ethnic groups. Electoral issues in the Constituent Assembly that framed the new constitution occasionally arrayed large states against small states. On revenue issues, rich states have argued that revenue should be spent where it is "derived"; resource-poor states, that revenue should be apportioned by population. Interethnic alliances are notable on both sides.

The new Nigerian federal framework thus utilized all five mechanisms of conflict reduction enumerated earlier. First, the proliferation of states dispersed some of the conflict into more parochial forums. Second, the new states provided arenas in which intraethnic conflict might also occur. Third, a result of this was to enhance the position of some political parties at the expense of others, especially in the North, paving the way for greater interethnic cooperation in the all-Nigerian arena. Fourth, as the new states fought to advance their interests, a few nonethnic issues and actors were also introduced. And, fifth, the separate state bureaucracies provided career opportunities for groups not well represented in the federal civil service. Using all these tools, the nineteen states readjusted, realigned, and complexified the Nigerian political system.

In many ways, of course, there was substantial continuity between the First and Second Republics. Yet, even in party politics, where that continuity was manifest, what is striking is the considerable importance of rather small changes in party support. To be sure, the electoral impact of the new states was abruptly terminated by the (nonethnic) military coup that occurred on the last day of 1983. Nevertheless, in the wake of all the failures of planned change in the developing world, the Nigerian arrangements had by then already demonstrated that it is possible to take deliberate action to restructure institutions so as to alter ethnic balances and alignments.

THE DESIGN OF TERRITORIAL STRUCTURES

The Nigerian experiment provides a demonstration of the importance of political context in shaping the manifestations of ethnic conflict. If the results are replicable, territorial design may prove a useful instrument of conflict reduction.

In spite of the small number of federal states in Asia and Africa, several conclusions from the Nigerian experience can be corroborated. There is already good, if limited, evidence on the ethnic impact of homogeneous and heterogeneous states, the consequences of alternative ways of drawing boundaries, and the costs of devolution in terms of ethnic conflict.

Homogeneous States

If groups are territorially separate and subethnic divisions are prominent, the case for ethnically homogeneous states is strong. (The term *homogeneous*, needless to say, does not preclude subethnic cleavages.) India, which moved toward "linguistic" states in the 1950s, provides abundant testimony. The classic case is Andhra Pradesh, a state of Tel-

ugu-speakers previously merged with Tamil-majority Madras. The Telugu movement for a separate state "assumed such an intensity that it
was unimaginable that within a decade language . . . would have to
contend with other claims."[16] Yet, after a separate Andhra was conceded
in 1953, language conflict was superseded by the unremitting struggle
between the Kamma and Reddi castes, both Telugu, to control the state,
not to mention the equally fervid struggle between the Telangana region
(which joined the state in 1956) and the Coastal region of Andhra.[17]
Subethnic differences have also preempted politics in other monolingual
Indian states. Kerala politics has revolved around the rivalry of Ezhavas,
Christians, Nairs, and Muslims, a quadrilateral configuration of caste
and religious conflict replicated in no other state.[18] Neighboring Karnataka, designed as a homogeneous Kannada-speaking state, "since its
inception has been a silent spectator of the uninterrupted virulent race
for power between Lingayats and Vokkaligars."[19] Bihar has its quarrels
between tribals and caste Hindus. In each case, broader territorial
boundaries would probably produce broader ethnic conflict, along the
lines of Tamil-Telugu conflict in pre-1953 Madras.

The complexity of Indian society has facilitated the flow of conflict in
linguistically homogeneous states into subethnic channels, just as it has
in Nigeria's homogeneous states. Under such circumstances, devolution
of a generous share of power upon largely homogeneous federal units
promises a dramatic reduction in conflict at the center. Many issues will
be contested within ethnic groups, rather than between them, simply
because many contested issues become state-level issues. It is difficult to
infer causality from Switzerland, because it has not had intense conflict,
but it has been argued that Swiss federalism, with its powerful and
mainly homogeneous cantons, is effective in dampening ethnic conflict
because of the sparseness of contentious issues at the confederal level of

16. Jyotirindra Das Gupta, "Ethnicity, Language Demands, and National Development in India," in Nathan Glazer and Daniel P. Moynihan, eds., *Ethnicity: Theory and
Experience* (Cambridge: Harvard Univ. Press, 1975), 485.
17. G. N. Sharma, "Aspects of Andhra Politics," in Iqbal Narain, ed., *State Politics in
India* (Meerut, India: Meenakshi Prakashan, 1968), 96–104.
18. Lloyd I. Rudolph and Susanne Hoeber Rudolph, *The Modernity of Tradition:
Political Development in India* (Chicago: Univ. of Chicago Press, 1967), 71–76; Selig
Harrison, *India: The Dangerous Decades* (Princeton: Princeton Univ. Press, 1960), 196–
99; V. K. S. Nayar, "Communal Interest Groups in Kerala," in Donald Eugene Smith, ed.,
South Asian Politics and Religion (Princeton: Princeton Univ. Press, 1966), chap. 8.
19. Sushil Kumar, "Panorama of State Politics," in Narain, ed., *State Politics in India*,
68.

politics and the "tranquilizing effect" of compartmentalizing them.[20] Whether or not this is what works in Switzerland, it certainly seems promising for countries with these attributes: serious conflict at the center, territorially separate groups, and significant subethnic divisions. It is essentially what was proposed for Nigeria by Ibo leaders on the eve of the Biafra secession: "Since the control of the Centre has been the main cause of friction and tensions between the different Regions, thereby threatening national solidarity and integrity, the distribution of functions between the Regions and the Centre should be reviewed and so arranged that only such subjects and functions as will engender the minimum of suspicion and friction among different groups are allowed in the hands of the Federal Government."[21] Few states in Asia and Africa, however, would be willing to accord as much power to constituent units as Switzerland does to its cantons.

Even less generous devolution, however, promises some results. The regional autonomy agreement put into effect for the Southern Sudan in 1972 carefully limited the powers of the People's Regional Assembly it created for the South, and the agreement specified that the regional Executive Council was to be responsible to Khartoum.[22] Limited though Southern authority was, it was sufficient to set in motion a contest for control of the region that brought to the fore all the intra-Southern differences that had been manifested during the civil war: between those who spent the war years in Khartoum and those who spent them in exile or in the bush, among the various Southern parties, and among the several main ethnic groups in the South. As the regional government began its work, new intra-Southern issues arose. Now it became imperative that bureaucratic appointments and expenditures not favor one group or area over another.[23] The autonomy agreement seems to have

20. Hans Daalder, "On Building Consociational Nations: The Cases of the Netherlands and Switzerland," in Kenneth D. McRae, ed., *Consociational Democracy: Political Accommodation in Segmented Societies* (Toronto: McClelland & Stewart, 1974), 110; André Siegfried, *Switzerland: A Democratic Way of Life*, trans. Edward Fitzgerald (New York: Duell, Sloan & Pearce, 1950), 161.
21. Statement of Lt. Col. Ojukwu to Diplomatic Representatives of the U.K. and U.S.A., Sept. 1966, reprinted in *Nigerian Crisis, 1966: Eastern Nigerian Viewpoint* (Enugu: Eastern Nigeria Ministry of Information, 1966), 42.
22. "The Addis Ababa Agreement on the Problem of South Sudan," Chaps. IV–VI, in *The Grass Curtain* (London) 2 (May 1972): 18–20.
23. Nelson Kasfir, "Southern Sudanese Politics Since the Addis Ababa Agreement," *African Affairs* 76 (Apr. 1977): 143–66; James E. Sulton, Jr., "Regional Autonomy in the Southern Sudan: A Study in Conflict Regulation" (Ph.D. diss., Johns Hopkins Univ., 1980), 200–03, 255–56, 410; *Sudanow* (Khartoum) 5 (June 1980): 12.

achieved some balance between North-South issues and intra-Southern issues, but the balance was undone by the controversial division of the South into three regions in 1983 and the resurgence of warfare thereafter.

The development councils adopted in Sri Lanka in 1980 are also centrally controlled, but they, too, augur some restructuring of conflict. Elected councils were set up in every administrative district. However, members of parliament comprise a majority of members of each council, and a centrally appointed district minister sits as a member of the council's executive committee. The councils operate as local authorities in rural areas and have limited powers of taxation, but the district minister and the central government he represents retain ultimate authority.[24] In order to make them more palatable to Sinhalese opinion, which fears Tamil separatism, the development councils were portrayed as mere adjuncts of the district ministers, useful for decentralizing development functions.[25] In fact, they were designed to be district legislatures. At the time of adoption, some policy planners spoke of the councils as a "settlement" with the Tamils, an arrangement for "quasi-federalism," or "24 states."[26] Plainly, the councils were intended to devolve power upon local authorities which, in the North and East, would be Tamil-dominated.

That, indeed, is how they were perceived by Muslim members of the commission appointed to make recommendations regarding the structure of the councils. In a concurring report, two Muslims pointedly opposed inclusion of the Muslim minority, heavily concentrated in the Eastern Province, within the jurisdiction of Tamil-dominated units; they also opposed elections to the councils.[27] Their apprehension reflects the

24. By the terms of the Development Councils Act, No. 35 of 1980, sections 61–63, the district minister is empowered to remove any council member or the chairman of the council for incompetence, mismanagement, abuse of power, unlawful behavior, or default in the performance of duty, while the president of Sri Lanka is authorized to dissolve a council's executive committee if there are differences between it and the district minister or to remove executive committee members for incompetence or mismanagement. For a survey of the councils, see Bruce Matthews, "District Development Councils in Sri Lanka," *Asian Survey* 22 (Nov. 1982): 1117–34.

25. See, e.g., *Far Eastern Economic Review* (Hong Kong), Aug. 17, 1979, p. 15. In an interview, however, President Jayewardene referred revealingly to district ministers as becoming "rather like the Chief Ministers who run Indian states." *Ceylon Observer* (Colombo), Apr. 6, 1980.

26. I am drawing here and elsewhere in this discussion on interviews I conducted with several members of the Presidential Commission on Development Councils and some leading politicians and policymakers, Sinhalese, Tamil, and Muslim, in Colombo in April 1980.

27. *Report of the Presidential Commission on Development Councils*, Sessional Paper No. V—1980 (Colombo: Government Publications Bureau, 1980), 83–95 (Note of Reservation by Mr. A. C. M. Ameer, Q.C., and Mr. M. A. Azeez).

fact that, as Tamils are outnumbered by Sinhalese in Sri Lanka, Muslims are outnumbered by Tamils in the Eastern Province. In the first elections to the councils, held in 1981, the Tamil United Liberation Front did indeed capture control over the six councils in the North and East.

Were it not for the severe anti-Tamil riots of 1983, as well as the continuing Tamil terrorism and army reprisals, it would seem safe to conclude that the Sri Lankan devolution might portend a good deal less Sinhalese-Tamil conflict at the center, in exchange for somewhat more intra-Tamil and Tamil-Muslim conflict in the districts of the East. This last, of course, is not subethnic, for the Muslims are not Tamils (though they are Tamil-speaking), but it is certainly conflict at a lower level and with different alignments. Where groups are territorially concentrated, devolution may have utility, not because it provides "self-determination," but because, once power is devolved, it becomes somewhat more difficult to determine who the self is.

That the riots and the terrorism occurred despite the devolution is, of course, no evidence against the efficacy of devolving power. The terrorism that precipitated the riots was, as I shall suggest in Chapter 16, the product of long-standing Tamil frustration. What the violence shows, once again, is the importance of timing: accommodation long delayed may be accommodation ultimately denied.

Heterogeneous States

Where groups are territorially intermixed, some reduction in conflict at the center may be achieved by the creation of heterogeneous states. The Malaysian federal system illustrates several purposes that may be fulfilled by carving out states with varying degrees of heterogeneity.

First, as the new states in Nigeria showed, federalism can create political compartments in which ethnically and subethnically differentiated parties can flourish. If ethnic ratios vary from state to state, a group that is a minority at the center may be a majority in one or more states and may be in a position to rule these states, thereby mitigating its reduced influence or even exclusion at the center. This was the theory behind the unwritten arrangement that gave the Chinese a preeminent voice in the Chinese-majority state of Penang. Like reserved offices—which it practically is—this arrangement tends to exacerbate subethnic divisions and promote intraethnic party competition.

Second, state governments provide opportunities for the development of interethnic elite relations that sometimes soften ethnic hostility among politicians. In Malaysia, land is a subject reserved to the states. Chinese businessmen who need land for development or who need state approval for other projects find it advantageous to develop close relations with the Malay chief minister or with members of the state executive council. A frequent result of these close business relations is that the Malay politicians involved become "much quieter" on ethnic issues.[28]

Third, though it may seem unlikely, even ethnically heterogeneous states may produce a quarantine effect for certain issues of ethnic conflict. Two of the worst outbreaks of ethnic violence in Malaysia—in Penang in 1967 and in Kuala Lumpur in 1969—were largely, though not entirely, confined to the states in which they began. The issues which precipitated the violence may have been seen as local or state issues; in the latter case, the precipitant was related to the results of the state elections. Quarantine effects seem more likely where state boundaries have some historical foundation, as they do in Malaysia, and are not merely convenient constructs. The creation of ethnically heterogeneous states may help scale down to the state level some divisive issues that might otherwise engulf the entire country.

If this is so, the benefits of heterogeneous states challenge the conventional wisdom that federalism is an apt prescription for ethnic conflict only when groups are territorially compact and therefore amenable to encapsulation in homogeneous units. In fact, the prospects for federalism are more complex than the conventional formula would indicate, for neither homogeneous nor heterogeneous units are useful under all conditions.

As I have noted, what makes homogeneous states useful in conflict control is the existence of lower-level cleavages that are activated in state politics. Without subethnic divisions or lower-level ethnic divisions than those that prevail in politics at the center—or *with* a structure that suppresses such lower-level divisions, as the old regional system did in Nigeria—homogeneous states are unlikely to reduce conflict at the center. Rather, they are likely to be, as the Nigerian regions were, springboards

---

28. The phrase is drawn from an interview I conducted with a Malay politician in Kuala Lumpur, Jan. 1968. Joseph S. Nye has pointed out that one function of corruption is sometimes to "overcome divisions in a ruling elite that might otherwise result in destructive conflict," and he specifically notes that elites based on power and on wealth sometimes have "assimilated each other" through corrupt payments. "Corruption and Political Development: A Cost-Benefit Analysis," *American Political Science Review* 61 (June 1967): 417–27, at 420. In Malaysia, interethnic elite relations at the state level are greatly facilitated by the multiethnic alliance that has long ruled the country and nearly all the states. Because of this party arrangement, state-level Malay and Chinese politicians simply must deal with each other.

to group power at the center. Especially if there are only a few units, homogeneous states on the model of the First Nigerian Republic will exacerbate rather than alleviate ethnic conflict. Consequently, not all homogeneous states are an improvement on no states at all.

On the other hand, heterogeneous states sometimes are a decided improvement on unitary government. However, as we shall see in a moment, heterogeneous states embracing territorially separate groups, each occupying a portion of the state, have some tendency to fission. In practical terms, therefore, heterogeneous states with the greatest potential for reducing ethnic conflict are those whose groups are intermixed or whose territorial boundaries have some long-standing binding force, as the Malaysian states (formerly sultanates) have.

In short, federalism is not for everybody. The federal judgment must be a differentiated and prudential one. Even so, it is safe to say that federalism or at least some devolution has conflict-reducing possibilities for many more countries than have so far contemplated it.

The Fine Art of Devolution

Whether to attempt to use homogeneous or heterogeneous states in conflict reduction, and how much power to devolve, depends on which of the underlying mechanisms of conflict reduction stands the best chance of functioning in a given environment. If intraethnic cleavages can be utilized to reduce the energy expended at the center in interethnic conflict, their availability points to homogeneous states and, as indicated earlier, a generous grant of power. Similarly, if group disparities coincident with region are so pronounced that the aim is to use federalism for distributive purposes, either within states or at the center by allocating opportunities by states, then, too, homogeneous states are called for; and if the aim is specifically to create state bureaucracies composed differently from the federal one, this argues for more state-level powers and functions. If the objective is simply to take the heat off an overheated center, then heterogeneous states may accomplish this and in the process help quarantine some conflict-producing issues that might otherwise be carried to the center. If, however, federalism is to foster interethnic cooperation, there are two routes to this. One is the Nigerian, which, using homogeneous and heterogeneous states, at first whittled down the power of the largest Northern group, thereby heightening incentives for interethnic cooperation at the federal level. The other route is the Malaysian, which proliferates the occasions for interethnic cooperation at the state level in mainly heterogeneous states, so that state politicians who find their way to the center have already had experience in dealing with leaders of other groups.

Generally, if states are heterogeneous, this points toward more cautious devolution, so as not to jeopardize interethnic cooperation that can be built up at the state level. Moreover, if significant goods can be obtained at the center, the possibility increases that some issues at the center will be defined in terms of state rather than ethnic interest, and competition for those goods will involve one ethnically heterogeneous unit against another. So again, if states are heterogeneous, a more powerful center is advisable.

More often than not, perhaps, homogeneous states will be indicated, but the availability of various mechanisms of conflict reduction—hence the attractiveness of one kind of unit or another—depends on the configuration of divisive issues, as well as the territorial distribution and internal structure of the groups. It needs to be underscored, however, that many regimes will be reluctant to devolve power on homogeneous regions that have exhibited separatist inclinations, and many more will be reluctant to weaken central authority by significant grants of power. More about these qualms shortly.

How many units are optimal for conflict reduction in a federal system is unanswerable for more than one reason. First of all, it depends on the size of groups relative to the state and relative to each other. The Hausa imbalance in Nigeria clearly called for a significant number of states if ethnic and subethnic divisions in the North were to be brought to bear in the creation of incentives to interethnic cooperation. The Southern Sudan did not present the same problem, and a single Southern region was sufficient to bring subethnicity into play. Equally important, it is difficult to forecast when an exercise in state creation will prove enduring. There is usually room for subsequent pressure to alter the number and boundaries of states. India and Nigeria have been through several waves of proliferating states, and in neither has the last word been spoken.

There has been a propensity for heterogeneous units within which groups are territorially concentrated to be somewhat more inclined to fission than are homogeneous units. In India, there has been the Andhra movement in Madras, the linguistic states movement in general, the division of Punjab into Haryana and a truncated Punjab, and the fragmentation of Assam into a half dozen units along ethnic lines. Strong

demands for new states in Nigeria also emanated from sharply heterogeneous states like Kaduna, Cross River, Rivers, and Bendel. But more
homogeneous states have not been immune from fissiparous tendencies—witness, in India, the Saurashtra movement in Gujarat and the
Mysore movement in Karnataka, or, in Nigeria, the Enugu movement in
Anambra and the Oshun movement in Oyo. Absent preexisting states,
principalities, emirates, or sultanates, to whose traditional boundaries
the new units may cleave, there is a tendency for ethnic groups and
prominent subethnic groups to advance claims to statehood that, if
granted, might result in a greater-than-anticipated number of largely
homogeneous states. Very often, however, such claims can be resisted or
placated with much less than separate statehood: strong separatist
movements are common but not universal.[29]

Within limits, the more states there are, the greater will be the tendency of ethnic and subethnic groups to be concerned with parochial
alignments and issues, and the greater will be their difficulty of combining across state lines to make coherent and divisive claims at the center.
All else being equal, therefore, it is probably better to have more rather
than fewer states.[30] Yet there is wisdom in Sir Geoffrey Vickers' observation that, in reorganizing institutions, "it is easiest to subdivide, more
difficult to combine and most difficult to carve up and regroup the constituents of a going concern."[31] It may be desirable to end up with a large
number of units but prudent to begin with fewer.

The Costs of Federalism

In most Asian and African states, there are so many obstacles to decentralization that one hardly needs to call attention to the costs of federalism here. Yet there *are* costs: duplication of function, expenses of build-

29. For an example of placation, see Howard Spodek, " 'Injustice to Saurashtra': A
Case Study of Regional Tensions and Harmonies in India," *Asian Survey* 12 (May 1972):
416–28.

30. There is a related question regarding when to encapsulate a whole group in a single
state and when to split it between two or more states. There may be a tradeoff here between
the need to break up a large group and the desire to quarantine conflict within state
boundaries. The former is aptly illustrated by the allocation of the Hausa, Yoruba, and Ibo
to more than one state each. The latter is illustrated by Indian federalism. In those Indian
states that encapsulate whole groups, a conflict that flares up typically does not spill across
state boundaries. Not all groups are so encapsulated, however. There are Bengalis in
Assam, as well as in West Bengal, and anti-Bengali agitation and violence in Assam cannot
be confined to that state. Likewise, tensions between "backward castes" and upper castes
in North India tend to cross state lines, particularly in Uttar Pradesh and Bihar, so that
conflicts in one state reverberate in the other.

31. Vickers, *The Art of Judgment* (London: Chapman & Hall, 1965), 59.

ing state capitals, various diseconomies of small scale. There is also, however, an ethnic conflict cost that should be underscored.

One of the strongest forces for devolution is the expectation that government offices in lower-level units will be composed differently from central bureaucracies. The assumption may simply be that, if nature takes its course, the composition of the state civil service will generally resemble the ethnic composition of the region or state. To make this happen, no discrimination is necessary—hence the appeal of devolution for achieving ethnically distributive goals—although a language of administration different from the central official language (Tamil in the Tamil districts of Sri Lanka, for example) may be a facilitating condition. In practice, however, ethnic discrimination may occur, affecting particularly the fortunes of well-educated groups willing to migrate in search of opportunities outside their own states. This has been a serious problem in Nigeria. Some states had hired out-of-state employees on limited-term contracts, rather than on the terms available to domiciliaries of the state. In the 1970s, the military government and then the new constitution put an end to discriminatory terms of employment, but there is no guarantee that applicants from out of state will be hired at all. The other side of this particular Nigerian coin was a growing parochialism, signified by an aphorism enjoining civil servants to serve in their own states: "Don't be a Peace Corps."[32]

Another form of discrimination is perhaps more likely where regional autonomy schemes are implemented. An assumption may grow that members of groups with "their own" regions have no claim to work in the central government or anywhere outside their region. Such a reaction was certainly feared by those Ceylon Tamils who consistently opposed federalism. Ethnic discrimination and its attendant inefficiencies are thus facilitated by territorial boundaries.

I shall deal more extensively with the costs and benefits of distributive policies later. Suffice it to say here that, to the extent that territorial arrangements have an ethnically distributive impact, they are not exempt from these costs and benefits.

DEVOLUTION TO AVERT SEPARATISM

Important as it is to ask how a regime of devolved power should be structured, it is also important to ask related questions: when and how

32. I am grateful to Dr. Martin Dent for a letter, Jan. 6, 1978, containing the quotation and a discussion of the problem and to Dr. Anthony Oyewole for a helpful conversation in Ife, Jan. 16, 1978.

devolution and other policies to counter separatism can be put in place and how they can avoid fostering the very secession they aim to prevent. Proposals for devolution abound, but more often than not devolution agreements are difficult to reach and, once reached, soon abort. Most such agreements are concluded against a background of secessionist warfare or terrorist violence. Where central authority is secure, as in India, the appropriate decisions can be made and implemented by the center. But, where the very question is how far the writ of the center will run, devolution is a matter of bilateral agreement, and an enduring agreement is an elusive thing.

The recent history of Arab-Kurdish relations in Iraq is laced with failed agreements for Kurdish autonomy—agreements unimplemented by Baghdad or later rejected by the Kurds when their prospects in warfare seemed better. The federation of Eritrea with Ethiopia was resisted from the first by Muslim Eritreans and was later undone by Addis Ababa, which forced Eritrean integration into the Empire. In the course of the Moro rebellion, the Philippine government put into effect a regional autonomy scheme; it was quickly rejected as inadequate by the Moro National Liberation Front that had sought it. Only slowly have some MNLF factions begun to accept it. Bad timing, reluctance to relinquish critical areas of central control, or the prospect of additional external assistance for the separatists can easily undo such arrangements.

It takes some special conditions to create a federal or regional autonomy arrangement that will take hold. A more general constitutional change provides an auspicious setting in which to consider new territorial arrangements to cope with ethnic problems. New states were created with alacrity as the Nigerian military began the process of turning power back to civilians. The democratization of Spain was a suitable occasion to provide for regional autonomy for the Basques, Catalans, and Galicians. In Sri Lanka, adoption of a new presidential constitution and the increasing role of district ministers comprised the background against which power could be confided to district-level development councils. A long period of warfare that brings home the destructive impact of unrestrained ethnic conflict can sometimes serve to catalyze change (Nigeria and the Sudan), but not always (Burma and Iraq). Where separatist warfare is ongoing, a decline in the capacities of the antagonists may be conducive to a regional autonomy settlement. The Sudanese regional autonomy agreement was concluded at a time when Uganda had limited Anyanya access to supplies. The Numeiry regime in Khartoum had barely survived a Communist coup attempt and had to contend with a continuing threat from the Ansar sect. Both sides therefore felt weaker than they previously had, and regional autonomy seemed more attractive than pursuing each side's preferred alternative, with its high costs and uncertain outcome.[33] Policymakers can search for opportunities, but it is difficult to create them out of whole cloth.

The problem is complicated, as the Sudanese example well shows, by the presence of two sides that must agree. Different techniques are applicable to securing the acquiescence of ethnic groups influential in the central government, on the one hand, and gaining the acceptance of the separatists, on the other.

Regional autonomy or federal arrangements are often viewed as undue concessions to separatist sentiment. They may entail a diminution of sovereignty, or confer what seem like special privileges on troublesome and disliked ethnic groups, or "strengthen centrifugal forces and play into the hands of the separatists."[34] The widespread fear that regionalism or statehood will merely feed the secession is difficult to dispel, but there are partial answers. One is for the central government to retain ultimate control over the powers of regional governments, as central governments were able to do in the Sudan, Sri Lanka, and Spain, without losing the cooperation of the beneficiary groups. Another way to reduce opposition to regional autonomy is to make it available not only to separatist regions but to all regions. The Sri Lankan development councils were to be operative throughout the country, and Spanish regional government has been offered to all regions on a referendum basis. The Sudanese scheme followed a local government law decentralizing authority to all the provinces.[35] Here, however, there is a tradeoff, exempli-

---

33. Numeiry had executed his Minister of Southern Affairs, who was a Communist, replacing him with another Southerner (Abel Alier) who came to enjoy his confidence. Even before the agreement, Numeiry signaled willingness to provide funds for the South and had enacted a Local Government Law that decentralized authority to the provincial level. On some difficult issues, such as language, the regional autonomy agreement was ambiguous but conciliatory to the South; and it made the regional council executive subject to Numeiry's authority. But the agreement also offered the separatist guerrillas the chance to join the Sudanese armed forces. See generally Sulton, "Regional Autonomy in the Southern Sudan"; Kasfir, "Southern Sudanese Politics Since the Addis Ababa Agreement"; John Howell, "Politics in the Southern Sudan," *African Affairs* 72 (Apr. 1973): 163–78.

34. Astri Suhrke, "The Muslims in Southern Thailand: An Analysis of Political Developments, 1968–78" (unpublished paper, Washington, D.C., Dec. 1978), 4.

35. Subsequently, the Sudanese devolution ran into difficulty partly because of asymmetry between the Northern and Southern regions. The Self-Government Act of 1972 created one region in the South. Five were created in the North. In the early 1980s, a move to divide the South into several regions, comparable to the Northern regions, created considerable apprehension in the South. See Dunstan Wai, "Geoethnicity and the Margin of Autonomy in the Sudan," in Donald Rothchild and Victor A. Olorunsola, eds., *State Versus Ethnic Claims: African Policy Dilemmas* (Boulder: Westview, 1983), 304–30.

fied by earlier Sri Lankan attempts to regionalize and resistance to regionalization in Spain. By universalizing regional autonomy, it is possible to dispel ethnic opposition to special concessions, only to solidify opposition based on the generalized fear of politicians that rival power centers are being created or that central authority will be dissipated altogether. Opposition based on either ground can doom the scheme.

The Sri Lanka scheme might not have been possible without changes in the structure of the central government. Previous attempts to devolve power on Tamil authorities had failed because Sinhalese opposition had produced back-bench revolts. Since 1978, however, Sri Lanka has had a presidential system and a constitutional provision that prevents legislators, elected on a party list system, from crossing the aisle without risking their seats.[36] As intended, the result is much greater latitude for "unpopular decisions"[37] between elections. The prospects for policies to reduce conflict are closely related to the character of broader structural arrangements.

Precautions such as a fixed presidential term may make it possible to offer regional autonomy or federalism, but they are no guarantee of its acceptance by separatists. Here some distinctions, based on timing and the character of the secession, are in order. An early, generous offer of autonomy, made before extreme separatist organizations outflank moderate leaders, may avert secession.[38] A similar offer, made after separatist violence has broken out, may well do what opponents of concessions fear: it may testify to the weakness or vacillation of the central government and the success of the separatists, thereby fortifying their will to

36. *The Constitution of the Democratic Socialist Republic of Sri Lanka*, section 99 (13) (Colombo: Department of Government Printing, 1978), as amended by the Second Amendment to the Constitution, Feb. 22, 1979.

37. "To ensure the stability of the Government between elections was very important because in all developing countries Governments had to take what may be termed unpopular decisions . . . ." Statement of H.E. Mr. J. R. Jayewardene, President of Sri Lanka, at the Commonwealth Heads of Government Regional Meeting, Sept. 1980 (mimeo., n.d.), 2.

38. For the succession of increasingly intransigent organizations, each outflanking the one that preceded it, see, e.g., Brian Crozier, *The Rebels: A Study of Post-War Insurrections* (Boston: Beacon Press, 1960), 85–89; Martin R. Doornbos, "Protest Movements in Western Uganda: Some Parallels and Contrasts," in Raymond L. Hall, ed., *Ethnic Autonomy—Comparative Dynamics: The Americas, Europe and the Developing World* (New York: Pergamon Press, 1979), 274. Somewhat the same thing can be said for a policy of repression. Early, decisive, and consistent use of force against separatism seems to deter separatist warfare; late, equivocal, or sporadic repression (alternating with concession) seems merely to strengthen the separatists' resolve, as it surely did in Burma and the Sudan. Cf. Joane Nagel, "The Conditions of Ethnic Separatism: The Kurds in Turkey, Iran, and Iraq," *Ethnicity* 7 (Sept. 1980): 279–97, esp. 295–96.

fight on. Years after warfare broke out in Chad, the Tombalbaye regime devolved revenue and judicial powers to the North, without any effect on separatism.[39] In addition, there is a greater chance that regional autonomy will reduce separatist sentiment among late, reluctant secessionists like the Ibo and the Ceylon Tamils than among early, eager secessionists like the Chadian Muslims, the Karens, and the Moros.[40] Policy latitude contracts much more quickly with early secessionists.

Federalism or regionalism will be most attractive if it is coupled with policies whose effect is to raise the costs of a successful secession. Here it is possible to learn something pertinent to policy from negative cases. Why is it that the Luo in Kenya, whose home is in the West and who resent the dominance of the Kikuyu, have never "seriously contemplated a Biafra-type secession"?[41] Clearly, it is because they hold influential positions in major Kenyan towns outside their region, especially Nairobi and Mombasa. Like the Lozi of Zambia, but unlike the Ibo, ethnic conflict has not forced them to return home. Secession is less attractive if it is likely to mean a forfeiture of abundant opportunities outside the home region.

This lesson has not been lost on some regimes seeking to counter separatism. Pakistan has continued the British practice of providing Pathans with opportunities in the army, frontier scouts, and militia, while at the same time expending disproportionate funds on investment in Pathan areas, so that other groups even speak sarcastically of the government as "Pathan Raj."[42] The Nagas have had similar treatment from the Indian government: a package of statehood, investment, and reserved offices outside of Nagaland.[43] Once again, structural and distributive policies are used in tandem.

In point of fact, the two principal disincentives to secession are dispersion of the separatist group's population outside of the separatist region, especially in lucrative opportunities, and the regional investments or subsidies that a separatist region would lose if it opted out. It is revealing that Kurdish demands in Iraq recurrently embody claims to increased

39. For a discussion of these matters, I am indebted to a conversation with a Chadian economist in Washington, D.C., July 19, 1971.

40. For the basic distinction between these two types of separatist groups, see Chapter 6, above.

41. David Parkin, "Congregational and Interpersonal Ideologies in Political Ethnicity," in Abner Cohen, ed., *Urban Ethnicity* (London: Tavistock, 1974), 142.

42. Hugh Tinker, *India and Pakistan: A Political Analysis*, rev. ed. (New York: Praeger, 1968), 146.

43. *Far Eastern Economic Review*, May 11, 1979, pp. 27–29. See also the report of Walter Schwarz, *Washington Post*, Mar. 3, 1974.

opportunities in Arab areas and to augmented expenditures in Kurdish areas, both in addition to autonomy.[44] Conversely, the 1980 "sovereignty-association" referendum in Quebec was defeated after a campaign that emphasized the post-separatist isolation that Francophones would suffer in Ontario, New Brunswick, and Manitoba, and that made telling points about tariff protection, federal subsidies, and the ratio of funds expended in Quebec to taxes collected there.[45] Even then, as a separatist leader argued, sovereignty was also a matter of "pride,"[46] and the referendum outcome was not foreordained.

Some secession-inhibiting policies are easy to carry out. For advanced, population-exporting groups, this is largely a matter of limiting discrimination and preventing violence against them outside their home region, so as to protect their diaspora. For advanced regions (such as the Basque country) that complain that they are subsidizing the rest of the country, the power confided to regional authorities probably needs to include an ample measure of freedom to tax and spend. For many regions, especially the more developed regions, financial policies in general may be used to create interregional entanglements and interdependence without explicit ethnic provisions. Beyond this, the problem becomes delicate, for policy may involve ethnically preferential expenditures that can simultaneously do too little to prevent separatism and yet so much as to provoke an ethnic reaction to the policies. (Here, again, we are up against the costs and benefits of preferential policies, a subject I shall deal with in Chapter 16.)

Territory constitutes a framework in which incentives and disincentives operate. These do not always determine group decisions to secede.

44. The Kurdish demand is usually for proportional representation in government positions and proportional per capita expenditure in Kurdish areas. Lorenzo Kent Kimball, *The Changing Pattern of Political Power in Iraq, 1958 to 1971* (New York: Robert Speller, 1972), 141–42; Charles M. Benjamin, "The Kurdish Non-State Nation" (unpublished paper presented at the 1975 annual meeting of the International Studies Association), 6; Abdul H. Raoof, "Kurdish Ethnic Nationalism and Political Development in Republican Iraq" (unpublished paper presented at the 1971 annual meeting of the Middle East Studies Association), 4, 10.

45. It was said that, if Quebec seceded, the Franco-Ontarians would become homeless "Palestinians of North America." *The Gazette* (Montreal), Apr. 22, 1980. To allay fears of Francophones in New Brunswick, the Parti Québécois (PQ) announced its support of a separate Acadian state there. Ibid., Feb. 1, 1980. Quebec's dependence on the Ontario market, on federal oil and health subsidies and pension supplements, and on spending in Quebec above Quebec's tax contributions were all stressed in the anti-separatist campaign. The PQ conceded the last point, but argued that the relevant measure was lower federal spending per capita compared to that in other provinces, rather than expenditures against revenues. *Financial Post* (Toronto), Mar. 8, 1980. I am indebted to Barbara G. Haskel for an array of press clippings on Quebec ethnic issues.

46. Jacques Parizeau, quoted in *The Gazette*, Jan. 22, 1980.

Moreover, different sorts of incentives and disincentives are apt for different kinds of separatist groups. Policy measures will not always work or may not work when policymakers are ready to have them work. Nonetheless, the broader point remains: the most potent way to assure that federalism or regional autonomy will not become just a step to secession is to reinforce those specific interests that groups have in the undivided state.

ELECTORAL SYSTEMS
AND CONFLICT REDUCTION

Electoral systems have a role in fostering or retarding ethnic conflict. The delimitation of constituencies, the electoral principle (such as proportional representation or first-past-the-post), the number of members per constituency, and the structure of the ballot all have a potential impact on ethnic alignments, ethnic electoral appeals, multiethnic coalitions, the growth of extremist parties, and policy outcomes.

Unfortunately, the development of this fertile field has been arrested by two fortuitous circumstances. First, in Asia and Africa, concern for minority electoral protection initially took the form of imposition of a separate electoral roll for Muslims in India and later for certain minorities elsewhere.[47] This began a long and sterile debate over whether the so-called communal roll widens or narrows existing gaps between ethnic groups.[48] Second, scholarly studies of electoral systems have had a completely different focus: whether proportional representation is more conducive to the proliferation of parties than is the first-past-the-post system

47. In 1906, the British in India were first confronted with a demand for a separate Muslim electoral roll, the first of many such demands they encountered in the colonies. See Sir Reginald Coupland, *The Indian Problem*, vol. 1 (London: Oxford Univ. Press, 1942), 28–36. Although they yielded in India, the British eventually resisted in other colonies, such as Ceylon, which had communal rolls until the Donoughmore Commission, in drafting the universal suffrage constitution adopted in 1931, set its face decisively against them. Ceylon Tamils accordingly boycotted the first elections under the constitution. Robert N. Kearney, *The Politics of Ceylon (Sri Lanka)* (Ithaca: Cornell Univ. Press, 1973), 28–33. As independence approached, the British tended to accede to separate rolls or seats only where white settlers insisted, as in Kenya, or where the British saw self-government as impossible without them, notably in Fiji and Cyprus. See Glen Wright, "Fiji Approaches Independence," *Race Today* (London), Apr. 1970, pp. 114–15; "Fijian Independence," *Current Notes on International Affairs* (Canberra) 41 (Sept. 1970): 461–64; Adamantia Pollis, "Intergroup Conflict and British Colonial Policy: The Case of Cyprus," *Comparative Politics* 5 (July 1973): 575–99.

48. The debate was sterile because it was abstruse and acontextual. A splendid example of the debate is W. J. M. Mackenzie, "Representation in Plural Societies," *Political Studies* 2 (Feb. 1954): 54–69.

of election.[49] Although this debate has some relevance to the impact of electoral formulae on ethnicity, it has scarcely touched explicitly on ethnic variables at all.[50]

Politicians have been more acutely aware of the ethnic impact of electoral provisions. Various forms of electoral manipulation and gerrymandering have been practiced in many countries to favor one group or another. More recently, electoral innovation has been used by a small but growing number of severely divided societies in Asia and Africa as a vehicle for ethnic accommodation.

There are several possible goals of such innovations, and there has not always been great clarity about them. All of the goals stem from the growth of ethnically based parties in severely divided societies.

Suppose, once again, that two groups, A and B, support their respective parties, A and B. Suppose further that Group A comprises 60 percent of the population and a majority of voters in 60 percent of the single-member electoral constituencies, with members elected on a first-past-the-post formula; Group B comprises a 40 percent minority overall and a majority in 40 percent of the constituencies. Clearly, as the election returns come in, Group A and its ethnic party appear to have gained power for the indefinite future. This, as we have seen, is a simplified version of the situation that prevailed in many Asian and African countries under free elections after independence. Ethnic parties developed, majorities took power, and minorities took shelter. It was a fearful situation, in which the prospect of minority exclusion from government, underpinned by ethnic voting, was potentially permanent. Variants of this situation were responsible for much of the instability in the post-colonial world in the first ten years of independence. Civil violence, military coups, and the advent of single-party regimes can all be traced to this problem of inclusion-exclusion. Now the question is whether anything can be done about it while free elections prevail.

In principle, there are three solutions to the pure form of the problem depicted by the 60–40 split. The first is an alternation scheme, such as

---

49. See Maurice Duverger, *L'Influence des systèmes électoraux sur la vie politique* (Paris: Armand Colin, 1954); Maurice Duverger, *Political Parties*, trans. Barbara North and Robert North (New York: John Wiley, 1954); Douglas W. Rae, *The Political Consequences of Electoral Laws*, rev. ed. (New Haven: Yale Univ. Press, 1971).

50. An outstanding exception is J. A. Laponce, "The Protection of Minorities by the Electoral System," *Western Political Quarterly* 10 (June 1957): 318–39. See also J. A. Laponce, *The Protection of Minorities* (Berkeley and Los Angeles: Univ. of California Press, 1960).

the rotating presidency that was attempted unsuccessfully among three groups in Benin in the 1960s and somewhat more successfully after civil war in Colombia. Where ethnic divisions are deep, it is unlikely that such an arrangement will prove enduring. The second possibility is an all-embracing "national government." This is what many single-party regimes said they were creating when they dissolved the opposition, but what they were actually doing was something quite different. In the absence of an external emergency of the sort that produced the wartime national government in Britain, such a contrivance is no solution for ethnically divided Asian and African countries. The third solution is to use the electoral system to encourage party fragmentation with a view to producing one of two outcomes: (1) a split in Party A, resulting in two parties for Group A, neither of them with a majority of seats—hence the need for an interethnic coalition; (2) splits in both Party A and Party B, resulting in much more fluidity and, depending on how seats are apportioned, perhaps as many as four possible interethnic coalitions. It should be noted, however, that both of these solutions depend on the capacity of the electoral system to induce splits in at least one of the parties (A). Party A, however, has the most to lose if it does split, and it is thus most likely to try to avoid splitting.

There are, however, more complex versions of the ascriptive majority-minority problem. For all of them, let us assume, as before, that ethnic voting prevails; that each group has a majority in a number of parliamentary constituencies that is proportionate to ethnic shares of the population; and that the electoral formula is first-past-the-post in single-member constituencies.

Suppose Group A is 80 percent of the population, and Group B is 20 percent, but Group A is divided into two parties competing for the A vote. This is a dangerous situation, in which ethnic outbidding can occur, but it is not necessarily solved by splitting the support of Group A, which is already split. More useful would be incentives for the parties of Group A to behave moderately toward Group B or—and the two may go together—a device that would make the votes of Group B essential for the formation of a government. An even balance between the two parties of Group A may be preferable for this purpose to a system that splits Group A's support further, perhaps enabling the strongest of the A parties to win a majority of seats by recurrent pluralities in three- or four-way contests.

Another variant of the ascriptive majority-minority problem, a common one in fact, entails a situation in which several ethnic groups, none a majority, are potential contenders for power. There are, however, affinities among Groups *A*, *B*, and *C*, on the one hand, and *D*, *E*, and *F*, on the other. Given the exigencies of forming governments under the parliamentary system, it is possible that the two clusters will form two ethnically based parties, thus producing a situation as polarized as the 60–40 situation. Two courses of prevention suggest themselves. One is to create incentives for multiethnic support that will cross the chasm between the two clusters, making consolidation into two parties less likely. The other is to make it less exigent for the existing groups to congeal into a majority. Perhaps there is an electoral formula that can help preserve a more fluid multigroup-multiparty system.

So far, for simplicity, I have hypothesized situations in which ethnic group percentages get translated into the same fractional shares of votes for the party or parties of each ethnic group, which then get translated into the same fractional shares of seats. Thus, a group with 60 percent of the population was hypothesized, first, to cast 60 percent of the total vote for its party, and that party was assumed, second, to win 60 percent of the seats. In point of fact, there is distortion at both interchanges. Demographic and behavioral differences account for the first distortion; the electoral system typically introduces the second.

Even in conditions of acute ethnic conflict, with ethnic parties, ethnic group percentages of a population do not convert perfectly into percentages of a vote. Three variables intervene: (1) relative shares of eligible voters, which, holding registration rates constant, is essentially a function of the age structure of each ethnic group (groups with the largest percentage of members under the age of eligibility obviously have a smaller share of voters than of population); (2) relative rates of voter turnout, which vary with party organization, urban or rural concentration, and certain cultural features (in some groups, for instance, it is more difficult to induce women to vote); and (3) relative rates of voting for ethnic parties (even in high-conflict cases, the incidence of ethnic voting varies marginally from group to group). There is not much an electoral system can do about these variables, which are typically not decisive in polarizing elections in any case, and I shall not consider them further. For the sake of the discussion, I shall simply assume no difference between shares of a population and shares of a vote.

The translation of votes into seats is a wholly different matter, and it gives rise to yet another majority-minority problem. Quite commonly, a party with a mere plurality of votes obtains a solid majority of seats.[51] Suppose, then, in a 60–40 situation, the support of Group A is divided equally between two parties, while Group B's support is given solidly to one party. In three-sided contests in single-member constituencies, under a first-past-the-post formula, Group B's party, with 40 percent of the vote, may end up with as much as 60 percent of the seats. So a cohesive minority group can govern a less cohesive majority group, or a group with a plurality of the vote can gain a majority of seats if the balance of the vote is at all fragmented. Both of these outcomes are generally perceived as instances of illegitimate minority-group rule. Where they occur, they tend to create explosive situations. Several very serious ethnic riots are traceable to electoral results of this kind. The question is whether the electoral system can be modified so that shares of votes are translated more faithfully into shares of seats.

These hypothetical examples give rise to essentially five possible aims for an electoral system that is to be harnessed to the goal of ethnic accommodation. An attempt can be made to utilize the electoral system to:

1.   Fragment the support of one or more ethnic groups, especially a majority group, to prevent it from achieving permanent domination.

2.   Induce an ethnic group, especially a majority, to behave moderately toward another group and engage in interethnic bargaining.

3.   Encourage the formation of multiethnic coalitions.

4.   Preserve a measure of fluidity or multipolar balance among several groups to prevent bifurcation and the permanent exclusion of the resulting minority.

5.   Reduce the disparity between votes won and seats won, so as to reduce the possibility that a minority or plurality ethnic group can, by itself, gain a majority of seats.

The available evidence indicates that many of these aims can probably be achieved. That the aims are vitally important cannot be gainsaid. The alternative frequently is for ethnic party systems of the exclusionary 60–40 sort to produce violent reactions and narrowly based military or

---

51. Rae, *The Political Consequences of Electoral Laws*, 75–76. In Rae's sample of Western countries, every party with more than 48 percent of the vote secured more than 50 percent of the seats. Sometimes a party with as little as 40 percent of the vote was able to gain more than 50 percent of the seats. Occasionally, a party could gain as much as 73 percent of the seats with less than half the votes. Ibid.

single-party regimes. I intend to consider the feasibility of the five aims through an examination of electoral arrangements in four severely divided societies in four different regions of the world: Lebanon, Nigeria, Sri Lanka, and Guyana.

FLUIDITY THROUGH FIXITY: LEBANON

From the National Pact of 1943 to the civil war that began in 1975–76, Lebanon had an electoral system that encouraged moderation, that practically required interethnic coalitions, and that prevented the crystallization of allegiances around the overarching affiliations of Muslim versus Christian. Four electoral provisions were conducive to these results: reserved offices, reserved seats, interethnic tickets, and interethnic voting.[52] All the major offices were reserved. The president was to be a Maronite, the prime minister a Sunni, the speaker of the house a Shiite, the vice-speaker a Greek Orthodox, and so on. By the same token, the ethnic composition of the legislature was prescribed by law; that of the cabinet, by custom. Although there were variations over time, generally most constituencies were multimember and multiethnic. The ethnic identity of each seat was specified. There was a common electoral roll, so that each voter, regardless of ethnic identity, cast a ballot for each seat. Candidates formed competing interethnic lists, appealing to the entire electorate.

Rarely in a severely divided society has there been a system that placed as high a premium on intraethnic competition and interethnic cooperation. That the major political offices were reserved for members of specified groups meant that it was not possible for members of other groups to aspire to the same office and use ethnic appeals to mobilize support. Sunni aspirants for the prime ministership sought to link up with Maronite aspirants for the presidency, each trading the support he could muster

52. For the structures of Lebanese politics, see Michael C. Hudson, *The Precarious Republic: Political Modernization in Lebanon* (New York: Random House, 1968); Leonard Binder, ed., *Politics in Lebanon* (New York: John Wiley, 1966); David R. Smock and Audrey C. Smock, *The Politics of Pluralism: A Comparative Study of Lebanon and Ghana* (New York: Elsevier, 1975); Ralph E. Crow, "Religious Sectarianism in the Lebanese Political System," *Journal of Politics* 24 (Aug. 1963): 489–520; Michael W. Suleiman, "The Role of Political Parties in a Confessional Democracy: The Lebanese Case," *Western Political Quarterly* 20 (Sept. 1967): 682–93; Michael C. Hudson, "Democracy and Social Mobilization in Lebanese Politics," *Comparative Politics* 1 (Jan. 1969): 245–63; Enver M. Koury, *Crisis in the Lebanese System: Confessionalism and Chaos* (Washington, D.C.: American Enterprise Institute, 1976); Riad B. Tabbarah, "Background to the Lebanese Conflict," *International Journal of Comparative Sociology* 20 (Mar.–June 1979): 101–21.

in his own group for the support of the other. Reserved offices reinforced tensions within each group, while solidifying ties between one group and another. The same was true of legislative elections. Reserved seats restricted competition to members of the same group. Mixed tickets in multimember constituencies with a common roll required agreements among politicians of various groups—underpinned, of course, by the need for every candidate to obtain votes of members of several groups. The fixed proportions of the system meant that it was impossible to increase the number of seats held by any group or for a group to occupy an office or seat assigned to another group. All that was left was to squabble over who, among members of a given group, would occupy a seat or office and, in the process of doing so, to maximize support from sources outside the group.

This was a system that depended upon and exacerbated preexisting subethnic cleavages, based on family, clan, and region. Lebanon is richly endowed with such distinctions, and so it was by no means artificial to force one Maronite faction to oppose another, for instance, or to induce the Chouf Druze to line up against their Druze rivals, the Yazbakis. Lebanese subgroups were tailor-made for this system, and they rose to its opportunities.

With half a dozen major groups and many subgroup factions, typically organized around strong leaders, there was much flux in the system. The cabinet was, of course, composed of fixed proportions of the various groups. There were many candidates competing for inclusion in it, and so it was possible for the president to maintain his power by reshuffling the cabinet frequently. This flux in appointments was a disincentive to extreme opposition. A Shiite, for example, excluded from the cabinet today might be required for a Shiite position in it tomorrow. Extreme behavior could only impair his future attractiveness. Consequently, the same system that made subethnic factions the most relevant political actors encouraged rotation in office and discouraged ethnic appeals that might alienate potential electoral, legislative, or cabinet allies.

Similar forces inhibited the growth of political parties. It was the individual leaders who, by dint of ethnic and subethnic identity, were asked to fill reserved places. This enhanced the position of notables who commanded factions. Occasionally, they called their faction by a party name. (Some fifteen to twenty "parties" could be identified in the 1960s.) But party organization would have deprived such leaders of the flexibility they needed to make and unmake electoral arrangements and to enter and leave cabinets as individuals.[53] Moreover, there was no acceptable ethnic basis for party organization. Since ethnic hostility was strong, it was not possible to create parties that were multiethnic in support. Yet, because of the constant need to forge links and secure votes across ethnic lines, neither was it possible to create ethnically based parties. The system had to be personalistic.

The Lebanese system provided a deeply divided society with a politics of conciliation for over thirty years.[54] It was undone by many forces, external and internal, most of them unrelated to the character of the electoral system.[55] Two, however, bear mention. Neither is inherent in a Lebanese type of system.

First, the absence of parties created an organizational vacuum, which facilitated the emergence of armed private militias. These gangs, some of them attached to parliamentary politicians, had much greater freedom than they would have had if real party organizations had existed and seen them early on as rivals for political authority. The notorious weakness of the Lebanese state, related to its ethnic structure, was also conducive to the flourishing of militias.

Second, as indicated in Chapter 14, the fixed ethnic proportions of the system were a given. Small adjustments in parliamentary representation were made from time to time, but the overall proportional shape of the system, with its reserved offices, could only be challenged by challenging the entire structure. In a sense, Lebanese electoral institutions created two options: moderation or civil war. The former was much more common, but the latter, when it came, was deadly.

MULTIETHNICITY THROUGH DISTRIBUTION: NIGERIA

A new constitution went into effect in Nigeria in 1979. It was abrogated by military intervention less than five years later. In the interval, however, a major electoral experiment went forward.

Determined to avoid a recurrence of the ethnically exclusionary politics that had produced the Biafra war, the framers of the new constitution attempted a far-reaching reconstruction of the political system. Nigeria's parliamentary system was replaced by American-style institu-

---

53. Hudson, *The Precarious Republic*, 148, 265–66.
54. The brief 1958 civil war was an exception, but it was largely brought on by a breach of the rules by the then-president.
55. See Richard Hrair Dekmejian, "Consociational Democracy in Crisis: The Case of Lebanon," *Comparative Politics* 10 (Jan. 1978): 251–65.

tions, replete with a separately elected president, a two-house National Assembly, and a strong separation of powers, together with comparable institutions in the nineteen states. The reasoning was that the parliamentary system had been conducive to ethnic divisions. Whereas any party with a parliamentary majority—even an ethnically limited majority—could form a government and rule the rest, a nationally elected president might be more broadly representative. Even if not, the separation of powers could prevent an ethnic group dominating one branch from controlling everything.

The framers of the Nigerian constitution aimed at a multiethnic party system. In this they did not succeed, but they did not wholly fail either. A mixed electoral system produced mixed results. And indeed the framers seem to have succeeded in something they did not quite intend: preserving the fluidity of a multiplicity of ethnic parties against the threat of a North-South bifurcation.

The principal device to encourage multiethnic parties was the presidential electoral formula.[56] To be elected president, a candidate was required to win a plurality of votes nationwide plus at least 25 percent of the vote in no fewer than two-thirds of the nineteen states. Since no one or two ethnic groups (even in combination) had voters distributed widely enough to meet this stringent requirement, the expectation was that it would produce a party system with a small number of parties, perhaps just two, each with broad multiethnic support. Otherwise, it might be impossible for any presidential candidate to get elected.[57]

This logic was not incorrect, but it was incomplete. Although the presidential electoral formula did create incentives to multiethnicity and party consolidation, by itself it was not sufficient to produce broadly multiethnic parties or only two parties. Other features of the constitutional structure created countervailing incentives to one or both of these goals.

56. There was also a formal requirement of geographical distribution of party membership, to discourage ethnically exclusive parties, but this, predictably, was easily satisfied and was no impediment to any of the ethnically based parties. For the new Nigerian constitution, see Donald L. Horowitz, "About-Face in Africa: The Return to Civilian Rule in Nigeria," *Yale Review* 68 (Winter 1979): 192–206. I am also drawing here on interviews I conducted in Nigeria in 1978 and 1980.

57. The framers were much concerned with the possibility of deadlock, and they considered a number of different presidential electoral formulae to minimize the possibility. See ibid., 197–201. In the end, they settled on a vote of federal and state legislators if no candidate won on the first ballot, but the departing military government prescribed a runoff election instead.

The proliferation of states, as we have seen, made it possible for minority parties in the North to control states in the 1979 elections, thereby fragmenting party support in the North and insuring party proliferation overall. In fostering multipolarity, the new states served a function similar to the Lebanese electoral arrangements.

The two major Nigerian innovations thus pulled in opposite directions: the presidential distribution requirement toward fewer parties, the new states toward more. Overall, the incentives to party consolidation were not strong. With more than two presidential candidates, only a plurality was required to win. The candidate who did win in 1979 had only a third of the total vote, and in 1983 he still had less than half. The winner had to have broadly distributed support, but the party system did not have to congeal into two or three parties to produce a winner. Once a plurality president was installed, he might have to arrange a legislative coalition to get his program through, for his or another party might only have a plurality in the National Assembly, but his appointment power gave him bargaining leverage to negotiate a coalition; and, after the 1979 election, this was done. The coalition, rather short-lived, resembled Nigeria's earlier coalition of convenience.

The incentives to multiethnicity were also countered. There was, to be sure, no ignoring the distribution requirement for presidential election. All parties sought support outside their core region, but two did this better than the others. In the two elections held under the new constitution, 1979 and 1983, the mainly-Ibo party (NPP) drew considerable support in a Middle Belt state, Plateau, where it was also able to elect a governor. The mainly-Hausa party (NPN) developed strong links outside the Muslim North—in Rivers, Cross River, and Benue states— and came in first or second in nearly every state, in both presidential and senatorial contests. The NPN candidate, Shehu Shagari, was the only presidential contender even to approach the 25 percent distribution requirement. In 1979, he had the largest number of votes, more than 25 percent in twelve states, and about 20 percent in the thirteenth state. This, the electoral commission decided, was tantamount to having 25 percent in two-thirds of the states.[58] In 1983, Shagari won at least 25 percent in sixteen states, but some of those results were doubtful.

58. Unofficial returns of the presidential election may be found in *West Africa*, Aug. 27, 1979, p. 1573. For an analysis, see Richard A. Joseph, "Democratization Under Military Tutelage: Crisis and Consensus in the Nigerian 1979 Elections," *Comparative Politics* 14 (Oct. 1981): 75–100. For the 1983 presidential results, see *West Africa*, Aug. 15, 1983, p. 1866.

The presidential election was not the only election, but it was the only one to have the distribution requirement. Both houses of the National Assembly were elected on a first-past-the-post formula in single-member constituencies. These constituencies generally were ethnically homogeneous or had a majority or large plurality ethnic group. A presidential candidate might take his constituency to be all of multiethnic Nigeria. A representative or senator could hardly do the same. Inevitably, most members of the legislature would arrive in Lagos as delegates of their ethnic groups and would expect their parties to be responsive to ethnic claims.

The party system that emerged from this interplay of ethnic groups and electoral incentives was mainly a somewhat realigned, expanded, and newly balanced version of the earlier ethnic party system. Indeed, it is significant that proto-parties began to emerge as divisive ethnic issues emerged in the Constituent Assembly that redrafted the constitution.[59] But the new system did not seem to have the dangerous tendency of the earlier ethnic party system to polarize into two parties—one Northern, one Southern—for four parties survived through two general elections.

The electoral system of the Second Republic was subject to strong cross-pressures. Shagari's party had a core of support in the Hausa-Fulani North. Yet, if Hausa-Fulani interests had been given untrammeled sway by the president, the support his party enjoyed outside the North would have eroded. That extraregional support was more important than it was for the predecessor NPC in the First Republic. The presidential electoral formula required it. Even if some of the opposition parties had merged, the NPN's strength in the South would have made North-South bifurcation an unlikely outcome. It is not surprising that the president emerged as a conciliatory pan-ethnic figure or that the legislature was a forum for the expression of ethnic demands.[60] The two electoral systems pushed those subject to them in different directions. Parties, which aimed to elect both legislators and presidents, were simultaneously pulled both ways. Electoral engineering in the Nigerian Second Republic modified but did not obliterate the ethnic basis of the party system. That was to be expected, since the engineers went to work only on the election of the president.

59. A split over a proposed Sharia court of appeals, favored by the Muslim North but opposed by the Middle Belt and South, helped draw the first party lines, but later splits increased the number of parties eventually formed.

60. On such matters, for example, as the composition of the civil and foreign service, which was occasionally debated angrily in the legislature.

MODERATION THROUGH ALTERNATIVE VOTES
AND PROPORTIONAL REPRESENTATION: SRI LANKA

As the Nigerians were drafting a new constitution, so were the Sri Lankans. Both chose a presidential form of government, the Nigerian resembling the American arrangements, the Sri Lankan somewhat resembling the French, with a prime minister as well as a president. Both constitutions attempted in different ways to make provision for reducing ethnic tensions. Like the Nigerian constitution of 1978, the Sri Lankan constitution of 1978 adopted a different formula for electing the president from that employed in electing the legislature. But, while the Nigerian presidential formula was devised for ethnic engineering purposes, the Sri Lankan formulae responded to somewhat different concerns. Neither the presidential nor the legislative electoral provisions adopted in Sri Lanka aimed at multiethnic parties. Nevertheless, both Sri Lankan formulae are likely to have important effects on ethnic accommodation.[61]

Whereas the Nigerians constructed a presidential electoral formula that, they anticipated, would produce party consolidation, the Sri Lankans took their multiplicity of parties as a given. With the few parties they envisioned and the stringent distributive formula they enacted, the Nigerians were content to elect a president on a plurality basis, rather than resort to the additional complexities required to construct a majority if there were more than two candidates. With at least several parties, however, plurality election of the president was less attractive to the Sri Lankans, for the plurality achieved by a candidate might be a small fraction of the total vote. Only once in seven Sri Lankan general elections since independence had any party secured more than 50 percent of the total vote. The strongest party generally polled 30–40 percent. Accordingly, it was provided that the president must have a majority. But how to arrive at a majority if there are several candidates? For this purpose, a preferential or alternative vote system was adopted. Where there are three candidates, each voter must specify his second preference; where

---

61. The electoral innovations are described in C. R. de Silva, "The Constitution of the Second Republic of Sri Lanka (1978) and Its Significance," *Journal of Commonwealth and Comparative Politics* 17 (July 1979): 192–209; James Manor, "A New Political Order for Sri Lanka," *The World Today* 35 (Sept. 1979): 377–86; K. M. de Silva, "Political and Constitutional Change in Sri Lanka," *The Round Table* 273 (Jan. 1979): 49–57; W. A. Wiswa Warnapala, "Sri Lanka 1978: Reversal of Policies and Strategies," *Asian Survey* 19 (Feb. 1979): 178–87. The provisions are contained in *The Constitution of the Democratic Socialist Republic of Sri Lanka*, chap. XIV.

more than three candidates, his second and third preferences. In the absence of an initial majority, all but the top two candidates are eliminated. The alternative preferences of voters whose first (or second) choices are not among the top two contenders but whose second (or third) choices are among the top two are reallocated to them to compute a majority.

Under the previous parliamentary system, Tamil parties occasionally held the balance between the two major Sinhalese parties and were able to gain concessions in exchange for Tamil votes in Sinhalese-majority constituencies and Tamil support in parliament. More often than not, however, a plurality for one of the Sinhalese parties could be translated into a majority of parliamentary seats, thus obviating the need for conciliating the Tamils.[62] Under the new system, however, presidential candidates cannot benefit from such a bonus. Consequently, interparty arrangements must be made in advance for second preference votes. Under ordinary conditions, this should give the Tamil United Liberation Front, which largely controls the Ceylon Tamil vote, and the Ceylon Workers' Congress, which controls most of the Indian Tamil vote, good bargaining power. If Tamil candidates run for president, they are unlikely to finish first or second. The second and third preferences of Tamil voters should thus become quite valuable commodities in political exchange.[63] A Sinhalese president elected on reallocated Tamil votes has a strong disincentive to extremism. The alternative vote is said to be conducive to a politics of bargaining and moderation,[64] and Sri Lanka's use of the technique will probably work in accordance with that view. Unfortunately, the evidence so far is not conclusive. Until the 1983 riots, Sri Lanka's first president, J. R. Jayewardene, was certainly more moderate on ethnic issues than his predecessors. But, in the first election under the

62. For a convenient summary of party votes and seats since 1947, see James Manor, "The Failure of Political Integration in Sri Lanka (Ceylon)," *Journal of Commonwealth and Comparative Politics* 17 (Mar. 1979): 23–46, at 45 n.99.

63. For similar assessments, see de Silva, "The Constitution of the Second Republic of Sri Lanka (1978) and Its Significance," 198–99; Manor, "A New Political Order for Sri Lanka," 381. A more cynical interpretation of the second preference system holds that Tamil second preferences will generally go to the United National Party, thus insuring election of its candidate. The constitution was promulgated by a UNP government. But this argument comes to the same thing, for if any other Sinhalese candidate wishes to be elected president, he will have to bid against the UNP for Tamil support. Under either interpretation, the provision encourages interethnic bargaining.

64. Palley, *Constitutional Law and Minorities*, .6–17. Cf. Laponce, "The Protection of Minorities by the Electoral System," 326–28.

new system, vote transfers were not necessary, since Jayewardene won 52 percent of the vote.[65]

Soon thereafter, the future of interparty accommodation was put in jeopardy by the riots. Precipitated by a Tamil terrorist ambush of an army unit, the violence was no reflection on the new constitutional arrangements, which had not really been tested. But the aftermath of the riots opened a breach that made all interethnic political relations problematic.

The legislative electoral system adopted for the Second Sri Lankan Republic would also be expected to have a moderating effect on ethnic politics. As in the case of the president, the probable fate of Sinhalese candidates was linked to Tamil votes.

The principal purpose of the proportional representation scheme that was adopted was to prevent small swings in votes from producing large swings in number of seats. Sri Lanka has had a change of government at virtually every parliamentary election, and shares of seats have frequently been far out of line with shares of the total vote. As Douglas W. Rae has shown, proportional representation, like first-past-the-post, tends to inflate the strongest party's share of seats at the expense of the weakest, but PR does this less prominently than first-past-the-post; and PR does not generally magnify changes in party support when legislative seats are allocated, so it is particularly responsive to the oscillation problem the framers of the Sri Lanka constitution were addressing.[66]

The system adopted in Sri Lanka was the party list system by multimember territorial constituencies. To avert the party proliferation that was feared—some say to dilute the strength of the small Marxist parties—any party with less than one-eighth of the vote in a constituency is awarded no seats there. This is a rather high cutoff that disadvantages those small parties whose strength is not territorially concentrated.

In ethnic terms, PR should be conducive to Sinhalese moderation. PR in multimember constituencies tends to reduce the seat advantage enjoyed by territorially concentrated minorities, such as the Tamils.[67] So, assuming the continuation of Tamil parliamentary participation, the Tamil United Liberation Front will generally not gain more seats under

---

65. For a report, see S. W. R. de A. Samarasinghe, "Sri Lanka in 1982: A Year of Elections," *Asian Survey* 23 (Feb. 1983): 158–64.
66. Rae, *The Political Consequences of Electoral Laws*, 88–92, 101.
67. Ibid., 170.

this formula than under first-past-the-post.[68] The conciliatory effects derive, rather, from the apportionment of Sinhalese seats, the character of the list system, and the probable nature of electoral appeals.

First of all, PR seems likely to achieve the intended effect of reducing the spread between shares of votes and seats. With Sinhalese seats more evenly divided between the two main parties, Tamil support should more often be pivotal to the formation and maintenance of parliamentary majorities than it has previously been.

In addition, though the Tamil parties do not gain seats under PR, there may well be an increase in the number of Tamil candidates. Indeed, in multimember constituencies with Tamil minorities, Tamil candidates might even appear on Sinhalese party lists. The constituency list system of PR makes it more attractive for parties to have Tamil candidates than it was under first-past-the-post.

Finally, for similar reasons, PR tends to encourage moderation in electoral appeals where minority voters in a constituency can be alienated by Sinhalese extremism. Under first-past-the-post, at least in some constituencies, minority voters could be ignored by Sinhalese parties without paying a penalty in seats. Now that every last vote counts, this is a less compelling strategy.

Once again, however, there has been no definitive test, for, after the 1982 presidential election, the government decided to prolong the life of parliament by six years, until 1989. This it did by winning a referendum required by the constitution. Consequently, there has yet to be a parliamentary election conducted under PR.

The new importance of Tamil second preferences, of Tamil votes for parliamentary candidates in the South, and of pivotal Tamil seats in parliament—all of which can be powerful influences in the competition between more evenly matched Sinhalese parties—should ultimately cement coalitions of commitment between the Tamil parties and the more conciliatory of the main Sinhalese parties. This, of course, assumes the continued vitality of two-party competition on the Sinhalese side. It also assumes that Tamil separatism does not break out into warfare and that Tamil parties are allowed to play a normal parliamentary role. These things can no longer be taken for granted in the aftermath of the 1983 riots, the continuing terrorism, and governmental and military hostility

68. For illustrations, see de Silva, "The Constitution of the Second Republic of Sri Lanka (1978) and Its Significance," 203; Robert N. Kearney, "The Political Party System in Sri Lanka," *Political Science Quarterly* 98 (Spring 1983): 17–33, at 32.

to the Tamils.[69] The electoral innovations are not too little, but they might be too late.

ETHNIC PROPORTIONALITY
THROUGH PR: GUYANA

There are times when first-past-the-post systems distort the electoral demography of ethnically divided societies. By inflating the share of seats obtained by an ethnic party with a majority of votes, first-past-the-post can reduce ethnic minority representation to below proportional levels. By the same process of inflation, the plurality share of the largest or most cohesive minority can be translated into a majority of seats, sometimes at the expense of a less cohesive majority of voters. In these circumstances, proportional representation can change the result in one of two ways. If it reduces the vote-seat disparity, PR can prevent ethnic minority rule by denying a majority of seats to a party with a mere plurality of votes. If, as frequently asserted, PR tends to proliferate parties, the resulting multiplicity of parties can deny every group a majority of seats, thus creating Lebanese-style fluidity and eliminating the problem of perpetual minority status. Both of these objectives—proportionality and fragmentation—were given a good test by the system designed for Guyana on the eve of its independence.[70]

To be sure, the unqualified assertion that PR tends to proliferate parties is not accurate, but a PR system can be designed, with large multimember constituencies and no minimum percentage cutoff, so as to maximize the chances of both strict proportionality and party fragmentation.[71] Precisely that was done in Guyana. The British moved from first-past-the-post in single-member constituencies in the 1961 election to PR, with the whole country a single constituency and each party putting up a single list, for the 1964 election. It should be noted that PR with one nationwide list per party is inimical to fostering coalitions of commitment or alliances, for it prevents vote pooling in a way that indi-

---

69. See the issue "Sri Lanka: Racism and the Authoritarian State," *Race and Class* 26 (Summer 1984).

70. What follows draws on interviews I conducted in Guyana in 1965. For election results, see *Report on the General Election of Members of the Legislative Assembly, 1961* (Georgetown: Government Printery, 1964); *Report on the House of Assembly General Election, 1964* (Georgetown: Government Printery, 1965). See also Peter Simms, *Trouble in Guyana* (London: Allen & Unwin, 1966); Cheddi Jagan, *The West on Trial: My Fight for Guyana's Freedom* (London: Michael Joseph, 1966); B. A. N. Collins, "The End of a Colony—II: British Guiana, 1965," *Political Quarterly* 36 (Oct. 1965): 406–16.

71. See Rae, *The Political Consequences of Electoral Laws*, 151–70.

vidual candidacies or constituency lists do not. But, in Guyana, that was
not its purpose—fragmentation was. It was forecast at the time that PR
would produce "a proliferation of splinter parties," that, "since each
minor group can have its own representation, the society will find its
many divisions increasing . . . ."[72] This forecast proved entirely wrong.
Fragmentation did not occur, but proportionality did.

The East Indian–dominated People's Progressive Party (PPP) of
Cheddi Jagan had won a solid majority of seats in 1961 on a 42.6 percent
plurality of the vote. East Indians were a majority of the population at
the time, but their population was disproportionately under the voting
age and slightly less cohesive in ethnic voting than was the Afro-Guyanese population, which voted heavily for the People's National Congress (PNC) of Forbes Burnham. A small third party, the United Force
(UF), got many votes from the mixed (Eurafrican) population and the
smaller groups of whites, Chinese, and Portuguese. Together the PNC
and UF had outvoted the PPP, but, since their votes tended to be more
urban and more concentrated than PPP votes were, these two parties
were consigned to minority status in the legislature. This result led to
considerable unrest in 1962–63.

With independence approaching, the British instituted a PR system.
Jagan's Marxism had alarmed the Kennedy administration in Washington, which had urged the British to change the electoral system to effect
a change of regime.[73] In this, the shift to PR was remarkably successful,
for it apportioned seats much more closely in accordance with votes and
made possible a PNC-UF coalition government, as Table 12 shows.[74]

At the same time, it was thought that PR might provide the necessary
inducements for Jagan's East Indian support to split into its component
parts: especially Hindu-Muslim, but perhaps also left-wing and right-
wing. Several parties did spring up to contest the 1964 elections. One of
them was an Indian Muslim party, another an ideologically moderate
Indian party. The two managed to obtain no seats and together only one

72. Peter Newman, *British Guiana: Problems of Cohesion in an Immigrant Society*
(London: Oxford Univ. Press, 1964), 97.
73. See Arthur M. Schlesinger, Jr., *A Thousand Days: John F. Kennedy in the White
House* (Boston: Houghton Mifflin, 1965), 645–49.
74. The PNC-UF coalition, though more or less multiethnic, did not really span the
main fault line of Guyanese politics: the Creole–East Indian division. Consequently, it was
not the sort of accommodative coalition I have been speaking of. It should also be noted,
in connection with Table 12, that the comparison is restricted to 1961 versus 1964, because
post-1964 election data in Guyana are not reliable.

TABLE 12   ELECTORAL OUTCOMES IN GUYANA, 1961 AND 1964
(by party; in percentages)

| | First-Past-the-Post: 1961 | | | Proportional Representation: 1964 | | |
Party	Votes	Seats	Seat–Vote Disparity	Votes	Seats	Seat–Vote Disparity
PPP	42.6	57.1	14.5	45.8	45.3	−0.5
PNC	41.0	31.4	−9.6	40.5	41.5	1.0
UF	16.4	11.4	−5.0	12.4	13.2	0.8
Total	100.0	99.9[a]	9.7[b]	98.7[c]	100.0	0.8[b]

[a] Total does not equal 100.0 because of rounding.
[b] Average disparity for the three parties.
[c] Total does not equal 100.0 because of rounding and minor party votes.

percent of the vote. The incentives existed, but, as we saw in Chapter 8, the electorate set its face against fragmentation.

In fact, the only third party with any significant strength, the United Force, lost votes under PR: four percentage points. This, however, had nothing to do with the electoral formula. In 1961, the UF had benefited from some votes that would otherwise have gone to the PPP in constituencies where the PPP did not put up a candidate because Indian voters were too few to make it worthwhile. Under the list system of 1964, these votes went back to the PPP.

With this insignificant exception, what is impressive about the Guyanese experience is how stable voting patterns remained despite the radical change in electoral system. This stability makes PR a feasible strategy to achieve proportionality where first-past-the-post has distorted the results, but it makes PR an unlikely vehicle to create a new fluidity. It is one thing to say that, starting from scratch, electoral incentives do or do not produce a given result. It is another to claim that they can rapidly undo a result already entrenched in the party system. Guyana is consistent with Maurice Duverger's conclusion that "on the whole P.R. maintains almost intact the structure of parties existing at the time of its appearance."[75]

75. *Political Parties*, 252.

These four experiments proceeded from various motivations. In Lebanon and Nigeria, ethnic accommodation was an explicit goal of electoral innovation. In Sri Lanka and Guyana, PR was invoked to reduce vote-seat disparities, though in Guyana for the special purpose of ousting and perhaps splitting the governing party. In Sri Lanka, the preferential vote was used to prevent capture of the presidency by a candidate with a low plurality. Such a prophylactic measure was perhaps less necessary in Nigeria, with its plurality plus distribution requirement. Although the purposes were various, the experiments illuminate the prospects for achieving the five accommodative aims enumerated earlier: *fragmentation, moderation, coalition, fluidity,* and *proportionality.*

1. Fragmentation of the support of a majority group to avert its permanent domination seems a difficult goal to achieve through electoral means. The Guyanese electoral system was as conducive to achieving this goal as any is likely to be; yet it had no significant effect on voting patterns. Of course, the structure of subgroup cleavages in Guyana was not propitious. East Indians were not significantly divided along Hindu-Muslim lines. Had there been Hindu and Muslim factions in Jagan's PPP, then PR might have had an impact. Even then, however, it needs to be remembered that the East Indians had powerful incentives to remain cohesive; had they split, they would have lost their majority status. As Duverger has noted, if a conflict is already bifurcated, party splits in response to PR are unlikely.[76] Group structure is an important variable influencing the response to electoral incentives, and group interest is a variable bearing on group structure.

Fragmentation was achieved in Northern Nigeria, but not by the electoral system *per se.* Rather, the federal system, by providing state-level arenas for electoral victory and for power to be exercised, laid the groundwork for a somewhat more fragmented ethnic party system. Fragmentation continued despite later-enacted, though incomplete, electoral incentives for party consolidation. In addition to group structure and group interest, features of the territorial environment also affect the response to electoral incentives. The division of territory is probably a more reliable way of fragmenting the support of dangerously large

76. Ibid., 244.

groups to achieve multipolar fluidity than is the introduction of a particular electoral formula.

2. The encouragement of moderation appears easier to achieve through the electoral system than is the restructuring of group support. Several approaches are possible. The elaborate Lebanese system of reserved offices and seats and mixed lists is certainly one way; the Nigerian geographic distribution requirement is another; and the Sri Lankan PR and preferential vote formulae seem to be yet another. Of course, the Nigerian provisions were tested only twice, and the Sri Lankan not yet at all. Still, the Nigerian provisions worked according to their conflicting logic, and Nigerian assumptions about a separately elected president in lieu of a prime minister were impressively confirmed. If a presidential system is designed so that the electoral formula encourages moderation and penalizes ethnic exclusivism, as it was in Nigeria and Sri Lanka, the potential for presidential systems to foster accommodation seems considerable.

3. Multiethnic parties are difficult to encourage in severely divided societies. Nigeria's electoral incentives were sufficiently mixed so as to reduce their value as a test of the possibilities on this score. Although at least two parties in the Second Republic—the NPN and, to a lesser extent, the NPP—were notably more multiethnic than their predecessors in the First Republic were, none of them spanned, with any degree of completeness, any two of the three largest groups. Even so, Nigerian parties were probably pushing close to the limits of their ethnic inclusiveness.

Multiethnic coalitions of ethnic parties are possible, however. The need for a majority of legislative seats may be sufficient to induce coalitions of convenience, but these, as we have seen, do not foster accommodation. More enduring arrangements—coalitions committed to ethnic accommodation as a policy goal—are more likely to be formed as a result of the dependence of each partner on popular votes commanded by the other, rather than just on an exchange of legislative seats.

There are at least three ways to encourage such party interdependence where it would not otherwise exist: preferential voting (Sri Lankan presidency), list-system PR in heterogeneous multimember constituencies (Sri Lankan parliament), and mixed lists in constituencies with a common electoral roll (Lebanon). Still another way is suggested by Malaysia: single-member constituencies, multiethnic in composition, so that coalition partners can provide marginal votes for each other's candidates on a reciprocal basis. This enumeration readily shows how, with a bit of imagination, the electoral system might be used to promote multiethnic coalitions.

4. The existing fluidity of a multipolar system of ethnic parties is easier to preserve than it is to create anew through efforts to fragment already consolidated parties. Not only the Nigerian experience, but the Lebanese experience, suggests this. Lebanon's subgroups were, to be sure, the main actors of politics, but there was also a tendency for higher levels of group identity to assume increasing importance. "In times of trouble," Michael C. Hudson remarks, "one is compelled to identify himself as a Christian or a non-Christian; in ordinary times it is often necessary for an individual to assert or exploit his membership in a particular sect, like the Sunnite (Muslim) or the Maronite (Christian)."[77] In a different electoral system, these ultimate identifications, Christian and Muslim, could have formed the basis of party loyalty and of a bifurcated, conflict-prone party system. Comparable North-South loyalties did exactly that in the First Nigerian Republic. The elaborate Lebanese electoral system did a remarkable job of keeping the center of gravity of Lebanese politics at the lower levels of the groups and subgroups. There it stayed even at the peak of the civil war of 1975–84. The Nigerian plurality election of the president and the proliferation of states also reduced the impulse to consolidate, and thus to bifurcate, the party system.

Proportional representation can also help in such cases, by making party consolidation in a fragmented system less attractive. Some light is cast on this possibility by a sideways glance at Belgium. For many decades, the Belgian party system was organized along Left-Right and clerical-secular lines, each of the three major parties spanning ethnic divisions, albeit in different proportions. When Fleming-Walloon conflict rose to the forefront of Belgian politics in the 1960s, so did explicitly ethnic parties on both sides. By 1971, these two parties had between them gained about 20 percent of the vote. Under a first-past-the-post system, the ethnic parties would have been submerged. Even under PR, the three major parties were long able to prevent ethnic claims from producing splinter ethnic parties with substantial electoral strength.[78] It

77. *The Precarious Republic*, 21.
78. Rae has shown that PR does not automatically make it easier for a new party to gain seats. *The Political Consequences of Electoral Laws*, 151–67.

took a major surge in ethnic tension to do this. Once five parties, rather than three, were in existence, however, PR helped them stay afloat, just as it had earlier kept the third party (the Liberals) alive, thereby preventing the consolidation of opinion into only two parties.[79] In multipolar countries like Belgium and like Nigeria from 1979 to 1983, governing is difficult, because a legislative majority is hard to find, but polarization is averted by the fluidity of relationships possible among contending forces. The electoral system cannot manufacture ethnic and subethnic divisions, but it certainly can help sustain them once they have crossed the threshold of political relevance.

5. Certain versions of PR can reduce the disparity between votes and seats. Sometimes the disparity is not great, and it makes no difference to the outcome. Sometimes the disparity is significant and perhaps desirable. In Malaysia, it has strengthened the position of a permanent multiethnic coalition against ethnically based flank parties. In six parliamentary elections, first-past-the-post has provided the ruling National Front and its predecessor, the Alliance, a bonus of between 18 and 30 percent of seats over votes.[80] First-past-the-post in this case countered centrifugal forces. But where all parties are ethnically based and a minority is seriously underrepresented because first-past-the-post provides a voting majority with a bonus in seats, or where a minority group rules because its plurality of votes translates into a majority of seats, then PR with a list system, large multimember constituencies, and low or no cutoffs for minor parties can help bring seats and votes into line.

There is a more intriguing question of ethnic accommodation lurking in the vote-seat disparity issue. Is it possible that this version of PR, imposed before a party system crystallizes, can actually prevent the emergence of ethnic parties? In the early evolution of ethnic parties, lines frequently are not clearly drawn. Ethnic voting may not approach 100 percent the first time around, but it may be high enough, in a first-past-the-post system, so that, if groups are territorially concentrated, the party that gains most of a group's votes will win all of its seats. This will make it fruitless for dissident members of the group to withhold support

79. George Armstrong Kelly, "Biculturalism and Party Systems in Belgium and Canada," *Public Policy* 16 (1967): 316–57, at 326.

80. In 1959, the Alliance won 71 percent of the seats with 52 percent of the votes; in 1964, 86 percent with 58 percent; in 1969, 64 percent with 49 percent; in 1978, 85 percent with 55 percent; in 1982, 86 percent with 61 percent. I have omitted 1974 because the National Front then included a Malay party, the PMIP, that in all other elections had been in opposition.

from that party. Rates of ethnic voting will increase, and the identification of each party with an ethnic group will be complete. Under PR, however, dissident votes will count, and perhaps it will be harder to complete the alignment of parties with groups.

Although the point is well worth a test, I am inclined to think that the process by which ethnic parties emerge in severely divided societies cannot be retarded once a strong majority of an ethnic group casts its support for one party. Two exceptions come to mind, however.

The first is where support for such a party is limited by subethnic cleavages. If a prominently demarcated subgroup withholds its support from a party purporting to represent the whole group, PR may be enough to fortify this reluctance. Very likely, however, this will not make for nonethnic or multiethnic parties; it will only mean that this particular ethnic group will be represented by more than one party.

The second is not really an exception, for it involves a case where ethnic divisions, though significant, are not so powerful as to be the only divisions. There are countervailing forces for moderation. A number of Western countries fit this description; fewer ethnically divided Asian and African countries do. In Canada, the vote-seat disparity has been so significant as to foster regional and ethnic polarization, and PR has been recommended. Under these conditions, the remedy should work.[81]

It should surprise no one that electoral reform cannot work magic on ethnic conflict. It cannot, for example, solve the pure form of the 60–40 problem posed at the outset. No electoral device can split Group *A*'s 60 percent, so that Group *B* will not be a perpetual minority. Yet it is extraordinary just how much an electoral system *can* do in what seems an

---

81. In the 1980 Canadian parliamentary elections, the victorious Liberals, with 23 percent of the vote in the Western provinces, gained only two seats there; the Conservatives, with only twice as many votes in the West, won twenty-five times the number of seats. In Quebec, the results were reversed: the Conservatives, with 13 percent of the vote, won just one seat; the Liberals, with two-thirds of the Quebec vote, won nearly all the seats there. *The Gazette* (Montreal), Mar. 1, 1980. The result was to make the Liberals appear to be—and to behave as—a wholly Eastern party and the Conservatives a wholly Anglophone party, thereby exacerbating ethnic and regional tensions. The remedy proposed is to supplement first-past-the-post seats with a minority of seats elected by provincial constituencies on a PR formula. The aim is to assure parties seats wherever they have significant votes and so to mitigate polarization. Alan C. Cairns, "The Strong Case for Modest Electoral Reform in Canada" (unpublished paper presented at the Harvard Univ. Seminar on Canada–United States Relations, Sept. 25, 1979). The regional distribution of party support was quite different, however, in the 1984 parliamentary elections.

intractable situation. Various combinations of electoral formula, ballot structure, and constituency delimitation can operate to preserve fluidity, promote moderation, induce coalition, and produce proportionality.

None of these effects is a matter of party reconstruction: no system examined here abolishes ethnic parties any more than it succeeds in fragmenting them. Many of the effects are matters of party posture more than structure. A party may remain ethnically based but become more moderate. But nothing in ethnic conflict in civilian regimes is more crucial than whether a party adopts a conciliatory posture on ethnic issues.

Similarly, the work of electoral systems is vulnerable to the offsetting effects of other variables: the strength of the conflict, the way territory has been carved up, the timing of innovation (did the proliferation of states, for example, precede the new electoral formula?). The electoral system is one part of the total framework of incentives and disincentives in which ethnic groups and parties operate. The Nigerian experiment shows with supreme clarity the extent to which countervailing incentives can produce mixed outcomes. What stands out, in spite of the limitations, is just how important a piece of the incentive structure the electoral system is and what a dearth of imagination there has been in most countries in utilizing its potential for ethnic accommodation.

THE SUBSTITUTABILITY OF TECHNIQUES

The analysis of territorial and electoral innovations makes clear that the political incentive structure is one package. We have seen that the operation of some pieces of that structure can offset results that might have been achieved by other parts of the structure. By the same token, there may be more than one way to achieve the same result. In the Nigerian federal system, it will be recalled, the proliferation of states helped bring to the fore subethnic divisions that catalyzed party formation in Northern Nigeria, thereby enhancing inducements to multiethnic party support. Lebanon reached a similar destination by a quite different route. By insisting on mixed tickets and reserved offices, the Lebanese electoral system required cooperation across ethnic lines, thereby channeling conflict in intraethnic directions. There is, then, a degree of substitutability of techniques.

The implications for policymakers are clear. A range of means is available to achieve particular ends. If the prospect of devolution arouses resistance, as it does in many countries, electoral change may seem less threatening. If there is fear that a regime may tinker with the electoral system in its own narrow interests, territorial realignment may prove a more promising course. Substitutability enhances the options open to policymakers in the quest for conflict reduction.

CHAPTER SIXTEEN

Preferential Policies
to Reduce Ethnic Conflict

Electoral policies have a short time frame from adoption to impact; preferential policies do not. A new electoral formula or constituency delimitation produces (or fails to produce) a political response in the next election or two. Any reduction in conflict behavior on the part of politicians will soon be visible. Policies to reduce ethnic disparities, by augmenting the representation of particular groups in, for example, modern-sector employment or higher education, do not have the same quality. Measuring changes in ethnic representation is more difficult than computing election results, and representational changes do not necessarily augur changes in ethnic conflict behavior. Then, too, the impact of preferential policies on ethnic relations may vary over time, compounding the difficulty of evaluation.

All of this may simply be to say that electoral and, for that matter, territorial changes do not really operate on the structure of society but on the epiphenomenal behavior of voters and politicians. Preferential policies have more far-reaching aims and are inherently more difficult to guide to their intended destination. The difference resembles the distinction developed by Martin Shapiro and James Q. Wilson between point and line decisions. "A point decision is one that involves a self-effectuating choice among competing alternatives; a line decision is one that requires the coordination by plan of the actions of many people extending over a substantial period of time." With point decisions, the consequences are "immediately and continuously felt."[1] With line decisions,

---

1. James Q. Wilson, "What Can Be Done?" (unpublished paper presented at the fourth annual Public Policy Week conference sponsored by the American Enterprise Institute, Washington, D.C., Dec. 10, 1980), 23.

they are more distant and liable to deflection. The adoption of a preferential policy is plainly a line decision.

THE RANGE OF
PREFERENTIAL PROGRAMS

Preferential policies are common in ethnically divided societies, but they vary in scope, formality, and explicitness. Some are limited to public-sector opportunities, while others extend to the private sector as well. Some reach broadly into business and education, in addition to employment. Others are confined to particular spheres, such as higher education or civil service positions. Some policies are formally stated and openly pursued, whereas many others are adopted *sub silentio*.

On the whole, the more ceremonious the adoption, the more extensive the policies tend to be. The Malaysian program is as extensive as any, and it has its roots, though not all of its branches, in the Malaysian constitution. The constitution recognizes the "special position" of the Malays and authorizes reserved shares of public service positions, scholarships and educational benefits, certain lands, and certain business permits.[2] The current Malaysian program lays down ambitious targets in share ownership and employment and extends also to licenses and contracts, as well as secondary school and university admission, all with the aim of restructuring the society to "reduce or actually eliminate the identification of race with economic function."[3] India's constitution reserves educational places, civil service positions, and legislative seats for "scheduled" castes and tribes.[4] The states may, as some have, also make provision for "backward" castes, and an increasing number of states have, in addition, enacted preferential policies to protect indigenes from competition from migrants.[5]

Not all broad preferential programs originate in constitutions, and not all constitutional provisions authorize broad programs. In the First

2. *Constitution of Malaysia*, sections 89, 153.

3. Government of Malaysia, *Second Malaysia Plan, 1971–1975* (Kuala Lumpur: Government Press, 1971), 1. For a good discussion of the Malaysian program, see Robert Klitgaard and Ruth Katz, "Overcoming Ethnic Inequalities: Lessons From Malaysia," *Journal of Policy Analysis and Management* 2 (Spring 1983): 333–49.

4. *Constitution of India*, articles 341–42. The scheduled castes are ex-untouchables. For the law of reservations in India, see Marc Galanter, *Competing Equalities: Law and the Backward Classes in India* (Berkeley and Los Angeles: Univ. of California Press, 1984).

5. Myron Weiner, *Sons of the Soil: Migration and Ethnic Conflict in India* (Princeton: Princeton Univ. Press, 1978).

Nigerian Republic, the former Northern Regional Government adopted a policy of "Northernization" that affected the tender of contracts and employment in the public service. The results were dramatic. In 1959, only one senior civil servant in eight in the region was a Northerner; by 1965, Northerners outnumbered expatriates and Southerners together.[6] At the national level, regional quotas were also used for recruitment to the officer corps of the army and for scholarships for higher education.[7] The Biafran war altered Nigerian thinking on such questions. In general, it strengthened the forces opposed to parochial discrimination. Before the return to civilian rule, the military regime overrode state policies that had permitted preferential terms of employment for indigenes of a state. Nevertheless, the constitution of the Second Republic contained provisions stating in general terms that public-sector appointments should "reflect the federal character of the country" and insure that "there shall be no predominance of persons from a few States or from a few ethnic or other sectional groups" in central government agencies.[8] On this basis, there were demands for a policy that would rectify the allegedly skewed composition of the Nigerian services.[9]

In the Southern Philippines, a quite extensive program to prefer Muslims for bank loans, scholarships, government employment, and university admissions has grown up with little formal acknowledgment. Principally, this has been the work of government officials, but large private employers in the South have also been induced to participate.[10] As is typical of such informal programs, the Philippine measures operate by exempting Muslim applicants from meeting formal requirements, such as credit-worthiness for loans or examinations for civil service entry.

A number of countries have adopted preferential programs targeted at particular sectors. In Fiji, nearly all the cultivable land has long been reserved to Fijians. In Sri Lanka, a policy of "standardization of marks" gave extra points to applicants for university admission who took their examinations in Sinhala, so that Sinhalese applicants were preferred to Tamils. In Indonesia, a specified percentage of the shares in new compa-

6. C. S. Whitaker, Jr., *The Politics of Tradition: Continuity and Change in Northern Nigeria, 1946–1966* (Princeton: Princeton Univ. Press, 1970), 390.

7. W. F. Gutteridge, *Military Regimes in Africa* (London: Methuen, 1975), 117; Omolade Adejuyigbe, "The Size of States and Political Stability in Nigeria," *African Studies Review* 16 (Sept. 1973): 157–82, at 172–73.

8. *Constitution of Nigeria*, sections 14(3), 157(5).

9. *Daily Times* (Lagos), Jan. 18, 1980.

10. These observations draw on interviews I conducted in the Southern Philippines in 1980.

nies must be held by *pribumis* (indigenes); there are comparable preferences for non-Chinese in government contracts and business loans,[11]
although in 1980 and 1984 these requirements were modified to refer to
"weak economic groups" (still mainly *pribumi*) in lieu of overt ethnic
designations. And in Andhra Pradesh, India, a fixed percentage of government positions was to be reserved for Telanganas. Land, education,
business, and employment—these are the most common subjects of targeted programs.

Programs also vary in the depth and specificity of their coverage.
Programs that prefer certain groups in employment may not prefer them
in promotions, though in practice the extension from one to the other is
frequently made. Programs that prefer certain groups in the generalist
services of government employment may or may not prefer them in the
professional and technical services. Programs that apply to positions
under a specified salary level may leave positions above that level
untouched.

Finally, preferential programs vary in the explicitness with which ethnic criteria are used to define the preferred category. Malaysia and Indonesia prefer ethnic groups deemed to be indigenous (*bumiputera* or *pribumi*). The "Northernization" policy in Nigeria, though framed in
territorial terms, had essentially the same meaning. Andhra Pradesh cast
its definition in terms of *mulkis*, meaning roughly "domiciliaries," leaving room for long-resident migrants from areas outside Telangana to
claim preferred status. Sri Lanka used language of examination as a
proxy for ethnicity. Zaire's preference for Lulua over Baluba in education takes the form of regional quotas for university admission.[12] Tanzania's regional equalization policy in secondary education also employs
region as a clear proxy for ethnic group: "If you talk about Moshi area,
you talk about tribes; if you talk about Didoma area, you talk about
tribes."[13] Whatever the formulation, the aim is to adjust rewards and
opportunities among ethnic groups.

The exact formulation matters a great deal in implementation. First,
an inclusive formulation increases the chance that the benefits of the
policy will accrue to those within the preferred category who need them

11. See Leo Suryadinata, "Indonesian Policies Toward the Chinese Minority Under the
New Order," *Asian Survey* 16 (Aug. 1976): 770–87.

12. Michael G. Schatzberg, "Ethnicity and Class at the Local Level: Bars and Bureaucrats in Lisala, Zaire," *Comparative Politics* 13 (July 1981): 461–78, at 470.

13. I am quoting an informed academic observer of the Tanzanian program, Dar es
Salaam, 1980.

least. The inclusion of all *pribumis* in the Indonesian policy opened the way for established entrepreneurial groups like the Minangkabau to improve their position through preferential access to share offerings and credit. Second, an ostensibly nonethnic definition of the preferred category allows room for evasion of the policy. That the Andhra preferences were cast in terms of domiciliaries rather than Telanganas created a brisk trade in false *"mulki* certificates," rendering large numbers of non-Telanganas eligible for employment preferences. Third, the same breadth of formulation allows for flexibility in enforcement so that countervailing policy objectives, such as enhancing productivity or conciliating political opposition, can be taken into account. Fourth, the way the preferred group is defined dictates the direction of what might be called the politics of preferential inclusion and exclusion. An amorphous formulation like "backward classes" that prevails in some Indian states encourages claims of backwardness. In one state, Karnataka, this went so far that every caste except Brahmins—including some wealthy landowning castes— was officially designated "backward" and accorded preferences, until the Supreme Court of India overrode that determination. The issue was eventually confided to a "Backward Classes Commission" to sort out. A more exact formulation may set in motion a struggle within the preferred group over the distribution of benefits. In Bihar, preferences for tribals have led to demands from non-Christian tribals that Christians be excluded from coverage, because Christians, better educated, were able to reap a disproportionate share of reserved positions.[14] The criteria of inclusion, in short, shape the way intraethnic politics develops.

THE ADOPTION OF PREFERENTIAL POLICIES

Virtually everywhere, policies of ethnic preference are regarded as exceptions, temporary expedients, often with a specified time limit. In a surprising number of countries that have made special provisions to enable particular ethnic groups to "catch up," such measures carry a heavy presumption of illegitimacy. The acknowledged norm remains equal treatment of all individuals. Provisions that depart from this norm are usually explained as distasteful concessions to the unfortunate inability of the preferred group to compete on equal terms without preferences.

14. Weiner, *Sons of the Soil*, 184–86.

In view of this ambivalence, why are such programs so frequently adopted? Two explanations are immediately obvious and pertinent. The first is the existence of influential political constituencies with an interest in the adoption of such policies. The adoption of preferential policies depends in part on how well organized and effective such groups are, and the scope of the policies reflects the sectors in which they are active.

The second is that preferential policies appear to be cheap. They require no initial outlay in expenditure. In education, the rectification of regional and ethnic disparities in examination results might entail considerable capital investment in facilities and personnel, even if the techniques required to reduce those disparities were known and readily available. Reallocating existing places in educational institutions by ethnic groups involves no incremental outlay. In employment, the same appears to be true: a labor force must be assembled, and its ethnic composition may be a secondary concern.

In the private sector, securing government good will is an additional incentive to adopt preferential policies. Vulnerable foreign firms see special advantages in such policies. If they do not know the host country well, they are susceptible to persuasion that ethnic employment quotas will minimize the political risks of their operations. They may, in some circumstances, be able to extract concessions from the host government in exchange for preferential employment policies, concessions such as training assistance or pressure on unions to moderate demands. Sometimes preferential employment policies are a condition of the tax concessions that are offered to attract foreign investment. But, even if the policy is not formally articulated, a variety of informal pressures is frequently brought to bear on foreign firms.[15]

The adoption of a formal preferential program by government usually involves something else: a conviction on the part of policymakers that ethnic preferences or quotas are required to achieve some larger purpose. That conviction is either part of their intellectual baggage at indepen-

---

15. Thus, one firm operating in ethnically sensitive Aceh, in Indonesia, was easily persuaded by politically powerful Acehnese to adopt a 50 percent Acehnese employment quota, over the objections of Javanese officials of the central government who were involved in the project. A firm operating in French Guyana adopted an elaborate ethnic division of labor for its operations. "Northernization" was also pressed on expatriate firms in Nigeria. Leonard Plotnicov, *Strangers to the City: Urban Man in Jos, Nigeria* (Pittsburgh: Univ. of Pittsburgh Press, 1967), 60. I have dealt with some of these issues in a short article, "Ethnic Demands Abroad," *The Wall Street Journal*, Dec. 18, 1978.

dence, as the need to enhance opportunities for scheduled castes and tribes was in India, or it is the product of dramatic events that happen later.

After the Malay-Chinese riots of 1969, a change came over Malaysian elites.[16] The belief spread that development policy had failed the Malays, that economic imbalances were at the root of ethnic hostility, that time was running out, and that the only way to insure peace was to embark on an extensive program to put the Malays in all sectors of the economy at all levels. A crucial role was played by young, Western-educated Malay civil servants and politicians who were able to persuade conservative Malay political leaders to make decisions they had earlier avoided. Two deputy prime ministers were pivotal actors: once they were convinced, the New Economic Policy, with its ambitious aims, was assured.

It was in this sense that the riots were described by more than one participant in this process as a "blessing in disguise," for they shocked the leadership into a realization of the need for drastic action. Indeed, the riots also had an impact on Chinese opinion, convincing some Chinese leaders, though they quibbled about details, that a new course was required. As disasters are often used by advocates of a policy to put it on the policymakers' agenda and to neutralize opposition,[17] the violence of 1969 performed these functions in Malaysia, making possible the adoption of policies previously shunned because they appeared ethnically biased and loaded against merit criteria.

The adoption of preferential policies is thus fostered by the confluence of several beliefs: (1) that preferential policies require little in the way of expenditure and hence are a low-cost strategy for coping with ethnic conflict; (2) that they are necessary, at least temporarily, if groups are ultimately going to be able to compete on equal terms; and (3) that the causes of ethnic conflict reside in objective economic disparities between groups that can be eliminated through policies aimed at those disparities. Beneath preferential policies lies a mind-set that sees ethnic conflict as the product of economic differences and ethnic harmony as the result of proportional distribution of all groups at all levels and in all functions of a society.

16. What follows draws upon extensive interviews I conducted in Malaysia in 1975. See also Karl von Vorys, *Democracy without Consensus: Communalism and Political Stability in Malaysia* (Princeton: Princeton Univ. Press, 1975), 398–412; R. S. Milne, "The Politics of Malaysia's New Economic Policy," *Pacific Affairs* 49 (Summer 1976): 235–62.

17. Jack L. Walker, "Setting the Agenda in the U.S. Senate: A Theory of Problem Selection," *British Journal of Political Science* 7 (Oct. 1977): 423–45.

THE SHORT-TERM IMPACT
OF PREFERENTIAL POLICIES

The late Wallace Sayre once said that the benefits of a reform are immediate, but the costs are cumulative. With preferential policies, there is reason to believe instead that the costs precede the benefits. Gains in the ability to compete and in the reduction of conflict appear much later, if they appear at all. In the long run, to be sure, it is possible that preferential policies may have a payoff in enlarging the pool of trained manpower and creating new pools of capital. Even if the first generation of new entrepreneurs, professionals, and bureaucrats is not efficient, subsequent generations may still benefit from the advantages the first generation is able to confer. Preferential policies, however, are not generally cast in these terms or geared so as to maximize the chances that long-term benefits will occur. The primary rationale of these policies is to reduce disparities in the present, and it is in the present that the costs show up.

The precise impact of preferential policies seems to vary with the field in which they operate. Because of this, it is useful to examine separately preferences in education, business, and employment.

PREFERENCES IN EDUCATION

Ethnic preferences in admission to schools and universities involve gate-keeper decisions. Consequently, in a short time, they can effect dramatic changes in the composition of student bodies. After the riots of 1969, the Malaysian government began to pay close attention to the ethnic composition of university student bodies, and the constitution was eventually amended to permit the government to control the admission of Malays to university education. Between 1970 and 1973, the percentage of Malays in degree-level courses rose from 39.7 to 52.7.[18] In Sri Lanka, Tamils comprised nearly half of all university admissions in medicine and engineering in 1969–70; Sinhalese comprised barely more than half. By 1974, after preferential policies were put into effect, Tamils comprised 16 percent of engineering admissions and 26 percent of medical admissions.[19] If representation in a student body is the goal, a formula

18. Bee-lan Chan Wang, "Governmental Intervention in Ethnic Stratification: Effects on the Distribution of Students Among Fields of Study," *Comparative Education Review* 21 (Feb. 1977): 110–23, at 111.

19. C. R. de Silva, "Weightage in University Admissions: Standardization and District Quotas in Sri Lanka," *Modern Ceylon Studies* 5 (July 1974): 151–78, at 178.

can be found to achieve it. As we shall see, this is much more straightforward than is the attainment of ethnic group representation in business.

Representation, however, does not end the matter. Preferential admissions policies have important consequences for the educational and political systems.

A principal effect is to shift applicants for places denied because of preferences at government institutions into the private sector of education or to create a private sector where there was none. Tanzania's regional equalization policy had precisely this effect.[20] Preferential policies are in force only for secondary-school admissions in Tanzania. Before regional equalization, advanced groups such as the Chagga and the Wahaya sent disproportionate numbers of students to government secondary schools. Under the equalization policy, secondary-school places are allocated to each region on the basis of its proportionate share of the total number of primary-school leavers eligible to attend secondary school. Within each regional allocation, candidates are selected by test scores. Since Chagga and Wahaya students tend to perform well, their cutoff scores tend to be significantly higher than those of students from other areas. To accommodate the demand for secondary education from capable but rejected students, a network of private secondary schools has sprung up.

A good many of these schools are in the Kilimanjaro region, where the Chagga live and support the schools through their coffee-growing cooperatives. With a small fraction of Tanzania's population (the Chagga are about 3 percent), Kilimanjaro has 28 percent of all its secondary schools. To prevent private schools from defeating the equalization policy, in 1979 the government began to require them to reserve 25 percent of their places for students from other regions. Socialist Tanzania thus finds that its equalization policy stimulates the private sector in education, which it then seeks to regulate.

Malaysia's preferential policies at the university level have had a comparable effect. Many able Chinese students, prevented from attending university in Malaysia, departed for universities in the West. By 1983, there were some 35,000 Malaysians, 60 percent of them Chinese, at universities outside Malaysia. Moreover, as university enrollment within Malaysia has expanded, enrollment outside has more than kept pace. For every degree candidate inside Malaysia, there is at least one outside.

20. What follows draws on interviews with government education officials and academics in Tanzania in 1980.

In terms of the total pool of university students, therefore, the Malaysian policies have altered the ethnic mix only in government institutions at home. In Malaysia, as in Tanzania, preferential policies gave a fillip to the private sector in education, as students sought ways to secure education outside the reach of government policy.

Within Tanzania, Sri Lanka, and Malaysia, the change in ethnic representation in public educational institutions, however, is undeniable. The cost in student performance, as measured by test scores, is also apparent. There are no reliable figures for Tanzania, but it was estimated that secondary-school admission for Kilimanjaro might require a score of 180, whereas admission from some other regions might be possible with a score of only 140. Much more precise data are available for Malaysia and Sri Lanka.

Among a sample of students in technical high school in Malaysia, ethnic differences in performance on the Lower Certificate of Education examination were marked. There were equal numbers of Malays and non-Malays (Chinese and Indians) among the students, roughly proportionate to ethnic group shares of the population. However, 91.7 percent of the non-Malay students scored 3.4 or better (a score of 1.0 is highest) in math and in the combined average of history, geography, math, and general science, whereas only 37.1 percent of the Malay students had such a high math score and only 34.3 percent of the Malays had average scores so high.[21] Preferential policies thus made it possible for Malays with distinctly poorer scores to secure admission to upper secondary school.

There was, in addition, some dampening of Chinese aspirations for higher education as university admission for non-Malays became more difficult. Survey data indicate that Malay students were somewhat more willing than Chinese students to forgo job opportunities in order to pursue Form 6 (pre-university) training. Test scores were much more strongly correlated with willingness to forgo a job in favor of Form 6 among Chinese than among Malays. Indeed, among Malays, there was practically no such correlation, largely because nearly all the Malay students in the sample expected to gain university entrance—such was the effect of preferences on the relationship of performance to aspirations.[22]

21. Wang, "Governmental Intervention in Ethnic Stratification," 113.
22. Bee-lan Chan Wang, "Sex and Ethnic Differences in Educational Investment in Malaysia: The Effect of Reward Structure," *Comparative Education Review* 24 (June 1980): S140–59.

In Sri Lanka, preferential policies were a reaction to the greater success of Tamil students in gaining university admission in the sciences, medicine, and engineering. Responding to unsubstantiated rumors that Tamil graders were unduly lenient with examination papers in the Tamil medium, the government in 1971 adjusted admissions for each ethnic group on an *ad hoc* basis and in subsequent years instituted a system of adjusting or "standardizing" grades on university entrance examinations. The scheme reflected "the ascendancy of a group of Sinhalese in the Ministry of Education, a group which firmly believed that some adjusting mechanism was necessary to give Sinhalese students a chance in competing for the coveted places in science-based courses at the University."[23] The effect was to reduce grades in the three examination media—English, Sinhala, and Tamil—to a common scale, so that the number of students qualifying for university admission from each medium would be proportionate to the number taking the examination in that medium.

This was the system adopted for 1973. It had its biggest impact in the two fields in which Tamil students outperformed Sinhalese students most strongly: pure and applied mathematics. In 1972, in pure math, for example, Tamil-medium candidates comprised just under one-third of those taking the exam; they had, however, a pass rate of 54 percent, compared to the Sinhalese pass rate of 40 percent, with the result that Tamil candidates comprised 39 percent of the total passes (and fully 54 percent of those with a grade of A). With standardization in effect the following year, this disparity between the percentage of Tamils taking the exam and those doing well on it was eliminated, with a concomitant decline in Tamil enrollment.[24]

The following year, this system was supplemented by district quotas. Standardization by medium of examination had only reduced Tamil admissions moderately, because the standard was the proportion of students taking the exam in each medium, and Tamil candidates took the exam far out of proportion to their share of population. However, weightage by district shares of population had an enormous impact on the Tamils, who are heavily concentrated in a few districts. The largest concentration is in Jaffna, where, in 1974, 398 students qualified to enter

23. C. R. de Silva, "The Politics of University Admission: A Review of Some Aspects of the Admissions Policy in Sri Lanka, 1971–1978," *Sri Lanka Journal of Social Sciences* 2 (June 1979): 85–123, at 89–90.
24. Computed from de Silva, "Weightage in University Admissions," 160, 162.

university medical and biological science courses and 575 qualified to enter engineering and physical science courses. By district quotas, only 34 and 37 places, respectively, were open to these candidates.[25]

The result of these measures was to alter raw scores dramatically. Even in 1971, when *ad hoc* adjustments of raw scores were first made and Tamils comprised more than 40 percent of engineering admissions, the minimum raw score for a Sinhalese student to be admitted to engineering was only 90 percent of the minimum Tamil raw score. Later adjustments of raw scores are not available, but the ethnic gap in minimum raw scores must have grown enormously, because the percentage of Tamils admitted to engineering declined precipitously—from 40.8 in 1970–71 to 34.7 in 1971–72 to 24.4 in 1973 to 16.3 in 1974, the year district quotas were introduced.[26] The inference is inescapable that significantly less qualified Sinhalese students were being admitted.

The Sri Lankan preferences do not appear to have stimulated private-sector educational alternatives. Whereas a good many Malaysian Chinese could afford to send their children abroad for university education, few Ceylon Tamils are in the same position. The situation was even more acute for them, because—in contrast to the significant Malaysian expansion in places available in higher education in the 1970s, when preferences were enforced—the number of places available in Sri Lanka remained constant for quite some time.

If in Malaysia it is conceivable that accelerated recruitment of Chinese to the ranks of the Communist guerrillas in the early and mid-1970s was linked to preferential educational admissions, in Sri Lanka a new wave of Tamil separatist violence, including the assassination of policemen and soldiers, rather clearly flowed from standardization of marks and district quotas. This admission system "convinced many Sri Lankan Tamils that it was futile to expect equality of treatment with the Sinhalese majority. It has immensely strengthened separatist forces within the Tamil United Front and contributed to the acceptance of a policy of campaigning for a separate state in early 1975."[27] It also, however, convinced the government to open a new campus at Jaffna, in the Tamil heartland. So, in the end, preferences indirectly operated in Sri Lanka, too, to expand the total number of university students.

In both Malaysia and Sri Lanka, preferential admissions reached a

25. Ibid., 164.
26. Ibid., 156; de Silva, "The Politics of University Admissions," 105–06.
27. De Silva, "Weightage in University Admissions," 166.

point at which the preferred group, formerly underrepresented, ended up being significantly overrepresented in university student bodies. In both, political reactions were strong enough to require modification, but in neither was there an end to preferential admissions.

Among Malaysian Chinese, a demand grew in 1978 for the establishment of a Chinese university to offset Malay admission preferences. The Malaysian Chinese Association, a component of the ruling coalition, stood firm against that demand while simultaneously threatening to leave the government unless a change in admissions policy were forthcoming. Eventually, it was agreed that the Chinese share of students in Malaysian universities would gradually rise until it approximated the Chinese share of the population. Preferences thus led, not to admission by test scores alone, but to proportionality.[28]

The Sri Lankan changes came in two parts. The first, adopted in 1975–76, allocated 70 percent of university places by standardized marks, based on medium of instruction, and 30 percent by district quotas, but with augmented quotas for Jaffna as well as Colombo. In 1977, the newly elected United National Party government had pledged to abolish preferential admissions altogether, but when grades were processed it was revealed that Tamil students would again outnumber Sinhalese in medicine and engineering. An uproar among Sinhalese students was followed by supplemental admissions of all who would have been admitted on the basis of standardized marks. (Note, again, the expansionary implications of preferences.) The formula that emerged in the second stage admitted 30 percent of all students on raw marks, 55 percent on district population quotas, and 15 percent for educationally backward districts. Tamil admissions are higher than under the system of standardized marks—for example, 28 percent of the engineering places in 1983–84[29]—but lower than under free competition. And the last word has not yet been spoken, for now there are demands from the educationally backward Muslim and Tamil-untouchable minorities for admissions proportionate to their populations. Preferences are difficult to abolish, and they tend to move toward proportional quotas.

These data are not as extensive as one might wish, but they do seem to point to some regularities in the consequences of educational prefer-

28. I am drawing on my interviews with leading politicians in Malaysia in 1980 and 1984. For the Chinese grievances, see *Far Eastern Economic Review* (Hong Kong), Apr. 10, 1981, p. 75.

29. S. W. R. de A. Samarasinghe, "Ethnic Conflict in Sri Lanka: A Brief Analysis," *Ethnic Studies Report* (Kandy, Sri Lanka) 2 (Jan. 1984): 11–20, at 15.

ences. To begin with, preferences in school and university admission are likely to be demanded where there are significant disparities in the educational performance of the affected ethnic groups. Preferential policies therefore result in the admission of students with significantly lower test scores. Applicants displaced by preferential admissions may simply lower their aspirations, but many seek admission to alternative institutions, either private-sector or foreign, in which preferential policies do not operate. Although it is percentages, rather than absolute numbers, of students that preferential admissions seek to regulate, in the end they tend to produce an unintended expansion of the total number of students. This may render the preferences less effective, but also less explosive; for otherwise the dissatisfaction they generate seems likely to be expressed in the form of ethnic extremism, especially if alternative educational opportunities are not available.

PREFERENCES IN BUSINESS

Judgments on the impact of preferential policies in the field of business licenses, contracts, and ownership are more difficult to make. The short-term costs are apparent, though their magnitude is not easy to gauge, whereas the long-term benefits are difficult to estimate.

Preferential policies in business lead to the widespread use of front men of the preferred ethnic group. Licenses are applied for in their name, title to land is conveyed to them, shares are issued to them, contract bids are signed by them, but they have no role in the enterprise beyond collecting a fee for the use of their name. In Malaysia and Indonesia, such arrangements are called Ali-Baba combinations, Ali being the *bumiputera* or *pribumi* front man and Baba the Chinese businessman.

Alternatively, preferential policies multiply opportunities for official corruption as businessmen make payments to secure immunity from enforcement of ethnic requirements. Transportation in Malaysia, for example, has been a sector long marked out for preferences to Malays in the award of licenses. In the mid-1970s, it became difficult for Chinese to secure transport licenses, with the result that a substantial bribe was sometimes offered for a taxi license and even more for a lorry license. Whether front men are recruited to achieve nominal compliance or corruption is employed to avoid compliance, preferential policies impose an added cost of doing business.[30] This raises the possibility that preferen-

---

30. In Fiji, where land was reserved to Fijians, it was leased to land-hungry Indians, who paid rents or premiums so high as to force them into overfarming and indebtedness. Adrian C. Mayer, *Indians in Fiji* (London: Oxford Univ. Press, 1963), 62.

tial requirements may discourage investment and even encourage the export of capital without necessarily strengthening the business class among members of the preferred group.

New business classes are not created overnight. In recognition of the magnitude of the task, the Malaysian government in the early 1970s embarked on an ambitious program designed to move Malay share ownership from less than 2 percent of all holdings to 30 percent in twenty years. Preferences were not abandoned; indeed, they tended to harden into 30 percent quotas, to be enforced more vigorously, and to be extended to new spheres as Malay businessmen and bureaucrats made their influence felt. It was, however, understood that expropriation was not permitted; only new opportunities were to be subject to the policy.

To implement the program, several new government agencies were established. Pernas, the "National Corporation," began to purchase assets to be held in trust for eventual distribution to the Malays. Initially, it was intended primarily to be a wholesaler to Malay merchants, but it has moved far afield in acquiring assets and operating businesses. UDA, the Urban Development Authority, was assigned the task of providing premises for new Malay businesses and also giving Malays a share in development in cities. The various states established state economic development corporations, which made investments in a variety of business ventures. MARA, the Indigenous People's Trust, was involved, even before the New Economic Policy was adopted, in training and making credit available to Malays on generous terms. Bank Bumiputera also antedates the New Economic Policy, but its activities expanded enormously after the policy was adopted. All of these organizations moved rapidly after 1971 to facilitate Malay entry into business.

The final verdict is by no means in on the activities of these entities. But several trends are already clear.

At least in Malaysia's expanding economy, these extraordinary efforts to foster Malay enterprise have not generally impinged on Chinese interests in politically significant ways. Preferential educational admissions and employment quotas are both more serious in their competitive impact. Chinese businessmen have largely adapted to the new requirements, treating them as a cost of doing business, and some have benefited from them. Many Chinese firms have been forced to "restructure" their share capital to provide for 30 percent Malay ownership, on financial terms very generous to the new shareholders. But some of these have managed to attract politically influential Malays, who have then lent their connections to the task of advancing the interests of the firm.

Chinese firms have also profited from participating in joint ventures with
UDA and Pernas, and they have sometimes been able, through such
partnerships, to obtain approval for projects that might otherwise not
have been approved readily. Chinese expertise has been essential to many
new ventures; especially in the 1970s, it was frequently called upon.

In at least one way, the effort to foster Malay entrepreneurship has
assuaged Malay-Chinese tensions. With the expansion of opportunities
targeted specifically for Malays, Malay politics has grown more complex, and Malay intraethnic competition has increased considerably.
Various groups of Malay businessmen have sought to maximize their
opportunities. In doing this, they have sometimes linked up with leading
Malay politicians in pursuit of their ambitions. To provide one example,
in 1975 a representative of the Malay Chambers of Commerce severely
criticized UDA for failing to help the Malays sufficiently. UDA was then
headed by the brother of a leading Malay politician who had been outspokenly critical of the selfishness of the Malay business class. The president of the Malay Chambers was another Malay political leader; the
two were rivals within the ruling party. The availability of an array of
benefits set in motion struggles to realize them.

If the new organizations do not yet seem to have cost much in terms
of ethnic conflict, their performance has not been free of difficulty. Their
mission of aiding Malay business has made it politically very difficult for
them to enforce business terms on Malay beneficiaries. Many of MARA's
loans have been in default, many of UDA's rents have been in arrears,
and many state development corporations have made decisions on other
than business criteria.

By 1983, government investment in trust for Malays represented
some 11.1 percent of total corporate ownership; individual Malays
owned an additional 7.6 percent.[31] For some years, there has been considerable discussion about how shares held in trust can be transferred to
individual Malay owners. There have been two fears: first, that because
most Malays are short of capital to purchase shares, distribution of these
assets will concentrate wealth unduly; and, second, that, especially if
shares are distributed at below-market value, they will quickly be resold
for capital gains, typically to non-Malay businessmen. If the latter were
to happen, the entire policy would be thwarted. Some state enterprises
have transferred their holdings to a national equity corporation, which

---

31. Government of Malaysia, *Mid-Term Review of the Fourth Malaysia Plan, 1981–
1985* (Kuala Lumpur: Jabatan Percetakan Negara, 1984), 101.

sells shares to individual Malays in a closely controlled national unit trust. So far, however, shares once purchased have not been made freely negotiable.

As the distribution debate suggests, there remains some question about whether new equity can be kept in the Malay community over time. At some point, restrictions on resale of these shares will have to be lifted.The real test of the success of the policy is, then, the long-term— indeed, the intergenerational—test of capital preservation.

PREFERENCES IN EMPLOYMENT

In some respects, the consequences of ethnic preferences in employment are a hybrid of the consequences of preferences in education and in business. They increase the cost of doing business in ways that business may be able to absorb, and they generate competitive resentments that find political expression. Competitive resentments, however, tend to be greater in employment than in education, because disappointed job applicants cannot generally seek places in a sector beyond the reach of preferences, as they often can in education. Consequently, the political costs of employment preferences tend to be high.

The representational impact of employment preferences is sometimes difficult to gauge. In their studies of preferential policies in India, Myron Weiner and Mary Fainsod Katzenstein have shown that the demand for preferences often follows the growth of an educated labor force; Maharashtrians, for example, were improving their employment position before preferential policies were adopted in Bombay, and it is not clear that later Maharashtrian gains in employment were a result of the policy.[32] Where, however, the policy is enforced vigorously and produces results beyond what would have occurred in the absence of preferences, the immediate consequences are quickly visible. Typically, the target is representation in proportion to total population. Often this is a quite unrealistic standard, since it takes no account of the widely varying demographic structure of ethnic groups.[33] A group that is significantly younger, less educated, and more rural will find it difficult to produce a

32. Myron Weiner and Mary Fainsod Katzenstein, *India's Preferential Policies: Migrants, the Middle Classes and Ethnic Equality* (Chicago: Univ. of Chicago Press, 1981), 120–35; Katzenstein, "Preferential Treatment and Ethnic Conflict in Bombay," *Public Policy* 25 (Summer 1977): 313–32.

33. In Lebanon, for example, Shiites long complained of their underrepresentation in the civil service. In proportion to population, they were underrepresented, but they were represented in numbers fully proportionate to their share of university graduates.

proportionate number of job applicants in the modern sector. Not surprisingly, the demand for qualified personnel of the preferred group quickly outstrips the supply. Unproductive employees may be added to the payroll to satisfy statistical requirements or, as in the case of representation in business, enforcement may be avoided through corruption.

The most detailed data on employment preferences come from Malaysia and India, which have the most extensive policies. The Malaysian evidence is particularly instructive on short-term effects.

Unlike share ownership, Malaysian employment targets have not been stated with great precision or fanfare. In general, the goal has been to have employment in the modern private sector mirror the composition of the population, so that firms have been pressed to aim at a 50 percent Malay work force at all levels. The Ministry of Labor oversees compliance, in conjunction with other government bodies. Sanctions for noncompliance have generally amounted to delays in the renewal of business or professional licenses.[34]

As a result of this policy, there has been heightened competition on the part of non-Malays to secure positions in what is seen as a declining share of the total job market. Employment grievances in the non-Malay middle class are long-standing and abundant. They relate both to hiring and promotion. Educational and employment preferences seem to produce somewhat opposite reactions, however. In education, the Chinese feel that they must perform well to be competitive now in a tight education market and later in a tight employment market. Malay students, who sense that their future is assured, feel less pressure to perform. On the job, however, the impact of preferences is to dampen the enthusiasm, and perhaps the performance, of the Chinese, as they observe younger Malays with brighter prospects.[35]

Malaysian policymakers, aware of these and other pressures, have had the latitude to be flexible. In recent years, while attention has been riveted on Malay share ownership and business opportunities, the government has been responsive to the complaints of businessmen that they

34. For the Malaysian policy and its effects, see Ozay Mehmet, "Malaysian Employment Restructuring Policies: Effectiveness and Prospects Under the Fourth Malaysian Plan," *Asian Survey* 22 (Oct. 1982): 978–87.

35. Similar descriptions of the morale of caste Hindus in Indian employment are available. There, places are reserved for scheduled castes, the employment and promotion of whom, it is said, hurt the interests of more qualified caste Hindus. See Sham Sunder Gupta, *Preferential Treatment in Public Employment and Equality of Opportunity* (Lucknow, India: Eastern Book Co., 1979).

cannot find qualified Malays to hire. Some policymakers have also felt that the heavy demand for Malay executive talent is excessive, that Malay executives have so much mobility that they do not stay in a job long enough to accumulate useful experience. Consequently, preferences have been implemented in a relaxed way. A firm with a reasonable explanation for a shortfall in Malays on its rolls will generally incur no penalty. This flexibility, though it does not wholly eliminate the grievances of non-Malay job applicants, may well have saved the Malaysian government some economic and political costs that a more strictly enforced policy might have incurred.

To a limited degree, the response of business and labor to preferential employment policies is comparable to the response to preferential education policies. As preferential admissions displace some of the demand for education onto the private sector, expanding the total number of students, so preferential hiring may result in a larger labor force. This can happen in two ways. Convinced that he must hire a less qualified member of the preferred ethnic group, an employer may hire that applicant as an extra and expect little of him. In addition, some disappointed applicants may displace their efforts into another labor market, by emigration. In India, Keralites, disproportionately educated and closed out of employment in some states that now prefer "sons of the soil," have sought employment in the Persian Gulf States.[36] In ordinary circumstances, however, neither of these adaptations would seem likely to be as pervasive as the displacement of students to the private sector. Emigration opportunities do not always exist, and the extent to which employers will expand their own rolls seems limited.

It is therefore not surprising that where employment preferences are implemented they produce "angry responses on the part of other ethnic groups."[37] Weiner and Katzenstein intimate that, in Bombay, Andhra, and Assam, employment preferences may also have aroused more ethnic conflict than they assuaged, particularly because proposals for preferences often emanate from "politicians not as a response to popular demands, but as a means of mobilizing political support."[38] Where groups are territorially differentiated, separatism is sometimes mooted among groups, such as the Ceylon Tamils, who feel the brunt of employment preferences.

36. Weiner and Katzenstein, *India's Preferential Policies*, 134.
37. Ibid., 147.
38. Ibid.

PREFERENCES AND SEPARATISM

In the preceding chapter, I noted that, for backward groups, such as India's Nagas or Pakistan's Pathans, an effective policy to avert secession might involve a measure of autonomy together with opportunities at the center. To insure commitment to the undivided state, preferential policies are sometimes used. And, in the case of the Nagas and the Pathans, the number of competitors affected by preferences is not so great as to constitute a major threat.

The relationship of preferences to separatism is a very delicate one, however. The same preferences that are used to convince backward groups on the periphery that their interests lie with the undivided state, if used against advanced groups on the periphery who would otherwise migrate to the center, tend to produce the very separatism that they might otherwise avert. And if, just as advanced groups sense that their interests are injured by preferences, backward groups become convinced that their own interests are inextricably bound up with the maintenance of preferences, a dilemma is created, for preferential policy has taken on a zero-sum aspect. Policymakers can neither enforce the preferences nor withdraw them.

Perhaps the best way to illustrate this dilemma is to examine in some detail a worst-case scenario, one in which preferences came to be seen as the most important symbolic issue and in which oscillating policies fed, not one, but two, complementary separatist movements. The case is Andhra Pradesh, India, in the 1960s and '70s. Barely a decade after the merger of several territories into a single Telugu-speaking state, Andhra Pradesh was torn by a separatist movement in Telangana. The policies adopted to respond to Telangana separatism led directly to a separatist reaction among Coastal Andhras, who had earlier been foremost among proponents of the unified state.[39]

39. My material on separatism in Andhra Pradesh is derived from conversations in Hyderabad in 1975 and from the following written sources: Duncan B. Forrester, "Subregionalism in India: The Case of Telangana," *Pacific Affairs* 43 (Spring 1970): 5–21; Hugh Gray, "The Demand for a Separate Telangana State in India," *Asian Survey* 11 (May 1971): 463–74; Rasheeduddin Khan, "Political Participation and Political Change in Andhra Pradesh (India)" (unpublished paper, Osmania Univ. Department of Political Science, June 1969); K. Seshadri, "The Rise and Fall of the Telangana Praja Samithi—A Case Study," *Journal of Constitutional and Parliamentary Studies* 5 (Oct.–Dec. 1971): 674–85; Myron Weiner, "The Socio-Political Consequences of Inter-State Migration in India" (unpublished paper, Massachusetts Institute of Technology, ca. 1971); *The Telangana Movement: An Investigative Focus* (Hyderabad: Anand Rao Thota, for the Telangana University and College Teachers' Convention, 1969); G. Ram Reddy, "Uni-Party Dominance in

Telanganas were the prototypical backward group in a backward region. With a literacy rate barely more than half that of the remainder of the state, with poorer soil and less development, Telangana joined Andhra Pradesh somewhat reluctantly, subject to a series of safeguards known as the "Gentlemen's Agreement." By its terms, only *mulkis* (Telanganas or residents of the region for at least fifteen years) were to be eligible for government positions in Telangana, with a few exceptions. There were also provisions restricting entry of non-*mulkis* to Telangana educational institutions, specifying Telangana proportions in the state cabinet, and apportioning revenue preferentially for Telangana. The position of Telangana and the *mulkis* was thus guaranteed by an elaborate system of preferences and quotas.

The unification of the state, however, had its own dynamic. With the capital at Hyderabad in Telangana, better-educated Coastal Andhras migrated there. Exceptions were made to the *mulki* rules, based on the alleged unavailability of qualified applicants. False "*mulki* certificates" were easily procured. Andhras were said to be favored in salaries and promotions; Telangana proportionality requirements were frequently honored in the breach.[40] Disparities in the price of land permitted enterprising Coastal Andhra farmers to sell a few acres in their home region and for the same sum acquire significantly more acreage in Telangana, which many did. The apprehension of Telanganas that they would be "swamped and exploited by the more advanced people of the coastal area"[41] was seemingly confirmed.

The result was a massive agitation for a Telangana state that began in 1969 and reached its apogee with the victory in ten out of fourteen Telangana parliamentary seats by the main separatist organization in 1971. Teachers, civil servants, and students were the most enthusiastic participants. The movement had a number of sources, but above all it was stimulated by the perceived failure of preferential policies de-

---

Centre-State Relations—Andhra Pradesh Experience," in B. L. Maheshwari, ed., *Centre-State Relations in the Seventies* (Calcutta: Minerva Associates, 1973), 1–32; Hugh Gray, "The Failure of the Demand for a Separate Andhra State," *Asian Survey* 14 (Apr. 1974): 338–49; "Telangana and Caste," *Economic and Political Weekly* (Bombay), Mar. 8, 1969, pp. 455–56; Weiner, *Sons of the Soil*, 217–64; Hugh Gray, "Andhra Pradesh," in Myron Weiner, ed., *State Politics in India* (Princeton: Princeton Univ. Press, 1968), 399–431; G. N. Sharma, "Aspects of Andhra Politics," in Iqbal Narain, ed., *State Politics in India* (Meerut, India: Meenakshi Prakashan, 1968), 96–104.

40. *The Telangana Movement* is replete with figures documenting alleged disparities and malpractices.

41. Ibid., 43.

signed to protect Telanganas from the "clever and cunning"[42] Coastal Andhras.

The Telangana movement died down for two main reasons. The first, which has to do with Indian federalism, is that the movement's leaders continued their ties with the Congress Party at the national level and aimed at factional advantages at the state level by unseating the Congress chief minister. When that was accomplished, it was in their interest to press their gains by rejoining Congress, rather than continuing the movement.

More important for present purposes was the second reason. The movement had been stimulated by a decision of the Supreme Court of India holding residence requirements for jobs in Telangana unconstitutional. The response to the movement, however, had been to grant a number of concessions to Telangana. A Telangana regional committee was set up; one of its functions was to increase employment opportunities for *mulkis*.[43] In 1972, the Supreme Court decided that the *mulki* rules were valid after all. Thereafter, some students continued to demand a separate Telangana, but the movement had been broken by major concessions to the preferential scheme. Employment preferences were the most important component of Telangana grievances.

What broke the movement in Telangana, however, created a new separatist movement in Coastal Andhra. The Telangana movement had produced a stream of migrant Andhras returning to their home region "telling stories of hardships, insults and physical violence"[44] suffered at the hands of the *mulkis*. When the Supreme Court validated the old *mulki* rules, grievances in Coastal Andhra ignited. Mrs. Gandhi proposed a compromise formula that restricted the application of the *mulki* rules only slightly. This added to the Andhra sense of grievance. Andhra ministers in the state cabinet resigned, government servants began a strike, and law and order deteriorated. The *mulki* rules and the discrimination they entailed produced a separatist reaction.

In an independent state, either of these movements would probably have led to armed secessionist warfare. Only the fact that Andhra Pradesh was a component state of a federation prevented this outcome, for the raw claims were utterly irreconcilable. In the end, the Andhra agita-

42. Reddy, "Uni-Party Dominance in Centre-State Relations—Andhra Pradesh Experience," 15.
43. Ramashray Roy, "India 1972: Fissures in the Fortress," *Asian Survey* 13 (Feb. 1973): 231–45, at 237.
44. Gray, "The Failure of the Demand for a Separate Andhra State," 339.

tion was brought under control by the central government through a formula that, while purporting to establish regional preferences, watered down domicile requirements and made murky the concept of *mulki*. It was the Andhra movement that the center had to cope with last, and Andhra's grievances dictated the outcome. Thereafter, Andhra Pradesh was administered more or less as an integrated state.[45]

Had it been possible to revive the Telangana movement while the Andhra movement was at its peak, the state would probably have been partitioned, as the Indian Punjab was in 1966. One of the most important reasons why this did not happen is inherent in complementary secessions: they are likely to be sequential, rather than simultaneous, because of the opposite grievances that bring them about. Enforcement of preferential policies breeds secession among advanced, population-exporting groups; the withdrawal of such policies breeds secession among backward groups. Andhra Pradesh experienced both types of separatism, one after the other, because it experienced oscillating policies.

Here, then, was a case where policymakers committed themselves firmly to preferential employment policy, simultaneously laying a foundation for grievance and depriving themselves of the flexibility to work their way out of the resulting conflict. Other policymakers who have gone down similar roads seem to be retracing their steps. Most notably, in Sri Lanka the Jayewardene government that came to power in 1977 embarked on an effort to reverse or modify twenty years of government employment preferences for Sinhalese. Language requirements were relaxed in government service, and there was a program to recruit Tamils to the police and armed forces.[46] The government had seen the face of Tamil separatist terrorism and connected it to preferential employment. The connection was not spurious, but it may have been grasped too late. By the time the new policies went into effect, many young Tamils had gotten the idea that government was against them. The "Tamil Tigers," who launched the terrorism, grew at the very time that ameliorative measures were being taken. A good case can be made that the separatist

45. The terms of the 1973 formula appear in ibid., 348–49. Not only were *mulki* rules abolished, but so was the redirection of revenue surpluses to Telangana under the Gentlemen's Agreement. The solution clearly favored the Andhras. Telanganas, many of whom felt betrayed by the political leaders of their earlier movement—who rejoined Congress as soon as the chief minister was unseated—were not up to beginning a new agitation, even if financing had been forthcoming, which apparently it no longer was. I am indebted for this information to several sources whom I consulted in Hyderabad in 1975.

46. The new language concessions were effective on July 9, 1980. See also *Ceylon Observer* (Colombo), Apr. 6, 1980.

terrorism that precipitated virulent anti-Tamil violence in 1983 was an indirect result of the earlier preferences.

THE COSTS AND BENEFITS
OF PREFERENTIAL POLICIES

It is too soon for a definitive evaluation of preferential policies, but it is not too soon for skepticism regarding their impact. The evidence is not all in, and the evidence available so far is much stronger on immediate consequences than on more distant ones. But it is precisely this imbalance that gives pause.

Preferential policies, if pursued vigorously, tend to generate dangerous reactions. The relatively mild response to educational preferences in Tanzania and Malaysia seems attributable to the existence of alternative educational outlets in the private sector or abroad, as well as to flexibility in implementation. Comparable alternatives were not available for several years in Sri Lanka, which experienced a much sharper reaction. The relatively mild reaction to employment preferences in Malaysia, in contrast to some Indian states, owes much to political sensitivity in enforcement. The Malaysian experience with business preferences suggests that these may be less provocative, although favorable Malaysian economic conditions and the expansion of business opportunities created by the new public authorities may have averted hostility that would otherwise have arisen. That preferential policies have not produced heavier short-run political costs is testimony to the frequent ability of those subject to them to circumvent or benefit from the policies and to the moderation of enforcement authorities as much as it is to the policies themselves. Especially with respect to education and employment, there is reason to expect most preferential policies to accentuate ethnic conflict over the short term.

In the medium term, there is an additional reason to expect preferential policies to increase ethnic conflict. As I noted in Chapter 3, the common pattern of occupational specialization by ethnic group channels career aspirations toward established ethnic niches. The ethnic division of labor thus fosters intraethnic rather than interethnic occupational competition. The same is initially true of preferences: if specific opportunities are reserved for members of one or another ethnic group, competition for them will take an intraethnic direction. But as preferences break down the ethnic division of labor, they open large fields of interethnic occupational competition previously shielded by segmented labor markets.[47]

Of course, costs in the short and medium run that now seem high may later seem worth bearing for benefits that are great. Ultimately, perhaps, there will be less ethnic conflict if all groups are proportionately represented at all levels in all sectors of the economy. One reason the truth of this proposition remains elusive is that few, if any, societies have ever approximated this description. And it remains problematical whether any but the most heavy-handed preferential policies, operating in a command economy, can actually move a society close to such a state. But even that does not conclude the matter. In Asia and Africa, the short run and the medium run are especially vulnerable to disturbances of interethnic tranquility, democratic stability, and economic development. Policies that impose heavy short-run costs, for the sake of heavy long-run benefits, should receive strict scrutiny—the more so if the benefits are speculative. In ethnic policy terms, there is a special sting to Keynes' quip that in the long run we are all dead.

What is needed are benefits in the present. It is because of their ability to produce short-term results that structural techniques seem so much more advantageous.

Preferential policies, to be sure, aim to reach deeper, to the very roots of intergroup hostility. But they fall short in two key respects. First, their social-class impact is usually skewed; and, second, they operate on the assumption that representational disparities alone are responsible for hostility between groups.

Preferences tend to respond to middle-class aspirations almost entirely. They do little or nothing about the resentments of those who do not aspire to attend secondary school or university, to enter the modern private sector or the bureaucracy, or to become businessmen. Although lower-class resentments are often profound—it is not, after all, the middle class that typically participates in ethnic violence—the resentments may have nothing to do with occupational mobility, and preferences do not address them. Indeed, by reducing disparities between ethnic groups, preferences are likely to increase disparities between classes within ethnic groups. This is a redistributive effect that has gone largely, though not entirely, unnoticed.[48] The magnification of social-class cleavages in

47. Weiner, *Sons of the Soil*, 352.
48. See Jacob Meerman, *Public Expenditure in Malaysia: Who Benefits and Why* (New York: Oxford Univ. Press, 1979), 37. Cf. Weiner, *Sons of the Soil*, 362.

an ethnically divided society is not necessarily conducive to the moderation of ethnic cleavages. On the contrary, it may encourage the displacement of lower-class aggression onto ethnic strangers.[49]

In attempting to rectify representational disparities alone, preferential
policies leave unattended the psycho-political concomitants of those disparities. Preferences would probably hold far more promise of conflict
reduction if they simultaneously were able to do something about the
felt inability to compete that is so commonly expressed by backward
groups. But here the very advantages of preferential policies are a limiting condition. Attractive because they require no public outlay of expenditure, preferential policies are designed to play a gatekeeper role. They
permit access to opportunities that would not ordinarily be open, but do
not necessarily contribute toward insuring success in the pursuit of those
opportunities. Sometimes governments have taken steps to redress this
deficiency, and sometimes firms have managed to extract government
help beyond the gatekeeper role—such as training assistance—but generally not. All too often, defaults on loans, insolvencies, and poor academic performance suggest that gatekeeper programs alone may supplement the fear of competing with a tangible experience of actual failure
in competition.

If preferential policies do not reduce beneficiary-group apprehensions, they may even contribute to what Erik Erikson has called "com-
pensation neuroses," ailments "unconsciously prolonged so as to secure
financial help."[50] Weiner and Katzenstein have noted that preferential
policies in India, intended to be temporary, tend, as they have in Malaysia and elsewhere, to become more and more permanent.[51] It is a mistake
to conclude from the entrenchment of preferences that liberal notions of
merit criteria and competition are cast aside, for they are very much on
the minds of leaders of the preferred groups, who typically intensify their
exhortations to group members to work hard, to justify government's
commitment to the policy by showing solid results, and to take advantage of special opportunities while they last, for they cannot last forever.[52] There is no close study of the impact on beneficiaries of these
pressures to compete, coupled with guilt about the need for special con-

49. See Donald L. Horowitz, "Direct, Displaced, and Cumulative Ethnic Aggression,"
Comparative Politics 6 (Oct. 1973): 1–16.
50. Childhood and Society, rev. ed. (New York: W. W. Norton, 1963), 44.
51. Weiner and Katzenstein, India's Preferential Policies, 18.
52. See, e.g., Mayer, Indians in Fiji, 82; Weiner, Sons of the Soil, 354; New Straits
Times (Kuala Lumpur), Mar. 29, 1980.

sideration, but it would be truly surprising if this explosive mixture did not heighten interethnic tensions. Representation is only a part of the problem, and not the most important part.

Preferential policies may proceed from a flawed theory of conflict, but it is nonetheless true that preferences once adopted are difficult to reverse, even when, as in Sri Lanka's university admissions, policymakers become convinced that reversal is warranted. Pressures for preferences, although not universal, are widespread. It is therefore pertinent to stress something policymakers rarely seem fully aware of—that different policies, even within the same general category of policy, have different benefit-cost ratios. Regimes that are committed to preferences still have choices to make, choices to enhance the likelihood of benefits or reduce the costs. Preferential employment policies can be coupled with training programs. Preferential admissions policies can make provision for alternative educational outlets for those excluded by them, lest displaced students make their own provision or turn to violent opposition. As preferential policies are not inevitable, neither is any particular version of preferences.

Where demands for preferences prove impossible to ignore, a promising approach might be to use territory in lieu of ethnicity to define the preferred category. In federal systems, this is most easily accomplished, but all states have district or provincial demarcations that can serve the same purpose. We have seen that the criteria of inclusion can make a difference in implementation. Territorial criteria have the advantage of being less rigidly and invidiously ascriptive than ethnic criteria, even when there is considerable overlap between territorial and ethnic boundaries. Proportionality by territorial unit or preference to underrepresented or backward regions does not foreordain who, within each unit, will be preferred. In a federal system, that can be left to each state to resolve, with potentially good results for the dispersal of conflict[53] and potentially variable costs in productivity. In unitary systems, the center may also implement territorial preferences in ways calculated to balance ethnic representation with productivity and conflict reduction goals. Rigid territorial quotas do raise serious problems of economic and political cost;[54] many backward regions cannot supply a proportionate number of able candidates, particularly for higher education. But that is an argument against firm quotas and against defining eligible territorial

53. See Chapter 15, above.
54. De Silva, "The Politics of University Admissions," 92–94.

units in terms of districts or other small areas that may include no urban centers.[55] If territorial criteria are used, flexibility can only be achieved and productivity costs minimized if territorial units are large.

Finally, policymakers need to know that there are alternatives to preferences that cost more in initial expenditure, but may cost less a short way down the road and yet bring greater benefits in both productivity and ethnic harmony. Many of the current economic disparities between ethnic groups are, as noted in Chapter 4, largely traceable to accidents of colonial location. Groups near a port, a missionary school, a colonial capital or commercial center obtained a head-start that they retained. Location policy and investment policy in general may well be more efficacious than preferential policies in reducing ethnic conflict. They have, in addition, the distinct political advantage that they spread the costs of redressing disparities widely and fairly, rather than inflicting the costs on individual competitors whose discontent can form the basis for serious political conflict.

55. Sri Lanka's territorial criteria scheme involved district quotas for admission to higher education. Some such quotas, in backward areas, were undersubscribed. Provincial quotas might have produced somewhat different results, and so would a standard more flexible than a numerical quota.

Afterword:
Ethnic Conflict
and Democracy

Democracy is exceptional in severely divided societies, and the claim has repeatedly been advanced that democracy cannot survive in the face of serious ethnic divisions. At least since John Stuart Mill pronounced in *Representative Government* that democracy is "next to impossible in a country made up of different nationalities,"[1] a respectable body of opinion has subscribed to such views.[2] In the 1960s, the sympathetic understanding that often followed as the Nkrumahs and Obotes of the new states dismantled their oppositions in the name of ethnic harmony bespoke an assumption that conflict-prone societies could ill afford, and might be better off without, democratic institutions.

Unless precautions are taken, democratic arrangements tend to unravel fairly predictably in ethnically divided societies, as we have seen in some detail. The propensity to form ethnically based parties manifests itself. If ethnic parties split off the flanks of a multiethnic party, the leadership of the multiethnic party may end the electoral process at that point by creating a single-party regime. Alternatively, ethnic parties contest divisive elections, which produce feelings of permanent exclusion on the part of those who are ascriptively locked out of office. These feelings are conducive to violent opposition: riots, plots, separatist movements. At this point, there is another chance to create a one-party state. If party

1. *Considerations on Representative Government*, in Mill, *Utilitarianism, Liberty, and Representative Government* (New York: E. P. Dutton, 1951; originally published in 1861), 486.
2. For an argument along these lines, see Alvin Rabushka and Kenneth A. Shepsle,, *Politics in Plural Societies: A Theory of Democratic Instability* (Columbus, Ohio: Charles E. Merrill, 1972), 74–92.

divisions persist, a seesaw coup may occur, provided the officer corps is composed differently from the civilian regime. Such a coup can also provoke violent opposition, civil or military, from ethnic groups that were formerly ascendant. Whether party leaders terminate elections, military leaders reverse election results, or separatist leaders attempt to constrict the area in which those results will prevail, it is clear that ethnic divisions strain, contort, and often transform democratic institutions.

We have also seen how regimes that dispense with the discipline of democratic elections, in the interest of preserving ethnic harmony, typically sacrifice harmony as well as democracy. Merely maintaining the electoral process in its original form is, of course, no answer to these problems. Since a majority can be obtained by setting half the state against the other half, elections commonly spur the very bifurcation that accelerates the slide away from democracy. The avoidance of bifurcation along ethnic lines thus becomes a critical task in the maintenance of democracy, as it is in the limitation of ethnic conflict.

There are no plausible shortcuts away from the problem of bifurcation. Its origins lie deep in the tendency to group comparison explored in Chapter 4, reinforced by the exigencies of attempting to form electoral majorities. We have seen in Chapter 6 that the prospects for greater homogeneity through secession or irredentas are not great; and, as Chapter 14 shows, neither the radical surgery of partition nor the plastic surgery of international regional integration seems much more promising for most severely divided societies. The answer to the problems of democracy and ethnic conflict is not to redraw the map of the world.

Consequently, we are relegated to internal political arrangements. Here the case for policy intervention is strong. We know from Chapter 15 that bifurcation can often be averted by prudent planning of electoral and territorial arrangements. Measures can be taken to avert the crystallization of ethnic allegiances at levels conducive to bifurcation and to encourage alignments that reach across the great cleavages that can rend a society. But if that is so, why are there not more democracies in severely divided societies than the few that exist?

The political difficulties underlying the precarious state of democracy in ethnically divided societies can be inferred from the experience of a few states that have taken deliberate action in the simultaneous service of democratic values and conflict reduction. One way to read this experience is to conclude that democratic experiments are subject to deflection by untoward events beyond the control of policymakers. The Nigerian Second Republic was overthrown at the end of 1983 by a military coup having little or nothing to do with ethnicity or with the accommodative provisions of the constitution.[3] The Nigerian coup was a blow to democratic institutions, but not necessarily an apt test of their durability in a severely divided society. The Lebanese arrangements were undone by a combination of external forces and long-term disaffection with some unfortunate features of the arrangements themselves. The Sri Lankan innovations were challenged soon after their adoption by separatists whose grievances antedated the innovations. Perhaps these instances suggest that democratic arrangements in conflict-prone societies go awry for reasons so various that the survival of democracy is merely a matter of chance.

Such an explanation, however, neglects the content of grievances in Lebanon and Sri Lanka. The frozen Lebanese quotas and the Sri Lankan preferences both comprised explicit ethnic policies that produced enough disaffection to jeopardize democratic arrangements. In other words, the effects of one set of policies can undo the effects of another.

The Nigerian and Sri Lankan cases prompt a more general observation about the timeliness of the arrangements. That innovations to foster democracy and reduce conflict tend to be adopted after the disruptive consequences of conflict have become all too apparent greatly increases the risk that the innovations will sweep too narrowly or come too late. In Nigeria, military intervention, after all, did not begin in 1983—it received its strongest impetus from the ethnic politics of the 1960s. Had they been in force at independence, the constitutional arrangements of 1978 might well have averted the coups of 1966. Instituted after three successful coups, a civil war that increased the importance of the armed forces, and thirteen years of military rule, the Nigerian arrangements were compelled to function under the shadow of a military poised to intervene. The Nigerian institutions were well designed, but their life chances would have been enhanced had they been born two decades earlier. In Sri Lanka, similarly, the 1978 constitution followed on the heels of seven years of governmental hostility to, and discrimination against, the Tamils. Had the new constitution come first, the governmental action to which the Tamils reacted would probably not have occurred, and the armed separatists would not have been entrenched. The matter resolves itself into a question of sequencing.

3. See Larry Diamond, "Nigeria in Search of Democracy," *Foreign Affairs* 62 (Spring 1984): 905–27.

Apt design and good timing are both required. Yet even such a formulation conceals almost as much as it reveals. Sequencing, in particular, is not a fortuitous element. Circularity is an integral part of the problem of sequencing: there will generally not be the requisite determination to enact appropriate measures until ethnic conflict has already advanced to a dangerous level; but by that time the measures that are adopted are more likely to be deflected or ineffective. Second chances to limit conflict by means of democratic institutions may come along, as they did in Nigeria and Sri Lanka, but the obstacles arrayed against them will be greater than they would have been earlier. These impediments add up to a problem of inducing policymakers to take action in time, for the irony is that it is more difficult to induce them to act when action promises better results.

To put the matter in these terms is to make clear that the principal impediments to democracy in severely divided societies do not derive from deficiencies of knowledge. The experience of conflict-prone societies is more revealing than might have been thought, on questions of conflict reduction and democratic institutions. The problems are not intellectual but political.

Still less can the problems be characterized as deriving from an unalterable human nature embodying elements of hostility to other ethnic groups so strong that it is likely to overwhelm any and all political arrangements. There are recurrent tendencies to ethnic cleavage and identifiable patterns of conflict, but the outcomes of conflict are various rather than uniform. There is no case to be made for the futility of democracy or the inevitability of uncontrolled conflict. Even in the most severely divided society, ties of blood do not lead ineluctably to rivers of blood.

Index

Compositor:	Wilsted & Taylor
Text:	10/13 Sabon
Display:	Sabon
Printer/binder:	The Maple-Vail Book Manufacturing Group